FIRST AID FOR THE USMLE STEP 1

UPDATED FOR 2000

A STUDENT TO STUDENT GUIDE

VIKAS BHUSHAN, MD
University of California, San Francisco, Class of 1991
Founder and CEO, Medschool.com

TAO LE, MD
University of California, San Francisco, Class of 1996
Founder and Chief Medical Officer, Medschool.com

CHIRAG AMIN, MD
University of Miami, Class of 1996
Vice President, Community and Content, Medschool.com

ANTONY CHU
Yale University, Class of 2002

ESTHER CHOO
Yale University, Class of 2001

JEAN SHEIN
2000 Student Editor
New York University, Class of 2001

McGraw-Hill
Medical Publishing Division

New York St. Louis San Francisco Auckland Bogotá Caracas Lisbon London
Madrid Mexico City Milan Montreal New Delhi San Juan
Singapore Sydney Tokyo Toronto

McGraw-Hill 

A Division of The **McGraw-Hill** *Companies*

Information and images from the following titles was incorporated into Section II: Database of High-Yield Facts, and was used with permission: Stobo J, *The Principles and Practice of Medicine*, 23rd ed., Appleton & Lange, 1996; McPhee S, *Pathophysiology of Disease*, 2nd ed., Appleton & Lange, 1997; Paulsen D, *Basic Histology*, 3rd ed., Appleton & Lange, 1996; Waxman S, *Correlative Neuroanatomy*, 24th ed., Appleton & Lange, 1999; Katzung BG (editor), *Basic & Clinical Pharmacology*, 7th ed., Appleton & Lange, 1997; Goldman HH, *Review of General Psychiatry*, 5th ed., Appleton & Lange, 1992; Ganong WF, *Review of Medical Physiology*, 18th ed., Appleton & Lange, 1996; Levinson W, *Medical Microbiology and Immunology: Examination and Board Review*, 5th ed., Appleton & Lange, 1998; Chandrasoma P, *Concise Pathology*, 3rd ed., Appleton & Lange, 1997; Milikowski C, *Color Atlas of Basic Histopathology*, Appleton & Lange, 1997; Bhushan V, *Underground Clinical Vignettes Internal Medicine, Vols. 1 & 11*, 1st ed., Blackwell Science, 1999; Costanzo L, *BRS Physiology*, 2nd ed., Williams & Wilkins, 1998; Klatt, WebPath website (http://www-medlib.med.utah.edu/ WebPath/webpath.html). The diagram on p. 202 was adapted from *Curr Opin Infect Dis* 1992; 5:214. Portions of the material in Section I are copyright © 2000 by The Federation of State Medical Boards of the United States, Inc., and the National Board of Medical Examiners.

First Aid for the USMLE Step 1 2000: A Student to Student Guide

0 1 2 3 4 5 6 7 8 9 0 DOCDOC 0 9 8 7 6 5 4 3 2 1 0

ISBN 0-07-135849-8

Notice

Medicine is an ever-changing science. As new research and clinical experience broaden our knowledge, changes in treatment and drug therapy are required. The authors and the publisher of this work have checked with sources believed to be reliable in their efforts to provide information that is complete and generally in accord with the standards accepted at the time of publication. However, in view of the possibility of human error or changes in medical sciences, neither the authors nor the publisher nor any other party who has been involved in the preparation or publication of this work warrants that the information contained herein is in every respect accurate or complete, and they disclaim all responsibility for any errors or omissions or for the results obtained from use of the information contained in this work. Readers are encouraged to confirm the information contained herein with other sources. For example and in particular, readers are advised to check the product information sheet included in the package of each drug they plan to administer to be certain that the information contained in this work is accurate and that changes have not been made in the recommended dose or in the contraindications for administration. This recommendation is of particular importance in connection with new or infrequently used drugs.

This book was set in Goudy by Rainbow Graphics, LLC.
The editors were John Dolan and Jeanmarie Roche.
Project Management was performed by Rainbow Graphics, LLC.
The production supervisor was Phil Galea.
The cover design is by Design Group Cook.
The interior design is by Elizabeth Sanders.

R.R. Donnelley & Sons was printer and binder.

This book is printed on acid-free paper.

To the contributors to this and future editions, who took
time to share their knowledge, insight, and
humor for the benefit of students.

&

To our families, friends, and loved ones, who endured
and assisted in the task of assembling this guide.

2000 Contributors

Fred Aslan
Contributing Author, High-Yield Facts
Yale University, Class of 2001

Soofia Rubbani
Contributing Author, High-Yield Facts
New York University, Class of 2001

Mital Sheth
Contributing Author, High-Yield Facts
New York University, Class of 2001

Isaac Sasson
Contributing Author, High-Yield Facts
Yale University, Class of 2004

2000 Associate Contributors

Steve Braunstein
New York University, Class of 2002

Peter Chien
New York University, Class of 2001

Manya Newton
New York University, Class of 2001

Lorraine Pan
New York University, Class of 2001

2000 Faculty Reviewers

Linda Costanzo, PhD
Professor of Physiology
Medical College of Virginia
Virginia Commonwealth University

William Ganong, MD
Lange Professor of Physiology Emeritus
University of California, San Francisco

Bertram Katzung, MD, PhD
Professor of Pharmacology
University of California, San Francisco

Henry Sanchez, MD
Assistant Clinical Professor of Pathology
University of California, San Francisco

William Stewart, PhD
Associate Professor of Surgery
Yale University School of Medicine

Warren Levinson, MD, PhD
Professor of Microbiology and Immunology
University of California, San Francisco

Contents

Preface to the 2000 Edition

With the 2000 edition of *First Aid for the USMLE Step 1*, we continue our commitment to providing students with the most useful and up-to-date preparation guide for the USMLE Step 1. The 2000 edition represents a thorough revision in many ways and includes:

- A completely revised and updated exam preparation guide for the new computerized USMLE Step 1. Includes detailed analysis as well as all new study and test-taking strategies for the new computer-based testing (CBT) format.
- Revisions and new material based on student experience with the 1999 administrations of the computerized USMLE Step 1.
- Expanded USMLE advice for international medical graduates, osteopathic medical students, podiatry students, and students with disabilities.
- An updated collection of over 90 high-yield glossy photos similar to those appearing on the USMLE Step 1 exam.
- More than 900 frequently tested facts and useful mnemonics, including more than 100 new or expanded entries with over 50 new diagrams and illustrations.
- Useful reference links to prototypical clinical cases from the popular *Underground Clinical Vignette* (UCV) series (S2S Medical Publishing).
- An updated listing of more than 100 high-yield clinical vignette topics that highlight key areas of basic science and clinical material recently emphasized on the USMLE Step 1.
- A completely revised, in-depth guide to over 280 basic science review and sample examination books, based on a random survey of thousands of third-year medical students across the country. Includes more than 30 new books and software titles.

The 2000 edition would not have been possible without the help of the hundreds of students and faculty members who contributed their feedback and suggestions. We invite students and faculty to continue sharing their thoughts and ideas to help us improve *First Aid for the USMLE Step 1*. (*See* How to Contribute, p. xvii, and User Survey, p. xxv.)

Los Angeles	Vikas Bhushan
Santa Monica	Tao Le
Santa Monica	Chirag Amin
Santa Monica	Antony Chu
Santa Monica	Esther Choo
New York	Jean Shein

February 2000

Foreword

January 1, 2000

Dear USMLE Step 1 Student,

A little history for the curious . . . in honor of the 10th edition.

In March of 1989, a classmate and I came to the sudden realization that with three short months to go until the boards, we were alarmingly unprepared. For the first two years at University of California, San Francisco (a pass/fail school), our motto had been "P"=MD. It had been deceptively easy to slide through classes, enjoy San Francisco, and postpone the inevitable and looming pain of studying for the boards.

We knew that cramming was the only option—the problem was that there was nothing all that "crammable" available. Our only hope was to do our own "high-yield" boards review, a term we coined and put to the test with our medical school careers on the line. We rapidly assembled a three-column database of crammable facts by sifting through class notes, review and Q & A books, and hand-me-down exam recollections from classmates. Every week, we printed out the latest cram list and circulated it among the members of our study group. We kept entries short (our Paradox database could only handle 255 characters in each field), added mnemonics, and focused only on testable facts.

The motivating sentiments at that point were primarily survival, fear of humiliation, and terror at the prospect of having to take the exam more than once. *Just let us pass*, we prayed, so that we would never, ever again have to take this exam. I never imagined that the USMLE, and helping students prepare for it, would become the primary focus of the next ten years of my professional and personal life.

Today, thanks to the contributions of thousands of medical students, *First Aid* has become the most popular single source for basic medical science review in the world. Over 250,000 students from nearly 80 countries have used the 10 consecutive editions of the book, and it has been enormously gratifying to receive notes of appreciation and contribution from *First Aid* readers.

In honor of our 10th edition, I'd like to thank some of the key players who helped each year, from 1991 to 1999, to make *First Aid* the collaborative institution that we are all so proud of.

Ted Hon (founding author)
Eddie Chu (founding author)
Jeffery Hansen (founding author)
Hatem Abou-Sayed
Taejoon Ahn
Shaun Anand
Alireza Atri
John Austin
Lisa Backus
Ross Berkeley
John Bethea, Jr.
Vishal Banthia
Peter Choi
Esther Choo
Antony Chu
M. Vaughn Emerson
Jose Fierro
Anthony Glaser
Stephen Gomperts
Robert Hosseini
Freddy Huang
Kassem Kahlil
Ketan Kapadia
Shin Kim
Kambiz Kosari
Rick Kulkarni
Thong Le
Ross Levine
Kathleen Liu
Hoang Nguyen
Kieu Nguyen
Christine Pham
Thao Pham
Michael Rizen
Archana Desai
Radhika Sekhri-Breaden
Judy Shih
Yi Chieh Shiuey
Vipal Soni
David Steensma
Jennifer Steinfeldt
Dax Swanson
Gary Ulaner
Matthew Voorsanger
Antonio Wong
Ziqiang Wu
Ronald Yap

This year the *First Aid* crew has embarked on a new and exciting parallel venture: Medschool.com. With the support of over 100 medical student representatives and a growing team of medical school deans and faculty, we aim to harness the power of multimedia and the Internet to provide the premier community and e-learning experience for medical students and professionals around the world.

Sincerely,

Vikas Bhushan, MD
Founder and CEO, Medschool.com

Acknowledgments

This has been a collaborative project from the start. We gratefully acknowledge the thoughtful comments, corrections, and advice of the many hundreds of medical students, international medical graduates, and faculty who have supported the authors in the continuing development of *First Aid for the USMLE Step 1*.

For submitting major contributions to the 2000 edition, often including dozens of new entries, book reviews, or entire annotated books, we give special thanks to Henry Nguyen, Maggie Marshall, Sarah Carroll, Rose Cohen, Carolina Takizawa, Jonathan Boxer, Pil Kang, Theodore Nicolaides, Eric Kenley, Miriam Segal, Chirag Kapadia. Special thanks to Dr. Raoul Fresco and Dr. Edward Klatt (WebPath, University of Utah) for their generous contributions to the glossy photo section.

Thanks to Melanie Nelson (NBME) for providing updated USMLE Step 1 information. For helping us obtain information concerning review books, we thank Barnes & Noble medical bookstore (New York City), Yale Co-op medical bookstore, and UCLA Health Sciences Bookstore. Thanks to Noam Maitless for the original book design, Evenson Design Group, Ashley Pound, and Elizabeth Sanders for design revisions, and Design Group Cook for the cover design.

For support and encouragement throughout the process, we are grateful to Kelly Ray, Thao Pham, and Jonathan Kirsch, Esq.

Thanks to our publisher, McGraw-Hill, for the valuable assistance of their staff. For enthusiasm, support, and commitment for this ongoing and ever-challenging project, thanks to our editor, John Dolan. For personal and last-minute production support, enormous thanks to Gianni Le Nguyen, Marinita Timban, Amy Elkavich, and our copy editors, Andrea Fellows and Elmarie Hutchinson. A special thanks to Jimmy and Bennie Sauls (Rainbow Graphics) for remarkable production work.

For submitting contributions, corrections, and book surveys for the 2000 edition, we thank Bradley Bragg, Mathew Pillsbury, Mohamed Adenwalla, Lynda Alvarado, Sean Amsbaugh, Eric Anderson, Lisa Anderson, Chris Andreoli, Mike Arch, Maryam Armin, Elyssa Aronson, Alfredo Arraut, Serena Aunon, Vijak Ayasanonda, Elizabeth Bailey, Aliessa Barnes, Geoff Bauer, Mindy Bauks, Sarina Bax DeBiaso, Mathew Bechtold, Mathew Bell, Ayanna Bennett, Sabrina Ben-Zion, Jennifer Berger, George Blanco, Jason Bogioli, D Bonnema, Elana Bornstein, Martin Boscarino, Gwendolyn Brophy, Jason Brown, Sara Buchdahl, Francois Cady, Jason Caeung, Erica Carnova, Jennifer Carpenter, Richelle Cerrone, S. Chai, Keith Chan, Jeff Chan, Sun Chaney, Richard Chang, Emery Chang, Cavahaim Chekins, Ting-hsu Chen, Linda Cheng, Regina Cho, Lisa Chu, Richard Cooke, Audrey Cox,

Theresa Cyr, Huey Dang, Sandeep Dang, Subinoy Das, Damon Davis, Kristina Delastro, Michael Do, Todd Duellman, Julia Eckersky, Bryan Edgington, Lee Epstien, Erica Evans, Vereen Farrar-Guillotte, Jennifer Fehser, Gary Fillmore, Natasha Fine, Shana Fogarty, Marcus Foos, Anne Forrest, Cary Foster, Jessica Frost, Randolph Fung, Charles Galaviz, Salvador Garfias, Aris Garro, Kathy Gater, Christina Gee, Barry Goetz, Kathleen Goings, Valerie Goldburt, Louise Gombako, Robert Goodman, Greg Gordon, Alison Gorman, Darin Gregory, Lora Grimes, Anna Grose, David Gross, Jason Gross, Verna Guo, Kavita Gupta, Aaron Guyer, Jerry Guzik, Mary Hamm, Faye Hant, Carl Hoegerl, Jeffrey Hohn, April Holmes, Angela Hsu, Jerry Hsu, Cindy Hsu, Jennie Huang, Kjell Hult, Kathleen Huth, Phung Huynh, Richard Isaacson, Amy Jarvis, Samuel Jean, Mathew Johnson, Daniel Jondle, Mathew Jordan, David Josephson, Nancy Kang, Patricia Kao, Hyung Kim, Brian Kit, Carl Knopke, M-Grace Knuttinen, Christian Koch, Lily Koo, Cindy Kraus, Karl Kronmann, Naveen Kumar, Karen Lamb, Eileen Lau, Marc Lee, Marie Catherine Lee, Sherri Lee, Timmy Lee, Robert Lehew, James Lehmann, Lenora Lehwald, Amanda Leino, Brian Leo, Sami Lewin, Carol Lewis, Felix Lin, Richard H.J. Lin, Wan-Tin Lin, Julie Lonze, John Lyons, Rob MacNeal, Elizabeth Mahoney, Jonrika Malone, Michele Manahan, Julie Martin, Ashley Matthews, Dipen Maun, Jennifer McBride, Phillip McKrevis, Nehal Mehta, Philip Mellen, Dawn Mersch, Mary Meux, Lorrie Miech, Rebecca Miksad, Wendy Molaska, Eleazar Morris, Pete Motolenich, Renee Mueller, Todd Myers, Eric Ng, Katherine Nguyen, Anne Nirupama, Gregory Novak, Bonnie Nowak, Jennifer Ochesner, Tessie October, Erin O'Fallon, Edward Oliver, Kevin Olson, Anjum Owaisi, Atman Pai, Amy Palese, Michael Papper, Sheel Patel, Neha Patel, Brenda Perez, Julie Phelan, Mary Pinder, Lym Rader, Jennifer Raffel, David Rahn, Fatima Rangwala, Dino Ravnic, Lynn Rebello, Amber Reeves-Daniel, Xiushui Ren, Patrick Renaud, Courtney Rhudy, Nasim Riazati, Christinia Riggs, Caroline Roberts, Eric Romriell, Sumita Roy, Tara Rubirias, Alexandra Rucker, Maria Rudisill, Chris Rupp, Rachel Saletel, John Samanich, Nancy Samolitis, Megan Schimpf, Greg Schmieder, Joel Schoffer, Jeff Schulman, Christina Seo, Gina Serraiocco, Amar Shah, Sonal Shah, Almaas Shaikh, Marina Shindell, Michelle Siefert, Josh Simmons, Alison Sistsky, Tanya Slick, Christopher Smith, Scott Smout, Yelena Sorduina, Jeffrey Spencer, Lowen Stewart, Pam Supanwanid, Scott Swanson, Yael Swica, Mark Takaki, Michael Takamura, Sriharsha Tanguturi, Stanley Tao, Eetein Tay, Elizabeth Thomas, Neeng Thomas, Dan Thuy Tran, Jody Tochterman, Therese Tomasoski, James Tomprand, Heather Toth, Nathan Troy-Tagg, Gladys Tse, Vanessa Urban, Claire Urbina, Raj Varma, Erin Vaughan, K Vaziri, Jason Vieder, Queng Vo, Nirav Vora, Jeremy Vos, Stephen Walsh, Joshua Walsh, John Walton, Raymond Wang, Kevin Weber, Anthony Wei, C Wendell, Brian Whang, John Wolen, Charles Woodall III, Michael Wu, Maria Wuebker, Alisa Yang, Stephen Yang, Aubrey Yao, Burt Yaszay, Robin Yates, David Yeh, David Yoo, Hsiang Michael Yu, Joyce Yu, Heather Zalusta, Andrea Zins. Our apologies if we omitted or misspelled your name.

Finally, thanks to Ted Hon, one of the founding authors of this book, for his vision in developing this guide on the computer.

Los Angeles Vikas Bhushan
Santa Monica Tao Le
Santa Monica Chirag Amin
Santa Monica Antony Chu
Santa Monica Esther Choo
New York Jean Shein

How to Contribute

This version of *First Aid for the USMLE Step 1* incorporates hundreds of contributions and changes suggested by faculty and student reviewers. We invite you to participate in this process. We also offer **paid internships** in medical education and publishing ranging from three months to one year (see next page for details).

Please send us your suggestions for:

- Study and test-taking strategies for the new computerized USMLE Step 1
- New facts, mnemonics, diagrams, and illustrations
- High-yield topics that may reappear on future Step 1 exams
- Personal ratings and comments on review books that you have examined

For each entry incorporated into the next edition, you will receive $10 cash per entry from the author group, as well as personal acknowledgment in the next edition. Diagrams, tables, partial entries, updates, corrections, and study hints are also appreciated, and significant contributions will be compensated at the discretion of the authors. Also let us know about material in this edition that you feel is low yield and should be deleted.

The preferred way to submit entries, suggestions, or corrections is via electronic mail. Please include name, address, school affiliation, phone number, and e-mail address (if different from address of origin). Please send submissions to:

2000step1@medschool.com

For *First Aid for the USMLE Step 1* updates and corrections, visit our Internet website at:

www.medschool.com

Otherwise, please send entries, neatly written or typed or on disk (Microsoft Word), to: **First Aid for the USMLE Step 1, 1015 Gayley Ave., #1113, Los Angeles, CA 90024, Attention: Contributions.** Please use the contribution and survey forms on the following pages. Each form constitutes an entry. (Attach additional pages as needed.)

Another option is to send in your entire annotated book. We will look through your additions and notes and will send you an honorarium based on the quantity and quality of any additions that we incorporate into the 2001 edition. Books will be returned upon request. Contributions received by July 15, 2000, receive priority consideration for the 2001 edition of *First Aid for the USMLE Step 1*.

Internship Opportunities

The author team of Bhushan, Le, and Amin is pleased to offer part-time and full-time paid internships in medical education and publishing to motivated medical students and physicians. Internships may range from three months (e.g., a summer) up to a full year. Participants will have an opportunity to author, edit, and earn academic credit on a wide variety of projects, including the popular *First Aid* series. Writing/editing experience, familiarity with Microsoft Word, and Internet access are desired. For more information, e-mail a résumé or a short description of your experience along with a cover letter to 2000step1@medschool.com.

Note to Contributors

All contributions become property of the authors and are subject to editing and reviewing. Please verify all data and spellings carefully. In the event that similar or duplicate entries are received, only the first entry received will be used. Include a reference to a standard textbook to facilitate verification of the fact. Please follow the style, punctuation, and format of this edition if possible.

Contribution Form I

For entries, mnemonics, facts, strategies, corrections, diagrams, etc.

Contributor Name: ______________________

School/Affiliation: ______________________
(no acronyms please)

Address: ______________________

____

Telephone: ______________________

E-mail: ______________________

Signature: ______________________

Topic:

Subject/Subsection:
Page number in '00 ed.:

Fact and Description:

Notes, Diagrams, and Mnemonics:

Reference:

Please return by July 15, 2000. You will receive personal acknowledgment and $10 cash for each entry that is used in future editions.

Please seal with tape only.
No staples or paper clips.

(fold here)

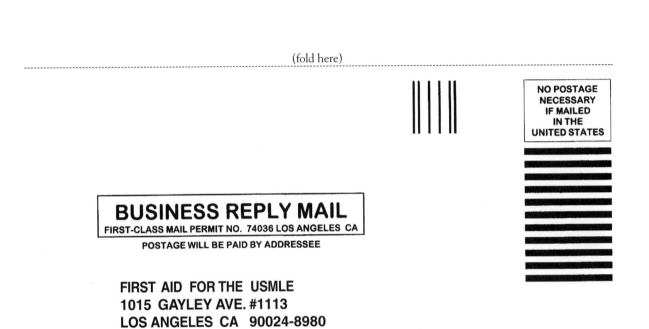

NO POSTAGE
NECESSARY
IF MAILED
IN THE
UNITED STATES

BUSINESS REPLY MAIL
FIRST-CLASS MAIL PERMIT NO. 74036 LOS ANGELES CA

POSTAGE WILL BE PAID BY ADDRESSEE

FIRST AID FOR THE USMLE
1015 GAYLEY AVE. #1113
LOS ANGELES CA 90024-8980

(fold here)

Contribution Form II

For entries, mnemonics, facts, strategies, corrections, diagrams, etc.

Contributor Name: ______________________________

School/Affiliation: ______________________________
(no acronyms please)

Address: ______________________________

____

Telephone: ______________________________

E-mail: ______________________________

Please place the subject heading (e.g., Anatomy) on the first line and the high-yield vignette or topic on the following two lines.

1. Subject: ____________________
   Vignette: ______________________________
   ____

2. Subject: ____________________
   Vignette: ______________________________
   ____

3. Subject: ____________________
   Vignette: ______________________________
   ____

4. Subject: ____________________
   Vignette: ______________________________
   ____

5. Subject: ____________________
   Vignette: ______________________________
   ____

6. Subject: ____________________
   Vignette: ______________________________
   ____

7. Subject: ____________________
   Vignette: ______________________________
   ____

8. Subject: ____________________
   Vignette: ______________________________
   ____

9. Subject: ____________________
   Vignette: ______________________________
   ____

10. Subject: ____________________
    Vignette: ______________________________
    ____

Please return by July 15, 2000. You will receive personal acknowledgment and $10 cash for each entry that is used in future editions.

Please seal with tape only.
No staples or paper clips.

(fold here)

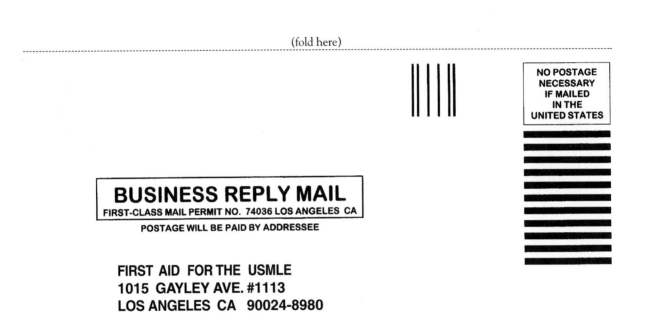

NO POSTAGE
NECESSARY
IF MAILED
IN THE
UNITED STATES

BUSINESS REPLY MAIL
FIRST-CLASS MAIL PERMIT NO. 74036 LOS ANGELES CA

POSTAGE WILL BE PAID BY ADDRESSEE

FIRST AID FOR THE USMLE
1015 GAYLEY AVE. #1113
LOS ANGELES CA 90024-8980

(fold here)

Contribution Form III

For entries, mnemonics, facts, strategies, corrections, diagrams, etc.

Contributor Name: ______________________

School/Affiliation: ______________________
(no acronyms please)
Address: ______________________

____

Telephone: ______________________

E-mail: ______________________

We welcome additional comments on review resources rated in Section III as well as reviews of resources not rated in Section III. Please fill out each review entry as completely as possible. Please do not leave "Comments" blank. Rate texts using the letter grading scale provided on p. 334, taking into consideration current ratings of other books on that subject.

1. ***Title/Author:*** ______________________ Days needed to read: ______________
   Publisher/Series: ______________________ ISBN Number: ______________
   Rating: ________ ***Comments:*** ______________________

2. ***Title/Author:*** ______________________ Days needed to read: ______________
   Publisher/Series: ______________________ ISBN Number: ______________
   Rating: ________ ***Comments:*** ______________________

3. ***Title/Author:*** ______________________ Days needed to read: ______________
   Publisher/Series: ______________________ ISBN Number: ______________
   Rating: ________ ***Comments:*** ______________________

4. ***Title/Author:*** ______________________ Days needed to read: ______________
   Publisher/Series: ______________________ ISBN Number: ______________
   Rating: ________ ***Comments:*** ______________________

5. ***Title/Author:*** ______________________ Days needed to read: ______________
   Publisher/Series: ______________________ ISBN Number: ______________
   Rating: ________ ***Comments:*** ______________________

Please return by July 15, 2000. You will receive personal acknowledgment and $10 cash for each entry that is used in future editions.

Please seal with tape only.
No staples or paper clips.

(fold here)

NO POSTAGE
NECESSARY
IF MAILED
IN THE
UNITED STATES

BUSINESS REPLY MAIL
FIRST-CLASS MAIL PERMIT NO. 74036 LOS ANGELES CA

POSTAGE WILL BE PAID BY ADDRESSEE

FIRST AID FOR THE USMLE
1015 GAYLEY AVE. #1113
LOS ANGELES CA 90024-8980

(fold here)

User Survey

Contributor Name: ______________________

School/Affiliation: ______________________
(no acronyms please)

Address: ______________________

____

Telephone: ______________________

E-mail: ______________________

What student-to-student advice would you give someone preparing for the computerized USMLE Step 1? What on-line resources, if any, did you use for Step 1 prep?

What commercial review courses have you been enrolled in, and what were your overall assessments of the courses?

What would you change about the study and test-taking strategies listed in Section I: Guide to Efficient Exam Preparation?

Were there any high-yield facts, topics, or vignettes in Section II that you think were inaccurate or should be deleted? Which ones and why? What would you change or add? What high-yield images would you like to see?

What review resources for the USMLE Step 1 are not covered in Section III? Would you change the rating of any of the review resources in Section III? If so, which one(s) and why?

What other suggestions do you have for improving *First Aid for the USMLE Step 1*? Any other comments or suggestions? What did you dislike most about the book? What did you like most?

Please return by July 15, 2000. You will receive personal acknowledgment and $10 cash for each entry that is used in future editions.

Please seal with tape only.
No staples or paper clips.

(fold here)

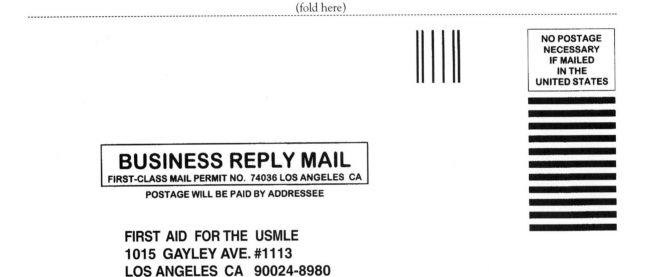

NO POSTAGE
NECESSARY
IF MAILED
IN THE
UNITED STATES

BUSINESS REPLY MAIL
FIRST-CLASS MAIL PERMIT NO. 74036 LOS ANGELES CA
POSTAGE WILL BE PAID BY ADDRESSEE

FIRST AID FOR THE USMLE
1015 GAYLEY AVE. #1113
LOS ANGELES CA 90024-8980

(fold here)

How to Use This Book

Medical students who have used previous editions of this guide have given us feedback on how best to make use of the book.

It is recommended that you begin using this book as early as possible when learning the basic medical sciences. You can use Section III to select first-year course review books, internet resources, and then use those books for review while taking your medical school classes.

Use different parts of the book at different stages in your preparation for the USMLE Step 1. Before you begin to study for the USMLE Step 1, we suggest that you read Section I: Guide to Efficient Exam Preparation and Section III: Database of Science Review Books. **If you are an international medical graduate student, an osteopathic medical student, a podiatry student, or a student with a disability,** refer to the appropriate Section I supplement for additional advice. Devise a study plan and decide what resources to buy. We strongly recommend that you invest in at least one or two top-rated review books in each subject. *First Aid* is not a comprehensive review book, and it is not a panacea for not studying during the first two years of medical school. Scanning Section II will give you an initial idea of the diverse range of topics covered on the USMLE Step 1.

As you study each discipline, **use the corresponding high-yield-fact section in *First Aid for the USMLE Step 1* as a way of consolidating the material and testing yourself** to see if you have covered some of the frequently tested items. Use the UCV reference links to see corresponding clinical vignettes. Work with the book to integrate important facts into your fund of knowledge. Using *First Aid for the USMLE Step 1* as a review can serve as both a self-test of your knowledge and a repetition of important facts to learn. High-yield topics and vignettes are abstracted from recent exams to help guide your preparation.

Return to Section II frequently during your preparation and fill your short-term memory with remaining high-yield facts a few days before the USMLE Step 1. The book can serve as a useful way of retaining key associations and keeping high-yield facts fresh in your memory just prior to the examination.

Reviewing the book immediately after the exam is probably the best way to **help us improve the book in the next edition.** Decide what was truly high and low yield and **send in the contribution forms or your entire annotated book.**

Illustration Credits

Illustrations were reproduced or adapted from the following sources with permission.

PAGE	ILLUSTRATION	REFERENCE
87	Fetal circulation	Ganong WF, *Review of Medical Physiology,* 18th ed., Appleton & Lange, 1996, Fig. 32–11, p. 600.
94	Coronary artery	Ibid., Fig. 32–21, p. 592.
96	Digestive tract anatomy	McPhee S, *Pathophysiology of Disease,* 2nd ed., Appleton & Lange, 1997, Fig. 13–2, p. 292.
97	Kidney and glomerulus	Ibid., Fig. 16–2, p. 376.
106	Cavernous sinus	Stobo J, *The Principles and Practice of Medicine,* 23rd ed., Appleton & Lange, 1996, Fig. 4.2–2, p. 277.
157	Lipoproteins	McPhee S, *Pathophysiology of Disease,* 2nd ed., Appleton & Lange, 1997, Fig. 14–6, p. 329.
170	Cell walls	Levinson W, *Medical Microbiology and Immunology: Examination and Board Review,* 5th ed., Appleton & Lange, 1998, Fig. 3–1, p. 6.
171	Bacterial growth	Ibid., Fig. 2–4, p. 14.
172	Endotoxin	Ibid., Fig. 7–4, p. 34.
180	Tuberculosis	Chandrasoma P, *Concise Pathology,* 3rd ed., Appleton & Lange, 1997, Fig. 34–13, p. 523.
187	DNA viruses	Levinson W, *Medical Microbiology and Immunology: Examination and Board Review,* 5th ed., Appleton & Lange, 1998, Table 31–1, p. 168.
188	RNA viruses	Ibid., Table 31–2, p. 170.
195	HIV	Ibid., Fig. 45–1, p. 252.
195	Time course of HIV infection	Ibid., Fig. 45–4, p. 255.
197	Hepatitis serology	Ibid., Fig. 41–2, p. 229.
200	Components of immune response	Ibid., Fig. 57–1, p. 314.
202	Complement	Ibid., Fig. 63–1, p. 355.
212	Tetralogy of Fallot	Chandrasoma P, *Concise Pathology,* 3rd ed., Appleton & Lange, 1997, Fig. 21–8, p. 345.
217	Neoplastic progression	McPhee S, *Pathophysiology of Disease,* 2nd ed., Appleton & Lange, 1997, Fig. 5–1, p. 83.
226	Multiple myeloma	Stobo J, *The Principles and Practice of Medicine,* 23rd ed., Appleton & Lange, 1996, Fig. 12.7–4, p. 806.
228	Hirschsprung's disease	Chandrasoma P, *Concise Pathology,* 3rd ed., Appleton & Lange, 1997, Fig. 39–6, p. 594.
228	Cirrhosis	McPhee S, *Pathophysiology of Disease,* 2nd ed., Appleton & Lange, 1997, Fig. 14–12, p. 349.
236	Osteoarthritis	Stobo J, *The Principles and Practice of Medicine,* 23rd ed., Appleton & Lange, 1996, Fig. 3.9–1, p. 241.
245	Evolution of MI	Chandrasoma P, *Pathology Notes,* 1st ed., Appleton & Lange, 1991, Fig. 23–1, p. 244.
256	Normal blood smear	McPhee S, *Pathophysiology of Disease,* 2nd ed., Appleton & Lange, 1997, Fig. 6–2, p. 100.
256	Microcytic hypochromic anemia	Stobo J, *The Principles and Practice of Medicine,* 23rd ed., Appleton & Lange, 1996, Fig. 11.2–2, p. 709.
256	Megaloblastic anemia	Ibid., Fig. 11.3–1, p. 713.
256	Target cells	Ibid., Fig. 11.1–1, p. 704.
256	Sickle cells	Ibid., Fig. 11.4–1, p. 719.
266	Penicillin	Katzung BG, *Basic & Clinical Pharmacology,* 7th ed., Appleton & Lange, 1997, Fig. 43–1, p. 725.
269	Sulfonamides	Ibid., Fig. 46–1, p. 340.
272	Antiviral chemotherapy	Ibid., Fig. 49–1, p. 789.
274	Central and peripheral nervous system	Ibid., Fig. 6–1, p. 74.
275	Autonomic drugs	Ibid., Fig. 6–2, p. 412.
277	Sympathomimetics	Ibid., Fig. 9–2, p. 72.
287	Diuretics: site of action	Ibid., Fig. 15–1, p. 243.
288	Anti-anginal therapy	Ibid., Fig. 12–7, p. 193.
289	Class I drugs	Ibid., Fig. 14–5, p. 118.
290	Class III drugs	Ibid., Fig. 14–6, p. 120.
291	Class IV drugs	Ibid., Fig. 14–7, p. 121.
292	Lipid lowering agents	Ibid., Fig. 35–2, p. 267.
301	Arachodonic acid products	Ibid., Fig. 18–1, p. 150.
302	Asthma drugs	Ibid., Figs. 20–4, 20–3, p. 159,161.
302	Immunosuppressive agents	Ibid., Fig. 56–7, p. 924.
307	Myocardial action potential	Ganong WF, *Review of Medical Physiology,* 18th ed., Appleton & Lange, 1996, Fig. 3–14, p. 74
307	Pacemaker action potential	Ibid., Fig. 28–2, p. 524.
309	Starling curve	Ibid., Fig. 29–8, p. 548.
313	Pressure volume loop	Ibid., Fig. 29–2, p. 540.
313	Cardiac cycle	Ibid., Fig. 29–3, p. 541.
314	EKG	Ibid., Fig. 28–1, p. 522.
315	Lung volumes	Ibid., Fig. 34–4, p. 622.
316	CO_2 transport	Ibid., Fig. 35–6, p. 638.
322	Relative concentration along renal tubule	Ibid., Fig. 38–9, p. 678.
323	Renin-angiotensin	Ibid., Fig. 39–2, p. 697.
325	Steroid/thyroid hormones	Ibid., Fig. 1–33, p. 36.

SECTION I

Guide to Efficient Exam Preparation

INTRODUCTION

Relax.

This section is intended to make your exam preparation easier, not harder. Our goal is to reduce your level of stress and help you make the most of your study effort by helping you understand more about the United States Medical Licensing Examination, Step 1 (USMLE Step 1)—especially what the new computer-based testing (CBT) is likely to mean for you. As a medical student, you are no doubt familiar with taking standardized examinations and absorbing large amounts of material. When you first confront the USMLE Step 1, however, you may find it easy to become sidetracked and not achieve your goal of studying with maximal effectiveness. Common mistakes that students make when studying for the boards include the following:

- "Stressing out" owing to an inadequate understanding of the new computer-based format
- Not understanding how scoring is performed or what your score means
- Starting *First Aid* too late
- Starting to study too late
- Using inefficient or inappropriate study methods
- Buying the wrong books or buying more books than you can ever use
- Buying only one publisher's review series for all subjects
- Not using practice examinations to maximum benefit
- Not using review books along with your classes
- Not analyzing and improving your test-taking strategies
- Getting bogged down by reviewing difficult topics excessively
- Studying material that is rarely tested on the USMLE Step 1
- Failing to master certain high-yield subjects due to overconfidence
- Using *First Aid* as your sole study resource

In this section, we offer advice to help you avoid these pitfalls and be more productive in your studies. To begin, it is important for you to understand what the examination involves.

USMLE STEP 1-THE CBT BASICS

The purpose of the USMLE Step 1 is to test your understanding and application of important concepts in basic biomedical sciences.[2]

Some degree of concern about your performance on the USMLE Step 1 examination is both expected and appropriate. All too often, however, medical students become unnecessarily anxious about the examination. It is therefore important to understand precisely what the USMLE Step 1 involves. As you become familiar with Step 1, you can translate your anxiety into more efficient preparation.

The USMLE Step 1 is the first of three examinations that you must pass in order to become a licensed physician in the United States.[1] The USMLE is a joint endeavor of the National Board of Medical Examiners (NBME) and the Federation of State Medical Boards (FSMB). In previous years, the examination was strictly organized around seven traditional disciplines: anatomy, behavioral science, biochemistry, microbiology, pathology, pharmacology, and physiology. In June 1991, the NBME began administering the "new" NBME Part I examination, which offers a more integrated and multidisciplinary format coupled with more clinically oriented questions.

Many students report that Step 1 is looking more and more like Step 2.

In 1992, the USMLE replaced both the Federation Licensing Examination (FLEX) and the certifying examinations of the NBME.[3] The USMLE now serves as the single examination system for United States medical students and International Medical Graduates (IMGs) seeking medical licensure in the United States.

How Will the CBT Be Structured?

In 1999, the traditional two-day paper-and-pencil exam gave way to an eight-hour computer-based test. The exam, administered by Sylvan Learning Systems, is now offered year-round at hundreds of sites around the world.

The CBT format of Step 1 is simply a computerized version of the former paper exam.

The CBT Step 1 exam consists of seven question "blocks" of 50 questions each (Fig. 1) for a total of 350 questions, timed at 60 minutes per block. A short 11-question survey follows the last question block. The computer begins the survey with a prompt to proceed to the next block of questions. Don't be fooled! "Block 8" is the NBME survey.

These blocks were designed to reduce eye strain and fatigue during the exam. Once an examinee finishes a particular block, he or she must click on a screen icon to continue to the next block. Examinees will **not** be able to go back and change answers to questions from any previously completed block. Changing answers, however, is allowed **within** a block of questions as long as time permits.

Don't be fooled! After the last question block comes the NBME survey ("Block 8").

Sylvan Technology Centers (STCs) offer Step 1 on a year-round basis, except for the first two weeks in January. The exam is given every day except Sunday at most centers. Some schools will eventually be able to administer the exam on their own campuses (see below).

FIGURE 1. Schematic of CBT Exam

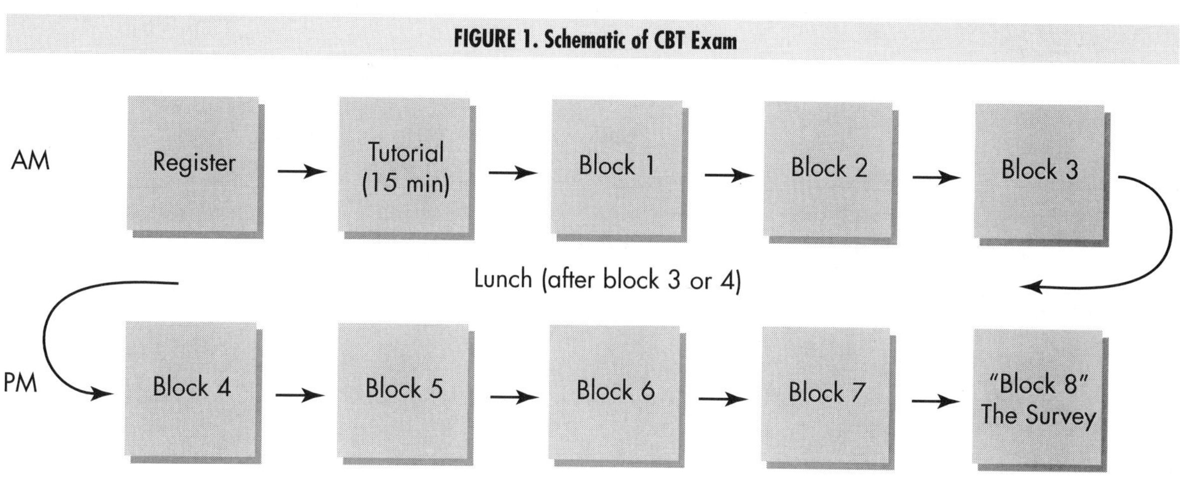

What Will the CBT Be Like?

Skip the tutorial and add 15 minutes to your break time!

Because of the unique environment of the CBT, it's important that you be familiar ahead of time with what your test-day conditions will be like. Familiarizing yourself with the testing interface before the exam can add 15 minutes to your break time! This is because a 15-minute tutorial, offered on exam day, may be skipped if you are already familiar with the exam procedures and the testing interface. The 15 minutes is added to your allotted break time (should you choose to skip the tutorial).

Pictures and text describing the Sylvan check-in procedure and testing environment are included on the free NBME CD-ROM, which is available from your medical school and the USMLE website (http://www.usmle.org). Here's what the Sylvan walk-through tour describes:

- The examinee enters a waiting room and signs in.
- The examinee waits in that room until the proctor calls him or her for "check-in."
- The examinee places personal belongings in a locker and follows the proctor into an office for official check-in activities. These include showing the proctor one's scheduling permit along with a signed photo identification. Next, the proctor takes a picture or "image capture" of the examinee with a digital camera. The examinee then receives two laminated boards and ink markers for scratch work. Earplugs are also offered at this time.
- The examinee is led into the testing area by the proctor. The testing workstation includes a computer, a monitor, a "banker's" lamp, and an adjustable chair. The monitor can be adjusted for contrast. (In fact, a color calibration is necessary preceding the exam to ensure accurate presentation of images.)
- Examinees are required to sign out with the proctor for breaks. The examinee can remove personal items from the locker during a break, but these items must be put back in the locker before the examinee returns to the testing area.
- Questions that arise during the exam period are answered by the proctor as soon as the examinee raises his or her hand.
- After the examinee completes the exam, test information is transmitted electronically to the NBME. The examinee then checks out and returns laminated boards and markers, after which he or she receives a written confirmation of exam completion.

For security reasons, examinees are not allowed to bring any personal electronic equipment into the testing area. This includes digital watches, watches with computer communication and/or memory capability, cellular telephones, and electronic paging devices. Food and beverages are also prohibited. The testing centers are monitored by audio and video surveillance equipment.

The typical question screen (Fig. 2) has a question followed by a number of choices on which an examinee can click, together with a number of navigational buttons at the bottom. There is also a button that allows the examinee

FIGURE 2. Typical Question Screen

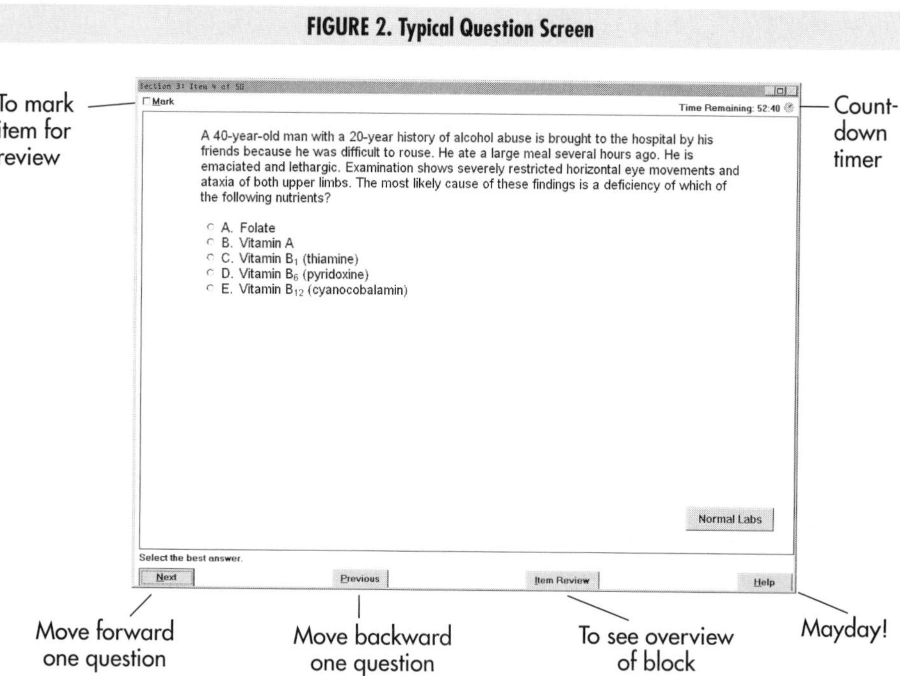

to mark the question for review. There is a countdown timer in the upper right-hand corner of the screen. If the question happens to be longer than the screen (very rare), a scroll bar appears on the right, allowing the examinee to see the rest of the question. Regardless of whether the examinee clicks on an answer or leaves it blank, he or she must click the "Next" button to advance to the next question.

Some questions contain figures or color illustrations (Fig. 3). These are typically situated to the right of the question. Although the contrast and bright-

FIGURE 3. Question Screen with Illustration

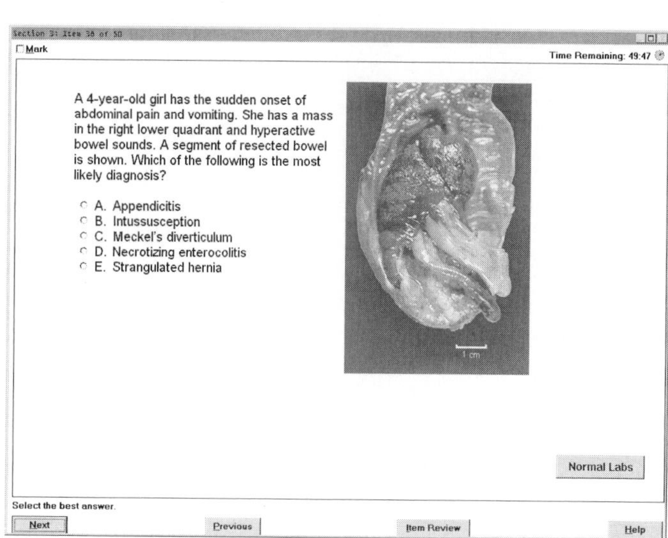

Test illustrations include:

- *Gross photos*
- *Histology slides*
- *Radiographs*
- *EMs*
- *Line drawings*

Keyboard shortcuts:

A–E—Letter choices

Enter or Alt–N—Move to next question

Alt–P—Move back one question

Alt–T—Countdown timers for current session and overall test.

ness of the screen can be adjusted, there are no other ways to manipulate the picture (e.g., no zooming or panning).

The examinee can call up a window displaying normal lab values (Fig. 4). However, if he or she does not press "Tile" on the normal-values screen, the normal-values window may obscure the question. The examinee may have to scroll down searching for the needed laboratory values. In the interest of time, it's worth memorizing common lab values.

Clicking "Item Review" at the bottom of the screen brings up a screen showing an overview of the block (Fig. 5). This screen allows the examinee to pinpoint questions marked for review as well as unanswered questions. This also serves as a quick way of navigating to any question in the block, even unmarked completed questions.

What Does the New CBT Format Mean for Me?

Ctrl-Alt-Delete are the keys of death during the exam. Don't touch them!

The significance to you of the CBT depends on the requirements of your school and your level of computer knowledge. If you hate computers and freak out whenever you see one, you might want to face your fears as soon as possible. Spend some time playing with a Windows-based system and pointing and clicking icons or buttons with a mouse. These are the absolute basics, and you won't want to waste valuable exam time figuring them out on test day. Your test taking will proceed by pointing and clicking, essentially without the use of the keyboard. The free CD is an excellent way to become familiar with the test interface.

For those who feel they would benefit, Sylvan offers an opportunity to take a simulated test, or "CBT Practice Session." Students are eligible to take the

FIGURE 4. Lab Values Screen—Floating and Tiled

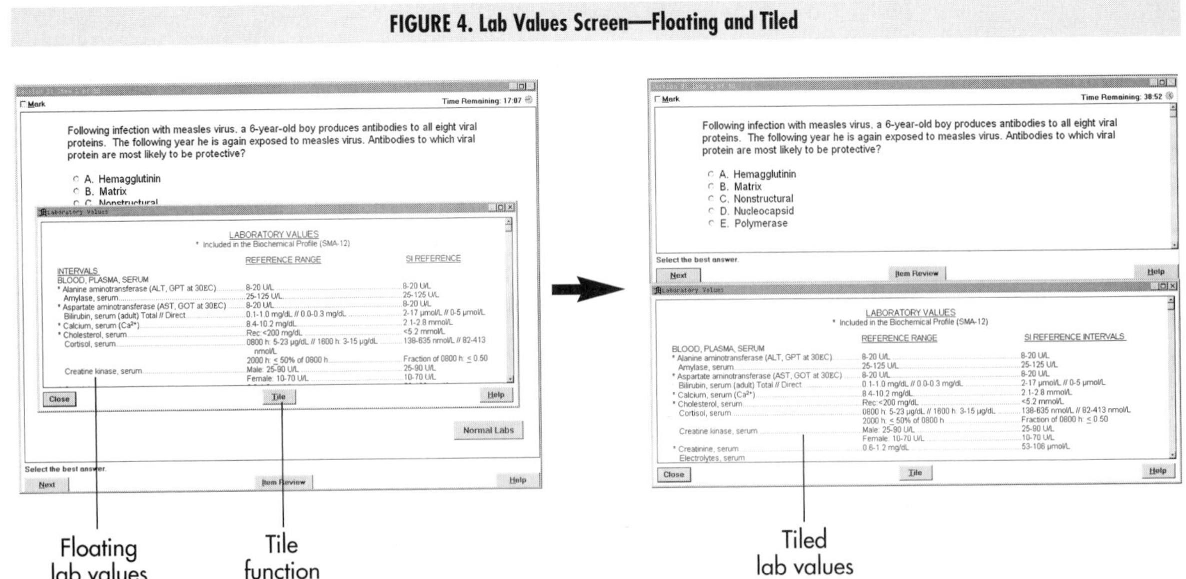

FIGURE 5. Item Review Screen

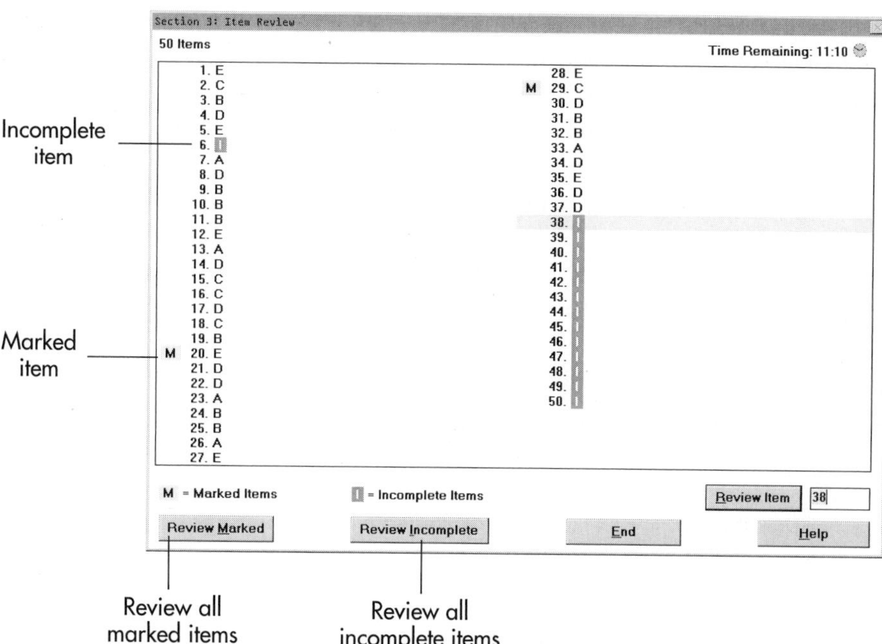

three and one-half-hour practice session after they have received their fluorescent orange scheduling permit (see below).

The same USMLE Step 1 sample test items (150 questions) provided to you in printed format and on the CD (available free on the CD or USMLE website: www.usmle.org) are used at these sessions. *No new items will be presented.* The session is divided into three one-hour blocks of 50 test items each and costs about $42. The student receives a printed percent-correct score after completing the session.

Contact your local STC to set up an appointment or register online at www.usmle.org.

How Do I Register to Take the Exam?

The preliminary registration process for the USMLE Step 1 is essentially unchanged, which is to say that students are required to complete registration forms and send exam fees to the NBME. The application allows applicants to select one of 12 overlapping three-month blocks in which to be tested (e.g., April/May/June, June/July/August). The application includes a photo ID form that must be certified by an official at your medical school to verify your enrollment. Your eligibility is re-verified prior to your scheduled test date. After the NBME processes your application, it will send you a fluorescent orange slip of paper called a scheduling permit.

The scheduling permit you receive from the NBME will contain your USMLE identification number, the eligibility period in which you may take the exam, and two unique numbers. One of these is known as your "scheduling number." You must have this number to make your exam appointment with Sylvan. The other number is known as the "candidate identification number." An examinee must enter their candidate identification number at the Sylvan workstation to access their exam. Sylvan has no access to the codes in advance. **Do not lose your permit!** You will not be allowed to take the boards unless you present this permit along with a photo identification with your signature. Make sure the name on your photo ID exactly matches the name appearing on your scheduling permit.

Test scheduling is on a "first-come, first-served" basis. It's important to call and schedule an exam date as soon as you receive your scheduling permit.

Once you receive your scheduling permit, you may call the Sylvan toll-free number to arrange a time to take the exam. Although requests for taking the exam may be completed more than six months before the test date, examinees will not receive their scheduling permits earlier than six months before the eligibility period. The eligibility period is the three-month period you have chosen to take the exam. Most medical students choose the May–July or June–August period. Because exams are scheduled on a "first-come, first-served" basis, it is recommended that you telephone Sylvan as soon as you have received your permit. After you've scheduled your exam, it's a good idea to confirm your exam appointment with Sylvan at least one week prior to your test date. Sylvan does not provide written confirmation of exam date, time, or location. Be sure to read the *2000 USMLE Bulletin of Information* for further details.

Register six months in advance for seating and scheduling preference.

When Should I Register for the Exam?

Although there are no deadlines for registering for Step 1, you should plan to register at least six months ahead of your desired test date. This will guarantee that you will get either your STC of choice or one within a 50-mile radius of your first choice. You will also be guaranteed a scheduled date within two weeks of your desired test date. For most US medical students, the desired date is in June, since most medical school curricula for the second year end in May or June. Thus, US medical students should plan to register before January for a June test date. For International Medical Graduates (IMGs), the timing of the exam is more flexible, as it is related only to when they finish exam preparations.

Choose your three-month eligibility period wisely. If you need to reschedule outside your initial three-month period, you must submit a new application along with another $340 application fee.

Where Can I Take the Exam?

There are two general locations available for taking the new computerized exam:

- **Sylvan Technology Centers.** If you register early, you can take the exam at your preferred site or at the next-closest testing center within a 50-mile radius. Note that there is a difference between Sylvan Learning Centers (SLCs) and Sylvan Technology Centers (STCs). Sylvan Technology Centers are add-on centers to the Sylvan Learning Centers. In other words, STCs cannot exist without an SLC, but not every SLC has an STC. The USMLE will be offered only at SLCs with an STC.

- **Medical schools.** The NBME has authorized a limited number of medical schools to serve as non-Sylvan testing centers. This means that some medical schools will dedicate some of their own computer resources for the administration of the new computer exam. Due to costs and limited resources, these sites will be limited (especially initially). Check with your student affairs office to find out if your school is administering USMLE.

Your testing location is arranged with Sylvan when you call for your test date (after you receive your scheduling permit). For a list of Sylvan locations nearest you, contact www.sylvanprometric.com.

How Long Will I Have to Wait Before I Get My Scores?

The USMLE is striving toward having scores ready for mailing two weeks after the examinee's test date. This time frame should be in place for 2000. Official information concerning the time required for score reporting is posted on the USMLE website.

What Did Other Students Like/Dislike About the CBT Format?

Feedback from students about the CBT format has been overwhelmingly positive. Students note that the testing environment was not as stressful as imagined and add that they enjoyed the test's point-and-click simplicity. "It's nice to be able to work at your own pace and take breaks whenever you want," commented one student.

Beware of the awkward lab-values screen, background noise, variable image quality, and eye strain.

Among the complaints expressed, students were most concerned with image quality, eye strain, temperature extremes (heat/cold) and background noise at the Sylvan center. Students noted that the quality of some images made it difficult to answer certain questions and that they would like to be able to enlarge images. Eye strain seemed to affect other test takers; taking a short break usually afforded relief. In addition, some students noted that the clicking of mice and keyboard chatter by other students bothered them. Earplugs helped but didn't completely block all such sounds.

What About Time?

Time is of special interest on the new CBT exam. The most critical time change, of course, lies in the consolidation of the exam into one day. Here's a breakdown of the exam schedule:

15 minutes	Tutorial (skip if familiar)
7 hours	60-minute question blocks
45 minutes	Break time (includes time for lunch)

The computer will keep track of how much time has elapsed. However, the computer will show you only how much time you have remaining in a given block. Therefore, it is up to you to determine if you are pacing yourself properly (at a rate of approximately one question per 72 seconds).

The computer will **not** warn you if you are spending more than your allotted time for a break. Taking long breaks between question blocks or for lunch may result in your not being able to take breaks later. You should budget your time so that you can take a short break when you need it and have time to eat.

Watch the clock on your break time.

You must be especially careful not to spend too much time in between blocks (you should keep track of how much time elapses from when you finish a block of questions to when you start the next block). After you finish one question block, you'll need to click the mouse when you are ready to proceed to the next block of questions.

Gain extra break time by skipping the tutorial or finishing a block early.

Forty-five minutes is the minimum break time for the day. You can gain extra break time (but not time for the question blocks) by skipping the tutorial or by finishing a block ahead of the allotted time.

For security reasons, digital watches are not allowed. This means that only analog watches are permitted. You should therefore get used to timing yourself with an analog watch so that you know exactly how much time you have left. Some analog watches come with a bevel that helps keep track of 60-minute periods. This may be useful for keeping track of break time.

If I Freak Out and Leave, What Happens to My Score?

Your scheduling permit shows a Candidate Identification Number (CIN) that you will enter onto your computer screen to start your exam. Entering the CIN is the same as breaking the seal on a test book, and you are considered to have started the exam. However, no score will be reported if you do not complete the exam. In fact, if you leave at any time from the start of the test to the last block, no score will be reported. However, the fact that you started but did not complete the exam will appear on your USMLE score transcript.

The exam ends when all blocks are completed or their time has expired. As you leave the testing center you receive a written test-completion notice to document your completion of the exam.

To receive an official score, you must finish the entire exam. This means that you must start and either finish or run out of time for each block of the exam. Again, if you do not complete all blocks, your exam is documented as an incomplete attempt and no score is reported.

What Types of Questions Are Asked?

Although numerous changes had to be made for the CBT format, the question types are the same as in previous years.

Nearly three-fourths of the 1999 Step 1 questions began with a description of a patient.

One-best-answer items have been the most commonly used multiple-choice format. Test takers report that every question was of this format. Most questions consist of a clinical scenario or a direct question followed by a list of five or more options. You are required to select the one best answer among the options. A number of options may be partially correct, in which case you must select the option that best answers the question or completes the statement.

How Is the Test Scored?

Each Step 1 examinee receives a score report that has the examinee's pass/fail status, two test scores, and a graphic depiction of the examinee's performance by discipline and organ system or subject area (Figs. 7A and 7B). The actual organ-system profiles reported may depend on the statistical characteristics of a given administration of the examination.

The mean Step 1 score for US medical students rose from 200 in 1991 to 215 in 1999.

For 1999, the NBME provided two overall test scores based on the total number of items answered correctly on the examination (Fig. 8). The first score, the three-digit score, was reported as a scaled score in which the mean was 215 and the standard deviation was 20. A score of 215 roughly corresponded to the 50th percentile, while a score of 235 roughly corresponded to the 85th percentile.[4] Percentile performance norms for 1995–96 were provided to medical schools and have been summarized in Figure 6. The second score scale, the two-digit score, defines 75 as the minimum passing score (equivalent to a score of 179 on the first scale). A score of 82 is equivalent to a score of 200 on the first score scale. To avoid confusion, we refer to scores using the three-digit scale with a mean of 215 and a standard deviation of 20.

In 1999, a score of 179 or higher was required to pass Step 1. Passing the CBT Step 1 is estimated to correspond to answering 55–65% of questions correctly. In 1998, 95% of all first-time test takers passed the June administration of the USMLE Step 1 (Fig. 9), up from previous years. These statistics prove it —you're much more likely to pass than fail.

Passing the CBT Step 1 is estimated to correspond to answering 55-65% of the questions correctly.

According to the USMLE, medical schools receive a listing of total scores and pass/fail results plus group summaries by discipline and organ systems. Students can withhold their scores from their medical school if they wish. Official USMLE transcripts, which can be sent on request to residency programs, include only total scores, not performance profiles.

Consult the latest USMLE publications, your medical school, or www.med-school.com for the most current and accurate information regarding the examination.

FIGURE 7A. Sample Score Report—Front Page

US·MLE
United States
Medical
Licensing
Examination™

UNITED STATES MEDICAL LICENSING EXAMINATION™

USMLE Step 1 is administered to students and graduates of U.S. and Canadian medical schools by the
NATIONAL BOARD OF MEDICAL EXAMINERS® (NBME®)
3750 Market Street, Philadelphia, Pennsylvania 19104-3190.
Telephone: (215) 590-9700

STEP 1 SCORE REPORT

Schmoe, Joe T
Anytown, CA 12345

USMLE ID: 1-234-567-8
Test Date: June 1999

The USMLE is a single examination program for all applicants for medical licensure in the United States; it replaces the Federation Licensing Examination (FLEX) and the certifying examinations of the National Board of Medical Examiners (NBME Parts I, II and III). The program consists of three Steps designed to assess an examinee's understanding of and ability to apply concepts and principles that are important in health and disease and that constitute the basis of safe and effective patient care. Step 1 is designed to assess whether an examinee understands and can apply key concepts of the basic biomedical sciences, with an emphasis on principles and mechanisms of health, disease and modes of therapy. The inclusion of **Step 1** in the USMLE sequence is intended to ensure mastery of not only the basic medical sciences undergirding the safe and competent practice of medicine in the present, but also the scientific principles required for maintenance of competence through lifelong learning. Results of the examination are reported to medical licensing authorities in the United States and its territories for use in granting an initial license to practice medicine. The two numeric scores shown below are equivalent; each state or territory may use either score in making licensing decisions. These scores represent your results for the administration of Step 1 on the test date shown above.

PASS	This result is based on the minimum passing score set by USMLE for Step 1. Individual licensing authorities may accept the USMLE-recommended pass/fail result or may establish a different passing score for their own jurisdictions.
215	This score is determined by your overall performance on Step 1. For recent administrations, the mean and standard deviation for first-time examinees from U.S. and Canadian medical schools are approximately 215 and 20, respectively, with most scores falling between 170 and 250. A score of 179 is set by USMLE to pass Step 1. The standard error of measurement (SEM)‡ for this scale is four points.
85	This score is also determined by your overall performance on the examination. A score of 82 on this scale is equivalent to a score of 200 on the scale described above. A score of 75 on this scale, which is equivalent to a score of 179 on the scale described above, is set by USMLE to pass Step 1. The SEM‡ for this scale is one point.

‡Your score is influenced both by your general understanding of the basic biomedical sciences and the specific set of items selected for this Step 1 examination. The SEM provides an estimate of the range within which your scores might be expected to vary by chance if you were tested repeatedly using similar tests.

121JP452

NOTE: Original score report has copy-resistant watermark.

FIGURE 6. Past Score to Percentile Conversion[5]

Three-Digit Score	95/96 Norms* (% ile)
248	99
244	97
240	94
235	90
230	83
225	75
220	67
215	58
210	48
205	40
200	31
195	24
190	19
185	14
180	10
176	**7**
170	5
165	3
160	2
156	2
154	1

* 1995/1996 US and Canadian 1st-time takers

What Does My Score Mean?

In May 1999, the NBME decided to eliminate the percentile correlation with Step 1 scores. This is because the exam uses a content-based standard for setting the passing score—theoretically, 100% could pass or fail. Since the exam is content-based and primarily intended to be used for determining minimal licensing standards, the NBME decided that providing percentiles only perpetuates the misuse of these scores as a cutoff for residency programs.

As a student, the most important point with the Step 1 score is passing versus failing. Passing essentially means, "Hey you're on your way to becoming a fully licensed doc."

FIGURE 7B. Sample Score Report—Back Page

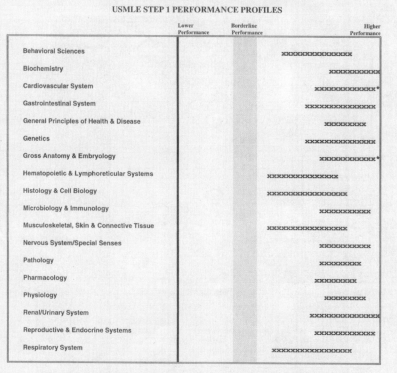

INFORMATION PROVIDED FOR EXAMINEE USE ONLY

The Performance Profile below is provided solely for the benefit of the examinee.
These profiles are developed as assessment tools for examinees only and will not be reported or verified to any third party.

USMLE STEP 1 PERFORMANCE PROFILES

	Lower Performance	Borderline Performance	Higher Performance
Behavioral Sciences			xxxxxxxxxxxxxxxx
Biochemistry			xxxxxxxxxxxx
Cardiovascular System			xxxxxxxxxxxxxx*
Gastrointestinal System			xxxxxxxxxxxxxxxx
General Principles of Health & Disease			xxxxxxxxx
Genetics			xxxxxxxxxxxxxxxx
Gross Anatomy & Embryology			xxxxxxxxxxxxx*
Hematopoietic & Lymphoreticular Systems			xxxxxxxxxxxxxxxx
Histology & Cell Biology			xxxxxxxxxxxxxxxxxx
Microbiology & Immunology			xxxxxxxxxxx
Musculoskeletal, Skin & Connective Tissue			xxxxxxxxxxxxxxxxxx
Nervous System/Special Senses			xxxxxxxxxxx
Pathology			xxxxxxxxx
Pharmacology			xxxxxxxxx
Physiology			xxxxxxxxx
Renal/Urinary System			xxxxxxxxxxxxxxxx
Reproductive & Endocrine Systems			xxxxxxxxxxxxxx
Respiratory System			xxxxxxxxxxxxxxxxxx

The above Performance Profile is provided to aid in self-assessment. The shaded area defines a borderline level of performance for each content area; borderline performance is comparable to a HIGH FAIL/LOW PASS on the total test.

Performance bands indicate areas of relative strength and weakness. Some bands are wider than others. The width of a performance band reflects the precision of measurement: narrower bands indicate greater precision. An asterisk indicates that your performance band extends beyond the displayed portion of the scale. Small differences in the location of bands should not be over interpreted. If two bands overlap, the performance in the associated areas should not be interpreted as significantly different.

This profile should not be compared to those from other Step 1 administrations.

Additional information concerning the topics covered in each content area can be found in the *USMLE Step 1 General Instructions, Content Description and Sample Items.*

452JP121

Beyond that, the main point of having a quantitative score is to give you a sense of how you've done beyond the fact that you've passed the exam. The two-digit or three-digit score compares how you have done relative to the content on the exam.

Since the content of the exam is what drives the score, the profile of the exam is what stays similar over the years. That is to say that each exam profile includes a certain number of "very hard" questions along with "medium" and "easy" ones. The questions vary, but the profile of the exam doesn't change much. This ensures that someone who scored 200 on the boards yesterday achieved a similar level of knowledge as the person who scored 200 four years ago.

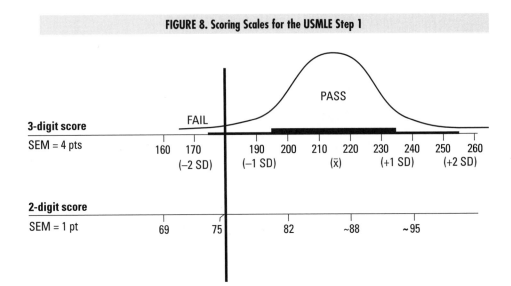

FIGURE 8. Scoring Scales for the USMLE Step 1

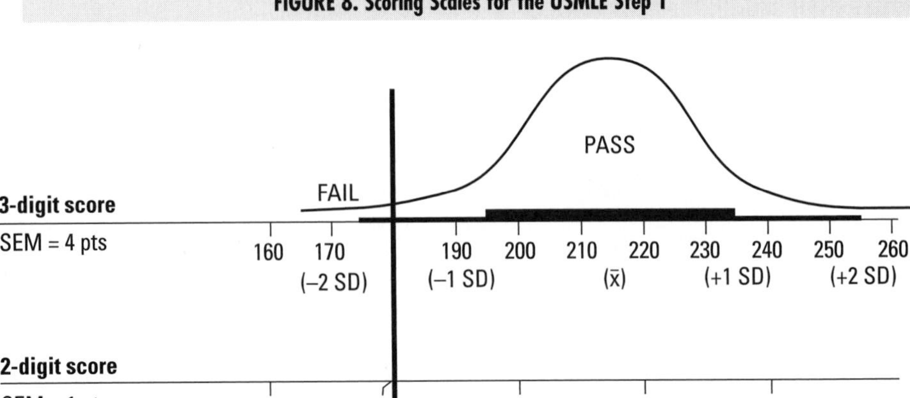

NBME/USMLE Publications

We strongly encourage students to use the free materials provided by the testing agencies (see p. 39), to study in detail the following NBME publications, and to retain them for future reference:

- *USMLE Step 1 2000 Computer-based Content and Sample Test Questions* (information given free to all examinees)

FIGURE 9. Passing Rates for 1998 USMLE Step 1[7]

	June 1998		October 1998		Total 1998	
	No. Tested	Passing (%)	No. Tested	Passing (%)	No. Tested	Passing (%)
NBME-Registered Examinees						
First-Time Takers	16,095	95	916	83	17,011	94
Repeaters	789	50	989	52	1,778	51
NBME Total	**16,884**	**93**	**1905**	**67**	**18,789**	**90**
ECFMG*-Registered Examinees						
First-Time Takers	8,392	66	5,204	56	13,596	62
Repeaters	6,479	33	4,167	30	10,646	32
ECFMG Total	**14,871**	**52**	**9,371**	**45**	**24,242**	**49**

* Educational Commission for Foreign Medical Graduates.

- *USMLE 2000 Bulletin of Information* (information given free to all examinees)
- USMLE CD-ROM
- USMLE website (http://www.usmle.org)

The *USMLE Step 1 2000 Content Description and Sample Test Questions* booklet contains approximately 150 questions that are similar in format and content to the questions on the actual USMLE Step 1. This practice test is one of the better methods for assessing your test-taking skills. However, it is not a computerized simulation and does not contain enough questions to simulate the full length of the examination, and its content represents a very limited sampling of the basic science material that may be covered on Step 1. Most students felt that the questions on the actual 1999 exam were more challenging than those contained in this booklet. Other students report encountering a few near-duplicates of these questions on the actual Step 1. Presumably, these are "experimental" questions, but who knows! Bottom line: Know these questions!

The extremely detailed, 20-page *Step 1 Content Outline* provided by the USMLE has not proved useful for students studying for the exam. The USMLE even states that ". . . the content outline is not intended as a guide for curriculum development or as a study guide."[6] We concur with this assessment.

The *USMLE 2000 Bulletin of Information* booklet accompanies application materials for the USMLE. This publication contains detailed procedural and policy information regarding the CBT, including descriptions of all three Steps, scoring of the exams, reporting of scores to medical schools and residency programs, procedures for score rechecks and other inquiries, policies for irregular behavior, and test dates.

The NBME offers test information and sample questions on a free USMLE web-based CD-ROM. The CD-ROM can run on Mac- or Windows-based computers. The CD-ROM includes 150 questions each for Step 1 and Step 2 of the USMLE, presented in a format that simulates actual exam questions. The sample test questions, however, must be downloaded to your computer and will run *only* on a Windows platform. These sample exam blocks can give you your best glimpse into the new computerized format. There is a separate CD for Step 3 that includes sample test questions as well as several computer-based case simulations.

The CD-ROM also comes with written instructions similar to those found in the NBME's print publications. In addition, it includes an electronic edition of the *USMLE 2000 Bulletin*, relevant website links, and information on test accommodations, scheduling, taking the test, STCs, and specific information for both US students and IMGs. All files are available for output to a printer.

Additional resources include the USMLE website, which contains up-to-date test information such as announcements regarding pass/fail standards and CBT. It is located at **http://www.nbme.org** or at **http://www.usmle.org.**

Still other publications may supplement the resources listed above. For example, the now-out-of-print *Retired NBME Basic Medical Sciences (Part I) Test Items* contains nearly 1000 "retired" questions, the content of which still may reappear on the new USMLE Step 1. This publication allows you to assess your performance on basic science topics as well as to identify potential areas of weakness. The retired test items include old NBME Part I questions of the K (multiple true/false) and C (A/B/both/neither) variety, neither of which appears on the USMLE Step 1. Although these question types are not found on the current version of the boards, the **content** of these questions is still relevant.

Another out-of-print NBME publication that may prove useful to students preparing for the USMLE Step 1 is the *Self-Test in the Part I Basic Medical Sciences*, which contains 630 questions drawn from the old NBME Part I item pool. It can be used in the same way as the *Retired NBME Basic Medical Sciences (Part I) Test Items*. There is some overlap in content between the two publications. Unfortunately, these question booklets are **no longer available from the NBME,** and the NBME does not grant permission to reprint these publications to individuals, medical schools, or organizations.[9] Some medical schools, however, still have old copies of these booklets available for their students. Ideally, a copy should be placed on reserve in the medical library. Another source would be third- and fourth-year students who have saved their copies.

The original questions are becoming more difficult to find every year. However, explanatory answers to all 1623 questions in the *Retired* and *Self-Test* booklets are available as an independent publication titled *Underground Step 1 Answers to the NBME Retired and Self-Test Questions*. This book, which is designed to be read alone or as a study guide to the NBME questions, is by the same authors as *First Aid for the USMLE Step 1* and is available for $22.95 plus shipping and handling at (800) 257-7341 (see Section III for a review).

The most productive way to use these study aids is to take the practice examinations and to identify the questions you missed or answered correctly by guessing. Try some questions early on to assess your strengths and weaknesses; save some questions for the few weeks before the exam to evaluate your progress. Students often find that many missed questions originate from a limited number of seemingly trivial topics (e.g., congenital diseases involving sphingolipid synthesis). It will prove worthwhile to study these subjects thoroughly, because student experience has shown that the topics covered in these retired questions (trivial or not) remain predictors of many topics tested on the new USMLE Step 1, even though the old NBME publications no longer approximate the style of questions appearing on the current USMLE Step 1 examinations. Thus, we suggest that you study these questions only if you are able to find them easily and only if you have the time.

Although the NBME Self-Test *and* Retired Test Items *are both out of print, they remain a good source of practice content for the USMLE Step 1.*

Adaptive Testing: The Next Generation

In the near future, the NBME plans to implement computer-adaptive sequential testing (CAST) in order to customize "the difficulty of the [USMLE] to the proficiency of each examinee across various stages of the examination." Essentially, this means that an "adaptive" boards exam will use the examinee's performance on a block of questions to determine the difficulty of the block that is presented to him or her next. This will allow the exam to assess proficiency accurately using fewer questions. Unlike most standardized exams you've seen, this means that all questions will certainly not be created equal (i.e., they will not be worth the same).

CAST will be implemented but no date has been set.

When the NBME field-tested a CAST version of Step 1, its exam algorithm (Fig. 10) selected an easy, moderate, or difficult block of 60 new items based on the examinee's answers to the previous block. Highly proficient examinees tended to get progressively harder test materials, whereas less proficient examinees tended to get progressively easier test materials.

Under CAST, the difficulty of the items is directly factored into each examinee's score. The NBME claims that "this process of customizing the test difficulty to each examinee's proficiency increases the overall accuracy of the scores and any related pass/fail decisions." The NBME adds, however, that although some examinees may receive more difficult blocks of questions, ". . . the score you achieve will not be affected by the difficulty of the question blocks selected for you." The NBME goes on to claim that "every examinee will be tested on equivalent content."

FIGURE 10. Simplified Schematic of CAST Algorithm

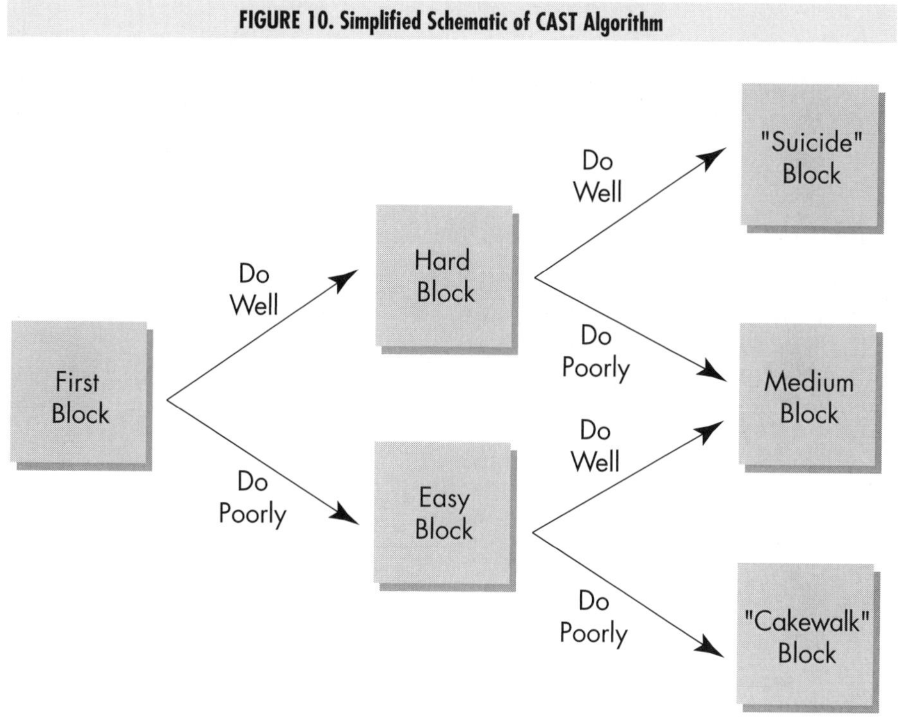

When will the new computerized USMLE be an "adaptive" exam? No one knows. After an initial CBT trial period, the NBME plans to change the exam to a CAST format, but no date has yet been set.

DEFINING YOUR GOAL

It is useful to define your own personal performance goal when approaching the USMLE Step 1. Your style and intensity of preparation can then be matched to your goal. Your goal may depend on your school's requirements, your specialty choice, your grades to date, and your personal assessment of the test's importance.

Comfortably Pass

As mentioned earlier, the USMLE Step 1 is the first of three standardized examinations that you must pass in order to become a licensed physician in the United States. Also, at many medical schools, passing the USMLE Step 1 is required before you can continue with your clinical training. The NBME, however, feels that medical schools should not use Step 1 as the sole determinant of advancement to the third year.[10] If you are headed for a "non-competitive" residency program and you have consulted advisers and fourth-year medical students in your area of interest, you may feel comfortable with this approach. Obviously, however, aiming for a 179 is a risky way to "comfortably pass" the exam.

Fourth-year medical students have the best feel for how Step 1 scores factor into residency applications.

Beat the Mean

Although the NBME warns against the misuse of examination scores to evaluate student qualifications for residency positions, some residency program directors continue to use Step 1 scores to screen applicants. Thus, many students feel it is important to score higher than the national average.

Internship and residency programs vary greatly in requesting scores. Some simply request your pass/fail status, whereas others ask for your total score. Some programs have even been known to request a photocopy of your score report to determine how well you performed on individual sections; however, this is unusual. It is unclear how the continuing changes in the USMLE Step 1 examination and score reporting will affect the application process for residency programs. The best sources of bottom-line information are fourth-year medical students who have recently completed the residency application process.

Several years ago, *First Aid for the USMLE Step 1* conducted a small, informal post-Match survey of fourth-year medical students at several US medical schools on the use of Step 1 scores. The results are summarized in Figure 11. Use this information only as a rough guide for goal-setting. Trends in certain specialties are evolving rapidly (see also Le, Bhushan, Amin: *First Aid for the Match*, and Iserson: *Getting into Residency*).

FIGURE 11. Informal Post-Match Survey: Step 1 Goals*

Comfortably Pass	Beat the Mean	Ace the Exam
Pediatrics →	Emergency Medicine	Dermatology
Family Practice →	OB/GYN	ENT
Internal Medicine →	←Radiology	Orthopedics
Anesthesiology	General Surgery	←Ophthalmology
Psychiatry		

* Based on the 1995 results of 110 respondents to an informal survey distributed to US fourth-year medical students at UCSF, UCLA, the University of Louisville, and the University of Miami. Arrows indicate perceived trends from 1996: → = increasing; ← = decreasing score.

Some medical students may wish to "beat the mean" for their own personal satisfaction. For these students, there may be a psychological advantage to scoring higher than the national average.

Ace the Exam

Certain highly competitive residency programs, such as those in otolaryngology and orthopedic surgery, have acknowledged their use of Step 1 scores in the selection process. In such residency programs, greater emphasis may be placed on attaining a high score, so students who wish to enter these programs may wish to consider aiming for a very high score on the USMLE Step 1. However, use of the USMLE scores for residency selection has been criticized because neither Step 1 nor Step 2 was designed for this purpose.[12] In addition, only a subset of the basic science facts and concepts that are tested is important to functioning well on the wards. Alternatively, some students may wish to score well in order to feel a sense of mastery. High scores are particularly important for IMGs applying in all specialties.

Some competitive residency programs use Step 1 scores in their selection process.

TIMELINE FOR STUDY

Make a Schedule

After you have defined your goals, map out a study schedule that is consistent with your objectives, your vacation time, and the difficulty of your ongoing coursework (Fig. 12). Determine whether you want to spread out your study time or concentrate it into 14-hour study days in the final weeks. Then factor in your own history in preparing for standardized examinations (e.g., SAT, MCAT).

Time management is key. Customize your schedule to your goals and available time following any final exams.

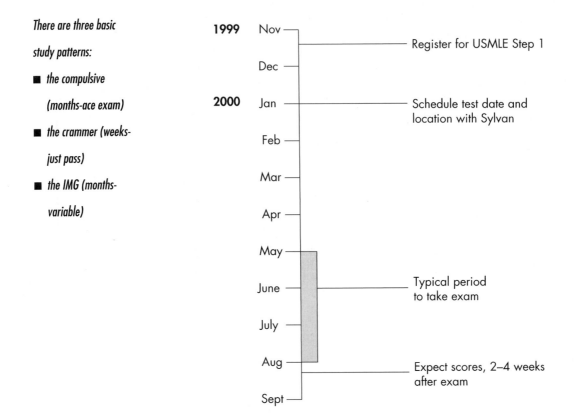

FIGURE 12. Typical Timeline for USMLE Step 1

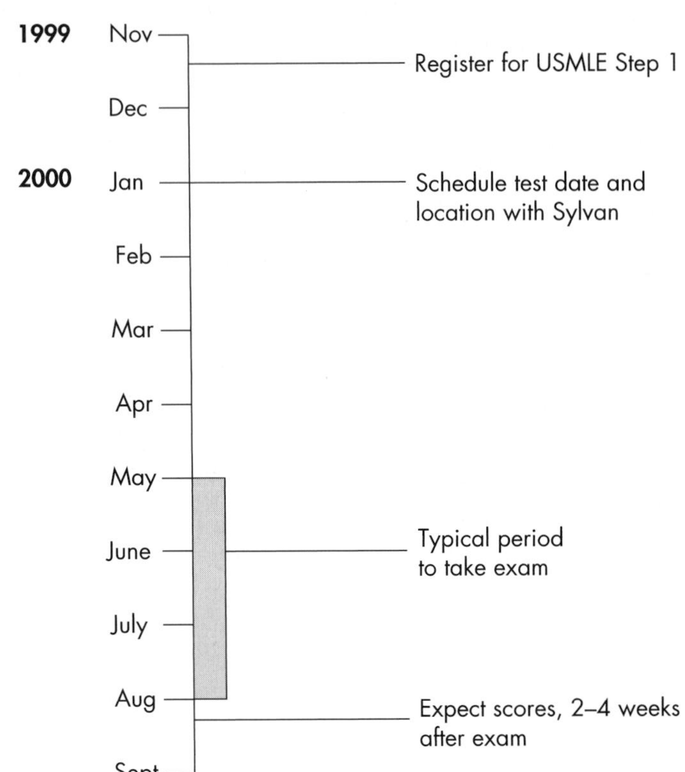

There are three basic study patterns:

- *the compulsive (months-ace exam)*
- *the crammer (weeks-just pass)*
- *the IMG (months-variable)*

"Crammable" subjects should be covered later and less crammable subjects earlier.

Another important consideration is when you will study each subject. Some subjects lend themselves to cramming, whereas others demand a substantial long-term commitment. The "crammable" subjects for Step 1 are those for which concise yet relatively complete review books are available. (See Section III for highly rated review and sample examination books.) Behavioral science and physiology are two subjects with concise review books. Three subjects with longer but quite complete review books are microbiology, pharmacology, and biochemistry. Thus, these subjects could be covered toward the end of your schedule, whereas other subjects (anatomy and pathology) require a longer time commitment and could be studied earlier. An increasing number of students report using a "systems-based" approach (e.g., GI, renal, CV) to integrate the material across basic science subjects.

Allow time in your study schedule for getting sidetracked by personal emergencies.

Practically speaking, spending a given amount of time on a crammable or high-yield subject (particularly in the last few days before the test) generally produces more correct answers on the examination than spending the same amount of time on a low-yield subject. Student opinion indicates that knowing the crammable subjects extremely well probably results in a higher overall score than knowing all subjects moderately well.

If you are having difficulty deciding when to start your test preparation, you may find the reverse-calendar approach helpful. Start with the day of the test and plan backward, setting deadlines for objectives to be met. Where the planning ends on your calendar defines a possible starting point.

Make your schedule realistic, and set achievable goals. Many students make the mistake of studying at a level of detail that requires too much time for a comprehensive review—reading Gray's Anatomy in a couple of days is not a realistic goal! Revise your schedule regularly based on your actual progress. Be careful not to lose focus. Beware of feelings of inadequacy when comparing study schedules and progress with your peers. **Avoid students who stress you out.** Focus on a few top-rated books that suit your learning style—not on some obscure books your friends may pass down to you. Do not set yourself up for frustration. Accept the fact that you cannot learn it all. Maintain your sanity throughout the process.

Avoid burnout. Maintain proper diet, exercise, and sleep habits.

You will need time for uninterrupted and focused study. Plan your personal affairs to minimize crisis situations near the date of the test. Allot an adequate number of breaks in your study schedule to avoid burnout. Maintain a healthy lifestyle with proper diet, exercise, and sleep.

Year(s) Prior

The USMLE asserts that the best preparation for the USMLE Step 1 resides in "broadly based learning that establishes a strong general foundation of understanding of concepts and principles in basic sciences."[13] We agree. Although you may be tempted to rely solely on cramming in the weeks and months before the test, you should not have to do so. The knowledge you gained during your first two years of medical school and even during your undergraduate years should provide the groundwork on which to base your test preparation. The preponderance of your boards preparation should thus involve resurrecting dormant information that you have stored away during the basic science years.

Some ways to help resurrect and integrate this information are as follows:

Buy review books early (first year) and use while studying for courses.

- Tutor first-year students during your second year.
- Review related first-year material in your second year. For example, review first-year cardiac physiology and histology while learning second-year cardiac pathology.
- At the end of each medical school course, compile and organize key tables, charts, and mnemonics into a "Step 1" binder. Then, when it comes time to study, you will have a head start with familiar high-yield material.
- Attend all "Introduction to Clinical Medicine" and "problem-based learning" classes and reviews to gain experience with clinical vignettes.
- Spend time using computer-based medical education software.

We also recommend that you buy highly rated review books early in your first year of medical school and use them as you study throughout the two years.

Review first-year material in parallel with related second-year topics.

When Step 1 comes along, the books will be familiar and personalized to the way in which you learn. It is risky to buy unfamiliar review books in the final two or three weeks.

You should talk with third- and fourth-year medical students to familiarize yourself with strengths and weaknesses in your school's curriculum. Identify subject areas in which you excel or with which you have difficulty. If you have any doubts concerning your reading speed, consider a speed-reading course. Content typically learned in the second year receives more coverage on Step 1 than do first-year topics owing to the emphasis placed on integration of basic science information across many courses.[14] Be aware of your school's testing format, and determine whether you have adequate exposure to multiple-choice and matching questions in the form of clinical vignettes.

Months Prior

Review test dates and the application procedure. In 2000, the testing for the USMLE Step 1 continues on a year-round basis (Fig. 13). Choose the most appropriate Sylvan testing site for optimal performance. Many US students simply take the exam at the closest site along with all their classmates. By contrast, a few students report a preference for traveling to more distant sites in the interests of privacy. Judge for yourself whether you find familiarity reassuring or stressful. If you have any disabilities or "special circumstances," contact the NBME as early as possible to discuss test accommodations (see p. 68, First Aid for the Student with a Disability).

Simulate the USMLE Step 1 under "real" conditions before beginning your studies.

Before you begin to study earnestly, simulate the USMLE Step 1 under "real" conditions (even down to the earplugs if you plan to use them during the real exam) to pinpoint strengths and weaknesses in your knowledge and test-taking skills. Be sure that you are well informed about the examination and that you have planned your strategy for studying. Consider what study methods you will use, the study materials you will need, and how you will obtain your materials. Some review books and software may not be available at your local bookstore, and you may have to order ahead of time to get copies (see the list of publisher contacts at the end of Section III). Plan ahead. Get advice from

FIGURE 13. 2000 USMLE Schedule

	Focus	No. of Questions/ No. of Blocks	Test Schedule Length of CBT Exam	Passing Score
Step 1	Basic mechanisms and principles	350/7	one day (eight hours)	179
Step 2	Clinical diagnosis and disease pathogenesis	400/8	one day (nine hours)	170
Step 3	Clinical management	—	two days (16 hours)	177 or 75

third- and fourth-year medical students who have recently taken the USMLE Step 1. There might be strengths and weaknesses in your school's curriculum that you should take into account in deciding where to focus your efforts. You might also choose to share books, notes, and study hints with classmates. That is how this book began.

Three Weeks Prior

Two to four weeks before the examination is a good time to resimulate the USMLE Step 1. You may want to do this earlier depending on the progress of your review, but do not do it later, when there will be little time to remedy defects in your knowledge or test-taking skills. Make use of remaining good-quality sample USMLE test questions, and try to simulate the computerized test conditions so that you gain a fair assessment of your test performance. Consider arranging a simulation at a local STC. Recognize, too, that time pressure is increasing as more and more questions are framed as clinical vignettes. Most sample exam questions are shorter than the real thing. Focus on reviewing the high-yield facts, your own notes, picture books, and very short review books.

In the final two weeks, focus on review and endurance. Avoid unfamiliar material.

One Week Prior

Make sure you have your candidate identification number (found on your scheduling permit) and other items necessary for the day of the examination, including a driver's license or other photo identification with signature (make sure your name on your ID matches *exactly* with that on your scheduling permit), an analog watch, and possibly earplugs. Confirm the Sylvan Testing Center location and test time. Work out how you will get to the STC and what parking and traffic problems you might encounter. Visit the testing site (if possible) to get a better idea of the testing conditions. Determine what you will do for lunch. Make sure you have everything you need to ensure that you will be comfortable and alert at the test site. Some students recommend loose earplugs to muffle distracting noises, with the caveat that you must be able to hear the directions. Sylvan will provide earplugs on request. Assess your pre-exam living and sleeping arrangements. Take aggressive measures to ensure an environment fit for concentration and sufficient sleep. If you must travel a long distance to the test site, consider arriving the day before and staying overnight with a friend or at a nearby hotel (make early hotel reservations).

One Day Prior

Try your best to relax and rest the night before the test. Double-check your admissions and test-taking materials as well as comfort measures as discussed earlier so you do not have to deal with such details the morning of the exam. Do not study any new material. If you feel compelled to study, then quickly review short-term-memory material (e.g., Section II: Database of High-Yield Facts) before going to sleep (the brain does a lot of information processing at night). However, do not quiz yourself, as you may risk becoming flustered and

Ensure that you will be comfortable and alert. You must be able to think, not just regurgitate.

confused. Remember that regardless of how hard you studied, you cannot know everything. There will be things on the exam that you have never even seen before, so do not panic. Do not underestimate your abilities.

No notes, books, calculators, pagers, recording devices, or digital watches are allowed in the testing area.

Many students report difficulty sleeping the night prior to the exam. This is often exacerbated by going to bed much earlier than usual. Do whatever it takes to ensure a good night's sleep (e.g., massage, exercise, warm milk). Do not change much about your daily routine prior to the exam. Exam day is not the day for a caffeine-withdrawal headache.

Morning of the Exam

Arrive at the STC 30 minutes before your scheduled exam time. If you arrive more than half an hour late, you will not be allowed to take the test.

Wake up at your regular time and eat a normal breakfast. Drink coffee, tea, or soda in moderation, or you may end up wasting exam time on bathroom breaks. Make sure you have your scheduling permit admission ticket, test-taking materials, and comfort measures as discussed earlier. Wear loose, comfortable clothing. Plan for a variable temperature in the testing center. Remember that you will arrive early in the morning, when it may be cool, and that you will not leave until late in the afternoon, when it may be warmer. Arrive at the test site 30 minutes before the time designated on the admission ticket; however, do not come too early, as this may increase your anxiety. Seating may be assigned, but ask to be reseated if necessary; you need to be seated in an area that will allow you to remain comfortable and to concentrate. Get to know your testing station, especially if you have never been in an STC before. Adjust your chair and the monitor. Test the mouse, keyboard, lamp, dry markers, and whiteboard to make sure everything is functioning properly before the exam starts. Listen to your proctors regarding any changes in instructions or testing procedures that may apply to your test site.

Remember that it is natural (and even beneficial) to be a little nervous. Focus on being mentally clear and alert. Avoid panic. Avoid panic. Avoid panic. When you are asked to begin the exam, take a deep breath, focus on the screen, and then begin. Keep an eye on the timer. Take advantage of breaks between blocks to stretch and relax for a moment.

Certain "theme" topics tend to recur throughout the exam.

The break for lunch is an excellent opportunity to relax, reorganize your thoughts, and regain composure if you are feeling overly stressed or panicked. Some students use the break to discuss questions with classmates or to look up information. Some students even recommend reviewing theme topics during lunch. However, do what feels comfortable as time will be short. If you decide to review the morning session, do not dwell on perceived mistakes.

After the Test

Have fun and relax regardless of the outcome. Taking the test is an achievement in itself. Enjoy the free time you have before your clerkships. Expect to experience some "reentry" phenomena as you try to regain a real life. Once you have recovered sufficiently from the test (or from partying), we invite you to send us your feedback, corrections, and suggestions for entries, facts, mnemonics, strategies, book ratings, and so on (see How to Contribute, p. xvii). Sharing your experience benefits fellow medical students and IMGs.

IF YOU THINK YOU FAILED

After the test, many examinees feel that they have failed, and most are at the very least unsure of their pass/fail status. There are several sensible steps you can take to plan for the future in the event that you do not achieve a passing score. First, save and organize all your study materials, including review books, practice tests, and notes. If you studied from borrowed materials, make sure you have immediate access to them. Review your school's policy regarding requirements for graduation and promotion to the third year. About one-half of the medical schools accredited by the Liaison Committee on Medical Education require passing Step 1 for promotion to the third year, and two-thirds require passing Step 1 as a requirement for graduation.[15] Familiarize yourself with the reapplication procedures for Step 1, including application deadlines and upcoming test dates. Instead of waiting four to eight months, the CBT format allows an examinee who fails to take the exam within 60 days of the last test date. Examinees will, however, be allowed to take the exam no more than three times within a twelve-month period should they repeatedly fail.

If you pass Step 1, you are not allowed to retake the exam in an attempt to raise your score.

The performance profiles on the back of the USMLE Step 1 score report provide valuable feedback concerning your relative strengths and weaknesses (see Fig. 7B). Study the performance profiles closely. Set up a study timeline to repair defects in knowledge as well as to maintain and improve what you already know. Do not neglect high-yield subjects. It is normal to feel somewhat anxious about retaking the test. If anxiety becomes a problem, however, seek appropriate counseling.

FIGURE 14. Pass Rates for USMLE Step 1 Repeaters 1996–97[16]

Score in June	% Pass Oct. 97	% Pass Oct. 98
176–178	—	85
173–175	88	76
170–172	80	66
165–169	73	52
160–164	49	33
150–159	21	12
<150	6	0
Overall	**67**	**60**

Fifty-two percent of the NBME-registered first-time takers who failed the June 1998 Step 1 repeated the exam in October 1998. The overall pass rate for that group in October was 60%. Eighty-five percent of those scoring near the old pass/fail mark of 176 (173–176) in June 1998 passed in October. However, pass rates varied widely depending on previous performance on the June 1998 administration (Fig. 14).

Although the NBME allows an unlimited number of attempts to pass Step 1, both the NBME and the FSMB recommend that licensing authorities allow a minimum of three and a maximum of six attempts for each Step examination.[17] Again, review your school's policy regarding retakes.

IF YOU FAILED

Even if you came out of the exam room feeling that you failed, seeing that failing grade can be traumatic, and it is natural to feel upset. Different people react in different ways: For some it is a stimulus to buckle down and study harder; for others it may "take the wind out of their sails" for a few days; and for still others it may lead to a reassessment of individual goals and abilities. In some instances, however, failure may trigger weeks or months of sadness, feelings of hopelessness, social withdrawal, and inability to concentrate—in other words, true clinical depression.

If you think you are depressed, seek help. Depression is a common yet potentially disabling and at times even fatal illness. Depression is also very treatable, so you must use the same resources that you plan to offer your patients. In other words, you must seek treatment, whether from a school counselor, a psychiatrist, or a psychologist. Do not "treat" yourself with alcohol, illicit drugs, or anything else; you need the same skilled help that anyone else with this problem warrants.

Near the failure threshold, each three-digit scale point is equivalent to about 1.5 questions answered correctly.[18]

As Figure 15 shows, the majority of people who fail Step 1 the first time pass on their second attempt, especially if they were near the passing threshold. If you repeatedly fail the exam despite maximum preparation, you may need to reevaluate your goals. Seek testing and career counseling early.

STUDY METHODS

It is important to have a set of study methods for preparing for the USMLE Step 1. There is too much material to justify a studying plan that is built on random reading and memorization. Experiment with different ways of studying. You do not know how effective something might be until you try it. This is best done months before the test to determine what works and what you enjoy. Possible study options include:

- Studying review material in groups
- Creating personal mnemonics, diagrams, and tables
- Using *First Aid* as a framework on which to add notes
- Taking practice computer as well as pencil-and-paper tests (see Section III for reviews)
- Attending faculty review sessions
- Making or sharing flashcards
- Reviewing old syllabi and notes
- Making cassette tapes of review material to study during commuting time
- Playing Trivial Pursuit–style games with facts and questions
- Getting away from home for an extended period to avoid distractions and to immerse yourself in studying

Study Groups

A good study group has many advantages. It can relieve stress, organize your time, and allow people with different strengths to exchange information. Study groups also allow you to pool resources and spend less money on review books and sample tests.

There are, however, potential problems associated with study groups. Above all, it is difficult to study with people who have different goals and study paces. Avoid large, unwieldy groups. Otherwise, studying can be inefficient and time-consuming. Avoid study groups that tend to socialize more than study.

Balance individual and group study.

If you choose not to belong to a study group, it may be a good idea to find a support group or a study partner simply to keep pace with and share study ideas. It is beneficial to get different perspectives from other students in evaluating what is and is not important to learn. Do not become intimidated or discouraged by interactions with a few overly compulsive students; everyone studies and learns differently.

Mnemonics and Memorizing

Cramming is a viable way of memorizing short-term information just before a test, but after one or two days you will find that much of that knowledge has dissipated. For that reason, cramming and memorization by repetition ("brute force") in the weeks before the exam are not ideal techniques for long-term memorization of the overwhelming body of information covered in Step 1. Mnemonics are memory aids that work by linking isolated facts or abstract ideas to acronyms, pictures, patterns, rhymes, and stories—information that the mind tends to store well.[19] The best mnemonics are your own, and developing them takes work. The first step to creating a mnemonic is understanding the information to be memorized. Play around with the information and look for unique features that help you remember it. In addition, make the mnemonic as colorful, humorous, or outlandish as you can; such mnemonics are the most memorable. Effective mnemonics should link the topic with the facts in as specific and unambiguous a manner as possible. In memorizing the mnemonic, engage as many senses as possible by repeating the fact aloud or by writing or acting it out. Keep the information fresh by quizzing yourself periodically with flashcards, in study groups, and so on. Do not make the common mistake of simply rereading highlighted review material. The material may start to look familiar, but that does not mean you will be able to remember it in another context during the exam.

Developing good mnemonics takes time and work. Quiz yourself periodically. Do not simply reread highlighted material.

Review Sessions

Faculty review sessions can also be helpful. Review sessions that are geared specifically toward the USMLE Step 1 tend to be more helpful than general review sessions. By contrast, open "question and answer" sessions tend to be inefficient and not worth the time. Focus on reviews given by faculty who are knowledgeable in the content and testing format of the USMLE Step 1.

Commercial Courses

Commercial preparation courses can be helpful for some students, but they are expensive and require significant time commitment. They are often effective in organizing study material for students who feel overwhelmed in preparing for Step 1 by the sheer volume of material. Note, however, that multi-week courses may be quite intense and may thus leave limited time for independent study. Note also that some commercial courses are designed for first-time test takers while others focus on students who are repeating the examination. Still other courses focus on IMGs, who must take all three Steps in a limited time period. See Section III for summarized data and excerpted information from several commercial review courses.

STUDY MATERIALS

Quality and Cost Considerations

Although an ever-increasing number of review books and software are now available on the market, the quality of such material is highly variable. Some common problems are as follows:

In 1999, many students felt that even the top-rated sample exams did not accurately reflect the clinical focus of the actual exam.

- Certain review books are too detailed for review in a reasonable amount of time or cover subtopics that are not emphasized on the exam (e.g., a 400-page histology book).
- Many sample question books were originally written years ago and have not been adequately updated to reflect trends on the revised USMLE Step 1.
- Many sample question books use poorly written questions or contain factual errors in their explanations.
- Explanations for sample questions range from nonexistent to overly detailed.
- The available review software is of highly variable quality, may be difficult to install, and may be fraught with bugs.

Basic Science Review Books

Most review books are the products of considerable effort by experienced educators. There are, however, many such books, so you must choose which ones to buy on the basis of their relative merits. Although recommendations from other medical students are useful, many students simply recommend whatever books they used without having compared them to other books on the same subject. Do not waste time with outdated "hand-me-down" review books. Some students blindly advocate one publisher's series without considering the broad range of quality encountered within most series. Weigh different opinions against each other, read the reviews and ratings in Section III of this guide, examine the books closely in the bookstore, and choose review books carefully. You are investing not only money but also your limited study time. Do not worry about finding the "perfect" book, as many subjects simply do not have one, and different students prefer different styles.

If a given review book is not working for you, stop using it, no matter how highly rated it may be.

There are two types of review books: books that are stand-alone titles and books that are part of a series. The books in a series generally have the same style, and you must decide if that style is helpful for you. However, a given style is not optimal for every subject. For example, charts and diagrams may be the best approach for physiology and biochemistry, whereas tables and outlines may be preferable for microbiology.

You should also find out which books are up to date. Some new editions represent major improvements, whereas others contain only cursory changes. Take into consideration how a book reflects the format of the USMLE Step 1. Note that some of the books reviewed in Section III have not been updated adequately to reflect the clinical emphasis and question format of the current USMLE Step 1. Books that emphasize obscure facts and minute details tend to be less helpful for the current USMLE Step 1 because there are now fewer "picky" questions and more problem-solving questions.

Many students regret not using the same books for medical school exam review and Step 1 review.

Practice Tests

Taking practice tests provides valuable information about potential strengths and weaknesses in your fund of knowledge and test-taking skills. Some students use practice examinations simply as a means of breaking up the monotony of studying and adding variety to their study schedule, whereas other students study almost solely from practice tests. There is, moreover, a wide range of quality in available practice material, and finding good practice exams is likely to become even more complicated with the introduction of the computerized Step 1. Your best preview of the new computerized exam can be found in the practice exams on the USMLE CD-ROM. The current generation of commercial software (both freestanding and bundled with books) poorly simulates the computerized Step 1, since most of the software was developed before design specifications for the computerized exam were finalized (see section III for reviews). In addition, students report that many current practice-exam books have questions that are, on average, shorter and less clinically oriented than the current USMLE Step 1. Many Step 1 questions demand fast reading skills and application of basic science facts in a problem-solving format. Approach sample examinations and simulation software critically, and do not waste time with low-quality questions until you have exhausted better sources.

Most practice exams are shorter and less clinical than the real thing.

After taking a practice test, try to identify concepts and areas of weakness, not just the facts that you missed. Do not panic if you miss a lot of questions on a practice examination; instead, use the experience you have gained to motivate your study and prioritize those areas in which you need the most work. Use quality practice examinations to improve your test-taking skills. Analyze your ability to pace yourself so that you have enough time to complete each block of 50 questions comfortably. Practice examinations are also a good means of training yourself to concentrate for long periods of time under appropriate time pressure. Consider taking practice tests with a friend or in a small group to increase motivation while simulating more accurately the format and schedule of the real examination. Analyze the pattern of your responses to questions to determine if you have made systematic errors in answering questions. Common mistakes are reading too much into the question, second-guessing your initial impression, and misinterpreting the question.

Use practice tests to identify concepts and areas of weakness, not just facts that you missed.

Clinical Review Books

Keep your eye out for more clinically oriented review books; purchase them early and begin to use them. A number of students are turning to Step 2 books, pathophysiology books, and case-based reviews to prepare for the clinical vignettes. Examples of such books include:

- *Blueprint* clinical series (Blackwell Science)
- *PreTest Physical Diagnosis* (McGraw-Hill)
- *Washington Manual* (Little, Brown)
- *Laboratory Medicine Case Book* (Appleton & Lange)
- Various USMLE Step 2 review books

Texts, Syllabi, and Notes

Limit your use of texts and syllabi for Step 1 review. Many textbooks are too detailed for high-yield review and include material that is generally not tested on the USMLE Step 1 (e.g., drug dosages, complex chemical structures). Syllabi, although familiar, are inconsistent and often reflect the emphasis of individual faculty, which often does not correspond to that of the USMLE Step 1 boards. Syllabi also tend to be less organized and to contain fewer diagrams and study questions than do top-rated review books. In our opinion, they are often a waste of time for the faculty to write and suboptimal for the student to read (when compared with the best review books). Make sure that your instructors are aware of the best books, and supplement your classes with case-based problem-solving curricula that reflect the current exam format. Your class notes have the advantage of presenting material in the way you learned it but suffer from the same disadvantages as syllabi.

When using texts or notes, engage in active learning by making tables, diagrams, new mnemonics, and conceptual associations whenever possible. Supplement incomplete or unclear material with reference to other appropriate textbooks. Keep a good medical dictionary at hand to sort out definitions.

GENERAL STUDY STRATEGIES

The USMLE Step 1 was created according to an integrated outline that organizes basic science material in a multidisciplinary approach. Broad-based knowledge is now more important than it was in the exams of prior years. The exam is designed to test basic science material and its application to clinical situations. A little over half of the questions include clinical situations, although some are brief. Some useful studying guidelines are as follows:

- Be familiar with the CBT tutorial. This will give you 15 minutes of extra break time.
- Use computerized practice tests in addition to paper exams.
- Consider doing a simulated test at a Sylvan center.
- Practice taking 60 questions in one-hour bursts.
- Be familiar with the Windows environment.
- Consider scheduling a light rotation for your first clinical block in case you get a test date later than you expected.

Familiarize yourself with the commonly tested normal laboratory values.

In spite of the change in the organization of the subject matter, the detailed Step 1 content outline provided by the USMLE has not proved useful for students. We feel that it is still best to approach the material along the lines of the seven traditional disciplines. In Section II, we provide suggestions on how to approach the material within each subject.

Practice questions that include case histories or descriptive vignettes are critical in preparing yourself for the clinical slant of the USMLE Step 1. The normal lab values provided on the computerized test are difficult to use and access. It's worth knowing the commonly encountered values so that you can answer questions faster. For this purpose, please refer to the table of high-yield lab values (see Fig. 15).

Practice questions that include case histories or descriptive vignettes are critical for Step 1 preparation.

TEST-TAKING STRATEGIES

Your test performance will be influenced by both your fund of knowledge and your test-taking skills. You can increase your performance by considering each of these factors. Test-taking skills and strategies should be developed and perfected well in advance of the test date so that you can concentrate on the test itself. We suggest that you try the following strategies to see if they might work for you.

Pacing

You have seven hours to complete 350 questions (down from 720). Note that each one-hour block can contain 50 questions. This works out to about 72 seconds per question. NBME officials note that time was not an issue for most takers of the CBT field test. However, pacing errors in the past have been

Practice and perfect test-taking skills and strategies well before the test date.

FIGURE 15. High-Yield Laboratory Values

* = Included in the Biochemical Profile (SMA-12)

Blood, Plasma, Serum	Reference Range	SI Reference Intervals
* Alanine aminotransferase (ALT, GPT at 30°C)	8–20 U/L	8–20 U/L
Amylase, serum	25–125 U/L	25–125 U/L
* Aspartate aminotransferase (AST, GOT at 30°C)	8–20 U/L	8–20 U/L
Bilirubin, serum (adult)		
Total // Direct	0.1–1.0 mg/dL // 0.0–0.3 mg/dL	2–17 μmol/L // 0–5 μmol/L
* Calcium, serum (Total)	8.4–10.2 mg/dL	2.1–2.8 mmol/L
* Cholesterol, serum	140–250 mg/dL	3.6–6.5 mmol/L
* Creatinine, serum (Total)	0.6–1.2 mg/dL	53–106 μmol/L
Electrolytes, serum		
Sodium	135–147 mEq/L	135–147 mmol/L
Chloride	95–105 mEq/L	95–105 mmol/L
* Potassium	3.5–5.0 mEq/L	3.5–5.0 mmol/L
Bicarbonate	22–28 mEq/L	22–28 mmol/L
Gases, arterial blood (room air)		
P_{O_2}	75–105 mm Hg	10.0–14.0 kPa
P_{CO_2}	33–44 mm Hg	4.4–5.9 kPa
pH	7.35–7.45	[H+] 36–44 nmol/L
* Glucose, serum	Fasting: 70–110 mg/dL	3.8–6.1 mmol/L
	2-h postprandial: < 120 mg/dL	< 6.6 mmol/L
Growth hormone - arginine stimulation	Fasting: < 5 ng/mL	< 5 μg/L
	provocative stimuli: > 7 ng/mL	> 7 μg/L
Osmolality, serum	275–295 mOsmol/kg	275–295 mOsmol/kg
* Phosphatase (alkaline), serum (p-NPP at 30°C)	20–70 U/L	20–70 U/L
* Phosphorus (inorganic), serum	3.0–4.5 mg/dL	1.0–1.5 mmol/L
* Proteins, serum		
Total (recumbent)	6.0–7.8 g/dL	60–78 g/L
Albumin	3.5–5.5 g/dL	35–55 g/L
Globulins	2.3–3.5 g/dL	23–35 g/L
* Urea nitrogen, serum (BUN)	7–18 mg/dL	1.2–3.0 mmol urea/L
* Uric acid, serum	3.0–8.2 mg/dL	0.18–0.48 mmol/L
Cerebrospinal Fluid		
Glucose	40–70 mg/dL	2.2–3.9 mmol/L
Hematologic		
Erythrocyte count	Male: 4.3–5.9 million/mm^3	4.3–5.9 × 10^{12}/L
	Female: 3.5–5.5 million/mm^3	3.5–5.5 × 10^{12}/L
Hematocrit	Male: 41–53%	0.41–0.53
	Female: 36–46%	0.36–0.46
Hemoglobin, blood	Male: 13.5–17.5 g/dL	2.09–2.71 mmol/L
	Female: 12.0–16.0 g/dL	1.86–2.48 mmol/L
Hemoglobin, plasma	1–4 mg/dL	0.16–0.62 μmol/L

FIGURE 15. High-Yield Laboratory Values (*continued*)

Blood, Plasma, Serum	Reference Range	SI Reference Intervals
Hematologic (*continued*)		
Leukocyte count and differential		
Leukocyte count	4500–11,000/mm^3	4.5–11.0 × 10^9/L
Segmented neutrophils	54–62%	0.54–0.62
Band forms	3–5%	0.03–0.05
Eosinophils	1–3%	0.01–0.03
Basophils	0–0.75%	0–0.0075
Lymphocytes	25–33%	0.25–0.33
Monocytes	3–7%	0.03–0.07
Mean corpuscular hemoglobin	25.4–34.6 pg/cell	0.39–0.54 fmol/cell
Platelet count	150,000–400,000/mm^3	150–400 × 10^9/L
Prothrombin time	11–15 seconds	11–15 seconds
Reticulocyte count	0.5–1.5% of red cells	0.005–0.015
Sedimentation rate, erythrocyte	Male: 0–15 mm/h	0–15 mm/h
(Westergren)	Female: 0–20 mm/h	0–20 mm/h
Proteins, total	< 150 mg/24 h	< 0.15 g/24 h

detrimental to the performance of even highly prepared examinees. The bottom line is to keep one eye on the clock at all times! If you find yourself running out of time, fill in all remaining blanks with C or B or your favorite letter, but also click on the "mark" button for each so that you can come back to them from the item review screen.

Dealing with Each Question

In 1999, students agreed that time management is an important skill for exam success.

There are several established techniques for efficiently approaching multiple-choice questions; see what works for you. One technique begins with identifying each question as easy, workable, or impossible. Your goal should be to answer all easy questions, work out all workable questions in a reasonable amount of time, and to make quick and intelligent guesses on all impossible questions. Most students read the stem, think of the answer, and turn immediately to the choices. A second technique is to first skim the answer choices and the last sentence of the question and then read through the passage quickly, extracting only relevant information to answer the question. Try a variety of techniques on practice exams and see what works best for you.

In general, when you eliminate an incorrect choice on a question, avoid rereading it unnecessarily. Move on. If you are unsure about a choice, mark it for later review. When you think you have determined the best answer, click on it and move on.

Difficult Questions

Questions on the USMLE Step 1 require varying amounts of time to answer. Some problem-solving questions take longer than simple, fact-recall questions. Because of the exam's clinical emphasis, you may find that many of the questions appear workable but take more time than is available to you. It can be tempting to dwell on such a question for an excessive amount of time because you feel you are on the verge of "figuring it out," but resist this temptation and budget your time. Answer the question with your best guess, mark it for review, and come back to it if you have time after you have completed the rest of the questions in the block. This will keep you from inadvertently leaving any questions blank in your efforts to "beat the clock." Remember to save a few minutes at the end to make sure that all questions have been answered.

Do not dwell excessively on questions that you are on the verge of "figuring out." Make your best guess and move on.

Inevitably, there will be some questions about which you will not have a clue (i.e., impossible questions). Do not be disturbed by these questions. Guess, mark them for later review, and move on. As a medical student, you are used to scoring well on standardized examinations (otherwise you would not be in medical school), so the USMLE Step 1 may be your first experience with facing lots of questions for which you do not know the answer. Prepare yourself for this. After narrowing down the answers as best you can, have a plan for guessing so that you do not waste time. Remember that you are not expected to know all the answers.

Another reason for not dwelling too long on any one question is that certain questions may be **experimental** or may be **printed incorrectly.** Moreover, not all questions are scored. Some questions serve as "embedded pretest items" that do not count toward your overall score.[20] In fact, anywhere from 10% to 20% of exam questions have been designated as experimental on past exams.

Students have also noted several printing errors in past USMLE Step 1 examinations. The lesson here is that you should not waste too much time with ambiguous or "flawed" questions. The reason you are having difficulty with a question may lie in the question itself, not with you!

Guessing

There is **no penalty** for wrong answers. Thus, no test block should be finished with unanswered questions. A hunch is probably better than a random guess. If you have to guess, we suggest selecting an answer you recognize over one that is totally unfamiliar. Go where the money is! If you have studied the subject and do not recognize a particular answer, then it is more likely a distractor than a correct answer.

Changing Your Answer

The conventional wisdom regarding "reconsidering" answers is not to change answers that you have already marked unless there is a convincing and logical reason to do so—in other words, go with your first hunch. You can test this strategy for yourself by keeping a running total of the questions on which you seriously considered changing your answer when taking practice exams. Experience eventually tells you how strongly to trust your first hunches. Remember, with the CBT format you can go back and change answers only within the question block you're working on. Once you move to the next block, you cannot return to questions in the previous block.

Do not terminate the block too early. Carefully review your answers if possible.

Fourth-Quarter Effect (Avoiding Burnout)

Pacing and endurance are important. Practice helps develop both. Fewer and fewer examinees are leaving the examination session early. Use any extra time you might have at the end of each block to return to marked questions or to recheck your answers; you cannot add the extra time to any remaining blocks of questions or to your break time. Do not be too casual in your review or you may overlook serious mistakes. A few students report that near the end of a section they suddenly remember facts that help answer questions they had guessed on earlier.

Remember your goals, and keep in mind the effort you have devoted to studying compared with the small additional effort to maintain focus and concentration throughout the examination.

Never give up. If you begin to feel frustrated, try taking a 30-second breather. Look away from the screen, breathe deeply, and slowly count to ten. Hopefully, you can return to the exam refreshed and clear. Every point you earn is to your advantage. The difference between passing and an average score is far fewer questions than you might think—about 25% of students who failed past exams were within 15 questions of passing.

CLINICAL VIGNETTE STRATEGIES

In recent years, the USMLE Step 1 has become increasingly clinically oriented. Students polled from 1999 exams report that nearly three-fourths of the questions were presented as clinical vignettes. This change mirrors the trend in medical education toward introducing students to clinical problem solving during the basic science years. The increasing clinical emphasis of the Step 1 may be challenging to those students who attend schools with a more traditional curriculum.

The first step toward approaching the clinical vignette is not to panic. The same basic science concepts are often being tested in the guise of a clinical vignette.

What Is a Clinical Vignette?

Be prepared to read fast and think on your feet!

A clinical vignette is a short (usually paragraph-long) description of a patient, including demographics, presenting symptoms, signs, and other information concerning the patient. Sometimes this paragraph is followed by a brief listing of the important physical findings and/or laboratory results. The task of assimilating all this information and answering the associated question in the span of one minute can be intimidating. Be prepared to read fast and think on your feet. Remember that the question is often indirectly asking something you already know.

Here are two examples of vignettes that appear complex but actually ask a relatively straightforward question.

Vignette #1

A 38-year-old African-American woman visits her physician. She explains that she has been experiencing palpitations, shortness of breath, and syncopal episodes for several months. In addition to a constant feeling of impending doom, she also has episodes of dizziness without nausea or vomiting. Her sleep pattern is normal. The physician's first course of action should be to:

A) provide psychotherapy
B) treat the patient with benzodiazepines
C) perform a physical examination
D) refer the patient to a psychiatrist
E) teach the patient self-hypnosis

Answer: C. Regardless of whether a psychiatric or organic disorder is present, a history and physical examination should always be performed during the first visit. As the history is summarized in the vignette, the physical exam would be the first course of action before considering any of the other answer choices.

Vignette #2

J.B. is a seven-year-old white male who complains of a chronic, persistent cough. The cough is often elicited by physical activity or cold exposure. His mother says that she had an uncomplicated, full-term pregnancy and that the child has been healthy except for one episode of pneumonia when he was five years old. She also notes that his appetite is variable and that he frequently has light-colored and foul-smelling stool. On physical exam, his weight was 20.5 kg (25th percentile) and his height was 119.5 cm (25th percentile). His physician orders a sweat chloride test (Cook–Gibson method) and receives the following results:

Right arm	103 mEq/L
Left arm	108 mEq/L
Normal	<70 mEq/L

What is the mode of inheritance of this disorder?

A) autosomal dominant
B) autosomal recessive
C) mitochondrial
D) X-linked recessive
E) none of the above

Answer: B.

Strategy

Remember that the Step 1 vignettes usually describe diseases or disorders in their most classic presentation. Look for buzzwords or cardinal signs (e.g., malar rash for SLE or nuchal rigidity for meningitis) in the narrative history. Sometimes the data from labs and the physical exam will help you confirm or reject possible diagnoses, thereby helping you rule answer choices in or out. In some cases, they will be a dead giveaway for the diagnosis.

Step 1 vignettes usually describe diseases or disorders in their most classic presentation.

Making a diagnosis from the history and data is often not the final answer. Not infrequently, the diagnosis is divulged at the end of the vignette, after you have just struggled through the narrative to come up with a diagnosis of your own. The question instead asks about a related aspect of the diagnosed disease.

One strategy that many students suggest is to skim the questions and answer choices before reading a vignette, especially if the vignette is lengthy. This focuses your attention on the relevant information and reduces the time spent on that vignette. Sometimes you may not need much of the information in the vignette to answer the question.

Sometimes making a diagnosis is not necessary at all.

For vignette #2, consider the following approach.

1. Take a look at the question and answer choices first. We see that a diagnosis of some inherited disease will likely have to be made to answer this question.
2. As in many vignettes, the first sentence presents the patient's age, sex, and race. This information can help direct your diagnosis. For the case above, you are looking for a genetic disease in a young white male, which may already tip you off to cystic fibrosis. If you are looking for an inherited anemia, sickle-cell disease would be more likely for an African-American patient. If, by contrast, the patient were Asian or Mediterranean, then thalassemia might be more likely.
3. Next, look for the chief complaint, in this case "chronic persistent cough."

"Two-step questions" are appearing with increasing frequency on the Step 1 exam.

4. Even if the diagnosis of cystic fibrosis is not apparent at this point, fear not! The vignette further describes other classic symptoms of the disease (e.g., fat malabsorption due to pancreatic insufficiency, growth retardation, elevated sweat chloride levels).
5. Instead of asking for the diagnosis, the question asks its mode of inheritance. Questions like this one require the test taker to go beyond the first stage in the reasoning process. **These "two-step questions" are appearing with increasing frequency on the Step 1 exam.**

IRREGULAR BEHAVIOR

During 1995, more than 75 examinees were reported by proctors to be suspicious of "irregular behavior," including continuing to work after being asked to stop, taking notes, talking with other examinees, looking at other examinees, falsifying score reports, and memorizing, reproducing, and disseminating test items. If a determination of irregular behavior is made, a permanent annotation is made on the individual's USMLE record.[21] Following the June 1997 administration of the USMLE Step 1, score results were delayed several weeks due to suspected cheating.

The CBT format may be accompanied by new possible exam infractions. For example, because Sylvan will not have "potty police" or escorts to follow you to the bathroom during the exam (as in previous years), if you leave the testing area for the bathroom during a block of questions, it may be recorded as "irregular behavior." We recommend against leaving the test during a block. The blocks are only one hour in duration—a period short enough to allow an examinee to complete the section and take a break between blocks. If there is an urgent situation during an exam block, raise your hand to consult with a proctor. All designations of "irregular behavior" are reviewed on an individual basis.

TESTING AGENCIES

National Board of Medical Examiners (NBME)
Department of Licensing Examination Services
3750 Market Street
Philadelphia, PA 19104-3190
(215) 590-9700
http://www.nbme.org

Educational Commission for Foreign Medical Graduates (ECFMG)
3624 Market Street, Fourth Floor
Philadelphia, PA 19104-2685
(215) 386-5900 or (202) 293-9320
Fax: (215) 386-9196
http://www.ecfmg.org

Federation of State Medical Boards (FSMB)
400 Fuller Wiser Road, Suite 300
Euless, TX 76039-3855
(817) 571-2949
Fax: (817) 868-4099
http://www.fsmb.org

USMLE Secretariat
3750 Market Street
Philadelphia, PA 19104-3190
(215) 590-9600
http://www.usmle.org

REFERENCES

1. Bidese, Catherine M., *U.S. Medical Licensure Statistics and Current Licensure Requirements 1995*, American Medical Association, 1995 (ISBN 0899707270).
2. National Board of Medical Examiners, *2000 USMLE Bulletin of Information, 1999*, Philadelphia, 1999.
3. National Board of Medical Examiners, *Bulletin of Information and Description of National Board Examinations, 1991*, Philadelphia, 1990.
4. "Highlights of the 1999 Annual Meeting: Standard Setting System, Score Reporting and Examinee Feedback Plan, USMLE Implementation Plans," *The National Board Examiner,* Spring 1999, Vol. 38, No. 2, pp. 1–6.
5. FSMB and NBME, *1998 Step 1 General Instructions, Content Description, and Sample Items* (http://www.usmle.org/stp1norm.htm).
6. FSMB and NBME, *USMLE: 1993 Step 1 General Instructions, Content Outline, and Sample Items*, op. cit.
7. http://www.usmle.org
8. National Board of Medical Examiners, *Summary of Examinee Performance*, Philadelphia, 1996.
9. http://www.nbme.org/usmleex.htm
10. Swanson, David B., Case, Susan M., Melnick, Donald E., et al., "Impact of the USMLE Step 1 on Teaching and Learning of the Basic Biomedical Sciences," *Academic Medicine*, September Supplement 1992, Vol. 67, No. 9, pp. 553–556.
11. Iserson, K., *Getting into Residency,* Tucson, AZ, Galen Press, 1996 (ISBN 1883620104).
12. Case, Susan M., and Swanson, David B., "Validity of NBME Part I and Part II Scores for Selection of Residents in Orthopaedic Surgery, Dermatology, and Preventive Medicine," *Academic Medicine*, February Supplement 1993, Vol. 68, No. 2, pp. S51–S56.

13. FSMB and NMBE, *USMLE: 1993 Step 1 General Instructions, Content Outline, and Sample Items*, op. cit.
14. Swanson et al., op. cit.
15. "Report on 1995 Examinations," op. cit.
16. "Report on 1996 Examinations," op. cit.
17. Swanson et al., op. cit.
18. O'Donnell, M.J., Obenshain, S. Scott, and Erdmann, James B., "I: Background Essential to the Proper Use of Results of Step 1 and Step 2 of the USMLE," *Academic Medicine*, October 1993, Vol. 68, No. 10, pp. 734–739.
19. Robinson, Adam, *What Smart Students Know*, New York, Crown Publishers, 1993 (ISBN 0517880857).
20. O'Donnell et al., op. cit.
21. http://www.usmle.org

Special Situations

FIRST AID FOR THE INTERNATIONAL MEDICAL GRADUATE

International Medical Graduate (IMG) is the term now used to describe any student or graduate of a non-US or non-Canadian medical school, regardless of whether he or she is a US citizen. The old term "Foreign Medical Graduate" (FMG) was replaced because it was misleading when applied to US citizens attending medical schools outside the United States.

The IMG's Steps to Licensure in the United States

If you are an IMG, you must go through the following steps (not necessarily in this order) to become licensed to practice in the United States. You must complete these steps even if you are already a practicing physician and have completed a residency program in your own country:

- Complete the basic sciences program of your medical school (equivalent to the first two years of US medical school).
- Take the USMLE Step 1. You can do this while still in school or after graduating, but in either case your medical school must certify that you completed the basic sciences part of your school's curriculum before taking the USMLE Step 1.
- Complete the clinical clerkship program of your medical school (equivalent to the third and fourth years of US medical school).
- Take the USMLE Step 2. If you are still in medical school, your school must certify that you are within one year of graduating for you to be allowed to take Step 2.
- Take the Test of English as a Foreign Language (TOEFL) recognized by the Educational Commission for Foreign Medical Graduates (ECFMG).
- Graduate with your medical degree.
- Obtain an ECFMG certificate; to do this, candidates must accomplish the following:
  —pass Step 1 and Step 2
  —pass TOEFL or the ECFMG English Test
  —pass the Clinical Skills Assessment (CSA) if the above 3 requirements were not met as of June 30, 1998
  —have medical credentials verified by ECFMG
- Then, to receive the ECFMG certificate, you send the ECFMG a copy of your degree, which they will verify with your medical school. You may have to wait eight weeks or more for the certificate. You must have the certificate if you wish to obtain a position in an accredited residency program; some programs do not allow you to apply unless you already have this certificate.
- Apply for residency positions in your field of interest, either directly or through the National Residency Matching Program ("the Match"). To be entered into the Match, you need to have passed all the examinations necessary for ECFMG certification (i.e., Step 1, Step 2, CSA and

the English test) by a certain deadline. If you do not pass these exams by the deadline, you will be withdrawn from the Match.

- Obtain a visa that will allow you to enter and work in the United States if you are not already a US citizen or green-card holder (permanent resident).
- If required for IMGs by the state in which your residency is located, obtain an educational/training/limited medical license. Your residency program may assist you with this application. Note that medical licensing is the prerogative of each individual state, not of the federal government, and that states vary with respect to their laws about licensing (although all 50 states recognize the USMLE).
- Take USMLE Step 3 during your residency, and then obtain a full medical license. Note that as an IMG you will not be able to take Step 3 and obtain an independent license until you have completed one, two, or three years of residency, depending on which state you live in (except in the 11 states that allow IMGs to take Step 3 at the beginning of residency). However, if you live in a state that requires two or three years of residency as a prerequisite to taking Step 3, you can take Step 3 and then obtain a license in another state. Once you have a license in any state, you are permitted to practice in federal institutions such as VA hospitals and Indian Health Service facilities in any state. This can open the door to "moonlighting" opportunities. For details on individual state rules, write to the licensing board in the state in question or contact the Federation of State Medical Boards (FSMB; see below).
- Complete your residency and then take the appropriate specialty board exams in order to become board certified (e.g., in internal medicine or surgery). If you already have a specialty certification in your home country (e.g., in surgery or cardiology), some specialty boards may grant you six months' or one year's credit toward your total residency time.
- Currently, many residency programs are accepting applications through ERAS (Electronic Residency Application Service). For more information, see *First Aid for the Match* or contact:

  ECFMG ERAS program
  P.O. BOX 13467
  Philadelphia, PA 19101–3467
  (215) 386-5900
  http://www.ecfmg.org/erasinfo.htm

Timing of the USMLE

For an IMG, the timing of a complete application is critical. It is extremely important that you send in your application early if you are to garner the maximum number of interview calls. A rough guide would be to complete all exam requirements by June of the year in which you wish to apply. This would translate into sending both your score sheets and your ECFMG certificate, which is imperative for an interview call, by this date.

Many IMGs also benefit from taking the USMLE Step 1 before Step 2 because a sizable portion of the Step 2 exam tests fundamental concepts of basic sciences. It should be added, however, that it is up to each candidate to arrive at his or her own time frame and to avoid procrastinating about taking these crucial tests.

USMLE Step 1 and the IMG

Developing good test-taking strategy is especially critical for the IMG.

The USMLE Step 1 is often the first—and, for most IMGs, the most challenging—hurdle to overcome. The USMLE is a standardized licensing system that gives IMGs a level playing field; it is the same exam series taken by US graduates, even though it is administered by the ECFMG rather than by the National Board of Medical Examiners (NBME). This means that pass marks for IMGs for both Step 1 and Step 2 are determined by a statistical process that is based on the scores of US medical students in 1991. In general, to pass Step 1, you will probably have to score higher than the bottom 8–10% of US and Canadian graduates. In 1998, however, only 62% of ECFMG candidates passed Step 1 on their first attempt, compared with 94% of US and Canadian medical students and graduates.

Of note, 1994–1995 data showed that USFMGs (US citizens attending non-US medical schools) performed 0.4 SD lower than IMGs (non-US citizens attending non-US medical schools). Although their overall scores were lower, USFMGs performed better than IMGs on behavioral sciences.

A good Step 1 score is key to a strong IMG application.

In general, students from non-US medical schools perform worst in behavioral science and biochemistry (1.9 and 1.5 SDs below US students) and comparatively better in gross anatomy and pathology (0.7 and 0.9 SDs below US students). Although they are derived from 1994–1995, these data may help you focus your studying efforts.

As an IMG, it is imperative to do your best on Step 1. Few if any students feel totally prepared to take Step 1, but IMGs in particular require serious study and preparation to reach their full potential on this exam. A poor score on Step 1 is a distinct disadvantage when applying for most residencies. Remember that if you pass Step 1, you cannot retake it to try to improve your score. Your goal should thus be to beat the mean, because you can then assert confidently that you have done better than average for US students. Good Step 1 scores will lend credibility to your residency application.

Do commercial review courses help improve your scores? Reports vary, and such courses can be expensive. Many IMGs decide to try the USMLE on their own first and then consider a review course only if they fail. Just keep in mind that many states require that you pass the USMLE within three attempts. (For more information on review courses, see Section III.)

USMLE Step 2 and the IMG

In the past, the Step 2 examination had a reputation for being much easier than Step 1, but this no longer seems to be the case for IMGs or US medical students. In August 1997–1998, 56% of ECFMG candidates passed Step 2 on the first attempt, compared with 95% of US and Canadian candidates. Also note that because this is a clinical sciences exam, cultural and geographic considerations play a greater role than is the case with Step 1. For example, if your medical education gave you a lot of exposure to malaria, brucellosis, and malnutrition but little to alcohol withdrawal, child abuse, and cholesterol screening, you must do some work to familiarize yourself with topics that are more heavily emphasized in US medicine. You must also have a basic understanding of the legal and social aspects of US medicine, because you will be asked questions about communicating with and advising patients.

There is a big difference between textbook learning of a language and actually being immersed in the culture that goes with it.

The English Language Test

If you did not pass the ECFMG English test by March 3, 1999, you will be required to pass the Test of English as a Foreign Language (TOEFL) to fulfill the English-language proficiency requirement for ECFMG certification. The administration date of a submitted TOEFL must be after March 3, 1999 to meet the requirement. A passing performance on the ECFMG English test taken prior to March 3, 1999, however, will continue to be accepted. For more information, check online at http://www.ecfmg.org/english.htm or www.toefl.org.

Native English-speaking IMGs are also required to take the English-language test.

Clinical Skills Assessment

Starting in June 1998, the ECFMG introduced the Clinical Skills Assessment (CSA), an interactive test with role-playing "patients," in an effort to level the disparities that existed among the more than 1400 medical schools worldwide in both curricula and educational standards. The goal of the CSA is to ensure that IMGs can gather and interpret histories, perform physical examinations, and communicate in the English language at a level comparable to that of US graduates.

The CSA simulates clinical encounters that are common in clinics, doctors' offices, and emergency departments. The test is standardized, which means that "standardized patients" (SPs)—i.e., laypeople who have been extensively trained to simulate various clinical problems—give the same responses to all candidates participating in the assessment. For quality assurance purposes, a videotape records all clinical encounters. Eleven cases are presented to the IMG that are mixed in terms of age, sex, ethnicity, organ system, and discipline. The five main areas emphasized are:

- Eye, ear, nose, throat, and musculoskeletal system
- General symptoms
- Cardiopulmonary system
- GI and GU systems
- Neuropsychiatry

Candidates are scored on only 10 of the 11 patient encounters. The non-scored encounter is added for research purposes, with results applied to future administration of the CSA.

Test Administration. Before entering a room to interact with an SP, you are given an opportunity to review preliminary information. This information, which is posted on the door of each room, includes the following:

- Patient characteristics (name, age, sex)
- Chief complaint and vitals (temperature, respiratory rate, pulse, BP)

After entering the room, you are given 15 minutes (with a warning bell sounded at 10 minutes) to perform the clinical encounter, which should include introducing yourself, obtaining an appropriate history, performing a focused clinical exam, formulating a differential diagnosis, and planning a diagnostic workup. You are expected to answer any questions the SP might ask as well as to discuss the diagnoses being considered and to advise the SP about their follow-up plans. After you leave the room, you have 10 minutes to write a patient note (PN).

"Do's and Don'ts." Ground rules for the clinical encounter are:

- Candidates are not permitted to perform rectal, pelvic/genital, or female breast exams. If a candidate feels that such examinations are warranted, he or she may suggest that they be conducted as part of the diagnostic workup.
- Candidates are not allowed to reenter a room once they have left it. It is therefore recommended that they obtain all the information they need before ending the clinical encounter.
- Time is not on the candidate's side, so it is advisable to "home in" on relevant problems and to conduct a focused clinical exam. For example, if a 40-year-old diabetic and smoker presents with chest pain, candidates should rule out problems of cardiopulmonary, gastrointestinal, and musculoskeletal origin to narrow the examination down to these systems. A CNS exam should therefore be the last one on the candidate's list in this particular example.

Scoring of the CSA. Your score will be based on the clinical encounter as a whole and on your overall communications skills.

- **Integrated Clinical Encounter (ICE) score.** The skills you demonstrate in the clinical encounter will be evaluated as follows:

1. Although SPs will not evaluate your performance, they will document your ability to gather data pertinent to the clinical encounter. Specifically, SPs will note on checklists whether you successfully obtained relevant information or correctly performed the physical exam. Your final DG score represents an average of your performance with all 10 SPs.
2. Health care professionals will score your PN according to predefined criteria, with your final PN score representing the average of your individual PN scores over all 10 clinical encounters. Your ICE score will then represent the sum of your DG and PN scores.

ICE = DG + PN

- **Communication (COM) score.** In addition to assessing your data-gathering skills, SPs will evaluate your interpersonal skills (IPS) and your proficiency in spoken English. Your IPS will be assessed on the following four criteria: rapport, interviewing skills, personal manner, and counseling. Your overall COM score is the sum of your averaged IPS scores and your spoken English proficiency rating.

The grade you receive on the CSA is either a "pass" or a "fail." The "pass" grade indicates you have met the standards set by experts for the ICE and COM. CSA scores, like those of all ECFMG tests, are mailed in six to eight weeks.

Applying for CSA. Applicants seeking to take the CSA must complete the four-part application form (Form 706—pink form) in full and mail to the ECFMG along with a $1200 registration fee. By calling (215) 386-5900 (Monday through Friday, 8 a.m. to 5:30 p.m. EST), you can have an operator help you schedule your test date. It is advisable to have several preferred dates in mind (all within one year of your notification of registration). The operator will formally schedule you on a mutually acceptable day, and your admissions permit will then be mailed to you. Alternatively, you can schedule your CSA date through the Internet at www.ecfmg.org. There is no application deadline, since the CSA is administered throughout the year (except on major US holidays).

After the ECFMG receives your fee and application form and determines that you are eligible to take the CSA, you must schedule your test date within four months and take the CSA within one year of the date indicated on your notification of registration.

Test Site Location. The CSA is administered at the following address:

ECFMG
3624 Market Street
CSA Center, 3rd Floor
Philadelphia, PA 19104-2685

If you are living outside the US, you will need to apply for a visa that will allow you lawful entry into the US in order to take the CSA. A B2 visa may be issued by a consulate. Documents that are recommended to facilitate this process include:

- The CSA admission permit and letter from ECFMG (explains why the applicant must enter the U.S.)
- Your medical diploma
- Transcripts from your medical school
- Your USMLE score sheets
- A sponsor letter or affidavit of support stating that you (if you are sponsoring yourself) or your sponsor will bear the expenses of your trip and that you have sufficient funds to meet that expense
- An alien status affidavit

Preparing for the CSA. You can prepare for the CSA by addressing common outpatient clinical issues. To improve doctor–patient communication skills, you can try "acting out" dialog with friends or relatives. Since time will be a major factor, do not forget to time the encounter as if it were a real test by giving yourself 15 minutes for data gathering and 10 minutes for the patient note. The following volumes may also be of use to you in your preparation for the CSA:

- *Manual of Family Practice*, Robert Taylor (Lippincott Williams & Wilkins)
- *Family Practice Review: Problem-Oriented Approach*, R. Swanson (Mosby)

Residencies and the IMG

It is becoming harder for IMGs to obtain residencies in the United States given the rising concerns about an oversupply of physicians in the US. Official bodies such as the Council on Graduate Medical Education (COGME) have recommended that the total number of residency slots be reduced from the current 144% of the number of US graduates to 110%. Furthermore, changes introduced in the 1996 immigration law are likely to make it much harder for noncitizens or legal residents of the US to remain in the country after completing a residency.

FIGURE 18. IMGs in the Match

IMG applicants	1998	1999
U.S. IMG citizens	1700	1821
% U.S. IMGs accepted	46%	47%
Non-U.S. citizens	7957	7977
% non-U.S. citizens accepted	31%	32%

In the residency Match, US-citizen IMG applications rose from 1700 in 1998 to 1821 in 1999, and the percentage of such IMGs accepted was 46% and 47%, an increase from 43.5% in 1997. For non-US-citizen IMGs, applications rose from 7957 in 1998 to 7977 in 1999, while the percentage accepted fell to 31% and 32%, from 34.5% in 1997. These percentages may continue to drop in the future, especially as some large hospitals that traditionally hire many IMGs (such as those in New York) cut back on their residency slots.

Visa Options for the IMG

As an IMG, you need a visa to work or train in the US unless you are a US citizen or a permanent resident (i.e, hold a green card). Two types of visas enable you to accept a residency appointment in the US: J1 and H1B. Most sponsoring residency programs (SRPs) prefer a J1 visa. Above all, this is because SRPs are authorized by the US Immigration and Naturalization Service (INS) to issue a Form IAP 66 directly to an IMG, whereas they have to go through considerable paperwork and an application to the Immigration and Labor Department to apply to the INS for an H1B visa on behalf of an IMG.

The J1 Visa. Also known as the Exchange Visitor Program, the J1 visa was introduced to give IMGs in diverse specialties the chance to use their training experience in the United States to improve conditions in their home countries. As mentioned above, the INS authorizes most SRPs to issue Form IAP 66 in the same manner that I20's are issued to regular international students in the US.

To enable an SRP to issue an IAP 66, you must obtain a certificate from the ECFMG indicating that you are eligible to participate in a residency program in the US. First, however, you must ask the Ministry of Health in your country to issue a statement indicating that your country needs physicians with the skills you propose to acquire by joining a US residency program. This statement, which must bear the seal of your country's government and must be signed by a duly designated government official, is intended to satisfy the U.S. Secretary of Health and Human Services that there is such a need. The Health Ministry in your country should send this statement to the ECFMG (or they may allow you to mail it to the ECFMG).

How can you find out if the government of your country will issue such a statement? In many countries, the Ministry of Health maintains a list of medical specialties in which there is a need for further training abroad. You can also consult seniors in your medical school. A word of caution: If you are applying for a residency in internal medicine and internists are not in short supply in your country, it may help to indicate an intention to pursue a subspecialty after completing your residency training.

The text of your statement of need should read as follows:

> Name of applicant for visa: _____________. There currently exists in _____________ (your country) a need for qualified medical practitioners in the specialty of _____________. (Name of applicant for visa) has filed a written assurance with the government of this country that he/she will return to _____________ (your country) upon completion of training in the United States and intends to enter the practice of medicine in the specialty for which training is being sought.
>
> Stamp (or seal and signature) of issuing official of named country.
> Dated____

To facilitate the issuing of such a statement by the Ministry of Health in your country, you should submit a certified copy of the agreement or contract from your SRP in the US. The agreement or contract must be signed by you and the residency program official responsible for the training.

Armed with Form IAP 66, you should go to the US consulate nearest to the residential address indicated in your passport. As for other nonimmigrant visas, you must show that you have a genuine nonimmigrant intent to return to your home country. You must also show that all your expenses will be paid.

When you enter the US, bring your Form IAP 66 along with your visa. You are usually admitted to the US for the length of the J1 program, designated as "D/S," or duration of status. The duration of your program is indicated on the IAP 66.

Duration of Participation. The duration of a resident's participation in a program of graduate medical education or training is limited to the time normally required to complete such a program. If you would like to get an idea of the typical training time for the various medical subspecialties, you may consult the *Directory of Medical Specialties*, published by Marquis Who's Who for the American Board of Medical Specialties. The authority charged with determining the duration of time required by an individual IMG is the United States Information Agency (USIA). This may change, however, because the USIA is likely to be merged into the State Department.

The maximum amount of time for participation in a training program is ordinarily limited to seven years unless the IMG has demonstrated to the satisfaction of the USIA director that his or her home country has an exceptional need for the specialty in which he or she will receive further training. The USIA director may grant an extension of stay in the event that an IMG needs to repeat a year of clinical medical training or needs time for training or education to enable him or her to take an exam required for board certification.

Requirements After Entry into the US. Each year, all IMGs participating in a residency program on a J1 visa must furnish the Attorney General of the United States with an affidavit (Form I-644) attesting that they are in good standing in the program of graduate medical education or training in which they are participating and that they will return to their home countries upon completion of the education or training for which they came to the United States.

Restrictions Under the J1 Visa. Not later than two years after the date of entry into the United States, an IMG participating in a residency program on a J1 visa is allowed one opportunity to change his or her designated program of graduate medical education or training if his or her director approves that change.

The J1 visa includes a condition called the "two-year foreign residence requirement." The relevant section of the Immigration and Nationality Act states:

> "Any exchange visitor physician coming to the United States on or after January 10, 1977, for the purpose of receiving graduate medical education or training is automatically subject to the two-year home-country physical presence requirement of section 212(e) of the Immigration and Nationality Act, as amended. Such physicians are not eligible to be considered for section 212(e) waivers on the basis of 'No Objection' statements issued by their governments."

The law thus requires that a J1 visa holder, upon completion of the training program, leave the US and reside in his or her home country for a period of at least two years. Currently there is pressure from the American Medical Association to extend this period to five years.

An IMG on a J1 visa is ordinarily not allowed to change from J1 to most other types of visas or (in most cases) to change from J1 to permanent residence while in the US until he or she has fulfilled the "foreign residence requirement." The purpose of the foreign residence requirement is to ensure that an IMG uses the training he or she obtained in the US for the benefit of his or her home country. The US government may, however, waive the two-year foreign residence requirement under the following circumstances:

- If you as an IMG can demonstrate a "well-founded fear of persecution" if forced to return to your country;
- If you as an IMG can prove that returning to your country would result in "exceptional hardship" to you or to members of your immediate family who are US citizens or permanent residents; or
- If you are sponsored by an "interested governmental agency."

Applying for a J1 Visa Waiver. IMGs who have sought a waiver based on the last alternative have found it beneficial to approach the following potentially "interested government agencies":

- **The Department of Health and Human Services (HHS).** HHS's considerations for a waiver have been as follows: (1) the program or activity in which the IMG is engaged is "of high priority and of national or international significance in an area of interest" to HHS (merely providing medical services in a medically underserved area would not be sufficient); (2) the IMG must be an "integral" part of the program or activity "so that the loss of his/her services would necessitate discontinuance of the program or a major phase of it"; and (3) the IMG "must possess outstanding qualifications, training, and experience well beyond the usually expected accomplishments at the graduate, postgraduate, and residency levels and must clearly demonstrate the capability to make original and significant contributions to the program."

In practice, HHS is more likely to recommend waivers for IMGs engaged in research than for those who treat patients. HHS waiver applications should be mailed to Joyce E. Jones, Executive Secretary, Exchange Visitor Review Board, Room 627-H, Hubert H. Humphrey Building, Department of Health and Human Services, 200 Independence Avenue, S.W., Washington, D.C. 20201.

- **The Veterans Administration (VA).** With over 170 health care facilities located in various parts of the US, the VA is a major employer of physicians in this country. In addition, many VA hospitals are affiliated with university medical centers. Unlike HHS, the VA sponsors IMGs working not only in research but also in patient care (regardless of specialty) and in teaching. The waiver applicant may engage in teaching and research in conjunction with clinical duties. The VA's latest guidelines (issued on June 22, 1994) provide that it will act as an interested government agency only when the loss of the IMG's services would necessitate the discontinuance of a program or a major phase of it and when recruitment efforts have failed to locate a US physician to fill the position.

  The procedure for obtaining a VA sponsorship for a J1 waiver is as follows: (1) the IMG should deal directly with the Human Resources Department at the local VA facility; and (2) the facility must request that the VA's chief medical director sponsor the IMG for a waiver. The waiver request should include the following documentation: (1) a letter from the director of the local facility describing the program, the IMG's immigration status, the health care needs of the facility, and the facility's recruitment efforts; (2) recruitment efforts, including copies of all job advertisements run within the preceding year; and (3) copies of the IMG's licenses, test results, board certifications, IAP 66 forms, etc.

  The VA contact person in Washington, D.C., Brian McVeigh, should be contacted by the local medical facility rather than by IMGs or their attorneys.

- **The Appalachian Regional Commission (ARC).** The ARC sponsors physicians in certain places in the eastern and southern US, namely, in the states of Alabama, Georgia, Kentucky, Maryland, Mississippi, New York, North Carolina, Ohio, Pennsylvania, South Carolina, Tennessee,

Virginia, and West Virginia. Since 1992, the ARC has sponsored approximately 200 primary care IMGs annually in counties within its jurisdiction that have been designated as Health Professional Shortage Areas (HPSA) by Health and Human Services (HHS).

In accordance with its February 1994 revision of its J1 waiver policies, the ARC requires that waiver requests be submitted initially to the ARC contact person in the state of intended employment. If the state concurs, a letter from the state's governor recommending the waiver must be addressed to Jesse J. White, Jr., the federal co-chairman of the ARC. The waiver request should include the following: (1) a letter from the facility to Mr. White stating the proposed dates of employment, the IMG's medical specialty, the address of the practice location, an assertion that the IMG will practice primary care for at least 40 hours per week in the HPSA, and details as to why the facility needs the services of the IMG; (2) a J1 Visa Data Sheet; (3) the ARC federal co-chairman's J1 Visa Waiver Policy and the J1 Visa Waiver Policy Affidavit and Agreement with the notarized signature of the IMG; (4) a contract of at least two years' duration; (5) evidence of the IMG's qualifications, including a resume, medical diplomas and licenses, and IAP 66 forms; and (6) evidence of recruitment efforts within the preceding six months. Copies of advertisements, copies of resumes received, and reasons for rejection must also be included. The ARC will not sponsor IMGs who have been out of status for six months or longer.

Requests for ARC waivers are processed in Washington, D.C. by Laura Dean Greathouse, ARC, 1666 Connecticut Avenue, N.W., Washington, D.C. 20235. ARC is usually able to forward a letter confirming that a waiver has been recommended to the USIA to the requesting facility or attorney within 30 days of the request.

- **The Department of Agriculture (USDA).** The USDA sponsors physicians who practice in family medicine, general surgery, pediatrics, obstetrics and gynecology, emergency medicine, internal medicine, and general psychiatry in rural areas. The USDA does not sponsor physicians to practice in areas located within the jurisdiction of the ARC.

For an area to be deemed "rural," the county in which the health care facility is located must have a population of less then 20,000 according to the last census. Also, the facility must be located in an HPSA. The IMG must sign a contract with a health care facility for a minimum period of three years. An IMG whose immigration status has lapsed for six months or more will not be considered for sponsorship by USDA.

Since August 1994, USDA has required that each request for a waiver be supported by a letter of concurrence ("no objection") from the Department of Health in the state of intended employment. A few states (e.g., Georgia, Mississippi, New York and Ohio) require that the USDA waiver request and accompanying documentation be submitted directly to them. If they concur with the request, they forward the entire packet together with a no-objection letter to USDA.

USDA waiver requests should be mailed to Linda Seckel, Program Manager, J1 Visa Residency Waiver Program, Bldg. 005, Room 320, BARC-West, 10300 Baltimore Blvd., Beltsville, MD 20705-2350. The current processing time is approximately four months.

- **State Departments of Public Health.** There is no application form for a state-sponsored J1 waiver. However, USIA regulations specify that an application must include the following documents: (1) a letter from the State Department of Public Health identifying the physician and specifying that it would be in the public interest to grant him a J1 waiver; (2) an employment contract that is valid for a minimum of three years and that states the name and address of the facility that will employ the physician and the geographic areas in which he or she will practice medicine; (3) evidence that these geographic areas are located within HPSAs; (4) a statement by the physician agreeing to the contractual requirements; (5) copies of all IAP 66 forms; and (6) a completed USIA Data Sheet. Applications are numbered in the order in which they are received, since only 20 physicians per year may be granted waivers in a particular state. Individual states may choose to participate or not to participate in this program. Participating states include Alabama, Alaska, Arkansas, Arizona, Delaware, Florida, Georgia, Illinois, Indiana, Iowa, Kentucky, Maine, Massachusetts, Michigan, Minnesota, Mississippi, Missouri, Nebraska, Nevada, New Hampshire, New Mexico, New York, North Carolina, North Dakota, Ohio, Oklahoma, Pennsylvania, Rhode Island, South Carolina, Vermont and Washington. Undecided states include California, Connecticut, New Jersey, Virginia and Wyoming. Nonparticipating states include Hawaii, Idaho, Kansas, Louisiana, Montana, Oregon, South Dakota, Tennessee, Texas, and Utah.

The H1B Visa. Since 1991, the law has allowed medical residency programs to sponsor foreign-born medical residents for H1B visas. There are no restrictions to changing the H1B visa to any other kind of visa, including permanent resident status (green card), through employer sponsorship or through close relatives who are US citizens or permanent residents. There was an overall ceiling of 65,000 H1B visas for professionals in all categories until mid-1998, when the number was raised to 95,000. It is advisable for SRPs to apply for H1B visas as soon as possible in the official year (beginning October 1) when the new quota officially opens up.

H1B visas are intended for "professionals" in a "specialty occupation." This means that an IMG intending to pursue a residency program in the US with an H1B visa needs to clear all three USMLE Steps before becoming eligible for the H1B. The ECFMG administers Step 1 and 2. Step 3 is conducted by the individual states. You will need to contact the FSMB or the medical board of the state where you intend to take the Step 3 for details.

USMLE Step 2 and the IMG

Basic eligibility requirements for USMLE Step 3 are as follows:

- Obtain the MD degree (or its equivalent) or a DO degree by the application deadline.
- Pass both USMLE Step 1 and Step 2 (or the equivalents). Applicants must receive notice of a passing score by the application deadline.
- Graduates of foreign medical schools should be ECFMG certified or successfully complete a "fifth pathway" program (at a date no later than the application deadline).
- Apply to the following states, which do not have postgraduate training as an eligibility requirement:

1. **California**
   Medical Board of California
   1426 Howe Ave., Suite 54
   Sacramento, CA 95825-3236
   www.medbd.ca.gov
   Phone: (916) 263-2389; Fax: (916) 263-2387
   Licensure inquiries: (916) 263-2499; (916) 263-2344

2. **Connecticut**
   Connecticut Department of Public Health
   PO Box 340308
   Hartford, CT 06134-0308
   Phone: (860) 509-7579; Fax: (860) 509-8457
   Step 3 inquiries: FSMB at (817) 571-2949

3. **Louisiana**
   Louisiana State Board of Medical Examiners
   PO Box 30250
   New Orleans, LA 70190-0250
   Phone: (504) 524-6763; Fax: (504) 568-8893

4. **Maryland**
   Maryland Board of Physician Quality Assurance
   PO Box 2571
   Baltimore, MD 21215-0095
   Phone: (410) 764-4777; Fax: (410) 764-2478
   Step 3 inquiries: (800) 877-3926

5. **Nebraska***
   Nebraska Department of Health
   PO Box 94986
   Lincoln, NE 68509-4986
   www.hhs.state.ne.us
   Phone: (402) 471-2118; Fax: (402) 471-3577
   Step 3 inquiries: FSMB at (817) 571-2949

*Nebraska requires that IMGs obtain a "valid indefinitely" ECFMG certificate.

6. **Nevada**
   Nevada State Board of Medical Examiners
   P.O. Box 7238
   Reno, NV 89510
   (702) 688-2559; Fax: (702) 688-2321
   Step 3 inquiries: FSMB at (817) 571-2949

7. **New York**
   New York State Board of Medicine
   Cultural Education Center, Room 3023
   Empire State Plaza
   Albany, NY 12230
   www.nysed.gov.opnme.html
   Phone: (518) 474-3841; Fax: (518) 473-6995

8. **Rhode Island**
   Rhode Island Board of Medical Licensure and Discipline
   Department of Health
   Cannon Building, Room 205
   Three Capitol Hill
   Providence, RI 02908-5097
   Phone: (401) 277-3855; Fax: (401) 277-2158
   Step 3 inquiries: FSMB at (817) 571-2949

9. **South Dakota**
   South Dakota State Board of Medical and Osteopathic Examiners
   1323 S. Minnesota Ave.
   Sioux Falls, SD 57105
   Phone: (605) 334-8343; Fax: (605) 336-0270
   Step 3 inquiries: FSMB at (817) 571-2949

10. **Tennessee**
    Tennessee Board of Medical Examiners
    425 5th Avenue North
    1st Floor, Cordell Hull Building
    Nashville, TN 37247-1010
    www.state.tn.us/health/downloads/dwnindex.htp
    Phone (615) 532-4384; Fax: (615) 532-5369
    Step 3 inquiries: FSMB at (817) 571-2949

11. **Utah**
    Utah Department of Commerce
    Division of Occupational & Professional Licensure
    PO Box 146741
    Salt Lake City, UT 84114-6741
    Phone: (801) 530-6628; Fax: (801) 530-6511

12. **West Virginia**
    West Virginia Board of Medicine
    101 Dee Dr.
    Charleston, WV 25311
    Phone (304) 558-2921; Fax: (304) 723-2877

H1B Application. An application for an H1B visa is not filed by the intending immigrating professional but by his or her employment sponsor—in your case, by the SRP in the US. If an SRP is willing to do so, you will be told about it at the time of your interview for the residency program.

Before filing an H1B application with the INS, an SRP must file an application with the US Labor Department affirming that the SRP will pay at least the normal salary for your job that a US professional would earn. After receiving approval from the Labor Department, your SRP should be ready to file the H1B application with the INS. The SRP's supporting letter is the most important part of the H1B application package; it must describe the job duties to make it clear that the physician is needed in a "specialty occupation" (resident) under the prevalent legal definition of that term.

Most SRPs prefer to issue an IAP 66 for a J1 visa rather than filing papers for an H1B visa, because of the burden of paperwork and the attorney costs involved in securing approval of an H1B visa application. Even so, a sizable number of SRPs are willing to go through the trouble, particularly if an IMG is an excellent candidate or if the SRP concerned finds it difficult to fill all the available residency slots (although this is becoming rarer with continuing cuts in residency slots). If an SRP is unwilling to file for an H1B visa because of attorney costs, you could suggest that you would be willing to bear the burden of such costs. The entire process of getting an H1B visa can take anywhere from 10 to 20 weeks.

Although an H1B visa can be stamped by any US consulate abroad, it is advisable to have it stamped at the US consulate where you first applied for a visitor visa to travel to the US for interviews.

Summary. Despite some significant obstacles, a number of viable methods are available to IMGs who seek to pursue a residency program or eventually practice medicine in the US.

There is no doubt that the best alternative for IMGs is to obtain H1B visas to pursue their medical residencies. However, in cases where an IMG joins a residency program with a J1 visa, there are some possibilities of obtaining waivers of the two-year foreign residency requirement, particularly for those who are willing to make a commitment to perform primary care medicine in medically underserved areas.

Resources for the IMG

- ECFMG
  3624 Market Street, Fourth Floor
  Philadelphia, PA 19104-2685
  (215) 386-5900 or (202) 293-9320
  Fax: (215) 386-9196
  http://www.ecfmg.org

The ECFMG telephone number is answered only between 9:00 AM and 12:30 PM and between 1:30 PM and 5:00 PM Monday through Friday EST. The ECFMG often takes a long time to answer the phone, which is frequently busy at peak times of the year, and then gives you a long voice-mail message, so it is better to write or fax early than to rely on a last-minute phone call. Do not contact the NBME, as all IMG exam matters are conducted by the ECFMG. The ECFMG also publishes the *Handbook for Foreign Medical Graduates and Information Booklet* on ECFMG certification and the USMLE program, which gives details on the dates and locations of forthcoming USMLE, CSA, and English tests for IMGs together with application forms. It is free of charge and is also available from the public affairs offices of US embassies and consulates worldwide, as well as from Overseas Educational Advisory Centers. Single copies of the handbook may also be ordered by calling (215) 386-5900, preferably on weekends or between 6 PM and 6 AM Philadelphia time, or by faxing to (215) 387-9963. Requests for multiple copies must be made by fax or mail on organizational letterhead. The full text of the booklet is also available on the ECFMG's website at http://www.ecfmg.org.

- Federation of State Medical Boards
  400 Fuller Wiser Road, Suite 300
  Euless, TX 76039-3855
  (817) 868-4000
  Fax: (817) 868-4099

  The FSMB publishes Exchange, Section I, which gives detailed information on examination and licensing requirements in all US jurisdictions. The 1996–1997 edition costs $25. (Texas residents must add 7.75% state sales tax.) To obtain publications, write to Federation Publications at the above address. All orders must be prepaid by a personal check drawn on a US bank, a cashier's check, or a money order payable to the Federation. Foreign orders must be accompanied by an international money order or the equivalent, payable in US dollars through a US bank or a US affiliate of a foreign bank. For Step 3 inquiries, the telephone number is (817) 868-4000, and the fax number is (817) 868-4099. The FSMB has a home page at http://www.fsmb.org.

- United States Information Agency
  301 4th Street, S.W.
  Washington, D.C. 20547
  (202) 619-6531
  http://www.ecfmg.org/evspusia.htm

  This website summarizes the Agency's policy regarding various program administration issues arising from the pursuit of graduate medical education or training in the U.S. by foreign medical graduates under the aegis of the Exchange Visitor Program.

- The Internet newsgroups misc.education.medical and bit.listserv.medforum can be valuable forums through which to exchange information on licensing exams, residency applications, and the like.
- Immigration information for IMGs is available from the sites of Siskind, Susser, Haas & Chang, a firm of attorneys specializing in immigration law:
  http://www.visalaw.com/~gsiskind/95feb/2feb95.html
  http://www.telalink.net/~gsiskind/95feb/index.html
- Another source of immigration information can be found on the website of the law offices of Carl Shusterman, a Los Angeles lawyer specializing in medical immigration law:
  http://shusterman.com
- International Medical Placement Ltd., a US company specializing in recruiting foreign physicians to work in the United States, has a site at http://www.intlmedicalplacement.com. This site includes ordering information for several publications by FMSG, Inc., including USMLE Study Guides and residency matching information, as well as details on USMLE lecture courses offered by the author of these publications, Stanley Zaslau. The site also has information on seminars held by the company in foreign countries for physicians who are thinking of moving to the United States.
- *The International Medical Graduates' Guide to U.S. Medicine: Negotiating the Maze* by Louise B. Ball (199 pages; ISBN 1883620163) can be obtained from:

  Galen Press
  PO Box 64400
  Tucson, AZ 85728-4400
  (800) 442-5369 (United States and Canada) or (520) 577-8363
  Fax: (520) 520-6459

  Price: $28.95 plus $3.00 shipping and handling, add $2.95 for priority mail (US dollars); Arizona residents add 7% sales tax.

  This book has a lot of detailed information and is particularly strong on the intricacies of immigration law as it applies to foreign-citizen IMGs who wish to practice in the United States—although this is a rapidly changing field, and some of the information is probably out of date already. Also note that much of the book's contents may be relevant only to some IMGs, as many chapters are geared toward specific problems or situations (e.g., how to sponsor a relative, how a small American town may try to sponsor a foreign physician, how a US faculty member can sponsor a foreign clinical research fellow), and there is considerable duplication across chapters.

  Bottom line: Great for foreign citizens who need help in understanding how to "negotiate the maze" of medical immigration regulations, but not necessarily high yield for many other IMGs.

What Is the COMLEX Level 1?

In 1995, the National Board of Osteopathic Medicine Examiners (NBOME) introduced a new assessment tool called the Comprehensive Osteopathic Medical Licensing Examination, or COMLEX. Like the former NBOME examination series, the COMLEX is administered over three levels. In 1995, only Level 3 was administered, but by 1998 all three levels were implemented. The COMLEX is now the only exam offered to osteopathic students. One of the goals of this changeover is to get all states to recognize this examination as equivalent to the USMLE, thereby allowing Doctor of Osteopathy (DO) students to use it for licensing. Another stated goal of the COMLEX Level 1 is to create a more primary-care-oriented exam that integrates osteopathic principles into clinical situations. To take the COMLEX Level 1, you must have satisfactorily completed at least half of your sophomore year in an American Osteopathic Association–approved medical school and must have the approval of your dean.

For all three levels of the COMLEX, raw scores are converted to a score ranging from 5 to 800. For Levels 1 and 2, a score of 400 is required to pass; for Level 3, a score of 350 is needed. The COMLEX are usually mailed 6–8 weeks after the test date. The mean score on the June 1999 exam was 500 with a standard deviation of 71.

If you pass a COMLEX examination, you are not allowed to retake it to improve your grade. If you fail, there is no specific limit to the number of times you can retake it in an effort to pass. However, Levels 2 and 3 must be passed in sequential order within seven years of passing Level 1. Figure 19 shows the upcoming examination dates for all levels of the COMLEX in 2000.

FIGURE 19. Test Dates for COMLEX in 2000

Level 1	June 6–7 October 24–25
Level 2	March 7–8 August 22–23
Level 3	February 8–9 June 13–14

What Is the Structure of the COMLEX Level 1?

The COMLEX Level 1 is a multiple-choice examination that is given over two days. In taking this test, you work through four booklets, each containing approximately 200 questions; you are given four hours to complete each. In the 1998 exam there were 800 questions in total. Since the number of questions may change, the best way to determine the number of questions you will encounter is to consult the most recent *Examination Guidelines and Sample Exam* (you should receive a copy when you register for the test).

The COMLEX Level 1 exam consists of one-best-answer questions, clinical vignettes, and matching sets. In the 1998 exam, approximately 50–60% of the questions were one-best-answer, 20–45% were clinical vignettes, and 3–5% were matching sets; there were no negatively phrased best-answer questions, answers such as "all the above" or "none of the above," or K-type questions. Each booklet had a similar breakdown; that is to say, at the end of each test booklet were approximately nine to ten clinical vignettes followed by approximately ten matching questions. Some of the clinical vignettes had four to five questions per case. Most single questions were also introduced with a short clinical vignette.

The exam includes color photos, with an accompanying brief clinical description and then a question asking for the diagnosis of the problem. For the 1999 exam, there were photos of an eye-movement deficit, one pathology specimen (mitral stenosis), one petri dish (hand drawing) and two EKGs. All photos appeared in the third booklet.

What Is the Difference Between the USMLE and the COMLEX?

Although the COMLEX and USMLE are similar in scope, content, and emphasis, some differences between the two are worth noting. For example, the COMLEX Level 1 tests osteopathic principles but does not emphasize lab techniques. In addition, although both exams often require that you apply and integrate knowledge over several areas of basic science to answer a given question, many students who took both tests in 1999 reported that the questions differed somewhat in style. Students reported, for example, that USMLE questions generally required that the test taker reason and draw from the information given (often a two-step process), whereas those on the COMLEX exam tended to be more straightforward. Furthermore, USMLE questions were on average found to be considerably longer than those on the COMLEX; therefore, many students who felt they had plenty of time on the COMLEX felt pressured while taking the USMLE.

Students also commented that the COMLEX made greater use of "buzzwords" (e.g., "rose spots" in typhoid fever), whereas the USMLE avoided buzzwords in favor of straightforward descriptions of clinical findings or symptoms (e.g., rose-colored papules on the abdomen instead of rose spots). Some students, however, thought that the 1999 COMLEX made limited use of buzzwords. Finally, the USMLE had many more photographs than did the COMLEX, but this difference may narrow in 2000. In general, the overall impression was that the USMLE was a more "thought-provoking" exam, while the COMLEX is a more "knowledge-based" one.

Who Should Take Both the USMLE and the COMLEX?

Aside from facing the COMLEX Level 1, you must decide if you will also take the USMLE Step 1. We recommend that you consider taking both the USMLE and the COMLEX under the following circumstances:

- **If you are applying to allopathic residencies.** Although there is growing acceptance of COMLEX certification on the part of allopathic residencies, some allopathic programs prefer or even require passage of the USMLE Step 1. These include many academic programs, programs in competitive specialties (e.g., orthopedics, ophthalmology, or ER) as well as programs in competitive geographic areas (such as California). Fourth-year DO students who have already matched may be a good source of information about which programs and specialties look for USMLE scores.
- **If you plan to practice in Louisiana.** The state of Louisiana requires that osteopathic physicians pass the USMLE system in order to obtain a license for practice. However, this state may have reciprocating agreements with other states that accept the COMLEX. Therefore, it may be possible for you to be licensed in another state and then petition to have your license transferred. We recently heard that the American Osteopathic Association (AOA) is pushing very hard to get Louisiana to accept the COMLEX.
- **If you are unsure about your postgraduate training plans.** Successful passage of both the COMLEX Level 1 and the USMLE Step 1 is certain to provide you with the greatest possible range of options when you are applying for internship and residency training.

The clinical coursework that most DO students receive during the summer of their third year (as opposed to their starting clerkships) is considered helpful in integrating basic science knowledge for the COMLEX or the USMLE.

How Do I Prepare for the COMLEX Level 1?

Student experience suggests that you should start studying for the COMLEX four to six months before the test is given, as an early start will allow you to spend up to a month on each subject. The recommendations made in Section I regarding study and testing methods, strategies, and resources, as well as the books suggested in Section III for the USMLE Step 1, hold true for the COMLEX as well.

Many students also believe that doing old test questions is a very good way to prepare for the test. SOMA, KCOM (Missouri), and PCOM (Philadelphia) have each put together a group of old test questions that provide an excellent means of gauging your studying skills. Many students reported that some questions from past exams appeared on the 1997 NBOME Part I. However, these old test review books may contain errors. It is therefore critical that you look up the information you missed.

Another important source of information is in the *Examination Guidelines and Sample Exam*, a booklet that discusses the breakdown of each subject while also providing sample questions. Many students, however, felt that this breakdown provided only a general guideline. For example, a number of students felt that more than 15% of the questions on anatomy (the stated percentage in the booklet) covered neuroanatomy. Also, the sample questions did not provide examples of clinical vignettes, which made up approximately 25% of the exam. You will receive this publication when you register for the COMLEX Level 1 exam, but you can also receive a copy and additional information by writing:

NBOME
8765 W. Higgins Rd. Suite 200
Chicago, IL 60631–4101
(773) 714-0622
(773) 714-0631 (fax)
http://www.nbome.org

The 1998 COMLEX exam consisted of 120 multiple-choice questions and 80 clinical vignette questions per test booklet. There were four test booklets, two of which had approximately 10 matching questions. Each multiple-choice question accompanied a small case (about one to two sentences long).

In 1999, students reported an emphasis in certain areas. For example:

- There was an increased emphasis on anatomy (lower limbs) and clinical neurology (especially lesions).
- High-yield osteopathic manipulative technique (OMT) topics on the 1999 exam included sacral testing/diagnosis, lumbar mechanics, spinal motion and diagnosis, and an emphasis on the sympathetic innervation of viscera.
- Specific topics were repeatedly tested on the exam. These included measles, rubella, diabetes, acid-base physiology, testicular cancer, porphyrias and alcohol metabolism. Thyroid and adrenal function, neurology (head injury), sexually transmitted diseases, specific drug treatments for bacterial infection and migraines/cluster headaches, and drug mechanisms also received heavy emphasis. All behavioral science questions were based on psychiatry.

- Since topics that were repeatedly tested appeared in all four booklets, students found it useful to review them in between the two test days. It is important to understand that the topics emphasized on the 1999 exam may not be stressed on the 2000 exam. However, since certain topics seem to be emphasized each year, it may be to your advantage to review such topics between test days.

The National Board of Podiatric Medical Examiners (NBPME) tests (see Fig. 20 for examination dates) are designed to assess whether a candidate possesses the knowledge required to practice as a minimally competent entry-level podiatrist. In all states that recognize them, the NBPME examinations are used as part of the licensing process governing the practice of podiatric medicine. Individual states use the examination scores differently; therefore, DPM candidates should refer to the information in the *NBPME Bulletin of 2000 Examinations*.

The NBPME Part I is generally taken after the completion of the second year of podiatric medical education. Unlike the USMLE Step 1, there is no behavioral science section. The exam does sample the seven basic science disciplines: general anatomy; lower extremity anatomy; biochemistry; physiology; medical microbiology and immunology; pathology; and pharmacology. Questions covering these content areas are interspersed throughout the test.

Candidates performing at extreme levels are passed or failed at 90 minutes.

Your NBPME Appointment

In early spring, your college registrar will have you fill out an application for the NBPME Part I. After your application and registration fees are received, you will be mailed the *NBPME Bulletin of 2000 Examinations*. This bulletin gives you a list of Sylvan Learning Centers across the country that are administering the exam. You may then find the location nearest you and set up an appointment to take the exam. We suggest that you do this as soon as you receive your *NBPME Bulletin*, because reservation slots fill up quickly, especially in the home cities of the seven podiatric medical schools.

On the day of the exam, be sure to arrive at the testing center at least 30 minutes before your scheduled appointment. At that time, you will be registered, escorted to a computer terminal, and given a tutorial to acquaint you with the format of the examination. At the end of the examination, you will be asked to complete a survey regarding your computer-based testing experience.

FIGURE 20. 2000 NBPME Examination Dates

Part 1	July 11–14 (Registration Deadline—May 7)
Part 1 (retake)	September 12–15

Computer-Based Testing

The NBPME Part I is a Computerized Mastery Test (CMT) whose format is multiple choice. Each candidate is administered a base test of 90 questions. The maximum amount of time permitted for this base test is 90 minutes. Following the base test, candidates performing at either extreme (either high or low) are passed or failed immediately. By contrast, candidates with an intermediate level of performance are administered additional "testlets" (consisting of 15 questions each), permitting them additional opportunity to demonstrate minimal competence. The maximum time allowed for each additional testlet is 15 minutes. You should try your best on each question, marking any questions that you would like to review should time permit. There is no penalty for guessing. No more than 180 questions are administered to a candidate.

Interpreting Your Score

After you complete the NBPME Part I, a pass/fail decision is reported on the computer. You need a scaled score of at least 75 to pass. Eighty-five percent of first-time test takers pass the NBPME Part I. In computing the scaled score, the number of questions varies from candidate to candidate; however, this is taken into consideration along with the number of questions answered correctly. Approximately two weeks after the examination, you will receive your official score report by mail. Passing candidates receive a message of congratulations but no numerical score. Failing candidates receive a report with one score between 55 and 74 in addition to diagnostic messages intended to help identify strengths or weaknesses in particular content areas. If you fail the NBPME Part I, you must retake the entire examination at a later date. There is no limit to the number of times you can retake the exam.

Preparation for the NBPME Part I

Students suggest that you begin studying for the NBPME Part I at least three months prior to the test date. Each of the colleges of podiatric medicine conducts a series of board reviews. Ask a third-year student which review sessions are most informative. The suggestions made in Section I regarding study and testing methods for the USMLE Step 1 can be applied to the NBPME as well. This book should, however, be used as a supplement and not as the sole source of information.

Know everything about lower extremity anatomy.

Approximately 24% of the NBPME Part I focuses on lower extremity anatomy. In this area, students should rely on the notes and material that they received from their class. Remember, lower extremity anatomy is the podiatrist's specialty—so everything about it is important. Do not forget to study osteology. Keep your old tests and look through old lower extremity class exams, because each of the podiatric colleges submits questions from its own exams. This strategy will give you an understanding of the types of questions that may be asked.

The NBPME, like the USMLE, requires that you apply and integrate knowledge over several areas of basic science to answer the questions. Students report that many questions emphasize clinical presentations; however, the facts in this book are very useful in helping students recall the different diseases and organisms. DPM candidates should expand on the high-yield pharmacology section and study antifungal drugs and treatment protocols for *Pseudomonas*, candidiasis, erythrasma, and so on. The high-yield section focusing on pathology is very useful; however, additional emphasis on diabetes mellitus and all its secondary manifestations should not be overlooked. Students should also focus on classic podiatric dermatopathologies, gout, and arthritis.

A sample set of questions is found in the *NBPME Bulletin of 2000 Examinations*. If you do not receive a *NBPME Bulletin* or if you have any questions regarding registration, fees, test centers, authorization forms, or score reports, please contact your college registrar or:

National Board of Podiatric Medical Examiners (NBPME)
PO Box 6516
Princeton, NJ 08541-6516
(609) 951-6335

Best of luck!

FIRST AID FOR THE STUDENT WITH A DISABILITY

The USMLE provides accommodations for students with documented disabilities. The basis for such accommodations is the Americans with Disabilities Act (ADA) of 1990. The ADA defines a disability as "a significant limitation in one or more major life activities." This includes both "observable/physical" disabilities (e.g., blindness, hearing loss, narcolepsy) and "hidden/mental disabilities" (e.g., attention deficit hyperactivity disorder, chronic fatigue syndrome, learning disabilities).

To provide appropriate support, the administrators of the USMLE must be informed of both the nature and the severity of an examinee's disability. Such documentation is required for an examinee to receive testing accommodations. Accommodations include extra time on tests, low-stimulation environments, assistance in completing answer sheets, extra or extended breaks, large-print exams, printed copies of the verbal instructions read by the proctor, and verbally administered tests.

Who Can Apply for Accommodations?

Students or graduates of a school in the US or Canada that is accredited by the Liaison Committee for Medical Education (LCME) or the AOA may apply for special accommodations directly from the National Board. Requests are granted only if they meet the ADA definition of a disability. If you are a disabled student or a disabled graduate of a foreign medical school, you must contact the ECFMG (see below).

Who Is Not Eligible for Accommodations?

Individuals who do not meet the ADA definition of disabled are not eligible for test accommodations. Difficulties not eligible for test accommodations include test anxiety, slow reading without an identified underlying cognitive deficit, English as a second language, or learning difficulties that have not been diagnosed as a medically recognized disability.

Understanding the Need for Documentation

Although most learning-disabled medical students are all too familiar with the often-exhausting process of providing documentation of their disability, you should realize that **applying for USMLE accommodation is different from these previous experiences.** This is because the National Board determines whether an individual is disabled solely on the basis of the guidelines set by the ADA.

Getting the Information

The first step in applying for USMLE special accommodations is to contact the NBME and obtain a guidelines and questionnaire booklet. This can be obtained by calling or writing to:

Testing Coordinator
Office of Test Accommodations
National Board of Medical Examiners
3750 Market Street
Philadelphia, PA 19104-3190
(215) 590-9700

Internet access to this information is also available at **www.ecfmg.org/adaintro.html.** This information is also relevant for IMGs, since the information is the same as that sent by the ECFMG.

Foreign graduates should contact the ECFMG to obtain information on special accommodations by calling or writing to:

ECFMG
3624 Market Street, fourth floor
Philadelphia, PA 19104-2685
(215) 386-5900

When you get this information, take some time to read it carefully. The guidelines are clear and explicit about what you need to do to obtain accommodations.

Applying for Accommodations

Although the accommodation guidelines cited above are fairly self-explanatory, here are some key points to keep in mind:

- **Produce a history.** Send the National Board extensive past records. Since almost all learning disabilities are present from birth, sending even the earliest records of your disability is invaluable in an assessment. Even if you were diagnosed at a late age, a "paper trail" of your learning disability should still be evident. Grade-school reports, tutoring letters, job reports, previous physician notes, report cards, teacher comments, medication history, and other documents will go a long way toward providing significant evidence of your learning disability.
- **Send your "official" documentation.** Most individuals who were diagnosed with a learning disability were tested with a specific battery of tests (an extensive list of these tests is given in the guidelines). Contact the physician who administered these tests and have the results sent to you. If you cannot locate that physician, obtain the documentation from the educational institutions you attended (college, high school, etc.). Verify that both the administering physician's clinical impressions and the results of your specific tests are included in your submitted material.

Reevaluating Your Disability

You might want to have your disability reevaluated for the USMLE. As stated previously, obtaining accommodations for the USMLE is different from any other process, as you are being evaluated solely on the basis of how well you meet the criteria specified by the ADA. Your evaluator should have this in mind when he or she performs the assessment. Sharing the information in the guidelines and questionnaire booklet with your evaluator will ensure that he or she is aware of this.

The purpose of a reevaluation is twofold. First of all, it is meant to produce further proof of the disability. In addition, it is meant to determine the need for accommodation based on the level of current functioning.

Reevaluation is not for everyone. An evaluation represents a considerable time commitment and is difficult to schedule during the hectic second year. An evaluation is also expensive, usually costing anywhere from $500 to $2000. Furthermore, since such a reevaluation is not being ordered for a strictly "medical reason" and since it is investigating a "previous condition," your insurance company may not cover it.

If you do decide to get reevaluated, the following is highly recommended:

- **Choose an expert.** You're in medical school. Use it! Most of the leading experts on learning disabilities are associated with medical school faculty. Ask around for the leading expert on learning disabilities affiliated with your medical school, and use that physician as your evaluator. Make sure you stress to the evaluator that he or she is functioning as an independent evaluator and not as a school advocate. Using someone at your school is also desirable from a cost perspective; a faculty member may charge you a lowered evaluation fee.
- **Undergo some testing.** If you have undergone previous cognitive testing, this step is probably not that important. However, you might want to undergo some basic tests that assess your current level of cognitive functioning. A purely clinical evaluation is commonly limited in both scope and ability. **If you have never undergone a full evaluation, a comprehensive diagnostic battery is essential.** Make sure that your evaluator is not just looking at one or two sessions or subtests but at the entire gestalt.
- **Share your previous history with the evaluator.** Even though the USMLE reviewer will examine your documentation, your evaluator should also have access to your medical history. In that way, he or she can highlight or emphasize certain aspects of your record.
- **Ask for a differential diagnosis.** Evaluators should offer a differential, not just a single diagnosis. Once the differential has been made, evidence for or against any alternative diagnosis should be presented.

Finally, it is highly advisable that you talk from the heart. Part of the application is an essay you write about your disability. This is your opportunity to shine. If you have problems with writing, just speak from your soul. No one else but you can truly describe your learning disability; view this as an opportunity to share your difficulties with a receptive audience.

The Accommodations

As previously mentioned, a wide variety of accommodations exist for the USMLE. By far the most commonly requested and granted accommodation is for extra time. The ADA requires that individuals with a disability be provided with "equal access" to the testing program. Therefore, the purpose of accommodations is to "cancel" the effect of the disability, not to provide extra help in passing an examination.

Because the same types of impairments often vary in severity and frequently restrict different people to different degrees or in different ways, each request is considered individually to determine the effect of the impairment on the life of the applicant and whether a particular accommodation is even appropriate for that person.

The following additional material is excerpted from the NBME World Wide Web site (http://www.nbme.org/testacco.htm) and is copyright 1996 by The Federation of State Medical Boards of the United States, Inc., and the National Board of Medical Examiners.

If I am requesting an accommodation from the NBME on Step 1 or Step 2, when should I send in my request and documentation?

Mail your request and supporting documentation for test accommodations to the NBME Office of Test Accommodations at the *same time* you submit your Step 1 application to the address shown in the registration materials.

Can my evaluator or my medical school send in my request for test accommodations?

No. A request for accommodations, by law, must be initiated by the person with a disability. Also, to protect your confidentiality, the NBME does not provide information concerning your request to third parties.

How does the NBME determine what is an appropriate accommodation for USMLE?

As part of the documentation, the examinee's evaluator should recommend appropriate accommodations to ease the impact of the impairment on the testing activity. Professional consultants in learning disabilities, attention deficit and hyperactivity disorder (ADHD), and various other psychiatric and physical conditions review the documentation and recommendations of evaluators to help match the type of assistance with the demonstrated need. The NBME consults with the examinee to determine what accommodations have been effectively used in the past.

If I apply for test accommodations on USMLE, does my disability evaluation have to be up to date?

For someone with a continuing history of accommodation, which would likely include high school and college as well as medical school, current testing is usually not necessary if objective documentation of the past accommodations is provided. However, the impact of the disability may change over time, and new testing may be necessary to demonstrate the current level of impairment and resulting need for accommodation. You will be advised if updated testing is needed.

What are some reasons my request for accommodations might not be approved?

Approximately 75% of the total number of requests for all Steps are approved.

- Insufficient documentation of a need for accommodation. Conditions such as learning disabilities and ADHD are permanent and lifelong. A diagnosis requires an objective history of chronic symptoms from childhood to adulthood as well as evidence of significant impairment currently.
- Lack of presence of a moderate to severe level of impairment attributable to the disorder.
- The identified difficulty is not considered to be a disability under the law, i.e., slow reading without evidence of an underlying language-processing disorder; language difficulties as a result of English as a second language.

Once my request for accommodations has been approved, do I need to arrange for accommodations the next time I register for a Step?

An examinee with a disability must request accommodations at the time of registration. NBME examinees must send a letter requesting accommodations to the Office of Test Accommodations. A repeated request must state whether any change in the accommodations is required, and if so, documentation of the needed change must be provided.

Accommodations are not granted automatically even if they were approved for previous Step administrations.

Miscellaneous Suggestions

- **Get your information to the USMLE early.** The earlier your information is received, the more time the USMLE will have for evaluating and considering your case. They will also have time to ask you for additional material should this prove necessary.
- **Use your winter holiday.** It is a lot easier to get this material ready for the USMLE when you are not in school. It is also immeasurably easier to be evaluated when you are not facing the pressures of the second year.

SECTION II

Database of High-Yield Facts

"There comes a time when for every addition of knowledge you forget something that you knew before. It is of the highest importance, therefore, not to have useless facts elbowing out the useful ones."
—*Arthur Conan Doyle, "A Study in Scarlet"*

"Never regard study as a duty, but as the enviable opportunity to learn."
—*Albert Einstein*

"Live as if you were to die tomorrow. Learn as if you were to live forever."
—*Gandhi*

HOW TO USE THE DATABASE

The 2000 edition of *First Aid for the USMLE Step 1* contains a revised and expanded database of basic science material that student authors and faculty have identified as high yield for boards review. The facts are loosely organized according to the seven traditional basic medical science disciplines (anatomy, behavioral science, biochemistry, microbiology, pathology, pharmacology, and physiology). Each discipline is then divided into smaller subsections of related facts. Individual facts are generally presented in a three-column format, with the **Title** of the fact in the first column, the **Description** of the fact in the second column, and the **Mnemonic** or **Special Note** in the third column. Some facts do not have a mnemonic and are presented in a two-column format. Others are presented in list or tabular form in order to emphasize key associations.

The database structure is useful for reviewing material already learned. This section is not ideal for learning complex or highly conceptual material for the first time. At the beginning of each basic science section we list supplementary high-yield clinical vignettes and topics that have appeared on recent exams in order to help focus your review.

Selected facts have embedded references to the nine titles in the Underground Clinical Vignettes (UCV) series (S2S Medical Publishing). These annotations link the high-yield fact to a corresponding vignette; illustrating how that fact may appear in a Step 1 clinical scenario. The following annotation, for example, refers to cases 23 and 45 from *UCV Anatomy:* UCV *Anat.23.45*

UCV REFERENCE LEGEND

UCV Title	Abbreviation
Anatomy	Anat
Behavioral Science	BehSci
Biochemistry	Bio
Microbiology, Vol. 1	Micro1
Microbiology, Vol. 2	Micro2
Pathophysiology, Vol. 1	Path1
Pathophysiology, Vol. 2	Path2
Pathophysiology, Vol. 3	Path3
Pharmacology	Pharm

The Database of High-Yield Facts is not comprehensive. Use it to complement your core study material and not as your primary study source. The facts and notes have been condensed and edited to emphasize the essential material, and as a result each entry is "incomplete." Work with the material, add your own notes and mnemonics, and recognize that not all memory techniques work for all students.

We update Section II annually to keep current with new trends in boards content as well as to expand our database of high-yield information. However, we must note that inevitably many other very high-yield entries and topics are not yet included in our database.

We actively encourage medical students and faculty to submit entries and mnemonics so that we may enhance the database for future students. We also solicit recommendations of alternate tools for study that may be useful in preparing for the examination, such as diagrams, charts, and computer-based tutorials (see How to Contribute, page xvii).

Disclaimer

The entries in this section reflect student opinions of what is high yield. Owing to the diverse sources of material, no attempt has been made to trace or reference the origins of entries individually. We have regarded mnemonics as essentially in the public domain. All errors and omissions will be gladly corrected if brought to the attention of the authors, either through the publisher or directly by e-mail.

NOTES

SECTION II

Anatomy

"Dispel from your mind the thought that an understanding of the human body in every aspect of its structure can be given in words ..."
—Leonardo da Vinci

Several topics fall under this heading, including embryology, gross anatomy, histology, and neuroanatomy. Do not memorize all the small details. However, do not ignore anatomy altogether. Review what you have already learned and what you wish you had learned. Many questions require two steps. The first step is to identify a structure on anatomic cross-section, electron micrograph, or photomicrograph. The second step may require an understanding of the clinical significance of the structure.

When studying, stress clinically important material. For example, be familiar with gross anatomy related to specific diseases (e.g., Pancoast's tumor, Horner's syndrome), traumatic injuries (e.g., fractures, sensory and motor nerve deficits), procedures (e.g., lumbar puncture), and common surgeries (e.g., cholecystectomy). There are also many questions on the exam involving x-rays, CT scans, and neuro MRI scans. Many students suggest browsing through a general radiology atlas, pathology atlas, and histology atlas. Focus on learning basic anatomy at key levels in the body (e.g., sagittal brain MRI; axial CT of midthorax, abdomen, and pelvis). Basic neuroanatomy (especially pathways, blood supply, and functional anatomy) also has good yield. Use this as an opportunity to learn associated neuropathology and neurophysiology. Basic embryology (especially congenital malformations) has good yield and is worth reviewing.

These abstracted case vignettes are designed to demonstrate the thought processes necessary to answer multistep clinical reasoning questions.

- Baby vomits milk when fed and has a gastric air bubble → what kind of fistula is present? → blind esophagus with lower segment of esophagus attached to trachea.
- 20-year-old dancer reports decreased plantar flexion and decreased sensation over the back of her thigh, calf, and lateral half of her foot → what spinal nerve is involved? → tibial.
- Patient presents with decreased pain and temperature sensation over the lateral aspects of both arms → what is the lesion? → syringomyelia.
- Penlight in patient's right eye produces bilateral pupillary constriction. When moved to the left eye, there is paradoxical bilateral pupillary dilatation → what is the defect? → atrophy of the left optic nerve.
- Patient describes decreased prick sensation on the lateral aspect of her leg and foot → a deficit in what muscular action can also be expected? → dorsiflexion of foot (common peroneal nerve).
- Elderly lady presents with arthritis and tingling over lateral digits of her right hand → what is the diagnosis? → carpal tunnel syndrome, median nerve compression.
- Woman involved in motor vehicle accident cannot turn head to the left and has right shoulder droop → what structure is damaged? → right CN XI (runs through jugular foramen with CN IX and X), innervating sternocleidomastoid and trapezius muscles.
- Man presents with one wild, flailing arm → where is the lesion? → contralateral subthalamic nucleus (hemiballismus).
- Pregnant woman in third trimester has normal blood pressure when standing and sitting. When supine, blood pressure drops to 90/50 → what is the diagnosis? → compression of the inferior vena cava.
- Soccer player who was kicked in the leg suffered a damaged medial meniscus → what else is likely to have been damaged? → anterior cruciate ligament.
- Gymnast dislocates her shoulder anteriorly → what nerve is most likely to have been damaged? → axillary nerve.
- Patient with cortical lesion does not know that he has a disease → where is the lesion? → right parietal lobe.
- Child presents with cleft lip → which embryologic process failed? → fusion of maxillary and medial processes.
- Patient cannot protrude tongue toward left side and has a right-sided spastic paralysis → where is the lesion? → left medulla, CN XII.
- Teen falls while rollerblading and hurts his elbow. He can't feel the median part of his palm → which nerve and what injury? → ulnar nerve due to broken medial condyle.
- 24-year-old male develops left testicular cancer → metastatic spread occurs by what route? → para-aortic lymph nodes (recall descent of testes during development).
- Field hockey player presents to the ER after falling on her arm during practice. X-ray shows midshaft break of humerus → which nerve and which artery are most likely damaged? → radial nerve and deep brachial artery, which run together.

- Carotid angiography → identify the anterior cerebral artery → occlusion of this artery will produce a deficit where? → contralateral leg.
- H&E of normal liver → identify the central vein, portal triad, bile canaliculi, etc.
- X-ray of fractured humerus → what nerve is most likely damaged? → radial nerve.
- X-ray of hip joint → what part undergoes avascular necrosis with fracture at the neck of the femur? → femoral head.
- Abdominal CT cross-section → obstruction of what structure results in enlarged kidneys? → inferior vena cava.
- Intravenous pyelogram with right ureter dilated → where is the obstruction and what is the likely cause? → ureterovesicular junction; stone.
- Illustration of fetal head → medial maxillary eminence gives rise to what? → primary palate.
- Abdominal MRI cross-section → locate the splenic artery, portal vein, etc.
- EM of cell → lysosomes (digestion of macromolecules), RER (protein synthesis), SER (steroid synthesis).
- Coronal MRI section of the head at the level of the eye → find the medial rectus muscle → what is its function? → medial gaze.
- Optic nerve path → defect where would cause diminished pupillary reflex in right eye? Defect where would cause right homonymous hemianopsia? → right optic nerve; left optic tract.
- Aortogram → identify adrenal artery, renal arteries, SMA, etc.
- Chest x-ray showing pleural effusion with layering → where is the fluid located? → costodiaphragmatic recess.
- MRI abdominal cross-section → what structure is derivative of the common cardinal veins? → inferior vena cava.
- Sagittal MRI of brain of patient with hyperphagia, increased CSF pressure, and visual problems → where is the lesion? → hypothalamus.

Embryology

1. Development of the heart, lung, liver, kidney (i.e., what are the embryologic structures that give rise to these organs?).
2. Etiology and clinical presentation of important congenital malformations (e.g., neural tube defects, cleft palate, tetralogy of Fallot, tracheoesophageal fistula, horseshoe kidney).
3. Development of the central nervous system (e.g., telencephalon, diencephalon, mesencephalon).
4. Derivatives of the foregut, midgut, and hindgut as well as their vascular supply.
5. Derivatives of the somites, and malformations associated with defects in somite migration.
6. Changes in the circulatory/respiratory system on the first breath of a newborn.
7. Development of the embryonic plate in weeks two and three.

Gross Anatomy

1. Anatomic landmarks in relation to medical procedures (e.g., direct and indirect hernia repair, lumbar puncture, pericardiocentesis).
2. Anatomic landmarks in relation to major organs (e.g., lungs, heart, kidneys).
3. Common injuries of the knee (including clinical examination), hip, shoulder, and clavicle; paying attention to the clinical deficits caused by these injuries (e.g., shoulder separation, hip fracture).
4. Clinical features and anatomic correlations of specific brachial plexus lesions (e.g., waiter's tip, wrist drop, claw hand, scapular winging).
5. Clinical features of common peripheral nerve injuries (e.g., common vs. deep peroneal nerve palsy, radial nerve palsy).
6. Etiology and clinical features of common diseases affecting the hands (e.g., carpal tunnel syndrome, cubital tunnel syndrome, Dupuytren's contracture).
7. Anatomic basis for the blood–testis barrier.
8. Major blood vessels and collateral circulatory pathways of the gastrointestinal tract (e.g., collaterals between the superior and inferior mesenteric arteries).
9. Bone structures (metaphysis, epiphysis, diaphysis), including histologic features; linear (epiphysis) and annular (diaphysis) bone growth.

Histology

1. Histology of the respiratory tract (i.e., differentiate between the bronchi, terminal bronchioles, respiratory bronchioles, and alveoli).
2. Structure, function, and electron microscopic (EM) appearance of major cellular organelles and structures (e.g., lysosomes, peroxisomes, glycogen, mitochondria, ER, Golgi apparatus, nucleus, nucleolus).
3. Structure, function, and EM appearance of cell–cell junctional structures (e.g., tight junctions, gap junctions, desmosomes).
4. Histology of lymphoid organs (e.g., lymph nodes, spleen).

5. Resident phagocytic cells of different organisms (e.g., Langerhans cells, Kupffer cells, alveolar macrophages, microglia).
6. Histology of muscle fibers and changes seen with muscle contraction (sarcomere structure, different bands, rigor mortis).

Neuroanatomy

1. Etiology and clinical features of important brain, cranial nerve, and spinal cord lesions (e.g., brain stem lesions and "crossed signs," dorsal root lesions, effects of schwannoma, Weber and Parinaud syndromes).
2. Production, circulation, and composition of cerebrospinal fluid.
3. Neuroanatomy of hearing (central and peripheral hearing loss).
4. Extraocular muscles (which muscle abducts, adducts, etc.) and their innervation.
5. Structure and function of a chemical synapse (e.g., neuromuscular junction).
6. Major neurotransmitters, receptors, second messengers, and effects.
7. Blood supply of the brain (anterior, middle, posterior cerebral arterial areas, "watershed" areas) and neurologic deficits corresponding to various vascular occlusions.
8. Functional anatomy of the basal ganglia (e.g., globus pallidus, caudate, putamen).
9. Anatomic landmarks near the pituitary gland.
10. Brain MRI/CT, including morphologic changes in disease states (e.g., Huntington's chorea, MS, aging).
11. Clinical exam of pupillary light reflex: pathway tested, important anatomic lesions, swinging light test.

Radiology

1. X-rays; plain films.
   a. Fractures (skull, humerus, etc.) and associated clinical findings.
   b. PA and lateral chest films, including important landmarks (costodiaphragmatic recess, major blood vessels, cardiac chambers, and abnormalities seen with different diseases [consolidation, pneumothorax, mitral stenosis, cardiomyopathy]).
   c. Abdominal films, including vasculature (locate important vessels in contrast films) and other important structures.
   d. Joint films (e.g., shoulder, wrist, knee, hip, spine), including important injuries/diseases (e.g., osteoarthritis, herniated disc).
2. CT/MRI studies.
   a. Brain cross-section (e.g., hematomas, brain lesions, extraocular muscles).
   b. Chest cross-section (e.g., superior vena cava, aortic arch, heart).
   c. Abdominal cross-section (e.g., liver, kidney, pancreas, aorta, inferior vena cava, rectus abdominis muscle, splenic artery).

ANATOMY—CELL TYPE

Erythrocyte 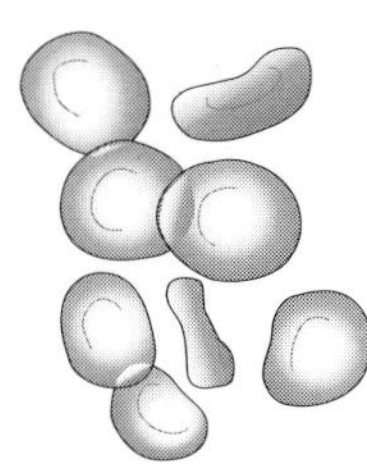	Anucleate, biconcave → large surface area: volume ratio → easy gas exchange (O_2 and CO_2). Source of energy = glucose (90% anaerobically degraded to lactate, 10% by HMP shunt). Survival time = 120 days. Membrane contains the chloride-bicarbonate antiport important in the "physiologic chloride shift," which allows the RBC to transport CO_2 from the periphery to the lungs for elimination.	*Eryth* = red; *cyte* = cell. Erythrocytosis = polycythemia = increased number of red cells Anisocytosis = varying sizes Poikilocytosis = varying shapes Reticulocyte = baby erythrocyte
Leukocyte	Types: granulocytes (basophils, eosinophils, neutrophils) and mononuclear cells (lymphocytes, monocytes). Responsible for defense against infections. Normally 4,000–10,000 per microliter.	*Leuk* = white; *cyte* = cell.
Basophil 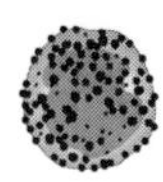 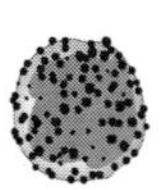	Mediates allergic reaction. <1% of all leukocytes. Bilobate nucleus. Densely basophilic granules containing heparin (anticoagulant), histamine (vasodilator) and other vasoactive amines, and SRS-A.	*Basophilic* = staining readily with *basic* stains.
Mast cell	Mediates allergic reaction. Degranulation = release of histamine, heparin, and eosinophil chemotactic factors. Can bind IgE to membrane. Mast cells resemble basophils structurally and functionally but are not the same cell type.	Involved in type I hypersensitivity reactions. Cromolyn sodium prevents mast cell degranulation. for asthma
Eosinophil 	1%–6% of all leukocytes. Bilobate nucleus. Packed with large eosinophilic granules of uniform size. Defends against helminthic and protozoan infections. Highly phagocytic for antigen–antibody complexes.	*Eosin* = a dye; *philic* = loving. Causes of eosinophilia = **NAACP:** **N**eoplastic **A**sthma **A**llergic processes **C**ollagen vascular diseases **P**arasites
Neutrophil 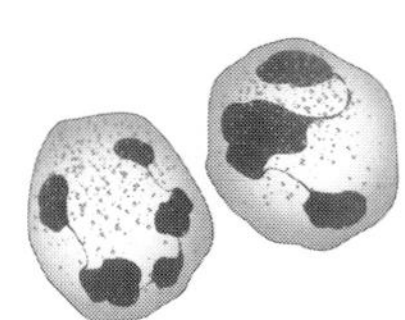	Acute inflammatory response cell. 40%–75% WBCs. Phagocytic. Multilobed nucleus. Large, spherical, azurophilic 1° granules (called lysosomes) contain hydrolytic enzymes, lysozyme, myeloperoxidase.	Hypersegmented polys are seen in vit. B_{12}/folate deficiency.

Monocyte 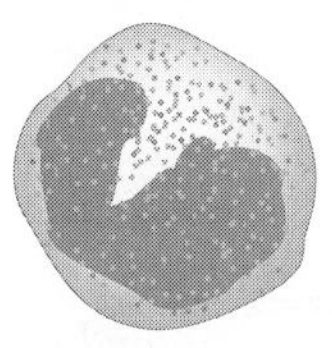	2%–10% of leukocytes. Large. Kidney-shaped nucleus. Extensive "frosted glass" cytoplasm. Differentiates into macrophages in tissues.	*Mono* = one, single; *cyte* = cell
Lymphocyte 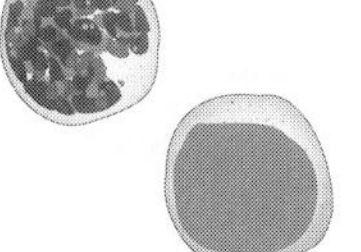	Small. Round, densely staining nucleus. Small amount of pale cytoplasm. B lymphocytes produce antibodies. T lymphocytes manifest the cellular immune response as well as regulate B lymphocytes and macrophages.	
B lymphocyte	Part of humoral immune response. Arises from stem cells in bone marrow. Matures in marrow. Migrates to peripheral lymphoid tissue (follicles of lymph nodes, white pulp of spleen, unencapsulated lymphoid tissue). When antigen is encountered, B cells differentiate into plasma cells and produce antibodies. Has memory. Can function as antigen-presenting cell (APC).	**B** = **B**one marrow.
Plasma cell	Off-center nucleus, clock-face chromatin distribution, abundant RER and well-developed Golgi apparatus. B cells differentiate into plasma cells, which can produce large amounts of antibody specific to a particular antigen.	Multiple myeloma is a plasma cell neoplasm.
T lymphocyte	Mediates cellular immune response. Originates from stem cells in the bone marrow, but matures in the thymus. T cells differentiate into cytotoxic T cells (MHC I, CD8), helper T cells (MHC II, CD4), suppressor T cells, delayed hypersensitivity T cells.	**T** is for **T**hymus. **CD** is for **C**luster of **D**ifferentiation. **MHC × CD = 8** (e.g., MHC 2 × CD4 = 8).
Macrophage	Phagocytizes bacteria, cell debris, and senescent red cells and scavenges damaged cells and tissues. Long life in tissues. Macrophages differentiate from circulating blood monocytes. Activated by γ-IFN. Can function as APC.	*Macro* = large; *phage* = eater.

Airway cells	Ciliated cells extend to the respiratory bronchioles; goblet cells extend only to the terminal bronchioles. Type I cells (97% of alveolar surfaces) line the alveoli. Type II cells (3%) secrete pulmonary surfactant (dipalmitoylphosphatidylcholine), which lowers the alveolar surface tension. Also serve as precursors to type I cells and other type II cells.	All the mucus secreted can be swept orally (ciliated cells run deeper). A lecithin:sphingomyelin ratio of > 1.5 in amniotic fluid is indicative of fetal lung maturity.
Juxtaglomerular apparatus (JGA)	JGA = JG cells (modified smooth muscle of afferent arteriole) and macula densa (Na^+ sensor, part of the distal convoluted tubule). JG cells secrete renin (leading to ↑ angiotensin II and aldosterone levels) in response to ↓ renal blood pressure, ↓ Na^+ delivery to distal tubule, and ↑ sympathetic tone. JG cells also secrete erythropoietin.	JGA defends glomerular filtration rate via the renin-angiotensin system. *Juxta* = close by.
Microglia 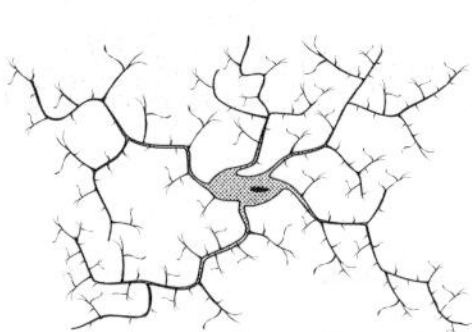	CNS phagocytes. Mesodermal origin. Not readily discernible in Nissl stains. Have small irregular nuclei and relatively little cytoplasm. In response to tissue damage, transform into large ameboid phagocytic cells.	HIV-infected microglia fuse to form multinucleated giant cells in the CNS.
Oligodendroglia 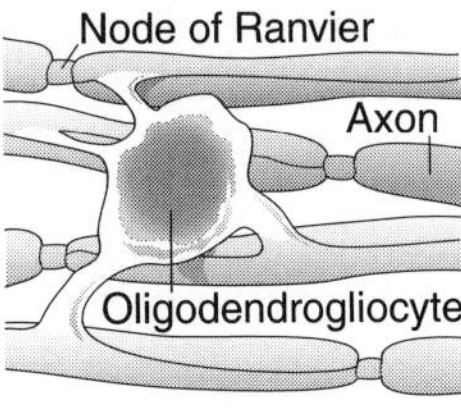	Function to myelinate multiple CNS axons. In Nissl stains, they appear as small nuclei with dark chromatin and little cytoplasm. Predominant type of glial cell in white matter.	These cells are destroyed in multiple sclerosis.
Schwann cells 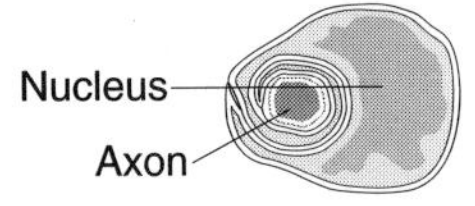	Function to myelinate PNS axons. Unlike oligodendroglia, a single Schwann cell myelinates only one PNS axon. Schwann cells promote axonal regeneration.	Acoustic neuroma is an example of a schwannoma.

Gas exchange barrier

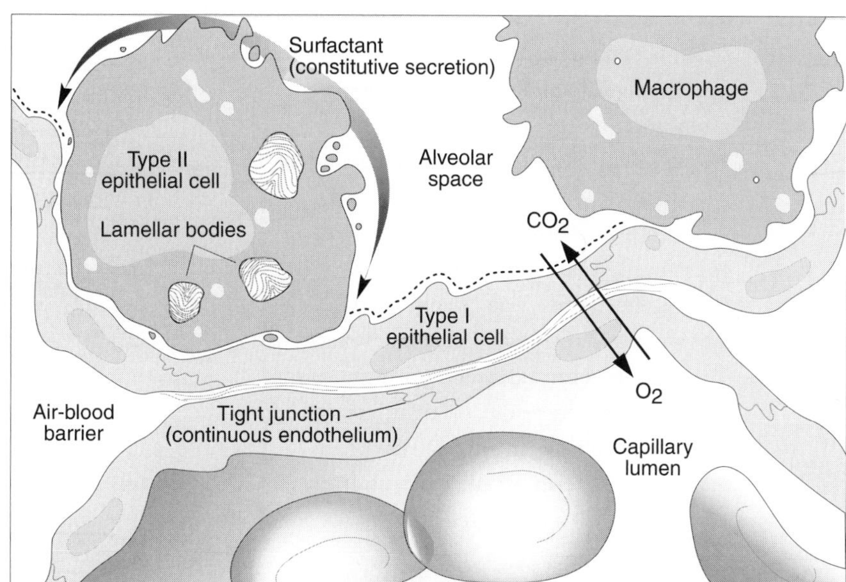

Type II epithelial cell also serves as progenitor for type I cells

ANATOMY—EMBRYOLOGY

Fetal Landmarks

Day 6	Implantation
Day 8	Bilaminar disk
Day 16	Gastrulation
Day 18	Primitive streak and neural plate begin to form
Weeks 3–8	Organogenesis
Week 4	Heart begins to beat, upper and lower limb buds begin to form
Week 10	Genitalia have male/female characteristics

Umbilical cord

3 vessels
2 Arteries
1 vein

Contains 2 umbilical arteries, which return deoxygenated blood from the fetus, and 1 umbilical vein, which supplies oxygenated blood from the placenta to the fetus.

Single umbilical artery is associated with congenital and chromosomal anomalies.

Embryologic derivatives

Ectoderm

Surface ectoderm	Adenohypophysis, lens of eye, epithelial linings, epidermis.
Neuroectoderm	Neurohypophysis, CNS neurons, oligodendrocytes, astrocytes, pineal gland.
Neural crest	ANS, dorsal root ganglia, melanocytes, chromaffin cells of adrenal medulla, enterochromaffin cells, pia, celiac ganglion, Schwann cells, odontoblasts, parafollicular (C) cells of thyroid.
Mesoderm	Dura connective tissue, muscle, bone, cardiovascular structures, lymphatics, blood, urogenital structures, and serous linings of body cavities (e.g., peritoneal), spleen, adrenal cortex.
Endoderm	Gut tube epithelium and derivatives (e.g., lungs, liver, pancreas, thymus, thyroid, parathyroid).
Notochord	Induces ectoderm to form neuroectoderm (neural plate). Its postnatal derivative is the nucleus pulposus of the intervertebral disc.

Early development Rule of 2's for 2nd week	2 germ layers (bilaminar disc): epiblast, hypoblast. 2 cavities: amniotic cavity, yolk sac. 2 components to placenta: cytotrophoblast, syncytiotrophoblast.	The epiblast (precursor to ectoderm) invaginates to form primitive streak. Cells from the primitive streak give rise to both intraembryonic mesoderm and endoderm.
Rule of 3's for 3rd week	3 germ layers (gastrula): ectoderm, mesoderm, endoderm.	

Aortic arch derivatives

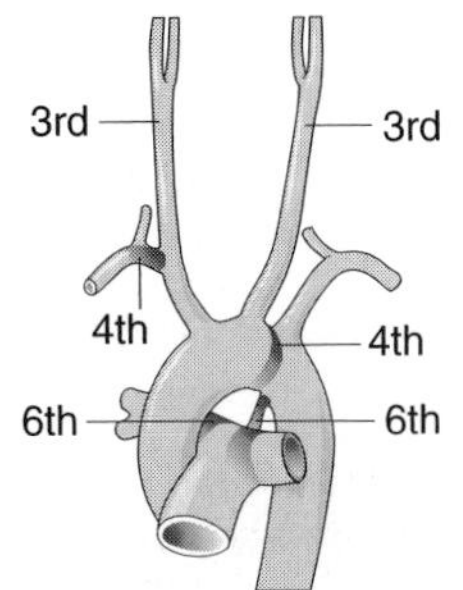

1st = part of **max**illary artery.	1st arch is **max**imal.
2nd = stapedial artery and hyoid artery.	Second = Stapedial.
3rd = common **C**arotid artery and proximal part of internal carotid artery.	**C** is 3rd letter of alphabet.
4th = on left, aortic arch; on right, proximal part of right subclavian artery.	4th arch (4 limbs) = systemic.
6th = proximal part of pulmonary arteries and (on left only) ductus arteriosus.	6th arch = pulmonary and the pulmonary-to-systemic shunt (ductus arteriosus).

Heart embryology

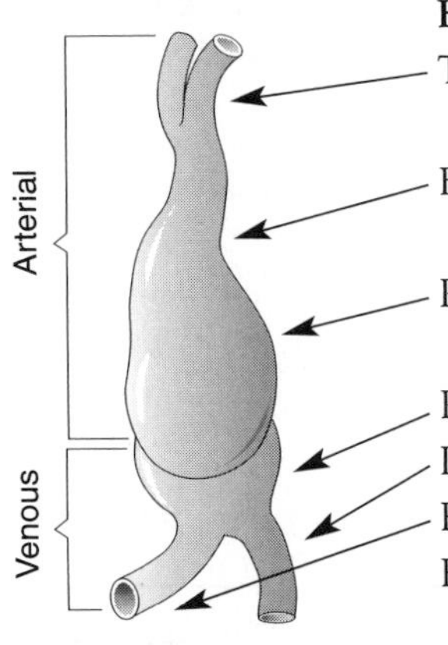

Embryonic structure	**Gives rise to**
Truncus arteriosus	Ascending aorta and pulmonary trunk
Bulbus cordis	Right ventricle and aortic outflow tract
Primitive ventricle	Left ventricle, except for the aortic outflow tract
Primitive atria	Auricular appendages
Left horn of sinus venosus	Coronary sinus
Right horn of sinus venosus	Smooth part of the right atrium
Right common cardinal vein and right anterior cardinal vein	Superior vena cava

Fetal erythropoiesis

Fetal erythropoiesis occurs in:

1. **Y**olk sac (3–8 wk)
2. **L**iver (6–30 wk)
3. **S**pleen (9–28 wk)
4. **B**one marrow (28 wk onward)

Young **L**iver **S**ynthesizes **B**lood.

Fetal circulation

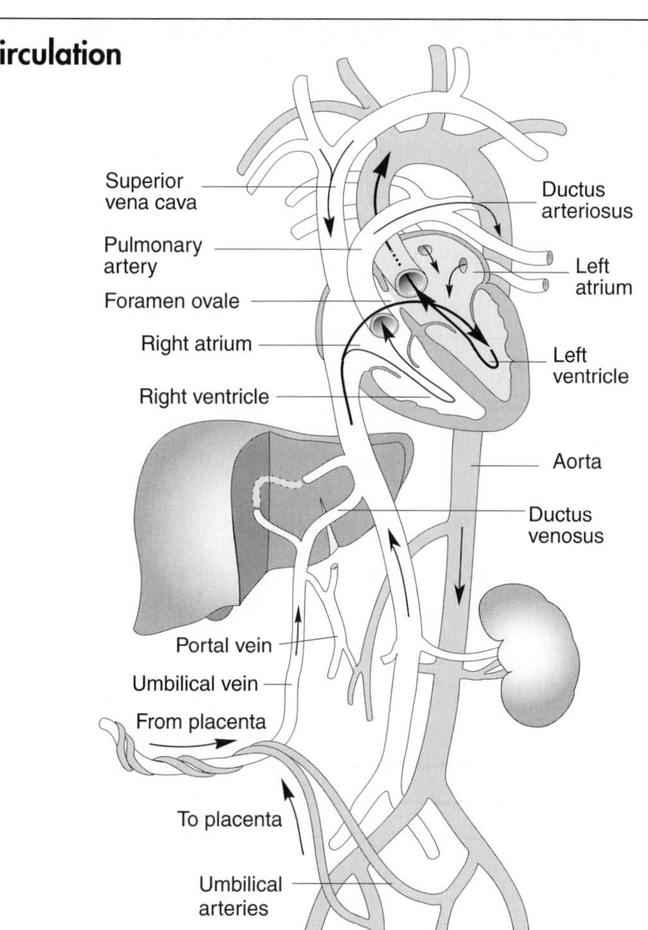

UCV Anat.6

Blood in umbilical vein is ≈ 80% saturated with O_2.

Most oxygenated blood reaching the heart via IVC is diverted through the foramen ovale and pumped out the aorta to the head.

Deoxygenated blood from the SVC is expelled into the pulmonary artery and ductus arteriosus to the lower body of the fetus.

At birth, infant takes a breath; ↓ resistance in pulmonary vasculature causes ↑ left atrial pressure vs. right atrial pressure; foramen ovale closes; ↑ in oxygen causes closure of ductus arteriosus.

Fetal-postnatal derivatives

1. Umbilical vein—ligamentum teres hepatis
2. Umbilical arteries—medial umbilical ligaments (2)
3. Ductus arteriosus—ligamentum arteriosum
4. Ductus venosus—ligamentum venosum
5. Foramen ovale—fossa ovalis
6. Allantois—urachus—median umbilical ligament
7. Notochord—nucleus pulposus

Urachal cyst or sinus is a remnant of the allantois (urine drainage from bladder).

Branchial apparatus

Branchial clefts are derived from ectoderm.

Branchial arches are derived from mesoderm and neural crests.

Branchial pouches are derived from endoderm.

CAP covers outside from inside (Clefts = ectoderm, Arches = mesoderm, Pouches = endoderm).

Branchial arch 1 derivatives

Meckel's cartilage: Mandible, Malleus, incus, sphenoMandibular ligament.

Muscles: Muscles of Mastication (temporalis, Masseter, lateral and Medial pterygoids), Mylohyoid, anterior belly of digastric, tensor tympani, tensor veli palatini.

Nerve: CN V_3

Branchial arch 2 derivatives

Reichert's cartilage: Stapes, Styloid process, lesser horn of hyoid, Stylohyoid ligament.

Muscles: muscles of facial expression, Stapedius, Stylohyoid, posterior belly of digastric.

Nerve: CN VII

HIGH-YIELD FACTS

Anatomy

Branchial arch 3 derivatives	Cartilage: greater horn of hyoid. Muscle: stylopharyngeus. Nerve: CN IX.	Think of pharynx: stylo**pharyngeus** innervated by glosso**pharyngeal** nerve.
Branchial arches 4 to 6 derivatives	Cartilages: thyroid, cricoid, arytenoids, corniculate, cuneiform. Muscles (4th arch): most pharyngeal constrictors, cricothyroid, levator veli palatini. Muscles (6th arch): all intrinsic muscles of larynx except cricothyroid. Nerve: 4th arch–CN X; 6th arch–CN X (recurrent laryngeal branch).	Arch 5 makes no major developmental contributions.
Branchial arch innervation	Arch 1 derivatives supplied by CN V_2 and V_3. Arch 2 derivatives supplied by CN VII. Arch 3 derivatives supplied by CN IX. Arch 4 and 6 derivatives supplied by CN X.	
Branchial cleft derivatives	1st cleft develops into external auditory meatus. 2nd through 4th clefts form temporary cervical sinuses, which are obliterated by proliferation of 2nd arch mesenchyme.	Persistent cervical sinus can lead to a branchial cyst in the neck.

Ear development

Bones	Muscles	Miscellaneous
Incus/malleus—1st arch	Tensor tympani (V_3)—1st arch	External auditory meatus—1st cleft
Stapes—2nd arch	Stapedius (VII)—2nd arch	Eardrum, eustachian tube—1st pouch

Pharyngeal pouch derivatives	1st pouch develops into middle ear cavity, eustachian tube, mastoid air cells. 2nd pouch develops into epithelial lining of palatine tonsil. 3rd pouch (dorsal wings) develops into **inferior** parathyroids. 3rd pouch (ventral wings) develops into thymus. 4th pouch develops into **superior** parathyroids. 5th pouch houses the ultimobranchial bodies, which become the C cells of the thyroid. arise from neural crest	1st pouch contributes to endoderm-lined structures of ear. 3rd pouch contributes to 3 structures (thymus, L and R inferior parathyroids). Ultimobranchial bodies arise from neural crest cells but migrate into 5th pouch.
Thymus UCV Anat.29	Site of T-cell maturation. Encapsulated. From epithelium of 3rd branchial pouches. Lymphocytes of mesenchymal origin. Cortex is dense with immature T cells; medulla is pale with mature T cells and epithelial reticular cells and contains Hassall's corpuscles. Positive and negative selection occurs at the corticomedullary junction.	Think of the **T**hymus as "finishing school" for **T** cells. They arrive immature and "dense" in the cortex; they are mature in the medulla.

Thyroid development

Thyroid diverticulum arises from floor of primitive pharynx, descends into neck. Connected to tongue by thyroglossal duct, which normally disappears but may persist as pyramidal lobe of thyroid. Foramen cecum is normal remnant of thyroglossal duct. Most common ectopic thyroid tissue site is the tongue.

UCV Anat.14

Tongue development

1st branchial arch forms anterior ⅔ (thus pain via CN V_3, taste via CN VII).
3rd and 4th arches form posterior ⅓ (thus pain and taste mainly via CN IX, extreme posterior via CN X).
Motor innervation is via CN XII.

Taste is CN VII, IX, X; pain is CN V_3, IX, X; motor is CN XII.

Cleft lip and cleft palate

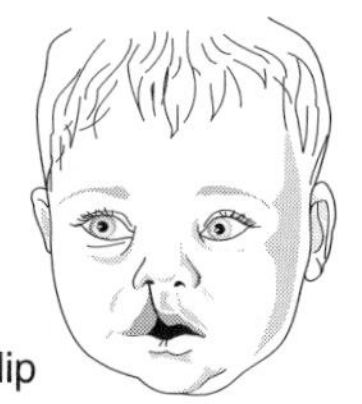
Cleft lip

Cleft lip—failure of fusion of the maxillary and medial nasal processes.
Cleft palate—failure of fusion of the lateral palatine processes, the nasal septum, and/or the median palatine process.

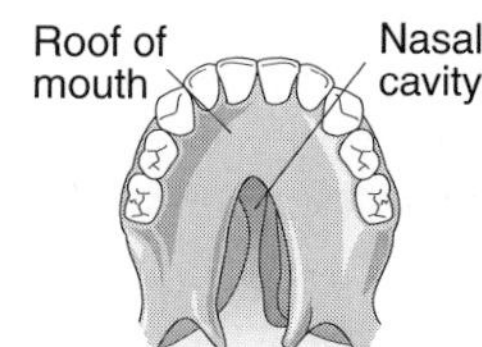

Cleft palate (partial)

Diaphragm embryology

Diaphragm is derived from:

1. **S**eptum transversum
2. **P**leuroperitoneal folds
3. **B**ody wall
4. **D**orsal mesentery of esophagus

Several **P**arts **B**uild **D**iaphragm.
Abdominal contents may herniate into the thorax due to incomplete development (hiatal hernia).

UCV Anat.18

Bone Formation

Intramembranous	Spontaneous bone formation without preexisting cartilage.
Endochondral	Ossification of cartilaginous molds. Long bones form by this type of ossification at primary and secondary centers.

Meckel's diverticulum

Persistence of the vitelline duct or yolk stalk. May contain ectopic acid–secreting gastric mucosa and/or pancreatic tissue. Most common congenital anomaly of the GI tract. Can cause bleeding or obstruction near the terminal ileum. Contrast with omphalomesenteric cyst = cystic dilatation of vitelline duct.

The five **2's**:
2 inches long.
2 feet from the ileocecal valve.
2% of population.
Commonly presents in first 2 years of life.
May have 2 types of epithelia.

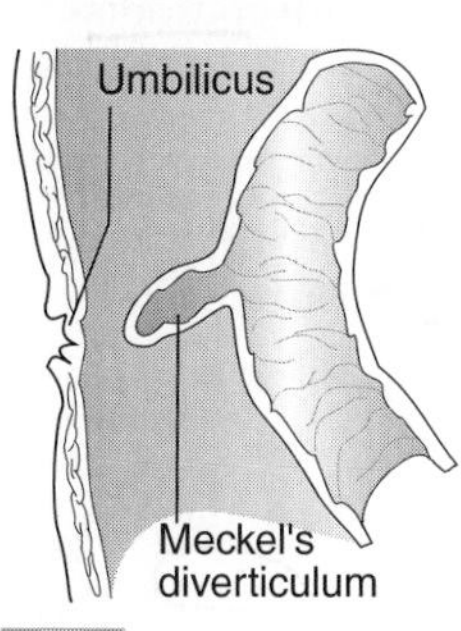

UCV Anat.89

Pancreas and spleen embryology

Pancreas is derived from the foregut. Ventral pancreatic bud becomes pancreatic head, uncinate process (lower half of head), and main pancreatic duct. Dorsal pancreatic bud becomes everything else (body, tail, isthmus, and accessory pancreatic duct).
Spleen arises from dorsal mesentery but is supplied by artery of foregut.

Genital ducts

Mesonephric (wolffian) duct	Develops into **S**eminal vesicles, **E**pididymis, **E**jaculatory duct, and **D**uctus deferens.	SEED
Paramesonephric (müllerian) duct	Develops into fallopian tube, uterus, and part of vagina.	
	Müllerian inhibiting substance secreted by testes suppresses development of paramesonephric ducts in males.	

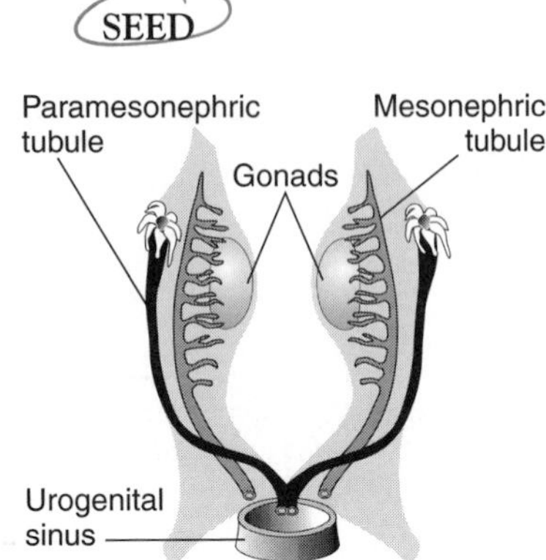

Bicornuate uterus

Results from incomplete fusion of the paramesonephric ducts. Associated with urinary tract abnormalities and infertility.

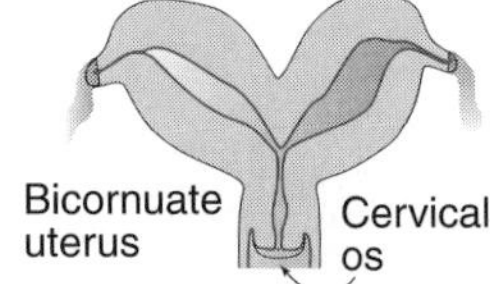

Male/female genital homologues

Corpus spongiosum ≈ vestibular bulbs.
Bulbourethral glands (of Cowper) ≈ greater vestibular glands (of Bartholin).
Prostate gland ≈ urethral and paraurethral glands (of Skene).
Glans penis ≈ glans clitoris.
Ventral shaft of the penis ≈ labia minora.
Scrotum ≈ labia majora.

Congenital penile abnormalities

Hypospadias	Abnormal opening of penile urethra on inferior (ventral) side of penis due to failure of urethral folds to close.	Hypospadias is more common than epispadias.
Epispadias	Abnormal opening of penile urethra on superior (dorsal) side of penis due to faulty positioning of genital tubercle.	Exstrophy of the bladder is associated with epispadias.

Sperm development

Spermatogenesis: spermatogonia → 1° spermatocyte → 2° spermatocyte → spermatid → (spermiogenesis) → spermatozoa. Full development takes 2 months. Spermatogenesis in **S**eminiferous tubules.

Derivation of sperm parts

Acrosome is derived from the Golgi apparatus and flagellum (tail) from one of the centrioles. Middle piece (neck) has **M**itochondria. Sperm food supply is fructose.

Meiosis and ovulation

1° oocytes begin meiosis I during fetal life and complete meiosis I just prior to ovulation.
Meiosis I is arrested in prOphase for years until Ovulation. Meiosis II is arrested in **MET**aphase until fertilization.

An egg **MET** a sperm.

Amniotic fluid abnormalities

Polyhydramnios	> 1.5–2 L of amniotic fluid; associated with esophageal/duodenal atresia, anencephaly.
Oligohydramnios	< 0.5 L of amniotic fluid; associated with bilateral renal agenesis or posterior urethral valves (in males).

Potter's syndrome

Bilateral renal agenesis → oligohydramnios → limb deformities, facial deformities, pulmonary hypoplasia.

Babies with Potter's can't "Pee" in utero.

ANATOMY—GROSS ANATOMY

Lumbar puncture

CSF obtained from lumbar subarachnoid space between L4 and L5 (at the level of iliac crests). Structures pierced as follows:

1. Skin/superficial fascia
2. Ligaments (supraspinous, interspinous, ligamentum flavum)
3. Epidural space
4. Dura mater
5. Subdural space
6. Arachnoid
7. Subarachnoid space—CSF

Pia is not pierced.

Lower extremity nerve injury

Nerve	Deficit in motion	Deficit in sensation
Common peroneal (L4–S2)	Loss of dorsiflexion (→ foot drop) *Anat.39*	PED = Peroneal Everts and Dorsiflexes.
Tibial (L4–S3)	Loss of plantar flexion	TIP = Tibial Inverts and Plantarflexes; if injured, can't stand on TIPtoes.
Femoral (L2–L4)	Loss of knee jerk *Anat.43*	
Obturator (L2–L4)	Loss of hip adduction	

UCV

Spinal cord lower extent

In adults, spinal cord extends to lower border of L1–L2; subarachnoid space extends to lower border of S2. Lumbar puncture is usually performed in L3–L4 or L4–L5 interspaces, at level of cauda equina.

To keep the cord alive, keep the spinal needle between L3 and L5.

Spinal nerves

There are 31 spinal nerves altogether: 8 cervical, 12 thoracic, 5 lumbar, 5 sacral, 1 coccygeal.

31, just like 31 flavors!

Landmark dermatomes

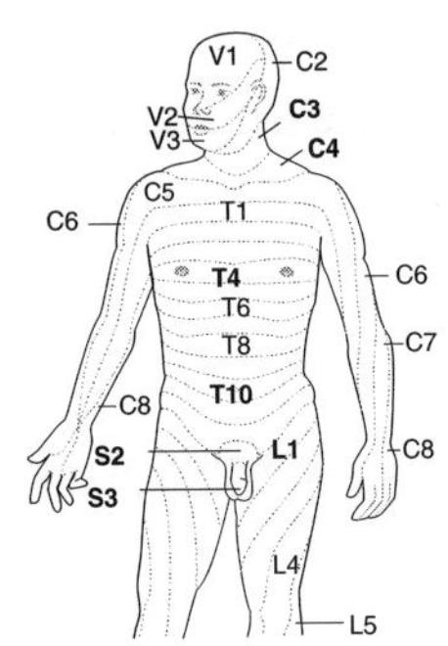

C2 is a posterior half of a skull "cap."
C3 is a high turtleneck shirt.
C4 is a low collar shirt.
T4 is at the nipple.
T7 is at the xiphoid process.
T10 is at the umbilicus (important for early appendicitis pain referral).
L1 is at the inguinal ligament.
L4 includes the kneecaps.
S2, S3, S4 erection and sensation of penile and anal zones.

Gallbladder pain referred to the right shoulder via the phrenic nerve.
T4 at the **teat pore.**
T10 at the belly but**TEN.**
L1 is **IL** (**I**nguinal **L**igament).
Down on **L4s (all fours).**
"**S2, 3, 4** keep the penis off the floor."

Rotator cuff muscles

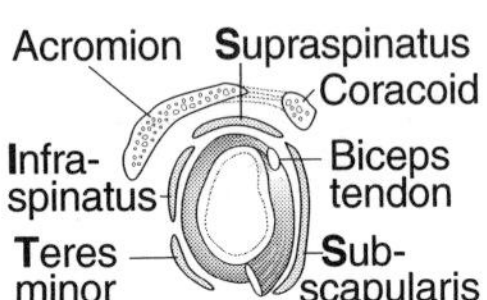

Shoulder muscles that form the rotator cuff: **S**upraspinatus, **I**nfraspinatus, **t**eres minor, **S**ubscapularis.

S I t S (small t is for teres minor).

Thenar-hypothenar muscles

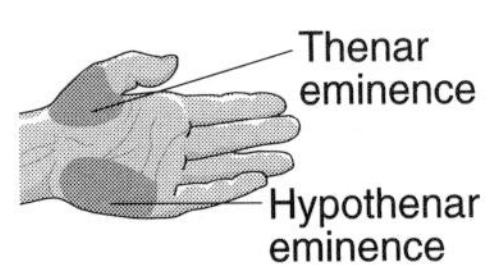

Thenar: **O**pponens pollicis, **A**bductor pollicis brevis, **F**lexor pollicis brevis.
Hypothenar: **O**pponens digiti minimi, **A**bductor digiti minimi, **F**lexor digiti minimi.

Both groups perform the same functions: **O**ppose, **A**bduct, and **F**lex **(OAF).**

Unhappy triad/ knee injury

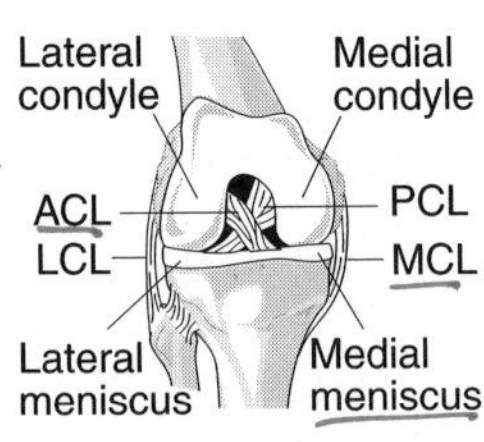

UCV Anat.68

This common football injury (caused by clipping from the lateral side) consists of damage to medial collateral ligament (MCL), medial meniscus, and anterior cruciate ligament (ACL).
PCL = posterior cruciate ligament. LCL = lateral collateral ligament.

Positive anterior drawer sign indicates tearing of the anterior cruciate ligament.
"Anterior" and "posterior" in ACL and PCL refer to sites of **tibial** attachment.

Femoral sheath

Femoral sheath contains femoral artery, femoral vein, and femoral canal (containing deep inguinal lymph nodes). Femoral nerve lies outside femoral sheath.

Lateral to medial: **N-(AVEL)** = **N**erve–(**A**rtery–**V**ein–**E**mpty space–**L**ymphatics).

Recurrent laryngeal nerve UCV Anat.12	Supplies all intrinsic muscles of the larynx except the cricothyroid muscle. Left recurrent laryngeal nerve wraps around the arch of the aorta and the ligamentum arteriosum. Right recurrent laryngeal nerve wraps around right subclavian artery. Damage results in hoarseness. Complication of thyroid surgery.	
Scalp and meninges: layers 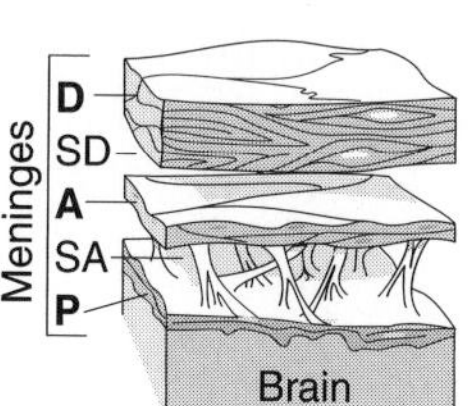 	Skin, Connective tissue, Aponeurosis, Loose connective tissue, Pericranium; skull. Dura mater, subdural (SD) space, Arachnoid, subarachnoid (SA) space, Pia mater, brain.	SCALP–skull–DAP. Loose connective tissue is vascular.
Trigeminal ganglion UCV Anat.54	Also called semilunar ganglion or gasserian ganglion. Located in the trigeminal cave (of Meckel). Trigeminal neuralgia = tic douloureux.	Trigeminal neuralgia can be treated with carbamazepine or surgical decompression.
Mastication muscles	Three muscles close jaw: **M**asseter, te**M**poralis, **M**edial pterygoid. One opens: lateral pterygoid. All are innervated by the trigeminal nerve (V_3).	**M**'s **M**unch. **L**ateral **L**owers (when speaking of pterygoids with respect to jaw motion).
Muscles with *glossus*	All muscles with root *glossus* in their names (except palatoglossus, innervated by vagus nerve) are innervated by *hypoglossal* nerve.	Palat: vagus nerve. *Glossus*: hypo*glossal* nerve.
Muscles with *palat*	All muscles with root *palat* in their names (except tensor veli palatini, innervated by mandibular branch of CN V) are innervated by vagus nerve.	Palat: vagus nerve (except tensor, who was too tense).
Carotid sheath	Three structures inside: 1. Internal jugular **V**ein (lateral) 2. Common carotid **A**rtery (medial) 3. Vagus **N**erve (posterior)	VAN
Diaphragm structures	Structures perforating diaphragm: At T**8**: IVC At T**10**: esophagus, vagus (two trunks) At T**12**: aorta (red), thoracic duct (white), azygous vein (blue) Diaphragm is innervated by **C3, 4, and 5** (phrenic nerve). Pain from the diaphragm can be referred to the shoulder. via phrenic	I 8 10 EGGs AT 12: **I** = Ivc @ **8th** vertebra; **E** = Esophagus, **G** = vaGus @ **10th** vertebra; **A** = Aorta, Azygous, **T** = Thoracic duct @ **12th** vertebra. "**C3, 4, 5** keeps the diaphragm alive."

HIGH-YIELD FACTS

Anatomy

RCA supply
· SA
· AV
· Inferior Ⓛ ventricle via PD

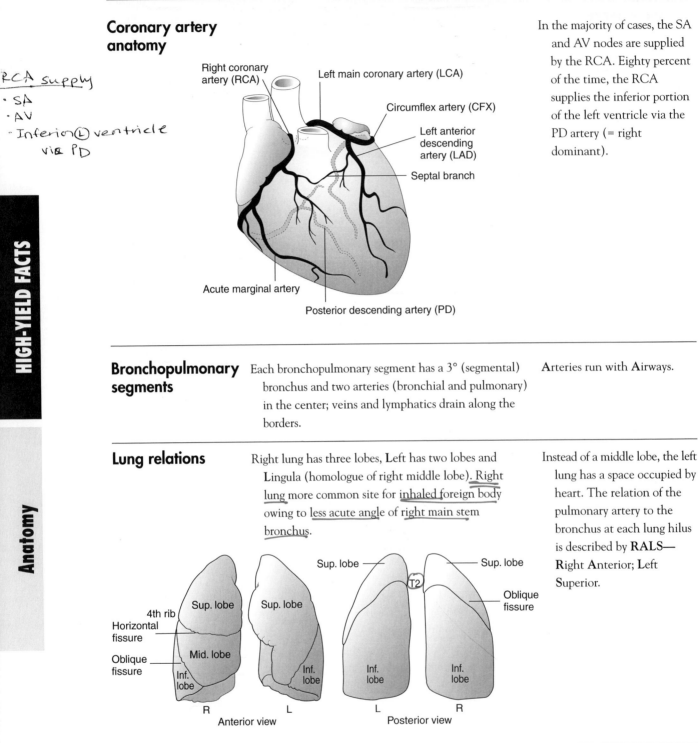

HIGH-YIELD FACTS

Anatomy

Coronary artery anatomy

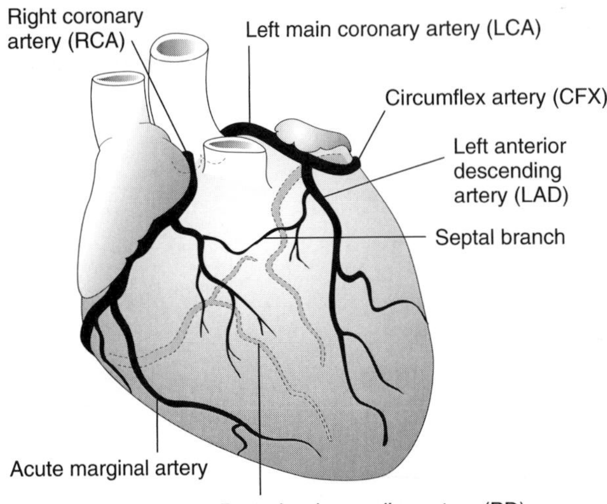

In the majority of cases, the SA and AV nodes are supplied by the RCA. Eighty percent of the time, the RCA supplies the inferior portion of the left ventricle via the PD artery (= right dominant).

Bronchopulmonary segments

Each bronchopulmonary segment has a 3° (segmental) bronchus and two arteries (bronchial and pulmonary) in the center; veins and lymphatics drain along the borders.

Arteries run with **A**irways.

Lung relations

Right lung has three lobes, **L**eft has two lobes and **L**ingula (homologue of right middle lobe). Right lung more common site for inhaled foreign body owing to less acute angle of right main stem bronchus.

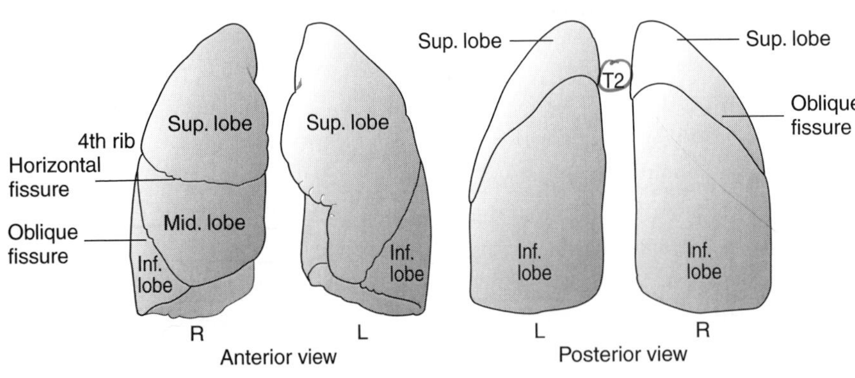

Instead of a middle lobe, the left lung has a space occupied by heart. The relation of the pulmonary artery to the bronchus at each lung hilus is described by **RALS**—**R**ight **A**nterior; **L**eft **S**uperior.

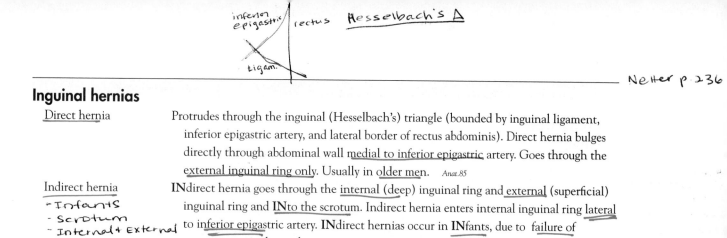

Inguinal hernias

Direct hernia	Protrudes through the inguinal (Hesselbach's) triangle (bounded by inguinal ligament, inferior epigastric artery, and lateral border of rectus abdominis). Direct hernia bulges directly through abdominal wall medial to inferior epigastric artery. Goes through the external inguinal ring only. Usually in older men. *Anat.85*
Indirect hernia	**IN**direct hernia goes through the internal (deep) inguinal ring and external (superficial) inguinal ring and **IN**to the scrotum. Indirect hernia enters internal inguinal ring lateral to inferior epigastric artery. **IN**direct hernias occur in **IN**fants, due to failure of processus vaginalis to close. *Anat.87*

UCV

Portal-systemic anastomoses

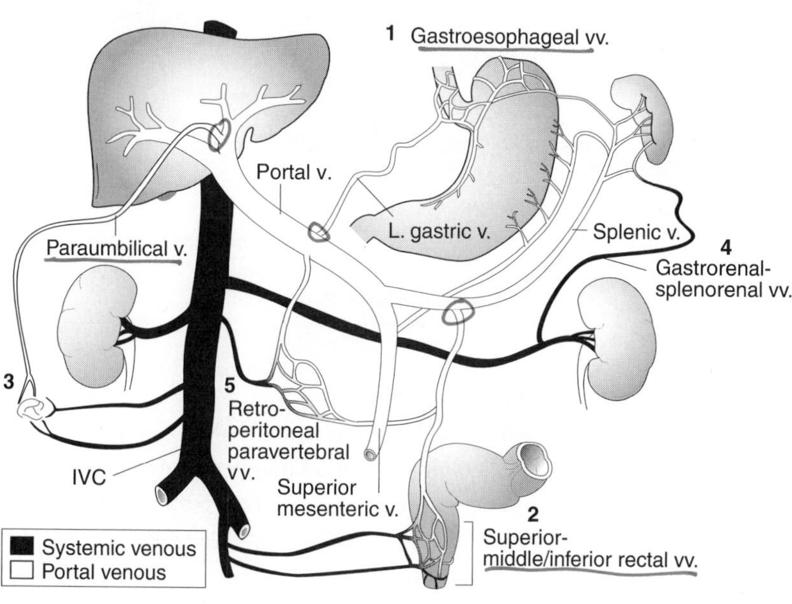

UCV *Anat.26*

1. Left gastric-azygous → **esophageal varices.**
2. Superior-middle/inferior rectal → **hemorrhoids.**
3. Paraumbilical-inferior epigastric → **caput medusae** (navel).
4. Retroperitoneal → renal.
5. Retroperitoneal → paravertebral.

Gut, butt, and caput, the anastomoses 3. Commonly seen in alcoholic cirrhosis.

Retroperitoneal structures

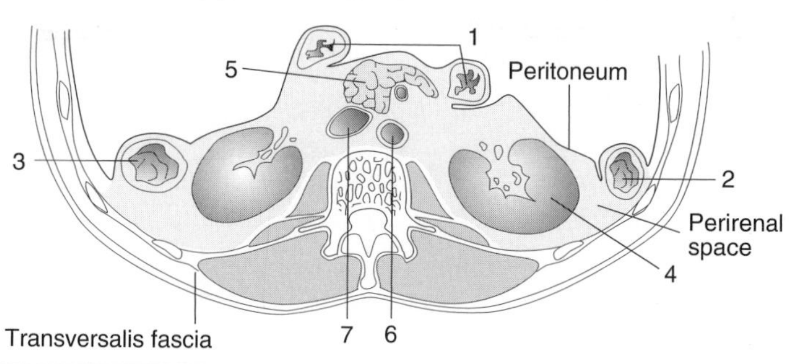

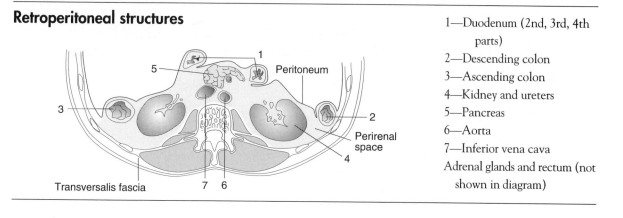

1—Duodenum (2nd, 3rd, 4th parts)
2—Descending colon
3—Ascending colon
4—Kidney and ureters
5—Pancreas
6—Aorta
7—Inferior vena cava
Adrenal glands and rectum (not shown in diagram)

Digestive tract anatomy

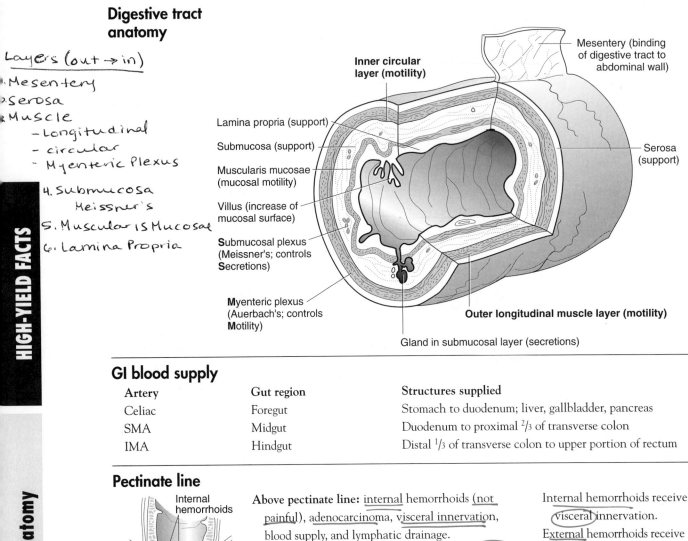

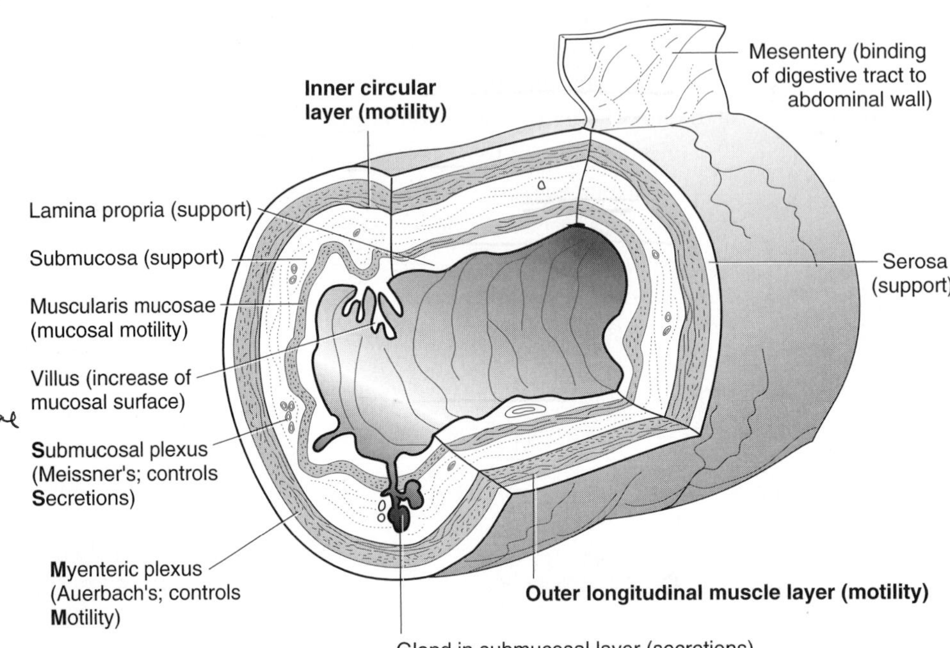

GI blood supply

Artery	Gut region	Structures supplied
Celiac	Foregut	Stomach to duodenum; liver, gallbladder, pancreas
SMA	Midgut	Duodenum to proximal $^2/_3$ of transverse colon
IMA	Hindgut	Distal $^1/_3$ of transverse colon to upper portion of rectum

Pectinate line

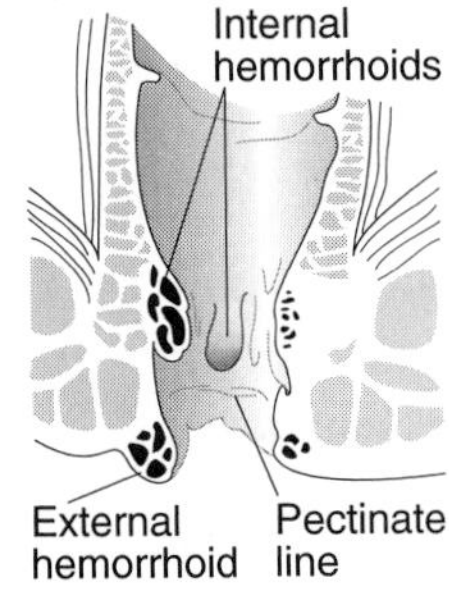

Above pectinate line: internal hemorrhoids (not painful), adenocarcinoma, visceral innervation, blood supply, and lymphatic drainage.

Below pectinate line: external hemorrhoids (painful), squamous cell carcinoma, somatic innervation, blood supply, and lymphatic drainage.

Internal hemorrhoids receive visceral innervation.

External hemorrhoids receive somatic innervation and are therefore painful.

UCV Anat.27

Kidney anatomy and glomerular structure

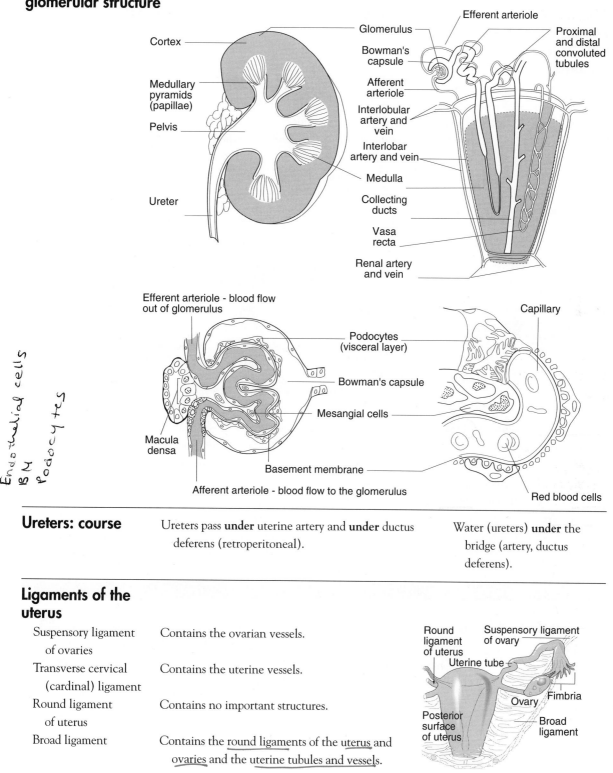

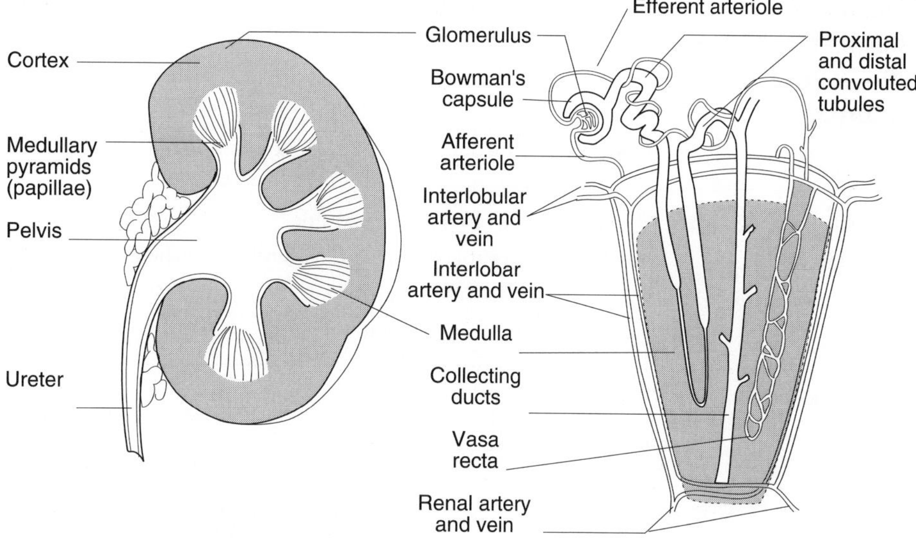

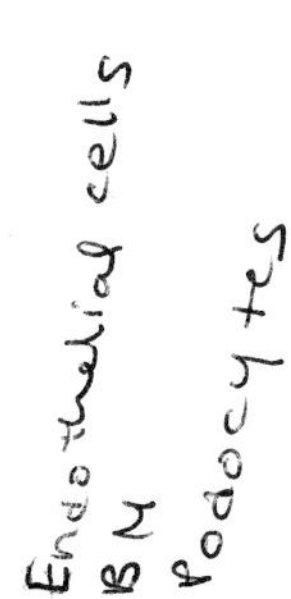

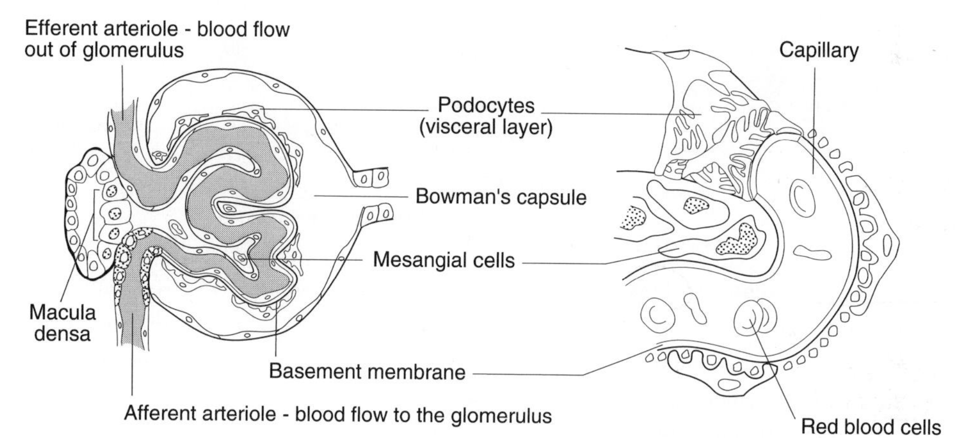

Ureters: course

Ureters: course	Ureters pass **under** uterine artery and **under** ductus deferens (retroperitoneal).	Water (ureters) **under** the bridge (artery, ductus deferens).

Ligaments of the uterus

Suspensory ligament of ovaries	Contains the ovarian vessels.
Transverse cervical (cardinal) ligament	Contains the uterine vessels.
Round ligament of uterus	Contains no important structures.
Broad ligament	Contains the round ligaments of the uterus and ovaries and the uterine tubules and vessels.

Round ligament of uterus
Suspensory ligament of ovary
Uterine tube
Fimbria
Ovary
Posterior surface of uterus
Broad ligament

Autonomic innervation of the male sexual response

Erection is mediated by the **P**arasympathetic nervous system.
Emission is mediated by the **S**ympathetic nervous system.
Ejaculation is mediated by visceral and somatic nerves.

Point and **S**hoot.

Clinically important landmarks

Pudendal nerve block—ischial spine.
Appendix—⅔ of the way from the umbilicus to the anterior superior iliac spine (McBurney's point).
Lumbar puncture—iliac crest.

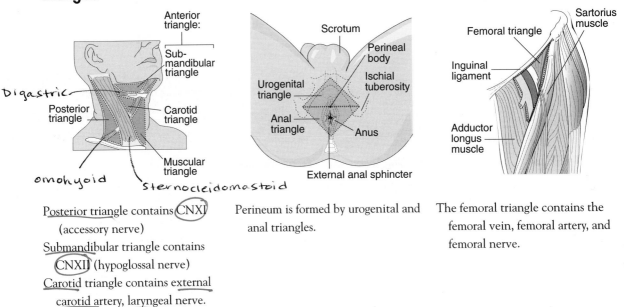

Triangles

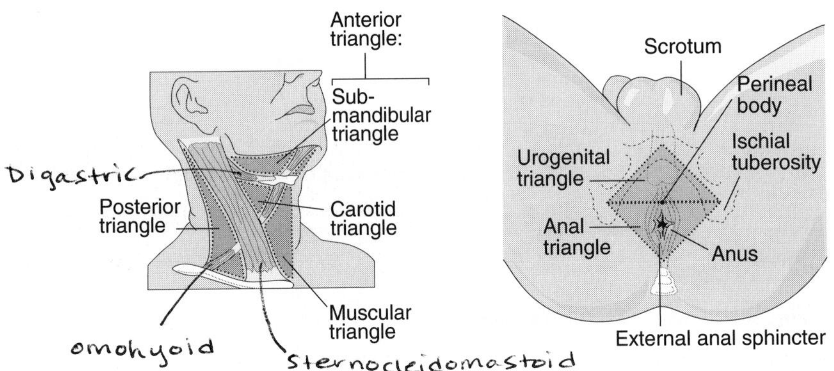

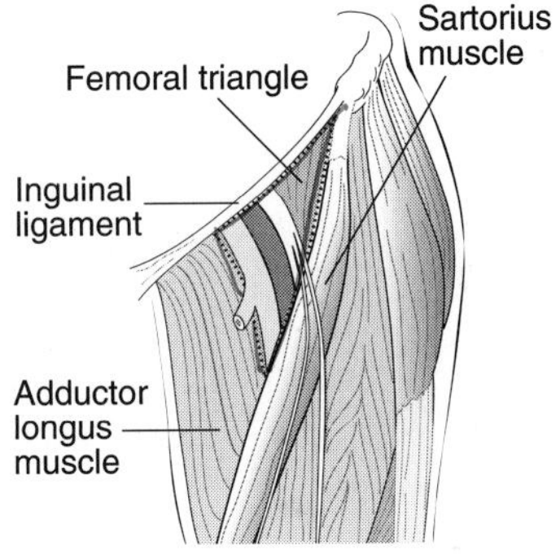

Posterior triangle contains CNXI (accessory nerve)
Submandibular triangle contains CNXII (hypoglossal nerve)
Carotid triangle contains external carotid artery, laryngeal nerve.

Perineum is formed by urogenital and anal triangles.

The femoral triangle contains the femoral vein, femoral artery, and femoral nerve.

ANATOMY—HISTOLOGY

Peripheral nerve layers

Endoneurium invests single nerve fiber.
Perineurium (permeability barrier) surrounds a fascicle of nerve fibers.
Epineurium (dense connective tissue) surrounds entire nerve (fascicles and blood vessels).

Perineurium = **P**ermeability barrier; must be rejoined in microsurgery for limb reattachment.
Endo = inner.
Peri = around.
Epi = outer.

Meissner's corpuscles

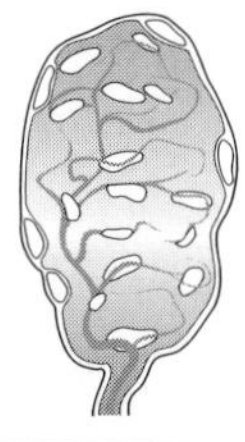

Small, encapsulated sensory receptors found in dermis of palm, soles, and digits of skin. Involved in light discriminatory touch of glabrous (hairless) skin.

Pacinian corpuscles

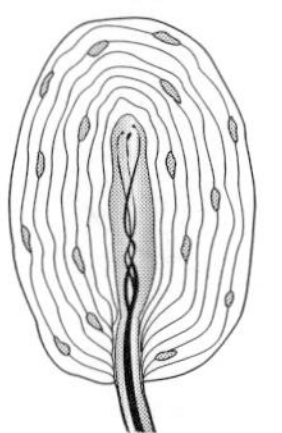

Large, encapsulated sensory receptors found in deeper layers of skin at ligaments, joint capsules, serous membranes, mesenteries. Involved in pressure, coarse touch, vibration, and tension.

Inner ear

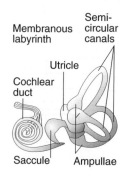

Membranous labyrinth
Semicircular canals
Utricle
Cochlear duct
Saccule
Ampullae

The bony labyrinth is filled with perilymph (Na^+ rich: similar to ECF) and includes the cochlea (hearing), the vestibule (linear acceleration), and the semicircular canals (angular acceleration).

The membranous labyrinth is filled with endolymph (K^+ rich: similar to ICF) and contains the cochlear duct, utricle, saccule, and semicircular canals. Hair cells are the sensory elements in both the cochlear and vestibular apparatus.

Peri—think outside of cell (Na^+).
Endo—think inside of cell (K^+).
Endolymph is made by the stria vascularis.
Utricle and saccule contain maculae: for linear acceleration.
Semicircular canals contain ampullae: angular acceleration.

Enteric plexuses

Myenteric — Coordinates Motility along entire gut wall. Also known as Auerbach's plexus. Contains cell bodies of some parasympathetic terminal effector neurons. Located between inner and outer layers of smooth muscle in GI tract wall.

Submucosal — Regulates local Secretions, blood flow, and absorption. Also known as Meissner's plexus. Contains cell bodies of some parasympathetic terminal effector neurons. Located between mucosa and inner layer of smooth muscle in GI tract wall.

Collagen types

Collagen is the most abundant protein in the human body.

Type I (90%): bone, tendon, skin, dentin, fascia, cornea, late wound repair. — Type **I**: BONE

Type II: cartilage (including hyaline), vitreous body, nucleus pulposus. — Type **II**: car**TWO**lage

Type III (reticulin): skin, blood vessels, uterus, fetal tissue, granulation tissue.

Type IV: basement membrane or basal lamina. — Type **IV**: Under the **floor** (basement membrane)

Type X: epiphyseal plate.

Epidermis layers

From surface to base: stratum **C**orneum, stratum **L**ucidum, stratum **G**ranulosum, stratum **S**pinosum, stratum **B**asalis.

Californians **L**ike **G**irls in **S**tring **B**ikinis.

Glomerular basement membrane

Formed from fused endothelial and podocyte basement membranes and coated with negatively charged heparan sulfate. Responsible for actual filtration of plasma according to net charge and size.

In **nephrotic syndrome**, **negative charge is lost** (and plasma protein is lost in urine as a consequence).

Cilia structure

9 + 2 arrangement of microtubules.
Dynein is an ATPase that links peripheral 9 doublets and causes bending of cilium by differential sliding of doublets.

Kartagener's syndrome is due to a dynein arm defect, resulting in immotile cilia.

UCV Bio.68

Intermediate filament

Permanent structure. Long fibrous molecules with 10-nm diameter linked to plasma membrane at desmosomes by desmoplakin. Very insoluble. Tissue specific. Rich in cysteine.

Tissue type	Intermediate filament protein
Epithelial cells	Contain cytokeratin.
Connective tissue	Contains vimentin.
Muscle cells	Contain desmin.
Neuroglia	Contain glial fibrillary acidic proteins (GFAP).
Neurons	Contain neurofilaments.
Nucleus	Contains nuclear lamin.

Nissl bodies

Nissl bodies (in neurons) = rough ER; not found in axon or axon hillock.
Synthesize enzymes (e.g., ChAT) and peptide neurotransmitters.

Functions of Golgi apparatus	1. Distribution center of proteins and lipids from ER to the plasma membrane, lysosomes, and secretory vesicles 2. Modifies N-oligosaccharides on asparagine. 3. Adds O-oligosaccharides to serine and threonine residues 4. Proteoglycan assembly from proteoglycan core proteins 5. Sulfation of sugars in proteoglycans and of selected tyrosine on proteins 6. Addition of mannose-6-phosphate to specific lysosomal proteins, which targets the protein to the lysosome (not outside cell)	I-cell disease is caused by the failure of addition of mannose-6-phosphate to lysosome proteins, causing these enzymes to be secreted outside the cell instead of being targeted to the lysosome.
Rough endoplasmic reticulum (RER)	RER is the site of synthesis of secretory (exported) proteins and of N-linked oligosaccharide addition to many proteins.	Mucus-secreting goblet cells of the small intestine and antibody-secreting plasma cells are rich in RER.
Smooth endoplasmic reticulum (SER)	SER is the site of steroid synthesis and detoxification of drugs and poisons.	Liver hepatocytes and steroid-hormone–producing cells of the adrenal cortex are rich in SER.
Sinusoids of liver	Irregular "capillaries" with round pores 100–200 nm in diameter. No basement membrane. Allows macromolecules of plasma full access to surface of liver cells through space of Disse.	
Sinusoids of spleen	Long, vascular channels in red pulp. With fenestrated "barrel hoop" basement membrane. Macrophages found nearby.	T cells are found in the PALS and the red pulp of the spleen. B cells are found in follicles within the white pulp of the spleen.
Pancreas endocrine cell types	Islets of Langerhans are collections of endocrine cells (most numerous in tail of pancreas). α = glucagon; β = insulin; δ = somatostatin. Islets arise from pancreatic buds.	

HIGH-YIELD FACTS

Anatomy

Adrenal cortex and medulla

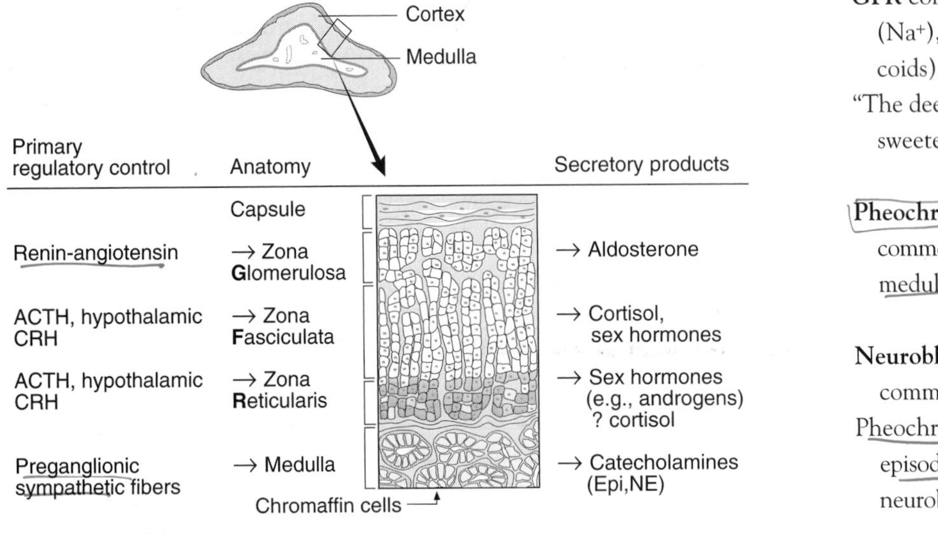

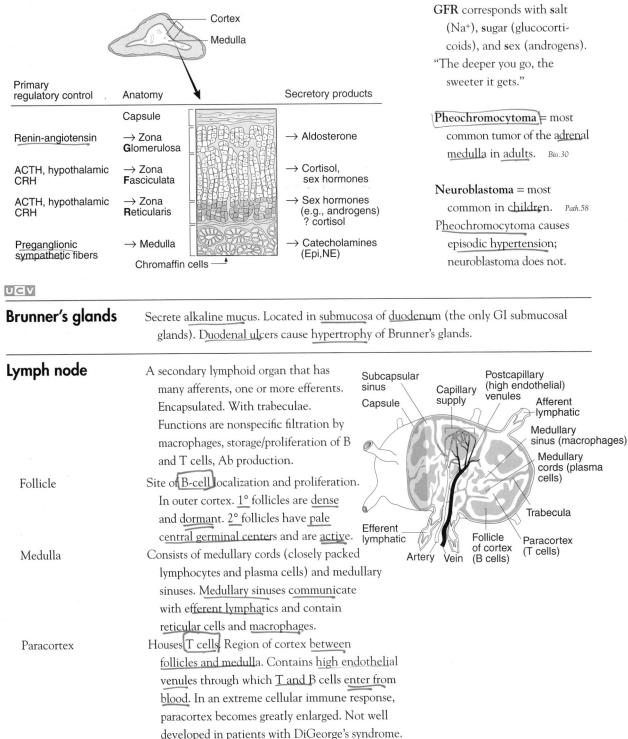

GFR corresponds with salt (Na+), sugar (glucocorticoids), and sex (androgens). "The deeper you go, the sweeter it gets."

Pheochromocytoma = most common tumor of the adrenal medulla in adults. *Bio.30*

Neuroblastoma = most common in children. *Path.58*

Pheochromocytoma causes episodic hypertension; neuroblastoma does not.

UCV

Brunner's glands — Secrete alkaline mucus. Located in submucosa of duodenum (the only GI submucosal glands). Duodenal ulcers cause hypertrophy of Brunner's glands.

Lymph node — A secondary lymphoid organ that has many afferents, one or more efferents. Encapsulated. With trabeculae. Functions are nonspecific filtration by macrophages, storage/proliferation of B and T cells, Ab production.

Follicle — Site of B-cell localization and proliferation. In outer cortex. 1° follicles are dense and dormant. 2° follicles have pale central germinal centers and are active.

Medulla — Consists of medullary cords (closely packed lymphocytes and plasma cells) and medullary sinuses. Medullary sinuses communicate with efferent lymphatics and contain reticular cells and macrophages.

Paracortex — Houses T cells. Region of cortex between follicles and medulla. Contains high endothelial venules through which T and B cells enter from blood. In an extreme cellular immune response, paracortex becomes greatly enlarged. Not well developed in patients with DiGeorge's syndrome.

Subcapsular sinus
Capsule
Capillary supply
Postcapillary (high endothelial) venules
Afferent lymphatic
Medullary sinus (macrophages)
Medullary cords (plasma cells)
Trabecula
Efferent lymphatic
Artery
Vein
Follicle of cortex (B cells)
Paracortex (T cells)

Peyer's patch	Unencapsulated lymphoid tissue found in lamina propria and submucosa of intestine. Covered by single layer of cuboidal enterocytes (no goblet cells) with specialized M cells interspersed. M cells take up antigen. Stimulated B cells leave Peyer's patch and travel through lymph and blood to lamina propria of intestine, where they differentiate to IgA-secreting plasma cells. IgA receives protective secretory piece, then is transported across epithelium to gut to deal with intraluminal Ag.	Think of **IgA,** the **I**ntra-**g**ut–**A**ntibody. And always say, "secretory IgA."

ANATOMY—NEUROANATOMY

Hypothalamus: functions	**T**hirst and water balance (supraoptic nucleus). **A**denohypophysis control via releasing factors. **N**eurohypophysis releases hormones synthesized in hypothalamic nuclei. **H**unger (lateral nucleus) and satiety (ventromedial nucleus). **A**utonomic regulation (anterior hypothalamus regulates parasympathetic activity), circadian rhythms (suprachiasmatic nucleus). **T**emperature regulation: Posterior hypothalamus—heat conservation and production when cold. Anterior hypothalamus—coordinates Cooling when hot. **S**exual urges and emotions (septate nucleus).	The hypothalamus wears **TAN HATS.** If you zap your **ventromedial** nucleus, you grow **ven**trally and **medial**ly (hyperphagia and obesity). If you zap your **P**osterior hypothalamus, you become a **P**oikilotherm (cold-blooded snake). **A/C** = anterior cooling.
Posterior pituitary (neurohypophysis)	Receives hypothalamic axonal projections from supraoptic (ADH) and paraventricular (oxytocin) nuclei.	Oxytocin: *oxys* = quick; *tocos* = birth.
Functions of thalamic nuclei	Lateral geniculate nucleus = visual. Medial geniculate nucleus = auditory. Ventral posterior nucleus, lateral part = body senses (proprioception, pressure, pain, touch vibration). Ventral posterior nucleus, medial part = facial sensation, including pain. Ventral anterior/lateral nuclei = motor.	**L**ateral to **L**ook. **M**edial for **M**usic.

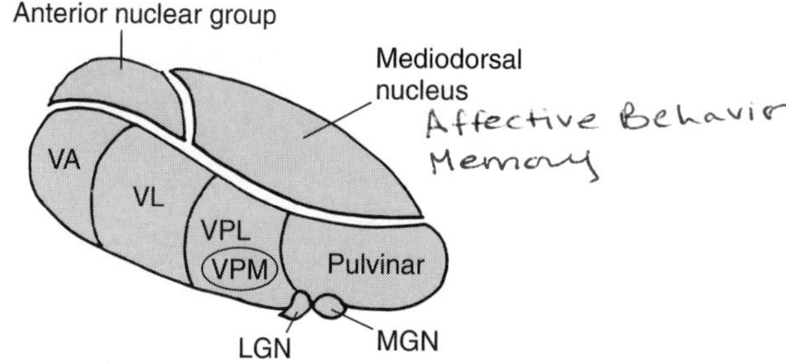

Anterior Nuclear Group- Input: Mamilary bodies
output: cingulate gyrus
→ Part of Papez circuit of emotion
- Limbic system

Hippocampus → Fornix → mamilary body → Anterior Nucle. Thalamus → cingulate gyrus → Hippocampus

Limbic system: functions	Responsible for **F**eeding, **F**ighting, **F**eeling, **F**light, and sex.	The famous **5 F's.**
CNS/PNS supportive cells	Astrocytes—physical support, repair, K^+ metabolism. Microglia—phagocytosis. Oligodendroglia—central myelin production. Schwann cells—peripheral myelin production. Ependymal cells—inner lining of ventricles.	
Blood–brain barrier	Formed by three structures: 1. **C**horoid plexus epithelium 2. **I**ntracerebral capillary endothelium 3. **A**rachnoid Glucose and amino acids cross by carrier-mediated transport mechanism. Nonpolar/lipid-soluble substances cross more readily than polar/water-soluble ones. L-dopa, rather than dopamine, is used to treat parkinsonism because dopamine does not cross the blood–brain barrier.	Blood–brain barrier guarded by **CIA** Other barriers include: 1. Blood–gas barrier 2. Blood–testis barrier
Chorea UCV Path3.52	Sudden, jerky, purposeless movements. Characteristic of basal ganglia lesion (e.g., Huntington's disease).	*Chorea* = dancing (Greek). Think choral dancing or choreography.
Athetosis	Slow, writhing movements, especially of fingers. Characteristic of basal ganglia lesion.	*Athetos* = not fixed (Greek). Think snakelike.
Hemiballismus UCV Path3.50	Sudden, wild flailing of one arm. Characteristic of contralateral subthalamic nucleus lesion.	Half ballistic (as in throwing a baseball).
Tremors: cerebellar versus basal	Cerebellar tremor = intention tremor. Basal ganglion tremor = resting tremor.	Basal = at rest (**Park**inson's disease) when **Park**ed.

HIGH-YIELD FACTS

Anatomy

Cerebral cortex functions

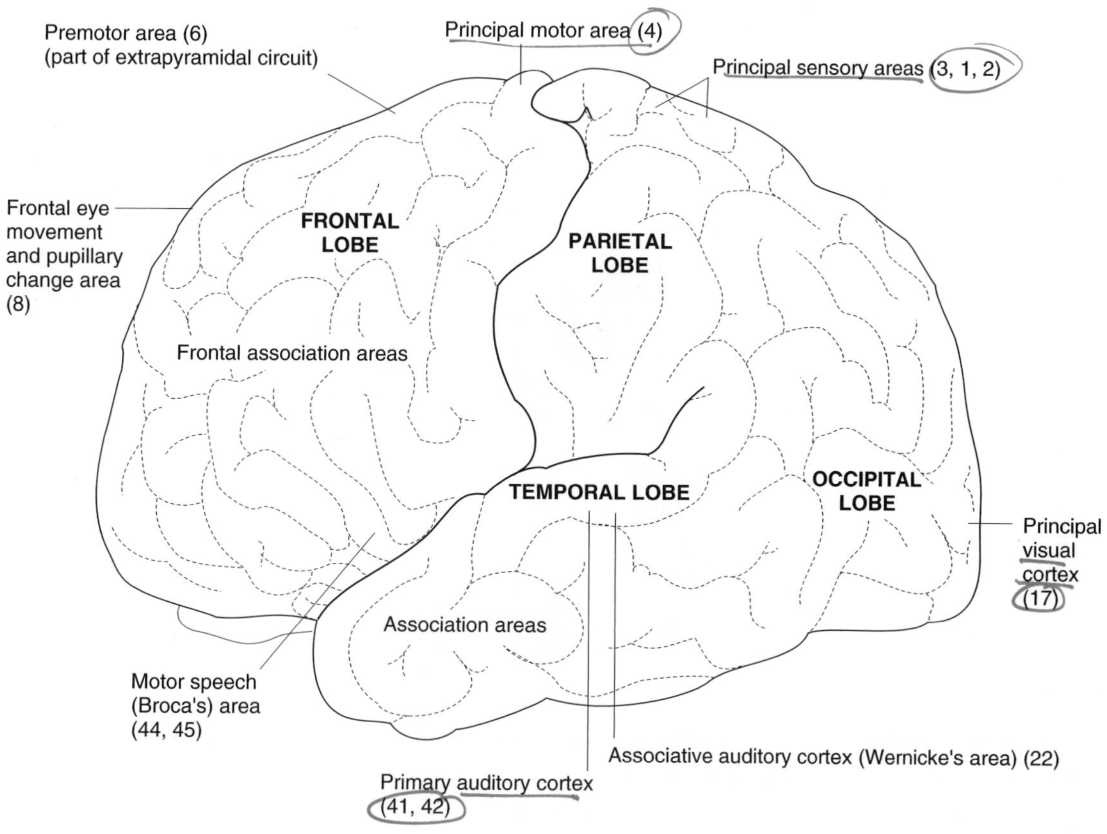

Brain lesions

Area of lesion	Consequence
Broca's area	Motor (expressive) aphasia *Path3.47*
Wernicke's area	Sensory (fluent/receptive) aphasia *Anat.56*
Amygdala (bilateral)	Klüver–Bucy syndrome (hyperorality, hypersexuality, disinhibited behavior) *Path3.54*
Frontal lobe	Frontal release signs (e.g., personality changes and deficits in concentration, orientation, judgment)
Right parietal lobe	Spatial neglect syndrome (agnosia of the contralateral side of the world)
Reticular activating system	Coma
Mamillary bodies (bilateral)	Wernicke–Korsakoff's encephalopathy (confabulations, anterograde amnesia) *BehSci.28*

BROca's is **BRO**ken speech.
Wernicke's is **W**ordy but makes no sense.

UCV

Cavernous sinus

CN III, IV, V_1, V_2, VI all pass through the cavernous sinus. Only CN VI is "free-floating." Cavernous portion of internal carotid artery also here.

The nerves that control extraocular muscles (plus V_1 and V_2) pass through the cavernous sinus.

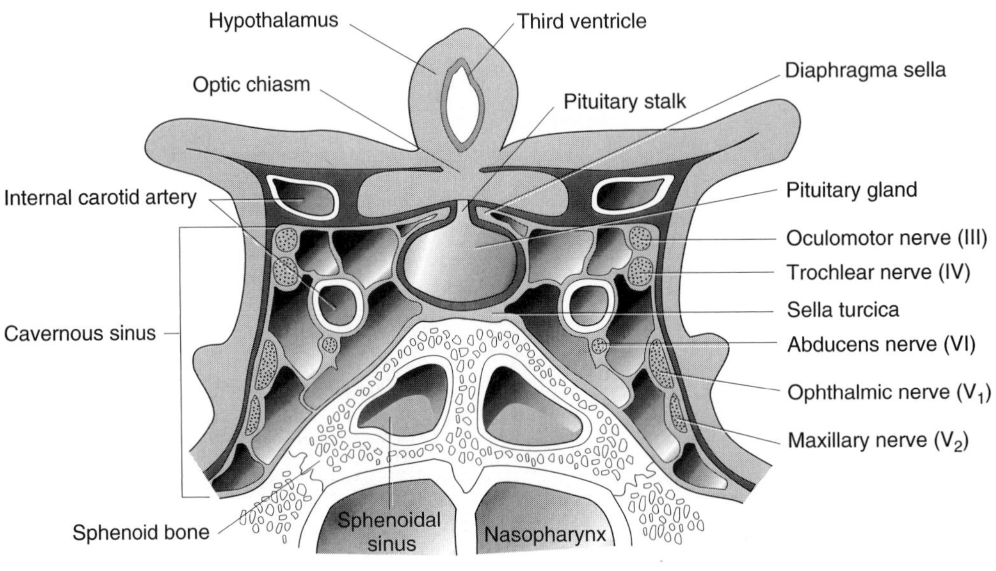

UCV Anat.38

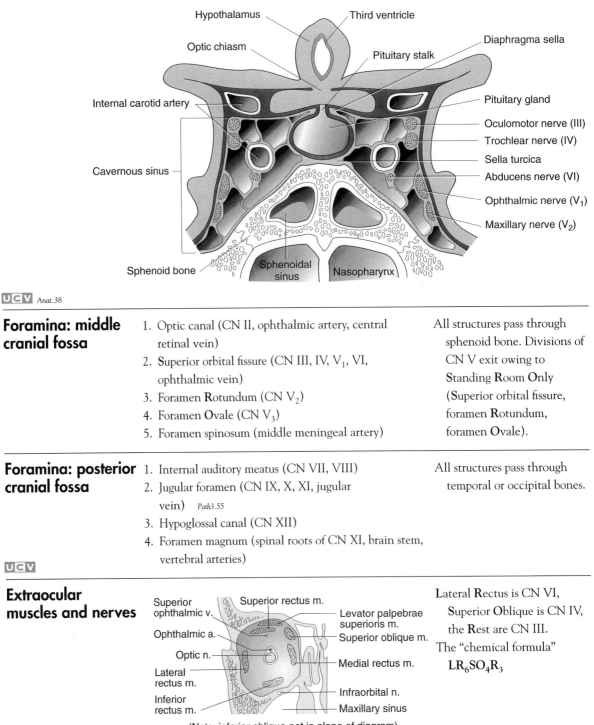

Foramina: middle cranial fossa

1. Optic canal (CN II, ophthalmic artery, central retinal vein)
2. Superior orbital fissure (CN III, IV, V_1, VI, ophthalmic vein)
3. Foramen **R**otundum (CN V_2)
4. Foramen **O**vale (CN V_3)
5. Foramen spinosum (middle meningeal artery)

All structures pass through sphenoid bone. Divisions of CN V exit owing to **S**tanding **R**oom **O**nly (**S**uperior orbital fissure, foramen **R**otundum, foramen **O**vale).

Foramina: posterior cranial fossa

1. Internal auditory meatus (CN VII, VIII)
2. Jugular foramen (CN IX, X, XI, jugular vein) Path3.55
3. Hypoglossal canal (CN XII)
4. Foramen magnum (spinal roots of CN XI, brain stem, vertebral arteries)

All structures pass through temporal or occipital bones.

UCV

Extraocular muscles and nerves

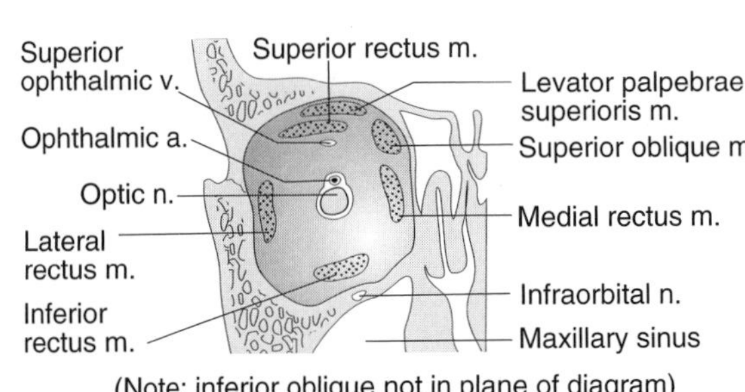

(Note: inferior oblique not in plane of diagram)

Lateral **R**ectus is CN VI, **S**uperior **O**blique is CN IV, the **R**est are CN III.
The "chemical formula" $LR_6SO_4R_3$

Internuclear ophthalmoplegia

Lesion in the medial longitudinal fasciculus (MLF). Results in medial rectus palsy on attempted lateral gaze. Nystagmus in abducting eye. Convergence is normal. MLF syndrome is seen in many patients with multiple sclerosis.

MLF = MS

UCV *Path2.20, Path3.53*

Cranial nerves

Nerve	CN	Function	Type	Mnemonic
Olfactory	I	Smell	Sensory	Some
Optic	II	Sight	Sensory	Say
Oculomotor	III	Eye movement, pupil constriction, accommodation, eyelid opening	Motor	Marry
Trochlear	IV	Eye movement	Motor	Money
Trigeminal	V	Mastication, facial sensation	Both	But
Abducens	VI	Eye movement	Motor	My
Facial	VII	Facial movement, anterior 2/3 taste, lacrimation, salivation (submaxillary and submandibular salivary glands)	Both	Brother
Vestibulocochlear	VIII	Hearing, balance	Sensory	Says
Glossopharyngeal	IX	Posterior 1/3 taste, swallowing, salivation (parotid gland), monitoring carotid body and sinus	Both	Big
Vagus	X	Taste, swallowing, palate elevation, talking, thoracoabdominal viscera	Both	Brains
Accessory	XI	Head turning, shoulder shrugging	Motor	Matter
Hypoglossal	XII	Tongue movements	Motor	Most

Cranial nerves and passageways

Cribriform plate	I
Optic canal	II
Superior orbital fissure	III, IV, V_1, VI
Foramen rotundum	V_2
Foramen ovale	V_3
Internal auditory meatus	VII, VIII
Jugular foramen	IX, X, XI
Hypoglossal canal	XII

Brain stem anatomy

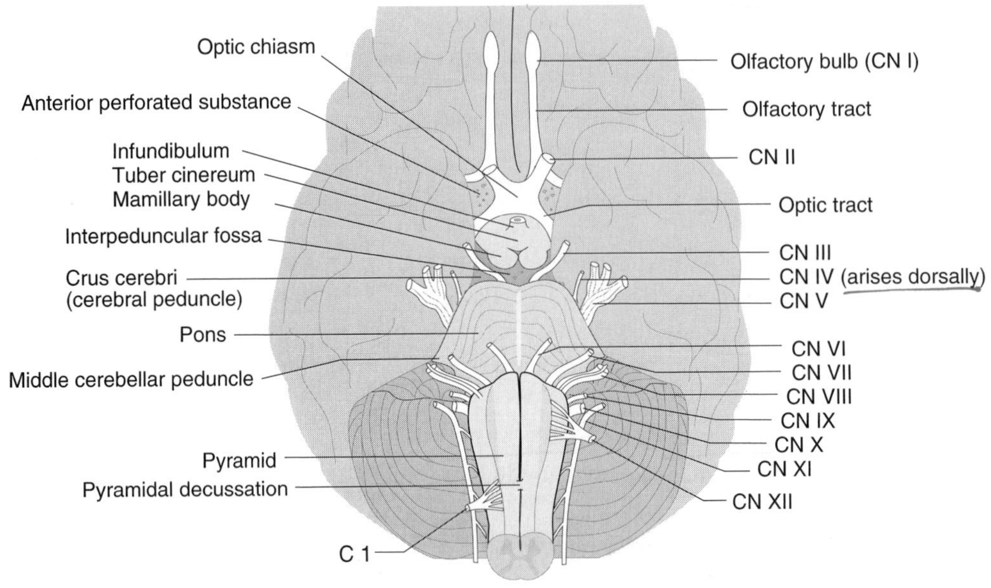

CNs that lie medially at brainstem: III, VI, XII. 3(×2) = 6(×2) = 12.

Homunculus

Topographical representation of sensory and motor areas in the cerebral cortex. Use to localize lesion (e.g., in blood supply) leading to specific defects.

For example, lower extremity deficit in sensation or movement indicates involvement of the anterior cerebral artery (see following entry).

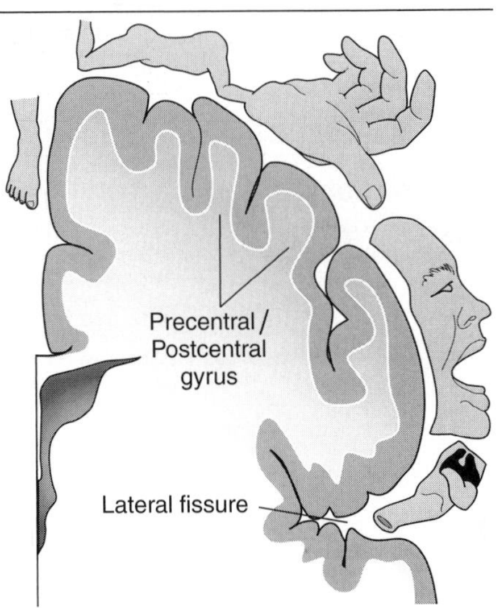

Circle of Willis

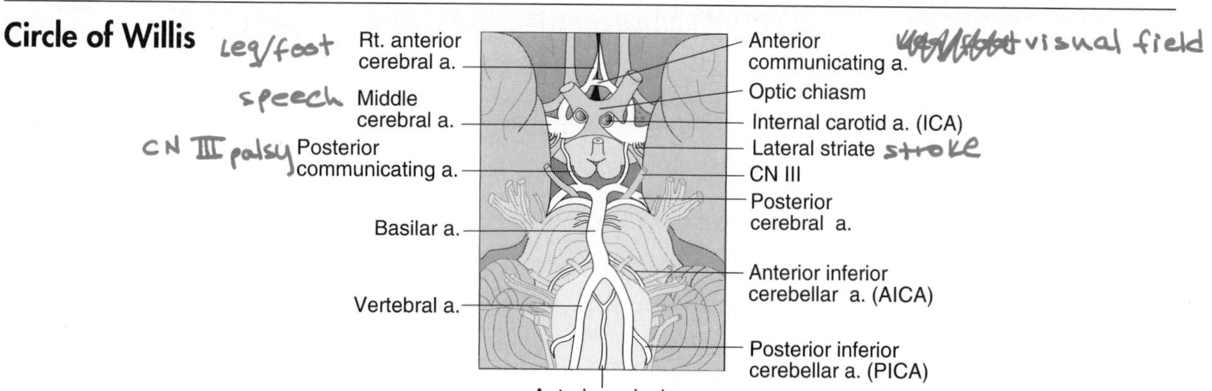

Anterior cerebral artery—supplies medial surface of the brain, leg–foot area of motor and sensory cortices.
Middle cerebral artery—supplies lateral aspect of brain, Broca's and Wernicke's speech areas.
Anterior communicating artery—most common circle of Willis aneurysm; may cause visual field defects.
Posterior communicating artery—common area of aneurysm; causes CN III palsy.
Lateral striate—"arteries of stroke"; supply internal capsule, caudate, putamen, globus pallidus.
In general, stroke of anterior circle → general sensory and motor dysfunction, aphasia; stroke of posterior circle → vertigo, ataxia, visual deficits, coma.

Visual field defects

1. Right anopsia
2. Bitemporal hemianopsia
3. Left homonymous hemianopsia
4. Left upper quadrantic anopsia (right temporal lesion)
5. Left lower quadrantic anopsia (right parietal lesion)
6. Left hemianopsia with macular sparing

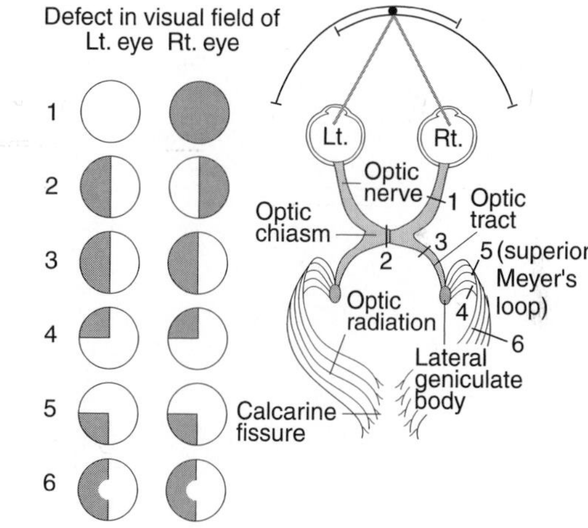

KLM sounds: kuh, la, mi

Kuh-kuh-kuh tests palate elevation (CN X—vagus).
La-la-la tests tongue (CN XII—hypoglossal).
Mi-mi-mi tests lips (CN VII—facial).

Say it aloud.

Vagal nuclei

Nucleus Solitarius	Visceral Sensory information (e.g., taste, gut distention, etc.).
Nucleus aMbiguus	Motor innervation of pharynx, larynx, and upper esophagus.
Dorsal motor nucleus	Sends autonomic (parasympathetic) fibers to heart, lungs, and upper GI.

Lesions and deviations

CN XII lesion (LMN): tongue deviates **toward** side of lesion (lick your wounds).
CN V motor lesion: jaw deviates **toward** side of lesion.
Unilateral lesion of cerebellum: patient tends to fall **toward** side of lesion.
CN X lesion: uvula deviates **away** from side of lesion.

Spinal cord and associated tracts

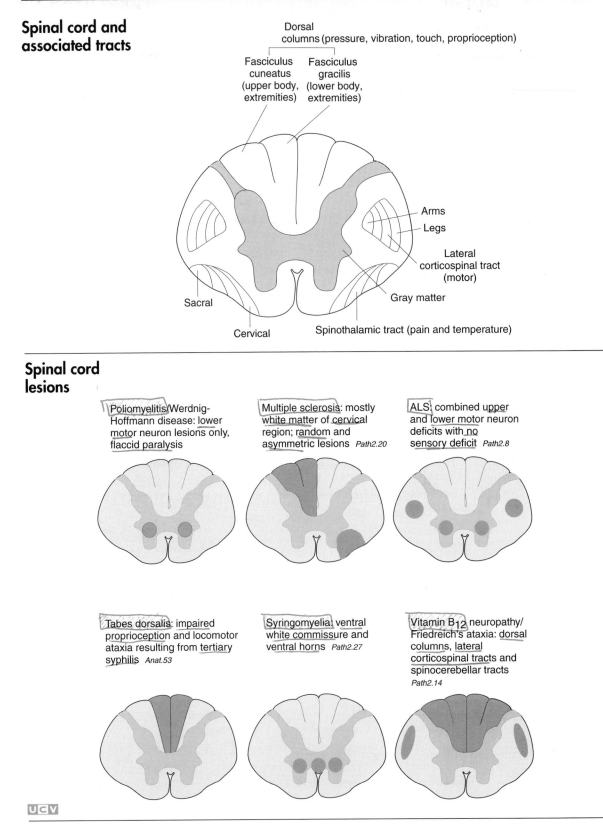

Dorsal columns (pressure, vibration, touch, proprioception)

Fasciculus cuneatus (upper body, extremities)

Fasciculus gracilis (lower body, extremities)

Arms

Legs

Lateral corticospinal tract (motor)

Gray matter

Sacral

Cervical

Spinothalamic tract (pain and temperature)

Spinal cord lesions

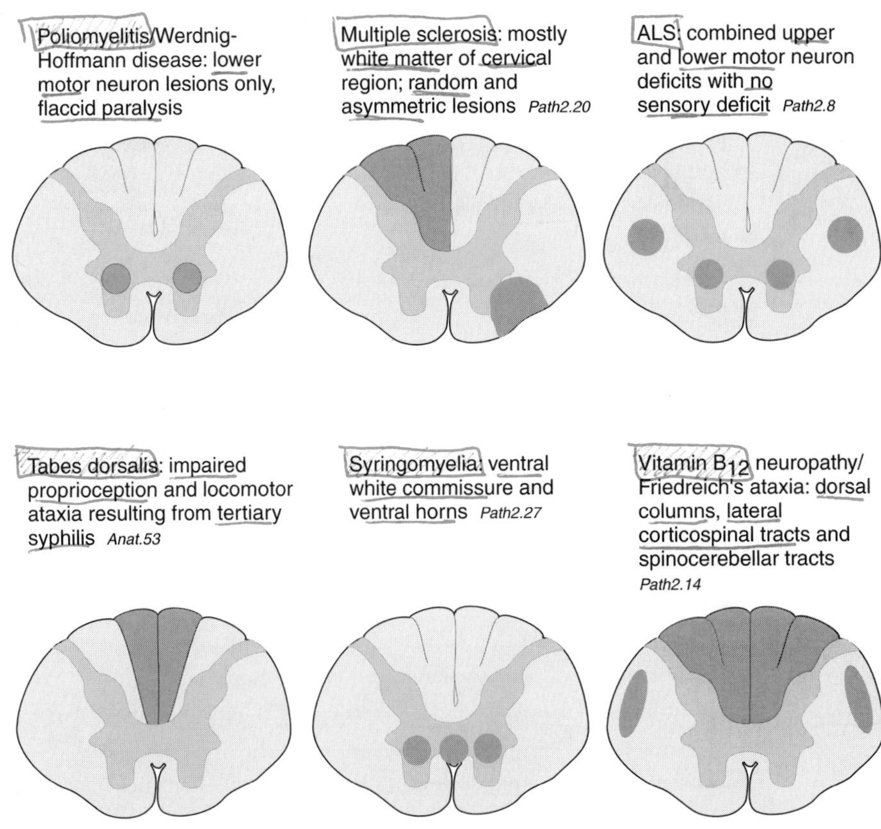

Poliomyelitis/Werdnig-Hoffmann disease: lower motor neuron lesions only, flaccid paralysis
Multiple sclerosis: mostly white matter of cervical region; random and asymmetric lesions Path2.20
ALS: combined upper and lower motor neuron deficits with no sensory deficit Path2.8
Tabes dorsalis: impaired proprioception and locomotor ataxia resulting from tertiary syphilis Anat.53
Syringomyelia: ventral white commissure and ventral horns Path2.27
Vitamin B12 neuropathy/ Friedreich's ataxia: dorsal columns, lateral corticospinal tracts and spinocerebellar tracts Path2.14

UCV

Dorsal column organization	In dorsal columns, lower limbs are inside to avoid crossing the upper limbs on the outside. Fasciculus gracilis = legs. Fasciculus cuneatus = arms.	Dorsal column is organized like you are, with hands at sides—arms outside and legs inside.
Brown-Séquard syndrome 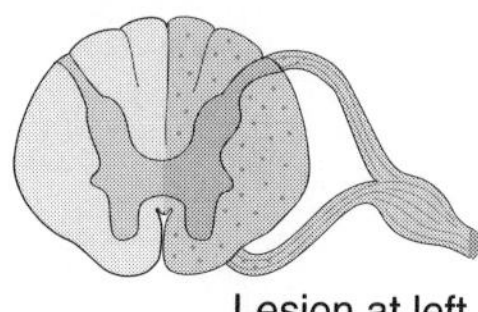 Lesion at left T10 level UCV Anat.37	Hemisection of spinal cord. Findings below the lesion: 1. Ipsilateral motor paralysis and spasticity (pyramidal tract)—not shown 2. Ipsilateral loss of tactile, vibration, proprioception sense (dorsal column) 3. Contralateral pain and temperature loss (spinothalamic tract) 4. Ipsilateral loss of all sensation at level of lesion	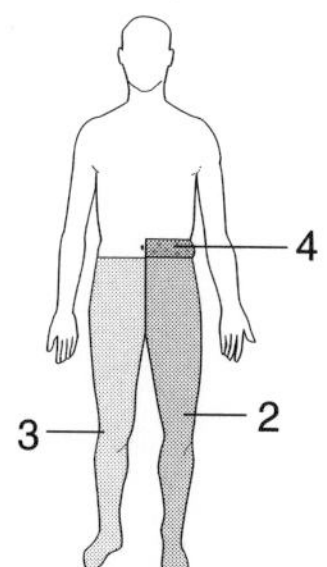
Lower motor neuron (LMN) signs	LMN injury signs: atrophy, flaccid paralysis, absent deep tendon reflexes. Fasciculations may be present.	**Lower** MN ≈ everything lowered (less muscle mass, decreased muscle tone, decreased reflexes, downgoing toes).
Upper motor neuron (UMN) signs	UMN injury signs: little atrophy, spastic paralysis (clonus), hyperactive deep tendon reflexes, possible positive Babinski.	**Upper** MN ≈ everything **up** (tone, DTRs, toes).
Facial lesion Central facial Bell's palsy UCV Anat.36, 42	Paralysis of the contralateral lower quadrant. Peripheral ipsilateral facial paralysis. Can occur idiopathically. Seen as a complication in **A**IDS, **L**yme disease, **S**arcoidosis, **T**umors, **D**iabetes. Complete destruction of the facial nucleus itself or its branchial efferent fibers (facial nerve proper) paralyzes all ipsilateral facial muscles.	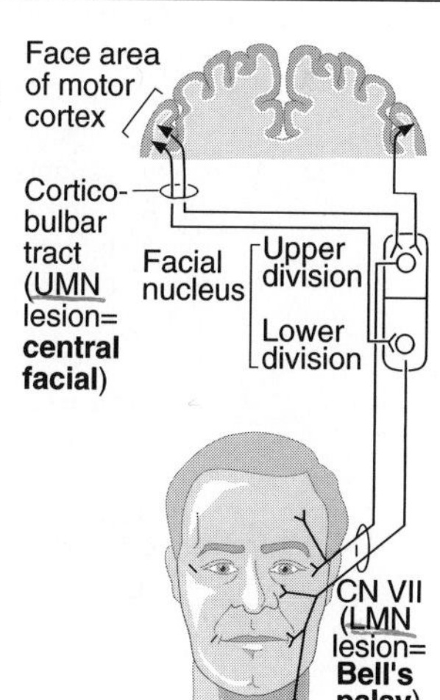 **AL**exander **Bell** with **STD**: **A**IDS, **L**yme, **S**arcoid, **T**umors, **D**iabetes

Spindle muscle control

Reflex arc	Muscle stretch → intrafusal stretch → stimulates Ia afferent→ stimulates α motor neuron → reflex extrafusal contraction
Gamma loop	CNS stimulates γ motor neuron → contracts intrafusal fiber → increased sensitivity of reflex arc

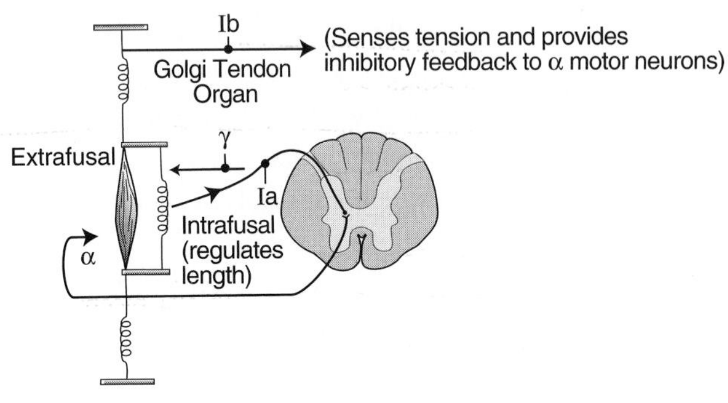

Brachial plexus

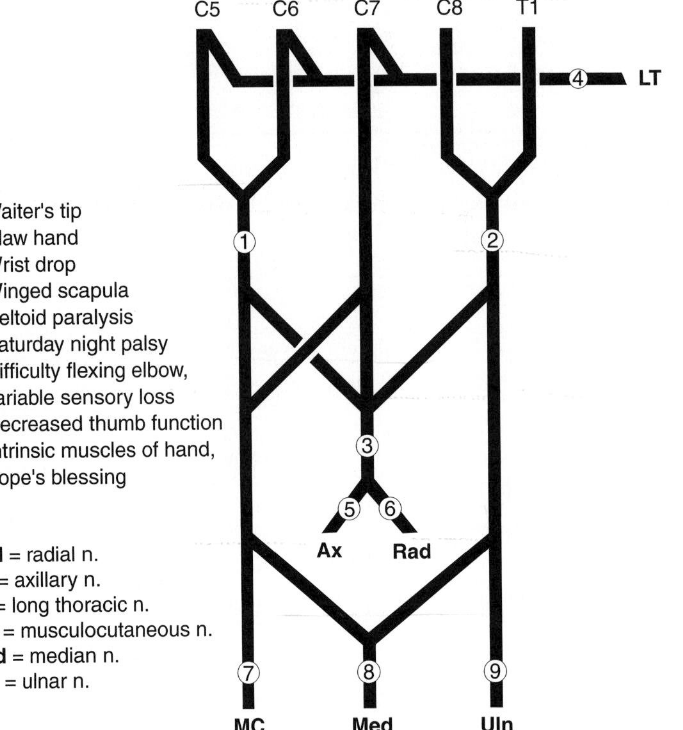

Median Nerve = C5, C6, C7, C8, T1
· carpal Tunnel

Upper limb nerve injury

	Deficit in motion	Deficit in sensation
Radial	Loss of triceps brachii (triceps reflex), brachioradialis (brachioradialis reflex), and extensor carpi radialis longus (→ wrist drop); often 2° to humerus fracture	Posterior brachial cutaneous Posterior antebrachial cutaneous
Median	No loss of power in any of the arm muscles; loss of forearm pronation, wrist flexion, finger flexion, and several thumb movements; eventually, thenar atrophy	Loss of sensation over the lateral palm and thumb and the radial $2^1/_2$ fingers
Ulnar	Impaired wrist flexion and adduction, and impaired adduction of thumb and the ulnar 2 fingers	Loss of sensation over the medial palm and ulnar $1^1/_2$ fingers
Axillary	Loss of deltoid action (shoulder dislocation)	
Musculocutaneous	Loss of function of coracobrachialis, biceps, and brachialis muscles (biceps reflex)	

Erb-Duchenne palsy

Traction or tear of the superior trunk of the brachial plexus (C5 and C6 roots); follows fall to shoulder or trauma during delivery.

Findings: limb hangs by side (paralysis of abductors), medially rotated (paralysis of lateral rotators), forearm is pronated (loss of biceps).

"Waiter's tip" owing to appearance of arm

UCV Anat.69

Radial nerve

Known as the "great extensor nerve." Provides innervation of the **B**rachioradialis, **E**xtensors of the wrist and fingers, **S**upinator, and **T**riceps.

Radial nerve innervates the **BEST!**

To **supinate** is to move as if carrying a bowl of **soup.**

UCV Anat.79

Cervical rib

An embryologic defect; can compress subclavian artery and inferior trunk of brachial plexus (C8, T1), resulting in thoracic outlet syndrome:

1. Atrophy of the thenar and hypothenar eminences
2. Atrophy of the interosseous muscles
3. Sensory deficits on the medial side of the forearm and hand
4. Disappearance of the radial pulse upon moving the head toward the opposite side

UCV Anat.67

Clinical reflexes

Biceps = C5 nerve root.

Triceps = C7 nerve root.

Patella = L4 nerve root.

Achilles = S1 nerve root.

Babinski = dorsiflexion of the big toe and fanning of other toes; sign of upper motor neuron lesion, but normal reflex in first year of life.

NOTES

SECTION II

Behavioral Science

"It's psychosomatic. You need a lobotomy. I'll get a saw."
—*Calvin*, Calvin & Hobbes

A heterogeneous mix of epidemiology/biostatistics, psychiatry, psychology, sociology, psychopharmacology, and more falls under this heading. Many medical students do not study this discipline diligently because the material is felt to be "easy" or "common sense." In our opinion, this is a missed opportunity. Each question gained in behavioral science is equal to a question in any other section in determining the overall score.

Many students feel that some behavioral science questions are less concrete and require awareness of social aspects of medicine. For example: If a patient does or says something, what should you do or say back? Medical ethics and medical law are also appearing with increasing frequency. In addition, the key aspects of the doctor–patient relationship (e.g., communication skills, open-ended questions, facilitation, silence) are high yield. Basic biostatistics and epidemiology are very learnable and high yield. Be able to apply biostatistical concepts such as specificity and predictive values in a problem-solving format. Also review the clinical presentation of personality disorders.

These abstracted case vignettes are designed to demonstrate the thought processes necessary to answer multistep clinical reasoning questions.

- Woman with anxiety about a gynecologic exam is told to relax and to imagine going through the steps of the exam → what process does this exemplify? → systematic desensitization.
- 65-year-old man is diagnosed with incurable metastatic pancreatic adenocarcinoma → his family asks you, the doctor, not to tell the patient → what do you do? → assess whether telling patient will negatively affect his health → if not, tell him.
- Man admitted for chest pain is medicated for ventricular tachycardia. The next day he jumps out of bed and does 50 pushups to show the nurses he has not had a heart attack → what defense mechanism is he using? → denial.
- A large group of people is followed over 10 years. Every two years, it is determined who develops heart disease and who does not → what type of study is this? → cohort study.
- Girl can speak in complete sentences, has an imaginary friend, and considers boys "yucky" → how old is she? → 6–11 years old.
- Man has flashbacks about his girlfriend's death two months following a hit-and-run accident. He often cries and wishes for the death of the culprit → what is the diagnosis? → normal bereavement.
- During a particular stage of sleep, man has variable blood pressure, penile tumescence, and variable EEG → what stage of sleep is he in? → REM sleep.
- 15-year-old girl of normal height and weight for age has enlarged parotid glands but no other complaints. The mother confides that she found laxatives in the daughter's closet → what is the diagnosis? → bulimia.
- 11-year-old girl exhibits Tanner stage 4 sexual development (almost full breasts and pubic hair) → what is the diagnosis? → advanced stage, early development.
- 4-year-old girl complains of a burning feeling in her genitalia; otherwise she behaves and sleeps normally. Smear of discharge shows *N. gonorrhoeae* → how was she infected? → sexual abuse.
- Person demands only the best and most famous doctor in town → what is the personality disorder? → narcissism.
- Nurse has episodes of hypoglycemia; blood analysis reveals no elevation in C-protein → what is the diagnosis? → factitious disorder; self-scripted insulin.
- 55-year-old businessman complains of lack of successful sexual contacts with women and lack of ability to reach full erection. Two years ago he had a heart attack → what might be the cause of his problem? → fear of sudden death during intercourse.

Epidemiology/Biostatistics

1. Differences in the incidence of disease among various ethnic groups.
2. Leading causes and types of cancers in men versus women.
3. Prevalence of common psychiatric disorders (e.g., alcoholism, major depression, schizophrenia).
4. Differences in mortality rates among ethnic and racial groups.
5. Definitions of morbidity, mortality, and case fatality rate.
6. Epidemiology of cigarette smoking, including prevalence and success rates for quitting.
7. Modes of human immunodeficiency virus (HIV) transmission among different populations (e.g., perinatal, heterosexual, homosexual, intravenous).
8. Simple pedigree analysis (understand symbols) for inheritance of genetic diseases (e.g., counseling, risk assessment).
9. Different types of studies (e.g., randomized clinical trial, cohort, case-control).
10. Definition and use of standard deviation, p value, r value, mean, mode, and median.
11. Effects of changing a test's criteria on number of false positives and number of false negatives.

Neurophysiology

1. Physiologic changes (e.g., neurotransmitter levels) in common neuropsychiatric disorders (e.g., Alzheimer's disease, Huntington's disease, schizophrenia, bipolar disorder).
2. Changes in cerebrospinal fluid composition with common psychiatric diseases (e.g., depression).
3. Physiologic, physical, and psychologic changes associated with aging (e.g., memory, lung capacity, glomerular filtration rate, muscle mass, pharmacokinetics of drugs).
4. Differences between anterior and posterior lobes of the pituitary gland (e.g., embryology, innervation, hormones).

Psychiatry/Psychology

1. Indicators of prognosis in psychiatric disorders (e.g., schizophrenia, bipolar disorder).
2. Genetic components of common psychiatric disorders (e.g., schizophrenia, bipolar disorder).
3. Diseases associated with different personality types.
4. Clinical features and treatment of phobias.
5. Clinical features of child abuse (shaken-baby syndrome).
6. Clinical features of common learning disorders (e.g., dyslexia, mental retardation).
7. Therapeutic application of learning theories (e.g., classical and operant conditioning) to psychiatric illnesses (e.g., disulfiram therapy for alcoholics).
8. Problems associated with the physician–patient relationship (e.g., reasons for patient noncompliance).
9. Management of the suicidal patient.
10. Addiction: risk factors, family history, behavior, factors contributing to relapse.
11. How physicians and medical students should help peers with substance abuse problems.

Prevalence versus incidence

Prevalence is total number of cases in a population at a given time.

Incidence is number of new cases in a population per unit time.

Incidence is new **incidents.**

Prevalence ≅ incidence × disease duration.

Prevalence > incidence for chronic diseases (e.g., diabetes).

Prevalence = incidence for acute disease (e.g., common cold.)

Sensitivity

Number of true positives divided by number of all people with the disease.

False negative ratio is equal to 1 – sensitivity.

High sensitivity is desirable for a screening test.

sensitivity Rules out

PID = **P**ositive **I**n **D**isease (note that PID is a **sensitive** topic).

SNOUT = **S**e**N**sitivity rules **OUT**.

Specificity

Number of true negatives divided by number of all people without the disease.

False positive ratio is equal to 1 – specificity.

High specificity is desirable for a confirmatory test.

NIH = **N**egative **I**n **H**ealth.

SPIN = **SP**ecificity rules **IN**.

Predictive value

Positive predictive value

Number of true positives divided by number of people who tested positive for the disease.

The probability of having a condition, given a positive test.

Negative predictive value

Number of true negatives divided by number of people who tested negative for the disease.

The probability of not having the condition, given a negative test.

Unlike sensitivity and specificity, predictive values are dependent on the prevalence of the disease.

The higher the prevalence of a disease, the higher the positive predictive value of the test.

Disease

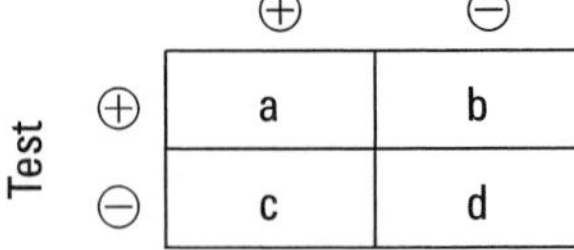

$$\text{Sensitivity} = \frac{a}{a+c}$$

$$\text{Specificity} = \frac{d}{b+d}$$

$$\text{PPV} = \frac{a}{a+b}$$

$$\text{NPV} = \frac{d}{c+d}$$

Odds ratio and relative risk

Odds ratio

Approximates the relative risk if the prevalence of the disease is not too high. Used for retrospective studies (e.g., case-control studies).

OR = ad / bc

Relative risk

Disease risk in exposed group/disease risk in unexposed group. Used for cohort studies.

Disease

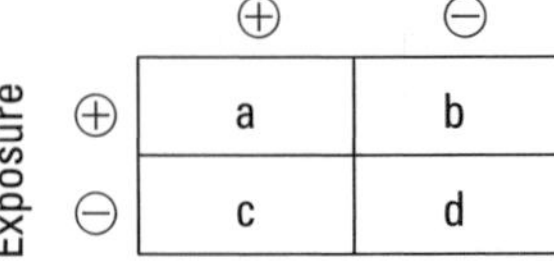

$$\text{RR} = \frac{\left[\frac{a}{a+b}\right]}{\left[\frac{c}{c+d}\right]} \qquad \text{Attributable Risk} = \left[\frac{a}{a+b}\right] - \left[\frac{c}{c+d}\right]$$

If the 95% confidence interval for OR or RR includes 1, the study is inconclusive.

Standard deviation versus error

n = sample size,
σ = standard deviation,
SEM = standard error of the mean,
$SEM = \sigma/\sqrt{n}$
Therefore, $SEM < \sigma$ and SEM ↓ as n ↑.

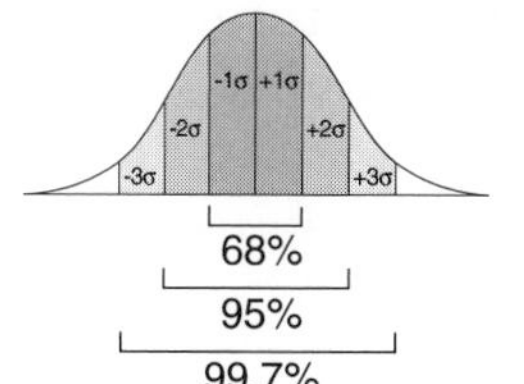

Statistical distribution

Terms that describe statistical distributions:
Normal ≈ Gaussian ≈ bell-shaped (mean = median = mode).

Bimodal is simply two humps.

Positive skew is asymmetry with tail on the right (mean > median > mode).

Negative skew has tail on the left (mean < median < mode).

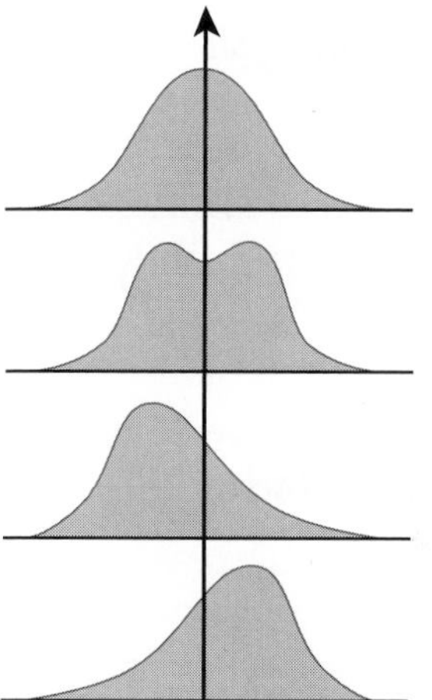

Precision vs. accuracy

Precision is:
1. The consistency and reproducibility of a test (reliability).
2. The absence of random variation in a test.

Accuracy is the trueness of test measurements.

Random error = reduced precision in a test.
Systematic error = reduced accuracy in a test.

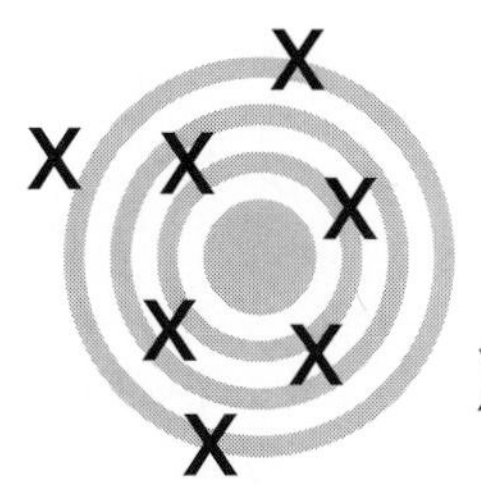
Accuracy

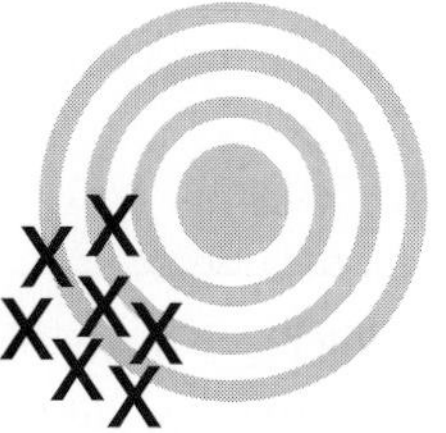
Precision

Accuracy and precision

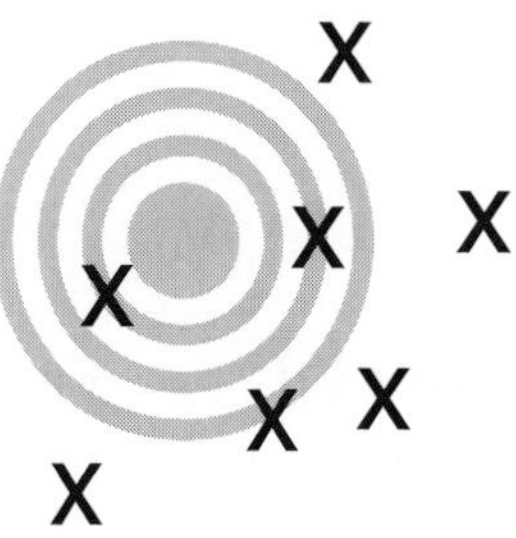
No accuracy, no precision

Reliability and validity

Reliability = Reproducibility (dependability) of a test.
Validity = whether the test truly measures what it purports to measure. Appropriateness of a test.

Test is reliable if repeat measurements are the same.
Test is valid if it measures what it is supposed to measure.

Correlation coefficient (r)

r is always between −1 and 1. Absolute value indicates strength of correlation.
Coefficient of determination = r^2.

***t*-test versus ANOVA versus χ^2**	*t*-test checks difference between two **means**. ANOVA analyzes variance of three or more variables. χ^2 checks difference between two or more percentages or proportions of categorical outcomes (not mean values).	Mr. **T** is **mean**. **ANOVA** = **AN**alysis **O**f **VA**riance of three or more variables. **%**^{2} = compare percentages (%) or proportions.
Meta-analysis	Pooling data from several studies (often via a literature search) to achieve greater statistical power.	Cannot overcome limitations of individual studies or bias in study selection.
Case-control study	Observational study. Sample chosen based on presence (cases) or absence (controls) of disease. Information collected about risk factors.	Often retrospective.
Cohort study	Observational study. Sample chosen based on presence or absence of risk factors. Subjects followed over time for development of disease.	The Framingham heart study was a large prospective cohort study.
Clinical trial	Experimental study. Compares therapeutic benefit of 2 or more treatments.	Highest-quality study.

Statistical hypotheses

Null (H_0)	Hypothesis of no difference (e.g., there is no association between the disease and the risk factor in the population).	
Alternative (H_1)	Hypothesis that there is some difference (e.g., there is some association between the disease and the risk factor in the population).	

Study results \ Reality	H_1	H_0
H_1	Power $(1-\beta)$	α
H_0	β	

Type I error (α)	Stating that there **is** an effect or difference when there really is not (to mistakenly accept the experimental hypothesis and reject the null hypothesis). α is the probability of making a type I error and is equal to p (usually $< .05$). p = probability of making a type I error.	If $p < .05$, then there is less than a 5% chance that the data will show something that is not really there. α = you "saw" a difference that did not exist—for example, convicting an innocent man.
Type II error (β)	Stating that there **is not** an effect or difference when there really is (to fail to reject the null hypothesis when in fact H_0 is false). β is the probability of making a type II error.	β = you did not "see" a difference that does exist—for example, setting a guilty man free. $1 - \beta$ is "power" of study, or probability that study will see a difference if it is there.

Power	Probability of rejecting null hypothesis when it is in fact false. It depends on: 1. Total number of end points experienced by population. 2. Difference in compliance between treatment groups (differences in the mean values between groups).	If you increase sample size, you increase power. There is power in numbers. Power = 1 – β.
Reportable diseases	Only some infectious diseases are reportable, including AIDS (but not HIV positivity), chickenpox, gonorrhea, hepatitis A and B, measles, mumps, rubella, salmonella, shigella, syphilis, tuberculosis.	

Leading causes of death in the US by age

Infants	Congenital anomalies, sudden infant death syndrome, short gestation/low birth weight, respiratory distress syndrome, maternal complications of pregnancy.
Age 1–14	Injuries, cancer, congenital anomalies, homicide, heart disease.
Age 15–24	Injuries, homicide, suicide, cancer, heart disease.
Age 25–64	Cancer, heart disease, injuries, stroke, suicide.
Age 65+	Heart disease, cancer, stroke, COPD, pneumonia.

Disease prevention

1°—Prevent disease occurrence (e.g., vaccination).
2°—Early detection of disease (e.g., Pap smear).
3°—Reduce disability from disease (e.g., exogenous insulin for diabetes).

Additional Services for Specific Groups

Risk factor	Preventive service(s) needed
Diabetes	Eye, foot exams; urine test
Drug abuse	HIV, TB tests; hepatitis immunization
Alcoholism	Influenza, pneumococcal immunizations; TB test
Overweight	Blood sugar test (test for diabetes mellitus)
Homeless, recent refugee or immigrant	TB test
High-risk sexual behavior	HIV, hep B, syphilis, gonorrhea, chlamydia tests

Elderly population in year 2000	In year 2000, estimated US population = 300,000,000. 35 million > 65 y old. Greatest increase in those > 85 y old.	In year 2000, 13% of US population > 65 y old (yet incur 30% of total medical costs).
Risk factors for suicide completion	White, male, alone, prior attempts, presence and lethality of plan, medical illness, alcohol or drug use, on 3 or more prescription medications.	SAD PERSONS: Sex (male), Age, Depression, Previous attempt, Ethanol, Rational thought, Sickness, Organized plan, No spouse, Social support lacking.

Most common surgeries	Abortion Dilation and curettage, hysterectomy, tonsillectomy, sterilization, hernia repair, oophorectomy, cesarean section, cholecystectomy.	Most done on women.
Divorce statistics	US has highest rate. Teenage marriages at high risk. More common when religions are mixed. Peaks at second/third year of marriage. Higher with low SES. Unrelated to industrialization. Divorcees remarry very frequently.	
Medicare, Medicaid	Medicare and Medicaid are federal programs that originated from amendments to the Social Security Act. Medicare Part A = hospital; Part B = supplemental. Medicaid is federal and state assistance for those on welfare or who are indigent.	MedicarE is for Elderly. MedicaiD is for Destitute.

BEHAVIORAL SCIENCE—ETHICS

Autonomy	Obligation to respect patients as individuals and to honor their preferences in medical care.	
Informed consent	Legally requires: 1. Discussion of pertinent information 2. Obtaining the patient's agreement to the plan of care 3. Freedom from coercion	Patients must understand the risks, benefits, and alternatives, which include no intervention.
Exceptions to informed consent	1. Patient lacks decision-making capacity (not legally competent) 2. Implied consent in an emergency 3. Therapeutic privilege—withholding information when disclosure would severely harm the patient or undermine informed decision-making capacity 4. Waiver—patient waives the right of informed consent	
Decision-making capacity	1. Patient makes and communicates a choice 2. Patient is informed 3. Decision is stable over time 4. Decision consistent with patient's values and goals 5. Decision not a result of delusions or hallucinations	The patient's family cannot require that a doctor withhold information from the patient.
Oral advance directive	Incapacitated patient's prior oral statements commonly used as guide. Problems arise from variance in interpretation of these statements. However, if patient was informed, directive is specific, patient makes a choice, and decision is repeated over time, the oral directive is more valid.	

Written advance directive

1. Living wills—patient directs physician to withhold or withdraw life-sustaining treatment if the patient develops a terminal disease or enters a persistent vegetative state.
2. Durable power of attorney—patient designates a surrogate to make medical decisions in the event that the patient loses decision-making capacity. Patient may also specify decisions in clinical situations. More flexible than a living will.

Nonmaleficence

"Do no harm." However, if benefits of an intervention outweigh the risks, a patient may make an informed decision to proceed.

Beneficence

Physicians have a special ethical responsibility to act in the patient's best interest (physician is a fiduciary). Patient autonomy may conflict with beneficence. If the patient makes an informed decision, ultimately the patient has the right to decide.

Confidentiality

Confidentiality respects patient privacy and autonomy. Disclosing information to family and friends should be guided by what the patient would want. The patient may also waive the right to confidentiality (e.g., insurance companies).

Exceptions to confidentiality

1. Potential harm to third parties is serious
2. Likelihood of harm is high
3. No alternative means exist to warn or to protect those at risk
4. Third party can take steps to prevent harm

Examples include:

1. Infectious diseases—physicians may have a duty to warn public officials and identifiable people at risk
2. The Tarasoff decision—law requiring physician to protect potential victim from harm; may involve breach of confidentiality
3. Child and/or elder abuse
4. Impaired automobile drivers
5. Suicidal/homicidal patient
6. Domestic violence

Malpractice

Civil suit under negligence requires:

1. Physician breach of duty to patient
2. Patient suffers harm
3. Breach of duty causes harm

Unlike a criminal suit, in which the burden of proof is "beyond a reasonable doubt," the burden of proof in a malpractice suit is "more likely than not."

Apgar score (at birth)

Score 0–2 at 1 and 5 min in each of five categories:
1. Color (blue/pale, trunk pink, all pink)
2. Heart rate (0, <100, 100+)
3. Reflex irritability (0, grimace, grimace + cough)
4. Muscle tone (limp, some, active)
5. Respiratory effort (0, irregular, regular)

10 is perfect score.

After Virginia **Apgar,** a famous anesthesiologist.
A = **A**ppearance (color)
P = **P**ulse
G = **G**rimace
A = **A**ctivity
R = **R**espiration

Low birth weight

Defined as under 2500 g. Associated with greater incidence of physical and emotional problems. Caused by prematurity or intrauterine growth retardation. Complications include infections, respiratory distress syndrome, necrotizing enterocolitis, and persistent fetal circulation.

Infant deprivation effects

Long-term deprivation of affection results in:
1. Decreased muscle tone
2. Poor language skills
3. Poor socialization skills
4. Lack of basic trust
5. Anaclitic depression
6. Weight loss
7. Physical illness

Severe deprivation can result in infant death.

Studied by René Spitz. The **4 W's:** **W**eak, **W**ordless, **W**anting (socially), **W**ary.
Deprivation for longer than 6 months can lead to irreversible changes.

Anaclitic depression

Anaclitic depression = depression in an infant owing to continued separation from caregiver. Can result in failure to thrive. Infant becomes withdrawn and unresponsive.

Regression in children

Children regress to younger behavior under stress: physical illness, punishment, birth of a new sibling, tiredness. An example is bedwetting in a child when hospitalized.

Child abuse

	Physical abuse	**Sexual abuse**
Evidence	Healed fractures on x-ray, cigarette burns, subdural hematomas, multiple bruises, retinal hemorrhage or detachment	Genital/anal trauma, STDs, UTIs
Abuser	Usually female and the primary caregiver	Known to victim, usually male
Epidemiology	~3000 deaths/yr in US	Peak incidence 9–12 yrs of age

UCV BehSci.96

Developmental milestones

	Approximate age	Milestone
Infant	3 mo	Holds head up, social smile, Moro reflex disappears
	4–5 mo	Rolls front to back, sits when propped
	7–9 mo	Stranger anxiety, sits alone, orients to voice
	12–14 mo	Upgoing Babinski disappears
	15 mo	Walking, few words, separation anxiety
Toddler	12–24 mo	Object permanence
	18–24 mo	Rapprochement
	24–48 mo	Parallel play
	24–36 mo	Core gender identity
Preschool	30–36 mo	Toilet training
	3 y	Group play, rides tricycle, copies line or circle drawing
	4 y	Cooperative play, simple drawings (stick figure), hops on one foot
School age	6–11 y	Development of conscience (superego), same-sex friends, identification with same-sex parent
Adolescence (puberty)	11 y (girls) 13 y (boys)	Abstract reasoning (formal operations), formation of personality

Changes in the elderly

1. Sexual changes
   Men: slower erection/ejaculation, longer refractory period
   Women: vaginal shortening, thinning, and dryness; sexual interest does not decrease
2. Sleep patterns: ↓ REM sleep, ↓ slow-wave sleep, ↑ sleep latency
3. Common medical conditions: arthritis, hypertension, heart disease
4. Psychiatric problems (e.g., depression) become more prevalent
5. Suicide rate increases

Kübler-Ross dying stages

Denial, Anger, Bargaining, Grieving, Acceptance. Stages do not necessarily occur in this order, and more than one stage can be present at once.

Death Arrives Bringing Grave Adjustments.

Grief

Normal bereavement characterized by shock, denial, guilt and somatic symptoms. Typically lasts 6 mo–1 yr. *BehSci.69*

Pathologic grief includes excessively intense or prolonged grief, or grief that is delayed, inhibited or denied. *BehSci.70*

UCV

Neurotransmitter changes with disease

Depression—decreased NE and serotonin (5-HT).
Alzheimer's dementia—decreased ACh.
Huntington's disease—decreased GABA, decreased ACh.
Schizophrenia—increased dopamine.
Parkinson's disease—decreased dopamine.

Frontal lobe functions

Concentration, orientation, language, abstraction, judgment, motor regulation, mood. Lack of social judgment is most notable in frontal lobe lesion.

Sleep stages

Stage (% of total sleep time in young adults)	Description	Waveform
	Awake (eyes open), alert, active mental concentration	Beta (highest frequency, lowest amplitude)
	Awake (eyes closed)	Alpha
1 (5%)	Light sleep	Theta
2 (45%)	Deeper sleep	Sleep spindles and K-complexes
3–4 (25%)	Deepest, non-REM sleep; sleepwalking; night terrors, bedwetting (slow-wave sleep)	Delta (lowest frequency, highest amplitude) slow wave
REM (25%)	Dreaming, loss of motor tone, possibly memory processing function, erections, ↑ brain O_2 use	Beta

At night, **B**ATS **D**rink **B**lood.

1. Serotonergic predominance of raphe nucleus key to initiating sleep
2. Norepinephrine reduces REM sleep
3. Extraocular movements during REM due to activity of PPRF (parapontine reticular formation/conjugate gaze center)
4. REM sleep having the same EEG pattern as while awake and alert has spawned the terms "paradoxical sleep" and "desynchronized sleep"
5. Benzodiazepines shorten stage 4 sleep; thus useful for night terrors and sleepwalking *BehSci.97, 98*
6. Imipramine is used to treat enuresis since it decreases stage 4 sleep *BehSci.62*

UCV

REM sleep

Increased and variable pulse, rapid eye movements (REM), increased and variable blood pressure, penile/clitoral tumescence. 25% of total sleep. Occurs every 90 minutes; duration increases through the night. REM sleep decreases with age. Acetylcholine is the principal neurotransmitter involved in REM sleep.

REM sleep is like sex: ↑ pulse, penile/clitoral tumescence, ↓ with age.

Sleep apnea

Central sleep apnea: no respiratory effort.
Obstructive sleep apnea: respiratory effort against airway obstruction.
Person stops breathing for at least 10 sec during sleep.
Associated with obesity, loud snoring, systemic/pulmonary hypertension, arrhythmias, and possibly sudden death.
Individuals may become chronically tired.

Narcolepsy

Person falls asleep suddenly. May include hypnagogic (just before sleep) or hypnopompic (with awakening) hallucinations. The person's nocturnal and narcoleptic sleep episodes start off with REM sleep. **Cataplexy** (sudden collapse while awake) in some patients. Strong genetic component. Treat with stimulants (e.g., amphetamines).

UCV *BehSci.23*

Sleep patterns of depressed patients

Patients with depression typically have the following changes in their sleep stages:

1. Reduced slow-wave sleep
2. Decreased REM latency
3. Early morning awakening (important screening question)

Stress effects

Stress induces production of free fatty acids, 17-OH corticosteroids, lipids, cholesterol, catecholamines; affects water absorption, muscular tonicity, gastrocolic reflex, and mucosal circulation.

Sexual dysfunction

Differential diagnosis includes:

1. Drugs (e.g., antihypertensives, neuroleptics, SSRIs, ethanol)
2. Diseases (e.g., depression, diabetes)
3. Psychological (e.g., performance anxiety)

UCV *BehSci.74*

BEHAVIORAL SCIENCE—PSYCHIATRY

Orientation

Is the patient aware of him- or herself as a person?
Does the patient know his or her own name?
Anosognosia = unaware that one is ill.
Autopagnosia = unable to locate one's own body parts.
Depersonalization = body seems unreal or dissociated.

Order of loss: first = time, second = place, last = person.

Amnesia types

*Antero*grade amnesia is being unable to remember things that occurred after a CNS insult (no new memory).

Antero = after

Korsakoff's amnesia is a classic anterograde amnesia that is caused by thiamine deficiency (bilateral destruction of the mamillary bodies), is seen in alcoholics, and is associated with confabulations.

UCV *BehSci.17, 28*

*Retro*grade amnesia is being unable to remember things that occurred before a CNS insult. Complication of ECT.

Retro = before

Substance dependence

Maladaptive pattern of substance use.
Defined as 3 or more of the following signs in 1 year:

1. Tolerance
2. Withdrawal
3. Substance taken in larger amounts than intended
4. Persistent desire or attempts to cut down
5. Lots of energy spent trying to obtain substance
6. Important social, occupational, or recreational activities given up or reduced because of substance use
7. Use continued in spite of knowing the problems that it causes

Substance abuse Maladaptive pattern leading to clinically significant impairment or distress. Symptoms have not met criteria for substance dependence. One or more of the following in 1 year:

1. Recurrent use resulting in failure to fulfill major obligations at work, school, or home
2. Recurrent use in physically hazardous situations
3. Recurrent substance-related legal problems
4. Continued use in spite of persistent problems caused by use

Signs and symptoms of substance abuse

Drug	Intoxication	Withdrawal
Alcohol	Disinhibition, emotional lability, slurred speech, ataxia, coma, blackouts. BehSci.41	Tremor, tachycardia, hypertension, malaise, nausea, seizures, delirium tremens (DTs), tremulousness, agitation, hallucinations.
Opioids	CNS depression, nausea and vomiting, constipation, pupillary constriction (pinpoint pupils), seizures (overdose is life-threatening).	Anxiety, insomnia, anorexia, sweating/ piloerection ("cold turkey"), fever, rhinorrhea, nausea, stomach cramps, diarrhea ("flu-like"symptoms), yawning.
Amphetamines	Psychomotor agitation, impaired judgment, pupillary dilation, hypertension, tachycardia, euphoria, prolonged wakefulness and attention, cardiac arrhythmias, delusions, hallucinations, fever. BehSci.42	Post-use "crash," including anxiety, lethargy, headache, stomach cramps, hunger, severe depression, dysphoric mood, fatigue, insomnia/hypersomnia.
Cocaine	Euphoria, psychomotor agitation, impaired judgment, tachycardia, pupillary dilation, hypertension, hallucinations (including tactile), paranoid ideations, angina and sudden cardiac death.	Hypersomnolence, fatigue, depression, malaise, severe craving, suicidality.
PCP	Belligerence, impulsiveness, fever, psychomotor agitation, vertical and horizontal nystagmus, tachycardia, ataxia, homicidality, psychosis, delirium. BehSci.79	Recurrence of intoxication symptoms due to reabsorption in GI tract; sudden onset of severe, random, homicidal violence.
LSD	Marked anxiety or depression, delusions, visual hallucinations, flashbacks.	
Marijuana	Euphoria, anxiety, paranoid delusions, perception of slowed time, impaired judgment, social withdrawal, increased appetite, dry mouth, hallucinations.	
Barbiturates	Low safety margin, respiratory depression.	Anxiety, seizures, delirium, life-threatening cardiovascular collapse.
Benzodiazepines	Amnesia, ataxia, somnolence, minor respiratory depression. Additive effects with alcohol.	Rebound anxiety, seizures, tremor, insomnia.
Caffeine	Restlessness, insomnia, increased diuresis, muscle twitching, cardiac arrhythmias.	Headache, lethargy, depression, weight gain.
Nicotine	Restlessness, insomnia, anxiety, arrhythmias.	Irritability, headache, anxiety, weight gain, craving, tachycardia.

UCV

Delirium tremens UCV BehSci.20	Severe alcohol withdrawal syndrome that peaks 2–5 d after last drink. In order of appearance: autonomic system hyperactivity (tachycardia, tremors, anxiety), psychotic symptoms (hallucinations, delusions), confusion.	
Heroin addiction	Approximately 500,000 US addicts. Heroin is schedule I (not prescribable). Evidence of addiction is narcotic abstinence syndrome (dilated pupils, lacrimation, rhinorrhea, sweating, yawning, irritability, and muscle aches). Also look for track marks (needle sticks in veins). Related diagnoses are hepatitis, abscesses, overdose, hemorrhoids, AIDS, and right-sided endocarditis.	Naloxone (Narcan) and naltrexone competitively inhibit opioids. Methadone (long-acting oral opiate) for heroin detoxification or long-term maintenance.
Delirium UCV BehSci.18-19	Decreased attention span and level of arousal, disorganized thinking, hallucination, illusions, misperceptions, disturbance in sleep–wake cycle, cognitive dysfunction. Key to diagnosis: waxing and waning level of consciousness, develops rapidly. Often due to substance use/abuse or medical illness.	Deli**rium** = changes in senso**rium.** Most common psychiatric illness on medical and surgical floors. Often reversible.
Dementia UCV BehSci.15-16	Development of multiple cognitive deficits: memory, aphasia, apraxia, agnosia, loss of abstract thought, behavioral/personality changes, impaired judgment. Key to diagnosis: rule out delirium—patient is alert, no change in level of consciousness. More often gradual onset. In elderly patients, depression may present like dementia.	De**mem**tia characterized by **mem**ory loss. Commonly irreversible.
Major depressive episode UCV BehSci.54-56, 61	Characterized by 5 of the following for 2 weeks, including (1) depressed mood or (2) anhedonia: 1. **S**leep disturbances 2. Loss of **I**nterest 3. **G**uilt 4. Loss of **E**nergy 5. Loss of **C**oncentration 6. Change in **A**ppetite 7. **P**sychomotor retardation 8. **S**uicidal ideations 9. Depressed mood Major depressive disorder, recurrent—requires 2 or more episodes with a symptom-free interval of 2 months. Lifetime prevalence = 13% male, 21% female. **Dysthymia** is a milder form of depression lasting at least two years.	SIG E CAPS

Manic episode

Distinct period of abnormally and persistently elevated, expansive or irritable mood lasting at least 1 week. During mood disturbance, 3 or more of the following:

1. **D**istractibility
2. **I**nsomnia: ↓ need for sleep
3. **G**randiosity: inflated self-esteem
4. **F**light of ideas
5. Increase in goal-directed **A**ctivity/psychomotor agitation
6. Pressured **S**peech
7. **T**houghtlessness: seeks pleasure without regard to consequences

DIG FAST

UCV BehSci.45

Hypomanic episode

Like manic episode except mood disturbance not severe enough to cause marked impairment in social and/or occupational functioning or to necessitate hospitalization, and there are no psychotic features.

Bipolar disorder

Six separate criteria sets exist for bipolar I disorders with combinations of manic, hypomanic, and depressed episodes. One manic or hypomanic episode defines bipolar disorder. Lithium is drug of choice.

Cyclothymic disorder is a milder form lasting at least 2 years.

UCV BehSci.45-46, 52

Malingering

Patient consciously fakes or claims to have a disorder in order to attain a specific gain (e.g., financial).

UCV BehSci.75

Factitious disorder

Consciously creates symptoms in order to assume "sick role" and to get medical attention. **Munchausen syndrome** is a subtype manifested by a chronic history of multiple hospital admissions and willingness to receive invasive procedures. **Munchausen syndrome-by-proxy** is seen when illness in a child is caused by the parent. Motivation is unconscious.

UCV BehSci.76

Somatoform disorders

Both illness production and motivation are unconscious drives. Several types:

1. Conversion—symptoms suggest motor or sensory neurologic or physical disorder but tests and physical exam are negative BehSci.51
2. Somatoform pain disorder—conversion disorder with pain as presenting complaint BehSci.101
3. Hypochondriasis—misinterpretation of normal physical findings, leading to preoccupation with and fear of having a serious illness in spite of medical reassurance BehSci.71
4. Somatization—variety of complaints in multiple organ systems BehSci.100
5. Body dysmorphic disorder—patient convinced that part of own anatomy is malformed BehSci.47
6. Pseudocyesis—false belief of being pregnant associated with objective signs of pregnancy BehSci.85

UCV

Gain: 1°, 2°, 3°

1° gain = what the symptom does for the patient's internal psychic economy.
2° gain = what the symptom gets the patient (sympathy, attention).
3° gain = what the caretaker gets (like an MD on an interesting case).

Panic disorder

Discrete periods of intense fear or discomfort peaking in 10 minutes with 4 of the following:

1. **P**alpitations
2. **A**bdominal distress
3. **N**ausea
4. **I**ncreased perspiration
5. **C**hest pain, chills, and choking

PANIC

Panic disorder must be diagnosed in context of occurrence (e.g., panic disorder with agoraphobia). High prevalence during Step 1 exam.

UCV *BehSci.78*

Specific phobia

Fear that is excessive or unreasonable, cued by presence or anticipation of a specific object or entity. Exposure provokes anxiety response. Person (not necessarily child) recognizes fear is excessive. Fear interferes with normal routine. Treatment options include systematic desensitization. Examples include:

1. Gamophobia (*gam* = gamete) = fear of marriage.
2. Algophobia (*alg* = pain) = fear of pain.
3. Acrophobia (*acro* = height) = fear of heights.
4. Agoraphobia (*agora* = open market) = fear of open places.

UCV *BehSci.99*

Post-traumatic stress disorder

Person experienced or witnessed event that involved actual or threatened death or serious injury. Response involves intense fear, helplessness, or horror. Traumatic event is persistently reexperienced, person persistently avoids stimuli associated with the trauma, and experiences persistent symptoms of increased arousal. Disturbance lasts longer than 1 month and causes distress or social/occupational impairment.

UCV *BehSci.81-82*

Personality

Personality trait—an enduring pattern of perceiving, relating to, and thinking about the environment and oneself that is exhibited in a wide range of important social and personal contexts.

Personality disorder—when these patterns become inflexible and maladaptive, causing impairment in social or occupational functioning or subjective distress.

Cluster A personality disorder

Odd or eccentric; cannot develop meaningful social relationships.

"Weird"

Types:

1. Paranoid—distrust and suspiciousness; projection is main defense mechanism
2. Schizoid—voluntary social withdrawal, no psychosis, limited emotional expression
3. Schizotypal—interpersonal awkwardness, odd thought patterns and appearance.

UCV *BehSci.36, 38, 39*

Cluster B personality disorder

Dramatic, emotional, or erratic. — "Wild"

Types:

1. Antisocial—disregard for and violation of rights of others, criminality; males > females
2. Borderline—unstable mood and behavior, impulsiveness, sense of emptiness; females > males
3. Histrionic—excessive emotionality, somatization, attention seeking, sexually provocative
4. Narcissistic—grandiosity, sense of entitlement, may demand "top" physician/best health care

UCV BehSci.29, 31, 33, 34

Cluster C personality disorder

Anxious or fearful. — "Worried"

Types:

1. Avoidant—sensitive to rejection, socially inhibited, timid, feelings of inadequacy
2. Obsessive-compulsive—preoccupation with order, perfectionism, and control
3. Dependent—submissive and clinging, excessive need to be taken care of, low self-confidence.

UCV BehSci.30, 32, 35, 37

Hallucination versus illusion versus delusion

Hallucinations are perceptions in the absence of external stimuli.

Illusions are misinterpretations of actual external stimuli.

Delusions are false beliefs not shared with other members of culture/subculture that are firmly maintained in spite of obvious proof to the contrary.

UCV BehSci.53

Delusion vs. loose association

A delusion is a disorder in the content of thought (the actual idea).

A loose association is a disorder in the form of thought (the way ideas are tied together).

Hallucination types

Visual hallucination is common in acute organic brain syndrome.

Auditory hallucination is common in schizophrenia.

Olfactory hallucination often occurs as an aura of a psychomotor epilepsy.

Gustatory hallucination is rare.

Tactile hallucination (e.g., formication) is common in delirium tremens. Also seen in cocaine abusers ("cocaine bugs").

Hypnagogic hallucination occurs while going to sleep.

Hypnopompic hallucination occurs while waking from sleep.

Schizophrenia

Waxing and waning vulnerability to psychosis.

Positive symptoms: hallucinations, delusions, strange behavior, loose associations.

Negative symptoms: flat affect, social withdrawal, thought blocking, lack of motivation.

The **4 A's** described by Bleuler:

1. **A**mbivalence (uncertainty)
2. **A**utism (self-preoccupation and lack of communication)
3. **A**ffect (blunted)
4. **A**ssociations (loose)

Fifth A should be **A**uditory hallucinations.

Genetic factors outweigh environmental factors in the etiology of schizophrenia.

Lifetime prevalence = 1.5% (males = females, blacks = whites). Presents earlier in men.

Five subtypes:

1. Disorganized
2. Catatonic
3. Paranoid
4. Undifferentiated
5. Residual

Schizoaffective disorder: a combination of schizophrenia and a mood disorder.

UCV *BehSci.86-92*

Electroconvulsive therapy

Treatment option for major depressive disorder refractory to other treatment. ECT is painless and produces a seizure with transient memory loss and disorientation. Complications can result from anesthesia. The major adverse effect of ECT is retrograde amnesia.

BEHAVIORAL SCIENCE—PSYCHOLOGY

Structural theory of the mind

Freud's three structures of the mind:

Id — Primal urges, sex, and aggression. (I want it.)

Superego — Moral values, conscience. (You know you can't have it.)

Ego — Bridge and mediator between the unconscious mind and the external world. (Deals with the conflict.)

Ego defenses

All ego defenses are automatic and unconscious reactions to psychological stress.

	Description	Example
MATURE		
Altruism	Guilty feelings alleviated by unsolicited generosity toward others.	Mafia boss makes large donation to charity.
Humor	Appreciating the amusing nature of an anxiety-provoking or adverse situation.	Nervous medical student jokes about the boards.
Sublimation	Process whereby one replaces an unacceptable wish with a course of action that is similar to the wish but does not conflict with one's value system.	Aggressive impulses used to succeed in business ventures.
Suppression	Voluntary (unlike other defenses) withholding of an idea or feeling from conscious awareness.	Choosing not to think about the USMLE until the week of the exam.
IMMATURE		
Acting out	Unacceptable feelings and thoughts are expressed through actions.	Tantrums.
Dissociation	Temporary, drastic change in personality, memory, consciousness, or motor behavior to avoid emotional stress.	Extreme forms can result in multiple personalities (dissociative identity disorder).
Denial	Avoidance of awareness of some painful reality.	A common reaction in newly diagnosed AIDS and cancer patients.
Displacement	Process whereby avoided ideas and feelings are transferred to some neutral person or object.	Mother yells at child because she is angry at her husband.
Fixation	Partially remaining at a more childish level of development.	Men fixating on sports games.
Identification	Modeling behavior after another person.	Spouse develops symptoms that deceased patient had.
Isolation	Separation of feelings from ideas and events.	Describing murder in graphic detail with no emotional response.
Projection	An unacceptable internal impulse is attributed to an external source.	A man who wants another woman thinks his wife is cheating on him.
Rationalization	Proclaiming logical reasons for actions actually performed for other reasons, usually to avoid self-blame.	Saying the job was not important anyway, after getting fired.
Reaction formation	Process whereby a warded-off idea or feeling is replaced by an (unconsciously derived) emphasis on its opposite.	A patient with libidinous thoughts enters a monastery.
Regression	Turning back the maturational clock and going back to earlier modes of dealing with the world.	Seen in children under stress (e.g., bedwetting) and in patients on peritoneal dialysis.
Repression	Involuntary withholding of an idea or feeling from conscious awareness. The basic mechanism underlying all others.	

UCV BehSci.1-13

Oedipus complex	Repressed sexual feelings of a child for the opposite-sex parent, accompanied by rivalry with same-sex parent. First described by Freud.	
Factors in hopelessness	Four dynamic factors in the development of hopelessness: 1. Sense of **I**mpotence (powerlessness) 2. Sense of **G**uilt 3. Sense of **A**nger 4. Sense of loss/**D**eprivation leading to depression	**IGAD!**
Classical conditioning	Learning in which a natural response (salivation) is elicited by a conditioned (learned) stimulus (bell) that previously was presented in conjunction with an unconditioned stimulus (food).	Programmed by habit, without any element of reward. As in Pavlov's classical experiments with dogs (ringing the bell provoked salivation).
Operant conditioning	Learning in which a particular action is elicited because it produces a reward. **Positive reinforcement:** desired reward produces action (mouse presses button to get food). **Negative reinforcement:** removal of aversive stimulus increases behavior (mouse presses button to avoid shock). Do not confuse with punishment.	

Reinforcement schedules

Continuous	Behavior shows the most rapid extinction when not rewarded.	This explains why people can get addicted to slot machines at casinos (variable ratio) and yet get upset when vending machines (continuous) don't work.
Variable ratio	Behavior shows the slowest extinction when not rewarded.	

Psychoanalysis	A form of insight therapy—intensive, lengthy, costly, great demands on patient, developed by Freud. May be appropriate for changing chronic character problems.
Topography (in psychoanalysis)	Conscious = what you are aware of. Preconscious = what you are able to make conscious with effort (like your phone number). Unconscious = what you are not aware of; the central goal of Freudian psychoanalysis is to make the patient aware of what is hidden in his/her unconscious.
Intelligence testing	Stanford–Binet and Wechsler are the most famous tests. Mean is defined at 100, with standard deviation of 15. IQ lower than 70 (or 2 standard deviations below the mean) is one of the criteria for diagnosis of mental retardation. IQ scores are correlated with genetic factors but are more highly correlated with school achievement. Intelligence tests are objective (not projective) tests.

NOTES

SECTION II

Biochemistry

"Biochemistry is the study of carbon compounds that crawl."
—Mike Adams

This high-yield material includes molecular biology, genetics, cell biology, and principles of metabolism (especially vitamins, cofactors, minerals, and single-enzyme-deficiency diseases). When studying metabolic pathways, emphasize important regulatory steps and enzyme deficiencies that result in disease. For example, understanding the defect in Lesch–Nyhan syndrome and its clinical consequences is higher yield than memorizing every intermediate in the purine salvage pathway. Do not spend time on hard-core organic chemistry, mechanisms, and physical chemistry. Detailed chemical structures are infrequently tested. Familiarity with the latest biochemical techniques that have medical relevance—such as enzyme-linked immunosorbent assay (ELISA), immunoelectrophoresis, Southern blotting, and PCR—is useful. Beware if you placed out of your medical school's biochemistry class, for the emphasis of the test differs from the emphasis of many undergraduate courses. Review the related biochemistry when studying pharmacology or genetic diseases as a way to reinforce and integrate the material.

BIOCHEMISTRY—HIGH-YIELD CLINICAL VIGNETTES

- Full-term neonate of uneventful delivery becomes mentally retarded and hyperactive and has a musty odor → what is the diagnosis? → PKU.
- A stressed executive comes home from work, consumes 7 or 8 martinis in rapid succession before dinner, and becomes hypoglycemic → what is the mechanisms? → NADH increase prevents gluconeogenesis by shunting pyruvate and oxaloacetate to lactate and malate.

BIOCHEMISTRY—HIGH-YIELD TOPICS

DNA/RNA/Protein

1. Molecular biology: tools and techniques (e.g., cloning, cDNA libraries, PCR, restriction fragment length polymorphism, restriction enzymes, sequencing).
2. Transcriptional regulation: the operon model (lac, trp operons) of transcription, eukaryotic transcription (e.g., TATA box, enhancers, effects of steroid hormones, transcription factors).
3. Protein synthesis: steps, regulation, energy (Which step requires ATP? GTP?), differences between prokaryotes and eukaryotes (N-formyl methionine), post-translational modification (targeting to organelles, secretion).
4. Acid–base titration curve of amino acids, proteins.

Genetic Errors

1. Inherited hyperlipidemias: types, clinical manifestations, specific changes in serum lipids.
2. Glycogen and lysosomal storage diseases (e.g., type III glycogen storage disease), I cell disease.
3. Porphyrias: defects, clinical presentation, effect of barbiturates.
4. Inherited defects in amino acid metabolism.

Metabolism

1. Glycogen synthesis: regulation, inherited defects.
2. Oxygen consumption, carbon dioxide production, and ATP production for fats, proteins, and carbohydrates.
3. Amino acid degradation pathways (urea cycle, tricarboxylic acid cycle).
4. Effect of enzyme phosphorylation on metabolic pathways.
5. Rate-limiting enzymes in different metabolic pathways (e.g., pyruvate decarboxylase).
6. Sites of different metabolic pathways (What organ? Where in the cell?).
7. Fed state versus fasting state: forms of energy used, direction of metabolic pathways.
8. Tyrosine kinases and their effects on metabolic pathways (insulin receptor, growth factor receptors).

9. Anti-insulin (gluconeogenic) hormones (e.g., glucagon, GH, cortisol).
10. Synthesis and metabolism of neurotransmitters (e.g., acetylcholine, epinephrine, norepinephrine, dopamine).
11. Purine/pyrimidine degradation.
12. Carnitine shuttle: function, inherited defects.
13. Cellular/organ effects of insulin secretion.

Chromatin structure	Condensed by (−) charged DNA looped twice around (+) charged H2A, H2B, H3, and H4 histones (nucleosome bead). H1 ties nucleosomes together in a string (30-nm fiber). In mitosis, DNA condenses to form mitotic chromosomes.	Think of beads on a string.
Heterochromatin	Condensed, transcriptionally inactive.	
Euchromatin	Less condensed, transcriptionally active.	*Eu* = true, "truly transcribed."
Nucleotides	Purines (**A, G**) have two rings. Pyrimidines (**C, T, U**) have one ring. Guanine has a ketone. Thymine has a methyl. Uracil found in RNA; thymine in DNA. G-C bond (3 H-bonds) stronger than A-T bond (2 H-bonds).	**PUR**e **A**s **G**old: **PUR**ines. **CUT** the **PY** (pie): **PY**rimidines. **THY**mine has a me**THY**l.

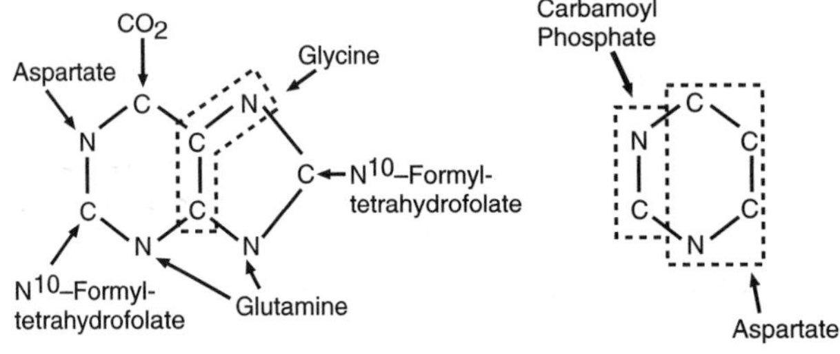

Start and stop codons	AUG (or rarely GUG) is the mRNA initiation codon. AUG codes for methionine, which may be removed before translation is completed. In prokaryotes the initial AUG codes for a formyl-methionine (f-met). Stop codons: UGA, UAA, UAG.	**AUG** in**AUG**urates protein synthesis. **UGA** = **U G**o **A**way **UAA** = **U A**re **A**way **UAG** = **U A**re **G**one
Genetic code: features	Unambiguous = each codon specifies only one amino acid. Degenerate = more than one codon may code for same amino acid. Commaless, nonoverlapping (except some viruses). Universal (exceptions include mitochondria, archaebacteria, *Mycoplasma*, and some yeasts).	
Mutations in DNA	Silent = same aa, often base change in third position of codon. Missense = changed aa (conservative = new aa is similar in chemical structure). Nonsense = change resulting in early stop codon. Frameshift = change resulting in misreading of all nucleotides downstream, usually resulting in a truncated protein.	Severity of damage: nonsense > missense > silent.

Transition versus transversion	Transition = substituting purine for purine or pyrimidine for pyrimidine. Transversion = substituting purine for pyrimidine or vice versa.	**Transversion** = **Trans**conversion (one type to another).
DNA replication	Origin of replication: continuous DNA synthesis on leading strand and discontinuous (Okazaki fragments) on lagging strand. **Primase** makes an RNA **primer** on which DNA polymerase can initiate replication. **DNA polymerase** reaches primer of preceding fragment; 5′ → 3′ exonuclease activity of DNA polymerase I degrades RNA primer; **DNA ligase** seals; 3′ → 5′ exonuclease activity of DNA polymerase "proofreads" each added nucleotide. DNA topoisomerases create a nick in the helix to relieve supercoils.	Eukaryotic genome has multiple origins of replication. Bacteria, viruses, and plasmids have only one origin of replication.

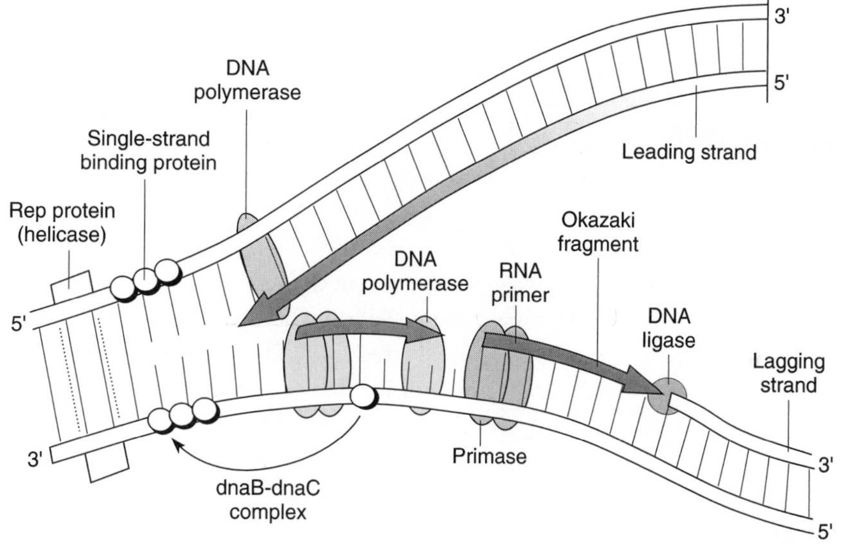

DNA repair: single strand	Single-strand, excision-repair–specific glycosylase recognizes and removes damaged base. Endonuclease makes a break several bases to the 5′ side. Exonuclease removes short stretch of nucleotides. DNA polymerase fills gap. DNA ligase seals.	If both strands are damaged, repair may proceed via recombination with undamaged homologous chromosome.
DNA/RNA/protein synthesis direction	DNA and RNA are both synthesized 5′ → 3′. Remember that the 5′ of the incoming nucleotide bears the triphosphate (energy source for bond). The 3′ hydroxyl of the nascent chain is the target. Protein synthesis also proceeds in the 5′ to 3′ direction.	Imagine the incoming nucleotide bringing a gift (triphosphate) to the 3′ host. "**BYOP** (phosphate) from **5** to **3**." Amino acids are linked N to C.
Types of RNA	mRNA is the **largest** type of RNA. rRNA is the most **abundant** type of RNA. tRNA is the **smallest** type of RNA.	**M**assive, **R**ampant, **T**iny.
Polymerases: RNA	**Eukaryotes:** RNA polymerase I makes **r**RNA. RNA polymerase II makes **m**RNA. RNA polymerase III makes **t**RNA. No proofreading function, but can initiate chains. RNA polymerase II opens DNA at promoter site (A-T-rich upstream sequence—TATA and CAAT). α-amanitin inhibits RNA polymerase II. **Prokaryotes:** RNA polymerase makes all three kinds of RNA.	I, II, and III are numbered as their products are used in protein synthesis. OR **1, 2, 3 = RMT** (rhyme).
Regulation of gene expression		
Promoter	Site where RNA polymerase and multiple other transcription factors bind to DNA upstream from gene locus.	Promoter mutation commonly results in dramatic decrease in amount of gene transcribed.
Enhancer	Stretch of DNA that alters gene expression by binding transcription factors. May be located close to, far from, or even within (in an intron) the gene whose expression it regulates.	
Introns versus exons	Exons contain the actual genetic information coding for protein. Introns are intervening noncoding segments of DNA.	**IN**trons stay **IN** the nucleus, whereas **EX**ons **EX**it and are **EX**pressed.

Splicing of mRNA	Introns are precisely spliced out of primary mRNA transcripts. A lariat-shaped intermediate is formed. Small nuclear ribonucleoprotein particles (snRNP) facilitate splicing by binding to primary mRNA transcripts and forming spliceosomes.	
RNA processing (eukaryotes)	Occurs in nucleus. After transcription: 1. Capping on 5′ end (7-methyl-G) 2. Polyadenylation on 3′ end (≈200 A's) 3. Splicing out of introns Initial transcript is called heterogeneous nuclear RNA (hnRNA). Capped and tailed transcript is called mRNA.	Only processed RNA is transported out of the nucleus.
tRNA structure	75–90 nucleotides, cloverleaf form, anticodon end is opposite 3′ aminoacyl end. All tRNAs, both eukaryotic and prokaryotic, have CCA at 3′ end along with a high percentage of chemically modified bases. The amino acid is covalently bound to the 3′ end of the tRNA.	
tRNA charging	Aminoacyl-tRNA synthetase (one per aa, uses ATP) scrutinizes aa before and after it binds to tRNA. If incorrect, bond is hydrolyzed by synthetase. The aa-tRNA bond has energy for formation of peptide bond. A mischarged tRNA reads usual codon but inserts wrong amino acid.	Aminoacyl-tRNA synthetase and binding of charged tRNA to the codon are responsible for accuracy of amino acid selection.
tRNA wobble	Accurate base pairing is required only in the first 2 nucleotide positions of an mRNA codon, so codons differing in the 3rd "wobble" position may code for the same tRNA/amino acid.	
Protein synthesis: ATP versus GTP	P site = peptidyl, A site = aminoacyl. ATP is used in tRNA charging, whereas GTP is used in binding of tRNA to ribosome and for translocation.	ATP = tRNA Activation. GTP = tRNA Gripping and Going places.

Polymerase chain reaction (PCR)

Molecular biology laboratory procedure that is used to synthesize many copies of a desired fragment of DNA.

Steps:

1. DNA is denatured by heating to generate 2 separate strands
2. During cooling, excess of premade primers anneal to a specific sequence on each strand to be amplified
3. Heat-stable DNA polymerase replicates the DNA sequence following each primer

These steps are repeated multiple times for DNA sequence amplification.

COMMON GENETIC DISEASES DETECTABLE BY PCR

Disease	Gene
SCID	Adenosine deaminase
Lesch–Nyhan syndrome	HGPRT
Cystic fibrosis	CFTR
Familial hypercholesterolemia	LDL-R
Retinoblastoma	Rb
Sickle cell anemia and β-thalassemia	β-globin gene
Hemophilia A and B	Factor VIII (A) and IX (B)
Von Willebrand's disease	VWF
Lysosomal storage diseases	See p. 153
Glycogen storage diseases	See p. 150

UCV Bio.53, 58, 70, 87, 94, 95, 96

Molecular biology techniques

Southern blot
A DNA sample is electrophoresed on a gel and then transferred to a filter. The filter is then soaked in a denaturant and subsequently exposed to a labeled DNA probe that recognizes and anneals to its complementary strand. The resulting double-stranded labeled piece of DNA is visualized when the filter is exposed to film.
DNA–DNA hybridization
Southern = Same

Northern blot
Similar technique, except that Northern blotting involves radioactive DNA probe binding to sample RNA.
DNA–RNA hybridization

Western blot
Sample protein is separated via gel electrophoresis and transferred to a filter. Labeled antibody is used to bind to relevant **protein.**
Antibody–protein hybridization

Southwestern blot
Protein sample is run on a gel, transferred to a filter, and exposed to labeled DNA. Used to detect DNA–protein interactions as with transcription factors (e.g., p53, *jun*).
DNA–protein interaction

Modes of inheritance

Autosomal dominant	Often due to defects in structural genes. Many generations, both male and female, affected.	Often pleiotropic and, in many cases, present clinically after puberty. Family history crucial to diagnosis.
Autosomal recessive	25% of offspring from 2 carrier parents are affected. Often due to enzyme deficiencies. Usually seen in only one generation.	Commonly more severe than dominant disorders; patients often present in childhood.
X-linked recessive	Sons of heterozygous mothers have a 50% chance of being affected. No male-to male transmission.	Commonly more severe in males. Heterozygous females may be affected.
Mitochondrial inheritance	Transmitted only through mother. All offspring of affected females may show signs of disease.	Leber's hereditary optic neuropathy, mitochondrial myopathies.

Genetic terms

Variable expression	Nature and severity of the phenotype varies from one individual to another.
Incomplete penetrance	Not all individuals with a mutant genotype show the mutant phenotype.
Pleiotropy	One gene has more than one effect on an individual's phenotype.
Imprinting	Differences in phenotype depend on whether the mutation is of maternal or paternal origin (e.g., Angelman's syndrome [maternal], Prader-Willi syndrome [paternal]).
Anticipation	Severity of disease worsens or age of onset of disease is earlier in succeeding generations (e.g., Huntington's disease).
Loss of heterozygosity	If a patient inherits or develops a mutation in a tumor suppressor gene, the complementary allele must be deleted/mutated before cancer develops. This is not true of oncogenes.

Hardy–Weinberg population genetics

If a population is in Hardy–Weinberg equilibrium, then:

$$p^2 + 2pq + q^2 = 1$$

$$p + q = 1$$

p and q are separate alleles; 2pq = heterozygote prevalence.

DNA repair defects

UCV Bio.60, 84

Xeroderma pigmentosum (skin sensitivity to UV light), ataxia-telangiectasia (x-rays), Bloom's syndrome (radiation), and Fanconi's anemia (cross-linking agents).

Xeroderma pigmentosum

UCV Bio.84

Defective excision repair such as uvr ABC exonuclease. Results in inability to repair thymidine dimers, which form in DNA when exposed to UV light.

Associated with dry skin and with melanoma and other cancers.

Fructose intolerance

UCV Bio.64

Hereditary deficiency of aldolase B. Fructose-1-phosphate accumulates, causing a decrease in available phosphate, which results in inhibition of glycogenolysis and gluconeogenesis.

Symptoms: hypoglycemia, jaundice, cirrhosis.

Treatment: must decrease intake of both fructose and sucrose (glucose + fructose).

HIGH-YIELD FACTS

Biochemistry

Galactosemia UCV Bio.62	Absence of galactose-1-phosphate uridyltransferase. Autosomal recessive. Damage is caused by accumulation of toxic substances (including galactitol) rather than absence of an essential compound. Symptoms: cataracts, hepatosplenomegaly, mental retardation. Treatment: exclude galactose and lactose (galactose + glucose) from diet.	
Lactase deficiency	Age-dependent and/or hereditary lactose intolerance (blacks, Asians). Symptoms: bloating, cramps, osmotic diarrhea. Treatment: avoid milk or add lactase pills to diet.	
Pyruvate dehydrogenase deficiency	Causes backup of substrate (pyruvate and alanine), resulting in lactic acidosis. Findings: neurologic defects. Treatment: increased intake of ketogenic nutrients.	Lysine and Leucine—the only purely ketogenic amino acids.
Glucose-6-phosphate dehydrogenase deficiency UCV Bio.86	G6PD is rate-limiting enzyme in HMP shunt (which yields NADPH). NADPH is necessary to keep glutathione reduced, which in turn detoxifies free radicals and peroxides. ↓ NADPH in RBCs leads to **hemolytic anemia** due to poor RBC defense against oxidizing agents (fava beans, sulfonamides, primaquine) and antituberculosis drugs. X-linked recessive disorder.	G6PD deficiency more prevalent among blacks. Heinz bodies: altered Hemoglobin precipitates within RBCs.
Glycolytic enzyme deficiency	Hexokinase, glucose-phosphate isomerase, aldolase, triose-phosphate isomerase, phosphate-glycerate kinase, enolase, and pyruvate kinase deficiencies are associated with hemolytic anemia.	RBCs metabolize glucose anaerobically (no mitochondria) and thus solely depend on glycolysis.
Glycogen storage diseases	12 types, all resulting in abnormal glycogen metabolism and an accumulation of glycogen within cells.	↑ Glycogen in Liver + Kidneys
Type I	Von Gierke's disease = glucose-6-phosphatase deficiency. Findings: severe fasting hypoglycemia, ↑↑ glycogen in liver. Bio.82	
Type II	Pompe's disease = lysosomal α-1,4-glucosidase deficiency. Findings: cardiomegaly and systemic findings, leading to early death. Bio.79	Pompe's trashes the Pump (heart, liver, and muscle).
Type III	Cori's = deficiency of debranching enzyme α-1,6-glucosidase.	
Type V UCV	McArdle's disease = skeletal muscle glycogen phosphorylase deficiency. Findings: ↑ glycogen in muscle but cannot break it down, leading to painful cramps, myoglobinuria with strenuous exercise.	McArdle's: Muscle. Very Poor Carbohydrate Metabolism.

Homocystinuria

UCV Bio.65

Defect in cystathionine synthase. Two forms:

1. Deficiency (treatment: ↓ Met and ↑ Cys in diet)
2. Decreased affinity of synthase for pyridoxal phosphate (treatment: ↑↑ vitamin B_6 in diet)

Results in excess homocystine in the urine. Cysteine becomes essential.

Cystinuria

UCV Bio.54

Common (1/7000) inherited defect of tubular amino acid transporter for **C**ystine, **O**rnithine, **L**ysine, and **A**rginine in kidneys. Excess cystine in urine can lead to the precipitation of cystine kidney stones.

COLA

Maple syrup urine disease

UCV Bio.71

Blocked degradation of **branched** amino acids (Ile, Val, Leu) due to ↓ α-ketoacid dehydrogenase. Causes severe CNS defects, mental retardation, and death.

Urine smells like maple syrup. Think of cutting (blocking) **branches** of a maple tree.

Amino acid derivatives

Phenylalanine → tyrosine → thyroxine

tyrosine → dopa → dopamine → NE → epi

dopamine → melanin

Tryptophan → niacin → $NAD^+/NADP^+$

Tryptophan → serotonin

Tryptophan → melatonin

Histidine → histamine

Glycine → porphyrin → heme

Arginine → creatine

Arginine → urea

Phenylketonuria

UCV Bio.77

Normally, phenylalanine is converted into tyrosine (nonessential aa). In PKU, there is ↓ phenylalanine hydroxylase or ↓ tetrahydrobiopterin cofactor. Tyrosine becomes essential and phenylalanine builds up, leading to excess phenylketones.

Findings: mental retardation, fair skin, eczema, musty body odor.

Treatment: ↓ phenylalanine (contained in Nutrasweet) and ↑ tyrosine in diet.

Screened for at birth.
Phenylketones = phenylacetate, phenyllactate, and phenylpyruvate in urine.

Alkaptonuria UCV Bio.51	Congenital deficiency of homogentisic acid oxidase in the degradative pathway of tyrosine. Resulting alkapton bodies cause **dark urine.** Also, the connective tissue is dark. Benign disease. May have arthralgias.	
Albinism UCV Bio.50	Congenital deficiency of tyrosinase. Results in an inability to synthesize melanin from tyrosine. Can result from a lack of migration of neural crest cells.	Lack of melanin results in an increased risk of skin cancer.
Adenosine deaminase deficiency	ADA deficiency can cause SCID. Excess ATP and dATP imbalances nucleotide pool via feedback inhibition of ribonucleotide reductase. This prevents DNA synthesis and thus lowers lymphocyte count. First disease to be treated by experimental human gene therapy.	SCID = severe combined (T and B) immunodeficiency disease. SCID happens to kids (remember "bubble boy").
Lesch–Nyhan syndrome UCV Bio.70	Purine salvage problem owing to absence of HGPRTase, which converts hypoxanthine to inosine monophosphate (IMP) and guanine to guanosine monophosphate (GMP). X-linked recessive. Results in excess uric acid production. Findings: retardation, self-mutilation, aggression, hyperuricemia, gout, and choreoathetosis.	**LNS** = **L**acks **N**ucleotide **S**alvage (purine).
Ehlers–Danlos syndrome UCV Bio.56	Faulty collagen synthesis causing: 1. Hyperextensible skin 2. Tendency to bleed 3. Hypermobile joints 10 types. Inheritance varies from autosomal dominant (type IV) to autosomal recessive (type VI) to X-linked recessive (type IX).	Sounds like "feller's damn loose" (loose joints).
Osteogenesis imperfecta UCV Bio.75	Clinically characterized by **multiple fractures** occurring with minimal trauma (brittle bone disease), which may occur during the birth process, as well as by **blue sclerae** due to the translucency of the connective tissue over the choroid. Caused by a variety of gene defects resulting in abnormal collagen synthesis. The most common form is autosomal-dominant with abnormal collagen type I synthesis.	May be confused with child abuse.

Sphingolipid components

Components of nerve tissue.

Lysosomal storage diseases

Each is caused by a deficiency in one of the many lysosomal enzymes.

Disease	Description	Inheritance
Fabry's disease	Caused by deficiency of α-galactosidase A, resulting in accumulation of ceramide trihexoside. Finding: renal failure. *Bio.57*	X-linked recessive.
Gaucher's disease	Caused by deficiency of β-glucocerebrosidase, leading to glucocerebroside accumulation in brain, liver, spleen, and bone marrow (Gaucher's cells with characteristic "crinkled paper" enlarged cytoplasm). Type I, the more common form, is compatible with a normal life span. *Bio.63*	Autosomal recessive.
Niemann–Pick disease	Deficiency of sphingomyelinase causes buildup of sphingomyelin and cholesterol in reticuloendothelial and parenchymal cells and tissues. Patients die by age 3. *Bio.73* Sphingomylin in lysosomes	Autosomal recessive. No man picks (Niemann–Pick) his nose with his sphinger.
Tay–Sachs disease	Absence of hexosaminidase A results in GM_2 ganglioside accumulation. Death occurs by age 3. Cherry-red spot visible on macula. Carrier rate is 1 in 30 in Jews of European descent (1 in 300 for others). *Bio.81* cells in CNS	Autosomal recessive. **Tay-saX** sounds like he**X**osaminidase.
Metachromatic leukodystrophy	Deficiency of arylsulfatase A results in the accumulation of sulfatide in the brain, kidney, liver, and peripheral nerves. *Bio.72*	Autosomal recessive.
Krabbe's disease	Absence of galactosylceramide β-galactosidase leads to the accumulation of galactocerebroside in the brain. Optic atrophy, spasticity, early death. *Bio.69*	Autosomal recessive.
Hurler's syndrome	Deficiency of α-L-iduronidase; results in corneal clouding and mental retardation. *Bio.67*	Autosomal recessive. { Chondroitin B sulfate, Heparan sulfate → in urine
Hunter's syndrome	Deficiency of iduronate sulfatase. Mild form of Hurler's with no corneal clouding and mild mental retardation. *Bio.66* ★ Deafness	X-linked recessive. ↑ urinary Heparan Sulfate; ↑ " Dermatan sulfate

UCV

HIGH-YIELD FACTS

Biochemistry

ATP

Base (adenine), ribose, 3 phosphoryls. 2 phosphoanhydride bonds, 7 kcal/mol each.
Aerobic metabolism of glucose produces 38 ATP via malate shuttle, 36 ATP via G3P shuttle.
Anaerobic glycolysis produces only 2 ATP per glucose molecule.
ATP hydrolysis can be coupled to energetically unfavorable reactions.

UCV Bio.54

Activated carriers

Phosphoryl (ATP)
Electrons (NADH, NADPH, $FADH_2$)
Acyl (coenzyme A, lipoamide)
CO_2 (biotin)
One-carbon units (tetrahydrofolates)
CH_3 groups (SAM)
Aldehydes (TPP)
Glucose (UDP-glucose)
Choline (CDP-choline)

G-protein-linked second messengers

Receptor	G protein class	Major functions
α_1	q	↑ vascular smooth muscle contraction
α_2	i	↓ sympathetic outflow, ↓ insulin release
β_1	s	↑ heart rate, ↑ contractility, ↑ renin release, ↑ lipolysis
β_2	s	Vasodilation, bronchodilation, ↑ glucagon release
M_1	q	CNS
M_2	i	↓ heart rate
M_3	q	↑ exocrine gland secretions

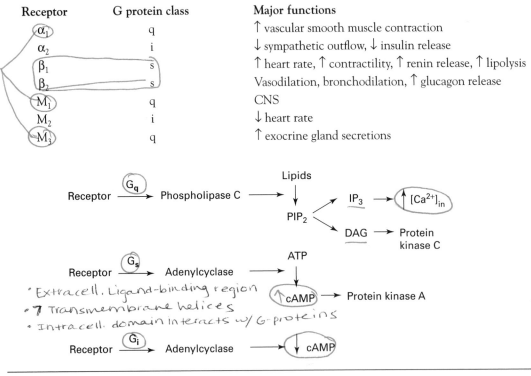

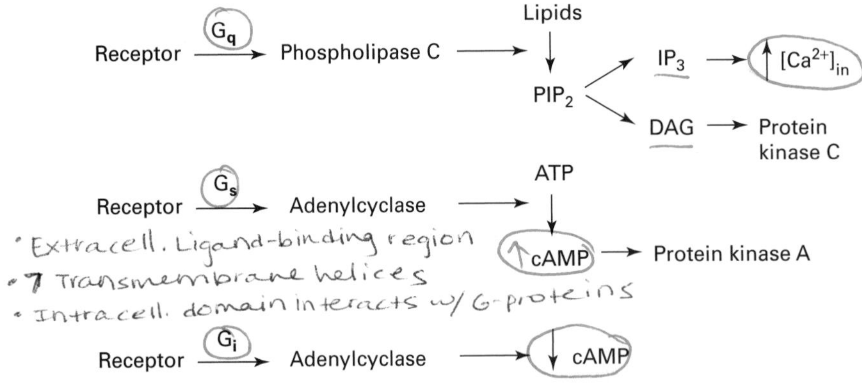

Signal molecule precursors

ATP → cAMP via adenylate cyclase.
GTP → cGMP via guanylate cyclase.
Glutamate → GABA via glutamate decarboxylase (requires vit. B_6).
Choline → ACh via choline acetyltransferase (ChAT).
Arachidonate → prostaglandins, thromboxanes, leukotrienes via cyclooxygenase/lipoxygenase.
Fructose-6-P → fructose-1,6-bis-P via phosphofructokinase (PFK), the rate-limiting enzyme of glycolysis.
1,3-BPG → 2,3-BPG via bisphosphoglycerate mutase.

NAD⁺/NADPH	NAD⁺ is generally used in **catabolic** processes to carry reducing equivalents away as NADH. NADPH is used in **anabolic** processes as a supply of reducing equivalents.	NADPH is a product of the HMP shunt and the malate dehydrogenase reaction.
***S*-adenosyl-methionine**	ATP + methionine → SAM. SAM transfers methyl units to a wide variety of acceptors (e.g., in synthesis of phosphocreatine, high-energy phosphate active in muscle ATP production). Regeneration of methionine (and thus SAM) is dependent on vitamin B_{12}.	SAM the methyl donor man. CH_3
Metabolism sites		
Mitochondria	Fatty acid **O**xidation (β-oxidation), **A**cetyl-CoA production, **K**rebs cycle.	**Mity OAK.**
Cytoplasm	Glycolysis, fatty acid synthesis, HMP shunt, protein synthesis (RER), steroid synthesis (SER).	
Both	Gluconeogenesis, urea cycle, heme synthesis.	
Hexokinase versus glucokinase	Hexokinase is found throughout body. Glucokinase (lower affinity [↑K_m] but higher capacity [↑V_{max}]) is predominantly found in the liver.	Only hexokinase is feedback inhibited by G6P.

	Hexokinase	Glucokinase
Tissue:	Most	Liver + β cells
K_m	Low	High
V_{max}	Low	High
Inhibited by Glucose-6-Phosph	YES	NO

Glucokinase works in Liver, when there is a lot of Glucose (↑Km) (after carbohydrate-rich meal) & it works fast (↑V_{max}) to prevent glucose from entering systemic circulation

HIGH-YIELD FACTS

Biochemistry

Regulation of metabolic pathways

Pathway	Major regulatory enzyme(s)	Activator	Inhibitor	Effector hormone	Remarks
Citric acid cycle	Citrate synthase		ATP, long-chain acyl-CoA		Regulated mainly by the need for ATP and therefore by the supply of NAD^+
Glycolysis and pyruvate oxidation	Phosphofructokinase	AMP, fructose 2,6-bisphosphate in liver, fructose-1,6-bisphosphate in muscle	Citrate (fatty acids, ketone bodies), ATP, cAMP	Glucagon ↓	Induced by insulin
	Pyruvate dehydrogenase	CoA, NAD, ADP, pyruvate	Acetyl-CoA, NADH, ATP (fatty acids, ketone bodies)	Insulin ↑ (in adipose tissue)	Also important in regulating the citric acid cycle
Gluconeogenesis	Pyruvate carboxylase Phosphoenolpyruvate carboxykinase	Acetyl-CoA cAMP?	ADP	Glucagon?	Induced by glucocorticoids, glucagon, cAMP
	Fructose-1,6-bisphosphatase	cAMP	AMP, fructose 2,6-bisphosphate	Glucagon	Suppressed by insulin
Glycogenesis	Glycogen synthase		Phosphorylase (in liver) cAMP, Ca^{2+} (muscle)	Insulin ↑ Glucagon ↓ (liver) Epinephrine ↓	Induced by insulin
Glycogenolysis	Phosphorylase	cAMP, Ca^{2+} (muscle)		Insulin ↓ Glucagon ↑ (liver) Epinephrine ↑	
Pentose phosphate pathway	Glucose-6-phosphate dehydrogenase	$NADP^+$	NADPH		Induced by insulin
Lipogenesis	Acetyl-CoA carboxylase	Citrate	Long-chain acyl-CoA, cAMP	Insulin ↑ Glucagon ↓ (liver)	Induced by insulin
Cholesterol synthesis	HMG-CoA reductase		Cholesterol, cAMP	Insulin ↑ Glucagon ↓ (liver)	Inhibited by certain drugs, eg, lovastatin

Metabolism in major organs

Organ	Major function	Major pathways	Main substrates	Major products	Specialist enzymes
Liver	Service for the other organs and tissues	Most represented, including gluconeogenesis; β-oxidation; ketogenesis; lipoprotein formation; urea, uric acid & bile acid formation; cholesterol synthesis	Free fatty acids, glucose (well fed), lactate, glycerol, fructose, amino acids (Ethanol)	Glucose, VLDL (triacylglycerol), HDL, ketone bodies, urea, uric acid, bile acids, plasma proteins (Acetate)	Glucokinase, glucose-6-phosphatase, glycerol kinase, phosphoenolpyruvate carboxykinase, fructokinase, arginase, HMG-CoA synthase and lyase, 7α-hydroxylase
Brain	Coordination of the nervous system	Glycolysis, amino acid metabolism	Glucose (main sub-, strate), amino acids, ketone bodies (in starvation) Polyunsaturated fatty acids in neonate	Lactate	
Heart	Pumping of blood	Aerobic pathways, eg, β-oxidation and citric acid cycle	Free fatty acids, lactate, ketone bodies, VLDL and chylomicron triacylglycerol, some glucose		Lipoprotein lipase Respiratory chain well developed
Adipose tissue	Storage and breakdown of triacylglycerol	Esterification of fatty acids and lipolysis	Glucose, lipoprotein triacylglycerol	Free fatty acids, glycerol	Lipoprotein lipase, hormone-sensitive lipase
Muscle Fast twitch Slow twitch	 Rapid movement Sustained movement	 Glycolysis Aerobic pathways, eg, β-oxidation and citric acid cycle	 Glucose Ketone bodies, triacylglycerol in VLDL and chylomicrons, free fatty acids	 Lactate	 Lipoprotein lipase Respiratory chain well developed

Glycolysis regulation, irreversible enzymes

Reaction	Enzyme	Regulation
D-glucose → Glucose-6-phosphate	Hexokinase/glucokinase*	Glucose-6-P ⊖
Fructose-6-P → Fructose-1,6-BP	Phosphofructokinase (rate-limiting step)	ATP ⊖, AMP ⊕, citrate ⊖, fructose 2, 6-BP ⊕
Phosphoenolpyruvate → Pyruvate	Pyruvate kinase	ATP ⊖, alanine ⊖, fructose-1,6-BP ⊕
Pyruvate → Acetyl-CoA	Pyruvate dehydrogenase	ATP ⊖, NADH ⊖, acetyl-CoA ⊖

* Glucokinase in liver; hexokinase in all other tissues.

Gluconeogenesis, irreversible enzymes

Pyruvate carboxylase	In mitochondria. Pyruvate → oxaloacetate.	Requires biotin, ATP. Activated by acetyl-CoA.
PEP carboxykinase	In cytosol. Oxaloacetate → phosphoenolpyruvate.	Requires GTP.
Fructose-1,6-bisphosphatase	In cytosol. Fructose-1,6-bisphosphate → fructose-6-P	**P**athway **P**roduces **F**resh **G**lucose.
Glucose-6-phosphatase	In cytosol. Glucose-6-P → glucose	

Above enzymes found only in liver, kidney, intestinal epithelium. Muscle cannot participate in gluconeogenesis.

Hypoglycemia is caused by a deficiency of these key gluconeogenic enzymes listed above (e.g., von Gierke's disease, which is caused by a lack of glucose-6-phosphatase in the liver). Bio.82

UCV

Pentose phosphate pathway

Produces ribose-5-P from G6P for nucleotide synthesis.

Produces NADPH from NADP+ for fatty acid and steroid biosynthesis and for maintaining reduced glutathione inside RBCs.

Part of HMP shunt.

All reactions of this pathway occur in the cytoplasm.

Sites: lactating mammary glands, liver, adrenal cortex—all sites of fatty acid or steroid synthesis.

Cori cycle

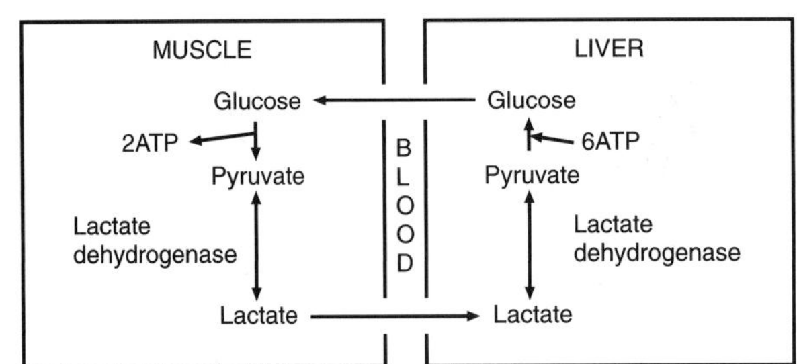

Transfers excess reducing equivalents from RBCs and muscle to liver, allowing muscle to function anaerobically (net 2 ATP).

-Lactate is released into blood by cells that do not have mitochondria (RBC's + exercising skeletal muscle)

Pyruvate dehydrogenase complex

The complex contains three enzymes that require five cofactors: pyrophosphate (from thiamine), lipoic acid, CoA (from pantothenate), FAD (riboflavin), NAD (niacin).

Reaction: pyruvate + NAD^+ + CoA → acetyl-CoA + CO_2 + NADH.

The complex is similar to the α-ketoglutarate dehydrogenase complex (same cofactors, similar substrate and action).

Cofactors are the first 4 B vitamins plus lipoic acid:

- B_1 (thiamine; TPP)
- B_2 (FAD) – Riboflavin
- B_3 (NAD) – Niacin
- B_5 (pantothenate → CoA)
- Lipoic acid

Pyruvate metabolism

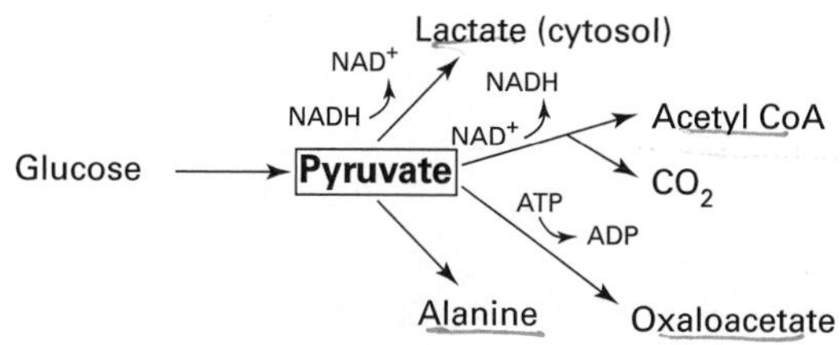

TCA cycle

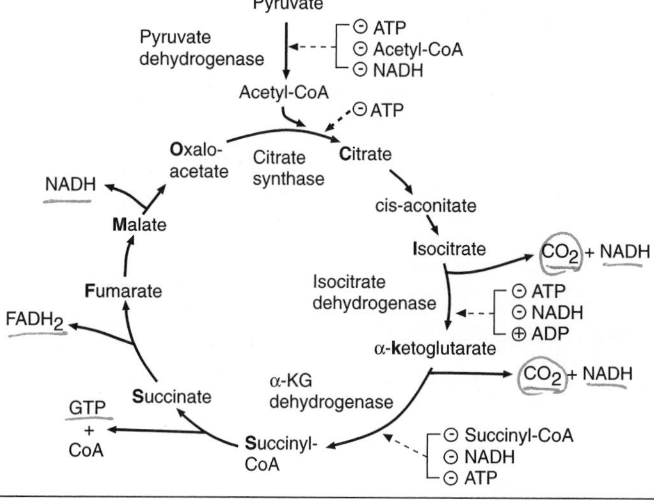

Produces 3NADH, $1FADH_2$, $2CO_2$, 1GTP per acetyl CoA = 12ATP/acetyl CoA (2× everything per glucose)

α-Ketoglutarate dehydrogenase complex requires same cofactors as the pyruvate dehydrogenase complex.

Cindy Is Kinky So She Fornicates More Often.

Electron transport chain and oxidative phosphorylation

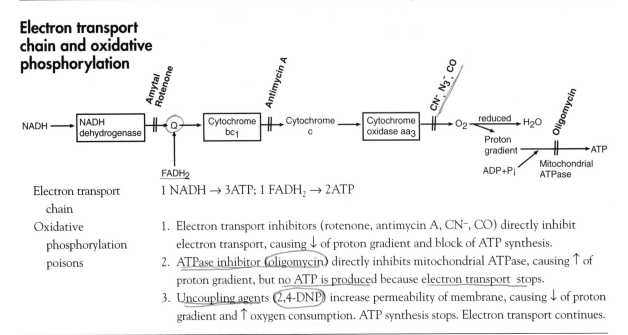

NADH → NADH dehydrogenase ‖ (Amytal, Rotenone) → Q ← $FADH_2$

Q → Cytochrome bc_1 ‖ (Antimycin A) → Cytochrome c → Cytochrome oxidase aa_3 ‖ (CN^-, N_3^-, CO) → O_2 —reduced→ H_2O

Proton gradient + ADP+P_i → Mitochondrial ATPase ‖ (Oligomycin) → ATP

Electron transport chain	1 NADH → 3ATP; 1 $FADH_2$ → 2ATP
Oxidative phosphorylation poisons	1. Electron transport inhibitors (rotenone, antimycin A, CN^-, CO) directly inhibit electron transport, causing ↓ of proton gradient and block of ATP synthesis. 2. ATPase inhibitor (oligomycin) directly inhibits mitochondrial ATPase, causing ↑ of proton gradient, but no ATP is produced because electron transport stops. 3. Uncoupling agents (2,4-DNP) increase permeability of membrane, causing ↓ of proton gradient and ↑ oxygen consumption. ATP synthesis stops. Electron transport continues.

Liver: fed state vs. fasting state

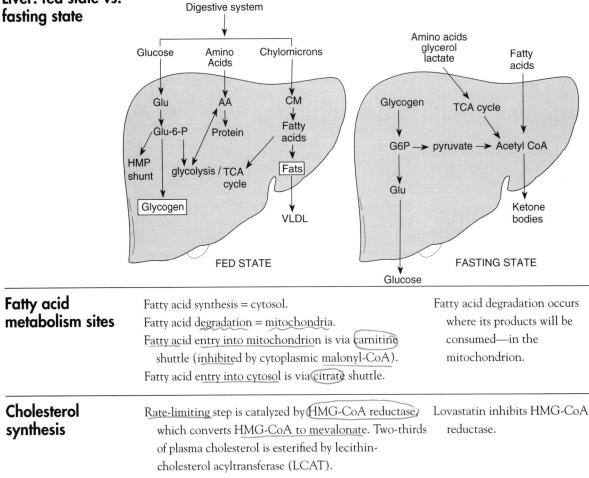

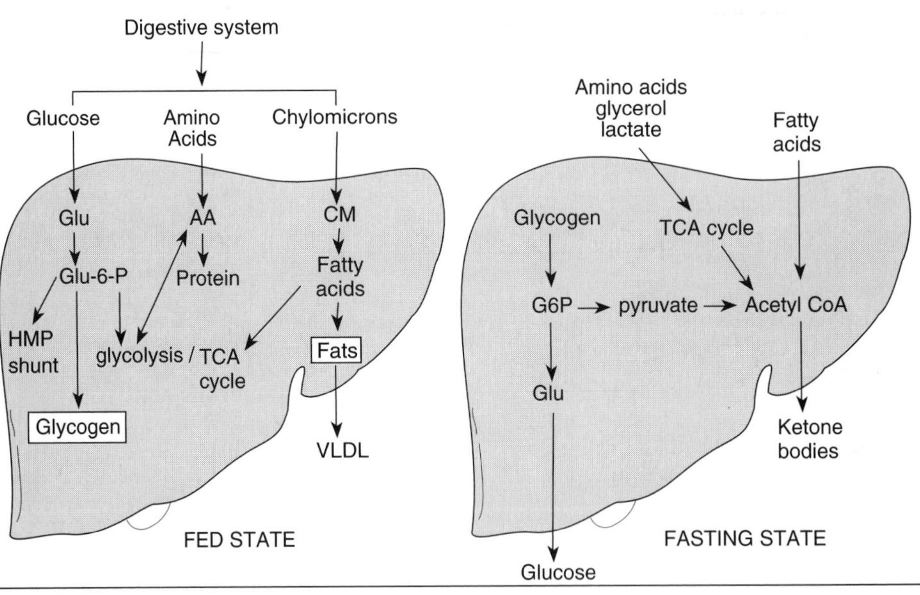

Fatty acid metabolism sites

Fatty acid synthesis = cytosol.
Fatty acid degradation = mitochondria.
Fatty acid entry into mitochondrion is via carnitine shuttle (inhibited by cytoplasmic malonyl-CoA).
Fatty acid entry into cytosol is via citrate shuttle.

Fatty acid degradation occurs where its products will be consumed—in the mitochondrion.

Cholesterol synthesis

Rate-limiting step is catalyzed by HMG-CoA reductase, which converts HMG-CoA to mevalonate. Two-thirds of plasma cholesterol is esterified by lecithin-cholesterol acyltransferase (LCAT).

Lovastatin inhibits HMG-CoA reductase.

Lipoproteins

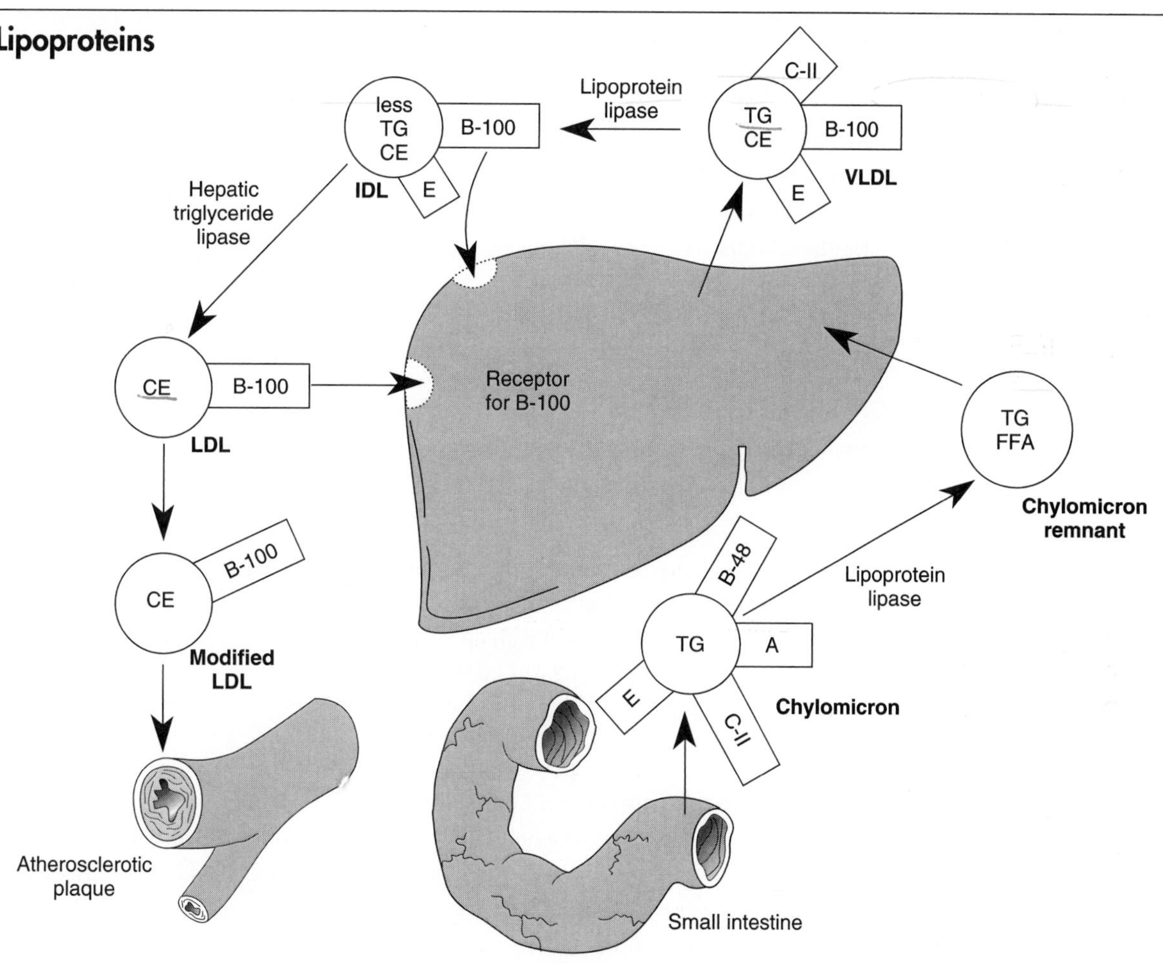

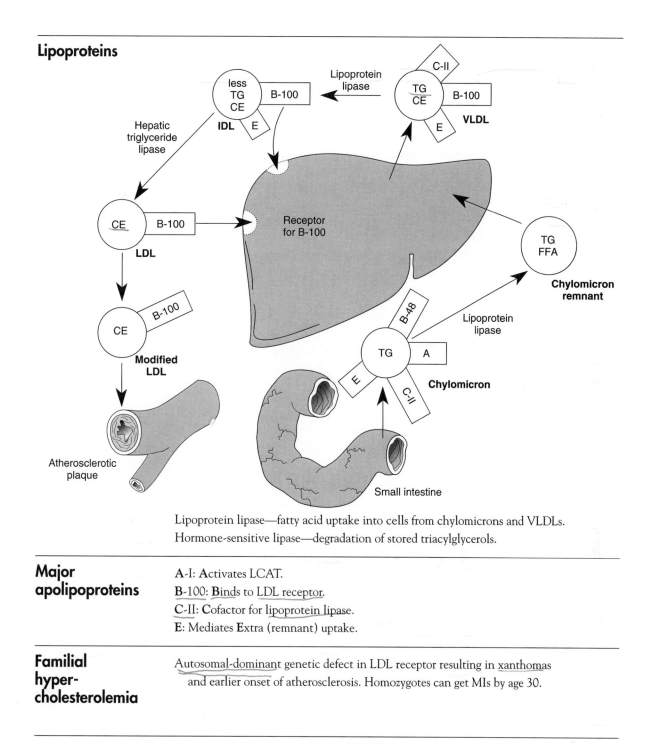

Lipoprotein lipase—fatty acid uptake into cells from chylomicrons and VLDLs.
Hormone-sensitive lipase—degradation of stored triacylglycerols.

Major apolipoproteins	A-I: Activates LCAT. B-100: Binds to LDL receptor. C-II: Cofactor for lipoprotein lipase. E: Mediates Extra (remnant) uptake.
Familial hyper-cholesterolemia	Autosomal-dominant genetic defect in LDL receptor resulting in xanthomas and earlier onset of atherosclerosis. Homozygotes can get MIs by age 30.

Lipoprotein functions

	Function and route	Apolipoproteins
Chylomicron	Delivers dietary triglycerides to peripheral tissues and dietary cholesterol to liver. Secreted by intestinal epithelial cells. Excess causes pancreatitis, lipemia retinalis, and eruptive xanthomas.	B-48 mediates secretion. A's are used for formation of new HDL. C-II activates lipoprotein lipase. E mediates remnant uptake by liver.
VLDL	Delivers hepatic triglycerides to peripheral tissues. Secreted by liver. Excess causes pancreatitis.	B-100 mediates secretion. C-II activates lipoprotein lipase. E mediates remnant uptake by liver.
LDL	Delivers hepatic cholesterol to peripheral tissues. Formed by lipoprotein lipase modification of VLDL in the peripheral tissue. Taken up by target cells via receptor-mediated endocytosis. Excess causes atherosclerosis, xanthomas, and arcus corneae.	B-100 mediates binding to cell surface receptor for endocytosis.
HDL	Mediates centripetal transport of cholesterol (reverse cholesterol transport, from periphery to liver). Acts as a repository for apoC and apoE (which are needed for chylomicron and VLDL metabolism). Secreted from both liver and intestine.	A's help form HDL structure. A-I in particular activates LCAT (which catalyzes esterification of cholesterol). CETP mediates transfer of cholesteryl esters to other lipoprotein particles.
	LDL and HDL carry most cholesterol. LDL transports cholesterol from liver to tissue; HDL transports it from periphery to liver.	**H**DL is **H**ealthy. **L**DL is **L**ousy.

Aminolevulinate (ALA) synthase

Rate-limiting step for heme synthesis. The end product (heme) feedback inhibits this enzyme. Found in the mitochondria, where it converts succinyl CoA and glycine to ALA.

Heme synthesis

P.260

Occurs in the liver and bone marrow. Committed step is glycine + succinyl CoA → δ-aminolevulinate. ALA Catalyzed by ALA synthase. Accumulation of intermediates causes porphyrias. Lead inhibits ALA dehydratase and ferrochelatase, preventing incorporation of iron and causing anemia and porphyria.

Underproduction of heme causes microcytic hypochromic anemia.

UCV Bio.49

Heme catabolism	Heme is scavenged from RBCs and Fe^{2+} is reused. Heme → biliverdin → bilirubin (sparingly water soluble, toxic to CNS, transported by albumin). Bilirubin is removed from blood by liver, conjugated with glucuronate and excreted in bile. In the intestine it is processed into its excreted form. Some urobilinogen, an intestinal intermediate, is reabsorbed into blood and excreted as urobilin into urine.	
Hyperbilirubinemia	From conjugated (direct; glucuronidated) and/or unconjugated (indirect) bilirubin. Causes: massive hemolysis, block in subsequent catabolism of heme, displacement from binding sites on albumin, decreased excretion (e.g., liver damage or bile duct obstruction). Bilirubin is yellow, causing jaundice.	UNconjugated is INdirect and INsoluble. Conjugated bilirubin is excreted in the urine.
Essential amino acids	Ketogenic: Leu, Lys. Glucogenic/ketogenic: Ile, Phe, Trp. Glucogenic: Met, Thr, Val, Arg, His.	All essential amino acids: **PriVaTe TIM HALL.** Arg and His are required during periods of growth.
Acidic and basic amino acids	At body pH (7.4), acidic amino acids Asp and Glu are negatively charged; basic amino acids Arg and Lys are positively charged. Basic amino acid His at pH 7.4 has no net charge. Arginine is the most basic amino acid. Arg and Lys are found in high amounts in histones, which bind to negatively charged DNA.	Asp = aspartic ACID, Glu = glutamic ACID. Arg and Lys have an extra NH_3 group. Basic
Urea cycle	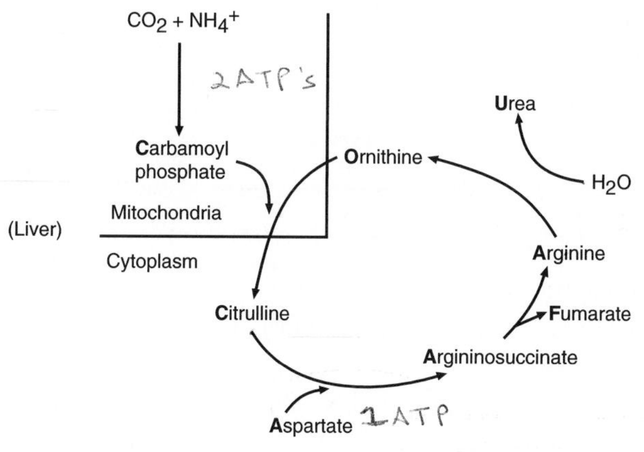	Ordinarily, Careless Crappers Are Also Frivolous About Urination.

Arachidonic acid products	Phospholipase A_2 liberates arachidonic acid from cell membrane. Lipoxygenase pathway yields Leukotrienes. LT B_4 is a neutrophil chemotactic agent. LT C_4, D_4, and E_4 (SRS-A) function in bronchoconstriction, vasoconstriction, contraction of smooth muscle, and increased vascular permeability. Cyclooxygenase pathway yields thromboxanes, prostaglandins, and prostacyclin. Tx A_2 stimulates platelet aggregation and vasoconstriction. **PG I_2** inhibits platelet aggregation and vasodilation.	**L** for **L**ipoxygenase and **L**eukotriene. **P**latelet-**G**athering **I**nhibitor
Insulin 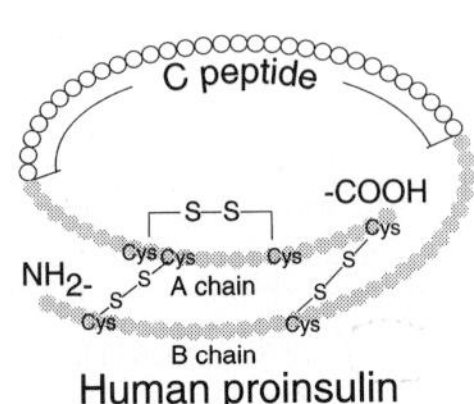 	Made in β cells of pancreas. No effect on glucose uptake by brain, RBCs, and hepatocytes. Required for adipose and skeletal muscle uptake of glucose. Inhibits glucagon release by α cells of pancreas. Serum C-peptide is not present with exogenous insulin intake.	Brain, liver, and RBCs take up glucose independent of insulin. **In**sulin moves glucose **In**to cells.
Ketone bodies UCV Bio.11	In liver: fatty acid and amino acids → acetoacetate + β-hydroxybutyrate (to be used in muscle and brain). Ketone bodies found in prolonged starvation and diabetic ketoacidosis. Excreted in urine. Made from HMG-CoA. Ketone bodies are metabolized by the brain to 2 molecules of acetyl CoA.	Breath smells like acetone (fruity odor). Urine test for ketones does not detect β-hydroxybutyrate (favored by high redox state).
Ethanol metabolism	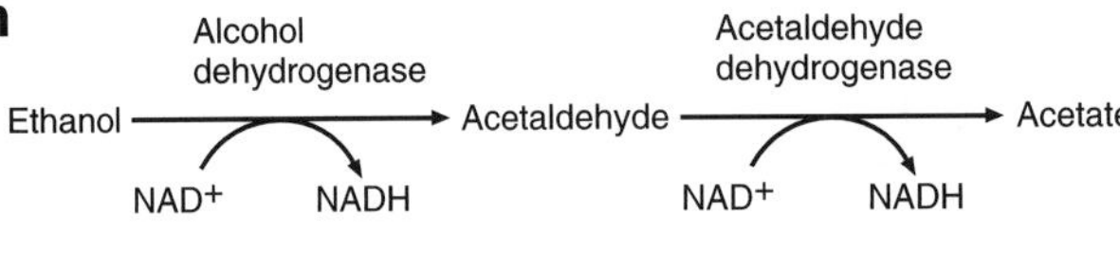 NAD^+ is the limiting reagent. Alcohol dehydrogenase operates via zero order kinetics.	Disulfiram (Antabuse) inhibits acetaldehyde dehydrogenase (acetaldehyde accumulates, contributing to hangover symptoms).
Ethanol hypoglycemia	Ethanol metabolism increases $NADH/NAD^+$ ratio in liver, causing diversion of pyruvate to lactate and OAA to malate, thereby inhibiting gluconeogenesis and leading to hypoglycemia. 1. Pyruvate —(NADH → NAD^+)→ lactate 2. Oxaloacetate —(NADH → NAD^+)→ malate	

Kwashiorkor versus marasmus

Kwashiorkor = protein malnutrition resulting in skin lesions, edema, liver malfunction (fatty change). Clinical picture is small child with swollen belly.

Marasmus = protein-calorie malnutrition resulting in tissue wasting.

Kwashiorkor results from a protein-deficient **MEAL:**
- Malabsorption
- Edema
- Anemia
- Liver (fatty)

UCV Bio.24

BIOCHEMISTRY—PROTEIN/CELL

Enzyme kinetics

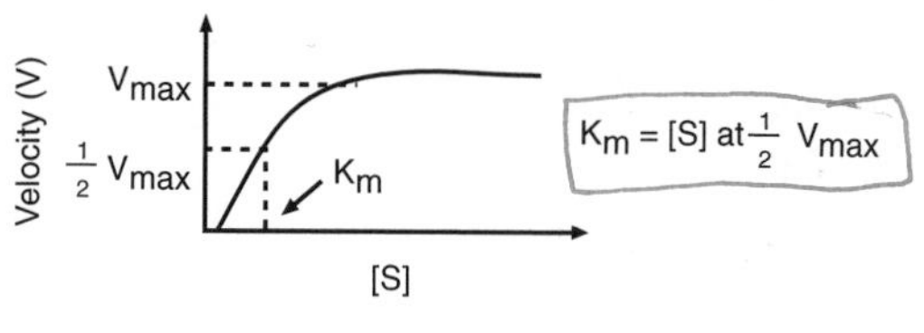

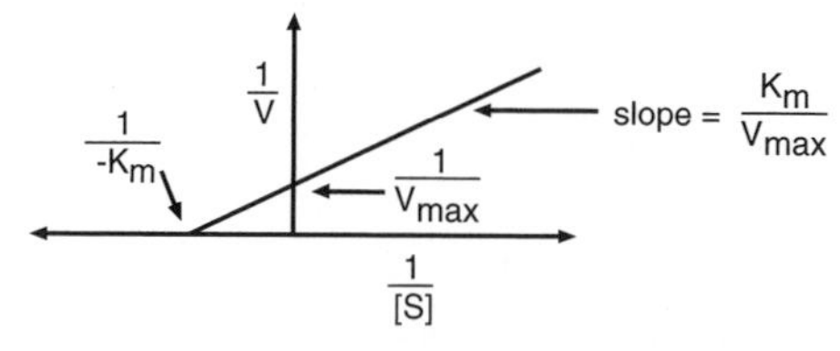

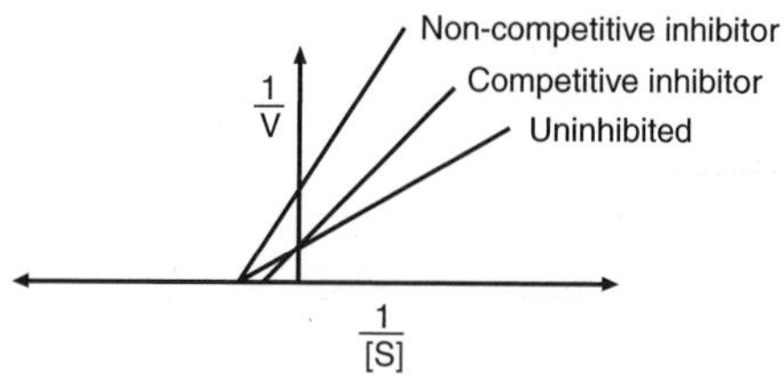

The lower the K_m, the higher the affinity.

Competitive inhibitors: Resemble substrates; bind reversibly to active sites of enzymes. High substrate concentration overcomes effect of inhibitor. V_{max} remains unchanged, K_m increases compared to uninhibited.

Noncompetitive inhibitors: Do not resemble substrate; bind to enzyme but not necessarily at active site. Inhibition cannot be overcome by high substrate concentration. V_{max} decreases, K_m remains unchanged compared to uninhibited.

Cell cycle phases

M (mitosis: prophase–metaphase–anaphase–telophase)

G_1 (growth)

S (synthesis of DNA)

G_2 (growth)

G_0 (quiescent G_1 phase)

G_1 and G_0 are of variable duration. Mitosis is usually shortest phase. Most cells are in G_0.

Rapidly dividing cells have a shorter G_1.

G stands for Gap or Growth; S for Synthesis.

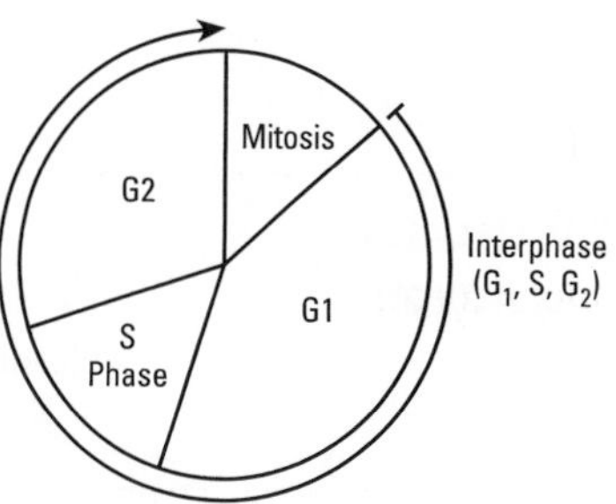

Plasma membrane composition

Plasma membranes contain cholesterol (≈50%, promotes membrane stability), phospholipids (≈50%), sphingolipids, glycolipids, and proteins. Only noncytoplasmic side of membrane contains glycosylated lipids or proteins (i.e., the plasma membrane is an asymmetric, fluid bilayer).

HIGH-YIELD FACTS

Biochemistry

P.39

Phosphatidylcholine function

Phosphatidylcholine (lecithin) is a major component of RBC membranes, of myelin, of bile, and of surfactant (DPPC–dipalmitoyl phosphatidylcholine). Also used in esterification of cholesterol.

Microtubule

Cylindrical structure 23 nm in diameter and of variable length. A helical array of polymerized dimers of α- and β-tubulin (13 per circumference). Each dimer has 2 GTP bound. Incorporated into flagella, cilia, mitotic spindles. Grows slowly, collapses quickly. Microtubules are also involved in slow axoplasmic transport in neurons.

Drugs that act on microtubules = **M**icro**T**ubules **G**row **V**ery slowly but **C**ollapse quickly:
- Mebendazole/thiabendazole (anti-helminthic)
- Taxol (anti-breast cancer)
- Griseofulvin (anti-fungal)
- Vincristine/Vinblastine (anti-cancer)
- Colchicine (anti-gout)

Collagen synthesis and structure

Hydroxylation of specific prolyl and lysyl residues in the endoplasmic reticulum requires vitamin C.

Procollagen molecules are exocytosed into extracellular space. Procollagen peptidases cleave terminal regions of procollagen, transforming procollagen into insoluble tropocollagen, which aggregates to form collagen fibrils.

Fibrillar structure is reinforced by the formation of covalent lysine-hydroxylysine cross-links between tropocollagen molecules.

Collagen fibril = many staggered collagen molecules (linked by lysyl oxidase). Collagen molecule = 3 collagen α chains (usually X-Y-Gly, X and Y = proline, hydroxyproline, or hydroxylysine).

Hemoglobin

Hemoglobin is composed of four polypeptide subunits (2α and 2β) and exists in two forms:
1. T (taut) form has low affinity for oxygen.
2. R (relaxed) form has high affinity for oxygen (300×). Hemoglobin exhibits positive cooperativity and negative allostery (accounts for the sigmoid-shaped O_2 dissociation curve for hemoglobin), unlike myoglobin.

Carbon monoxide has a 200× greater affinity for hemoglobin than oxygen.

Hb structure regulation

Increased Cl^-, H^+, CO_2, DPG, and temperature favor **T** form over **R** form (shifts dissociation curve to right, leading to ↑ O_2 unloading). T form has low affinity for O_2.

When you're **R**elaxed, you do your job better (carry O_2).

Methemoglobinemia

Iron in hemoglobin is in a reduced state (ferrous, Fe^{2+}). Methemoglobin is an oxidized form of hemoglobin (ferric, Fe^{3+}) that does not bind oxygen as readily.

UCV Bio.90

CO_2 transport in blood	CO_2 binds to amino acids in globin chain (at N terminus) but not to heme. CO_2 binding favors T (taut) form of hemoglobin (and thus promotes O_2 unloading).	CO_2 must be transported from tissue to lungs, the reverse of O_2.
Muscle activation: calcium	In skeletal muscle, calcium ions activate troponin, which moves tropomyosin, which exposes actin and allows actin-myosin interaction. In smooth muscle, Ca^{2+} activates contraction by binding to calmodulin (no troponins).	
Sodium pump	Na^+-K^+ATPase is located in the plasma membrane with ATP site on cytoplasmic side. For each ATP consumed, 3 Na^+ go out and 2 K^+ come in. During cycle, pump is phosphorylated (inhibited by vanadate). Ouabain inhibits by binding to K^+ site. Cardiac glycosides (digoxin, digitoxin) also inhibit the Na^+-K^+ATPase, causing increased cardiac contractility.	
Enzyme regulation methods	Enzyme concentration alteration (synthesis and/or destruction), covalent modification (e.g., phosphorylation), proteolytic modification (zymogen), allosteric regulation (e.g., feedback inhibition), and transcriptional regulation (e.g., steroid hormones).	

BIOCHEMISTRY—VITAMINS

Vitamins

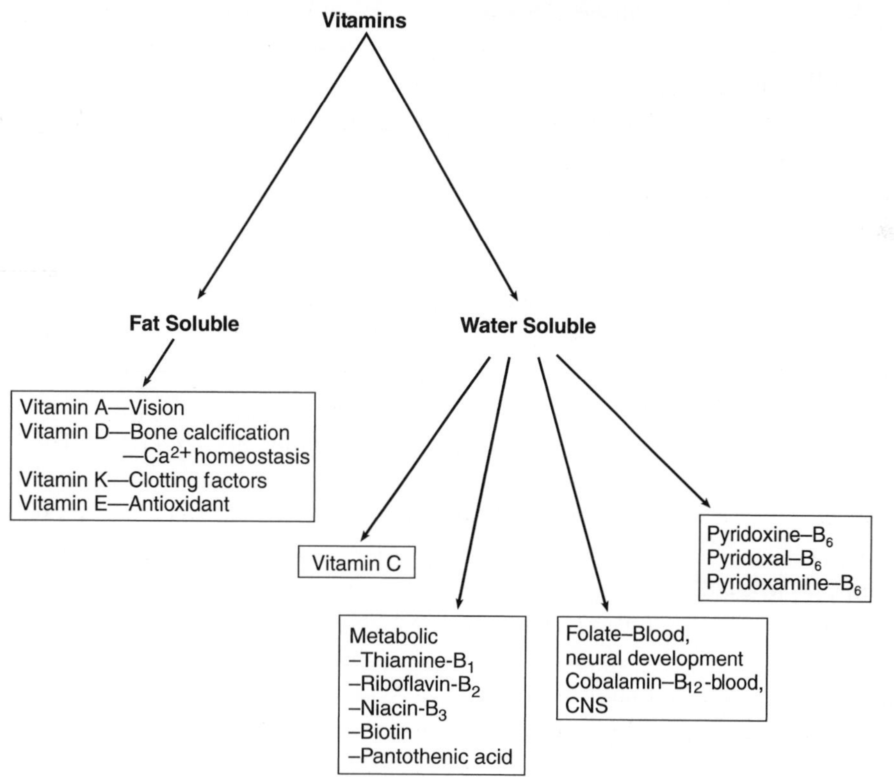

HIGH-YIELD FACTS

Biochemistry

Vitamins: fat soluble	A, D, E, K. Absorption dependent on gut (ileum) and pancreas. Toxicity more common than for water-soluble vitamins, because these accumulate in fat.	Malabsorption syndromes (steatorrhea), such as cystic fibrosis and sprue, or mineral oil intake can cause fat-soluble vitamin deficiencies.
Vitamins: water soluble	B_1 (Thiamine: TPP) B_2 (**R**iboflavin: FAD, FMN) B_3 (**N**iacin: NAD^+) B_5 (**P**antothenate: CoA) B_6 (**P**yridoxine: PP) B_{12} (**C**obalamin) C (ascorbic acid) Biotin Folate	All wash out easily from body except B_{12} (stored in liver). B complex vitamins: **T**he **R**ich **N**ever **P**ay **C**ash.

Vitamin A (retinol)

Deficiency	Night blindness and dry skin.	Retinol is vitamin A, so think Retin-A (used topically for wrinkles and acne).
Function	Constituent of visual pigments (retinal).	
Excess	Arthralgias, fatigue, headaches, skin changes, sore throat, alopecia.	

UCV Bio.42

Vitamin B_1 (thiamine)

Deficiency	Beriberi and Wernicke–Korsakoff syndrome. Seen in alcoholism and malnutrition.	Beriberi: characterized by polyneuritis, cardiac pathology, and edema. Spell beriberi as **Ber1Ber1.** Wet beriberi may lead to high output cardiac failure (dilated cardiomyopathy).
Function	In thiamine pyrophosphate, a cofactor for oxidative decarboxylation of α-keto acids (pyruvate, α-ketoglutarate) and a cofactor for transketolase in the HMP shunt.	

UCV Bio.7

Vitamin B_2 (riboflavin)

Deficiency	Angular stomatitis, **C**heilosis, **C**orneal vascularization.	The 2 **C**'s
Function	Cofactor in oxidation and reduction (e.g., $FADH_2$).	**F**AD and **F**MN are derived from ribo**F**lavin (B_2 = 2 ATP).

Vitamin B_3 (niacin)

Deficiency	Pellagra can be caused by Hartnup disease, malignant carcinoid syndrome and INH.	Pellagra's symptoms are the 3 **D's:** **D**iarrhea, **D**ermatitis, **D**ementia (also beefy glossitis).
Function	Constituent of NAD^+, $NADP^+$ (used in redox reactions). Derived from tryptophan.	**N**AD derived from **N**iacin (B_3 = 3 ATP).

UCV Bio.29

Vitamin B_5 (pantothenate)

Deficiency	Dermatitis, enteritis, alopecia, adrenal insufficiency.	
Function	Constituent of CoA, part of fatty acid synthase. Cofactor for acyl transfers.	Pantothen-**A** is in Co-**A.**

Vitamin B_6 (pyridoxine)

Deficiency	Convulsions, hyperirritability (deficiency inducible by INH).
Function	Converted to pyridoxal phosphate, a cofactor used in transamination (e.g., ALT and AST), decarboxylation, and trans-sulfuration.

Biotin

Deficiency	Dermatitis, enteritis. Caused by antibiotic use, ingestion of raw eggs.	
Function	Cofactor for carboxylations (pyruvate carboxylase, acetyl-CoA carboxylase, propionyl-CoA carboxylase) but not decarboxylations.	"Buy-a-tin of CO_2" for carboxylations.

Folic acid

Deficiency	Most common vitamin deficiency in US. Macrocytic, megaloblastic anemia (often no neurologic symptoms), sprue.	**F**olate from **F**oliage. Eat green leaves (because folic acid is not stored very long).
Function	Coenzyme for one-carbon transfer; involved in methylation reactions. Important for the synthesis of nitrogenous bases in DNA and RNA.	Supplemental folic acid in early pregnancy reduces neural tube defects. PABA is the folic acid precursor in bacteria. Sulfa drugs and dapsone are PABA analogs.

UCV *Bio.85*

Vitamin B_{12} (cobalamin)

Deficiency	Macrocytic, megaloblastic anemia; neurologic symptoms (optic neuropathy, subacute combined degeneration, paresthesia); glossitis.	Found only in animal products. Vit. B_{12} deficiency is usually caused by malabsorption (sprue, enteritis, *Diphyllobothrium latum*), lack of intrinsic factor (pernicious anemia), or absence of terminal ileum (Crohn's disease).
Function	Cofactor for homocysteine methylation and methylmalonyl-CoA handling. Stored primarily in the liver. Synthesized only by microorganisms.	Use Schilling test to detect deficiency.

Vitamin C (ascorbic acid)

Deficiency	Scurvy.	Vitamin **C** **C**ross-links
Function	Necessary for hydroxylation of proline and lysine in collagen synthesis. Scurvy findings: swollen gums, bruising, anemia, poor wound healing.	**C**ollagen. British sailors carried limes to prevent scurvy (origin of the word "limey").

UCV *Bio.36*

Vitamin D	D_2 = ergocalciferol, consumed in milk. D_3 = cholecalciferol, formed in sun-exposed skin. 25-OH D_3 = storage form. 1,25 $(OH)_2$ D_3 = active form.	Remember that drinking milk (fortified with vitamin D) is good for bones.
Deficiency	Rickets in children (bending bones), osteomalacia in adults (soft bones), and hypocalcemic tetany.	
Function	Increases intestinal absorption of calcium and phosphate.	
Excess	Hypercalcemia, loss of appetite, stupor. Seen in sarcoidosis, a disease where the epithelioid macrophages convert vit. D into its active form.	
UCV Bio.28, 35		

Vitamin E		
Deficiency	Increased fragility of erythrocytes.	Vitamin **E** is for **E**rythrocytes.
Function	Antioxidant (protects erythrocytes from hemolysis).	

Vitamin K		
Deficiency	Neonatal hemorrhage with ↑ PT, ↑ aPTT, but normal bleeding time.	**K** for **K**oagulation. Note that the vitamin K–dependent clotting factors are II, VII, IX, X, and protein C and S. Warfarin is a vitamin K antagonist.
Function	Catalyzes γ-carboxylation of glutamic acid residues on various proteins concerned with blood clotting. Synthesized by intestinal flora. Therefore, vit. K deficiency can occur after the prolonged use of broad-spectrum antibiotics.	
UCV Bio.43		

SECTION II

Microbiology

"What lies behind us and what lies ahead of us are tiny matters compared to what lives within us."
—Oliver Wendell Holmes

This high-yield material covers the basic concepts of microbiology and immunology. The emphasis in previous examinations has been approximately 40% bacteriology (20% basic, 20% quasi-clinical), 25% immunology, 25% virology (10% basic, 15% quasi-clinical), 5% parasitology, and 5% mycology. Learning the distinguishing characteristics, target organs, and method of spread of—as well as relevant laboratory tests for—major pathogens can improve your score substantially.

Many students preparing for this part of the boards make the mistake of studying bacteriology very well without devoting sufficient time to the other topics. For this reason, learning immunology and virology well is high yield. Learn the components and mechanistic details of the immune response, including T cells, B cells, and the structure and function of immunoglobulins. Also learn the major immunodeficiency diseases (e.g., AIDS, agammaglobulinemia, DiGeorge's syndrome). Knowledge of viral structures and genomes remains important as well.

MICROBIOLOGY—HIGH-YIELD CLINICAL VIGNETTES

These abstracted case vignettes are designed to demonstrate the thought processes necessary to answer multistep clinical reasoning questions.

- An alcoholic vomits gastric contents and develops foul-smelling sputum → what organisms are most likely? → anaerobes.
- Middle-age male presents with acute-onset monoarticular joint pain and bilateral Bell's palsy → what is the likely disease and how did he get it? → Lyme disease, *Ixodes* tick vector.
- Patient with *Mycoplasma pneumoniae* exhibits cryoagglutinins during recovery phase → what types of immunoglobulins are reacting? → IgM.
- Urinalysis of patient shows WBC casts → what is the diagnosis? → pyelonephritis.
- Young child presents with tetany and candidiasis. Hypocalcemia and immunosuppression are found → what cell is deficient? → T-cell (DiGeorge's).
- Patient presents with rose gardener's scenario (thorn prick with ulcers along lymphatic drainage) → what is the infectious bug? → *Sporothrix schenckii*.
- 25-year-old medical student from the Midwest has a burning feeling in his gut after meals. Biopsy of gastric mucosa shows gram-negative rods → what is the likely organism? → *H. pylori*.
- 32-year-old male has cauliflower lesions. Tissue biopsy shows broad-based budding yeasts → what is the likely organism? → *Blastomyces*.
- Breast-feeding woman suddenly develops redness and swelling of her right breast. On examination, it is found to be a fluctuant mass → what is the diagnosis? → mastitis caused by *S. aureus*.
- Young child has recurrent lung infections and granulomatous lesions → what is the defect in neutrophils? → NADPH oxidase.
- 20-year-old college student presents with lymphadenopathy, fever, and hepatosplenomegaly. His serum agglutinates sheep red blood cells → what cell is infected? → B cell (EBV; infectious mononucleosis).
- One hour after eating custard at a picnic, a whole family began to vomit. After 10 hours, they were all right → what is the organism? → *S. aureus*.
- Infant becomes flaccid after eating honey → what gram-positive rod is implicated? → *Clostridium botulinum* → what is the mechanism of action? → inhibited release of acetylcholine.
- Man with squamous cell carcinoma of penis had exposure to what virus? → HPV.
- Patient develops endocarditis three weeks after receiving prosthetic heart valve → what organism is suspected? → *S. aureus* or *S. epidermidis*.

MICROBIOLOGY—HIGH-YIELD GLOSSY MATERIAL

1. Patient who visited Mexico presents with bloody diarrhea → what infectious form is found in the stool? → erythrocyte-ingesting trophozoite → *Entamoeba histolytica*.
2. Glossy photograph of cardiac valve with cauliflower growth → diagnosis? → bacterial endocarditis.
3. Adolescent with cough and rusty sputum → what does Gram stain of sputum show? → gram-positive diplococci (*Streptococcus pneumoniae*/*pneumococci*).
4. HIV-positive patient with CSF showing 75/mm^3 lymphocytes suddenly dies. Picture of yeast in meninges → diagnosis? → cryptococcal meningitis.

Microbiology

1. Principles and interpretation of bacteriologic lab tests (culture, drug sensitivity, specific growth requirements).
2. Dermatologic manifestations of bacterial and viral infections (e.g., syphilis, Rocky Mountain spotted fever, meningococcemia, herpes zoster, coxsackievirus infection).
3. Common sexually transmitted diseases (e.g., syphilis, AIDS, HSV, gonorrhea, chlamydia).
4. Viral gastroenteritis in the pediatric and adult populations.
5. Common causes of community-acquired and nosocomial pneumonia.
6. Protozoa that frequently cause disease in the U.S. (e.g., *Entamoeba histolytica, Giardia*).
7. Parasites (protozoa, helminths) that cause disease more commonly outside the U.S. (e.g., malaria, Chagas' disease, elephantiasis).
8. Herpes simplex encephalitis (temporal lobe lesion, mental status changes, treat with acyclovir).
9. Tests available for diagnosis of viral infections (e.g., plaque assay, PCR).
10. Microscopic appearance of organisms.

Immunology

1. Principles and interpretation of immunologic tests (e.g., ELISA, complement-fixation tests, direct and indirect Coombs' test).
2. Immune complex diseases (e.g., post strep glomerulonephritis, systemic lupus erythematosus, serum sickness).
3. Genetics of immunoglobulin variety and specificity (class switching, VDJ recombination, affinity maturation).
4. Mechanisms of antigenic variation and immune system evasion employed by bacteria, fungi, protozoa, and viruses.
5. How different types of immune deficiencies lead to different susceptibilities to infection (e.g., T-cell defects and viral/fungal infection; splenectomy and encapsulated organisms).
6. MHC/HLA serotypes: transplant compatibility, disease associations, familial inheritance.
7. Allergies: common antigens, antigen-IgE-mast cell complex, presumed mechanism of immunotherapy (blocking antibodies).
8. Granulomas: role of macrophages, foreign body versus immune granulomas, caseating (TB) versus noncaseating (sarcoid) granulomas, common causes (e.g., TB, sarcoid, fungi).
9. Components of vaccines and how they produce immunity.
10. Characteristics and functions of macrophages and NK (natural killer) cells.

Bacterial structures

Structure	Function	Chemical composition
Peptidoglycan	Gives rigid support, protects against osmotic pressure	Sugar backbone with cross-linked peptide side chains
Cell wall/cell membrane (gram positives)	Major surface antigen	Teichoic acid induces TNF and IL-1
Outer membrane (gram negatives)	Site of endotoxin (lipopolysaccharide); major surface antigen	Lipid A induces TNF and IL-1; polysaccharide is the antigen
Plasma membrane	Site of oxidative and transport enzymes	Lipoprotein bilayer
Ribosome	Protein synthesis	RNA and protein in 50S and 30S subunits
Periplasm	Space between the cytoplasmic membrane and outer membrane in gram-negative bacteria	Contains many hydrolytic enzymes, including β-lactamases
Capsule	Protects against phagocytosis	Polysaccharide (except *Bacillus anthracis*, which contains D-glutamate)
Pilus/fimbria	Mediates adherence of bacteria to cell surface; sex pilus forms attachment between 2 bacteria during conjugation	Glycoprotein
Flagellum	Motility	Protein
Spore	Provides resistance to dehydration, heat, and chemicals	Keratin-like coat; dipicolinic acid
Plasmid	Contains a variety of genes for antibiotic resistance, enzymes, and toxins	DNA
Glycocalyx	Mediates adherence to surfaces, especially foreign surfaces (e.g., indwelling catheters)	Polysaccharide

Cell walls

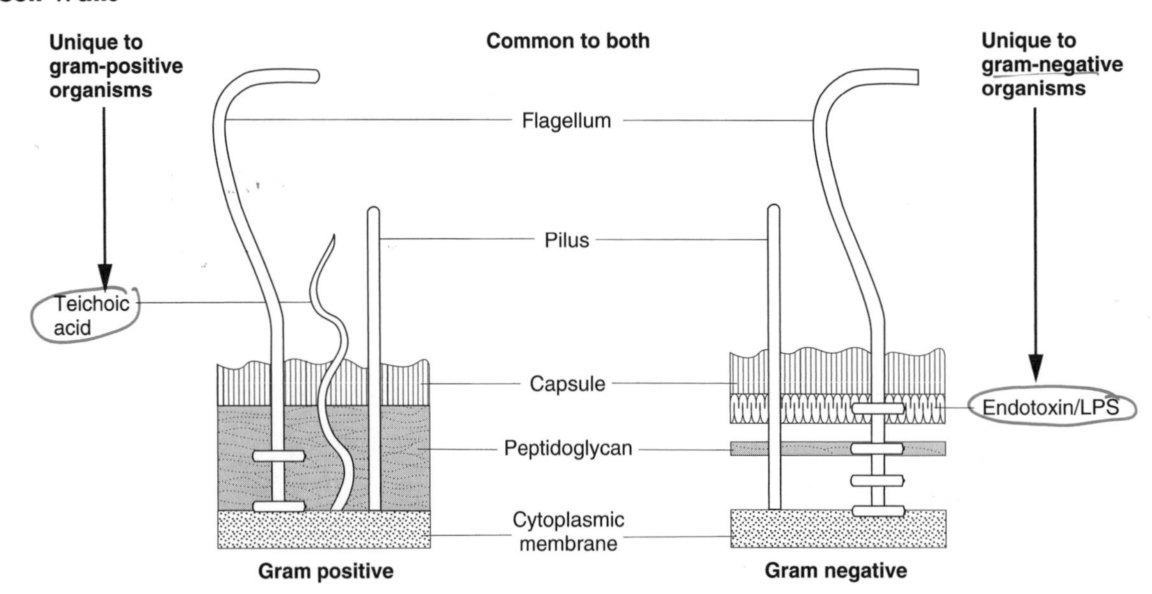

Bacterial growth curve

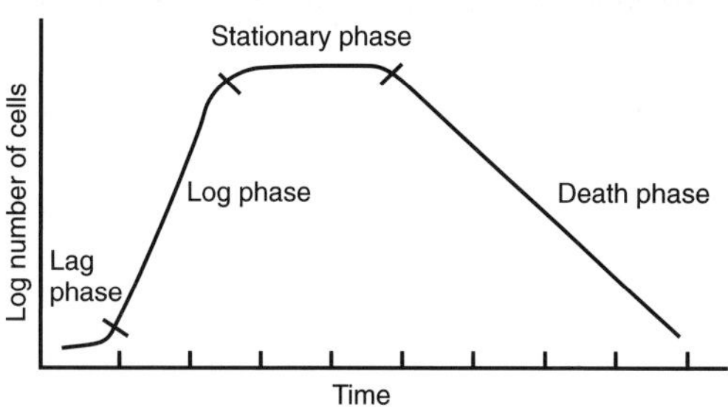

Exotoxins

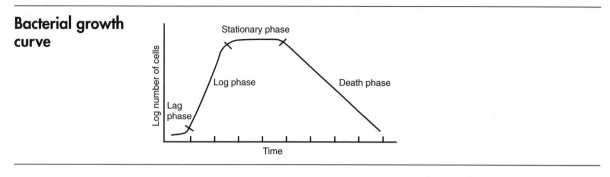

Peptides that are excreted by both gram-positive and gram-negative bugs. They are highly antigenic and generally not associated with fever. They are relatively unstable to heat, are highly toxic, and have specific receptors. Usually encoded by lysogenic phage DNA.

EXotoxins are EXcreted. Examples include tetanospasmin, botulinum toxin, and diphtheria toxin.

Bugs with exotoxins

Gram-positive bugs	Mode of action
Corynebacterium diphtheriae	Inactivates EF-2 by ADP ribosylation; causes mild exudative pharyngitis , Myocarditis EF-2 : Elongation Factor → translation of Human mRNA → Protein
Clostridium tetani	Blocks the release of the inhibitory neurotransmitter glycine
Clostridium botulinum	Blocks the release of acetylcholine: causes anticholinergic symptoms, CNS paralysis; spores found in canned food, honey (causes floppy baby)
Clostridium perfringens	Alpha toxin is a lecithinase in gas gangrene; get double zone of hemolysis on blood agar
Bacillus anthracis	One toxin in the toxin complex is an adenylate cyclase
Staphylococcus aureus	Toxin is a superantigen that binds to class II MHC protein and T-cell receptor, inducing IL-1 and IL-2 synthesis in toxic shock syndrome; also causes food poisoning
Streptococcus pyogenes	Erythrogenic toxin (causes rash of scarlet fever) and streptolysin O (antigen for ASO-antibody is found in rheumatic fever). Erythrogenic toxin is a superantigen; streptolysin O is a hemolysin
Gram-negative bugs	
Escherichia coli	Heat-labile toxin stimulates adenylate cyclase by ADP ribosylation of G protein Heat-stable toxin stimulates guanylate cyclase
Vibrio cholerae	Stimulates adenylate cyclase by ADP ribosylation of G protein; ↑ pumping of Cl^- and H_2O into gut; causes voluminous rice-water diarrhea ↑ cAMP Actives G_s
Bordetella pertussis	Stimulates adenylate cyclase by ADP ribosylation; causes whooping cough, inhibits chemokine receptor causing lymphocytosis Inhibits G_i : ↑ cAMP

- Bacillus anthracis : Edema Factor
  Lethal Factor
  Protective Antigen

- C. dificile
- P. aeruginosa - Exotoxin A : inhibits EF-2 (Liver)

Endotoxin

A lipopolysaccharide found in cell wall of gram-negative bacteria.

N-dotoxin is an integral part of gram-Negative cell wall. Endotoxin is heat stable.

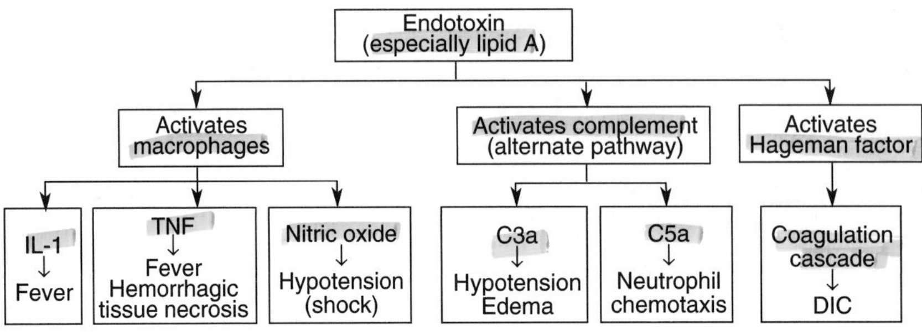

Endotoxins vs. exotoxins

	Exotoxin	Endotoxin
Source	Some gram-positive and gram-negative bacteria	Cell wall of most gram-negative bacteria
Secreted from cell	Yes	No
Composition	Polypeptide	Lipopolysaccharide (LPS)
Location of genes	Plasmid, bacteriophage, or bacterial chromosome	Bacterial chromosome
Clinical effects	Various effects	Fever, shock, DIC
Mode of action	Various modes	Induces TNF and IL-1 synthesis
Vaccines	Toxoids used as vaccines (highly antigenic), e.g., DPT	No toxoids formed and no vaccine available (poorly antigenic)

Gram stain limitations

These bugs do not Gram stain well:

These Rascals May Microscopically Lack Color.

Treponema (too thin to be visualized)

Treponemes—darkfield microscopy and fluorescent antibody staining.

Rickettsia (intracellular parasite)

Mycobacteria (high-lipid-content cell wall requires acid-fast stain)

Mycobacteria—acid fast.

M. tuberculosis

Mycoplasma (no cell wall)

Legionella pneumophila (primarily intracellular)

Legionella—silver stain.

Chlamydia (intracellular parasite)

Pigment-producing bacteria

Staphylococcus aureus produces a yellow pigment.
Pseudomonas aeruginosa produces a blue-green pigment.
Serratia marcescens produces a red pigment.

Aureus (Latin) = gold.
Serratia marcescens = maraschino cherries are red.

IgA proteases

IgA proteases allow these organisms to colonize mucosal surfaces: *Streptococcus pneumoniae*, *Neisseria meningitidis*, *Neisseria gonorrhoeae*, *Haemophilus influenzae*.

Gram-positive lab algorithm

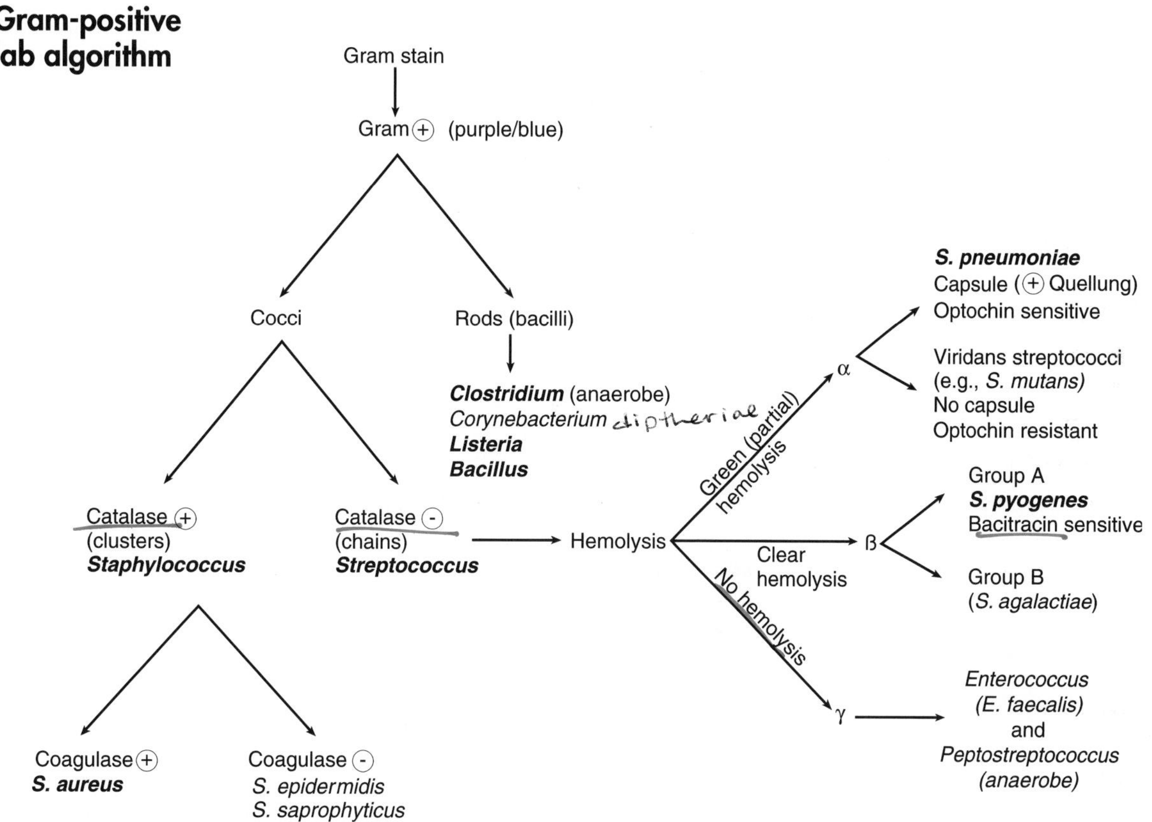

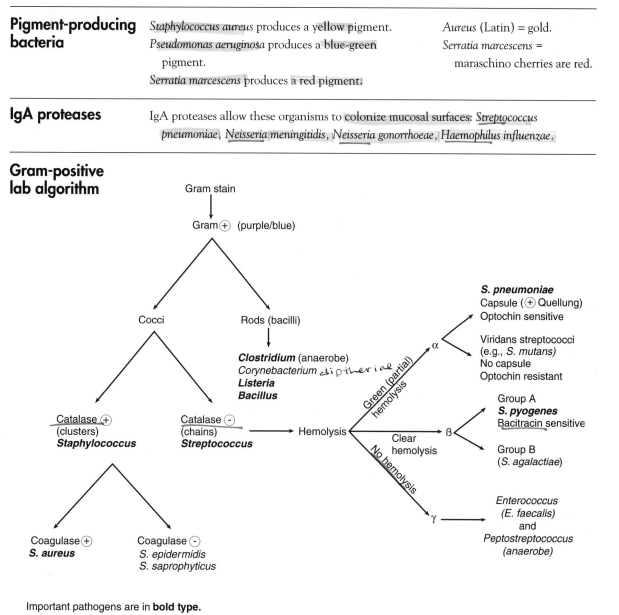

Important pathogens are in **bold type.**
Note: *Enterococcus* is either α- or γ-hemolytic.

Gram-negative lab algorithm

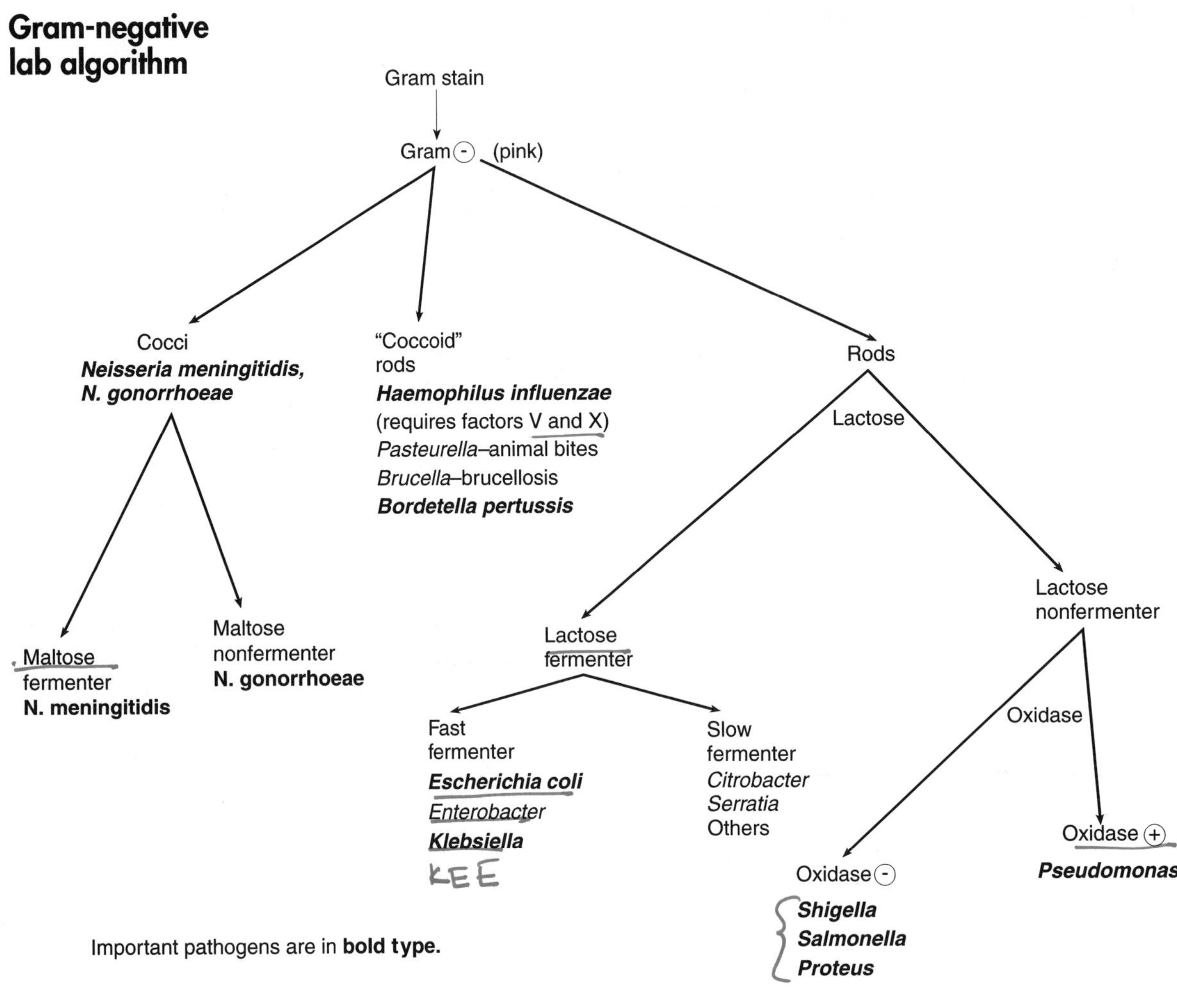

Important pathogens are in **bold type.**

Special culture requirements

Bug	Media used for isolation
H. influenzae	Chocolate agar with factors V (NAD) and X (hematin)
N. gonorrhoeae	Thayer–Martin media
B. pertussis	Bordet–Gengou (potato) agar
C. diphtheriae	Tellurite agar
M. tuberculosis	Löwenstein–Jensen agar
Lactose-fermenting enterics (e.g., *Escherichia*, *Klebsiella*, and *Enterobacter*) KEE	Pink colonies on MacConkey's agar
Legionella pneumophila	Charcoal yeast extract agar buffered with ↑ iron and cysteine
Fungi	Sabouraud's agar

Bacterial genetic transfer	Conjugation ≡ direct DNA transfer via sex (fertility, F) pilus. Transduction ≡ DNA transfer via bacteriophage vector. Transformation ≡ uptake of naked DNA (which is vulnerable to DNAse) from environment. Transposons ≡ "jumping genes," DNA sequences that jump from one site on the bacterial DNA to another site on the same DNA or from the bacterial DNA to plasmid DNA.	*Con* = with *jugate* = joining

MICROBIOLOGY—BACTERIOLOGY

Obligate aerobes	Use an O_2-dependent system to generate ATP. Examples include *Pseudomonas aeruginosa*, *Mycobacterium tuberculosis*, and *Nocardia*. *Mycobacterium tuberculosis* has a predilection for the apices of the lung, which have the highest PO_2.	*P.* ***AER****uginosa* is an **AER**obe seen in burn wounds, nosocomial pneumonia, and pneumonias in cystic fibrosis patients.
Obligate anaerobes UCV Micro2.30	Examples include *Clostridium*, *Bacteroides*, and *Actinomyces*. They lack catalase and/or superoxide dismutase and thus are susceptible to oxidative damage. They are generally foul-smelling (short-chain fatty acids), are difficult to culture, and produce gas in tissue (CO_2 and H_2).	Anaerobes are normal flora in GI tract, pathogenic elsewhere. Amin$\mathbf{O_2}$glycosides are ineffective against anaerobes because these antibiotics require $\mathbf{O_2}$ to enter into bacterial cell.
Encapsulated bacteria	Examples are *Streptococcus pneumoniae* (pneumococcus), *Haemophilus influenzae* (especially b serotype), *Neisseria meningitidis* (meningococcus), and *Klebsiella pneumoniae*. Polysaccharide capsule is an antiphagocytic virulence factor. Positive **Quellung** reaction: if encapsulated bug is present, capsule **swells** when specific anticapsular antisera are added.	IgG_2 necessary for immune response. Capsule serves as antigen in vaccines (Pneumovax, *H. influenzae* b, meningococcal vaccines). **Quellung** = capsular **"swellung."** Pneumococcus associated with "rusty" sputum, sepsis in sickle cell anemia and splenectomy.
Spores: bacterial	Only certain gram-positive rods form spores when nutrients are limited. Spores are highly resistant to destruction by heat and chemicals. Have dipicolinic acid in their core. Have no metabolic activity. Must autoclave to kill spores (as is done to surgical equipment).	Gram-positive soil bugs ≈ spore formers (*Bacillus anthracis*, *Clostridium perfringens*, *C. tetani*).
α-hemolytic bacteria	Include the following organisms: 1. *Streptococcus pneumoniae* (catalase-negative and optochin-sensitive) 2. Viridans streptococci (catalase-negative and optochin-resistant)	

β-hemolytic bacteria

Include the following organisms:

1. *Staphylococcus aureus* (catalase- and coagulase-positive)
2. *Streptococcus pyogenes* (catalase-negative and bacitracin-sensitive)
3. *Streptococcus agalactiae* (catalase-negative and bacitracin-resistant)
4. *Listeria monocytogenes* (tumbling motility, meningitis in newborns, unpasteurized milk)

Catalase/coagulase (gram-positive cocci)

Catalase degrades H_2O_2, an antimicrobial product of PMNs.

Staphylococci make catalase, whereas streptococci do not.

S. *aureus* makes coagulase, whereas S. *epidermidis* does not.

Staph make catalase because they have more "staff." Bad staph (*aureus*, because *epidermidis* is skin flora) make coagulase and toxins.

Staphylococcus aureus

UCV Micro2.98

Protein A (virulence factor) binds Fc-IgG, inhibiting complement fixation and phagocytosis.

Causes:

1. Inflammatory disease—skin infections, organ abscesses, pneumonia
2. Toxin-mediated disease—toxic shock syndrome (TSST-1 toxin), scalded skin syndrome (exfoliative toxin), rapid-onset food poisoning (enterotoxins)

TSST is a superantigen that binds to class II MHC and T-cell receptor, resulting in polyclonal T-cell activation.

S. *aureus* food poisoning is due to ingestion of preformed toxin. Micro2.18

Streptococcus pyogenes (Group A β-hemolytic streptococci) sequelae

UCV Micro1.83, Micro2.103

Causes:

1. Pyogenic—pharyngitis, cellulitis, skin infection
2. Toxigenic—scarlet fever, TSS
3. Immunologic—rheumatic fever, acute glomerulonephritis

Bacitracin sensitive. Antibody to **M protein** enhances host defenses against S. *pyogenes*.

Pharyngitis gives you rheumatic "phever."

Rheumatic fever = PECCS: Polyarthritis, Erythema marginatum, Chorea, Carditis, Subcutaneous nodules.

Enterococci

Enterococci (*Enterococcus faecalis* and E. *faecium*) are penicillin G-resistant and cause UTI and subacute endocarditis. Lancefield group D includes the enterococci and the nonenterococcal group D streptococci. Lancefield grouping is based on differences in the C-carbohydrate on the bacterial cell wall.

Entero = intestine, *faecalis* = feces, *strepto* = twisted (chains), *coccus* = berry. Enterococci, hardier than nonenterococcal group D, can thus grow in 6.5% NaCl (lab test).

Viridans group streptococci

Viridans streptococci are α-hemolytic. They are normal flora of the oropharynx and cause dental caries (*Streptococcus mutans*) and bacterial endocarditis (S. *sanguis*). Resistant to optochin, differentiating them from S. *pneumoniae*, which is α-hemolytic but is optochin sensitive.

Sanguis (Latin) = blood. There is lots of blood in the heart (endocarditis). Viridans group strep live in the mouth because they are not afraid of-the-chin (op-to-chin resistant).

Clostridia (with exotoxins) UCV	Gram-positive, spore-forming, anaerobic bacilli. *Clostridium tetani* produces an exotoxin causing tetanus. Micro1.89 *C. botulinum* produces a preformed, heat-labile toxin that inhibits ACh release, causing botulism. Micro1.30 *C. perfringens* produces α toxin, a hemolytic lecithinase that causes myonecrosis or gas gangrene. Micro2.79 *C. difficile* produces a cytotoxin, an exotoxin that kills enterocytes, causing pseudomembranous colitis. Often secondary to antibiotic use, especially clindamycin or ampicillin. Micro2.15	**Tet**anus is **tet**anic paralysis (blocks glycine, an inhibitory neurotransmitter). ***Bot**ulinum* is from bad **bot**tles of food (causes a flaccid paralysis). ***Perf**ringens* **perf**orates a gangrenous leg. ***Di**fficile* causes **di**arrhea. Treat with metronidazole.
Diphtheria (and exotoxin) UCV Micro1.41	Caused by *Corynebacterium diphtheriae* via exotoxin encoded by β-prophage. Potent exotoxin inhibits protein synthesis via ADP-ribosylation of EF-2. Symptoms include pseudomembranous pharyngitis (grayish-white membrane) with lymphadenopathy. Lab diagnosis based on gram-positive rods with metachromatic granules.	*Coryne* = club shaped. Grows on tellurite agar. **ABCDEFG:** **A**DP-ribosylation **B**eta-prophage **C**orynebacterium **D**iphtheriae **E**longation **F**actor 2 **G**ranules
Anthrax UCV Micro1.28	Caused by *Bacillus anthracis*, a gram-positive, spore-forming rod that produces anthrax toxin. Contact → malignant pustule (painless ulcer); can progress to bacteremia and death. Inhalation of spores can cause life-threatening pneumonia (woolsorters' disease).	
Actinomyces* versus *Nocardia UCV Micro1.67, Micro2.30	Both are gram-positive rods forming long branching filaments resembling fungi. *Actinomyces israelii*, a gram-positive anaerobe, causes oral/facial abscesses with "sulfur granules" that may drain through sinus tracts in skin. Normal oral flora. *Nocardia asteroides*, a gram-positive and also a weakly acid-fast aerobe in soil, causes pulmonary infection in immunocompromised patients.	*A. israelii* forms "sulfur" granules in sinus tracts.
Penicillin and gram-negative bugs	Gram-negative bugs are resistant to benzyl penicillin G but may be susceptible to penicillin derivatives like ampicillin. The gram-negative outer membrane layer inhibits entry of penicillin G and vancomycin.	
Bugs causing food poisoning	*Vibrio parahaemolyticus* and *Vibrio vulnificus* in contaminated seafood. *Bacillus cereus* in reheated rice. *Staphylococcus aureus* in meats, mayonnaise, custard. *Clostridium perfringens* in reheated meat dishes.	**V**omit **B**ig **S**melly **C**hunks. *Staphylococcus aureus* food poisoning starts quickly, ends quickly. "Food poisoning from reheated rice? Be serious!" (*B. cereus*) -pre-formed toxin

Diarrhea

Species	Typical findings	Fever/leukocytosis
Escherichia coli	Ferments lactose	No
Vibrio cholerae	Comma-shaped organisms	No
Salmonella	Does not ferment lactose, motile	Yes
Shigella	Does not ferment lactose, nonmotile, very low ID_{50}	Yes
Campylobacter jejuni	Comma- or S-shaped organisms; growth at 42°C	Yes
Vibrio parahaemolyticus	Transmitted by seafood	Yes
Yersinia enterocolitica	Usually transmitted from pet feces (e.g., puppies)	Yes

Bugs causing watery diarrhea

Include *Vibrio cholerae* (associated with rice-water stools), enterotoxigenic *E. coli*, viruses (e.g., rotaviruses), and protozoans (e.g., *Cryptosporidium* and *Giardia*).

Bugs causing bloody diarrhea

Include *Salmonella*, *Shigella*, *Campylobacter jejuni*, enterohemorrhagic/enteroinvasive *E. coli*, *Yersinia enterocolitica*, and *Entamoeba histolytica* (a protozoan).

Enterobacteriaceae

Diverse family including *E. coli*, *Salmonella*, *Klebsiella*, *Enterobacter*, *Serratia*, *Proteus*.
All species have somatic (O) antigen (which is the polysaccharide of endotoxin). The capsular (K) antigen is related to the virulence of the bug. The flagellar (H) antigen is found in motile species. All ferment glucose and are oxidase negative.

Think **COFFEe:**
- **C**apsular
- **O**-antigen
- **F**lagellar antigen
- **F**erment glucose
- **E**nterobacteriaceae
- e

Haemophilus influenzae

*Ha***EMOP***hilus* causes **E**piglottitis, **M**eningitis, **O**titis media, and **P**neumonia. Small gram-negative (coccobacillary) rod. Aerosol transmission. Most invasive disease caused by capsular type b. Produces IgA protease. Culture on chocolate agar requires factors **V** (NAD) and **X** (hemin) for growth. Treat meningitis with ceftriaxone. Rifampin prophylaxis in close contacts. Does not cause the flu (influenza virus does).

When a child has "flu," mom goes to five (**V**) and dime (**X**) store to buy some chocolate.
Vaccine contains type b capsular polysaccharide conjugated to diphtheria toxoid or other protein. Given between 2 and 18 months of age.

UCV Micro1.45, 70, Micro2.51

Legionella pneumophila

Legionnaires' disease. Gram-negative rod. Gram stains poorly—use silver stain. Grow on charcoal yeast extract culture with iron and cysteine. Aerosol transmission from environmental water source habitat. No person-to-person transmission. Treat with erythromycin.

Think of a French legionnaire (soldier) with his silver helmet, sitting around a campfire (charcoal) with his iron dagger—he is no sissy (cysteine).

UCV Micro1.54

Pseudomonas aeruginosa

PSEUdomonas causes wound and burn infections, Pneumonia (especially in cystic fibrosis), Sepsis (black lesions on skin), External otitis (swimmer's ear), UTI, and hot tub folliculitis. Aerobic gram-negative rod. Non–lactose fermenting, oxidase positive. Produces pyocyanin (blue-green) pigment. Water source. Produces endotoxin (fever, shock) and exotoxin A (inactivates EF-2). Treat with aminoglycoside plus extended-spectrum penicillin (e.g., piperacillin, ticarcillin).

AERuginosa—AERobic. Think water connection and blue-green pigment. Think *Pseudomonas* in burn victims.

Helicobacter pylori

Causes gastritis and up to 90% of duodenal ulcers. Risk factor for peptic ulcer and gastric carcinoma. Gram-negative rod. Urease positive (e.g., urease breath test). Creates alkaline environment. Treat with triple therapy: 1. bismuth (Pepto-Bismol), metronidazole, and either tetracycline or amoxicillin; 2. (more costly) metronidazole, omeprazole, clarithromycin.

Pylori—think pylorus of stomach. *Proteus* and *H. pylori* are both urease positive (cleave urea to ammonia).

UCV Micro2.9

Lactose-fermenting enteric bacteria

These bacteria grow pink colonies on MacConkey's agar. Examples include ***K**lebsiella*, ***E**. coli*, ***E**nterobacter*, and *Citrobacter*.

Lactose is **KEE**.

Salmonella versus *Shigella*

Both are non–lactose fermenters; both invade intestinal mucosa and can cause bloody diarrhea. Only *Salmonella* is motile and can invade further and disseminate hematogenously. Symptoms of salmonellosis may be prolonged with antibiotic treatments. *Shigella* is more virulent (10^1 organisms) than *Salmonella* (10^5 organisms).

Salmon swim (motile and disseminate). *Salmonella* has an animal reservoir; *Shigella* does not and is transmitted via "food, fingers, feces, and flies."

UCV Micro1.81, Micro2.17, 74

Cholera and pertussis toxins

Vibrio cholerae toxin permanently activates G_s, causing rice-water diarrhea. Micro1.35

Pertussis toxin permanently disables G_i, causing whooping cough. Micro1.96

Both toxins act via ADP ribosylation that permanently activates adenyl cyclase (resulting in ↑ cAMP).

Cholera turns the "on" on. Pertussis turns the "off" off. Pertussis toxin also promotes lymphocytosis.

UCV

Zoonotic bacteria

Species	Disease	Transmission and source
Borrelia burgdorferi	Lyme disease	Tick bite; *Ixodes* ticks that live on deer and mice
Brucella spp.	Brucellosis/ Undulant fever	Dairy products, contact with animals
Francisella tularensis	Tularemia	Tick bite; rabbits, deer
Yersinia pestis	Plague	Flea bite; rodents, especially prairie dogs
Pasteurella multocida	Cellulitis	Animal bite; cats, dogs

Bugs From Your Pet

Undulates and Unpasteurized dairy products give you Undulant fever.

Intracellular bugs

Obligate intracellular	*Rickettsia*, *Chlamydia*. Can't make own ATP.	Stay inside (cells) when it is **R**eally **C**old.
Facultative intracellular	*Mycobacterium*, *Brucella*, *Francisella*, *Listeria*	

1° and 2° tuberculosis

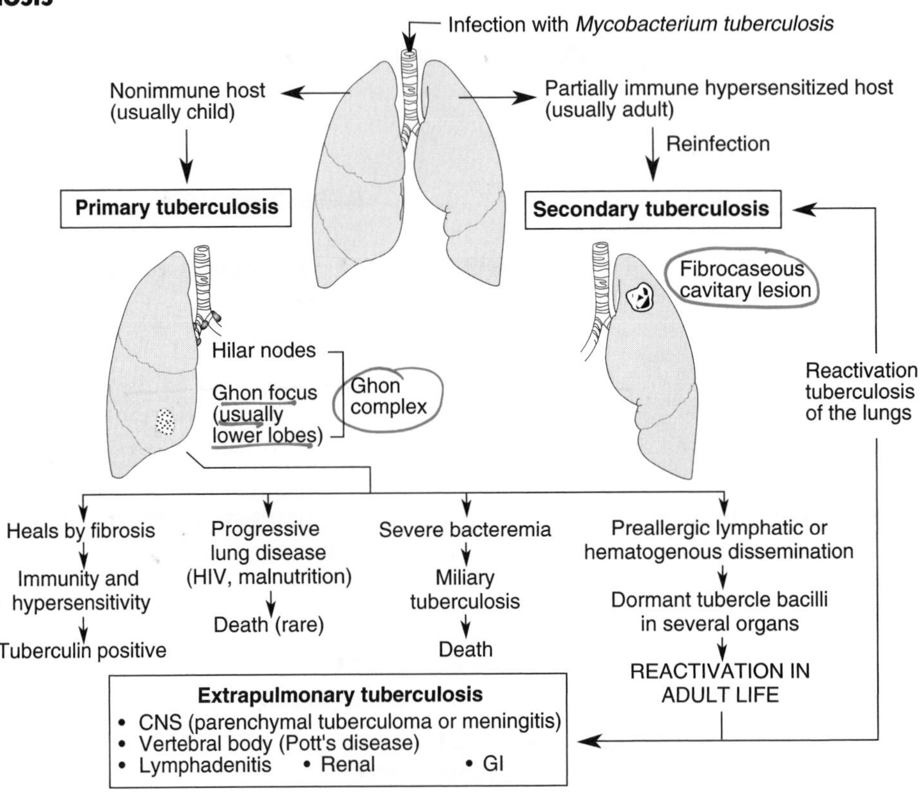

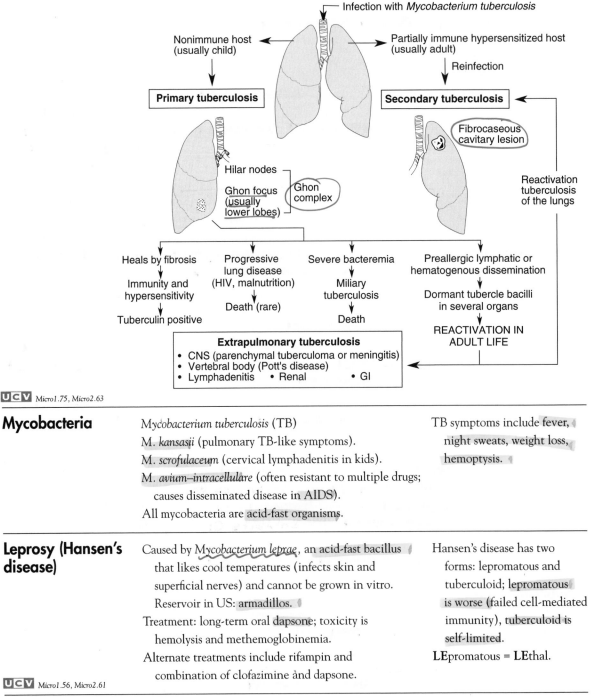

UCV Micro1.75, Micro2.63

Mycobacteria

Mycobacterium tuberculosis (TB)
M. *kansasii* (pulmonary TB-like symptoms).
M. *scrofulaceum* (cervical lymphadenitis in kids).
M. *avium–intracellulare* (often resistant to multiple drugs; causes disseminated disease in AIDS).
All mycobacteria are acid-fast organisms.

TB symptoms include fever, night sweats, weight loss, hemoptysis.

Leprosy (Hansen's disease)

Caused by *Mycobacterium leprae*, an acid-fast bacillus that likes cool temperatures (infects skin and superficial nerves) and cannot be grown in vitro. Reservoir in US: armadillos.
Treatment: long-term oral dapsone; toxicity is hemolysis and methemoglobinemia.
Alternate treatments include rifampin and combination of clofazimine and dapsone.

Hansen's disease has two forms: lepromatous and tuberculoid; lepromatous is worse (failed cell-mediated immunity), tuberculoid is self-limited.
LEpromatous = **LE**thal.

UCV Micro1.56, Micro2.61

Rickettsiae

Rickettsiae are obligate intracellular parasites (except *R. quintana*) and need CoA and NAD. All except *Coxiella* are transmitted by an arthropod vector and cause headache, fever, and rash; *Coxiella* is an atypical rickettsia, because it is transmitted by aerosol.

Tetracycline is the treatment of choice for most rickettsial infections.

Classic triad: headache, fever, rash (vasculitis).

Rickettsial diseases and vectors

Rocky Mountain spotted fever (tick): *Rickettsia rickettsii*

Endemic typhus (fleas): *R. typhi*

Epidemic typhus (human body louse): *R. prowazekii*

Q fever (inhaled aerosols): *Coxiella burnetii*

Treatment for all: tetracycline.

TyPHus has centriPHugal (outward) spread of rash, sPotted fever is centriPetal (inward). Q fever is Queer because it has no rash, has no vector, has negative Weil–Felix, and its causative organism can survive outside for a long time and does not have *Rickettsia* as its genus name.

Rocky Mountain spotted fever

Caused by *Rickettsia rickettsii.*

Symptoms: rash on palms and soles (migrating to wrists, ankles, then trunk), headache, fever.

Endemic to East Coast (in spite of name).

Palm and sole rash is seen in Rocky Mountain spotted fever, syphilis, and coxsackievirus infection (hand, foot, and mouth disease).

UCV Micro1.7

Weil–Felix reaction

Weil–Felix reaction assays for antirickettsial antibodies, which cross-react with *Proteus* antigen. Weil–Felix is usually positive for typhus and Rocky Mountain spotted fever but negative for Q fever.

Mycoplasma pneumoniae

Classic cause of atypical "walking" pneumonia (insidious onset, headache, nonproductive cough). X-ray looks worse than patient. High titer of cold agglutinins. Grown on Eaton's agar.

Treatment: tetracycline or erythromycin (bugs are penicillin resistant because they have no cell wall).

No cell wall.

Only bacterial membrane containing cholesterol.

Mycoplasma pneumonia is more common in patients younger than age 30.

Frequent outbreaks in military recruits and prisons.

UCV Micro1.66

Chlamydiae

Chlamydiae are obligate intracellular parasites that cause mucosal infections. Two forms:

1. Elementary body (small, dense), which Enters cell via endocytosis
2. Initial or Reticulate body, which Replicates in cell by fission

Chlamydiae cause arthritis, conjunctivitis, pneumonia, and nongonococcal urethritis. The peptidoglycan wall is unusual in that it lacks muramic acid.

Treatment: erythromycin or tetracycline.

Chlamys = cloak (intracellular).

Chlamydia psittaci notable for an avian reservoir.

C. *trachomatis* infects only humans.

Lab diagnosis: cytoplasmic inclusions seen on Giemsa or fluorescent-antibody stained smear.

***Chlamydia trachomatis* serotypes** UCV Micro1.60, 2.78	Types A, B, and C: chronic infection, causes blindness in Africa. Types D–K: urethritis/PID, neonatal pneumonia, or neonatal conjunctivitis. Types L1, L2, and L3: lymphogranuloma venereum (acute lymphadenitis: positive Frei test). TWAR = new strain, pneumonia. Now called *C. pneumoniae*. Acquired by aerosol.	**ABC** = **A**frica/**B**lindness/**C**hronic infection. **L**1–3 = **L**ymphogranuloma venereum. D–K = everything else. Neonatal disease acquired by passage through infected birth canal.
Spirochetes	The spirochetes are spiral-shaped bacteria with axial filaments and include ***B**orrelia* (big size), ***L**eptospira*, and ***T**reponema*. Only *Borrelia* can be visualized using aniline dyes (Wright's or Giemsa stain) in light microscopy. *Treponema* is visualized by dark-field microscopy.	**BLT. B** is **B**ig.
Lyme disease UCV Micro1.58	Classic symptom is erythema chronicum migrans, an expanding "bull's eye" red rash with central clearing. Also affects joints, CNS, and heart. Caused by *Borrelia burgdorferi*, which is transmitted by the tick *Ixodes*. Mice are important reservoirs. Deer required for tick life cycle. Treat with tetracycline. Named after Lyme, Connecticut; disease is common in northeastern US. Transmission is most common in summer months.	3 stages of Lyme disease: Stage 1: Erythema chronicum migrans, flu-like symptoms Stage 2: Neurologic and cardiac manifestations Stage 3: Autoimmune migratory polyarthritis
Treponemal disease	Treponemes are spirochetes. *Treponema pallidum* causes syphilis. *T. pertenue* causes yaws (a tropical infection that is not an STD, although VDRL test is positive).	
Syphilis	Caused by spirochete *Treponema pallidum*.	Treat with penicillin G.
1° syphilis	Presents with painless chancre.	
2° syphilis	Constitutional symptoms, maculopapular rash, condylomata lata	**S**econdary syphilis = **S**ystemic.
3° syphilis UCV Micro1.86-88, 104	Gummas, aortitis, neurosyphilis (tabes dorsalis) Argyll Robertson pupil.	

VDRL versus FTA-ABS	FTA-ABS is specific for treponemes, turns positive earliest in disease, and remains positive longest during disease. VDRL is less specific.	**FTA-ABS** = **F**ind **T**he **A**ntibody-**ABS**olutely: 1. Most specific 2. Earliest positive 3. Remains positive the longest
VDRL false positives	VDRL detects nonspecific Ab that reacts with beef cardiolipin. Used for diagnosis of syphilis, but many biologic false positives, including viral infection (mononucleosis, hepatitis), some drugs, rheumatic fever, rheumatoid arthritis, SLE, and leprosy.	

MICROBIOLOGY—MYCOLOGY

Spores: fungal	Most fungal spores are asexual. Both coccidioidomycosis and histoplasmosis are transmitted by inhalation of asexual spores.	Conidia ≡ asexual fungal spores (e.g., blastoconidia, arthroconidia).
Candida albicans UCV Micro1.33	Systemic or superficial fungal infection (budding yeast with pseudohyphae, germ tube formation at 37°C). Thrush in throat with immunocompromised patients (neonates, steroids, diabetes, AIDS), endocarditis in IV drug users, vaginitis (post-antibiotic), diaper rash. Treatment: nystatin for superficial infection; amphotericin B for serious systemic infection.	*Alba* = white.

Systemic mycoses

Disease	Endemic location	Notes
Coccidioidomycosis	Southwestern US, California. Micro1.36	San Joaquin Valley or desert (desert bumps) "Valley fever"
Histoplasmosis	Mississippi and Ohio river valleys Micro1.50	Bird or bat droppings; intracellular (frequently seen inside macrophages)
Paracoccidioidomycosis	Rural Latin America	"Captain's wheel" appearance
Blastomycosis	States east of Mississippi River and Central America Micro2.37	**B**ig, **B**road-**B**ased **B**udding

Broad-based budding

All of the above are caused by **dimorphic** fungi, which are mold in soil (at lower temperature) and yeast in tissue (at higher/body temperature: 37°C) except coccidioidomycosis, which is a spherule in tissue. You can treat with fluconazole or ketoconazole for local infection; amphotericin B for systemic infection.

Cold = Mold.
Heat = Yeast.
Culture on Sabouraud's agar.

UCV

Opportunistic fungal infections

Candida albicans	Thrush in immunocompromised (neonates, steroids, diabetes, AIDS), vulvovaginitis (high pH, diabetes, use of antibiotics), disseminated candidiasis (to any organ), chronic mucocutaneous candidiasis. Micro1.33
Aspergillus fumigatus	Ear fungus, lung cavity aspergilloma ("fungus ball"), invasive aspergillosis. **Mold** with septate hyphae that branch at a V-shaped (45°) angle. Not dimorphic. Micro1.29, Micro2.33
Cryptococcus neoformans	Cryptococcal meningitis, cryptococcosis. Heavily encapsulated **yeast.** Not dimorphic. Found in soil, pigeon droppings. Culture of Sabouraud's agar. Stains with India ink. Latex agglutination test detects polysaccharide capsular antigen.
Mucor and *Rhizopus* species	Mucormycosis. **Mold** with irregular nonseptate hyphae branching at wide angles (≥ 90°). Disease mostly in ketoacidotic diabetic and leukemic patients. Micro1.64

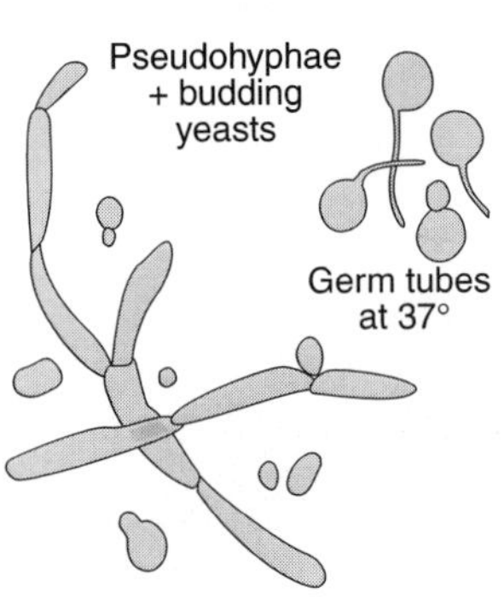

CANDIDA

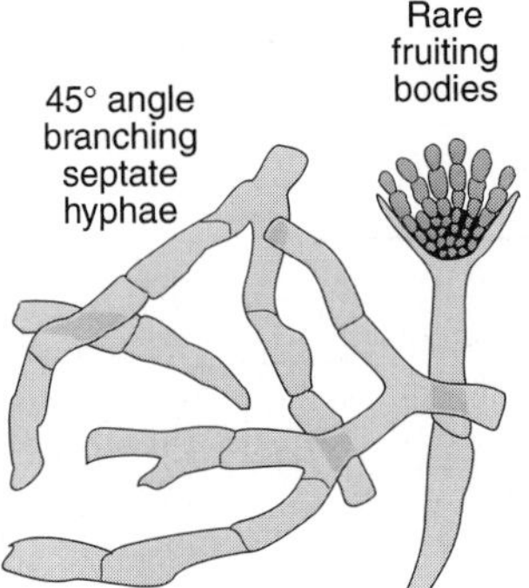

ASPERGILLUS

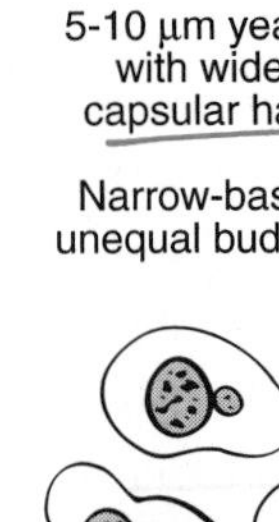

CRYPTOCOCCUS

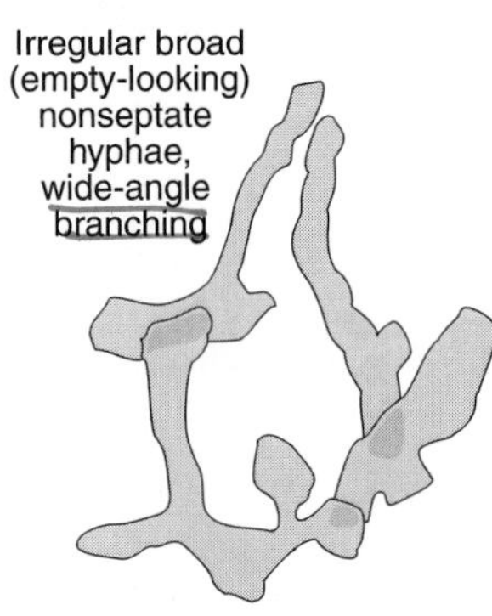

MUCOR

Pneumocystis carinii

Causes pneumonia (PCP). Yeast (originally classified as protozoan). Inhaled. Most infections asymptomatic. Immunosuppression (e.g., AIDS) predisposes to disease. Silver stain of lung tissue. Treat with TMP-SMX, pentamidine. Start prophylaxis when CD4 drops below 200 cells/mL in HIV patients.

UCV Micro1.74

Sporothrix schenckii

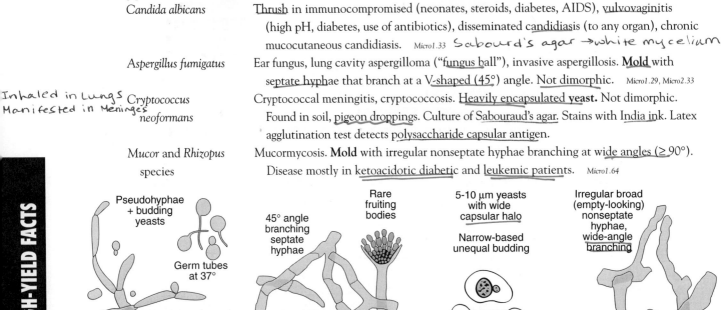

Sporotrichosis. Dimorphic fungus that lives on vegetation. When traumatically introduced into the skin, typically by a thorn ("rose gardener's" disease), causes local pustule or ulcer with nodules along draining lymphatics. Little systemic illness. Cigar-shaped budding yeast visible in pus. Treat with itraconazole or potassium iodide.

UCV Micro1.82

Medically important protozoa

Organism	Disease	Mode of Transmission	Diagnosis	Treatment
Entamoeba histolytica Micro2.11	Amebiasis Bloody diarrhea (dysentery) Liver abscess RUQ pain	Cysts in water	Serology and/or trophozoites or cysts in stool	Metronidazole and iodoquinol
Giardia lamblia Micro1.46	Giardiasis Bloating Flatulence Foul-smelling diarrhea	Cysts in water	Trophozoites or cysts in stool	Metronidazole
Cryptosporidium Micro1.38	Severe diarrhea in AIDS Mild disease (watery diarrhea) in non-HIV	Cysts in water	Cysts on acid-fast stain	None
Toxoplasma Micro1.90	Brain abscess in HIV Birth defects	Cysts in meat or cat feces	Serology, biopsy	Sulfonamide + pyrimethamine
Pneumocystis carinii Micro1.74	Diffuse interstitial pneumonia in HIV	Inhalation	Lung biopsy or lavage; methenamine silver stain	TMP-SMX or dapsone or pentamidine
Plasmodium *vivax* *ovale* *malariae* *falciparum* Micro1.61	Malaria Cyclic fever Headache Anemia Splenomegaly Malaria —severe (cerebral)	Mosquito (*Anopheles*)	Blood smear	Chloroquine (primaquine for *vivax, ovale*) Chloroquine Mefloquine Quinine
Trichomonas vaginalis	Vaginitis Foul-smelling, greenish discharge Itching and burning	Sexual	Trophozoites on wet mount	Metronidazole
Trypanosoma cruzi	Chagas' disease (heart disease) Micro1.34	Reduviid bug	Blood smear	Nifurtimox
Trypanosoma gambiense and *rhodesiense*	African sleeping sickness Micro1.25	Tsetse fly	Blood smear	Suramin for blood-borne disease or melarsoprol for CNS penetration

UCV

Medically important helminths

	Transmission/disease	Treatment
Cestodes (tapeworms)		
Taenia solium Micro1.102	Undercooked pork tapeworm. Causes mass lesions in the brain. Cysticercosis.	Praziquantel/Niclosamide Albendazole for cysticercosis
Echinococcus granulosus Micro1.42	Eggs in dog feces cause cysts in liver. Causes anaphylaxis if echinococcal antigens are released from cysts.	Albendazole
Trematodes (flukes)		
Schistosoma Micro1.80, 2.104	Snails are host. Cercariae penetrate skin of humans. Causes granulomas, fibrosis, and inflammation of the spleen and liver.	Praziquantel
Clonorchis sinensis	Undercooked fish. Causes inflammation of the biliary tract.	Praziquantel
Paragonimus westermani	Undercooked crab meat. Causes inflammation and secondary bacterial infection of the lung.	Praziquantel
Nematodes (roundworms)		
Ancylostoma duodenale Micro2.25 (hookworm)	Larvae penetrate skin of feet. Intestinal infection can cause anemia.	Mebendazole/Pyrantel pamoate
Ascaris lumbricoides	Eggs are visible in feces. Intestinal infection.	Mebendazole/Pyrantel pamoate
Enterobius vermicularis Micro2.14 (pinworm)	Food contaminated with eggs. Intestinal infection. Causes anal pruritis.	Mebendazole/Pyrantel pamoate
Strongyloides stercoralis Micro1.84	Larvae in soil penetrate the skin. Intestinal infection.	Thiabendazole
Trichinella spiralis Micro1.91	Undercooked meat, usually pork. Inflammation of muscle, periorbital edema.	Thiabendazole
Dracunculus medinensis	In drinking water. Skin inflammation and ulceration.	Niridazole
Loa loa	Transmitted by deer fly. Causes swelling in skin (can see worm crawling in conjunctiva).	Diethylcarbamazine
Onchocerca volvulus Micro1.68	Transmitted by female blackflies. Causes river blindness.	Ivermectin
Toxocara canis	Food contaminated with eggs. Causes granulomas (if in retina → blindness).	Diethylcarbamazine
Wuchereria bancrofti Micro1.59	Female mosquito. Causes blockage of lymphatic vessels (elephantiasis).	Diethylcarbamazine

DNA viral genomes	All DNA viruses except the Parvoviridae are dsDNA. All are linear except papovaviruses and hepadnaviruses (circular).	All are dsDNA (like our cells) except "part-of-a-virus" (parvovirus) is ssDNA.
RNA viral genomes	All RNA viruses except Reoviridae are ssRNA.	All are ssRNA (like our mRNA), except "**re**peatovirus" (**re**ovirus) is dsRNA.

DNA viruses

DNA viruses are **HHAPPP**y viruses.

Viral family	Envelope?	DNA structure	Medical importance
Hepadnavirus *Micro1.13*	Yes	DS-partial circular	Hepatitis B virus Acute or chronic hepatitis Vaccine available—use has ↑ tremendously Not a retrovirus but has reverse transcriptase
Herpesviruses	Yes	DS-linear	HSV 1—oral (and some genital) lesions HSV 2—genital (and some oral) lesions Varicella-zoster virus—chickenpox, zoster, shingles Epstein-Barr virus—mononucleosis, Burkitt's lymphoma Cytomegalovirus—infection in immunosuppressed patients, esp. transplant recipients HHV 6—roseola HHV 7—monkey bites (fatal in humans) HHV 8 (KSHV)—Kaposi's sarcoma–associated herpesvirus
Adenovirus *Micro2.31*	No	DS-linear	Febrile pharyngitis—sore throat Pneumonia Conjunctivitis—"pink eye"
Parvovirus *Micro2.29*	No	SS-linear	B19 virus—aplastic crises in sickle cell disease —"slapped cheeks" rash—erythema infectiosum AAV—adeno-associated virus
Papovavirus	No	DS-circular	HPV—warts, CIN, cervical cancer JC—progressive multifocal leukoencephalopathy in HIV BK—in kidney transplant patients
Poxvirus	Yes	DS-linear	Smallpox eradication Vaccinia—cowpox ("milkmaid's blisters")

UCV

RNA viruses

Viral family	Envelope?	RNA structure	Capsid symmetry	Medical importance
Picornaviruses	No	SS + linear	Icosahedral	**P**oliovirus—polio-Salk/Sabin vaccines KPV/OPV **E**chovirus—aseptic meningitis **R**hinovirus—"common cold" **C**oxsackievirus—aseptic meningitis Herpangina—febrile pharyngitis "Hand, foot, and mouth" disease Myocarditis **H**epatitis A—acute viral hepatitis Micro1.12
Caliciviruses	No	SS + linear	Icosahedral	Hepatitis E Norwalk virus—viral gastroenteritis
Reoviruses	No	DS linear Segmented	Icosahedral (double)	Reovirus—Colorado tick fever Rotavirus—#1 cause of fatal diarrhea in children
Flaviviruses	Yes	SS + linear	Icosahedral	Hepatitis C Micro1.14 Yellow fever Micro1.97 Dengue Micro2.44 St. Louis encephalitis Micro2.90
Togaviruses	Yes	SS + linear	Icosahedral	Rubella (German measles) Micro1.78 Eastern equine encephalitis Western equine encephalitis
Retroviruses	Yes	SS + linear	Icosahedral	Have reverse transcriptase HIV—AIDS HTLV—T-cell leukemia Micro1.52
Orthomyxoviruses	Yes	SS – linear Segmented	Helical	Influenza virus Micro2.58
Paramyxoviruses	Yes	SS – linear Nonsegmented	Helical	**P**a**R**a**M**yxovirus: **P**arainfluenza—croup Micro2.43 **R**SV—bronchiolitis in babies; Rx–ribavirin Micro1.31 **M**easles Micro1.62 **M**umps Micro1.65
Rhabdoviruses	Yes	SS – linear	Helical	Rabies Micro1.76
Filoviruses	Yes	SS – linear	Helical	Ebola/Marburg hemorrhagic fever—often fatal! Micro2.45
Coronaviruses	Yes	SS + linear	Helical	Coronavirus—"common cold"
Arenaviruses	Yes	SS – circular	Helical	LCV—lymphocytic choriomeningitis Meningitis—spread by mice
Bunyaviruses	Yes	SS – circular	Helical	California encephalitis Sandfly/Rift Valley fevers Crimea-Congo hemorrhagic fever Micro2.42 Hantavirus—hemorrhagic fever, pneumonia

SS, single-stranded; DS, double-stranded; +, + polarity; –, – polarity

UCV

Naked viral genome infectivity	Naked nucleic acids of most dsDNA (except poxviruses and HBV) and (+) strand ssRNA (≈mRNA) Viruses are infectious. Naked nucleic acids of (−) strand ssRNA and dsRNA viruses are not infectious. **Naked** (nonenveloped) RNA viruses include **C**alicivirus, **P**icornavirus, and **R**eovirus.	Viral nucleic acids with the same structure as host nucleic acids are infective alone; others require special enzymes (contained in intact virion). **Naked CPR.**
Enveloped viruses	Generally, enveloped viruses acquire their envelopes from plasma membrane when they exit from cell. Exceptions are herpesviruses, which acquire envelopes from nuclear membrane.	
Virus ploidy	All viruses are haploid (with one copy of DNA or RNA) except retroviruses, which have two identical ssRNA molecules (≈ diploid).	
Viral replication		
DNA viruses	All replicate in the nucleus (except poxvirus).	
RNA viruses	All replicate in the cytoplasm (except influenza virus and retroviruses).	
Viral vaccines	Live attenuated vaccines induce humoral and cell-mediated immunity but have reverted to virulence on rare occasions. Killed vaccines induce only humoral immunity but are stable. Live attenuated: measles, mumps, rubella, Sabin polio, VZV, yellow fever. Killed: rabies, influenza, hepatitis A, and Salk polio vaccines. Recombinant: HBV (antigen = recombinant HBsAg).	Dangerous to give live vaccines to immunocompromised patients or their close contacts. MMR = measles, mumps, rubella. Sal**K** = **K**illed.
Viral genetics		
Recombination	Exchange of genes between 2 chromosomes by crossing over within regions of significant base sequence homology.	
Reassortment	When viruses with segmented genomes (e.g., influenza virus) exchange segments. High-frequency recombination.	
Complementation	When one of 2 viruses that infects the cell has a mutation that results in a nonfunctional protein. The nonmutated virus "complements" the mutated one by making a functional protein that serves both viruses.	
Phenotypic mixing	Genome of virus A can be coated with the surface proteins of virus B. Type B protein coat determines the infectivity of the phenotypically mixed virus. However, the progeny from this infection has a type A coat and is encoded by its type A genetic material.	

Viral pathogens

Structure	Viruses
DNA enveloped viruses	Herpesviruses (herpes simplex virus types 1 and 2, varicella-zoster virus, cytomegalovirus, Epstein-Barr virus), hepatitis B virus, smallpox virus
DNA nucleocapsid viruses	Adenovirus, papillomaviruses
RNA enveloped viruses	Influenza virus, parainfluenza virus, respiratory syncytial virus, measles virus, mumps virus, rubella virus, rabies virus, human T-cell leukemia virus, human immunodeficiency virus
RNA nucleocapsid viruses	Enteroviruses (poliovirus, coxsackievirus, echovirus, hepatitis A virus), rhinovirus, reovirus

Slow virus infections UCV Micro2.87	Virus exists in patient for months to years before it manifests as clinical disease. SSPE (late sequela of measles), PML (reactivation of JC virus) in immunocompromised patients.	
Segmented viruses	All are RNA viruses. They include **B**unyaviruses, **O**rthomyxoviruses (influenza viruses), **A**renaviruses, and **R**eoviruses. Influenza virus consists of 8 segments of negative-stranded RNA. These segments can undergo reassortment, causing worldwide epidemics of the flu.	**BOAR**
Picornavirus	Includes poliovirus, rhinovirus, coxsackievirus, echovirus, hepatitis A virus. RNA is translated into one large polypeptide that is cleaved by proteases into many small proteins. Can cause aseptic meningitis (except rhinovirus and hep A virus).	Pico**RNA**virus = small **RNA** virus.
Rhinovirus UCV Micro1.37	Nonenveloped RNA virus. Cause of common cold: more than 100 serologic types.	**Rhino** has a runny nose.
Rotavirus UCV Micro2.16	Rotavirus, the most important global cause of infantile gastroenteritis, is a segmented dsRNA virus (a reovirus). Major cause of acute diarrhea in US during winter.	**ROTA** = **R**ight **O**ut **T**he **A**nus.
Paramyxoviruses	Paramyxoviruses include those that cause parainfluenza (croup), mumps, and measles as well as RSV, which causes respiratory tract infection (bronchiolitis, pneumonia) in infants. Paramyxoviruses cause disease in children. All paramyxoviruses have 1 serotype except parainfluenza virus, which has 4.	

Mumps virus UCV Micro1.65	A paramyxovirus with one serotype. Symptoms: aseptic Meningitis, Orchitis (inflammation of testes), and Parotitis. Can cause sterility (especially after puberty).	**Mumps** gives you **bumps** (parotitis). **MOP**
Measles virus UCV Micro1.62	A paramyxovirus that causes measles. Koplik spots (bluish-gray spots on buccal mucosa) are diagnostic. SSPE, encephalitis (1 in 2000), or giant cell pneumonia (rarely, in immunosuppressed) are possible sequelae.	**3 C's** of measles: Cough Coryza Conjunctivitis Also look for Koplik spots.
Influenza viruses	Enveloped, single-stranded RNA viruses with segmented genome. Contain hemagglutinin and neuraminidase antigens. Responsible for worldwide influenza epidemics; patients at risk for fatal bacterial superinfection. Rapid genetic changes.	Killed viral vaccine is major mode of protection; reformulated vaccine offered each fall to elderly, health-care workers, etc.
Genetic shift	Reassortment of viral genome (such as when human flu virus recombines with swine flu virus).	Amantadine and rimantadine are approved for use against influenza A (especially prophylaxis) but are not useful against influenza B or C.
Genetic drift UCV Micro2.58	Minor changes based on random mutation.	
Rabies virus UCV Micro1.76	Negri bodies are characteristic cytoplasmic inclusions in neurons infected by rabies virus. Has bullet-shaped capsid. Rabies has long incubation period (weeks to 3 mo). Causes fatal encephalitis with seizures and hydrophobia. More commonly from bat, raccoon, and skunk bites than from dog bites.	Travels to the CNS by migrating in a retrograde fashion up nerve axons.
Arboviruses	Transmitted by arthropods (mosquitoes, ticks). Classic examples are dengue fever (also known as break-bone fever) and yellow fever. A variant of dengue fever in Southeast Asia is hemorrhagic shock syndrome.	**Arbo** virus = **Ar**thropod-**bo**rne virus
Yellow fever UCV Micro1.97	Caused by flavivirus, an arbovirus transmitted by *Aedes* mosquitos. Virus has a monkey or human reservoir. Symptoms: high fever, black vomitus, and jaundice. Councilman bodies (acidophilic inclusions) may be seen in liver.	*Flavi* = yellow.

HIGH-YIELD FACTS

Microbiology

Herpesviruses

	Diseases	Route of transmission	
HSV-1	Gingivostomatitis, temporal lobe encephalitis, herpes labialis *Micro2.83*	Respiratory secretions, saliva	Get herpes in a CHEVrolet: CMV, **HSV**, EBV, VZV.
HSV-2	Herpes genitalis, neonatal herpes *Micro1.49*	Sexual contact, perinatal	
VZV	Varicella zoster (shingles), encephalitis, pneumonia *Micro1.94, 95*	Respiratory secretions	
EBV	Infectious mononucleosis, Burkitt's lymphoma *Micro1.53*	Respiratory secretions, saliva	
CMV	Congenital infection, mononucleosis, pneumonia *Micro1.39, 40, 101*	Congenital, transfusion, sexual contact, saliva, urine, transplant	
HHV8	Kaposi's sarcoma (HIV patients)	Sexual contact	

UCV

Mononucleosis

Caused by EBV, a herpesvirus. Characterized by fever, hepatosplenomegaly, pharyngitis, and lymphadenopathy (especially posterior auricular nodes).

Peak incidence 15–20 y old. Positive heterophil Ab test. Abnormal circulating cytotoxic T cells (atypical lymphocytes).

Most common during peak kissing years ("kissing disease").

UCV *Micro1.53*

Tzanck test

A smear of an opened skin vesicle to detect multinucleated giant cells. Used to assay for herpesvirus.

Tzanck heavens I do not have herpes.

Hepatitis transmission		
	HAV (RNA virus) is transmitted primarily by fecal–oral route. Short incubation (3 wk). No carriers. Micro1.12	Hep **A**: **A**symptomatic (usually)
	HBV (DNA virus) is transmitted primarily by parenteral, sexual, and maternal–fetal routes. Long incubation (3 mo). Carriers. Reverse transcription occurs; however, the virion enzyme is a DNA-dependent DNA polymerase. Micro1.13	Hep **B**: **B**lood-borne
	HCV is transmitted primarily via blood and resembles HBV in its course and severity. Carriers. Common cause of posttransfusion and IV drug use hepatitis in the United States. Micro1.14	Hep **C**: **C**hronic, **C**irrhosis, **C**arcinoma, **C**arriers
	HDV (delta agent) is a defective virus that requires HBsAg as its envelope. Carriers.	Hep **D**: **D**efective, **D**ependent on HBV
	HEV is transmitted enterically and causes water-borne epidemics. Resembles HAV in course, severity, incubation. High mortality rate in pregnant women.	Hep **E**: **E**nteric, **E**xpectant mothers
	Both HBV and HCV predispose a patient to hepatocellular carcinoma.	A and E by fecal-oral route: "The **vowels** hit your **bowels.**"

Hepatitis serologic markers

	Description
IgM HAVAb	IgM antibody to HAV; best test to detect active hepatitis A.
HBsAg	Antigen found on surface of HBV; continued presence indicates carrier state.
HBsAb	Antibody to HBsAg; **provides immunity** to hepatitis B.
HBcAg	Antigen associated with core of HBV.
HBcAb	Antibody to HBcAg; positive during **window period.** IgM HBcAb is an indicator of recent disease.
HBeAg	A second, different antigenic determinant in the HBV core. Important indicator of transmissibility. (**BE**ware!)
HBeAb	Antibody to e antigen; indicates low transmissibility.

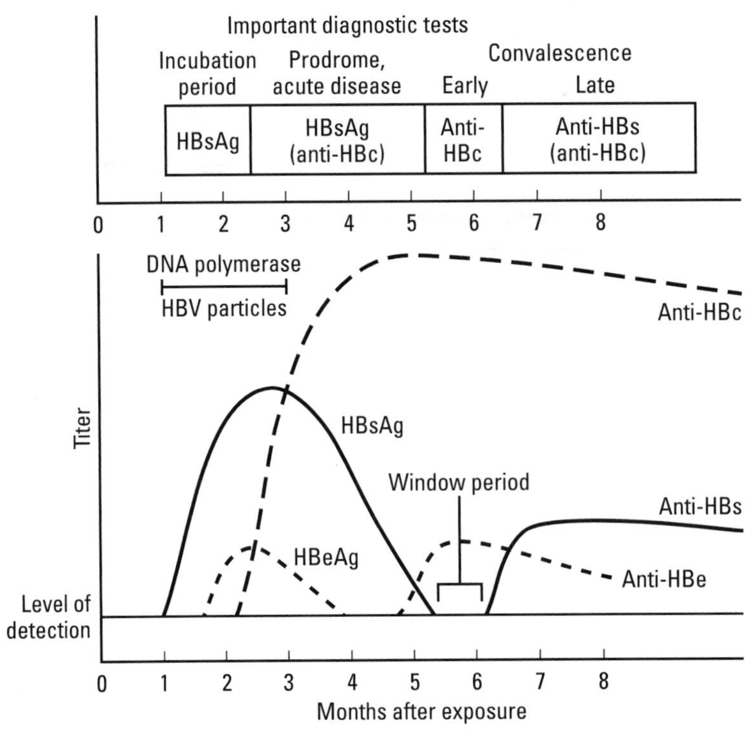

HIV

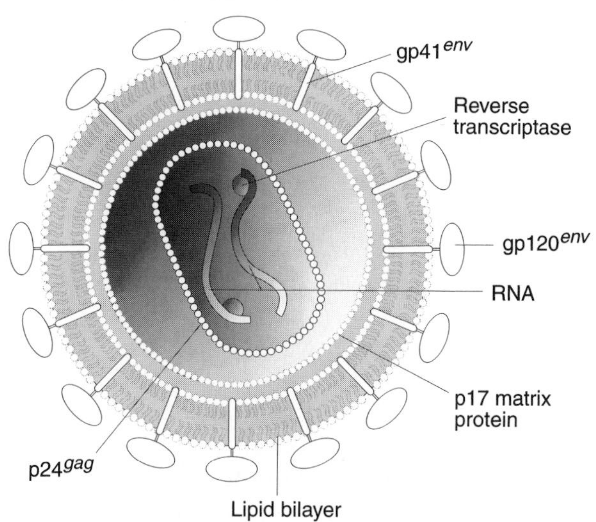

Diploid genome (2 molecules of RNA).

p24 = rectangular nucleocapsid protein.

gp41 and gp120 = envelope proteins.

HIV diagnosis

Presumptive diagnosis made with ELISA (sensitive); positive results are then confirmed with Western blot assay (specific).

HIV PCR/viral load tests are increasing in popularity; they allow physician to monitor the effect of drug therapy on viral load.

ELISA/Western blot tests look for antibodies to viral proteins; these tests are often falsely negative in the first 1–2 months of HIV infection.

Time course of HIV infection

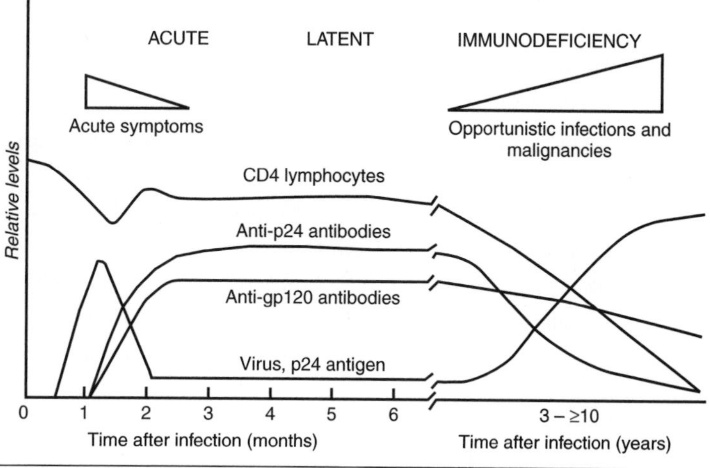

HIGH-YIELD FACTS

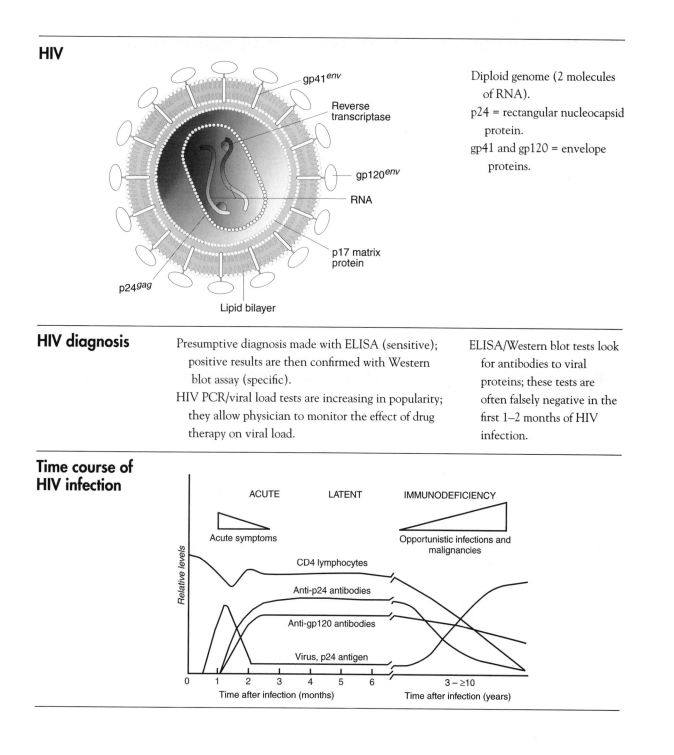

Microbiology

Opportunistic infections in AIDS

Bacterial	Tuberculosis, M. *avium–intracellulare* complex. Micro1.75	Alphabet soup: TB, MAC, HSV, VZV, CMV, PCP.
Viral	Herpes simplex, varicella-zoster virus, cytomegalovirus, progressive multifocal leukoencephalopathy (JC virus). Micro1.40, 49, 94, 95, 101	
Fungal	Thrush (*Candida albicans*), cryptococcosis (cryptococcal meningitis), histoplasmosis, *Pneumocystis* pneumonia. Micro1.33, 50, 74	
Protozoan	Toxoplasmosis, cryptosporidiosis. Micro1.38, 90	

UCV

Prions

Infectious agents that do not contain RNA or DNA (consist only of proteins); diseases include Creutzfeldt–Jakob disease (CJD: rapid progressive dementia), kuru, scrapie (sheep), and "mad cow disease."

Normal flora: dominant

Skin–S. *epidermidis*
Nose–S. *aureus*
Oropharynx–Viridans streptococci
Dental plaque–S. *mutans*
Colon–B. *fragilis* > E. *coli*
Vagina–*Lactobacillus*, E. *coli*, group B strep

Neonates delivered by cesarean section have no flora but are rapidly colonized after birth.

Common causes of pneumonia

Children (6 wk–18 y) ➤	**Adults (18–40 y)** ➤	**Adults (40–65 y)** ➤	**Elderly**
Viruses (RSV)	***Mycoplasma***	S. *pneumoniae*	**S. *pneumoniae***
Mycoplasma	C. *pneumoniae*	H. *influenzae*	Anaerobes
Chlamydia pneumoniae	S. *pneumoniae*	Anaerobes	H. *influenzae*
S. *pneumoniae*		Viruses	Gram-negative rods
		Mycoplasma	**Viruses**

Special groups	
Nosocomial (hospital acquired)	*Staphylococcus*, gram-negative rods
Immunocompromised	*Staphylococcus*, gram-negative rods, **fungi,** viruses, ***Pneumocystis carinii*—with HIV**
Aspiration	Anaerobes
Alcoholic/IV drug user	S. *pneumoniae*, *Klebsiella*, *Staphylococcus*
Postviral	*Staphylococcus*, H. *influenzae*
Neonate	Group B streptococci, E. *coli*
Atypical	*Mycoplasma*, *Legionella*, *Chlamydia*

Causes of meningitis

Newborn (0–6 mo) ⟶	Children (6 mo–6 y) ⟶	6 y–60 y ⟶	60 y +
Group B streptococci	*H. influenzae* B	***N. meningitidis***	***S. pneumoniae***
E. coli	*S. pneumoniae*	Enteroviruses	Gram-negative rods
Listeria	*N. meningitidis*	*S. pneumoniae*	*Listeria*
	Enteroviruses	HSV	

In HIV—*Cryptococcus*, CMV, toxoplasmosis (brain abscess), JC virus (PML)

Note: Incidence of *H. influenzae* meningitis has ↓ greatly with introduction of *H. influenzae* vaccine in last 10–15 years.

UCV Micro1.57, 63, Micro2.85

CSF findings in meningitis

Bacterial: ↑pressure, ↑polys, ↑proteins, ↓sugar.

Viral: pressure normal/↑, ↑lymphs, proteins **normal,** sugar **normal.**

TB/fungal: ↑pressure, ↑lymphs, ↑proteins, ↓sugar.

Osteomyelitis

Most people: *S. aureus*

Sexually active: *N. gonorrhoeae* (rare: septic arthritis more common)

Drug addicts: *Pseudomonas aeruginosa*

Sickle cell: *Salmonella*

Hip replacement: *S. aureus* and *S. epidermidis*

Assume *S. aureus* if no other information.

Most osteomyelitis occurs in children.

Elevated ESR.

UCV Micro1.69

Urinary tract infections

Ambulatory: *E. coli* (50–80%), *Klebsiella* (8–10%).

Staphylococcus saprophyticus (10–30%) is the second most common cause of UTI in young ambulatory women.

Hospital: *E. coli, Proteus, Klebsiella, Serratia, Pseudomonas.*

Epidemiology: women to men = 30 to 1 (short urethra colonized by fecal flora).

UTIs mostly caused by ascending infections. In males: babies with congenital defects; elderly with enlarged prostates.

UTI: dysuria, frequency, urgency, suprapubic pain.

Pyelonephritis: fever, chills and flank pain.

UCV Micro1.109, Micro2.105

UTI bugs

Species	Features of the organism	
Serratia marcescens	Some strains produce a red pigment; often nosocomial and drug-resistant; "red-diaper syndrome"	**SEEK PP**
Staphylococcus saprophyticus	Second leading cause of community-acquired UTI in sexually active women.	
Escherichia coli	Leading cause of UTI. Colonies show metallic sheen on EMB agar.	
Enterobacter cloacae	Often nosocomial and drug-resistant	
Klebsiella pneumoniae	Large mucoid capsule and viscous colonies	
Proteus mirabilis	Motility causes "swarming" on agar; produces urease; associated with struvite stones	
Pseudomonas aeruginosa	Blue-green pigment and fruity odor; usually nosocomial and drug-resistant	

HIGH-YIELD FACTS

Microbiology

Sexually transmitted diseases

Disease	Clinical features	Organism
Gonorrhea	Urethritis, cervicitis, PID, prostatitis, epididymitis, arthritis Micro1.48	*Neisseria gonorrhoeae*
Primary syphilis	Painless chancre Micro1.87	*Treponema pallidum*
Secondary syphilis	Fever, lymphadenopathy, skin rashes, condylomata lata Micro1.88	
Tertiary syphilis	Gummas, tabes dorsalis, general paresis, aortitis, Argyll Robertson pupil	
Genital herpes	Painful penile, vulvar, or cervical ulcers Micro1.49	HSV-2
Chlamydia	Urethritis, cervicitis, conjunctivitis, Reiter's syndrome, PID Path2.79	*Chlamydia trachomatis* (D–K)
Lymphogranuloma venereum	Ulcers, lymphadenopathy, rectal strictures Micro1.60	*Chlamydia trachomatis* (L1–L3)
Trichomoniasis	Vaginitis	*Trichomonas vaginalis*
AIDS	Opportunistic infections, Kaposi's sarcoma, lymphoma	HIV
Condylomata acuminata	Genital warts, koilocytes	HPV 6 and 11
Hepatitis B	Jaundice Micro1.13	HBV

UCV

Pelvic inflammatory disease

Top bugs: *Chlamydia trachomatis* (subacute, often undiagnosed), *N. gonorrhoeae* (acute, high fever). *C. trachomatis* is the most common STD in the US (3–4 million cases per year). Cervical motion tenderness, purulent cervical discharge. PID may include salpingitis, endometritis, hydrosalpinx, and tubo-ovarian abscess.

Salpingitis is a risk factor for ectopic pregnancy, infertility, chronic pelvic pain, and adhesions.
Other STDs include *Gardnerella* (clue cells) and *Trichomonas* (motile on wet prep).

UCV Micro2.97

Nosocomial infections

By risk factor:
Newborn nursery: CMV, RSV
Urinary catheterization: *E. coli*, *Proteus mirabilis*

Respiratory therapy equipment: *P. aeruginosa*
Work in renal dialysis unit: HBV
Hyperalimentation: *Candida albicans*
Water aerosols: *Legionella*

The two most common causes of nosocomial infections are *E. coli* (UTI) and *S. aureus* (wound infection).
Presume *Pseudomonas* ***air**-uginosa* when **air** or burns are involved.
Legionella when water source is involved.

Infections dangerous in pregnancy

ToRCHeS = Toxoplasma, Rubella, CMV, HSV, Syphilis.

Bug hints (if all else fails)

Pus, empyema, abscess: *S. aureus*
Pediatric infection: *H. influenzae* (including epiglottitis)
Pneumonia in CF, burn infection: *P. aeruginosa*
Branching rods in oral infection: *Actinomyces israelii*
Traumatic open wound: *C. perfringens*
Surgical wound: *S. aureus*
Dog or cat bite: *Pasteurella multocida*
Currant jelly sputum: *Klebsiella*

MICROBIOLOGY—IMMUNOLOGY

Antibody structure Variable part of L and H chains recognizes antigens. Constant part of H chain of IgM and IgG fixes complement. Heavy chain contributes to Fc and Fab fractions. Light chain contributes only to Fab fraction.

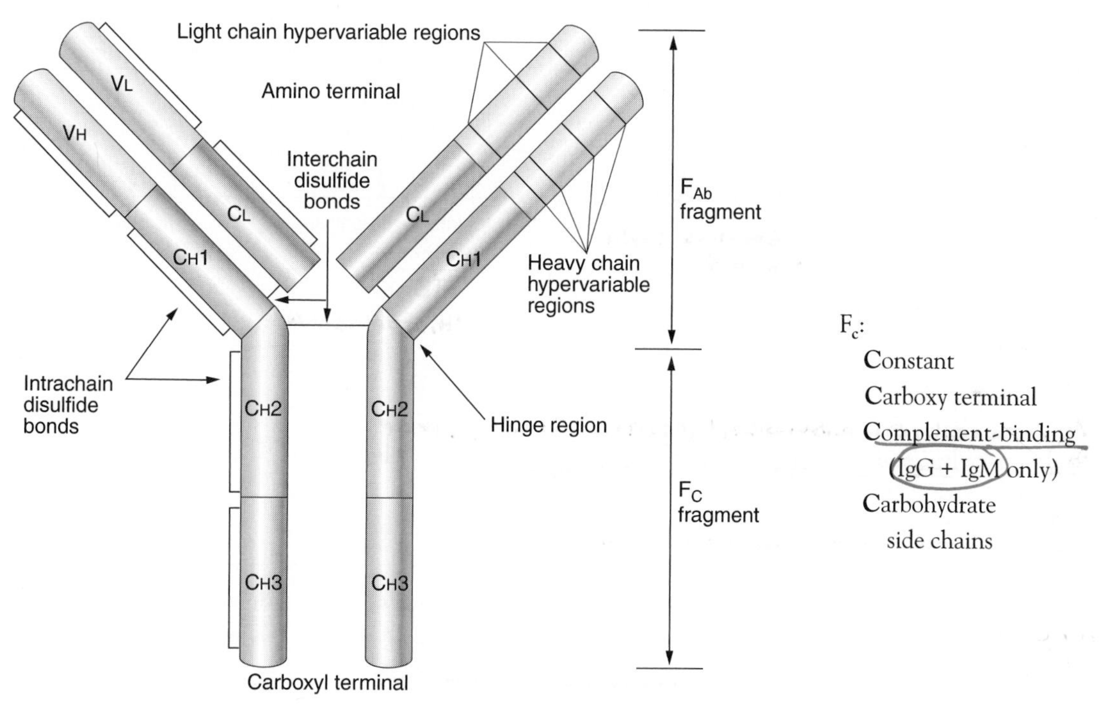

F_c:
Constant
Carboxy terminal
Complement-binding (IgG + IgM only)
Carbohydrate side chains

Immunoglobulin isotypes

IgG	Most abundant. Opsonizes bacteria, fixes complement, neutralizes bacterial toxins and viruses, crosses the placenta.
IgA	Prevents attachment of bacteria and viruses to mucous membranes, does not fix complement. Monomer or dimer. Found in secretions. Picks up secretory component from epithelial cells before secretion.
IgM	Produced in the primary response to an antigen. Fixes complement but does not cross the placenta. Antigen receptor on the surface of B cells. Monomer or pentamer.
IgD	Unclear function. Found on the surface of many B cells and in serum.
IgE	Mediates immediate (type I) hypersensitivity by inducing the release of mediators from mast cells and basophils when exposed to allergen. Mediates immunity to worms.

Ig epitopes

Allotype (polymorphism) = Ig epitope that differs among members of same species. Can be on light chain or heavy chain.

Isotype (IgG, IgA, etc.) = Ig epitope common to a single class of Ig (five classes, determined by heavy chain).

Isotype = Iso (same). Common to same class.

Idiotype (specific for a given Ag) = Ig epitope determined by antigen-binding site.

Idiotype = Idio (unique). Hypervariable region is unique.

Components of immune response

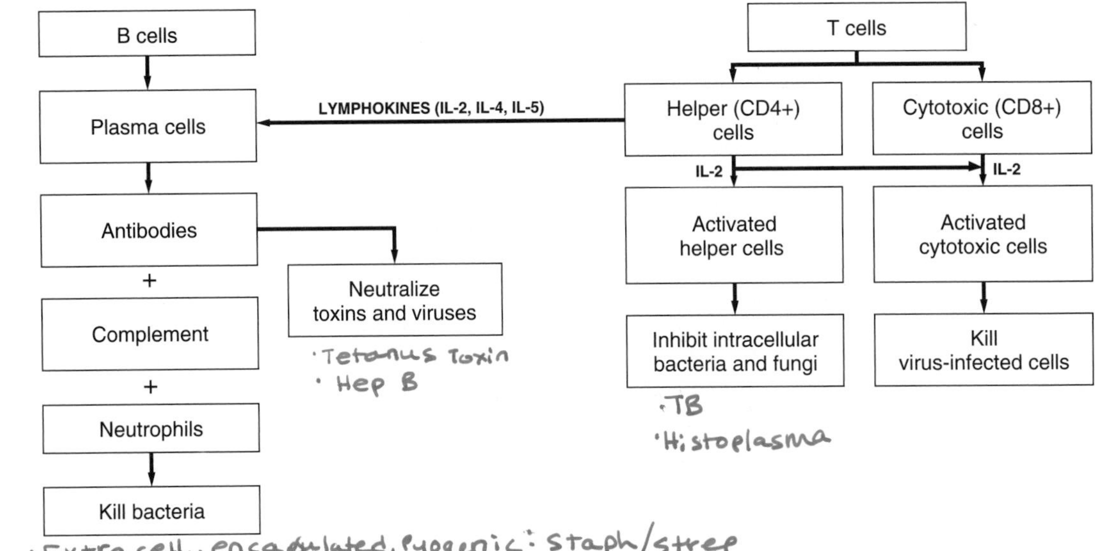

T_H1 cells (produce IL-2 and γ-interferon): activate macrophages (increase killing efficiency of intracellular bacteria) and T_c cells.

T_H2 cells (produce IL-4 and IL-5): help B cells make Ab (B = 2nd letter of alphabet).

Adjuvant definition

Adjuvants are nonspecific stimulators of the immune response but are not immunogenic by themselves. Adjuvants are given with a weak immunogen to enhance response. Human vaccines contain aluminum hydroxide or lipid adjuvants.

Adjuvant = that which aids another.

MHC I and II

MHC = major histocompatibility complex. Consists of 3 class I genes (A, B, C) and 3 class II genes (DP, DQ, DR). All nucleated cells have class I MHC proteins.

Antigen-presenting cells (e.g., macrophages) also have class II MHC proteins.

Class II are the main determinants of organ rejection.

MHC I Ag loading occurs in rER (viral antigens).

MHC II Ag loading occurs in acidified endosome.

Class I = 1 polypeptide, with β_2-microglobulin.

Class II = 2 polypeptides, an α and a β chain.

T-cell glycoproteins

Helper T cells have CD4, which binds to class II MHC on antigen-presenting cells. Cytotoxic T cells have CD8, which binds to class I MHC on virus-infected cells.

Product of CD and MHC = 8. (CD4 × MHC **II** = **8** = CD8 × MHC **I**).

CD3 complex = cluster of polypeptides associated with a T-cell receptor. Important in signal transduction.

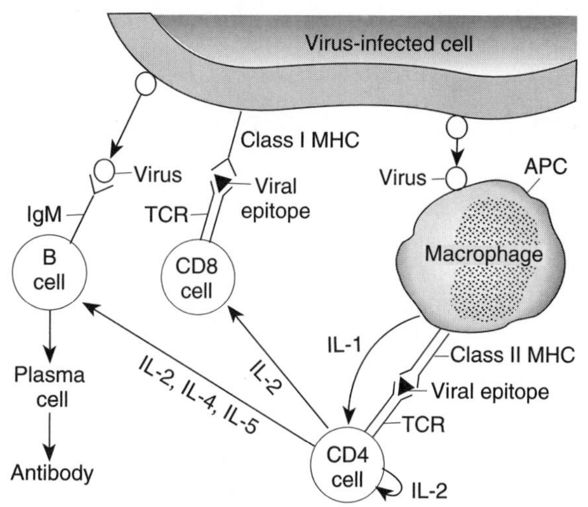

Important cytokines

IL-1
Secreted by macrophages. Stimulates T cells, B cells, neutrophils, fibroblasts, epithelial cells to grow, differentiate, or synthesize specific products. Is an endogenous pyrogen.

IL-2
Secreted by helper T cells. Stimulates growth of helper and cytotoxic T cells.

IL-3
Secreted by activated T cells. Supports the growth and differentiation of bone marrow stem cells. Has a function similar to GM-CSF.

IL-4
Secreted by helper T cells. Promotes growth of B cells. Enhances the synthesis of IgE and IgG.

IL-5
Secreted by helper T cells. Promotes differentiation of B cells. Enhances the synthesis of IgA. Stimulates production and activation of eosinophils.

Gamma interferon
Secreted by helper T cells. Stimulates macrophages.

TNF-α
Secreted by macrophages. ↑ IL-2 receptor synthesis by helper T cells. ↑ B-cell proliferation. Attracts and activates neutrophils.

TNF-β
Secreted by activated T lymphocytes. Functions similar to those of TNF-α.

"Hot T-bone stEAk":
- IL-1: fever **(hot)**
- IL-2: stimulates **T** cells
- IL-3: stimulates **bone** marrow
- IL-4: stimulates Ig**E** production
- IL-5: stimulates Ig**A** production

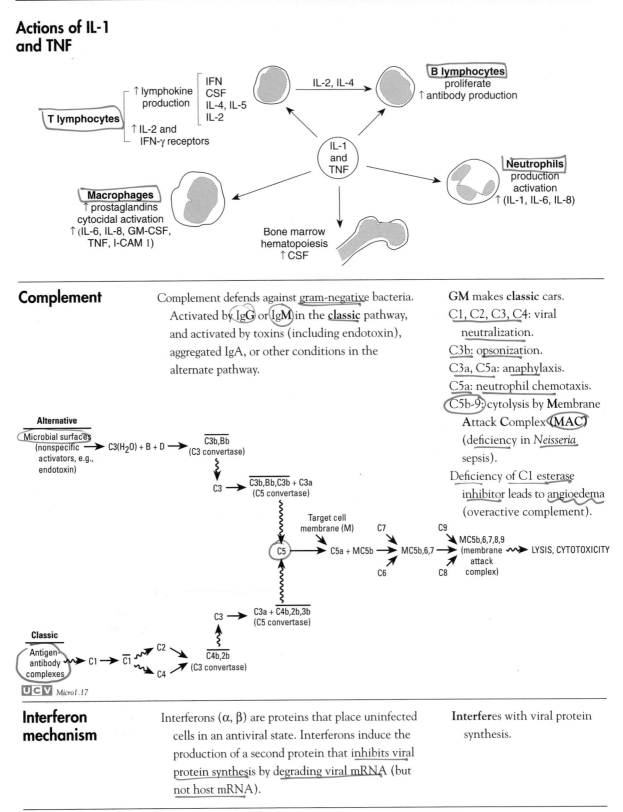

Actions of IL-1 and TNF

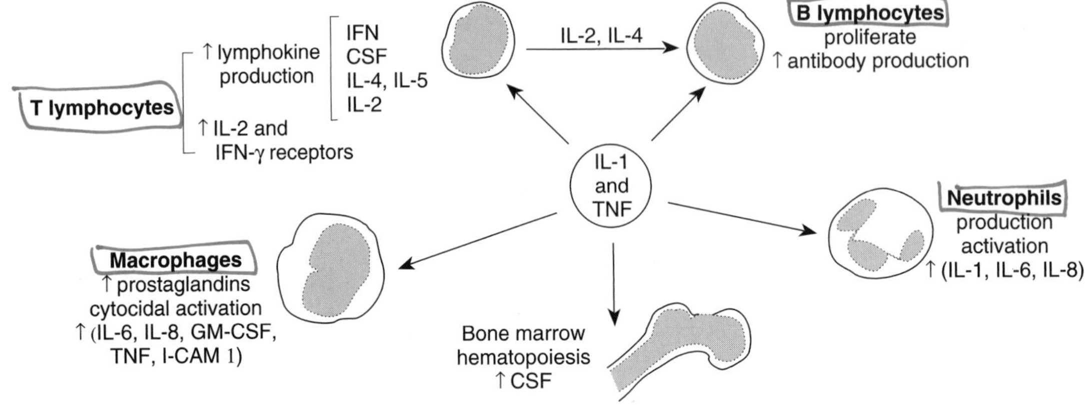

Complement

Complement defends against gram-negative bacteria. Activated by IgG or IgM in the **classic** pathway, and activated by toxins (including endotoxin), aggregated IgA, or other conditions in the alternate pathway.

GM makes **classic** cars.
C1, C2, C3, C4: viral neutralization.
C3b: opsonization.
C3a, C5a: anaphylaxis.
C5a: neutrophil chemotaxis.
C5b-9: cytolysis by **M**embrane **A**ttack **C**omplex (MAC) (deficiency in *Neisseria* sepsis).
Deficiency of C1 esterase inhibitor leads to angioedema (overactive complement).

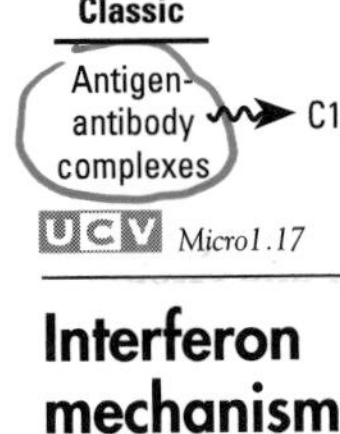

UCV Micro1.17

Interferon mechanism

Interferons (α, β) are proteins that place uninfected cells in an antiviral state. Interferons induce the production of a second protein that inhibits viral protein synthesis by degrading viral mRNA (but not host mRNA).

Interferes with viral protein synthesis.

Hypersensitivity

Type I

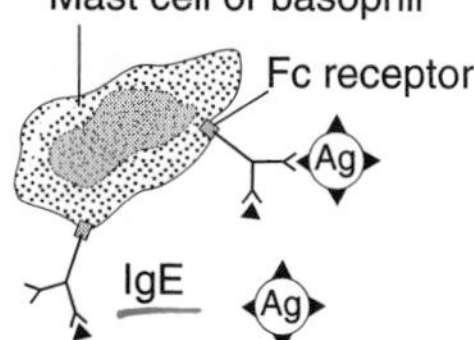

Anaphylactic and atopic: Ag cross-links IgE on presensitized mast cells and basophils, triggering release of vasoactive amines. Reaction develops rapidly after Ag exposure due to preformed Ab. Possible manifestations include anaphylaxis, asthma, or local wheal and flare.

First and **F**ast (anaphylaxis). I, II, and III are all antibody mediated. IV : T helper

Type II

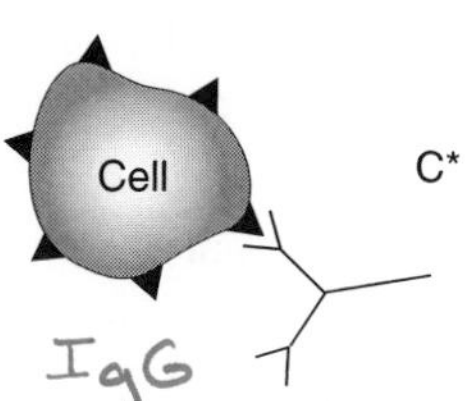

Cytotoxic: IgM, IgG bind to Ag on "enemy" cell, leading to lysis (by complement) or phagocytosis. Examples include autoimmune hemolytic anemia, Rh disease (erythroblastosis fetalis), Goodpasture's syndrome.

Cy-**2**-toxic. Antibody and complement mediated.

Type III

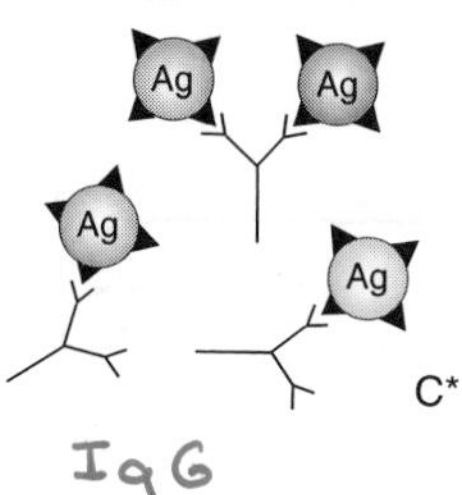

Immune complex: Ag-Ab complexes activate complement, which attracts neutrophils; neutrophils release lysosomal enzymes (e.g., PAN, immune complex GN).

Imagine an immune complex as **three** things stuck together: Ag–Ab–complement. GN RA SLE

Serum sickness: an immune complex disease (type III) in which Abs to the foreign proteins are produced (takes 5 days). Immune complexes form and are deposited in membranes, where they fix complement (leads to tissue damage). More common than Arthus reaction. *Path1.98*

Most serum sickness is now caused by drugs (not serum). Fever, urticaria, arthralgias, proteinuria lymphadenopathy 5–10 days after Ag exposure.

Arthus reaction: a local subacute Ab-mediated hypersensitivity (type III) reaction. Intradermal injection of Ag induces antibodies, which form Ag-Ab complexes in the skin. Characterized by edema, necrosis, and activation of complement.

Ag-Ab complexes cause the Arthus reaction.

Type IV

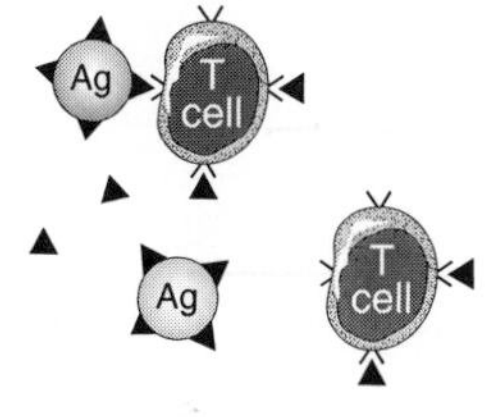

Delayed (cell-mediated) type: Sensitized T lymphocytes encounter antigen and then release lymphokines (leads to macrophage activation). Examples include TB skin test, transplant rejection, contact dermatitis (e.g., poison ivy, poison oak). *Micro1.4*

4th and last = delayed. Cell mediated; therefore, it is not transferable by serum.

C* = complement

ACID =
Anaphylactic and **A**topic (type I)
Cytotoxic (type II)
Immune complex (type III)
Delayed (cell-mediated) (type IV)

UCV

Passive versus active immunity

Active	Induced after exposure to foreign antigens. Slow onset. Long-lasting protection (memory).	After exposure to Tetanus toxin, Botulinum toxin, HBV, or Rabies, patients are given preformed antibodies (passive)— To Be Healed Rapidly.
Passive	Based on receiving preformed antibodies from another host. Rapid onset. Short life span of antibodies.	

Antigen variation

Classic examples:
Bacteria: *Salmonella* (two flagellar variants), *Borrelia* (relapsing fever), *Neisseria gonorrhoeae* (pilus protein).
Virus: influenza (major = shift, minor = drift).
Parasites: trypanosomes (programmed rearrangement).

Some mechanisms for variation include DNA rearrangement and RNA segment rearrangement (e.g., influenza major shift).

Immune deficiencies

Bruton's agammaglobulinemia	B-cell deficiency. X-linked recessive defect in a tyrosine-kinase gene associated with low levels of all classes of immunoglobulins. Associated with recurrent Bacterial infections after 6 months of age, when levels of maternal IgG antibody decline. Occurs in Boys (X-linked). Micro1.21
Thymic aplasia (DiGeorge's syndrome)	T-cell deficiency. Thymus and parathyroids fail to develop owing to failure of development of the 3rd and 4th pharyngeal pouches. Presents with Tetany owing to hypocalcemia. Congenital defects of heart and great vessels. Recurrent viral, fungal, and protozoal infections. Anat.29
Chronic mucocutaneous candidiasis	T-cell dysfunction specifically against *Candida albicans*.
Severe combined immunodeficiency (SCID)	B- and T-cell deficiency. Defect in early stem-cell differentiation. Presents with recurrent viral, bacterial, fungal, and protozoal infections. May have multiple causes (e.g., failure to synthesize class II MHC antigens, defective IL-2 receptors, or adenosine deaminase deficiency). Micro2.24
Wiskott–Aldrich syndrome	B- and T-cell deficiency. Defect in the ability to mount an IgM response to capsular polysaccharides of bacteria. Associated with elevated IgA levels, normal IgE levels, and low IgM levels. Triad of symptoms includes recurrent pyogenic infections, eczema, and thrombocytopenia.
Ataxia–telangiectasia	B- and T-cell deficiency, with associated IgA deficiency. Presents with cerebellar problems (ataxia) and spider angiomas (telangiectasia).
Selective immunoglobulin deficiency	Deficiency in a specific class of immunoglobulins. Possibly due to a defect in isotype switching. Selective IgA deficiency is the most common selective immunoglobulin deficiency. Micro1.20
Chronic granulomatous disease	Phagocyte deficiency. Defect in phagocytosis of neutrophils owing to lack of NADPH oxidase activity or similar enzymes. Presents with marked susceptibility to opportunistic infections with bacteria, especially *S. aureus* and *E. coli*, and *Aspergillus*. Micro1.19
Chédiak–Higashi disease	Autosomal recessive defect in phagocytosis that results from microtubular and lysosomal defects of phagocytic cells. Presents with recurrent pyogenic infections by staphylococci and streptococci. Micro1.18, Micro2.27
Job's syndrome	Neutrophils fail to respond to chemotactic stimuli. Associated with high levels of IgE. Presents with recurrent cold staphylococcal abscesses.

UCV

Autoantibodies

Autoantibody	Disease
Anti-nuclear antibodies (ANA)	Systemic lupus
Anti-ds DNA	Specific for systemic lupus
Anti-histone	Drug-induced lupus
Anti-IgM (rheumatoid factor)	Rheumatoid arthritis
Anti-neutrophil	Vasculitis
Anti-centromere	Scleroderma (CREST)
Anti-mitochondria	Primary biliary cirrhosis
Anti-gliadin	Celiac disease
Anti-basement membrane	Goodpasture's syndrome
Anti-epithelial cell	Pemphigus vulgaris

Transplant rejection

Hyperacute rejection—Antibody mediated due to the presence of preformed anti-donor antibodies in the transplant recipient. Occurs within minutes after transplantation.

Acute rejection—Cell mediated due to cytotoxic T lymphocytes reacting against foreign MHCs. Occurs weeks after transplantation. Reversible with immunosuppressants such as cyclosporin and OKT3.

Chronic rejection—Antibody-mediated vascular damage (fibrinoid necrosis); occurs months to years after transplantation. Irreversible.

HIGH-YIELD FACTS

Microbiology

NOTES

SECTION II

Pathology

"The begining of health is to know the disease."
—Spanish Proverb

Questions dealing with this discipline are difficult to prepare for because of sheer volume of material. Review the basic principles and hallmark characteristics of each key disease. Given the increasingly clinical orientation of Step 1, it is no longer enough to know the "trigger words" or key associations of certain diseases (e.g., café-au-lait macules and neurofibromatosis); you must also know the clinical descriptions of these findings.

With the increasingly clinical slant of the USMLE Step 1, it is also important to review the classic presenting signs and symptoms of diseases as well as their associated laboratory findings. Delve into the signs, symptoms, and pathophysiology of the major diseases having a high prevalence in the US (e.g., alcoholism, diabetes, hypertension, heart failure, ischemic heart disease, infectious disease). Be prepared to think one step beyond the simple diagnosis to treatment or complication.

The examination includes a number of color photomicrographs and photographs of gross specimens, which are presented in the setting of a brief clinical history. However, read the question and the choices carefully before looking at the illustration, because the history will help you identify the pathologic process. Flip through your illustrated pathology textbook, color atlases, and appropriate web sites in order to look at the pictures in the days before the exam. Pay attention to potential clues such as age, sex, ethnicity, occupation, specialized lab tests, and activity.

These abstracted case vignettes are designed to demonstrate the thought processes necessary to answer multistep clinical reasoning questions.

- Patient has multiple fractures, anemia, cranial nerve deficits → in which of the following cell types is there a defect? → osteoclasts (e.g., osteopetrosis).
- 35-year-old man has high blood pressure in arms and low pressure in legs → what is the diagnosis? → coarctation of the aorta.
- Woman presents with diffuse goiter and hyperthyroidism → what are the expected values of TSH and thyroid hormones? → low TSH and high thyroid hormones.
- Patient exhibits an extended expiratory phase → what is the disease process? → obstructive lung disease.
- Woman presents with headache, visual disturbance, galactorrhea, and amenorrhea → what is the diagnosis? → prolactinoma. *Path1.37*
- Baby has foul-smelling stool and recurrent pulmonary infections → what is the diagnosis, and what test is used? → cystic fibrosis, chloride sweat test.
- Obese woman presents with hirsutism and increased levels of serum testosterone → what is the diagnosis? → polycystic ovarian syndrome.
- Man presents with extensive destruction of knees, subcutaneous nodules, and exquisite pain in the metatarsophalangeal joint → biopsy shows needle-like crystals → what is the diagnosis? → gouty arthritis.
- 48-year-old female with progressive lethargy and cold intolerance → what is the diagnosis? → hypothyroidism. *Path1.33*
- Patient with elevated serum cortisol levels undergoes dexamethasone suppression test. One milligram of dexamethasone does not decrease cortisol levels; 8 mg does → what is the diagnosis? → pituitary tumor.
- During a game, a young basketball player collapses and dies immediately → what type of cardiac disease? → hypertrophic cardiomyopathy. *Path1.10*
- Child has been anemic since birth. Splenectomy would result in increased hematocrit in what disease? → spherocytosis.
- 43-year-old man experiences dizziness and tinnitus. CT shows enlarged internal acoustic meatus → what is the diagnosis? → schwannoma.
- Child exhibits weakness and enlarged calves → what is the disease, and how is it inherited? → Duchenne's muscular dystrophy, X-linked recessive.
- 25-year-old female presents with sudden uniocular vision loss and slightly slurred speech. She has a history of weakness and paresthesias that have resolved → what is the diagnosis? → MS.
- Teenager presents with nephritic syndrome and hearing loss → what is his disease? → Alport's syndrome.
- Tall, thin male teenager has abrupt-onset dyspnea and left-sided chest pain. There is hyperresonant percussion on the affected side, and breath sounds are diminished. → what is the diagnosis? → pneumothorax.
- Young man is concerned about his wife's inability to conceive and her recurrent URIs. She has dextrocardia → which of her proteins is defective? → dynein (Kartagener's).

UCV

- 55-year-old man who is a smoker and a heavy drinker presents with a new cough and flu-like symptoms → Gram stain shows no organisms; silver stain of sputum shows gram-negative rods → what is the diagnosis? → *Legionella*.
- Patient has a stroke after incurring multiple long bone fractures in MVA trauma → what caused the infarct? → fat emboli.
- 25-year-old woman presents with a low-grade fever and a rash across her nose that gets worse when she is out in the sun → you are concerned about what disease? → SLE.
- 50-year-old man complains of diarrhea; on physical exam his face seems plethoric and a heart murmur is detected → what is the diagnosis? → carcinoid syndrome.
- Elderly woman presents with a headache and jaw pain → labs show elevated ESR → what is the diagnosis? → temporal arteritis.
- Pregnant woman at 16 weeks of gestation presents with an atypically large abdomen → what abnormality might be seen on blood test, and what is the disorder? → high hCG; hydatidiform mole.
- 80-year-old man presents with a systolic crescendo-decrescendo murmur → what is the most likely cause? → aortic stenosis.
- Woman of short stature presents with shortened 4th and 5th metacarpals → what endocrine disorder comes to mind? → Albright's hereditary osteodystrophy, or pseudohypoparathyroidism.
- After a stressful life event, 30-year-old man has diarrhea and blood per rectum; intestinal biopsy shows transmural inflammation → what is the diagnosis? → Crohn's.
- Young man presents with mental deterioration and tremors. He has brown pigmentation in a ring around the periphery of his cornea and altered LFTs → what treatment should he receive? → penicillamine for Wilson's disease.
- Patient presents with signs of vitamin B_{12} deficiency → why not give folate? → masks signs of neural damage.
- 10-year-old child "spaces out" in class (e.g., stops talking midsentence and then continues as if nothing had happened). During spells, there is slight quivering of lips → what is the diagnosis? → absence seizure.

PATHOLOGY—HIGH-YIELD GLOSSY MATERIAL

- Gross photograph of abdominal aorta with aneurysm → what is the most likely process? → atherosclerosis.
- Gross photograph of hydatidiform mole ("bunch of grapes") → high levels of what substance are present? → hCG.
- Gross photograph of focally hemorrhagic small intestine of weight lifter → what is the process responsible for this? → strangulation of a hernia.
- Chest x-ray shows collapse of middle lobe of right lung; recurrent pneumonia and growth in bronchus → what is the diagnosis? → bronchogenic carcinoma.
- Middle-aged woman with intermittent syncope has a mass removed from the right atrium → H&E shows wispy, mucus-like tissue → what is the diagnosis? → myxoma.
- Chest x-ray shows pneumothorax → what are the clinical findings? → pleuritic chest pain.
- 1-year-old baby presents with big red splotch on face → what is the likely course of this lesion? → regression vs. Sturge–Weber.

PATHOLOGY—HIGH-YIELD GLOSSY MATERIAL (*Countinued*)

- Gross photograph of lung with caseous necrosis → what is the diagnosis? → TB.
- H&E of lung biopsy from plumber shows elongated structures in tissue (ferruginous bodies) → what is the diagnosis? increased risk for what? → asbestosis; malignant mesothelioma.
- H&E of glomerulus → looks like Kimmelstiel–Wilson nodules → lesion is indicative of what disease? → diabetes mellitus.
- H&E of granuloma → what is activated? → macrophages.
- Softball player develops back pain and lost sensation in a dermatome of the leg → what is the diagnosis? → herniated lumbar disk.
- Karyotype with three 21 chromosomes → what features would patient have? → flat facies, simian crease, epicanthal folds.
- Gross photograph of polycystic kidneys in adult male → what is the mode of inheritance? → autosomal dominant.
- Patient with anemia, hypercalcemia, and bony pain on palpation; bone marrow biopsy shows lots of plasma cells → what is the diagnosis? → multiple myeloma.

PATHOLOGY—HIGH-YIELD TOPICS

Congenital

1. Maternal complications of birth (e.g., Sheehan's syndrome, puerperal infection).
2. Failure to thrive: common causes.
3. Causes of kernicterus (hemolytic disease of the newborn).

Neoplasia

1. Bone and cartilage tumors (e.g., osteosarcoma, giant cell tumor, Ewing's sarcoma).
2. Clinical features of lymphomas (Burkitt's and other non-Hodgkin's lymphomas).
3. Risk factors for common carcinomas (e.g., lung, breast).
4. Chemical carcinogens (e.g., vinyl chloride, nitrosamines, aflatoxin) and mechanisms of carcinogenesis (e.g., initiator vs. promoter).
5. Malignancies associated with pneumoconioses (e.g., asbestos, silicosis).
6. AIDS-associated neoplasms (Kaposi's sarcoma, B-cell lymphoma).
7. Pituitary tumors (e.g., prolactinoma) and other sellar lesions (e.g., craniopharyngioma).
8. Tumors of the mouth, pharynx, and larynx (e.g., vocal cord tumors in smokers).
9. Modes of spread of certain cancers (e.g., transitional cell carcinoma).
10. Clinical features of leukemias (e.g., demographics, pathology, prognosis).

Nervous System

1. Hydrocephalus: types (e.g., communicating, obstructive), sequelae.
2. CNS manifestations of viral infections (e.g., HIV, HSV).
3. Spinal muscular atrophies (e.g., Werdnig–Hoffmann disease, ALS).

Rheumatic/Autoimmune

1. Transplant rejection (hyperacute, acute, chronic).
2. Differences between rheumatoid arthritis and graft-versus-host disease.
3. Psoriasis: skin/joint involvement.
4. Autoantibodies (e.g., antimicrosomal) and disease associations.

Vascular/Hematology

1. Common hematologic diseases (e.g., thrombocytopenia, clotting factor deficiencies, lymphoma, leukemia).
2. Valvular heart disease (e.g., mitral stenosis, mitral regurgitation, aortic stenosis, aortic regurgitation, tricuspid regurgitation), including clinical presentation, associated murmurs, and cardiac catheterization results.
3. Thoracic and abdominal aortic aneurysms: similarities and differences.
4. Polycythemia: primary (polycythemia vera) and secondary (e.g., hypoxia) causes, clinical manifestations (e.g., pruritus, fatigue).

General

1. Common clinical features of AIDS (e.g., CNS, pulmonary, GI, dermatologic manifestations).
2. Dermatologic manifestations of systemic disease (e.g., neoplasia, inflammatory bowel disease, meningococcemia, systemic lupus erythematosus).
3. Geriatric pathology: diseases common in the elderly, normal physiologic changes with age.
4. Renal failure: acute versus chronic, features of uremia.
5. Acid–base disturbances, including renal tubular acidosis.
6. Wound repair.
7. Dehydration (e.g., hyponatremic vs. isotonic vs. hypernatremic), including appropriate treatment.
8. Gynecologic pathology (e.g., menstrual disorders).
9. Cell injury and death.
10. Malabsorption (e.g., celiac sprue, bacterial overgrowth, disaccharidase deficiency).

Common congenital malformations

1. Heart defects (congenital rubella)
2. Hypospadias
3. Cleft lip with or without cleft palate
4. Congenital hip dislocation
5. Spina bifida
6. Anencephaly
7. Pyloric stenosis (associated with polyhydramnios); projectile vomiting

Neural tube defects (spina bifida and anencephaly) are associated with increased levels of α-FP (in the amniotic fluid and maternal serum). Their incidence is decreased with maternal folate ingestion during pregnancy.

Congenital heart disease

R-to-L shunts (early cyanosis) "blue babies"

1. **T**etralogy of Fallot (most common cause of early cyanosis)
2. **T**ransposition of great vessels
3. **T**runcus arteriosus

The **3 T**'s:
Tetralogy
Transposition
Truncus
Children may squat to ↑ venous return.

L-to-R shunts (late cyanosis) "blue kids"

1. VSD (most common congenital cardiac anomaly)
2. ASD
3. PDA (close with indomethacin)

Frequency: VSD > ASD > PDA
↑ pulmonary resistance due to arteriolar thickening.
→ progressive pulmonary hypertension.

Tetralogy of Fallot

1. **P**ulmonary stenosis
2. **R**VH
3. **O**verriding aorta (overrides the VSD)
4. **V**SD

This leads to early cyanosis from a R-to-L shunt across the VSD. On x-ray, boot-shaped heart due to RVH. Patients suffer "cyanotic spells."

The cause of tetralogy of Fallot is anterosuperior displacement of the infundibular septum.

PROVe

Anat.7

Transposition of great vessels

Aorta leaves RV (anterior) and pulmonary trunk leaves LV (posterior) → separation of systemic and pulmonary circulations. Not compatible with life unless a shunt is present to allow adequate mixing of blood (e.g., VSD, PDA, or patent foramen ovale).

Without surgical correction, most infants die within the first months of life. Common congenital heart disease in offspring of diabetic mothers.

Coarctation of aorta

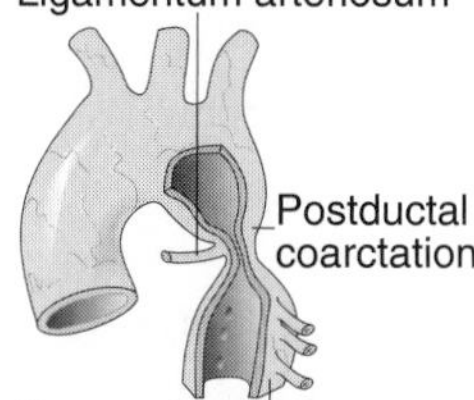

Infantile type: aortic stenosis proximal to insertion of ductus arteriosus (preductal).

Adult type: stenosis is distal to ductus arteriosus (postductal). Associated with notching of the ribs, hypertension in upper extremities, weak pulses in lower extremities.

UCV Anat.4

Affects males:females 3:1.

Check femoral pulses on physical exam.

INfantile: **IN** close to the heart. (Associated with Turner's syndrome.) **AD**ult: **D**istal to **D**uctus.

Patent ductus arteriosus

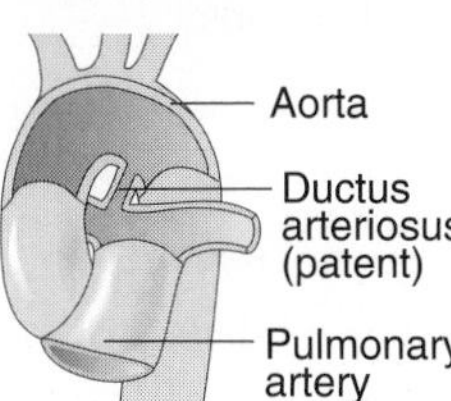

In fetal period, shunt is R-to-L (normal). In neonatal period, lung resistance decreases and shunt becomes L-to-R with subsequent RV hypertrophy and failure (abnormal). Associated with a continuous, "machine-like" murmur. Patency is maintained by PGE synthesis and low oxygen tension.

UCV Anat.6

Indomethacin is used to close a PDA. PGE is used to keep a PDA open, which may be necessary to sustain life in conditions such as transposition of the great vessels.

Eisenmenger's syndrome

UCV Path3.4

Uncorrected VSD, ASD, or PDA leads to progressive pulmonary hypertension. As pulmonary resistance increases, the shunt changes from L → R to R → L, which causes late cyanosis (clubbing and polycythemia).

Autosomal trisomies

Down's syndrome (trisomy 21), 1:700	Most common chromosomal disorder and cause of congenital mental retardation. Findings: mental retardation, flat facial profile, prominent epicanthal folds, simian crease, duodenal atresia, congenital heart disease (most common malformation is endocardial cushion defect), Alzheimer's disease in affected individuals ≥ 35 years old, associated with an increased risk of ALL. Ninety-five percent of cases are due to meiotic nondisjunction of homologous chromosomes, 4% of cases are due to Robertsonian translocation, and 1% of cases are due to Down mosaicism. Associated with advanced maternal age (from 1:1500 in women under 20 to 1:25 in women over 45).	Drinking age (21)
Edwards' syndrome (trisomy 18), 1:8000	Findings: severe mental retardation, rocker bottom feet, low-set ears, micrognathia, congenital heart disease, clenched hands (flexion of fingers), prominent occiput. Death usually occurs within 1 year of birth.	Election age (18)
Patau's syndrome (trisomy 13), 1:6000	Findings: severe mental retardation, microphthalmia, microcephaly, cleft lip/palate, abnormal forebrain structures, polydactyly, congenital heart disease. Death usually occurs within 1 year of birth.	Puberty (13)

UCV Path2.2

Genetic gender disorders

Klinefelter's syndrome [male] (XXY), 1:850 *Path2.4, Bio.23*	Testicular atrophy, eunuchoid body shape, tall, long extremities, gynecomastia, female hair distribution. Presence of inactivated X chromosome (Barr body).	One of the most common causes of hypogonadism in males.
Turner's syndrome [female] (XO), 1:3000 *Path2.6*	Short stature, ovarian dysgenesis, webbing of neck, coarctation of the aorta, most common cause of primary amenorrhea. No Barr body.	"Hugs & kisses" (XO) from Tina **Turner** (female).
Double Y males [male] (XYY), 1:1000	Phenotypically normal, very tall, severe acne, antisocial behavior (seen in 1–2% of XYY males).	Observed with increased frequency among inmates of penal institutions.

UCV

Pseudohermaphroditism

	Disagreement between the phenotypic (external genitalia) and gonadal (testes vs. ovaries) sex.	Gender identity is based on external genitalia and sex of upbringing.
Female pseudo-hermaphrodite (XX)	Ovaries present, but external genitalia are virilized or ambiguous. Due to excessive and inappropriate exposure to androgenic steroids during early gestation (i.e., congenital adrenal hyperplasia or exogenous administration of androgens during pregnancy).	
Male pseudo-hermaphrodite (XY)	Testes present, but external genitalia are female or ambiguous. Most common form is testicular feminization (**androgen insensitivity**), which results from a mutation in the androgen receptor gene (X-linked recessive); blind-end vagina.	

Cri-du-chat syndrome

Congenital deletion of short arm of chromosome 5 (46 XX or XY, 5p–).

Findings: microcephaly, severe mental retardation, high-pitched crying/mewing, epicanthal folds, cardiac abnormalities.

Cri-du-chat = cry of the cat

Fragile X syndrome

X-linked defect affecting the methylation and expression of the *FMR 1* gene. It is the second most common cause of genetic mental retardation (the most common cause is Down's syndrome). Associated with macro-orchidism (enlarged testes), long face with a large jaw, large everted ears, and autism.

Triplet repeat disorder $(CGG)_n$ that may show genetic anticipation.

UCV *Bio.61*

Duchenne's and Becker's muscular dystrophies

Duchenne's MD is an X-linked recessive muscular disease featuring a deleted dystrophin gene, leading to accelerated muscle breakdown. Onset before 5 years of age. Weakness begins in pelvic girdle muscles and progresses superiorly. Pseudohypertrophy of calf muscles due to fibro-fatty replacement of muscle; cardiac myopathy. The use of Gower's maneuver, requiring assistance of the upper extremities to stand up, is characteristic but not specific (indicates proximal lower limb weakness). Becker's muscular dystrophy is due to dystrophin gene mutations (not deletions) and is less severe. Diagnosis by muscle biopsy.

UCV *Bio.55*

Cystic fibrosis

Autosomal recessive defect in CFTR gene on chromosome 7. Defective Cl^- channel → secretion of abnormally thick mucus that plugs lungs, pancreas, and liver → recurrent pulmonary infections (*Pseudomonas* species and *Staphylococcus aureus*), chronic bronchitis, bronchiectasis, pancreatic insufficiency (malabsorption and steatorrhea), meconium ileus in newborns. Increased concentration of Cl^- ions in sweat test is diagnostic.

Infertility in males. Fat-soluble vitamin deficiencies (A, D, E, K). Can present as failure to thrive in infancy.

UCV Path2.1

Autosomal dominant diseases

Adult polycystic kidney disease Path2.84 — Bilateral massive enlargement of kidneys due to multiple large cysts. Patients present with pain, hematuria, hypertension, progressive renal failure. Ninety percent of cases are due to mutation in APKD1 (chromosome 16). Associated with polycystic liver disease, **berry aneurysms,** mitral valve prolapse. Juvenile form is recessive.

Familial hypercholesterolemia — Elevated LDL owing to defective or absent LDL receptor. Heterozygotes (1 in 500) have cholesterol ≈ 300 mg/dL. Homozygotes (very rare) have cholesterol ≈ 700+ mg/dL, severe atherosclerotic disease early in life, and tendon xanthomas (classically in the Achilles tendon). Myocardial infarction may develop before age 20.

Marfan's syndrome Path2.5 — Fibrillin gene mutation → connective tissue disorders.

- Skeletal abnormalities: tall with long extremities, hyperextensive joints, and long, tapering fingers and toes
- Cardiovascular: cystic medial necrosis of aorta → aortic incompetence and dissecting aortic aneurysms. Floppy mitral valve.
- Ocular: subluxation of lenses.

Von Recklinghausen's disease (NFT1) — Findings: café-au-lait spots, neural tumors, Lisch nodules (pigmented iris hamartomas). On long arm of chromosome 17; 17 letters in von Recklinghausen.

Von Hippel–Lindau disease Path2.28 — Findings: hemangioblastomas of retina/cerebellum/medulla; about half of affected individuals develop multiple bilateral renal cell carcinomas and other tumors. Associated with deletion of VHL gene (tumor suppressor) on chromosome 3 (3p).

Huntington's disease — Findings: depression, progressive dementia, choreiform movements, caudate atrophy and decreased levels of GABA and acetylcholine in the brain. Symptoms manifest in affected individuals between the ages of 20 and 50. Gene located on chromosome 4; triplet repeat disorder.

Familial Adenomatous Polyposis Path1.45 — Colon becomes covered with adenomatous polyps after puberty. Features: deletion on chromosome Five; Autosomal dominant inheritance; Positively will get colon cancer (100% without resection).

Hereditary spherocytosis — Spheroid erythrocytes; hemolytic anemia; increased MCHC. Splenectomy is curative.

UCV

Autosomal-recessive diseases

Cystic fibrosis, albinism, α_1-antitrypsin deficiency, phenylketonuria, thalassemias, sickle cell anemias, glycogen storage diseases, mucopolysaccharidoses (except Hunter's), sphingolipidoses (except Fabry's), infant polycystic kidney disease, hemochromatosis.

X-linked recessive disorders

Fragile X, Duchenne's muscular dystrophy, hemophilia A and B, Fabry's, G6PD deficiency, Hunter's syndrome, ocular albinism, Lesch–Nyhan syndrome, Bruton's agammaglobulinemia, Wiskott–Aldrich syndrome.

Female carriers of x-linked recessive disorders are rarely affected because of random inactivation of x chromosomes in each cell.

Neural tube defects

Associated with low folic acid intake during pregnancy. Elevated α-fetoprotein in amniotic fluid.

Spina bifida occulta: failure of bony spinal canal to close, but no structural herniation. Usually seen at lower vertebral levels.

Meningocele: meninges herniate through spinal canal defect.

Meningomyelocele: meninges and spinal cord herniate through spinal canal defect.

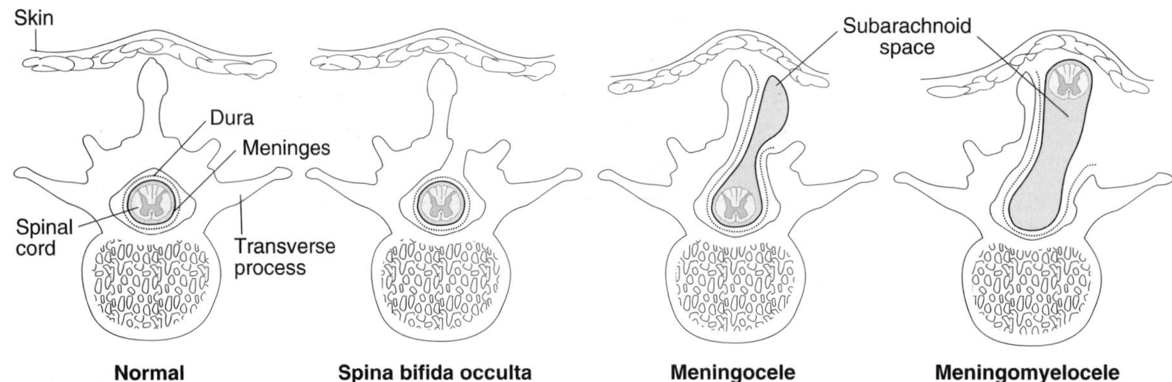

UCV Anat.51

Teratogens

Most susceptible in 3rd–8th week of pregnancy.

Examples	Effects
ACE inhibitors	Renal damage
Cocaine	Abnormal fetal development and fetal addiction
DES	Vaginal clear cell adenocarcinoma
Iodide	Congenital goiter or hypothyroidism
13-cis-retinoic acid	Extremely high risk for birth defects
Thalidomide	Limb defects
Warfarin, x-rays	Multiple anomalies

Fetal infections can also cause congenital malformations. (Other medications contraindicated in pregnancy are shown in the pharmacology section.)

Fetal alcohol syndrome

Newborns of mothers who consumed significant amounts of alcohol (teratogen) during pregnancy (highest risk at 3–8 weeks) have a higher incidence of congenital abnormalities, including pre- and post-natal developmental retardation, microcephaly, facial abnormalities, limb dislocation, and heart and lung fistulas. Mechanism may include inhibition of cell migration. The number one cause of congenital malformations in the United States.

UCV Pharm.50

Neoplastic progression

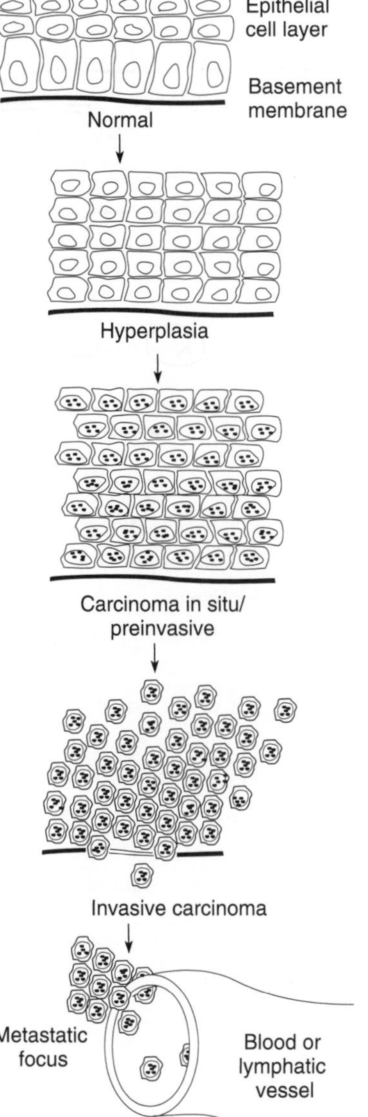

- Normal cells with basal → apical differentiation

- Cells have ↑ in number - **hyperplasia**
- Abnormal proliferation of cells with loss of size, shape, and orientation - **dysplasia**

- **In situ carcinoma**
- Neoplastic cells have not invaded basement membrane
- High nuclear/cytoplasmic ratio and clumped chromatin

- Cells have invaded basement membrane using **collagenases** and **hydrolases**
- Will metastasize if they reach a blood or lymphatic vessel

Metastasis - spread to distant organ

- Must survive immune attack
- "Seed and soil" theory of metastasis
  - Seed = tumor embolus
  - Soil = target organ—liver, lungs, bone, brain ...

-plasia definitions

Hyperplasia = increase in number of cells (reversible).

Metaplasia = one adult cell type is replaced by another (reversible). Often secondary to irritation and/or environmental exposure (e.g., squamous metaplasia in trachea and bronchi of smokers).

Dysplasia = abnormal growth with loss of cellular orientation, shape, and size in comparison to normal tissue maturation, commonly preneoplastic (reversible).

Anaplasia = abnormal cells lacking differentiation; like primitive cells of same tissue, often equated with undifferentiated malignant neoplasms. Tumor giant cells may be formed.

Neoplasia = a clonal proliferation of cells that is uncontrolled and excessive.

Tumor grade versus stage

Grade: Histologic appearance of tumor. Usually graded I–IV based on degree of differentiation and number of mitoses per high-power field.

Stage: Based on site and size of primary lesion, spread to regional lymph nodes, presence of metastases.

Stage has more prognostic value than grade.

TNM staging system:

T = size of **T**umor
N = **N**ode involvement
M = **M**etastases

Tumor nomenclature

Cell type	Benign	Malignant
Epithelium	Adenoma, papilloma	Adenocarcinoma, papillary carcinoma
Mesenchyme		
Blood cells		Leukemia, lymphoma
Blood vessels	Hemangioma	Angiosarcoma
Smooth muscle	Leiomyoma	Leiomyosarcoma
Skeletal muscle	Rhabdomyoma	Rhabdomyosarcoma
Bone	Osteoma	Osteosarcoma
More than one cell type	Mature teratoma	Immature teratoma

Conditions associated with neoplasms

Condition	Neoplasm
1. **Down's** syndrome	1. **A**cute **L**ymphoblastic **L**eukemia. "We will **ALL** go **DOWN** together."
2. Xeroderma pigmentosum	2. Squamous cell and basal cell carcinomas of skin
3. Chronic atrophic gastritis, pernicious anemia, postsurgical gastric remnants	3. Gastric adenocarcinoma
4. Tuberous sclerosis (facial angiofibroma, seizures, mental retardation)	4. Astrocytoma and cardiac rhabdomyoma
5. Actinic keratosis	5. Squamous cell carcinoma of skin
6. Barrett's esophagus (chronic GI reflux)	6. Esophageal adenocarcinoma
7. Plummer–Vinson syndrome (atrophic glossitis, esophageal webs, anemia; all due to iron deficiency)	7. Squamous cell carcinoma of esophagus
8. Cirrhosis (alcoholic, hepatitis B or C)	8. Hepatocellular carcinoma
9. Ulcerative colitis	9. Colonic adenocarcinoma
10. Paget's disease of bone	10. Secondary osteosarcoma and fibrosarcoma
11. Immunodeficiency states	11. Malignant lymphomas
12. AIDS	12. Aggressive malignant lymphomas and Kaposi's sarcoma
13. Autoimmune diseases (e.g., Hashimoto's thyroiditis, myasthenia gravis)	13. Benign and malignant thymomas
14. Acanthosis nigricans (hyperpigmentation and epidermal thickening)	14. Visceral malignancy (stomach, lung, breast, uterus)

Oncogenes

Gain of function.

Gene	Associated tumor
c-myc	Burkitt's lymphoma
bcl-2	Follicular and undifferentiated lymphomas (inhibits apoptosis)
erb-B2	Breast, ovarian, and gastric carcinomas
ras	Colon carcinoma

Tumor suppressor genes

Loss of function; both alleles must be lost for expression of disease.

Gene	Chromosome	Associated tumor
Rb	13q	Retinoblastoma, osteosarcoma
BRCA-1&2	17q, 13q	Breast and ovarian cancer
p53	17p	Most human cancers, Li–Fraumeni syndrome

Tumor markers

Marker	Associated tumors
PSA, prostatic acid phosphatase	Prostatic carcinoma
CEA	Carcinoembryonic antigen. Very nonspecific but produced by ~70% of colorectal and pancreatic cancers; also by gastric and breast carcinomas.
α-fetoprotein	Normally made by fetus. Hepatocellular carcinomas. Nonseminomatous germ cell tumors of the testis (e.g., yolk sac tumor).
β-hCG	Hydatidiform moles, Choriocarcinomas, and Gestational trophoblastic tumors.
α_1-antitrypsin	Liver and yolk sac tumors.
CA-125	Ovarian, malignant epithelial tumors.
S-100	Melanoma, neural tumors, astrocytomas.
Alkaline phosphatase	Metastases to bone, obstructive biliary disease, Paget's disease of bone.

Tumor markers should not be used as the primary tool for cancer diagnosis. They may be used to confirm diagnosis, to monitor for tumor recurrence, and to monitor response to therapy.

Oncogenic viruses

Virus	Associated cancer
HTLV-1	Adult T-cell leukemia
HBV, HCV	Hepatocellular carcinoma
EBV	Burkitt's lymphoma, nasopharyngeal carcinoma
HPV	Cervical carcinoma, penile/anal carcinoma
HHV 8 (Kaposi's sarcoma–associated herpesvirus)	Kaposi's sarcoma

Chemical Carcinogens

Toxin	Affected Organ
Aflatoxins, vinyl chloride	Liver
Nitrosamines	Esophagus, stomach
Asbestos	Lung (mesothelioma)
Arsenic	Skin (squamous cell)

Local effects of tumors	Local effect	Cause
	Mass	Tissue lump or tumor.
	Nonhealing ulcer	Destruction of epithelial surfaces (e.g., stomach, colon, mouth, bronchus).
	Hemorrhage	From ulcerated area or eroded vessel.
	Pain	Any site with sensory nerve endings. Tumors in brain are initially painless.
	Seizures	Tumor mass in brain.
	Obstruction	Of bronchus → pneumonia. Of biliary tree → jaundice. Of left colon → constipation.
	Perforation	Of ulcer in viscera → peritonitis, free air.
	Bone destruction	Pathologic fracture, collapse of bone.
	Inflammation	Of serosal surface → pleural effusion, pericardial effusion, ascites.
	Space-occupying lesion	Raised intracranial pressure with brain neoplasms. Anemia due to bone marrow replacement.
	Localized loss of sensory or motor function	Compression or destruction of nerve (e.g., recurrent laryngeal nerve by lung or thyroid cancer, with hoarseness).
	Edema	Venous or lymphatic obstruction.

Prostatic adenocarcinoma

Common in men over age 50. Arises most often from the posterior lobe (peripheral zone) of the prostate gland and is most frequently diagnosed by digital rectal examination (hard nodule) and prostate biopsy. Prostatic acid phosphatase and prostate-specific antigen (PSA) are useful tumor markers. Osteoblastic metastases in bone may develop in late stages, as indicated by an increase in serum alkaline phosphatase and PSA.

UCV Path2.95

Skin cancer

Squamous cell carcinoma	Very common. Associated with excessive exposure to sunlight. Commonly appear on hands and face. Locally invasive, but rarely metastasizes. Anat.32	Actinic keratosis is a precursor to squamous cell carcinoma. Path1.20 Keratin "pearls." Arsenic exposure.
Basal cell carcinoma	Most common in sun-exposed areas of body. Locally invasive, but almost never metastasizes. Gross pathology: pearly papules. Path1.21	Basal cell tumors have "palisading" nuclei.
Melanoma	Common tumor with significant risk of metastasis. Associated with sunlight exposure. Incidence increasing. Depth of tumor correlates with risk of metastasis. Path1.23	Increased risk in fair-skinned persons. Dysplastic nevus is a precursor to melanoma. → Mole

UCV

Metastasis to brain

Primary tumors that metastasize to brain: Lung, Breast, Skin (melanoma), Kidney (renal cell carcinoma), GI. Overall, approximately 50% of brain tumors are from metastases.

Lots of Bad Stuff Kills Glia

UCV Path2.19

HIGH-YIELD FACTS

Pathology

Metastasis to liver	The liver and lung are the most common sites of metastasis after the regional lymph nodes. Primary tumors that metastasize to the liver: Colon > Stomach > Pancreas > Breast > Lung.	Metastases >> 1° liver tumors. Cancer Sometimes Penetrates Benign Liver.
UCV Path1.65		
Metastasis to bone	These primary tumors metastasize to bone: **K**idney, **T**hyroid, **T**estes, **L**ung, **P**rostate, **B**reast. Metastasis from breast and prostate are most common. Metastatic bone tumors are far more common than 1° bone tumors.	**K**iller **T**umors **T**hat **L**ove **P**enetrating **B**one Lung = Lytic Prostate = blastic Breast = Both lytic and blastic

Paraneoplastic effects of tumors

Neoplasm	Causes	Effect
Small cell lung carcinoma	ACTH or ACTH-like peptide.	Cushing's syndrome
Small cell lung carcinoma and intracranial neoplasms	ADH or ANP.	SIADH
Squamous cell lung carcinoma, renal cell carcinoma, breast carcinoma, multiple myeloma, and bone metastasis (lysed bone)	PTH-related peptide, TGF-α, TNF-α, IL-2.	Hypercalcemia
Renal cell carcinoma	Erythropoietin.	Polycythemia
Thymoma, bronchogenic carcinoma	Antibodies against presynaptic Ca^{2+} channels at NMJ.	Lambert–Eaton syndrome
Various neoplasms	Hyperuricemia due to excess nucleic acid turnover (i.e., cytotoxic therapy).	Gout

Cancer epidemiology

	Male	Female	
Incidence	Prostate (32%)	Breast (32%)	Deaths from lung cancer have plateaued in males, but deaths continue to increase in females.
	Lung (16%)	Lung (13%)	
	Colon and rectum (12%)	Colon and rectum (13%)	
Mortality	Lung (33%)	Lung (23%)	Cancer is the second leading cause of death in the U.S. (heart disease is first).
	Prostate (13%)	Breast (18%)	

Anemia

Type	Etiology
Microcytic, hypochromic	Iron deficiency: ↑ TIBC, ↓ ferritin, ↓ serum iron *Bio.89*
	Thalassemias
	Lead poisoning
Macrocytic	Megaloblastic: Vitamin B_{12}/folate deficiency
	Drugs that block DNA synthesis (e.g., sulfa drugs, AZT)
	Marked reticulocytosis
Normocytic, normochromic	Hemorrhage
	Enzyme defects (e.g., G6PD deficiency, PK deficiency)
	RBC membrane defects (e.g., hereditary spherocytosis)
	Bone marrow disorders (e.g., aplastic anemia, leukemia)
	Hemoglobinopathies (e.g., sickle cell disease)
	Autoimmune hemolytic anemia
	Anemia of chronic disease: ↓ TIBC, ↑ ferritin, ↓ serum iron, ↑ storage iron in marrow macrophages

Vit. B_{12} and folate deficiencies are associated with hypersegmented PMNs. Unlike folate deficiency, vit. B_{12} deficiency is associated with neurologic problems.

Serum haptoglobin and serum LDH are used to determine RBC hemolysis. Direct Coombs' test is used to distinguish between immune vs. nonimmune mediated RBC hemolysis.

UCV

Aplastic anemia

Pancytopenia characterized by severe anemia, neutropenia, and thrombocytopenia caused by failure or destruction of multipotent myeloid stem cells, with inadequate production or release of differentiated cell lines.

Causes	Radiation, benzene, chloramphenicol, alkylating agents, antimetabolites, viral agents (HCV, CMV, EBV, herpes zoster-varicella), Fanconi's anemia, idiopathic (immune-mediated, primary stem-cell defect).
Symptoms	Fatigue, malaise, pallor, purpura, mucosal bleeding, petechiae, infection.
Pathologic features	Pancytopenia with normal cell morphology; hypocellular bone marrow with fatty infiltration.
Treatment	Withdrawal of offending agent, allogenic bone marrow transplantation, RBC and platelet transfusion, G-CSF or GM-CSF.

UCV *Path1.77*

Hemolytic Anemia

- ↑ uncongugated (Indirect) Billirubin
- ↓ serum Haptoglobin
  (Haptoglobin combines w/ liberated Hb)

HIGH-YIELD FACTS

Pathology

Blood dyscrasias

Sickle cell anemia	HbS mutation is a single amino acid replacement in β-chain (substitution of normal glutamic acid with valine). Low O_2 or dehydration precipitates sickling. Heterozygotes (sickle cell trait) are relatively malaria-resistant (balanced polymorphism). Complications in homozygotes (sickle cell disease) include aplastic crisis (due to B19 parvovirus infection), autosplenectomy, ↑ risk of encapsulated organism infection, *Salmonella* osteomyelitis, painful crisis (vaso-occlusive), and splenic sequestration crisis. HbC defect is a different β chain mutation; patients with Hb^c or Hb^{sc} (1 of each mutant gene) have milder disease than Hb^{ss} patients. New therapies for sickle cell anemia include hydroxyurea (↑ HbF) and bone marrow transplantation. *Bio.94, Path3.43*	Eight percent of African-Americans carry the HbS trait. 0.2% have the disease. Sickled cells are crescent-shaped RBCs.
α-thalassemia	There are four α-globin genes. In α-thalassemia, the α-globin chain is underproduced (as a function of number of bad genes, one to four). There is no compensatory increase of any other chains. HbH ($β_4$-tetramers, lacks three α-globin genes). Hb Barts ($γ_4$-tetramers, lacks all four α-globin genes) results in hydrops fetalis and intrauterine fetal death.	Thalassemia is prevalent in Mediterranean populations (*thalassa* = sea). Think of thala**SEA**mia.
β-thalassemia UCV	In β-minor thalassemia (heterozygote), the β-chain is underproduced; in β-major (homozygote), the β-chain is absent. In both cases, fetal hemoglobin production is compensatorily increased but is inadequate. HbS/β-thalassemia heterozygote has mild to moderate disease. *Bio.95, Path3.37*	β-thalassemia major results in severe anemia requiring blood transfusions. Cardiac failure due to secondary hemochromatosis.

Diagnosis of hematologic defects

Heinz bodies are seen in G6PD deficiency.
Ham's test is used to diagnose paroxysmal nocturnal hemoglobinuria (PNH).
Osmotic fragility test is used to diagnose hereditary spherocytosis (treat with splenectomy).

DIC

Activation of coagulation cascade, leading to microthrombi and global consumption of platelets, fibrin, and coagulation factors. Causes: septicemia, pregnancy, transfusion, trauma, malignancy, acute pancreatitis, nephrotic syndrome. Lab findings: ↑ PT, PTT, ↑ fibrin split products; ↓ platelet count.

UCV *Path1.82*

Bleeding disorders

Platelet abnormalities (microhemorrhage)	Mucous membrane bleeding Petechiae Purpura Prolonged bleeding time	Causes include ITP (antiplatelet antibodies and ↑ megakaryocytes), TTP (schistocytes), drugs, and DIC (↑ fibrin split products).
Coagulation factor defects (macrohemorrhage)	Hemarthroses (bleeding into joints) Easy bruising Prolonged PT and/or aPTT	Coagulopathies include hemophilia A (factor VIII deficiency), hemophilia B (factor IX deficiency), and von Willebrand's disease (deficiency of von Willebrand's antigen), the most common bleeding disorder.

Leukemias

General considerations: ↑ number of circulating leukocytes in blood; bone marrow infiltrates of leukemic cells; marrow failure can cause anemia (↓RBCs), infections (↓WBCs), and hemorrhage (↓platelets); leukemic cell infiltrates in liver, spleen, and lymph nodes are common.

ALL—children; lymphoblasts; most responsive to therapy.

AML—Auer rods; myeloblasts; adults.

CLL—older adults; lymphadenopathy; hepatosplenomegaly; few symptoms; indolent course; ↑ smudge cells in peripheral blood smear; warm Ab autoimmune hemolytic anemia; very similar to SLL (small lymphocytic lymphoma).

CML—most commonly associated with Philadelphia chromosome [t(9;22), *bcr-abl*]; myeloid stem cell proliferation; may accelerate to AML ("blast crisis").

LEUKEMIA
↑ Leukocytes
Full bone marrow

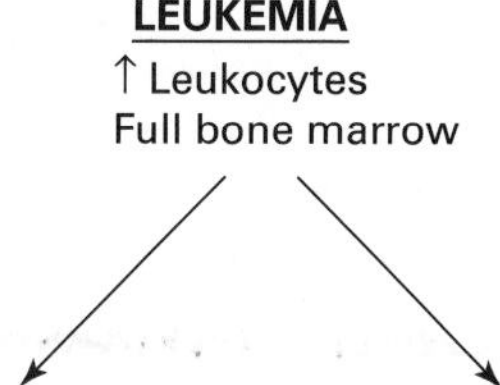

ACUTE LEUKEMIAS
Blasts predominate
Children or elderly
Short and drastic course

CHRONIC LEUKEMIAS
More mature cells
Midlife age range
Longer, less devastating course

ALL
Lymphoblasts
(pre–B or pre–T)

AML
Myeloblasts

CLL
Lymphocytes
Non–Ab-producing B cells

CML
Myeloid stem cells

UCV Path1.75, 76, 80, 81

Chromosomal translocations

t(9;22), or the Philadelphia chromosome, is associated with CML (*bcr-abl* hybrid).
t(8;14) is associated with Burkitt's lymphoma (*c-myc* activation).
t(14;18) is associated with follicular lymphomas (*bcl-2* activation).

Multiple myeloma

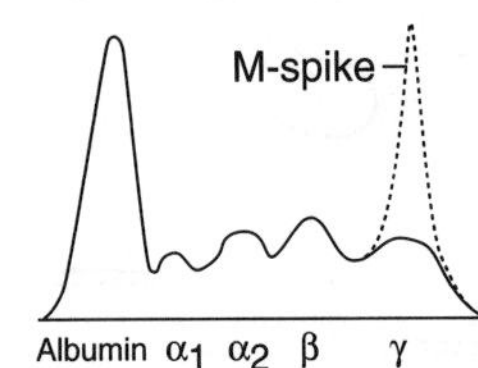

UCV Path1.90

Monoclonal plasma cell ("fried-egg" appearance) cancer that arises in the marrow and produces large amounts of IgG (55%) or IgA (25%). Most common 1° tumor arising within bone in adults. Destructive bone lesions and consequent hypercalcemia. Renal insufficiency, ↑ susceptibility to infection, and anemia. Ig light chains in urine (Bence Jones protein). Associated with primary amyloidosis and punched-out lytic bone lesions on x-ray. Characterized by monoclonal immunoglobulin spike (M protein) on serum protein electrophoresis. Blood smear shows RBCs stacked like poker chips (rouleau formation).

PATHOLOGY—GASTROINTESTINAL

Achalasia

Failure of relaxation of lower esophageal sphincter due to loss of myenteric (Auerbach's) plexus. Causes progressive dysphagia. Barium swallow shows dilated esophagus with an area of distal stenosis. Associated with an increased risk of esophageal carcinoma.

A-chalasia = absence of relaxation.
2° achalasia may arise from Chagas' disease.
"Bird beak" on barium swallow.

UCV Path1.40

Barrett's esophagus

Glandular (columnar epithelial) metaplasia—replacement of stratified squamous epithelium with gastric (columnar) epithelium in the distal esophagus.

BARRett's = **B**ecomes **A**deno-carcinoma, **R**esults from **R**eflux.

UCV Path3.29

Esophageal cancer

Risk factors for esophageal cancer are:

- Achalasia
- Barrett's esophagus
- Corrosive esophagitis
- Diverticuli
- Esophageal web
- Familial

ABCDEF

UCV Path1.54

Chronic gastritis

(non-erosive) chronic inflammation, atrophy of parietal cells

Type A — Autoimmune disorder characterized by Autoantibodies to parietal cells, pernicious Anemia, and Achlorhydria. Type **A** = **4 A's**

Type B — Caused by *H. pylori* infection. Type **B** = a **B**ug, *H. pylori*

UCV Path3.31

Peptic ulcer disease

Gastric ulcer	Pain Greater with meals: weight loss *H. pylori* infection in 70%; NSAID use also implicated Due to ↓ mucosal protection against gastric acid
Duodenal ulcer	Pain Decreases with meals: weight gain Almost 100% have *H. pylori* infection Due to ↑ gastric acid secretion or ↓ mucosal protection

Potential complications include bleeding, penetration, perforation, and obstruction.

H. pylori infection can be treated with "triple therapy" (metronidazole, bismuth salicylate, and either amoxicillin or tetracycline) with or without a proton pump inhibitor.

Incidence of peptic ulcer disease is twice as great in smokers.

UCV Anat.25, Path1.42, 69

Inflammatory bowel disease

	Crohn's disease	**Ulcerative colitis**
Location	May involve any portion of the GI tract, usually the terminal ileum, small intestine, and colon. **Skip** lesions, rectal sparing.	*Colitis* = colon inflammation. Continuous lesions with rectal involvement.
Gross morphology	Transmural inflammation. **Cobblestone** mucosa, creeping **fat,** bowel wall thickening ("string sign" on x-ray), linear ulcers, fissures.	Mucosal inflammation. Friable mucosal pseudopolyps with freely hanging mesentery.
Microscopic morphology	Noncaseating granulomas.	Crypt abcesses and ulcers.
Complications	Strictures, fistulas, perianal disease, malabsorption–nutritional depletion.	Severe stenosis, toxic megacolon, **colorectal carcinoma.**
Extraintestinal manifestations	Migratory polyarthritis, erythema nodosum.	Pyoderma gangrenosum, sclerosing cholangitis.

For **Crohn's,** think of a **fat** old **crone skipping** down a **cobblestone** road.

UCV Path3.32, 35

Diverticular disease

Diverticulum	Blind pouch leading off the alimentary tract, lined by mucosa, muscularis, and serosa, that communicates with the lumen of the gut. Most diverticula (esophagus, stomach, duodenum, colon) are acquired and are termed "false" in that they lack or have an attenuated muscularis propria.
Diverticulosis	The prevalence of diverticulosis (many diverticula) in patients over age 60 approaches 50%. Caused by increased intraluminal pressure and focal weakness in the colonic wall. Most frequently involves the sigmoid colon. Associated with low-fiber diets. Most often asymptomatic or associated with vague discomfort.
Diverticulitis	Inflammation of diverticula classically causing LLQ pain. May be complicated by perforation, peritonitis, abscess formation, or bowel stenosis.

UCV Path1.53

Hirschsprung's disease

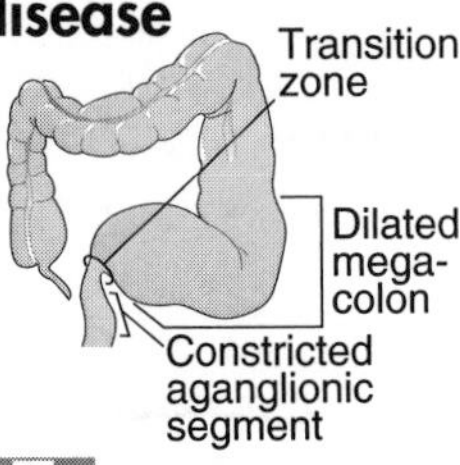

UCV Anat.21

Congenital megacolon characterized by absence of parasympathetic ganglion cells (Auerbach's and Meissner's plexuses) on intestinal biopsy. Due to failure of neural crest cell migration. Presents as chronic constipation early in life. Dilated portion of the colon proximal to the aganglionic segment, resulting in a "transition zone."

Think of a giant spring that has **sprung** in the colon.

Colorectal cancer risk factors

UCV Path1.50

Risk factors for carcinoma of colon: colorectal villous adenomas, chronic inflammatory bowel disease, low-fiber diet, increasing age, familial adenomatous polyposis (FAP), hereditary nonpolyposis colorectal cancer (HNPCC), personal and family history of colon cancer. Screen patients > 50 years old with stool occult blood test.

Associated w/ ↑ CEA

Cirrhosis/ portal hypertension

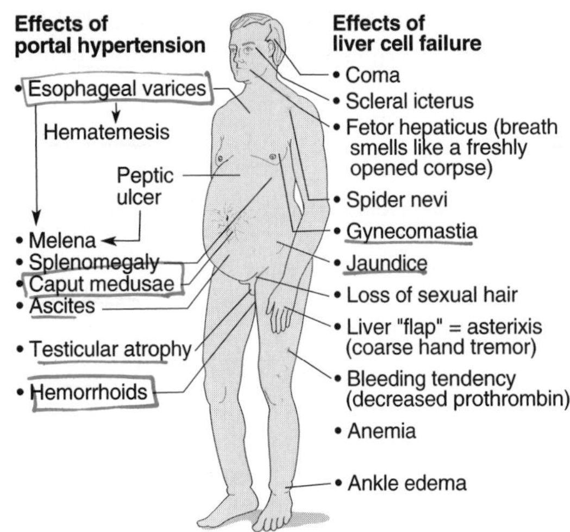

Cirrho (Greek) = tawny yellow.

Diffuse fibrosis of liver, destroys normal architecture.

Nodular regeneration.

Micronodular: nodules < 3 mm, uniform size. Due to metabolic insult (e.g., alcohol).

Macronodular: nodules > 3 mm, varied size. Usually due to significant liver injury leading to hepatic necrosis (e.g., postinfectious or drug-induced hepatitis). Increased risk of hepatocellular carcinoma.

↑ Hepatocell. CA

UCV Anat.26, Path1.60

Alcoholic hepatitis

UCV Path3.28

Swollen and necrotic hepatocytes, neutrophil infiltration, Mallory bodies (hyaline), fatty change, and sclerosis around central vein. SGOT (AST) to SGPT (ALT) ratio is usually greater than 1.5.

A Scotch and **T**onic: AST elevated (>ALT) >1.5 with alcoholic hepatitis.

Budd–Chiari syndrome

UCV Path3.30

Occlusion of IVC or hepatic veins with centrilobular congestion and necrosis, leading to congestive liver disease (hepatomegaly, ascites, abdominal pain, and eventual liver failure). Associated with polycythemia vera, pregnancy, hepatocellular carcinoma.

Wilson's disease	Due to failure of copper to enter circulation in the form of ceruloplasmin. Leads to copper accumulation, especially in liver, brain, cornea. Also known as hepatolenticular degeneration. Wilson's disease is characterized by: Asterixis Basal ganglia degeneration Ceruloplasmin ↓, Cirrhosis, Corneal deposits (Kayser–Fleischer rings), Copper accumulation, Carcinoma (hepatocellular), Choreiform movements Dementia	Treat with penicillamine. ABCD
UCV Bio.83, Path1.72		
Hemochromatosis	Increased iron deposition in many organs. Classic triad of micronodular pigment cirrhosis, "bronze" diabetes, skin pigmentation. Results in CHF and an increased risk of hepatocellular carcinoma. Disease may be a primary (autosomal recessive) disorder or secondary to chronic transfusion therapy. ↑ ferritin, ↑ transferrin saturation.	Total body iron may reach 50 g, enough to set off the metal detectors at airports. Treat with repeated phlebotomy, deferoxamine.
UCV Path1.59, Path3.42		
Hereditary hyperbilirubinemias		
Crigler–Najjar syndrome, type I	Absent UDP-glucuronyl transferase. Presents early in life; patients die within a few years. Bio.46 Findings: jaundice, kernicterus (bilirubin deposition in brain), ↑ unconjugated bilirubin. Treatment: plasmapheresis and phototherapy.	Crigler–Najjar type I is a severe disease.
Gilbert's syndrome	Mildly ↓ UDP-glucuronyl transferase. Asymptomatic, but unconjugated bilirubin is elevated without overt hemolysis. Associated with stress. Bio.48	Gilbert's may represent a milder form.
Dubin–Johnson syndrome	Conjugated hyperbilirubinemia due to defective liver excretion. Grossly black liver. Bio.47	Rotor's syndrome is similar but less severe and does not cause black liver.
UCV		
Hepatocellular carcinoma	Also called hepatoma. Most common primary malignant tumor of the liver in adults. Increased incidence of hepatocellular carcinoma is associated with hepatitis B and C, Wilson's disease, hemochromatosis, α_1-antitrypsin deficiency, alcoholic cirrhosis, and carcinogens (e.g., aflatoxin B1).	Hepatocellular carcinoma, like renal cell carcinoma, is commonly spread by hematogenous dissemination.
UCV Path1.61		
Reye's syndrome	Rare, often fatal childhood hepatoencephalopathy. Findings: fatty liver (microvesicular fatty change), hypoglycemia, coma. Associated with viral infection (especially VZV and influenza B) and salicylates; thus aspirin is no longer recommended for children (use acetaminophen, with caution).	"Don't give your baby a baby aspirin."
UCV Pharm.95		

Gallstones

Form when solubilizing bile acids and lecithin are overwhelmed by increased cholesterol and/or bilirubin.

Three types of stones:

1. Cholesterol stones: associated with obesity, Crohn's disease, cystic fibrosis, advanced age, clofibrate, estrogens, multiparity, rapid weight loss, and Native American origin.
2. Mixed stones: have both cholesterol and pigment components. Most common type.
3. Pigment stones: seen in patients with chronic RBC hemolysis, alcoholic cirrhosis, advanced age, and biliary infection.

Diagnose with ultrasound. Treat with cholecystectomy.

Risk factors (**4 F's**):

1. **F**emale
2. **F**at
3. **F**ertile
4. **F**orty

May present with "Charcot's triad" of epigastric/RUQ pain, fever, nausea/emesis.

Acute pancreatitis

Causes: **G**allstones, **E**thanol, **T**rauma, **S**teroids, **M**umps, **A**utoimmune disease; **S**corpion sting, **H**yperlipidemia, **D**rugs.

Clinical presentation: epigastric abdominal pain radiating to back.

Labs: elevated amylase, lipase.

Can lead to DIC, ARDS, diffuse fat necrosis, hypocalcemia, and pseudocyst formation.

Chronic pancreatitis is strongly associated with alcoholism.

GET SMASHeD

UCV Path1.44

Pancreatic adenocarcinoma

Prognosis averages 6 months or less; very aggressive; usually already metastasized at presentation; tumors more common in pancreatic head (obstructive jaundice).

Often presents with:

1. Abdominal pain radiating to back
2. Weight loss
3. Anorexia
4. Migratory thrombophlebitis (Trousseau's syndrome)
5. Pancreatic duct obstruction (malabsorption with palpable gallbladder)

UCV Path1.66

Obstructive lung disease

Obstruction of air flow, resulting in air trapping in the lungs. Pulmonary function tests: decreased FEV_1/FVC ratio (hallmark).

Types:

1. **Chronic Bronchitis** ("Blue Bloater")—productive cough for greater than 3 consecutive months in two or more years. Hypertrophy of mucus-secreting glands in the bronchioles (Reid index > 50%). Leading cause is smoking. Findings: wheezing, crackles, cyanosis. *Path2.54*
2. **Emphysema** ("pink puffer")—enlargement of air spaces and decreased recoil resulting from destruction of alveolar walls. Caused by smoking (centriacinar emphysema) and α_1-antitrypsin deficiency (panacinar emphysema and liver cirrhosis) → ↑ elastase activity. Findings: dyspnea, ↓ breath sounds, tachycardia, ↓ I/E ratio. *Path2.54, 3.91*
3. **Asthma**—bronchial hyper-responsiveness causes reversible bronchoconstriction. Can be triggered by viral URIs, allergens, and stress. Findings: cough, wheezing, dyspnea, tachypnea, hypoxemia, ↓ I/E ratio, pulsus paradoxus. *Path2.53*
4. **Bronchiectasis**—chronic necrotizing infection of bronchi → dilated airways, purulent sputum, recurrent infections, hemoptysis. Associated with bronchial obstruction, cystic fibrosis, poor ciliary motility.

UCV *Path2.55*

Restrictive lung disease

Restricted lung expansion causes decreased lung volumes (decreased VC and TLC). PFTs: FEV/FVC ratio > 80%.

Types:

1. Poor breathing mechanics (extrapulmonary):
   a. Poor muscular effort: polio, myasthenia gravis.
   b. Poor apparatus: scoliosis.
2. Poor lung expansion (pulmonary):
   a. Defective alveolar filling: pneumonia, ARDS, pulmonary edema. *Bio97, Path2.52*
   b. Interstitial fibrosis: causes increased recoil (decreased compliance), thereby limiting alveolar expansion. Complications include cor pulmonale. Can be seen in diffuse interstitial pulmonary fibrosis and bleomycin toxicity. Symptoms include gradual progressive dyspnea and cough. *Path3.93*

UCV

Pulmonary flow volume loops

	Resistance	FVC	FEV_1	$(FEV_1/FVC) \times 100$
Normal	–	–	–	>80%
Restrictive	↓	↓	↓	>80%
Obstructive	↑	↓	↓↓	<80%

Asbestosis

Diffuse pulmonary interstitial fibrosis caused by inhaled asbestos fibers. Increased risk of pleural mesothelioma and bronchogenic carcinoma. Long latency. Ferruginous bodies in lung (asbestos fibers coated with hemosiderin). Ivory-white pleural plaques.

Smokers have synergistically higher risk of cancer. Seen in ship builders and plumbers.

UCV *Path2.58*

Neonatal respiratory distress syndrome

Surfactant deficiency leading to ↑ surface tension, resulting in alveolar collapse. Surfactant is made by type II pneumocytes most abundantly after 35th wk of gestation. The lecithin-to-sphingomyelin ratio in the amniotic fluid, a measure of lung maturity, is usually less than 1.5 in neonatal respiratory distress syndrome.

Surfactant: dipalmitoyl phosphatidylcholine.

Prevention: maternal steroids before birth; artificial surfactant for infant.

UCV Bio.101

Kartagener's syndrome

Immotile cilia due to a dynein arm defect. Results in situs inversus, sterility (sperm also immotile), and bronchiectasis and recurrent sinusitis (bacteria and particles not pushed out).

UCV Bio.68

Lung cancer

Bronchogenic carcinoma

Tumors that arise centrally:

1. Squamous cell carcinoma—clear link to Smoking
2. Small cell carcinoma—clear link to Smoking; associated with ectopic hormone production

Tumors that arise peripherally:

1. Adenocarcinoma
2. Bronchioalveolar carcinoma (thought not to be related to smoking)
3. Large cell carcinoma—undifferentiated

Carcinoid tumor

Can cause carcinoid syndrome.

Metastases

Very common. Brain (epilepsy), bone (pathologic fracture), and liver (jaundice, hepatomegaly).

Lung cancer is the leading cause of cancer death.

Presentation: cough, hemoptysis, bronchial obstruction, wheezing, pneumonic "coin" lesion on x-ray.

SPHERE of complications:

- Superior vena caval syndrome
- Pancoast's tumor
- Horner's syndrome
- Endocrine (paraneoplastic)
- Recurrent laryngeal symptoms (hoarseness)
- Effusions (pleural or pericardial)

UCV Path2.57

Pneumonia

Type	Organism(s)	Characteristics
Lobar	Pneumococcus most frequently	Intra-alveolar exudate → consolidation; may involve entire lung
Bronchopneumonia	*S. aureus*, *H. flu*, *Klebsiella*, *S. pyogenes*	Acute inflammatory infiltrates from bronchioles into adjacent alveoli; patchy distribution involving ≥ 1 lobes.
Interstitial pneumonia	Viruses, *Mycoplasma*, *Legionella*	Diffuse patchy inflammation localized to interstitial areas at alveolar walls; distribution involving ≥ 1 lobes

Pancoast's tumor

Carcinoma that occurs in apex of lung and may affect cervical sympathetic plexus, causing Horner's syndrome.

Horner's syndrome: ptosis, miosis, anhidrosis.

Degenerative diseases

Cerebral cortex	**Alzheimer's disease:** most common cause of dementia in the elderly. Associated with senile plaques (β amyloid core) and neurofibrillary tangles (abnormally phosphorylated tau protein). Familial form (10%) associated with genes on chromosomes 1, 14, 19 (Apo-E4 allele), and 21 (p-App gene). *Path3.45*	Multi-infarct dementia is the second most common cause of dementia in the elderly.
	Pick's disease: associated with Pick bodies and is specific for the frontal and temporal lobes.	
Basal ganglia and brainstem	**Huntington's disease:** autosomal dominant inheritance, chorea, dementia. Atrophy of caudate nucleus. *Path3.52*	
	Parkinson's disease: associated with Lewy bodies and depigmentation of the substantia nigra. Rare cases have been linked to exposure to MPTP, a contaminant in illicit street drugs. *Anat.50, Path2.23*	TRAP = **T**remor (at rest), cogwheel **R**igidity, **A**kinesia, and **P**ostural instability (you are **TRAP**ped in your body).
Spinocerebellar	**Olivopontocerebellar atrophy**	
	Friedreich's ataxia *Path2.14*	
Motor neuron	**Amyotrophic lateral sclerosis (ALS):** is associated with both lower and upper motor neuron signs. *Path2.8*	Commonly known as Lou Gehrig's disease.
	Werdnig–Hoffmann disease: presents at birth as a "floppy baby"; tongue fasciculations.	
	Polio: lower motor neuron signs.	

UCV

Brain tumors

Adult	Seventy percent above tentorium (e.g., cerebral hemispheres). Incidence: metastases > astrocytoma (including glioblastoma) > meningioma.	Glioblastoma multiforme: necrosis, hemorrhage, and pseudo-palisading; "butterfly" glioma; very poor prognosis.
Childhood	Seventy percent below tentorium (e.g., cerebellum). Incidence: astrocytoma > medulloblastoma > ependymoma.	

UCV *Anat.35, Path2.15, 18, 19, Path3.56*

Intracranial hemorrhage

Epidural hematoma	Rupture of middle meningeal artery, often 2° to fracture of temporal bone. Lucid interval.
Subdural hematoma	Rupture of bridging veins. Venous bleeding (less pressure) with delayed onset of symptoms. Seen in elderly individuals, alcoholics, blunt trauma.
Subarachnoid hemorrhage	Rupture of an aneurysm (usually berry aneurysm) or an AVM. Patients complain of "worst headache of my life." Bloody or xanthochromic spinal tap.
Parenchymal hematoma	Caused by hypertension, amyloid angiopathy, diabetes mellitus, and tumor.

UCV *Path2.13, 25, 26*

Berry aneurysms

Berry aneurysms occur at the bifurcations in the circle of Willis. Most common site is bifurcation of the anterior communicating artery. Rupture (most common complication) leads to hemorrhagic stroke. Associated with adult polycystic kidney disease, Ehlers–Danlos syndrome and Marfan's disease.

UCV *Path2.9*

Demyelinating and dysmyelinating diseases

1. **Multiple sclerosis (MS)**—higher prevalence with greater distance from the equator; periventricular plaques, preservation of axons, loss of oligodendrocytes, reactive astrocytic gliosis; ↑ protein (IgG) in CSF. Many patients have a relapsing–remitting course. Patients can present with optic neuritis (loss of vision), MLF syndrome (internuclear ophthalmoplegia), hemiparesis, hemisensory symptoms, or bladder/bowel incontinence. *Path2.20*
2. **Progressive multifocal leukoencephalopathy (PML)**—associated with JC virus and seen in 2–4% of AIDS patients (reactivation of latent viral infection). *Micro2.87*
3. **Postinfectious encephalomyelitis**
4. **Metachromatic leukodystrophy** (a sphingolipidosis) *Bio.72*
5. **Guillain–Barré syndrome**—inflammation and demyelination of peripheral nerves; ascending muscle weakness and paralysis beginning in distal lower extremities. In some cases it follows herpesvirus or *C. jejuni* infection. CSF shows ↑ protein and normal cells. *Path2.16*

Classic triad of **MS** is a **SIN:**
Scanning speech
Intention tremor
Nystagmus

UCV

Guillain–Barré syndrome (acute idiopathic polyneuritis)

Sensory and motor neuron loss at the level of the peripheral nerves and motor fibers of the ventral roots (sensory effect less severe than motor), causing symmetric weakness with variable paresthesia or dysesthesia. Facial diplegia in 50% of cases. Autonomic function may be severely affected (e.g., cardiac irregularities, hypertension, or hypotension).

Findings: elevated CSF protein with normal cell count.

Associated with viral infections, inoculations, and stress, but no definitive link to pathogens.

UCV *Path2.16*

Poliomyelitis

Caused by poliovirus, which is transmitted by the fecal-oral route. Replicates in the oropharynx and small intestine before spreading through the bloodstream to the CNS, where it leads to the destruction of cells in the anterior horn of the spinal cord, leading in turn to LMN destruction.

Symptoms: malaise, headache, fever, nausea, abdominal pain, sore throat. Signs of LMN lesions: muscle weakness and atrophy, fasciculations, fibrillation, and hyporeflexia.

Findings: CSF with lymphocytic pleocytosis with slight elevation of protein. Virus recovered from stool or throat.

UCV

Seizures	Partial seizures: one area of the brain. 1. Simple partial (awareness intact): motor, sensory, autonomic, psychic. 2. Complex partial (impaired awareness). Generalized seizures: diffuse. 1. Absence: blank stare (petit mal). 2. Myoclonic: quick, repetitive jerks. 3. Tonic-clonic: alternating stiffening and movement (grand mal). 4. Tonic: stiffening. 5. Atonic: "drop" seizures.	Epilepsy is a disorder of recurrent seizures (febrile seizures are not epilepsy). Partial seizures can secondarily generalize. Causes of seizures by age: Children: genetic, infection, trauma, congenital, metabolic. Adults: tumors, trauma, stroke, infection. Elderly: stroke, tumor, trauma, metabolic, infection.
Broca's versus Wernicke's aphasia UCV Path3.47	Broca's is nonfluent aphasia with intact comprehension (expressive aphasia). Wernicke's is fluent aphasia with impaired comprehension (receptive aphasia). Broca's area = inferior frontal gyrus. Wernicke's area = superior temporal gyrus.	**BRO**ca's is **BRO**ken speech; Wernicke's is Wordy but makes no sense.
Horner's syndrome	Sympathectomy of face: 1. Ptosis (slight drooping of eyelid) 2. Miosis (pupil constriction) 3. Anhidrosis (absence of sweating) and flushing (rubor) of affected side of face Associated with Pancoast's tumor.	
Syringomyelia UCV Path2.27	Softening and cavitation around central canal of spinal cord. Crossing fibers of spinothalamic tract are damaged. Bilateral loss of pain and temperature sensation in upper extremities with preservation of touch sensation.	*Syrinx* (Greek) = tube, as in syringe. Often presents in patients with Arnold–Chiari malformation.
Tabes dorsalis UCV Anat.53	Degeneration of dorsal columns and dorsal roots due to 3° syphilis, resulting in impaired proprioception and locomotor ataxia. Associated with Charcot joints, shooting (lightning) pain, Argyll–Robertson pupils, and absence of deep tendon reflexes.	

Osteoarthritis	Mechanical: wear and tear of joints leads to destruction of articular cartilage, subchondral bone formation, sclerosis, osteophytes, eburnation, and Heberden's nodes (DIP). Common in older patients. Classic presentation: pain in weight-bearing joints after use (e.g., at the end of the day), improving with rest. No systemic symptoms.

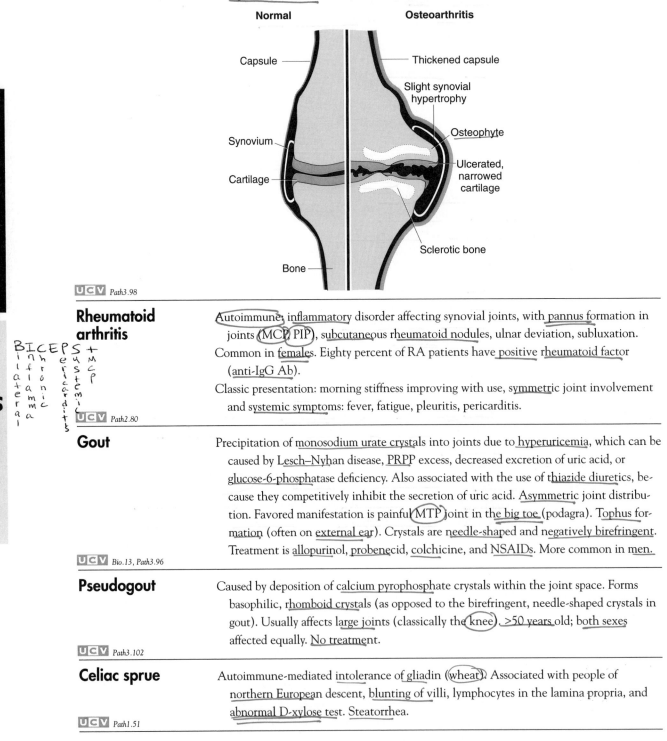

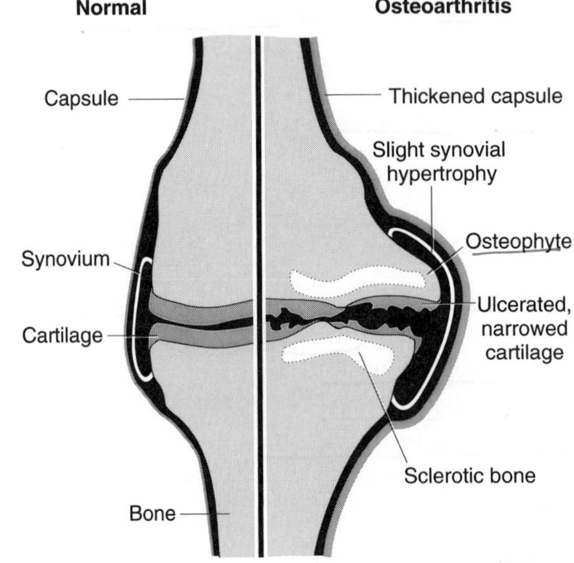

UCV Path3.98

Rheumatoid arthritis UCV Path2.80	Autoimmune inflammatory disorder affecting synovial joints, with pannus formation in joints (MCP, PIP), subcutaneous rheumatoid nodules, ulnar deviation, subluxation. Common in females. Eighty percent of RA patients have positive rheumatoid factor (anti-IgG Ab). Classic presentation: morning stiffness improving with use, symmetric joint involvement and systemic symptoms: fever, fatigue, pleuritis, pericarditis.
Gout UCV Bio.13, Path3.96	Precipitation of monosodium urate crystals into joints due to hyperuricemia, which can be caused by Lesch–Nyhan disease, PRPP excess, decreased excretion of uric acid, or glucose-6-phosphatase deficiency. Also associated with the use of thiazide diuretics, because they competitively inhibit the secretion of uric acid. Asymmetric joint distribution. Favored manifestation is painful MTP joint in the big toe (podagra). Tophus formation (often on external ear). Crystals are needle-shaped and negatively birefringent. Treatment is allopurinol, probenecid, colchicine, and NSAIDs. More common in men.
Pseudogout UCV Path3.102	Caused by deposition of calcium pyrophosphate crystals within the joint space. Forms basophilic, rhomboid crystals (as opposed to the birefringent, needle-shaped crystals in gout). Usually affects large joints (classically the knee). >50 years old; both sexes affected equally. No treatment.
Celiac sprue UCV Path1.51	Autoimmune-mediated intolerance of gliadin (wheat). Associated with people of northern European descent, blunting of villi, lymphocytes in the lamina propria, and abnormal D-xylose test. Steatorrhea.

Systemic lupus erythematosus UCV Path2.82, Path3.107	90% are female and between ages 14 and 45. Fever, fatigue, weight loss. Joint pain, malar rash, photosensitivity, pleuritis, pericarditis, nonbacterial verrucous endocarditis, Raynaud's phenomenon. **Wire loop** lesions in kidney with immune complex deposition (with nephrotic syndrome); death from renal failure and infections. False positives on syphilis tests (RPR/VDRL). Lab tests detect presence of: 1. Antinuclear antibodies (ANA): sensitive, but not specific for SLE 2. Antibodies to double-stranded DNA (anti-ds DNA): very specific 3. Anti-Smith antibodies (anti-Sm): very specific	**SLE** causes **LSE** (**L**ibman–**S**acks **E**ndocarditis). Most common and severe in black females. Drugs (procainamide, INH, phenytoin, hydralazine) can produce an SLE-like syndrome that is commonly reversible. Pharm.77
Sarcoidosis UCV Path3.94	Associated with restrictive lung disease, bilateral hilar lymphadenopathy, erythema nodosum, Bell's palsy, epithelial granulomas containing microscopic Schaumann and asteroid bodies, uveoparotitis, and hypercalcemia (due to elevated conversion of vit. D to its active form in epithelioid macrophages). Also associated with immune-mediated, widespread noncaseating granulomas and elevated serum ACE levels. Common in **black females.**	**GRAIN:** **G**ammaglobulinemia **R**heumatoid arthritis **A**CE ↑ **I**nterstitial fibrosis **N**oncaseating granulomas
Reiter's syndrome UCV Path2.79	A seronegative spondyloarthropathy. Strong HLA-B27 link. Classic triad: 1. Urethritis 2. Conjunctivitis and anterior uveitis 3. Arthritis Has a strong predilection for **males.**	"Can't see (anterior uveitis/conjunctivitis), can't pee (urethritis), can't climb a tree (arthritis)." Post-GI or chlamydia infections.
Sjögren's syndrome UCV Path2.81	Classic triad: dry eyes (conjunctivitis, xerophthalmia), dry mouth (dysphagia, xerostomia), arthritis. Parotid enlargement, ↑ risk of B-cell lymphoma. Predominantly affects **females** between 40 and 60 years of age.	Associated with rheumatoid arthritis. Sicca syndrome: dry eyes, dry mouth, nasal and vaginal dryness, chronic bronchitis, reflux esophagitis.
Scleroderma (progressive systemic sclerosis–PSS) UCV Path2.78	Excessive fibrosis and collagen deposition throughout the body. 75% female. Commonly sclerosis of skin but also of cardiovascular and GI systems and kidney. Two major categories: 1. Diffuse scleroderma: widespread skin involvement, rapid progression, early visceral involvement. Associated with anti-Scl-70 antibody. 2. **CREST** syndrome: **C**alcinosis, **R**aynaud's phenomenon, **E**sophageal dysmotility, **S**clerodactyly, and **T**elangiectasia. Limited skin involvement, often confined to fingers and face. More benign clinical course. Associated with anticentromere antibody.	

Goodpasture's syndrome	Findings: pulmonary hemorrhages, renal lesions, hemoptysis, hematuria, anemia, crescentic glomerulonephritis. Anti-glomerular basement membrane antibodies produce linear staining on immunofluorescence.	There are **two** **G**ood **P**astures for this disease: Glomerulus and Pulmonary. Also, a type **II** hypersensitivity disease. Most common in men 20–40 yo.
UCV Path2.67		

PATHOLOGY—ENDOCRINE/REPRODUCTIVE

Cushing's syndrome

Increased cortisol due to a variety of causes.
Etiologies include:

1. Cushing's disease (1° pituitary adenoma); ↑ ACTH
2. 1° adrenal (hyperplasia/neoplasia); ↓ ACTH
3. Ectopic ACTH production (eg, carcinoid); ↑ ACTH
4. Iatrogenic; ↓ ACTH

The clinical picture includes hypertension, weight gain, moon facies, truncal obesity, buffalo hump, hyperglycemia (insulin resistance), skin changes (thinning, striae), osteoporosis, and immune suppression.

Hyperaldosteronism

Primary (Conn's syndrome) Low Renin	Caused by an aldosterone-secreting tumor, resulting in hypertension, hypokalemia, metabolic alkalosis, and **low** plasma renin.	Treatment includes spironolactone, a diuretic that works by acting as an aldosterone antagonist.
Secondary High Renin	Due to renal artery stenosis, chronic renal failure, CHF, cirrhosis, or nephrotic syndrome. Kidney perception of low intravascular volume results in an overactive renin-angiotensin system. Therefore, it is associated with **high** plasma renin.	
UCV Bio.8, Path3.35		

Addison's disease

Deficiency of aldosterone and cortisol due to adrenal atrophy, causing hypotension (hyponatremic volume contraction) and skin hyperpigmentation (↑ MSH). Characterized by **A**drenal **A**trophy and **A**bsence of hormone production; involves **A**ll three cortical divisions.

UCV Bio.5, Path3.23

Tumors of the adrenal medulla	**Pheochromocytoma** is the most common tumor of the adrenal medulla in adults. **Neuroblastoma** is the most common tumor of the adrenal medulla in children, but it can occur anywhere along the sympathetic chain.	Pheochromocytomas may be associated with neurofibromatosis, MEN type II, and MEN type III.

Pheochromocytoma	Most of these neoplasms secrete a combination of norepinephrine and epinephrine. Urinary VMA levels and plasma catecholamines are elevated. Associated with MEN type II and type III. Treated with α antagonists, especially phenoxybenzamine, a nonselective, **irreversible** α blocker. Episodic hyperadrenergic symptoms **(5 P's):** Pressure (elevated blood pressure) Pain (headache) Perspiration Palpitations Pallor/diaphoresis	Rule of 10s: 10% malignant 10% bilateral 10% extraadrenal 10% calcify 10% kids 10% familial \# Phenoxybenzamine · α antagonist
UCV Bio.30		
Hypothyroidism and hyperthyroidism		
Hypothyroidism	Cold intolerance, hypoactivity, weight gain, fatigue, lethargy, ↓ appetite, constipation, weakness, ↓ reflexes, myxedema (facial/periorbital), dry, cool skin, and coarse, brittle hair. Path1.33	↑ TSH (sensitive test for 1° hypothyroidism), ↓ total T4, ↓ free T4, ↓ T3 uptake.
Hyperthyroidism	Heat intolerance, hyperactivity, weight loss, chest pain/ palpitations, arrhythmias, diarrhea, ↑ reflexes, warm, moist skin, and fine hair. Path1.30	↓ TSH (if 1°), ↑ total T4, ↑ free T4, ↑ T3 uptake.
Graves' disease	Ophthalmopathy (proptosis, EOM swelling), pretibial myxedema, diffuse goiter. Bio.14, Path3.25	An autoimmune hyperthyroidism with thyroid stimulating/TSH receptor antibodies.
UCV		
Cretinism	Endemic cretinism occurs wherever endemic goiter is prevalent (lack of dietary iodine); sporadic cretinism is caused by defect in T4 formation or developmental failure in thyroid formation. Findings: pot-bellied, pale, puffy-faced child with protruding umbilicus and protuberant tongue.	Cretin means Christ-like (French *chrétien*). Those affected were considered so mentally retarded as to be incapable of sinning. Still common in China.
UCV Path1.25		

Diabetes mellitus

Acute manifestations	Polydipsia, polyuria, polyphagia, weight loss, DKA (IDDM), hyperosmolar coma (NIDDM), unopposed secretion of GH and epinephrine (exacerbating hyperglycemia).

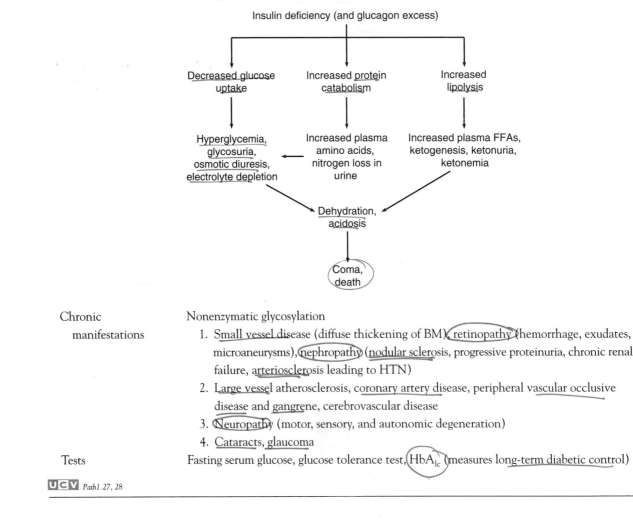

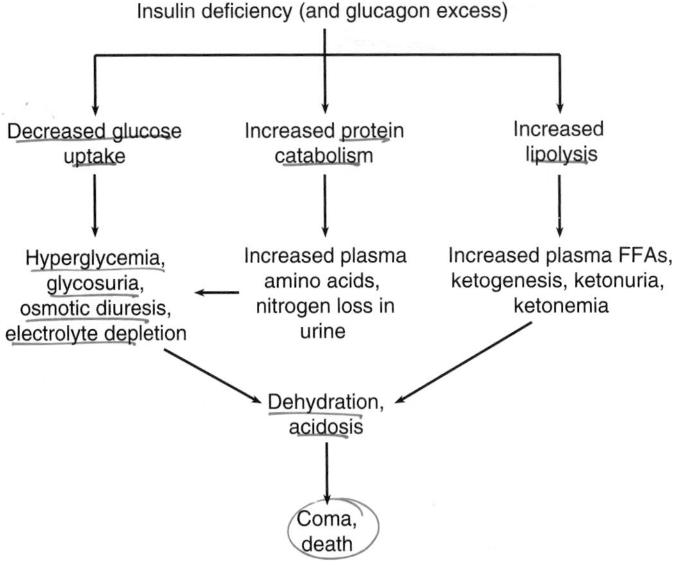

Chronic manifestations	Nonenzymatic glycosylation 1. Small vessel disease (diffuse thickening of BM), retinopathy (hemorrhage, exudates, microaneurysms), nephropathy (nodular sclerosis, progressive proteinuria, chronic renal failure, arteriosclerosis leading to HTN) 2. Large vessel atherosclerosis, coronary artery disease, peripheral vascular occlusive disease and gangrene, cerebrovascular disease 3. Neuropathy (motor, sensory, and autonomic degeneration) 4. Cataracts, glaucoma
Tests	Fasting serum glucose, glucose tolerance test, HbA_{1c} (measures long-term diabetic control)

UCV Path1.27, 28

Type I vs. type II diabetes mellitus

	Type I—juvenile onset (IDDM)	Type II—adult onset (NIDDM)
Incidence	15%	85%
Insulin necessary in treatment	Always	Sometimes
Age (exceptions commonly occur)	Under 30	Over 40
Association with obesity	No	Yes
Genetic predisposition	Weak, polygenic	Strong, polygenic
Association with HLA system	Yes (HLA DR 3 & 4)	No
Glucose intolerance	Severe	Mild to moderate
Ketoacidosis	Common	Rare
Beta cell numbers in the islets	Reduced	Variable
Serum insulin level	Reduced	Variable
Classic symptoms of polyuria, polydipsia, thirst, weight loss	Common	Sometimes
Basic cause	?Viral or immune destruction of beta cells	?Increased resistance to insulin

Diabetes insipidus

Characterized by intensive thirst and polyuria together with an inability to concentrate urine with fluid restriction owing to lack of ADH (central DI) or to a lack of renal response to ADH (nephrogenic DI). Caused by lithium or demeclocycline.

Findings: Urine specific gravity < 1.006; serum osmolality > 290 mOsm/L.

Treatment: Adequate fluid intake. For central DI: intranasal desmopressin (ADH analog) once or twice daily. For nephrogenic DI: hydrochlorothiazide, indomethacin, or amiloride.

UCV Bio.10

SIADH

Syndrome of inappropriate antidiuretic hormone secretion:

- Excessive water retention
- Hyponatremia
- Serum hypo-osmolarity with urine osmolarity > serum osmolarity

Very low serum sodium levels can lead to seizures.

Causes include:

- Ectopic ADH (small cell lung cancer)
- CNS disorders/head trauma
- Pulmonary disease
- Drugs

UCV Bio.38

Carcinoid syndrome

Rare syndrome caused by carcinoid tumors, especially those of the small bowel; the tumors secrete high levels of serotonin (5HT) that does not get metabolized by the liver due to liver metastases. Results in recurrent **diarrhea, cutaneous flushing,** asthmatic wheezing, and carcinoid heart disease. ↑ 5-HIAA in urine.

Rule of 1/3s:

- 1/3 metastasize
- 1/3 present with second malignancy
- 1/3 multiple

Treat with octreotide.

UCV Bio.45, Path3.49

Zollinger–Ellison syndrome

Gastrin-secreting tumor that is usually located in the pancreas. Causes recurrent ulcers. May be associated with MEN syndrome type I.

UCV Path1.73

Multiple endocrine neoplasias (MEN)

MEN type I (Wermer's syndrome)–pancreas (e.g., ZE syndrome, insulinomas, VIPomas), parathyroid and pituitary tumors.

MEN type II (Sipple's syndrome)–medullary carcinoma of the thyroid, pheochromocytoma, parathyroid tumor or adenoma.

MEN type III (formerly MEN IIb)–medullary carcinoma of the thyroid, pheochromocytoma, and oral and intestinal ganglioneuromatosis (mucosal neuromas).

MEN I = 3 "P" organs (**P**ancreas, **P**ituitary, and **P**arathyroid).

All MEN syndromes are autosomal dominantly inherited.

Osteoporosis

Reduction of bone mass in spite of normal bone mineralization.

Affects whites > blacks > Asians.

Type I

Postmenopausal (10–15 years after menopause); ↑ bone resorption due to ↓ estrogen levels. Treated with estrogen replacement.

Vertebral crush fractures: acute back pain, loss of height, kyphosis.

Type II

Senile osteoporosis—affects men and women > 70 years.

Distal radius (Colles') fractures, vertebral wedge fractures.

UCV Path3.100

Benign prostatic hypertrophy

Common in men over age 50. May be due to an age-related increase in estradiol with possible sensitization of the prostate to the growth-promoting effects of DHT. Characterized by a nodular enlargement of the periurethral (lateral and middle) lobes of the prostate gland, compressing the urethra into a vertical slit. Often presents with increased frequency of urination, nocturia, difficulty starting and stopping the stream of urine, and dysuria. May lead to distention and hypertrophy of the bladder, hydronephrosis, and urinary tract infections. **Not considered a premalignant lesion.**

UCV Path2.86

Hydatidiform mole

A pathologic ovum ("empty egg"—ovum with no DNA) resulting in cystic swelling of chorionic villi and proliferation of chorionic epithelium (trophoblast). Most common precursor of choriocarcinoma. High β-HCG. "Honeycombed uterus," "cluster of grapes" appearance. Genotype of a **complete mole** is 46, XX and is **purely paternal** in origin (no maternal chromosomes); no associated fetus. **Partial mole** is commonly **triploid** or **tetraploid.**

UCV Path2.40

Breast disease

Type	Characteristics
Fibrocystic disease	Presents with diffuse breast pain and multiple lesions, often bilateral. Biopsy shows fibrocystic elements. Usually does not indicate increased risk of carcinoma. Histologic types:
Cystic	Fluid-filled.
Epithelial hyperplasia	Increase in number of epithelial cell layers in terminal duct lobule. **Increased risk of carcinoma** with atypical cells. Occurs >30 yrs.
Fibrosis	Hyperplasia of breast stroma.
Sclerosing	Increased acini and intralobular fibrosis.
Benign tumors	
Cystosarcoma phyllodes	Large, bulky mass of connective tissue and cysts. Breast surface has "leaflike" appearance.
Fibroadenoma	Most common tumor < 25 years. Small, mobile, firm mass with sharp edges. ↑ size and tenderness with pregnancy.
Intraductal papilloma	Tumor of lactiferous ducts; presents with nipple discharge.
Malignant tumors (carcinoma):	Common postmenopause. Arise from mammary duct epithelium or lobular glands. Examples of histologic types:
Comedocarcinoma	Cheesy consistency of tumor tissue due to central necrosis.
Infiltrating ductal	Most common carcinoma. Firm, fibrous mass.
Inflammatory	Lymphatic involvement; poor prognosis.
Paget's disease	Eczematous patches on nipple.

PATHOLOGY—VASCULAR/CARDIAC

Hypertension

Risk factors	↑ age, obesity, diabetes, smoking, genetics, Black > White > Asian.
Features	90% of HTN is primary (essential) and related to ↑ CO or ↑ TPR; remaining 10% mostly 2° to renal disease.
Predisposes to	Coronary heart disease, cerebrovascular accidents, CHF, renal failure, and aortic dissection.
Pathology	Hyaline thickening and atherosclerosis.

Pregnancy-induced hypertension (preeclampsia-eclampsia)

Preeclampsia is the triad of hypertension, proteinuria, and edema; eclampsia is the addition of seizures to the triad. Affects 7% of pregnant women from 20 weeks' gestation to 6 weeks postpartum. Increased incidence in patients with preexisting hypertension, diabetes, chronic renal disease, and autoimmune disorders.

Clinical features	Headache, blurred vision, abdominal pain, edema of face and extremities, altered mentation, hyperreflexia; lab findings may include thrombocytopenia, hyperuricemia.
Treatment	Delivery of fetus as soon as viable. Otherwise bed rest, salt restriction, and monitoring and treatment of hypertension. For eclampsia, a medical emergency, IV magnesium sulfate and diazepam.

UCV Path2.49

Atherosclerosis

Disease of elastic arteries and large and medium-sized muscular arteries.

Risk factors: smoking, hypertension, diabetes mellitus, hyperlipidemia.

Progression: fatty streaks → proliferative plaque → complex atheromas.

Complications: aneurysms, ischemia, infarcts, peripheral vascular disease, thrombus, emboli.

Location: abdominal aorta > coronary artery > popliteal artery > carotid artery.

Symptoms: angina, claudication, but can be asymptomatic.

UCV Path1.5

Ischemic heart disease

Possible manifestations:

1. **Angina**–
   Stable: mostly 2° to atherosclerosis (retrosternal chest pain with exertion)
   Prinzmetal's variant: occurs at rest, 2° to coronary artery spasm
   Unstable/crescendo: thrombosis in a branch (worsening chest pain) MI
2. **Myocardial infarction**—most often occurs in CAD involving the left anterior descending artery
3. **Sudden cardiac death**—death from cardiac causes within 1 hour of onset of symptoms, most commonly due to a lethal arrhythmia
4. **Chronic ischemic heart disease**—progressive onset of congestive heart failure over many years due to chronic ischemic myocardial damage

Infarcts: red versus pale

Red (hemorrhagic) infarcts occur in loose tissues with collaterals, such as lungs, intestine, or following reperfusion.

Pale infarcts occur in solid tissues with single blood supply, such as brain, heart, kidney, and spleen.

REd = **RE**perfusion.

Atheroma = central core + Fibrous cap

1. central core
   - cholesterol
   - cholesterol esters
   - Lipid laden ø, "Foam cells"
   - Ca^{2+}
2. Fibrous cap
   - smooth muscle cells
   - Foam cells
   - Fibrin
   - coagulation proteins
   - Extracell. matrix

MI

0-6 hrs : CPK ↑
>12 hrs : AST ↑ (non-specific: Heart, Liver, skeletal muscle)
24 hrs : CPK peaks
24-48 : AST peaks, LDH ↑
2-3 days : LDH peaks &
7 day : LDH persists
CPK normal.

Evolution of MI

Coronary artery occlusion: LAD > RCA > circumflex.

Symptoms: severe retrosternal pain, pain in left arm and/or jaw, shortness of breath, fatigue, adrenergic symptoms.

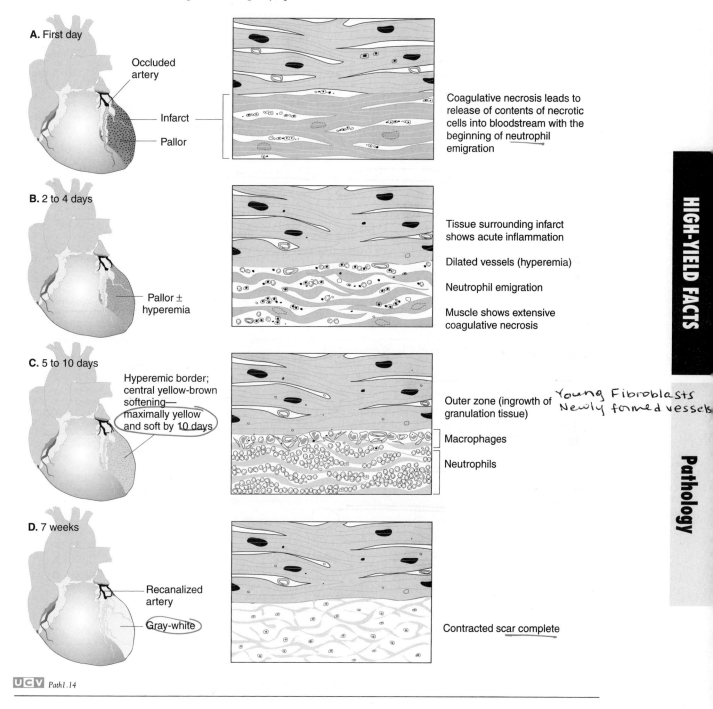

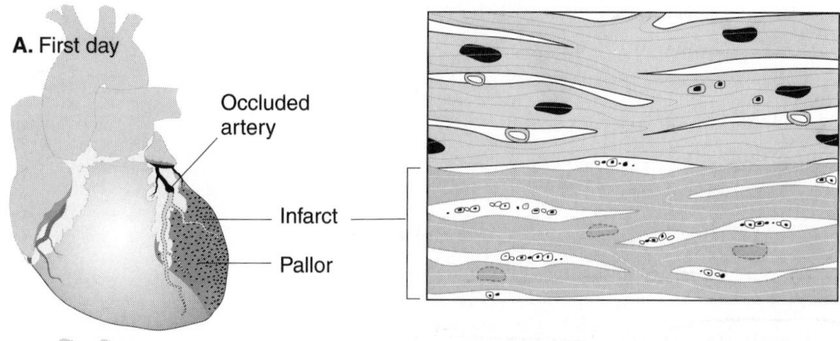

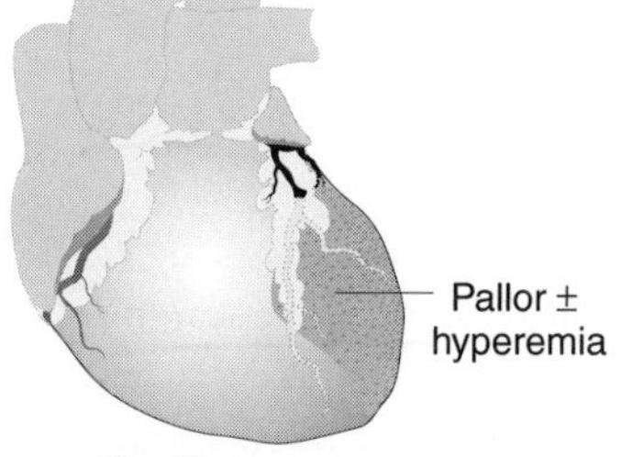

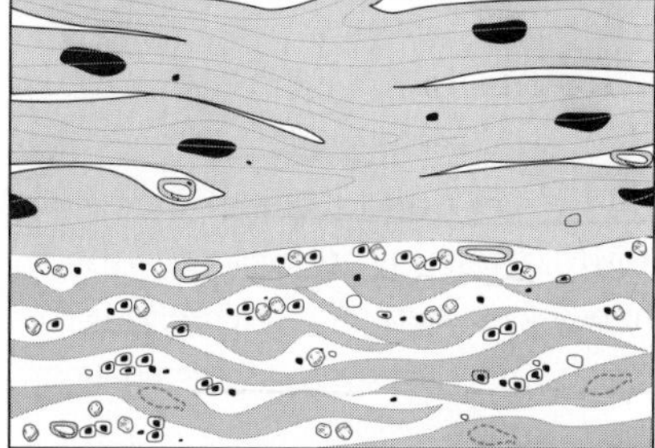

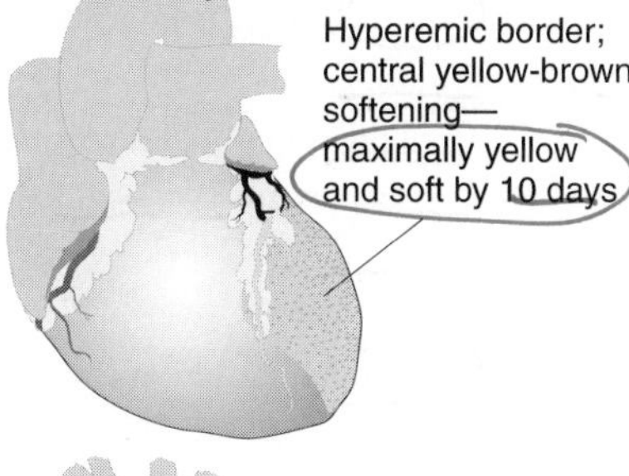

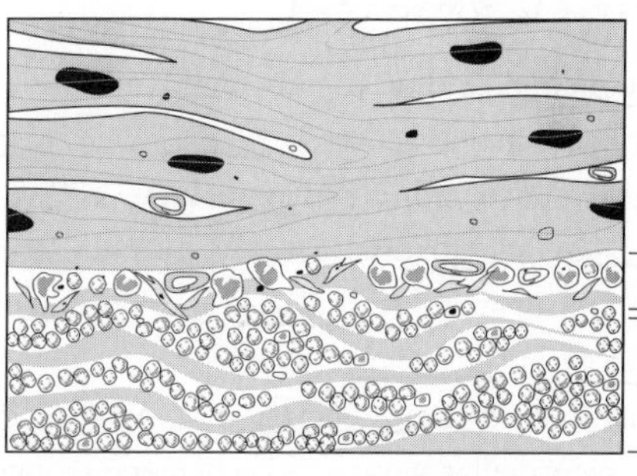

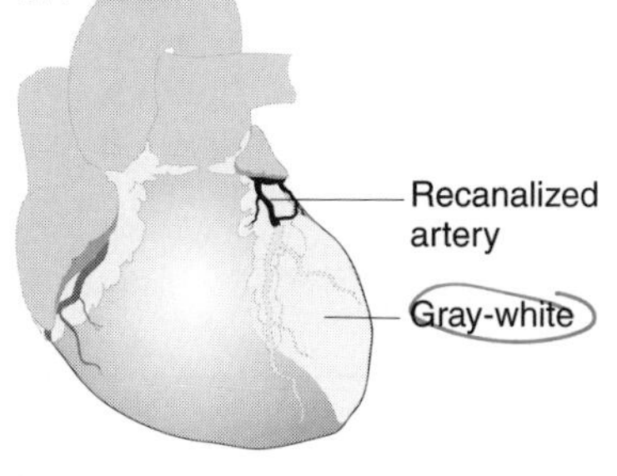

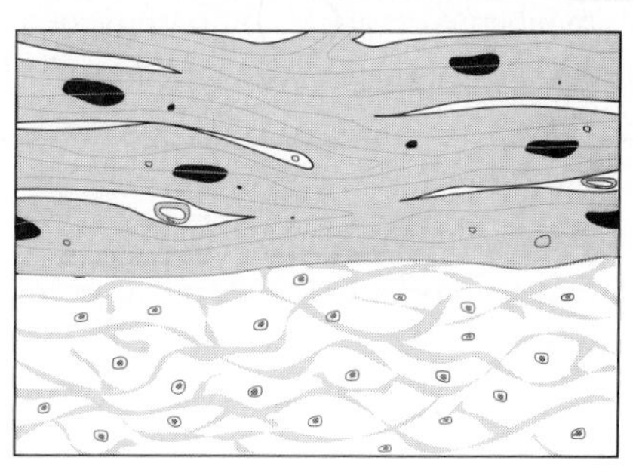

UCV Path1.14

Diagnosis of MI

In the first six hours, EKG is the gold standard.
Cardiac troponin I is used within the first 8 hours up to 7 to 10 days; more specific than other protein markers.
CK-MB is test of choice in the first 24 hours post-MI.
LDH_1 (former test of choice) is also elevated from 2 to 7 days post-MI.
AST is nonspecific and can be found in cardiac, liver, and skeletal muscle cells.
EKG changes can include ST elevation (transmural ischemia) and Q waves (transmural infarct).

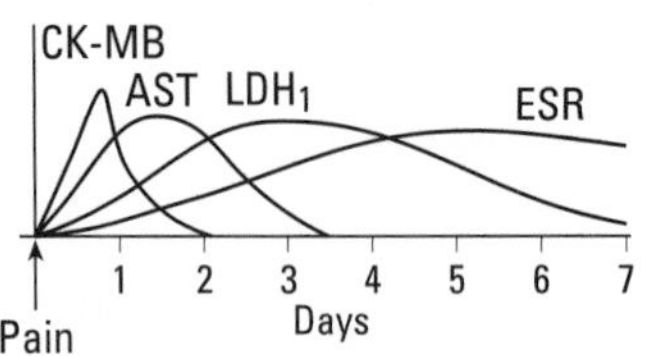

MI complications

1. Cardiac arrhythmia (90%)
2. LV failure and pulmonary edema (60%)
3. Thromboembolism: mural thrombus
4. Cardiogenic shock (large infarct: high risk of mortality)
5. Rupture of ventricular free wall, interventricular septum, papillary muscle (4–10 days post-MI), cardiac tamponade
6. Fibrinous pericarditis: friction rub (3–5 days post-MI)
7. Dressler's syndrome: autoimmune phenomenon resulting in fibrinous pericarditis (several weeks post-MI)

Cardiomyopathies

Dilated (congestive) cardiomyopathy Path1.9	Most common cardiomyopathy (90% of cases). Etiologies include chronic Alcohol abuse, Beriberi, postviral myocarditis by Coxsackievirus B, chronic Cocaine use, Doxorubicin toxicity, peripartum cardiomyopathy. Heart dilates and looks like a balloon on chest x-ray.	Systolic dysfunction ensues. Alcohol Beriberi (wet) Coxsackievirus B, Cocaine Doxorubicin
Hypertrophic cardiomyopathy (formerly IHSS) Path1.10	Hypertrophy often asymmetric and involving the intraventricular septum. 50% of cases are familial and are inherited as an AD trait. Cause of sudden death in young athletes. Walls of LV are thickened and chamber becomes banana-shaped on echocardiogram.	Diastolic dysfunction ensues.
Restrictive/obliterative cardiomyopathy	Major causes include sarcoidosis, amyloidosis, endocardial fibroelastosis, and endomyocardial fibrosis (Löffler's).	

UCV Path3.3

Heart murmurs

Aortic stenosis	Crescendo-decrescendo systolic ejection murmur, with LV >> aortic pressure during systole.
Aortic regurgitation	High-pitched "blowing" diastolic murmur. Wide pulse pressure.
Mitral stenosis	Rumbling late diastolic murmurs. LA >> LV pressure during diastole. Opening snap.
Mitral regurgitation	High-pitched "blowing" holosystolic murmur.
Mitral prolapse	Systolic murmur with midsystolic click. Most frequent valvular lesion, especially in young women.
VSD	Holosystolic murmur.
PDA	Continuous machine-like murmur.

UCV Anat.2, 8, Path1.4, 12, 13

Cardiac tumors

Myxomas are the most common 1° cardiac tumor in adults. Ninety percent occur in the atria (mostly LA). Myxomas are usually described as a "ball-valve" obstruction in the LA. Rhabdomyomas are the most frequent 1° cardiac tumor in children.

UCV Path3.1

CHF

Abnormality	Cause
Ankle, sacral edema	RV failure → increased venous pressure → fluid transudation.
Hepatomegaly (nutmeg liver)	Increased central venous pressure → increased resistance to portal flow. Rarely, leads to "cardiac cirrhosis."
Pulmonary congestion	LV failure → increased pulmonary venous pressure → pulmonary venous distention and transudation of fluid. Presence of hemosiderin-laden macrophages ("heart failure" cells).
Dyspnea on exertion	Failure of left ventricular output to increase during exercise.
Paroxysmal nocturnal dyspnea, pulmonary edema	Failure of left heart output to keep up with right heart output → acute rise in pulmonary venous and capillary pressure → transudation of fluid.
Orthopnea (shortness of breath when supine)	Pooling of blood in lungs in supine position adds volume to congested pulmonary vascular system; increased venous return not put out by left ventricle.
Cardiac dilation	Greater ventricular end-diastolic volume.

cor pulmonale

Decreased myocardial contractility
Decreased cardiac output
↓ Effective arterial blood volume
↑ Sympathetic nervous outflow
↑ Renin release
Maintains blood pressure
Angiotensin II
↑ Venous pressure
Renal vasconstriction
↑ Aldosterone secretion
↓ GFR
↑ Tubular reabsorption of Na^+ and H_2O
↓ Urinary excretion of Na^+ and H_2O
↑ Total body Na^+ and H_2O
Edema

UCV Path1.7

Right-sided heart failure = Distention of Neck veins

Embolus types

Fat, Air, Thrombus, Bacteria, Amniotic fluid, Tumor. Fat emboli are associated with long bone fractures and liposuction. Amniotic fluid emboli can lead to DIC, especially postpartum. Pulmonary embolus: chest pain, tachypnea, dyspnea.

An embolus moves like a **FAT BAT.** Approximately 95% of pulmonary emboli arise from deep leg veins.

Deep venous thrombosis

Predisposed by Virchow's triad:
1. Stasis
2. Hypercoagulability
3. Endothelial damage

- Formed in areas of Less Active Blood flow
- Dark Red
  Absent Lines of Zahn

Bacterial endocarditis

·Osler's Nodes
· Roth's spots
· Janeway Lesion
·Splinter hemorrhage

New murmur, anemia, fever, Osler nodes (tender raised lesions on finger or toe pads), Roth's spots (round white spots on retina surrounded by hemorrhage), Janeway lesions (small erythematous lesions on palm or sole), splinter hemorrhages on nailbed. Multiple blood cultures necessary for diagnosis (continuous bacteremia).

1. Acute: *Staphylococcus aureus* (high virulence). Large vegetations on previously normal valves. Rapid onset.
2. Subacute: *Streptococcus viridans* (low virulence). Smaller vegetations on congenitally abnormal or diseased valves. Sequela of dental procedures. More insidious onset.

Endocarditis may also be nonbacterial secondary to metastasis or renal failure (marantic/thrombotic endocarditis). Path3.5

Mitral valve is most frequently involved. Tricuspid valve endocarditis is associated with IV drug abuse.

UCV Micro.1.2

Rheumatic fever/ rheumatic heart disease

Rheumatic fever is a consequence of pharyngeal infection with group A, β-hemolytic streptococci. Late sequelae includes rheumatic heart disease, which affects heart valves: mitral > aortic >> tricuspid (high-pressure valves affected most). Associated with Aschoff bodies, migratory polyarthritis, erythema marginatum, elevated ASO titers.

Due to cross-reactivity, not direct effect of bacteria

FEVERSS:
Fever
Erythema marginatum
Valvular damage
ESR ↑
Red-hot joints (polyarthritis)
Subcutaneous nodules
St. Vitus' dance (chorea)

UCV Micro.1.23

Pericarditis

Causes: infection (viruses, TB, pyogenic bacteria; often by direct spread from lung or mediastinal lymph nodes), ischemic heart disease, chronic renal failure → uremia, and connective tissue disease.

Effusions are usually serous; hemorrhagic effusions are associated with TB and malignancy. Renal failure causes serous or fibrinous effusions.

Findings: pericardial pain, friction rub, EKG changes, pulsus paradoxus.

Can resolve without scarring or lead to chronic adhesive or chronic constrictive pericarditis.

UCV Micro1.1, Path3.3

Syphilitic heart disease

Tertiary syphilis disrupts the vasa vasorum of aorta via endarteritis obliterans and disrupts elastica (with consequent dilation of aorta and valve ring). Often affects the aortic root and ascending aorta.

Associated with a tree-bark appearance of the aorta.

Can result in aneurysm of ascending aorta or aortic arch and aortic valve incompetence.

UCV Path1.17

Buerger's disease

Known as **smoker's disease** and thromboangiitis obliterans; idiopathic, segmental, thrombosing vasculitis of intermediate and small peripheral arteries and veins.

Findings: intermittent claudication, superficial nodular phlebitis, cold sensitivity (Raynaud's phenomenon), severe pain in affected part; may lead to gangrene.

Treatment: quit smoking.

UCV Path1.19

Takayasu's arteritis	Known as "**pulseless disease**": thickening of aortic arch and/or proximal great vessels, causing weak pulses in upper extremities and ocular disturbances. Associated with an elevated ESR. Primarily affects young Asian females. **F**ever, **A**rthritis, **N**ight sweats, **MY**algia, **SKIN** nodules.	Affects medium and large arteries. **FAN MY SKIN.**
Temporal arteritis UCV Path1.18	Most common vasculitis that affects medium and small arteries, usually branches of carotid artery. Findings include unilateral headache, jaw claudication, impaired vision (occlusion of ophthalmic artery, which can lead to blindness). Half of patients have systemic involvement and syndrome of polymyalgia rheumatica. Associated with elevated ESR.	**Temp**oral = signs near **Temp**les. ESR is markedly elevated. Also known as giant cell arteritis. Affects elderly females.
Polyarteritis nodosa	Characterized by necrotizing immune complex inflammation of small or medium-sized muscular arteries, typically involving renal and visceral vessels.	PAN = P-ANca
Symptoms	Fever, weight loss, malaise, abdominal pain, headache, myalgia, hypertension.	
Findings	Cotton-wool spots, microaneurysms, pericarditis, myocarditis, palpable purpura. Increased ESR. Associated with hepatitis B infection in 30% of patients. **P-ANCA** (perinuclear pattern of antineutrophil cytoplasmic antibodies) is often present in the serum and correlates with disease activity, primarily in small vessel disease.	
Treatment UCV Path2.76	Corticosteroids, azathioprine, and/or cyclophosphamide.	
Wegener's granulomatosis	Characterized by focal necrotizing vasculitis and necrotizing granulomas in the lung and upper airway and by necrotizing glomerulonephritis.	
Symptoms	Perforation of nasal septum, chronic sinusitis, otitis media, mastoiditis, cough, dyspnea, hemoptysis.	
Findings	C-ANCA is a strong marker of disease; CXR may reveal large nodular densities; hematuria and red cell casts.	
Treatment UCV Path2.66	Cyclophosphamide, corticosteroids, and/or methotrexate.	

Glomerular pathology

Nephritic syndrome: hematuria, hypertension, oliguria.

1. Acute poststreptococcal glomerulonephritis
   LM: glomeruli enlarged and hypercellular; neutrophils; "lumpy-bumpy." EM: subepithelial humps. IF: granular pattern.
   Most frequently seen in children. Peripheral, periorbital edema. Resolves spontaneously.
2. Rapidly progressive (crescentic) glomerulonephritis
   LM and IF: crescent-moon shape.
   Rapid course to renal failure from one of many causes.
3. Goodpasture's syndrome
   IF: linear pattern; anti-GBM antibodies.
   Hemoptysis, hematuria.
4. Membranoproliferative glomerulonephritis
   EM: subendothelial humps; "tram track."
   Slowly progresses to renal failure.
5. IgA nephropathy (Berger's disease)
   IF and EM: mesangial deposits of IgA.
   Mild disease.

Nephrotic syndrome: massive proteinuria, hypoalbuminemia, generalized edema, hyperlipidemia.

IgG C3

1. Membranous glomerulonephritis
   LM: diffuse capillary thickening. IF: granular pattern. "spiked dome" subepithelial
   A common cause of adult nephrotic syndrome.
2. Minimal change disease (lipoid nephrosis)
   LM: normal glomeruli. EM: foot process effacement.
   Most common cause of childhood nephrotic syndrome.
3. Focal segmental glomerular sclerosis
   LM: segmental sclerosis and hyalinosis.
   More severe disease in HIV patients.
4. Diabetic nephropathy
   LM: Kimmelstiel–Wilson lesions. – Nodular glomerulosclerosis
5. SLE (5 patterns of renal involvement)
   LM: Wire loop appearance with extensive granular subendothelial basement-membrane deposits in membranous glomerulonephritis pattern.

(LM = light microscopy; EM = electron microscopy; IF = immunofluorescence)

UCV Path2.87-92, 3.107

Kidney stones

Can lead to severe complications such as hydronephrosis and pyelonephritis.
Four major types:

Calcium — Comprises the majority of kidney stones (80-85%). Calcium oxalate or calcium phosphate or both. Stones are radiopaque. Disorders or conditions that cause hypercalcemia (e.g., cancer, increased PTH, increased vitamin D, milk-alkali syndrome) can all lead to hypercalciuria and stones.

Ammonium magnesium phosphate — Second most common kidney stone. Radiolucent and formed in alkaline urine by urease-positive bugs such as *Proteus vulgaris* or *Staphylococcus*. Can form large struvite calculi that can be a nidus for UTIs.

Uric acid — Strong association with hyperuricemia (e.g., gout). Often seen as a result of diseases with increased cell proliferation and turnover, such as leukemia and myeloproliferative disorders.

Cystine — Most often secondary to cystinuria.

UCV Path2.98

Acid-base physiology

	pH	P_{CO_2}	$[HCO_3^-]$	Cause	Compensatory response
Metabolic acidosis	↓	↓	**↓**	Diabetic ketoacidosis; diarrhea; lactic acidosis; salicylate OD; acetazolamide OD	Hyperventilation
Respiratory acidosis	↓	**↑**	↑	COPD; airway obstruction	Renal $[HCO_3^-]$ reabsorption
Respiratory alkalosis	↑	**↓**	↓	High altitude; hyperventilation	Renal $[HCO_3^-]$ secretion
Metabolic alkalosis	↑	↑	**↑**	Vomiting	Hypoventilation

Henderson–Hasselbalch equation: $pH = pKa + \log \frac{[HCO_3^-]}{0.03\ P_{CO_2}}$

Key: **↑ ↓** = primary disturbance; ↓ ↑ = compensatory response.

Acidosis/alkalosis

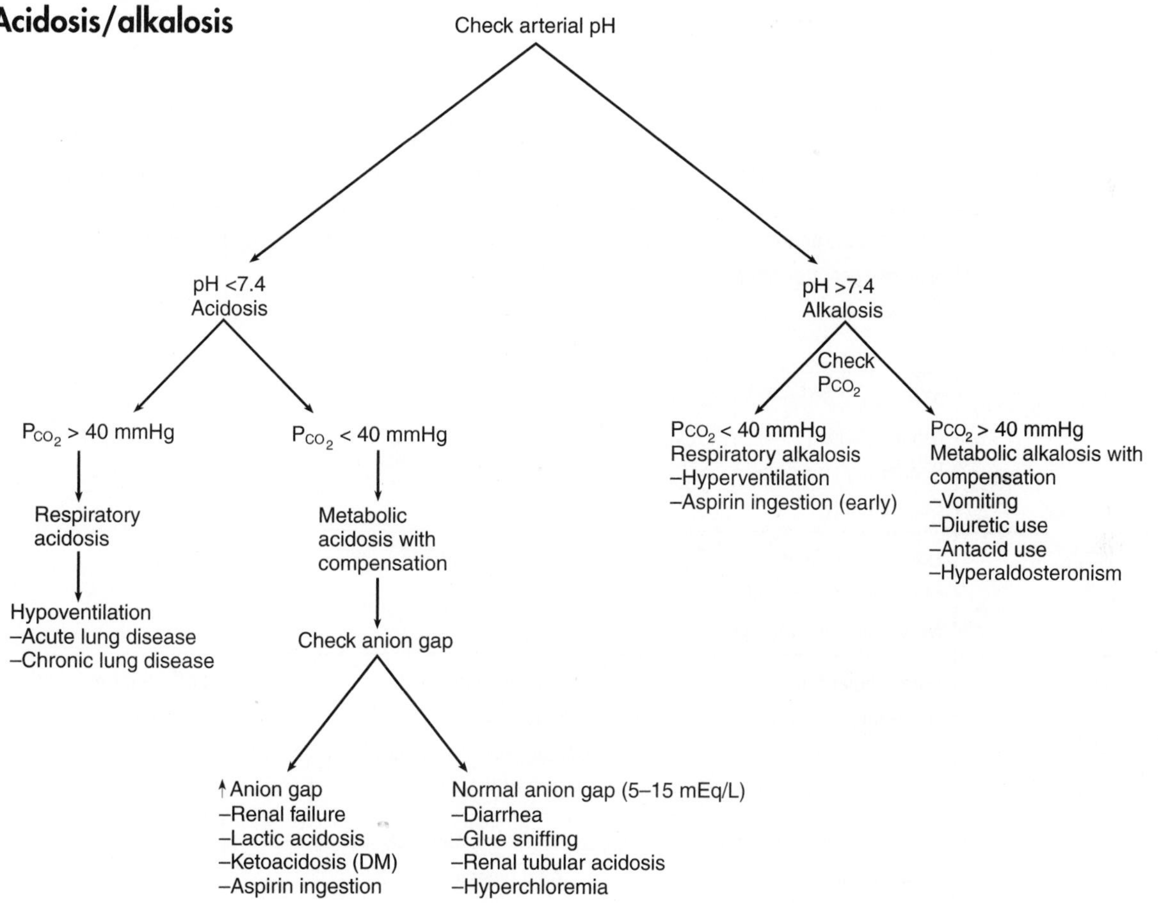

UCV *Bio.9, 11, 25, 34, Path2.99*

Anion gap acidosis

Gap is $Na^+ - (Cl^- + HCO_3^-)$ = 8 to 12 mEq/L.

If elevated, may be due to:

Methanol
Uremia
Diabetic ketoacidosis
Paraldehyde or **P**henformin
Iron tablets or **I**NH
Lactic acidosis (CN^-, CO, shock)
Ethanol or **E**thylene glycol
Salicylates

MUD PILES

Renal failure

Failure to make urine and excrete nitrogenous wastes. Consequences:

1. Anemia (failure of erythropoietin production)
2. Renal osteodystrophy (failure of active vitamin D production) Hypokalcemia
3. Hyperkalemia, which can lead to cardiac arrhythmias
4. Metabolic acidosis due to ↓ acid secretion and ↓ generation of HCO_3^-
5. Uremia (increased BUN, creatinine)
6. Sodium and H_2O excess → CHF and pulmonary edema

Two forms of renal failure: acute renal failure (often due to hypoxia) and chronic renal failure.

Electrolytes

Electrolyte	Functions	Causes and signs of deficiency	Causes and signs of toxicity
Ca^{2+} *Bio.15, 17*	Muscle contraction Neurotransmitter release Bones, teeth	Kids–rickets Adults–osteomalacia Contributes to osteoporosis Tetany	Delirium
PO_4^{3-}	ATP Nucleic acids Phosphorylation Bones, teeth	Kids–rickets Adults–osteomalacia	Low serum Ca^{2+} Can cause bone loss Renal stones
Na^+ *Bio.20*	Extracellular fluid Maintains plasma volume Nerve/muscle function	2° to injury or illness	Delirium
K^+ *Bio.18*	Intracellular fluid Nerve/muscle function	2° to injury, illness, or diuretics Causes weakness, paralysis, confusion	EKG changes Arrhythmia
Cl^-	Fluid/electrolyte balance Gastric acid HCO_3^-/Cl^- shift in RBC	2° to emesis, diuretics, renal disease	None that are clinically significant
Mg^{2+} *Bio.19*	Bones, teeth Enzyme cofactor	2° to malabsorption Diarrhea, alcoholism	↓ Reflexes ↓ Respiration

UCV

Azotemia = ↑ BUN + ↑ serum creatinine

① Pre-Renal
↑↑ Bun
↑ creatinine
• CHF
• Shock

② Renal
• Gentamycin Toxicity
• Progressive Glomeruloneph.

③ Post Renal
• Bladder outlet obstruction

Alcoholism

Physiologic tolerance and dependence with symptoms of withdrawal (tremor, tachycardia, hypertension, malaise, nausea, delirium tremens) when intake is interrupted. Continued drinking despite medical and social contraindications and life disruptions.

Treatment: disulfiram to condition the patient negatively against alcohol use. Supportive treatment of other systemic manifestations. Alcoholics Anonymous and other peer support groups are most successful in sustaining abstinence.

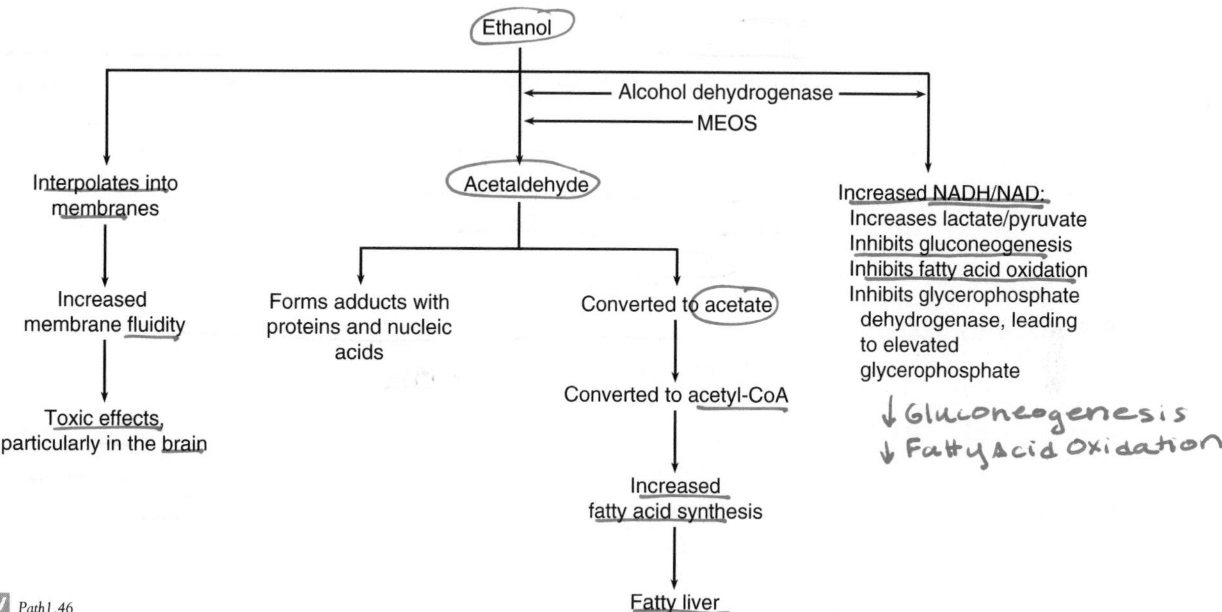

UCV Path1.46

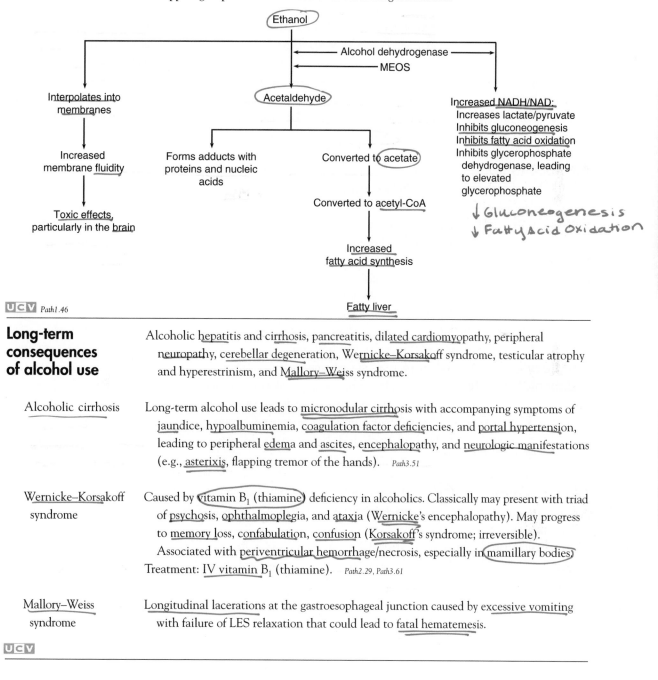

Long-term consequences of alcohol use

Alcoholic hepatitis and cirrhosis, pancreatitis, dilated cardiomyopathy, peripheral neuropathy, cerebellar degeneration, Wernicke–Korsakoff syndrome, testicular atrophy and hyperestrinism, and Mallory–Weiss syndrome.

Alcoholic cirrhosis

Long-term alcohol use leads to micronodular cirrhosis with accompanying symptoms of jaundice, hypoalbuminemia, coagulation factor deficiencies, and portal hypertension, leading to peripheral edema and ascites, encephalopathy, and neurologic manifestations (e.g., asterixis, flapping tremor of the hands). *Path3.51*

Wernicke–Korsakoff syndrome

Caused by vitamin B_1 (thiamine) deficiency in alcoholics. Classically may present with triad of psychosis, ophthalmoplegia, and ataxia (Wernicke's encephalopathy). May progress to memory loss, confabulation, confusion (Korsakoff's syndrome; irreversible). Associated with periventricular hemorrhage/necrosis, especially in mamillary bodies.

Treatment: IV vitamin B_1 (thiamine). *Path2.29, Path3.61*

Mallory–Weiss syndrome

Longitudinal lacerations at the gastroesophageal junction caused by excessive vomiting with failure of LES relaxation that could lead to fatal hematemesis.

UCV

Argyll–Robertson pupil	Argyll–Robertson pupil constricts with accommodation but is not reactive to light. Pathognomonic for 3° syphilis.	Argyll–Robertson Pupil **ARP:** **A**ccommodation **R**esponse **P**resent.
Amyloidosis UCV Path2.94	Primary (light chain deposition) seen with multiple myeloma or Waldenström's macroglobulinemia; secondary (amyloid-associated) can cause nephrotic syndrome in kidney. Apple-green birefringence on Congo red stain.	Alzheimer's disease associated with β-amyloid deposition in the cerebral cortex; islet cell amyloid deposition characteristic of diabetes mellitus type II.
Aschoff body	Aschoff bodies (granuloma with giant cells) and Anitschkow's cells (activated histiocytes) are found in rheumatic heart disease.	Think of two **RH**ussians with **RH**eumatic heart disease (Aschoff and Anitschkow).
Auer bodies (rods)	Auer rods are cytoplasmic inclusions in granulocytes and myeloblasts. Primarily seen in acute promyelocytic leukemia.	
Casts	Casts of nephron: RBC casts = glomerular inflammation, ischemia, or malignant hypertension. WBC casts = inflammation in renal interstitium, tubules, and glomeruli. Hyaline casts often seen in normal urine. Waxy casts seen in chronic renal failure.	Presence of casts indicates that hematuria/pyuria is of renal origin.
Erythrocyte sedimentation rate	Very nonspecific test that measures acute-phase reactants. Dramatically increased with infection, malignancy, connective tissue disease. Also increased with pregnancy, inflammatory disease, anemia. Decreased with sickle cell anemia, polycythemia, congestive heart failure.	Simple, cheap, but nonspecific. Should not be used for asymptomatic screening; can be used to diagnose and monitor temporal arteritis and polymyalgia rheumatica.
Ghon complex	TB granulomas with lobar or perihilar lymph node involvement (Ghon focus and lymph node involvement). Reflects primary infection or exposure.	
Hyperlipidemia signs	Atheromata = plaques in blood vessel walls. Xantheloma = plaques or nodules composed of lipid-laden histiocytes in the skin, especially the eyelids. Tendinous xanthoma = lipid deposit in tendon, especially Achilles. Corneal arcus = lipid deposit in cornea, nonspecific (arcus senilis).	

Psammoma bodies	Laminated, concentric, calcific spherules seen in: 1. Papillary adenocarcinoma of thyroid 2. Serous papillary cystadenocarcinoma of ovary 3. Meningioma 4. Malignant mesothelioma	 **P**apillary (thyroid) **S**erous (ovary) **a** **M**eningioma **M**esothelioma
RBC forms	Biconcave = normal. Spherocytes = hereditary spherocytosis, autoimmune hemolysis. Elliptocyte = hereditary elliptocytosis. Macro-ovalocyte = megaloblastic anemia, marrow failure. Helmet cell, schistocyte = DIC, traumatic hemolysis. Sickle cell = sickle cell anemia. Teardrop cell = myeloid metaplasia with myelofibrosis. Acanthocyte = spiny appearance in abetalipoproteinemia. Target cell = thalassemia, liver disease, HbC. Poikilocytes = nonuniform shapes in TTP/HUS, microvascular damage, DIC. Burr cell = TTP/HUS.	
HLA-B27	Associated with **P**soriasis, **A**nkylosing spondylitis, **I**nflammatory bowel disease, **R**eiter's syndrome. Ninety-fold greater chance of developing ankylosing spondylitis with HLA-B27.	**PAIR**
Reed–Sternberg cells	Distinctive tumor giant cell seen in Hodgkin's disease; large cell that is binucleate or bilobed with the 2 halves as mirror images ("owl's eyes"). Necessary but not sufficient for a diagnosis of Hodgkin's disease.	There are 4 types of Hodgkin's disease; nodular sclerosis variant is the only one seen in women > men (excellent prognosis).
Virchow's (sentinel) node	A firm supraclavicular lymph node, often on left side, easily palpable (can be detected by medical students), also known as "jugular gland." Presumptive evidence of malignant visceral neoplasm (classically stomach).	

Peripheral blood smears

Normal

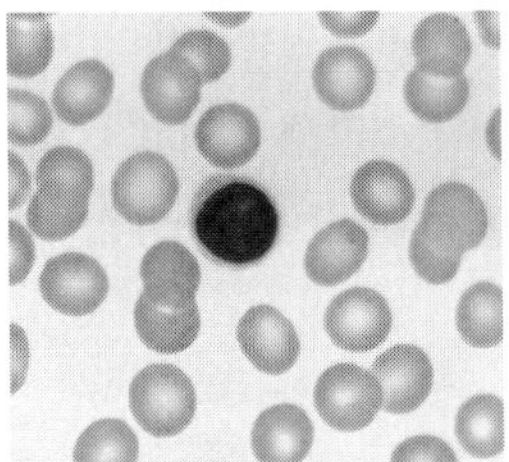

—normal

Microcytic hypochromic anemia

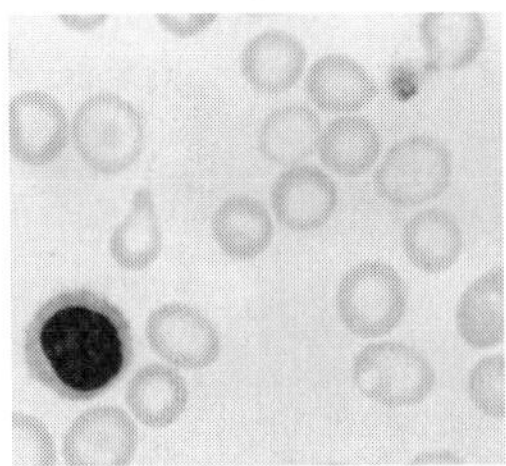

—normally 2° to **iron deficiency**
—low serum ferritin
—elevated serum iron binding capacity

Megaloblastic anemia

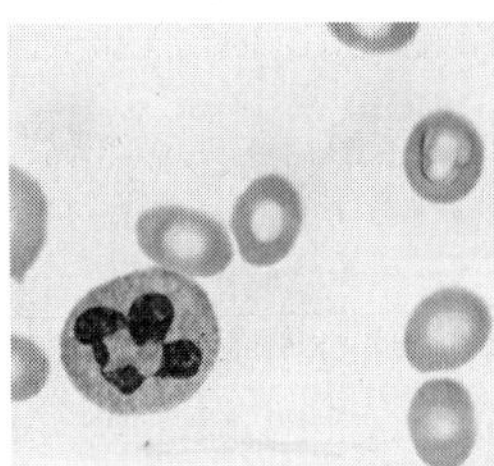

—2° to **folate or B_{12} deficiency**
—hypersegmented (5–7 lobes) PMNs
—large red blood cells (MCV > 100)
—**never** give folate to a patient who is deficient in B_{12}
—**pernicious anemia**—autoimmune disease which causes B_{12} deficiency by depleting **intrinsic factor,** which is needed to absorb B_{12} in **terminal ileum**

Target cells

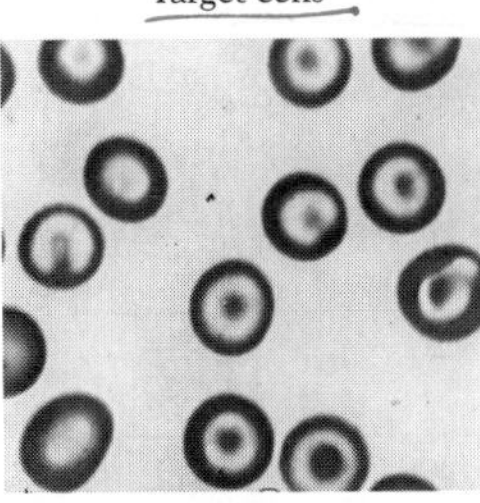

—thalassemia
—hemoglobin C disease
—liver disease

Hemoglobin SS with sickle cells

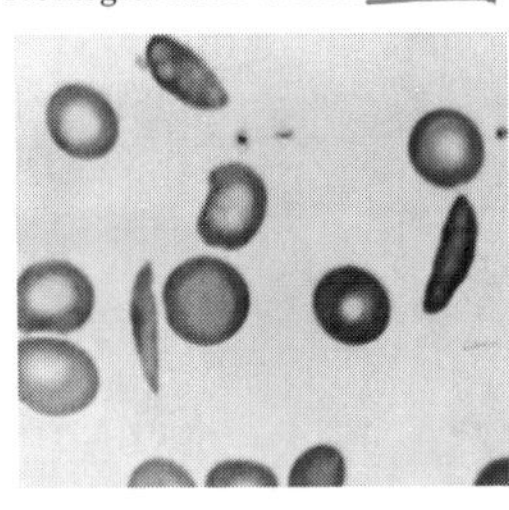

—**HbS**—β-globin GLU → VAL at #6; 8% of US blacks are HbS carriers
—cells will sickle 2° to hypoxia, dehydration, and ↑ blood viscosity
—anemia
—vaso-occlusive crises +/– chest pain
—aplastic crises (B19 virus)
—splenic sequestration crises
—strokes

Enzyme markers

Serum enzyme	Major diagnostic use
Aminotransferases (AST and ALT)	Myocardial infarction (AST only) Viral hepatitis (ALT > AST) Alcoholic hepatitis (AST > ALT)
Amylase	Acute pancreatitis, mumps
Ceruloplasmin (decreased)	Wilson's disease
CPK (creatine phosphokinase)	Muscle disorders (e.g., DMD) and myocardial infarction (CPK-MB)
GGT (γ-glutamyl transpeptidase)	Various liver diseases
LDH-1 (lactate dehydrogenase fraction 1)	Myocardial infarction (LDH1 > LDH2)
Lipase	Acute pancreatitis
Alkaline phosphatase	Bone disease, obstructive liver disease

NOTES

NOTES

NOTES

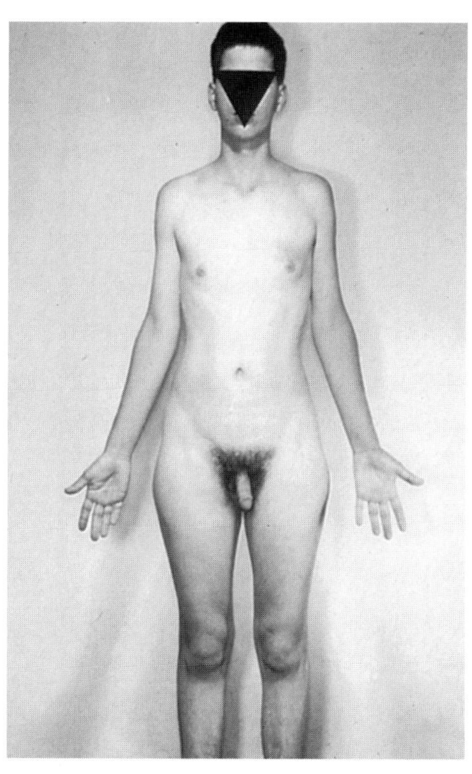

Klinefelter's syndrome (XXY). Phenotype includes a female fat distribution with male external genitalia.

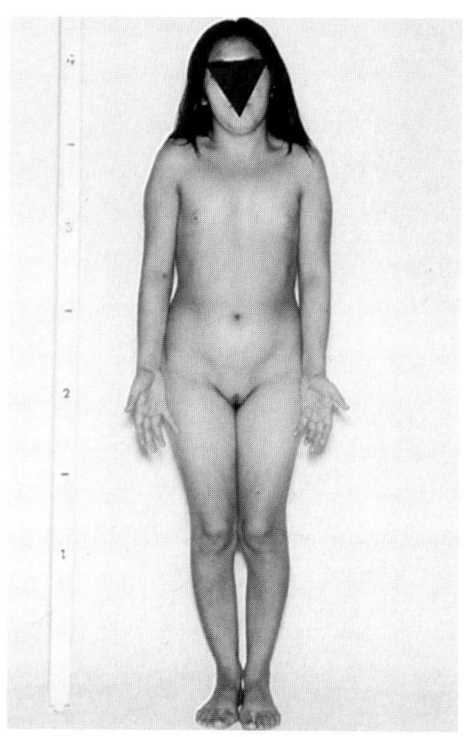

Turner's syndrome (XO). Phenotype includes short stature, webbing of the neck, and poorly developed secondary sex characteristics.

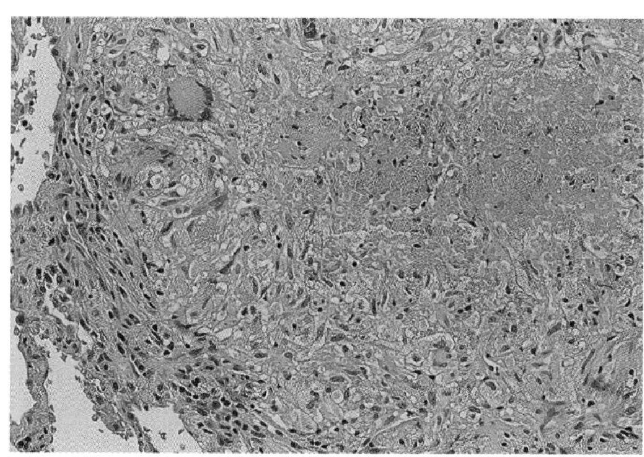

Granulomatous inflammation with Langhan's giant cell, epithelioid cells, and caseous necrosis, microscopic.

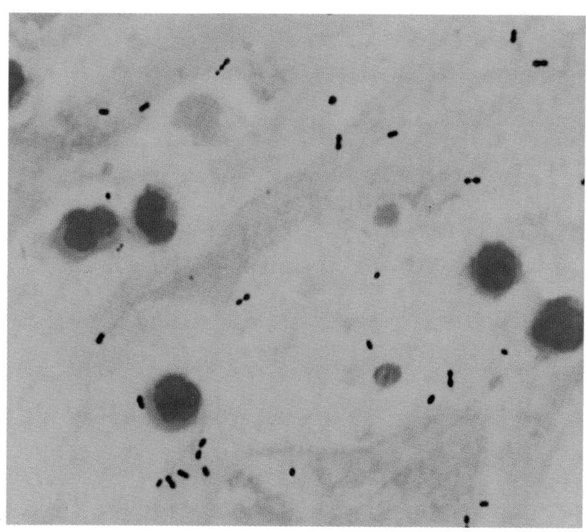

Streptococcus pneumoniae. Sputum sample from a patient with pneumonia shows gram-positive diplococci.

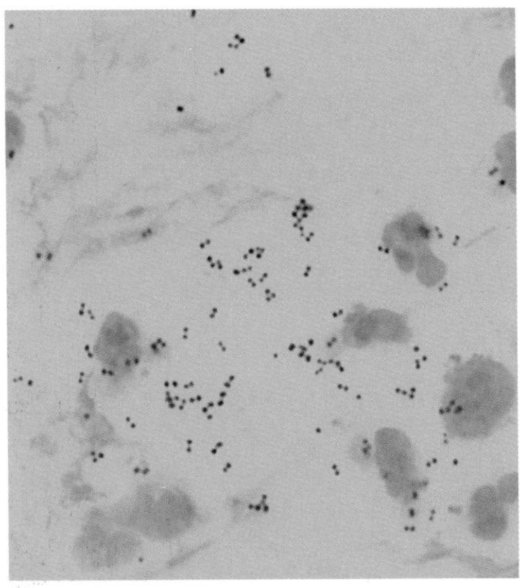

Staphylococcus aureus. Sputum sample from another patient with pneumonia shows gram-positive cocci in clusters.

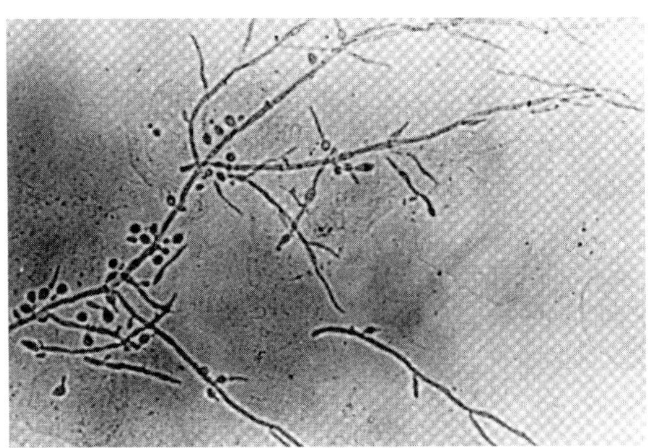

Candidal vaginitis. Branched and budding *Candida albicans* visable on KOH preparation of whitish vaginal discharge.

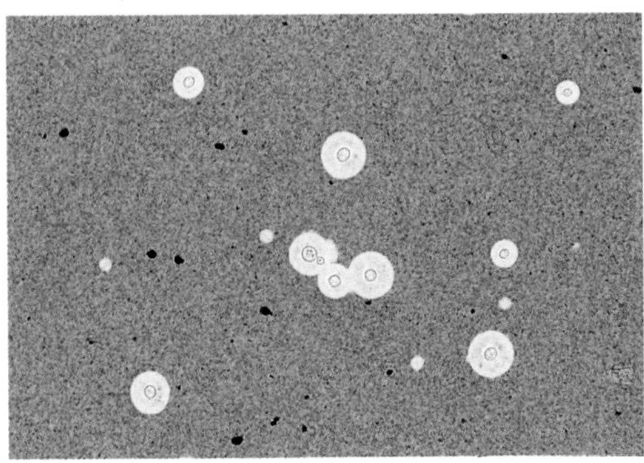

Cryptococcus neoformans, polysaccaride capsule visible by India ink preparation, in CSF from an AIDS patient with meningoencephalitis.

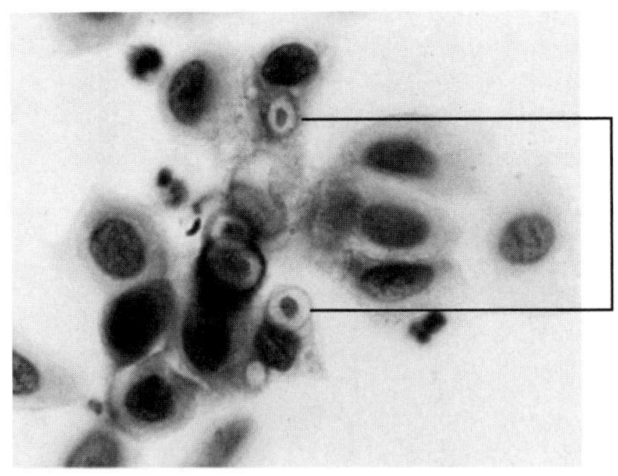

Trophozoites of ***Trichomonas vaginalis*** by Giemsa stain.

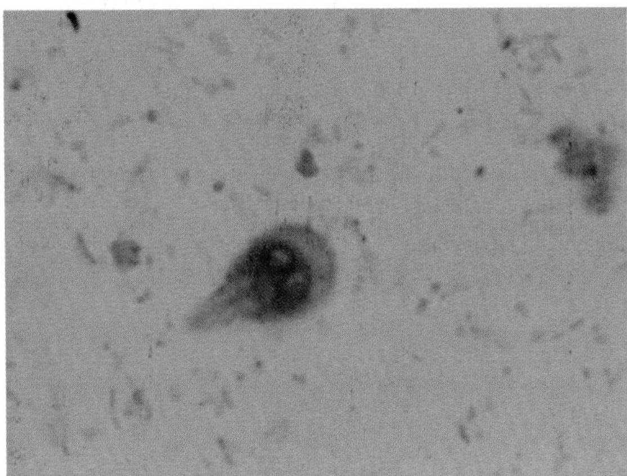

Giardia lamblia, small intestine, microscopic. Trophozoite has a classic pear shape with double nuclei giving an owl's eye appearance.

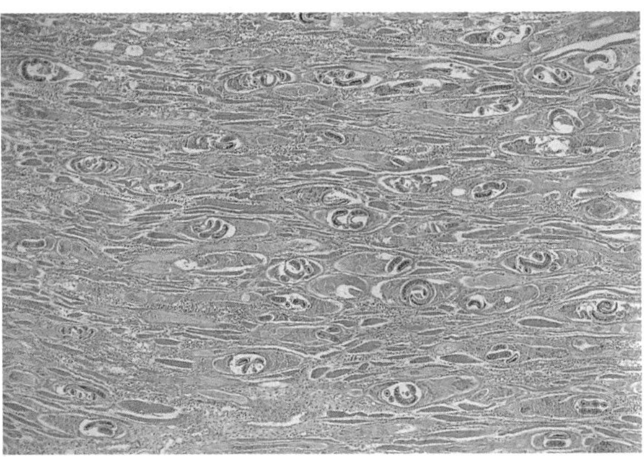

Taenia solium, the pig tapeworm, infesting porcine myocardium. When humans injest this meat, the larvae attach to the wall of the small intestine and mature to adult worms.

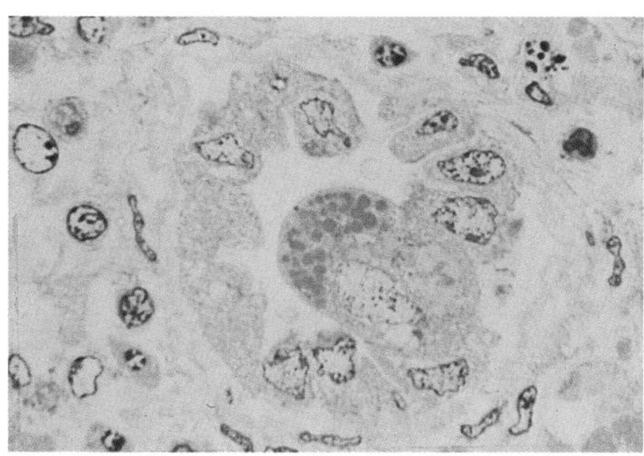

Cytomegalovirus (CMV) giant cell with multiple hyaline inclusions in a renal tubule. Of special concern in HIV patients (CMV retinitis) and organ transplant patients (as here, in a transplanted kidney); however, CMV can infect almost anything. Treatment is ganciclovir or foscarnet.

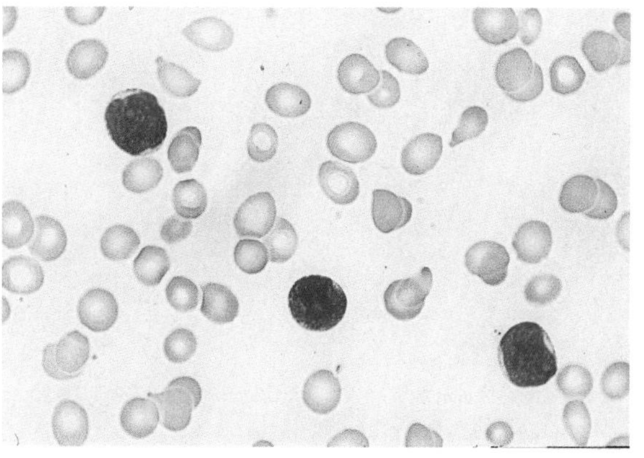

Acute lymphocytic leukemia, peripheral blood smear, from a 10-year old child.

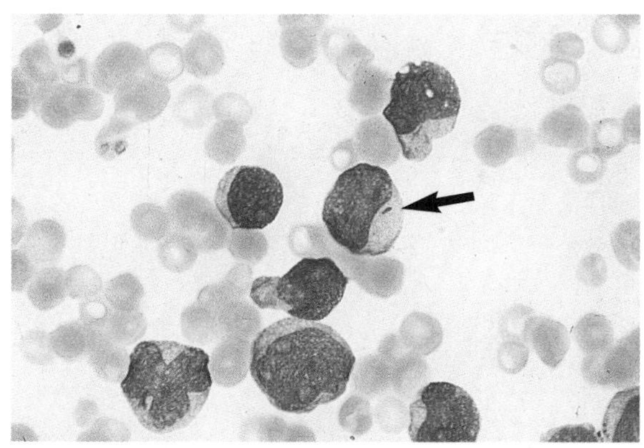

Acute myelogenous leukemia with Auer rod (arrow), peripheral blood smear.

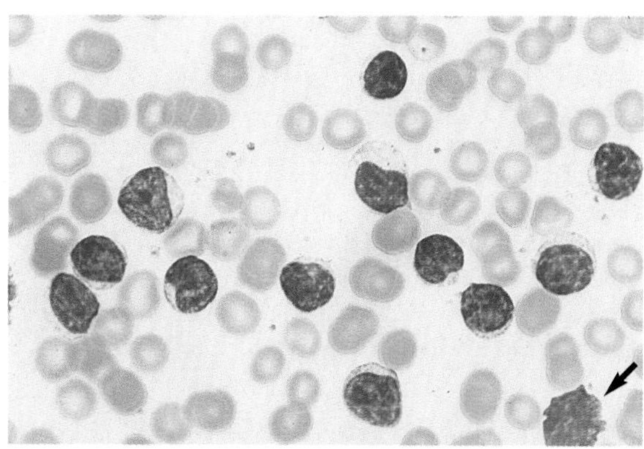

Chronic lymphocytic leukemia, peripheral blood smear, microscopic. In **CLL,** the lymphocytes are excessively fragile. These lymphocytes are easily disrupted during slide preparation, forming "smudge cells" (arrow).

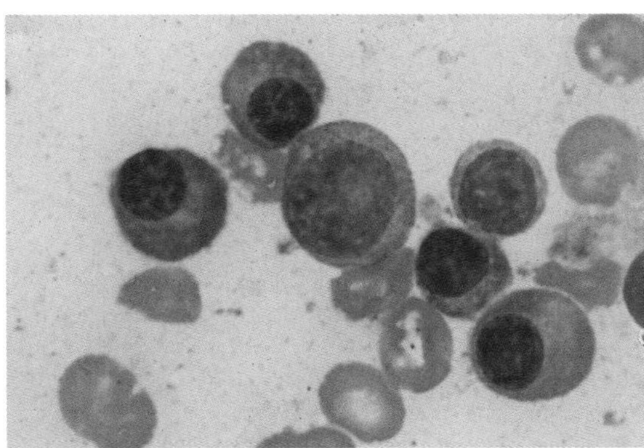

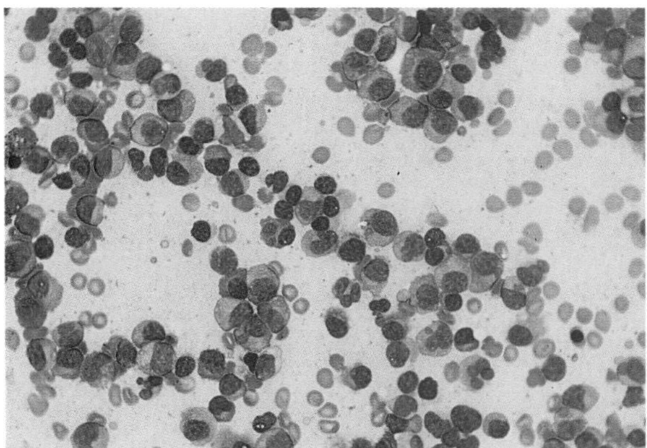

Smears from a patient with **multiple myeloma,** displaying an abundance of plasma cells. RBCs will often be seen in rouleaux formation, stacked like poker chips. Multiple myeloma is associated with hypercalcemia, lytic bone lesions, and renal insufficiency due to Bence Jones (light-chain) proteinuria.

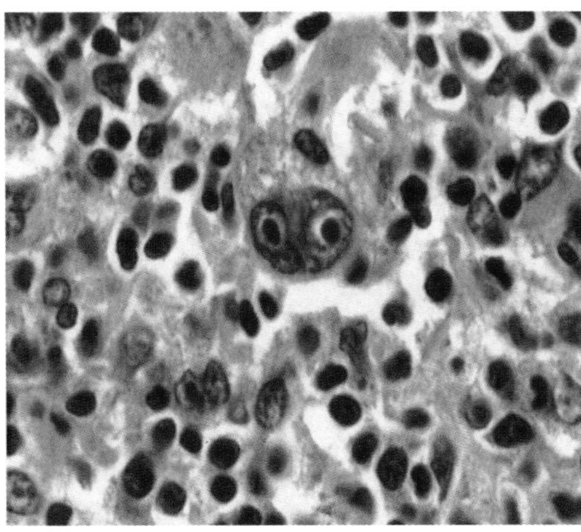

Hodgkin's disease (Reed-Sternberg cells). Binucleate RS cells displaying prominent inclusion-like nucleoli surrounded by lymphocytes and other reacting inflammatory cells. The RS cell is a necessary but insufficient pathologic finding for the diagnosis of Hodgkin's disease.

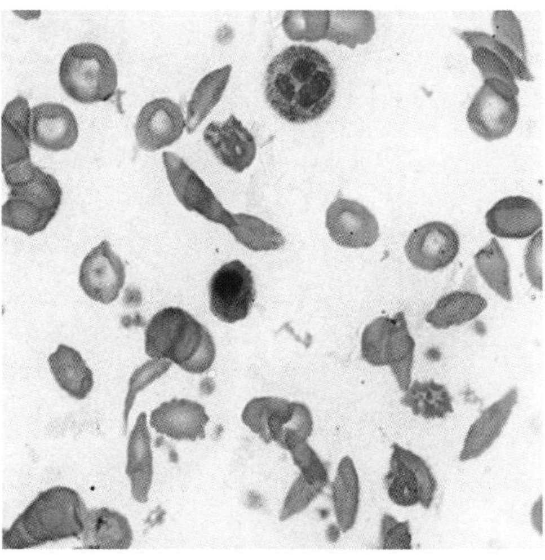

Sickle cell anemia: note the sickled cells as well as anisocytosis, poikilocytosis, and nucleated RBCs.

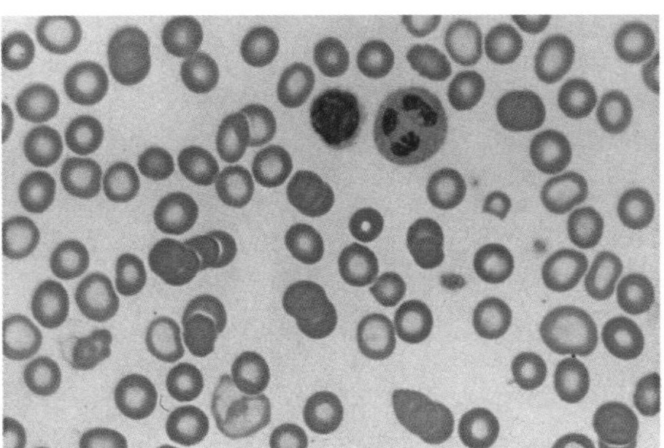

Iron deficiency anemia: microcytosis and hypochromia.

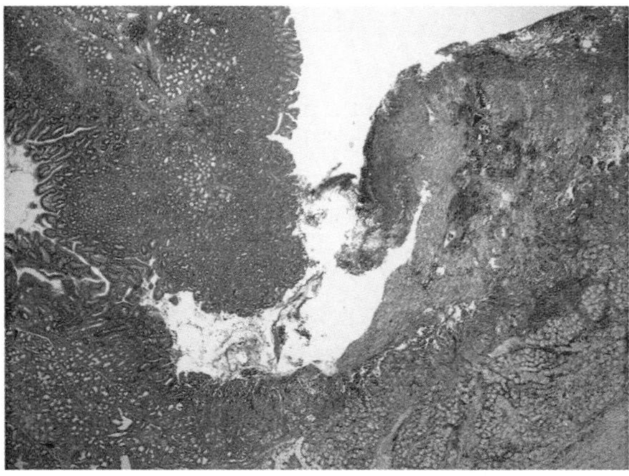

Duodenal ulcer: the epithelium is ulcerated, and the lamina propria is infiltrated with inflammatory cells. Necrotic debris is present in the ulcer crater.

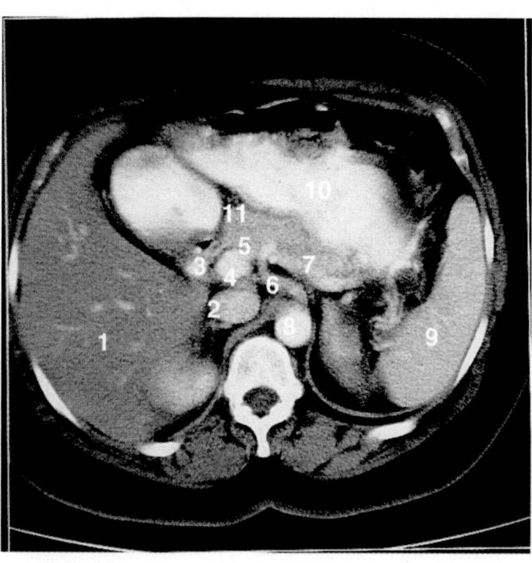

CT abdomen with contrast—normal anatomy.

1 Liver
2 Inferior vena cava
3 Portal vein
4 Hepatic artery
5 Gastroduodenal artery
6 Celiac trunk
7 Splenic vein
8 Aorta
9 Spleen
10 Stomach
11 Pancreas

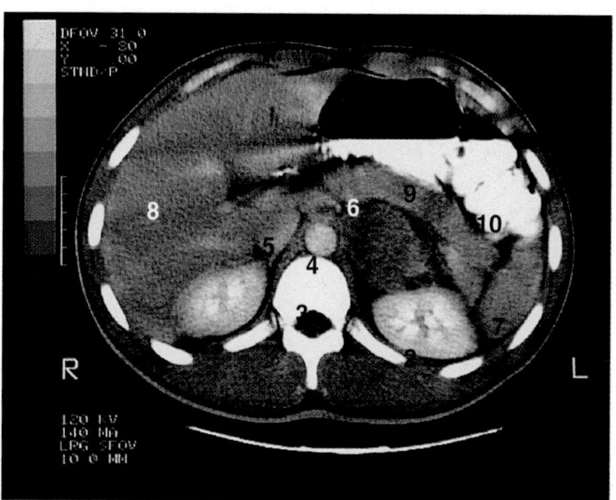

Left adrenal mass.

1 Large left adrenal mass
2 Kidney
3 Vertebral body
4 Aorta
5 IVC
6 Pancreas
7 Spleen
8 Liver
9 Stomach with air and contrast
10 Colon–splenic flexure

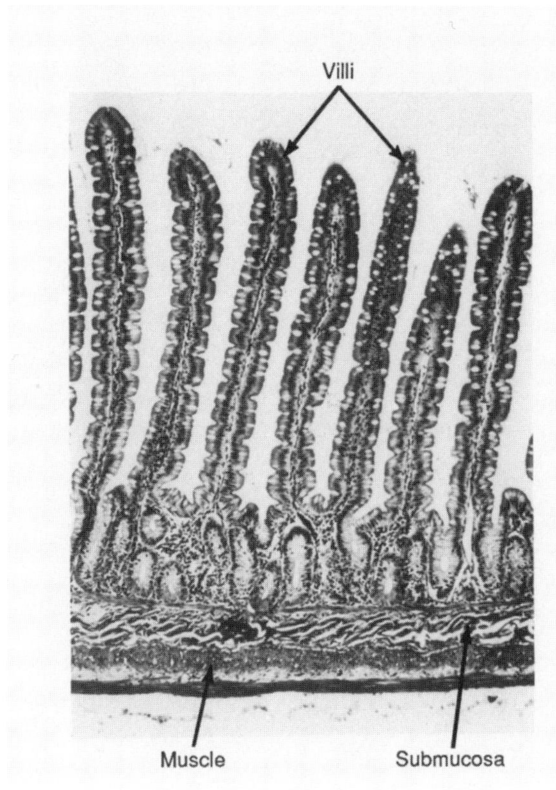

Photomicrograph of the small intestine.

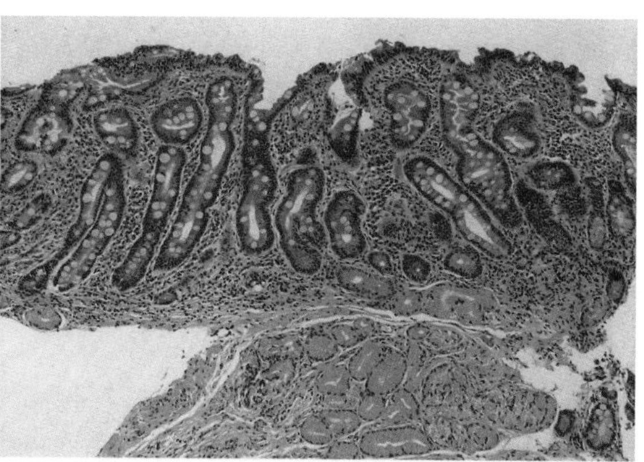

Celiac sprue (gluten-sensitive enteropathy): histology shows blunting of villi and crypt hyperplasia.

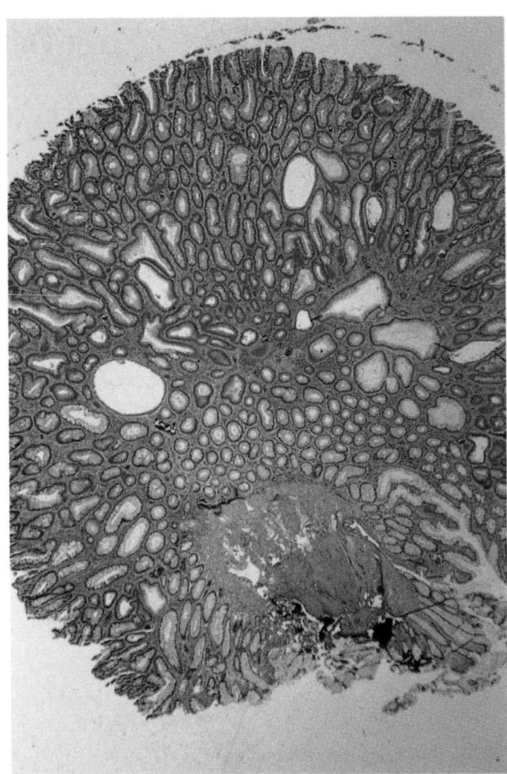

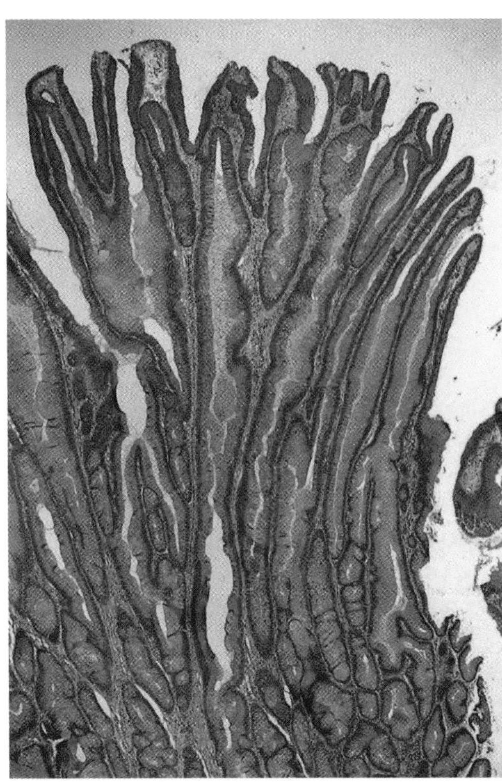

A B

Colonic polyps. Tubular adenomas (A) are smaller and rounded in morphology, and have less malignant potential than **villous adenomas (B),** which are composed of long, finger-like projections.

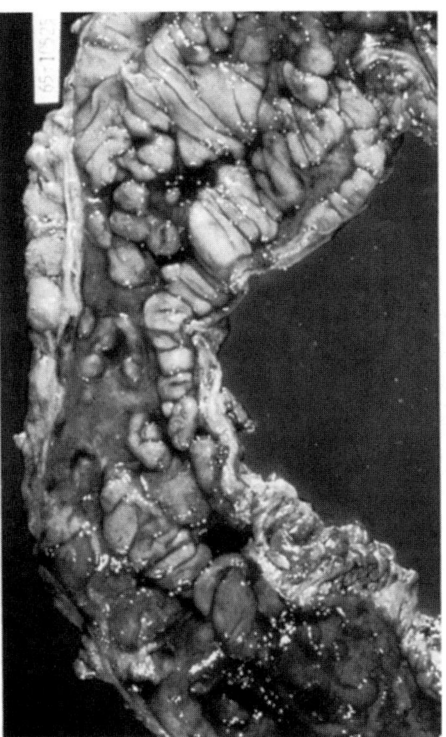

A B

Inflammatory Bowel Disease (IBD). In **Crohn's disease (A),** the juxtaposition of ulcerated and normal mucosa gives a "cobblestone" appearance. In acute **ulcerative colitis (B),** the intestinal mucosa is inflamed and edematous and has a pseudopolypoid appearance. Chronically, ulcerative colitis has a more atrophic appearance.

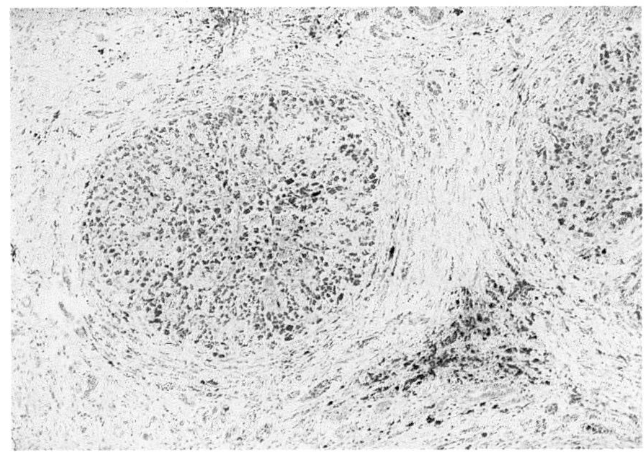

Hemochromatosis with cirrhosis, Prussian blue iron stain showing hemosiderin in the liver parenchyma. Such deposition occurs throughout the body, causing organ damage and the characteristic darkening of the skin.

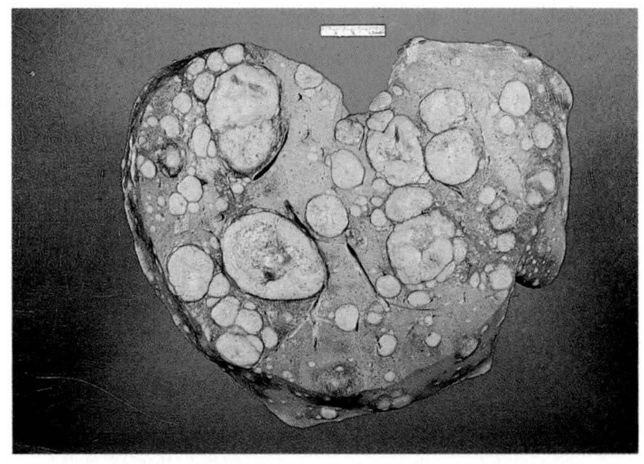

Metastatic carcinoma to liver: most common primary sites are colon, breast or lung.

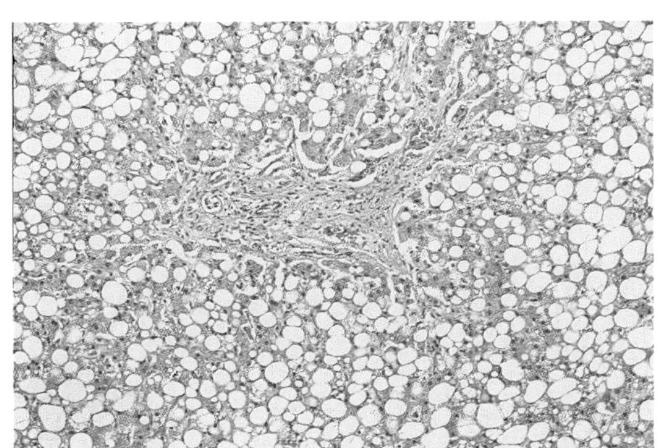

Fatty metamorphosis (macrovesicular steatosis) of liver, microscopic. Early reversible change associated with alcohol consumption; there are abundant fat-filled vacuoles but no inflammation or fibrosis of more serious alcoholic liver damage (yet).

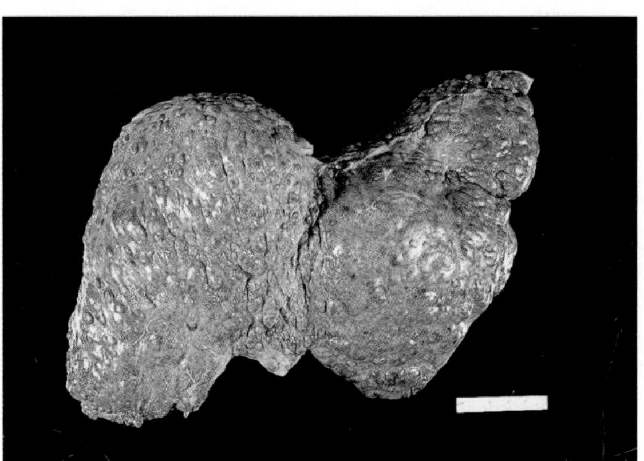

Micronodular cirrhosis of liver, gross, from an alcoholic patient. Liver is approximately normal in size, with a fine granular appearance. Later stages of disease result in an irregularly shrunken liver with larger nodules.

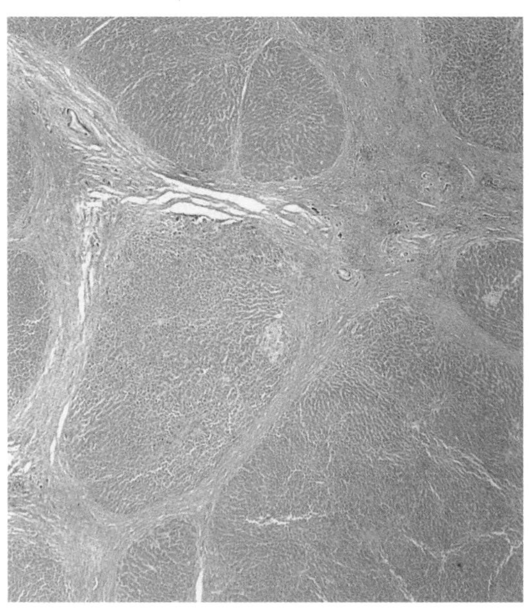

Cirrhosis, microscopic: regenerative lesions are surrounded by fibrotic bands of collagen, forming the characteristic nodularity.

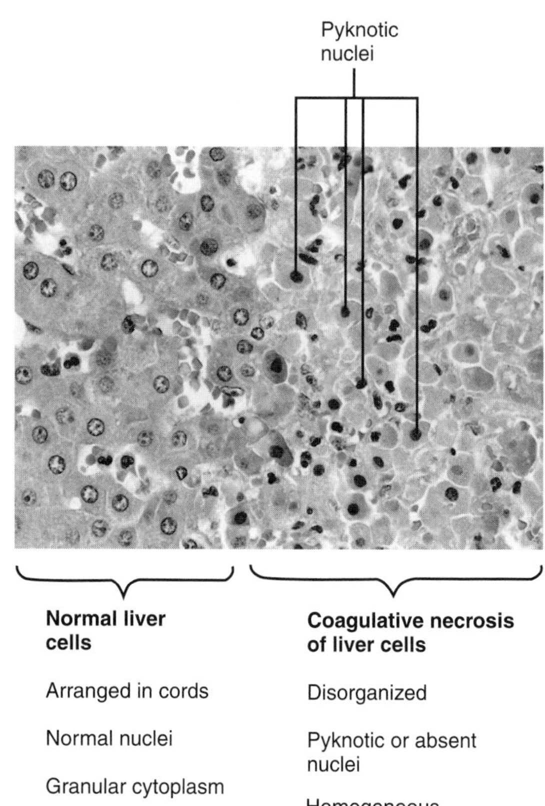

Coagulative necrosis of hepatocytes.

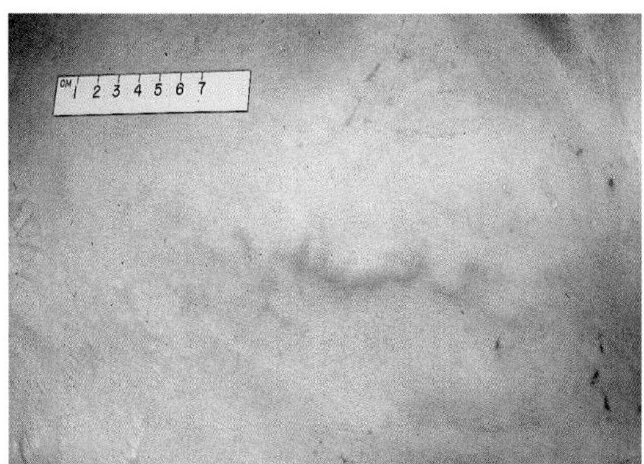

Caput medusae (periumbilical venous distension) with portal hypertension, in a patient with cirrhosis.

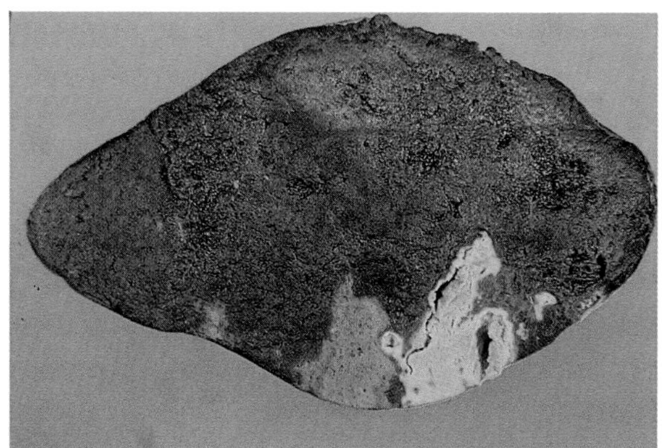

Splenic infarction. The splenic artery lacks collateral supply, making the spleen particularly susceptible to ischemic damage. Coagulative necrosis has occurred in a wedge shape, along the pattern of vascular supply.

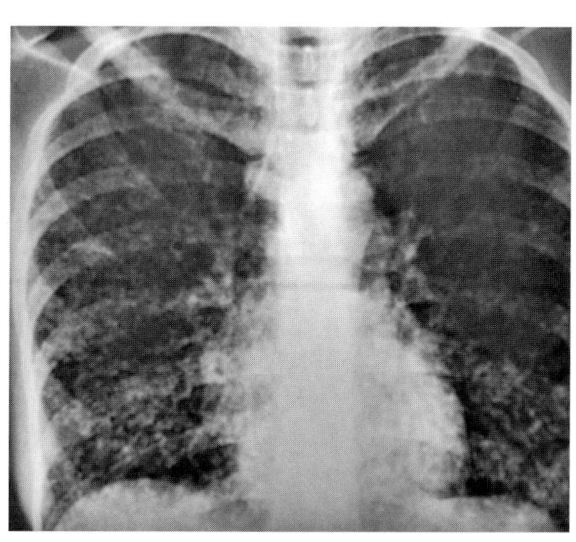

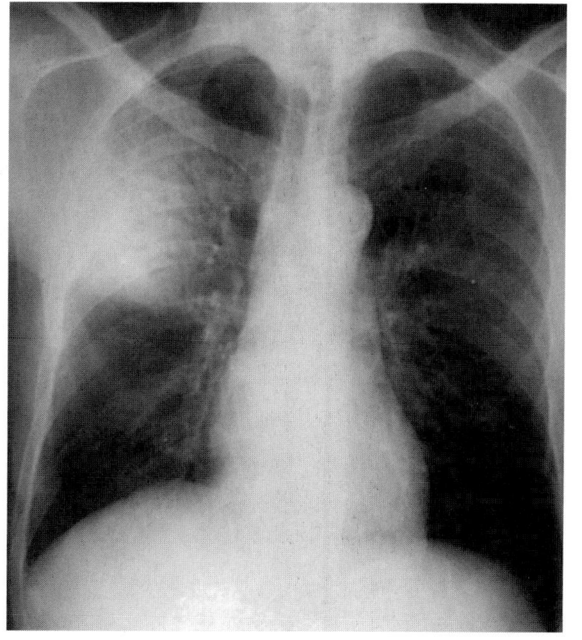

A **B**

Compare the diffuse, patchy, bilateral infiltrates of "atypical" **interstitial pneumonia (A),** with the localized dense lesion of **lobar pneumonia (B)**.

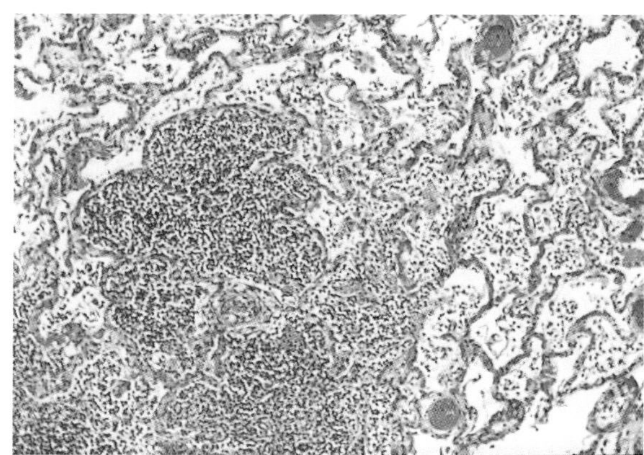

Bronchopneumonia with neutrophils in alveolar spaces, microscopic.

Bronchopneumonia, gross: note the large area of consolidation at the base plus multiple small areas of consolidation (pale) involving bronchioles and surrounding alveolar sacs throughout the lung.

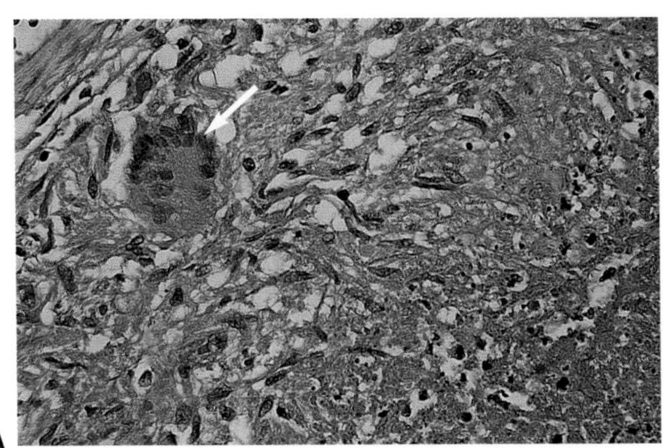

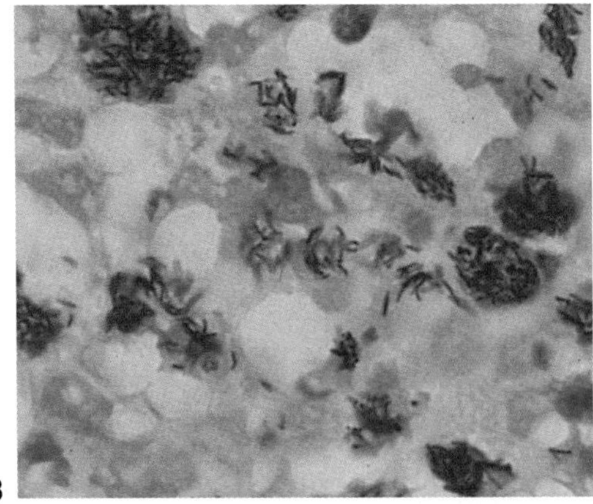

Microscopically, **tuberculosis (A)** is characterized by caseating granulomas containing Langhan's giant cells, which have a "horseshoe" pattern of nuclei (see arrow). Organisms **(B)** are identified by their red color on acid-fast staining ("red snappers").

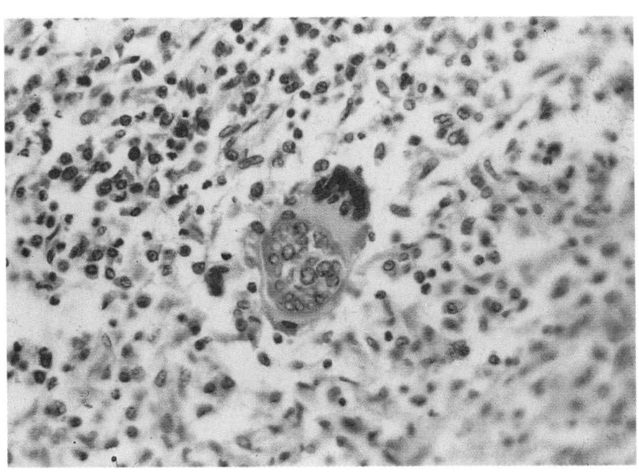

Coccioidomycosis: endospores within a spherule in infected lung parenchyma. Initial infection usually resolves spontaneously, but when immunity is compromised, dissemination to almost any organ can occur. Endemic in Southwest U.S.

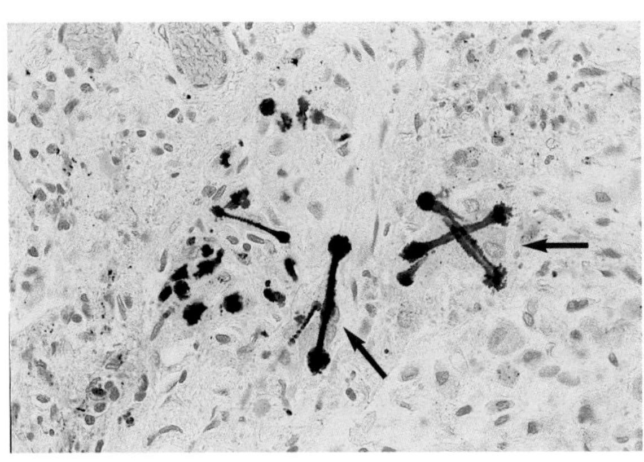

Asbestosis: ferruginous bodies (asbestos bodies with Prussian blue iron stain) in lung, microscopic. Inhaled asbestos fibers are injested by macrophages.

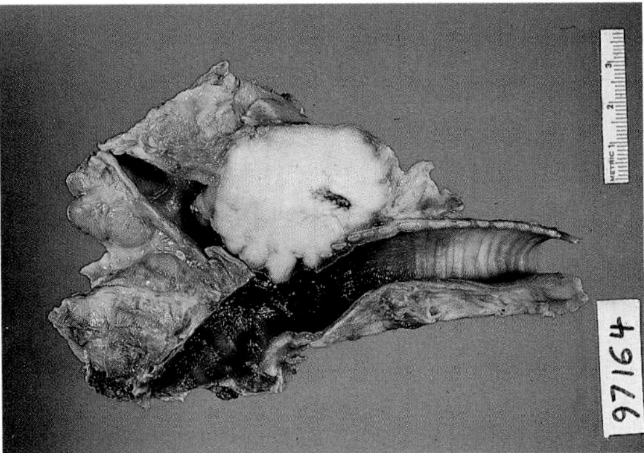

Squamous cell carcinoma of lung, gross, from a patient with a long smoking history. This tumor arises from the bronchial epithelium and is centrally located.

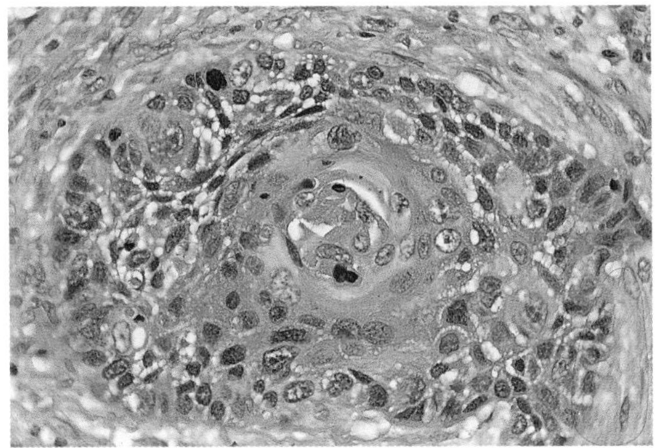

Squamous cell carcinoma, histologic: a nest of polygonal cells with pink cytoplasm and hyperchromatic nuclei.

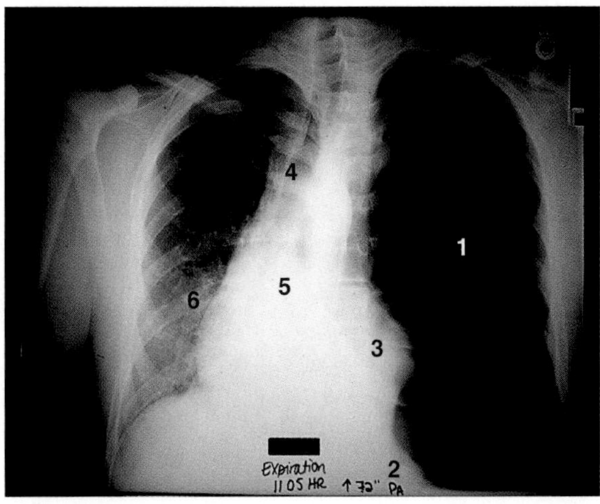

Tension pneumothorax.

Note these features:

1 Hyperlucent lung field
2 Hyperexpansion lowers diaphragm
3 Collapsed lung
4 Deviation of trachea
5 Mediastinal shift
6 Compression of opposite lung

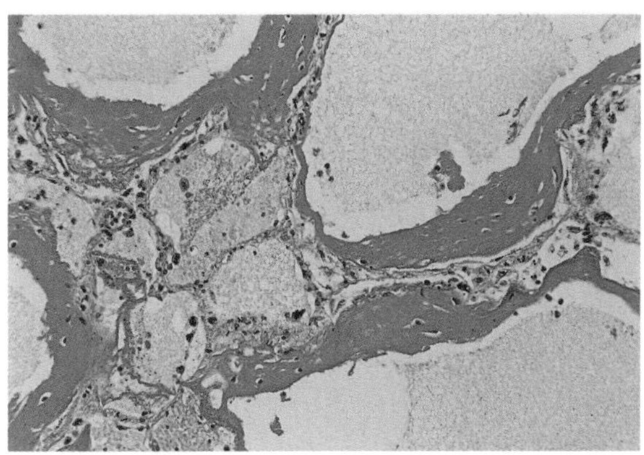

Acute respiratory distress syndrome (ARDS). Persistent inflammation leads to poor pulmonary compliance and edema; note both alveolar fluid and hyaline membranes.

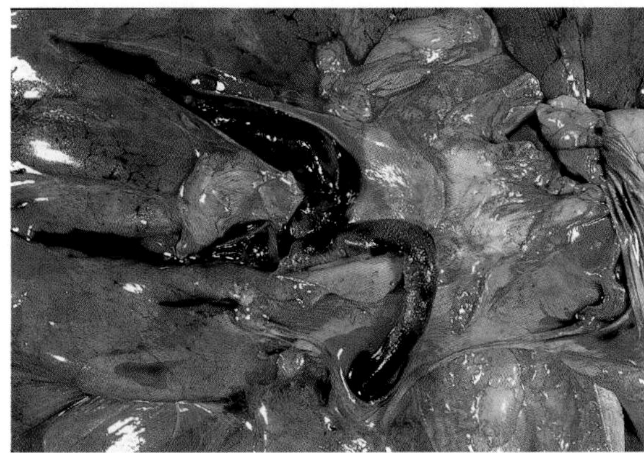

Saddle pulmonary thromboembolus, gross. Most often arises from deep venous thrombosis.

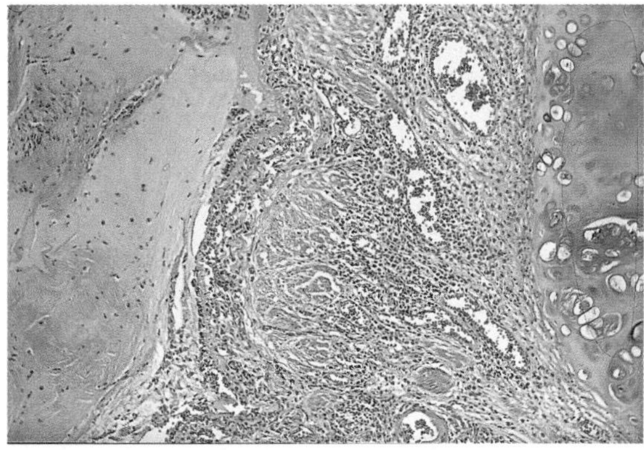

Inflammation and smooth muscle hypertrophy in **bronchial asthma.**

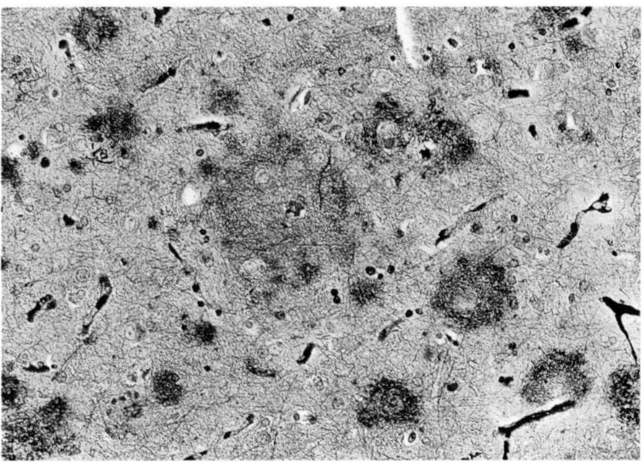

Brain with neuritic plaques indicative of **Alzheimer's disease,** Bielschowsky silver stain, microscopic.

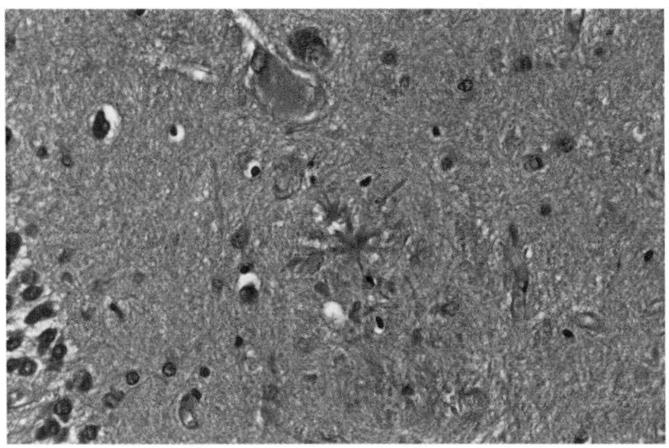

1.

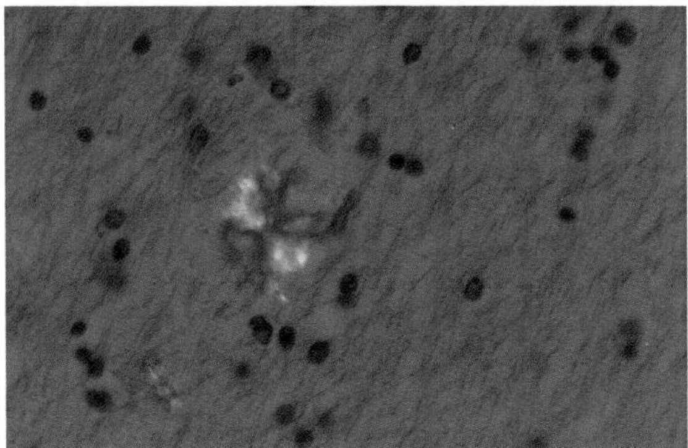

2.

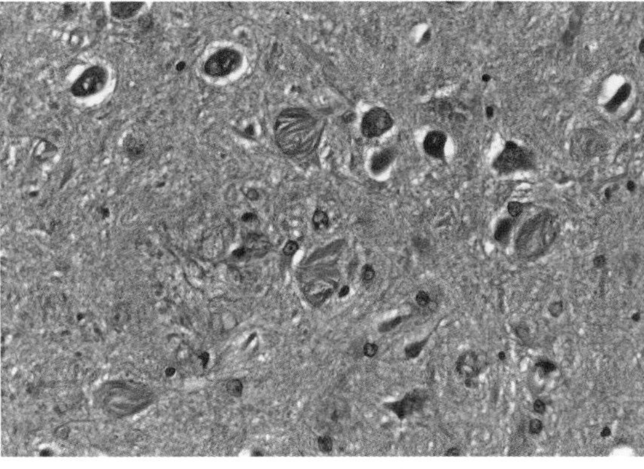

3.

Alzheimer's disease. Key histologic features include "senile plaques" **(1),** focal masses of interwoven neuronal processes around an amyloid core. The amyloid core stains with Congo red dye and shows apple-green birefringence under polarized light **(2).** Neurofibrillary tangles **(3),** the remnants of neuronal degeneration, are also associated with Alzheimer's disease, the most common cause of dementia in older persons.

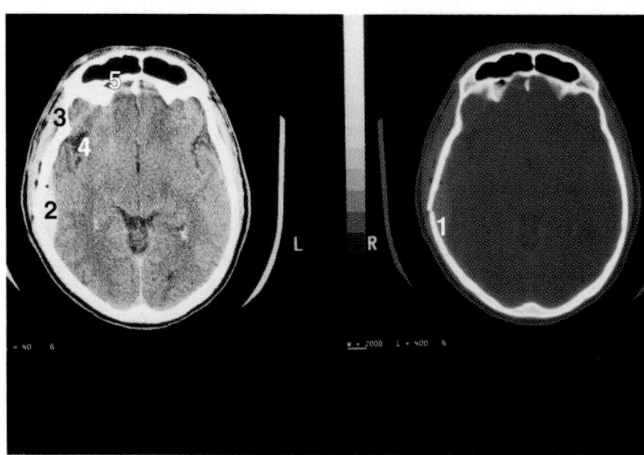

Epidural hematoma from skull fracture. Note lens-shaped (biconcave) dense blood next to fracture. 1 Skull fracture; 2 Hematoma in epidural space; 3 Temporalis muscle; 4 Sylvian fissure; 5 Frontal sinus.

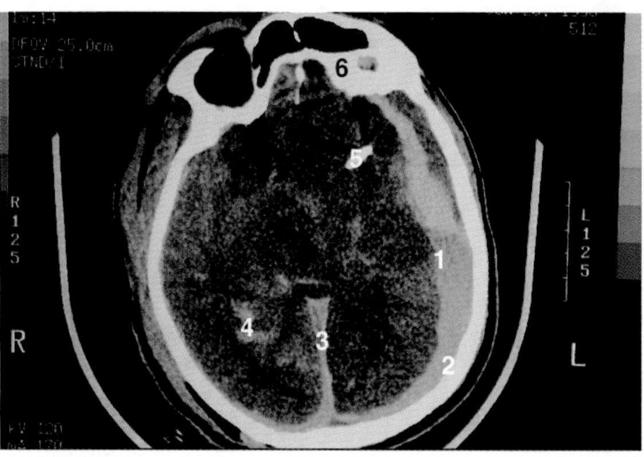

Subdural hemorrhage. Note hyperdense extra-axial blood on the left side. Concomitant subarachnoid hemorrhage. 1 Subdural blood, layering; 2 Skull; 3 Falx; 4 Subarachnoid blood; 5 Shunt catheter; 6 Frontal sinus.

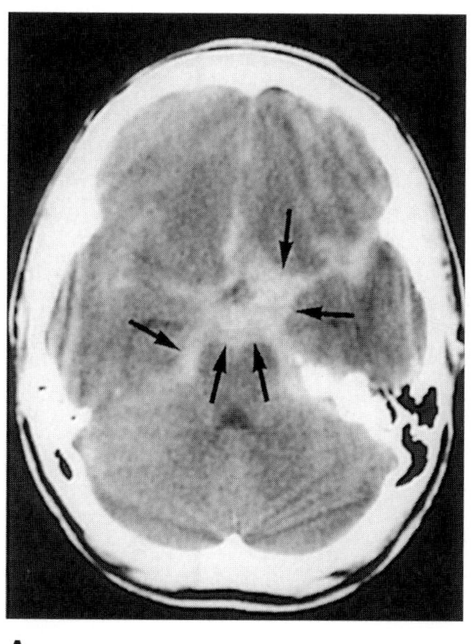

A

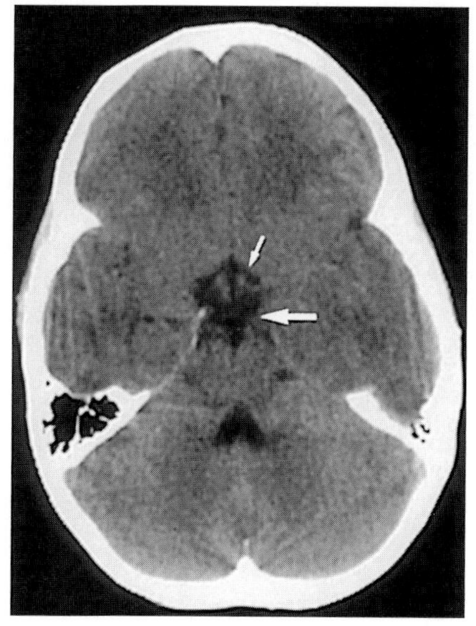

B

Subarachnoid hemorrhage. CT scan with contrast reveals blood in the subarachnoid space at the base of the brain.

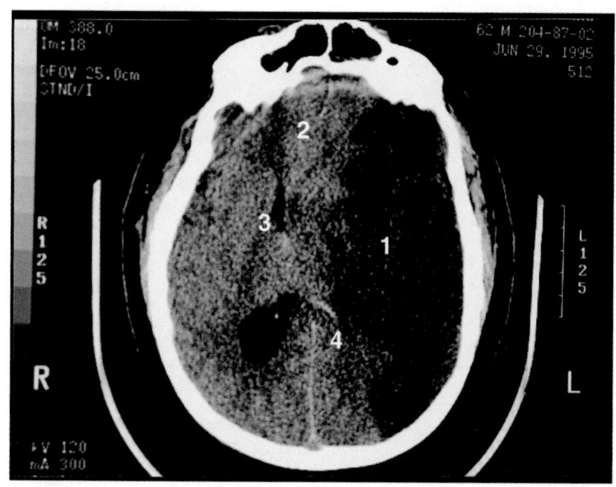

Left MCA stroke. Large left MCA territory stroke with edema and mass effect, but no visible hemorrhage. Patient experienced deficits in speech and in the right side of the face and upper extremities. 1 Ischemic brain parenchyma; 2 Subtle midline shift to the right; 3 Right frontal horn of lateral ventricle; 4 Left lateral ventricles obliterated by edema.

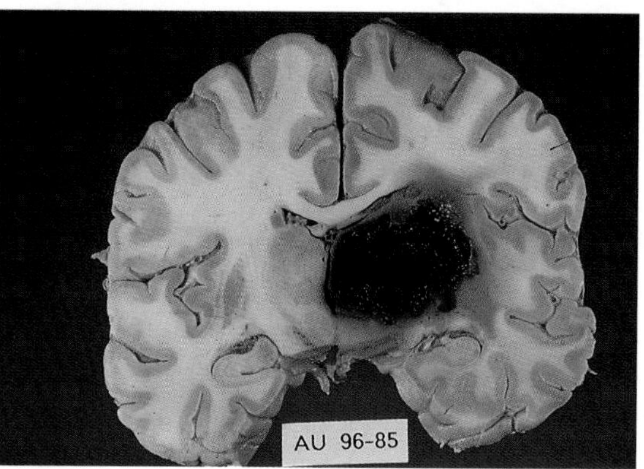

Brain with hypertensive hemorrhage in the region of the basal ganglia, gross.

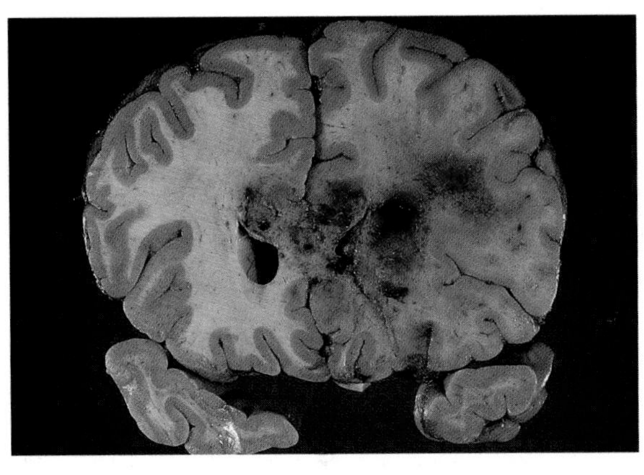

A

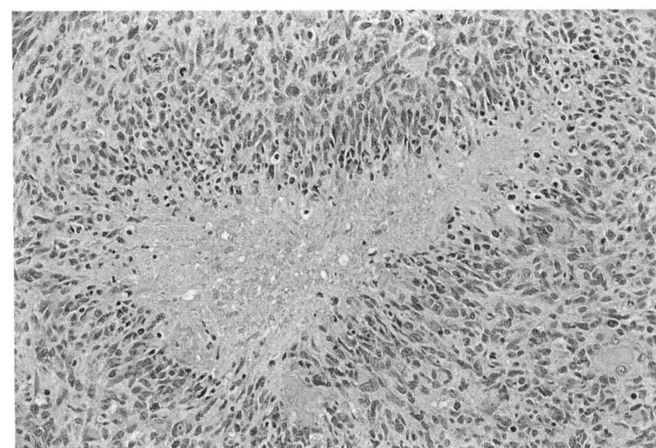

B

Glioblastoma multiforme extending across the midline of cerebral cortex, gross **(A).** Histologically **(B),** tumor cells have a "pseudopalisading" appearance around the necrotic tumor.

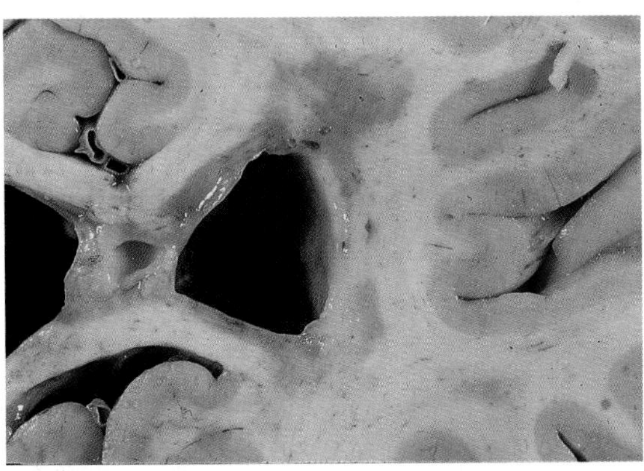

Brain with periventricular white matter plaques of demyelination due to **multiple sclerosis,** gross. Demyelination occurs in a bilateral asymmetric distribution. Classic clinical findings are nystagmus, scanning speech, and intention tremor.

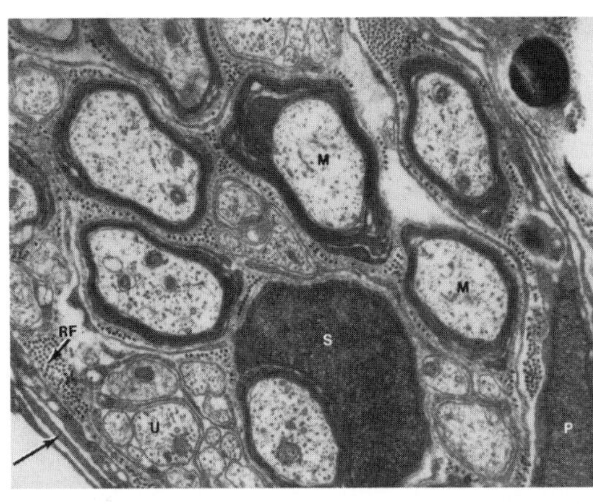

Electron micrograph of a peripheral nerve. (M) myelinated and (U) unmyelinated nerve fibers. (RF) reticular fibers (part of the endoneurium), (S) Schwann cell nucleus, (P, arrows) perineurial cells.

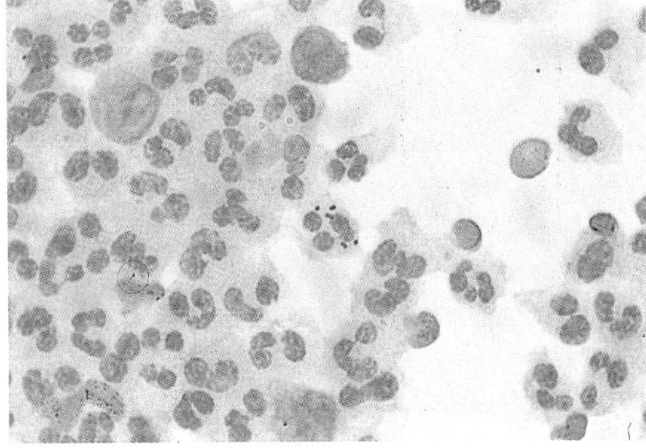

Gram negative diplococci of ***Neisseria meningitidis*** within a neutrophil, from CSF.

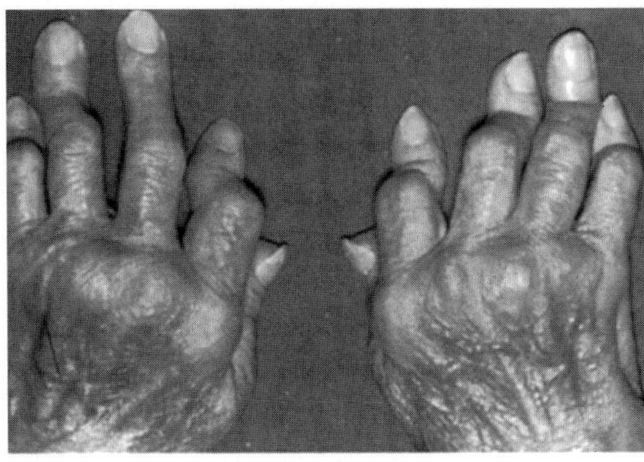

Rheumatoid arthritis: notice the swan-neck deformities of the digits and severe, symmetric involvement of the proximal interphalangeal (PIP) joints.

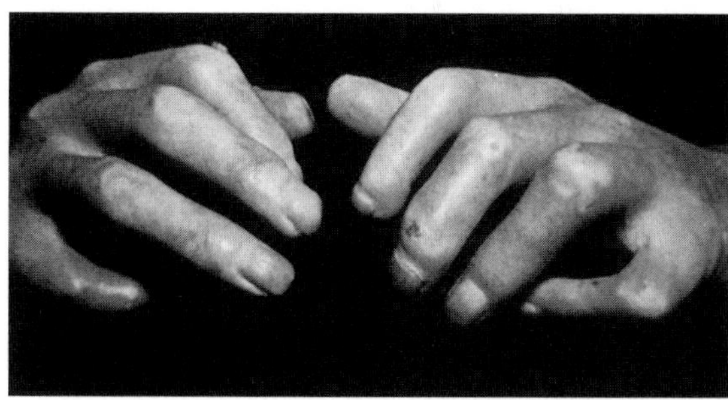

Scleroderma. The progressive "tightening" of the skin has contracted the fingers and eliminated creases over the knuckles. Fibrosis is widespread and may also involve the esophagus (dysphagia), lung (restrictive disease), and small vessels of the kidney (hypertension).

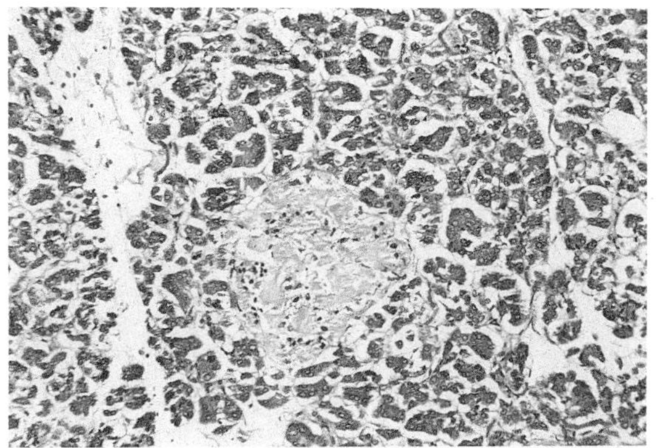

Pancreatic islet cells in **DM Type I.** In patients with diabetes mellitus type I, autoantibodies against B cells cause a chronic inflammation until, over time, islet cells are entirely replaced by amyloid.

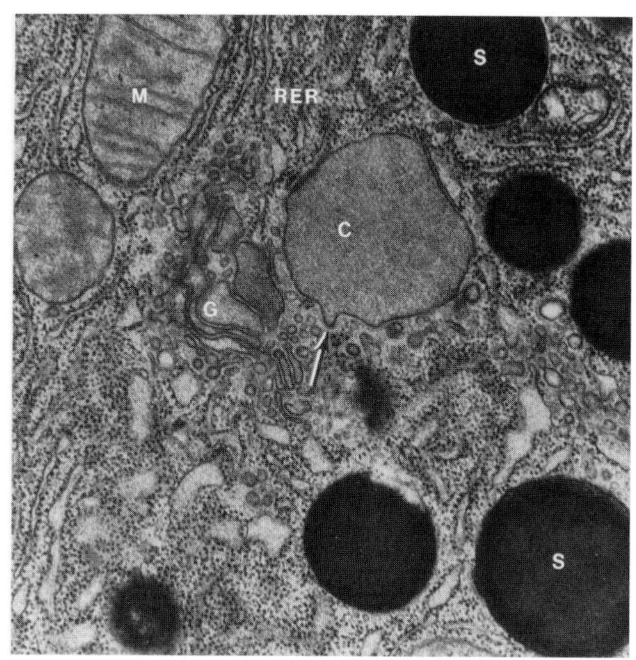

Electron micrograph of a **pancreatic acinar cell.** A condensing vacuole (C) is receiving secretory product (arrow) from the Golgi complex (G). Mitochondrion (M); rough endoplasmic reticulum (RER); mature condensed secretory zymogen granules (S).

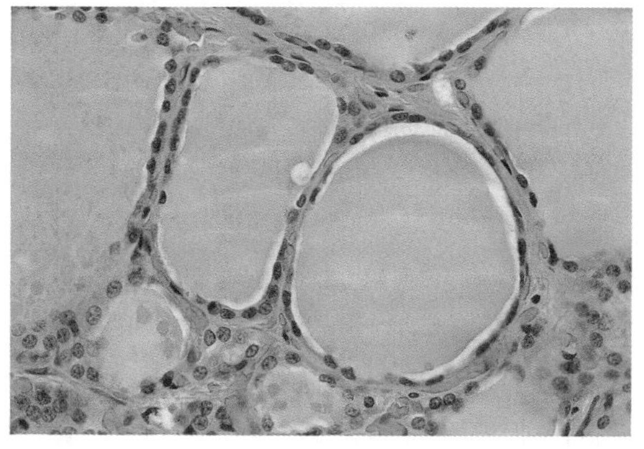

A

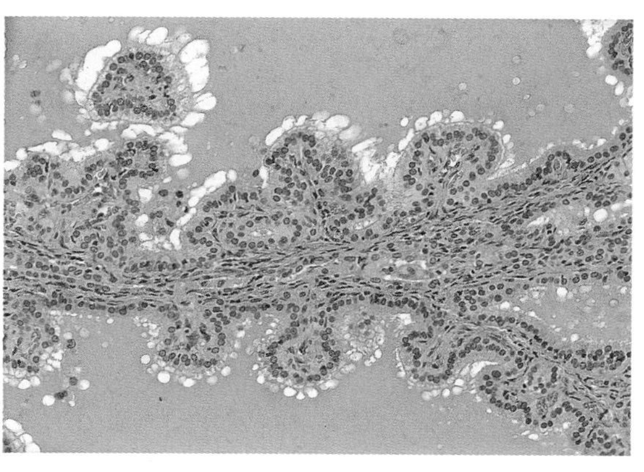

B

In **Graves' disease,** stimulation of follicular cells by TSH causes the normal uniform architecture to be replaced by hyperplastic papillary, involuted borders, and decreased colloid **(A, B).** Typical medical therapy is propylthiouracil, which inhibits production of thyroid hormone as well as peripheral conversion of T4 to T3.

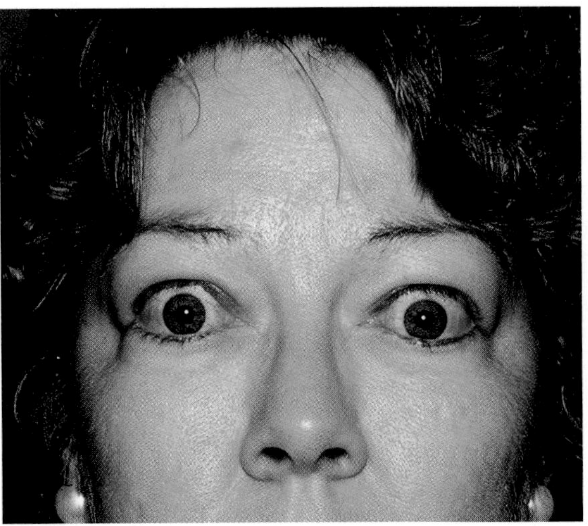

Exophthalmos in a patient with **Graves' disease,** with proptosis and periorbital edema.

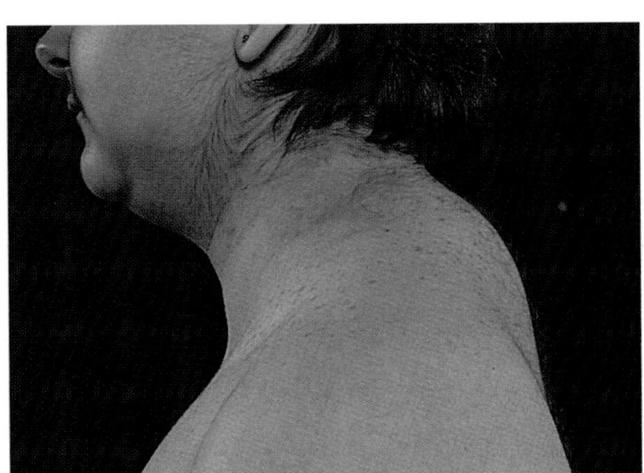

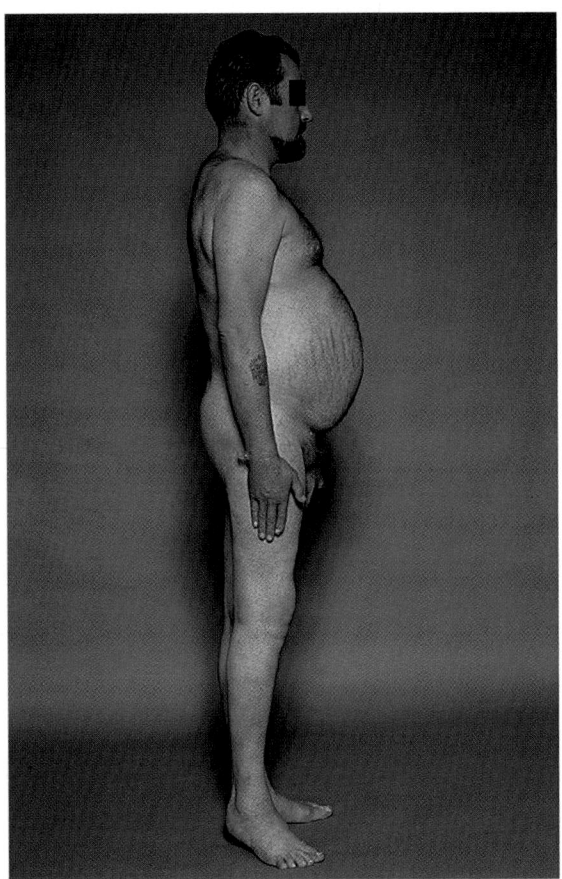

A B

Cushing's disease. The clinical picture includes **(A)** moon facies and buffalo hump and **(B)** truncal obesity and abdominal striae.

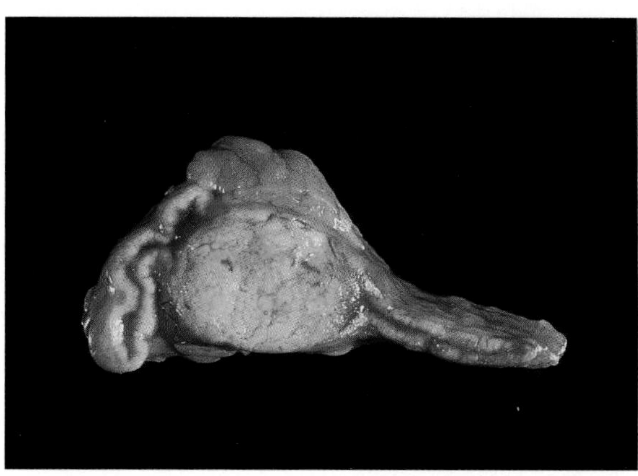

Adrenal cortical adenoma, gross. Cause of hypercortisolism (Cushing's syndrome) or hyperaldosteronism (Conn's syndrome).

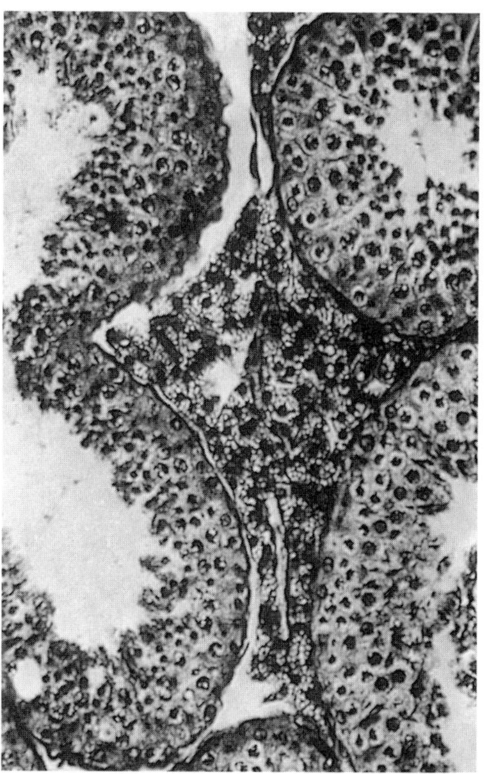

In the **seminiferous tubules,** Sertoli cells play a supportive and protective role for spermatogenesis. Note cells in various stages of differentiation, with spermatogonia near the basal lamina and more mature forms near the lumen.

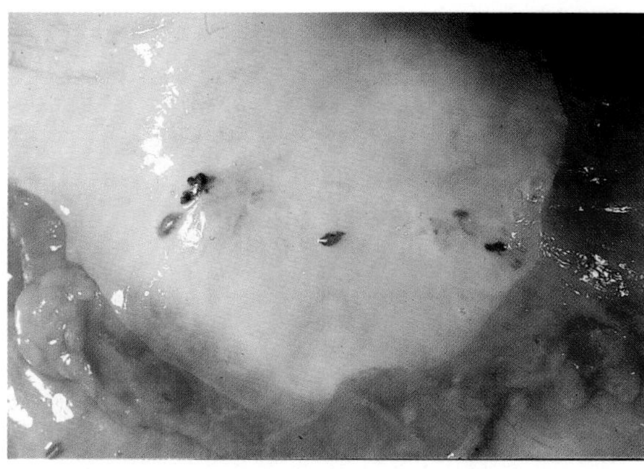

Serosal surface of uterus with "powder burn" lesions of **endometriosis,** gross. Ovarian chocolate cysts, due to bleeding of ectopic endometrial tissue, are another characteristic finding. Patients experience pain with menstruation.

Hydatidiform mole: the characteristic gross appearance is a "bunch of grapes." Hydatidiform moles are the most common precursors of choriocarcinoma. Complete moles usually display a 46, XX diploid pattern with all the chromosomes derived from the sperm. In partial moles, the karyotype is triploid or tetraploid, and fetal parts may be present.

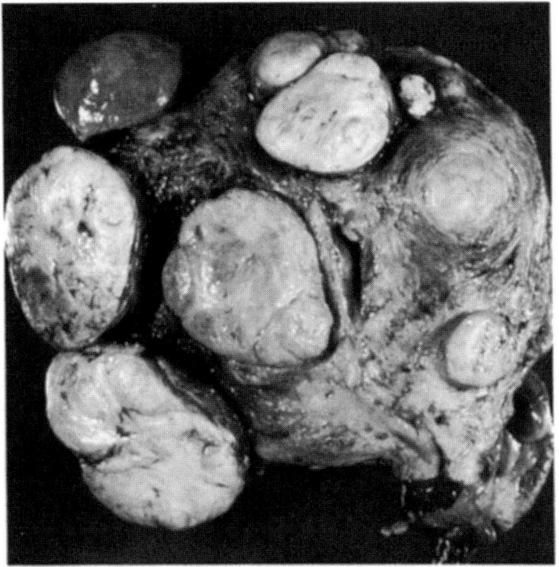

Multiple **leiomyomas** (fibroids) of the uterus. Common benign uterine tumor. Fibroids beneath the endometrium may present with vaginal bleeding; they also develop subserosally or within the myometrium.

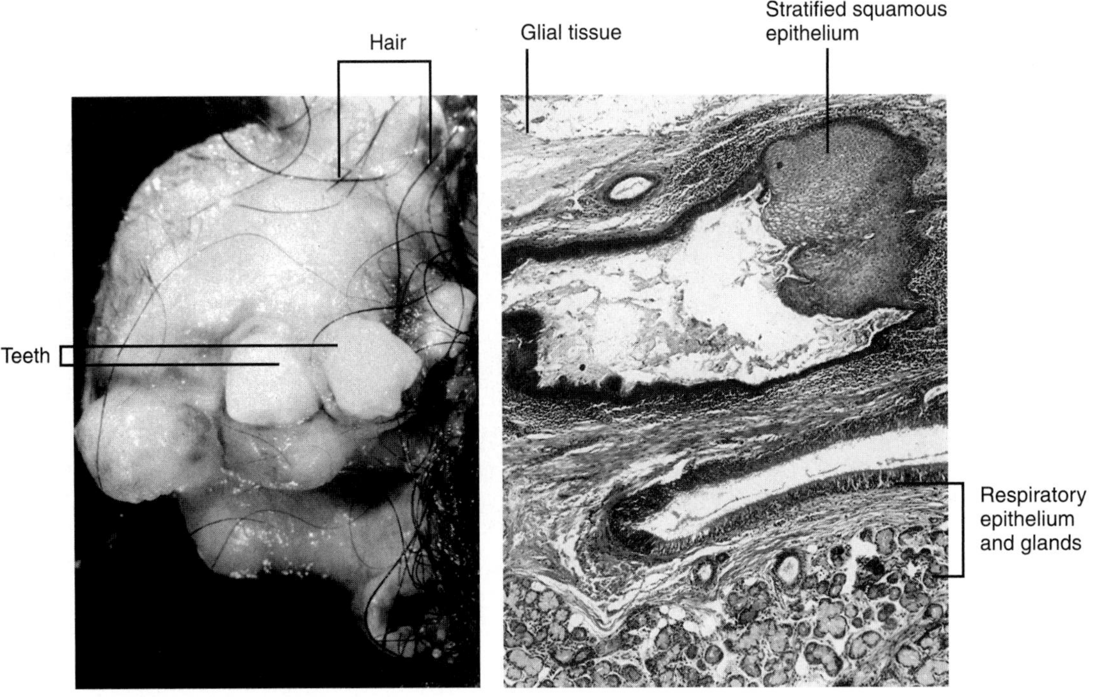

A benign **teratoma** of the ovary, containing teeth and hair, an incidental finding during abdominal surgery. In females, teratomas are generally benign, while in males, they account for about 30% of testicular tumors.

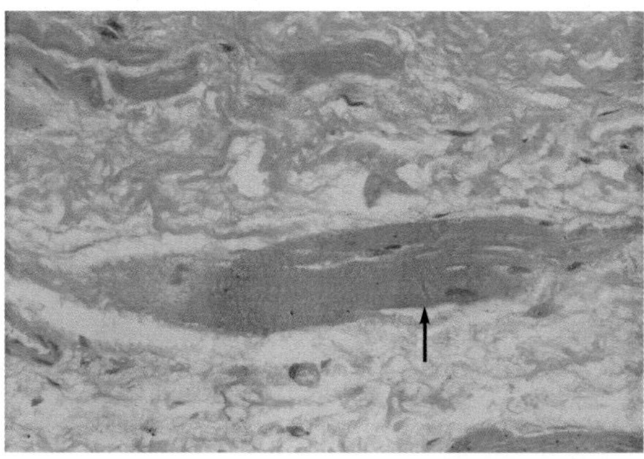

1.

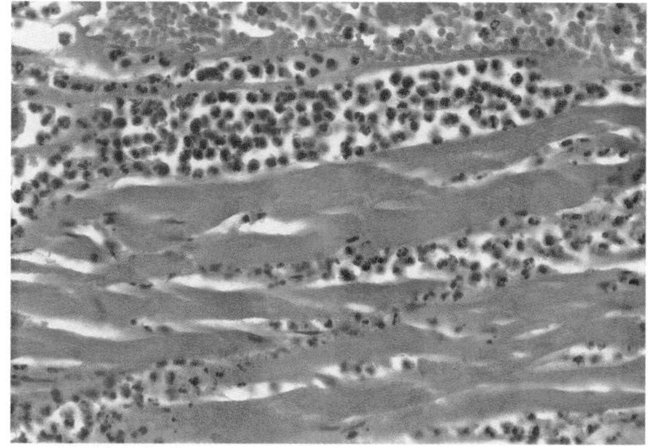

2.

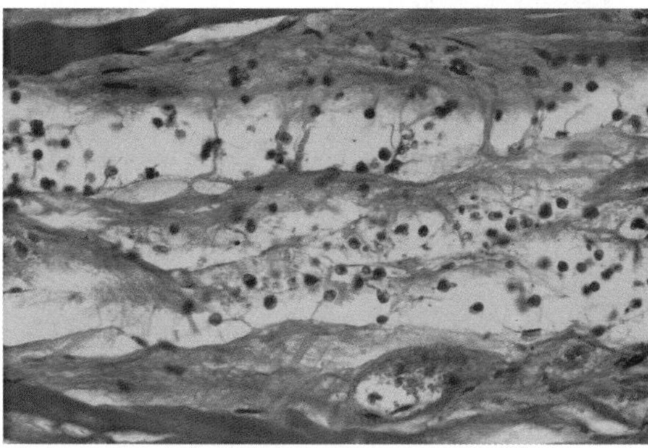

3.

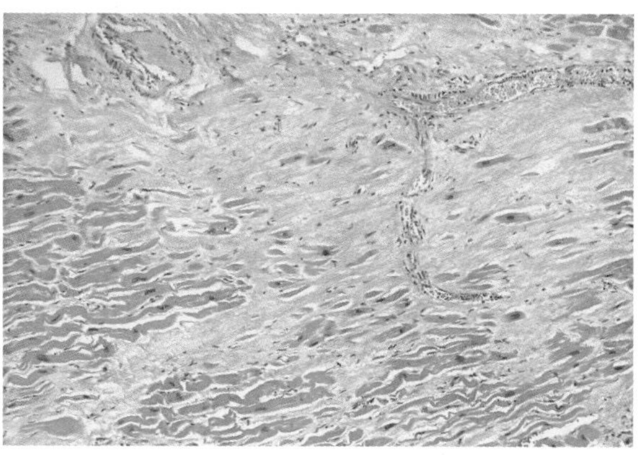

4.

Evolution of a **myocardial infarction:** **(1)** Contraction band necrosis is the first visible change, occurring in 1–2 hours. **(2)** In the first 3 days, neutrophilic infiltration and coagulation necrosis occur. **(3)** By 3–7 days, neutrophils have been replaced by macrophages, and clearing of myocyte debris has begun. **(4)** Within weeks, granulation and scarring occur.

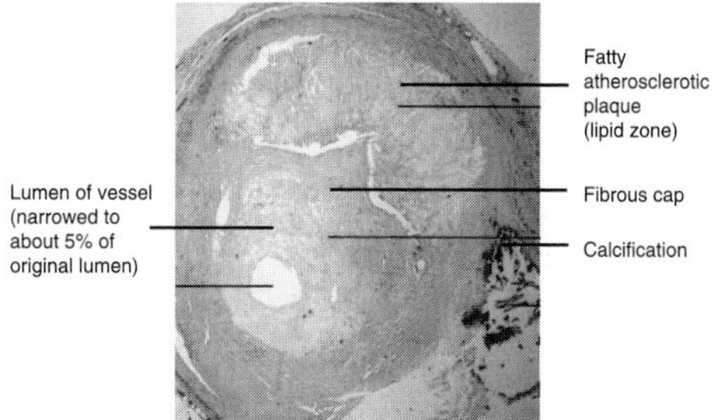

Atherosclerosis in a coronary vessel. Calcified plaques have narrowed the lumen of the artery, increasing the risk for occlusion, ie, myocardial infarction.

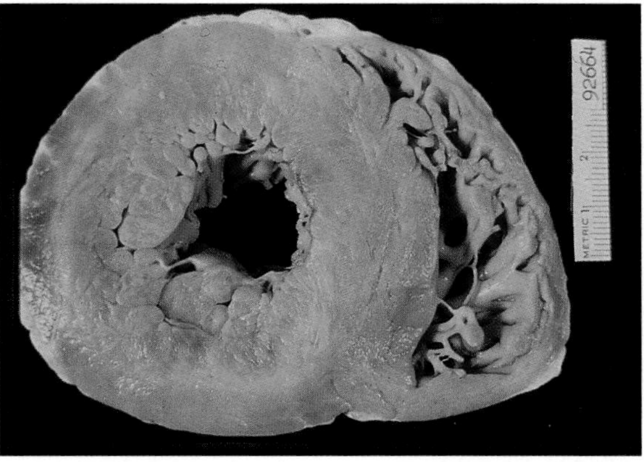

Heart with marked left ventricular hypertrophy from hypertension, gross.

Aortic dissection, with blood compressing the aortic lumen. A tear in the intima allowed blood to surge through the muscular layer to the adventitia. Risk factors are hypertension, Marfan's syndrome, pregnancy.

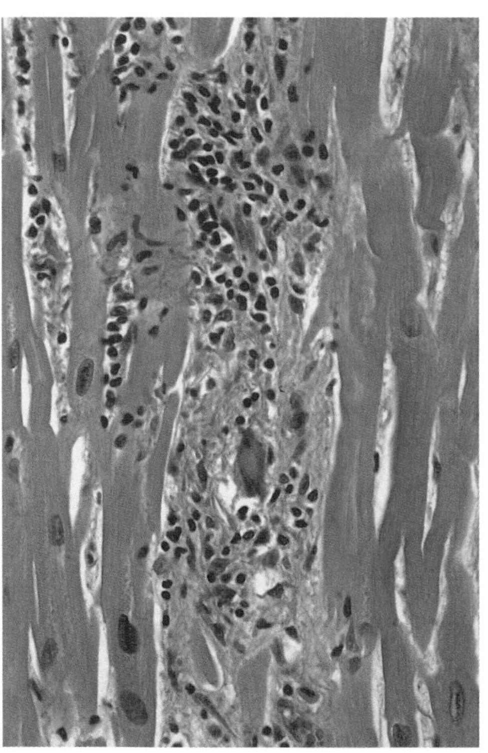

The Aschoff body, an area of fibrinoid necrosis surrounded by mononuclear and multinucleated giant cells, is pathognomonic for **rheumatic heart disease.** The mitral valve is most commonly affected.

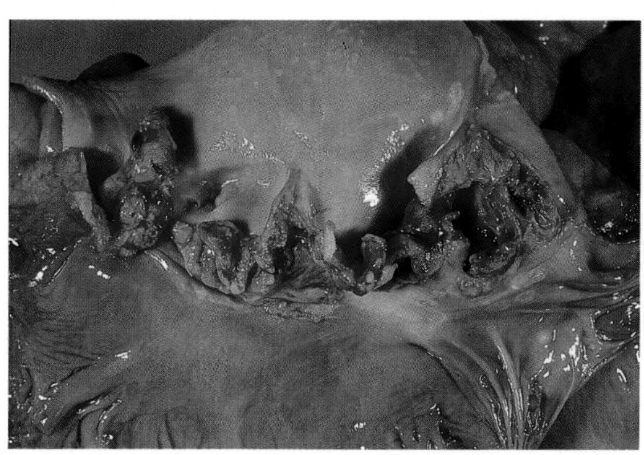

Acute bacterial endocarditis: virulent organisms (e.g., ***Staphylococcus aureus***) infect previously normal valves, causing marked damage (here, in the aortic valve) and potentially giving rise to septic emboli.

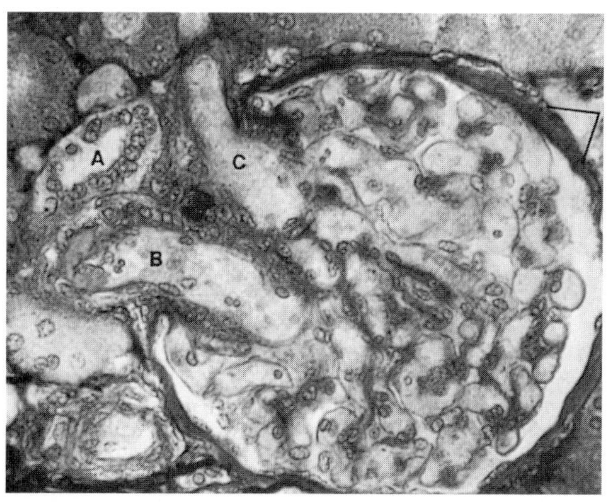

Normal glomerulus, microscopic, with (A) macula densa, (B) afferent and (C) efferent arterioles.

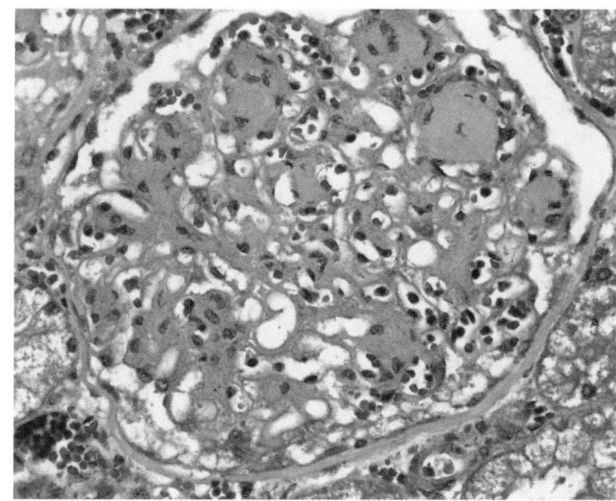

Diabetic nodular glomerulosclerosis. The nodular Kimmelstiel-Wilson lesions at the periphery of the glomerulus are pathognomonic for diabetic GS.

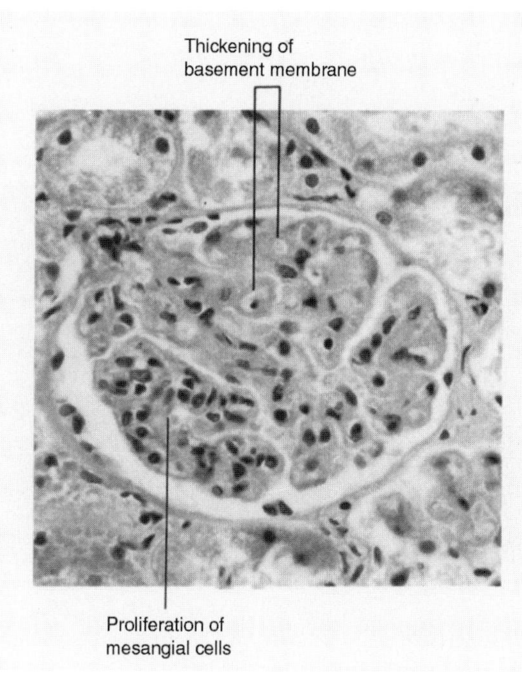

Systemic lupus erythematosus: kidney pathology. In the membranous glomerulonephritic pattern, "wire-loop" thickening occurs due to subendothelial immune complex deposition.

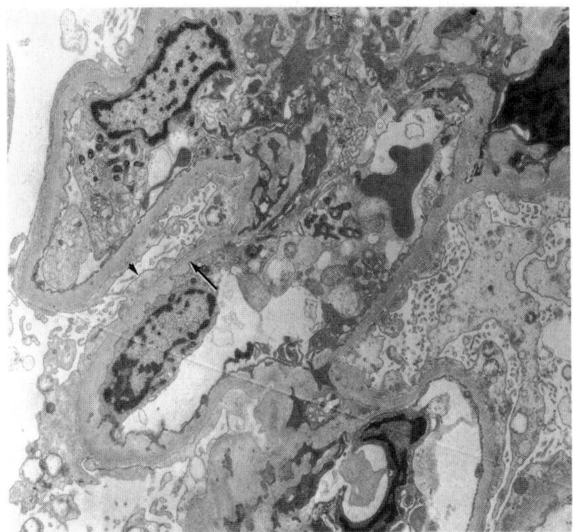

Minimal change disease (lipoid nephrosis) shows normal glomeruli on light microscopy but effacement of foot processes on EM (arrowhead). The full arrow points to a normal foot process.

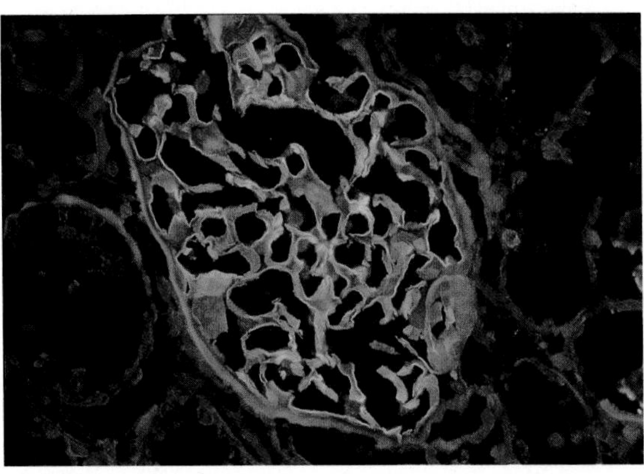

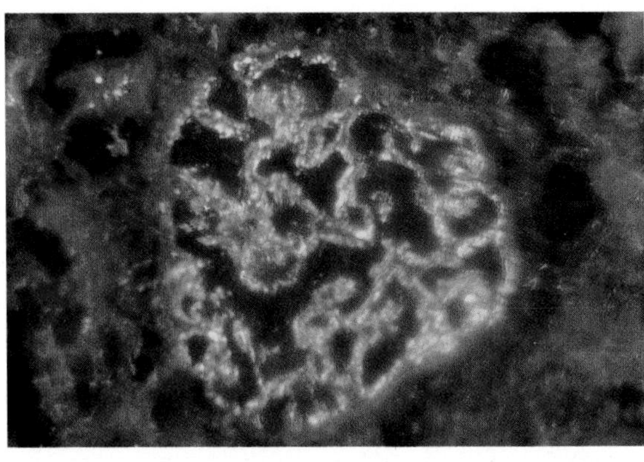

A **B**

In **Goodpasture's syndrome (A),** antiglomerular basement membrane antibody creates a linear pattern by immunofluorescence (microscopic); compare with the granular immune deposits seen by immunofluorescence in **poststreptococcal glomerulonephritis (B).**

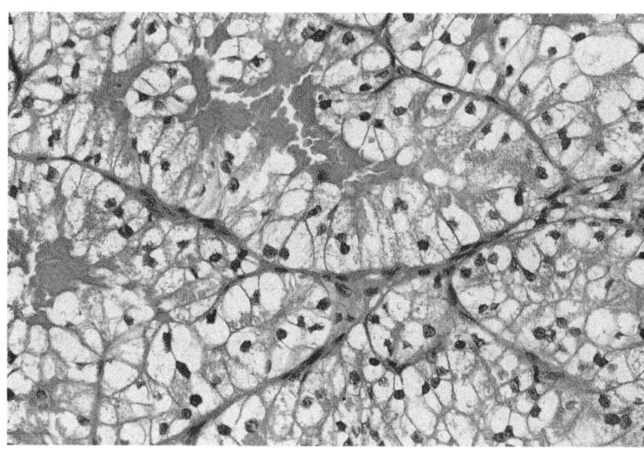

Renal cell carcinoma, microscopic. Glycogen and lipid-filled clear cells are derived from tubular epithelium.

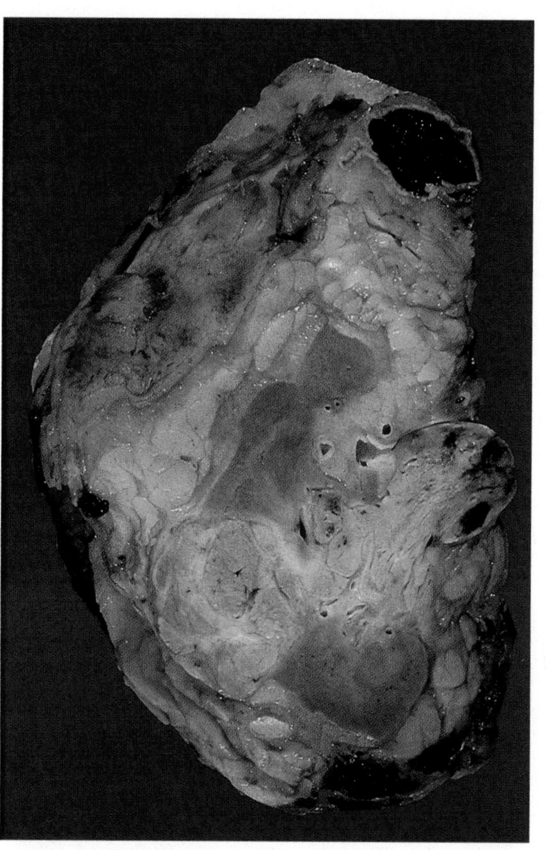

Renal cell carcinoma, gross. Notably, tumor may extend into the renal vein and IVC and spread hematogenously.

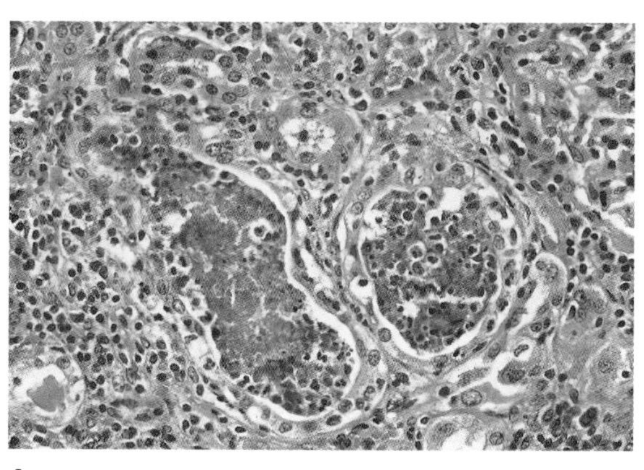

A

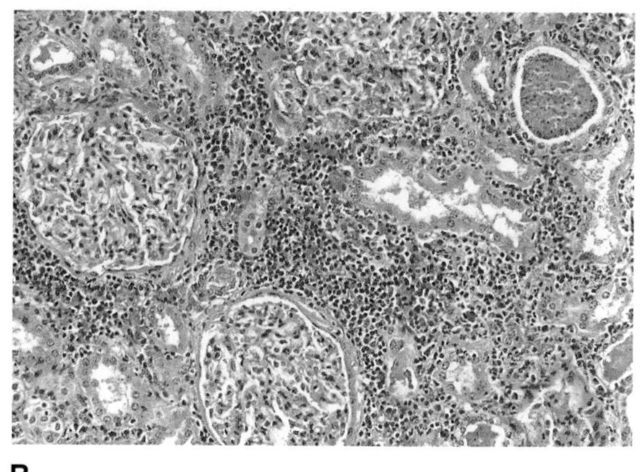

B

Acute pyelonephritis (A) is characterized by neutrophilic infiltration and abcess formation within the renal interstitum. Abcesses may rupture, introducing collections of white cells to the tubular lumen (arrow). In contrast, **chronic pyelonephritis (B)** has a lymphocytic invasion with fibrosis.

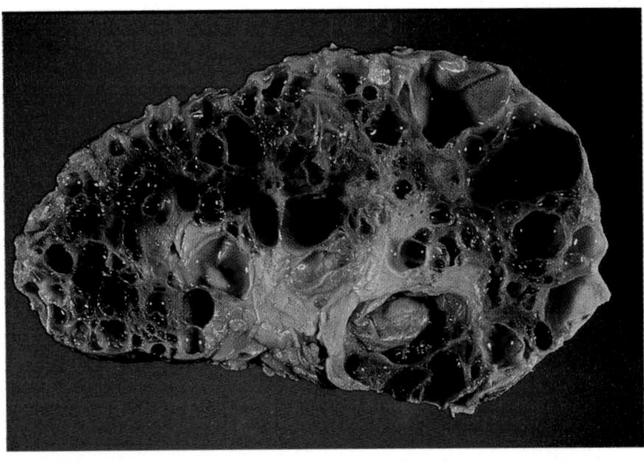

Autosomal-dominant polycystic kidney disease, gross. Disease occurs bilaterally and presents with flank pain and hematuria.

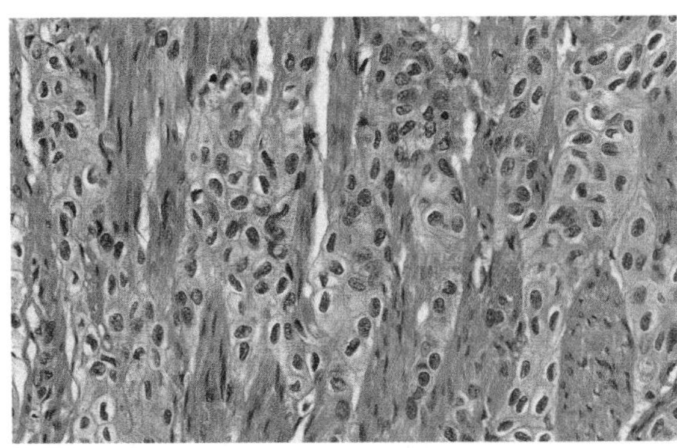

Transitional cell carcinoma of the urinary bladder, microscopic. Malignant urothelial cells have invaded the muscular layer of the bladder wall.

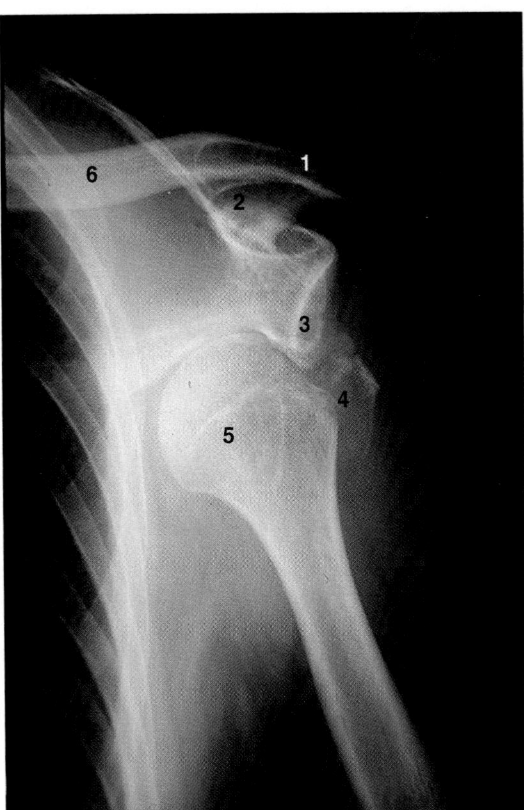

Anterior shoulder dislocation. Note humeral head inferior and medial to glenoid fossa and fracture fragments from greater tuberosity.

1 Acromion
2 Coracoid
3 Glenoid fossa
4 Fracture fragments
5 Humeral head
6 Clavicle

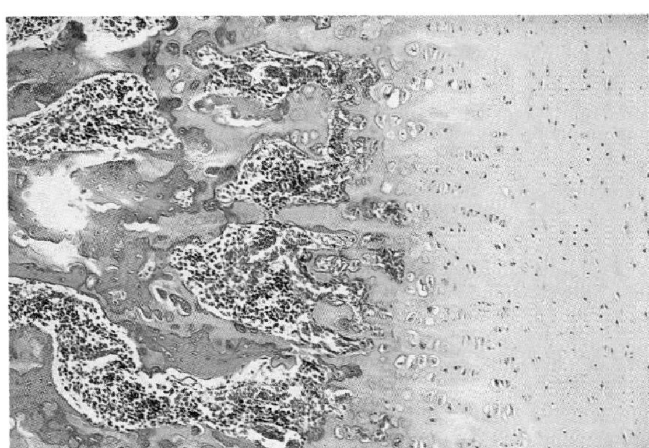

Fetal bone growth plate, endochondral bone formation in long bone. At the transitional zone, osteoblasts congregate to replace cartilage with bone.

Pharmacology

"Take me, I am the drug; take me, I am hallucinogenic."
—Salvador Dali

"I was under medication when I made the decision not to burn the tapes."
—Richard Nixon

Preparation for questions on pharmacology is straightforward. Memorizing all the key drugs and their characteristics (e.g., mechanisms, clinical use, and important side effects) is high yield. Focus on understanding the prototype drugs in each class. Avoid memorizing obscure derivatives. Learn the "classic" and distinguishing toxicities of the major drugs. Do not bother with drug dosages or trade names. Reviewing associated biochemistry, physiology, and microbiology can be useful while studying pharmacology. There is a strong emphasis on autonomic nervous system, central nervous system, antimicrobial, and cardiovascular agents as well as on NSAIDs. Much of the material is clinically relevant. Newer drugs on the market are also fair game.

These abstracted case vignettes are designed to demonstrate the thought processes necessary to answer multistep clinical reasoning questions.

- 28-year-old chemist presents with MPTP exposure → what neurotransmitter is depleted? → dopamine. Pharm.53
- Woman taking tetracycline exhibits photosensitivity → what are the clinical manifestations? → rash on sun-exposed regions of the body. Pharm.15
- Young girl with congenital valve disease is given penicillin prophylactically. She develops bacterial endocarditis → what do you give now? → beta-lactamase-resistant penicillin. Pharm.44
- Nondiabetic patient presents with hypoglycemia but low levels of C peptide → what is the diagnosis? → surreptitious insulin injection . Pharm.20
- African-American man who goes to Africa develops anemia after taking prophylactic medicine → what is the enzyme deficiency? → glucose-6-phosphate dehydrogenase.
- 27-year-old female with a history of psychiatric illness now has urinary retention due to a neuroleptic → what do you treat it with? → bethanechol.
- Farmer presents with dyspnea, salivation, miosis, diarrhea, cramping, and blurry vision → what caused this? what is the mechanism of action? → insecticide poisoning; inhibition of acetylcholinesterase.
- 55-year-old man undergoing treatment for BPH has decreased levels of testosterone and DHT as well as gynecomastia and edema → what is the drug? → estrogen (DES).
- Patient with recent kidney transplant is on cyclosporine for immunosuppression. Requires antifungal agent for candidiasis → what drug would result in cyclosporine toxicity? → ketoconazole. Pharm.43
- Man on several medications, including antidepressants and antihypertensives, has mydriasis and becomes constipated → what is the cause of his symptoms? → tricyclic antidepressant. Pharm.60
- Patient presents with renal insufficiency → what alterations in doses of digoxin and digitoxin, respectively? → decreased, same.
- 55-year-old postmenopausal woman is on tamoxifen therapy → what is she at increased risk of acquiring? → endometrial carcinoma.
- Woman on MAO inhibitor has hypertensive crisis after a meal → what did she ingest? → tyramine (wine or cheese). Pharm.6
- After taking clindamycin, patient develops toxic megacolon and diarrhea → what is the mechanism of diarrhea? → *C. difficile* overgrowth.
- Man starts a medication for hyperlipidemia. He then develops a rash, pruritus, and GI upset → what drug was it? → niacin. Pharm.8
- Patient is on carbamazepine → what routine workup should always be done? → LFTs. Pharm.49
- 23-year-old female who is on rifampin for TB prophylaxis and on birth control (estrogen) gets pregnant → why? → rifampin affects estrogen metabolism in the liver. Pharm.45
- Older female goes into OR for emergency surgery; after administration of succinylcholine, she requires respiratory support for over 4 hours. Later it is determined that she is receiving medication for glaucoma → what is she on? → acetylcholinesterase inhibitor.
- Patient develops cough and must discontinue captopril → what is a good replacement drug, and why doesn't it have the same side effects? → losartan, an ATII receptor antagonist, does not ↑ bradykinin as captopril does.

UCV

Mechanism, clinical use, and toxicity of:

1. Motion sickness drugs (e.g., scopolamine).
2. Antipsychotics (neuroleptics), low and high potency.
3. Opiates (e.g., analgesic, antidiarrheal, antitussive), receptor types, agonists, mixed agonist–antagonists.
4. Myasthenia gravis drugs.
5. Hormonal treatments of cancer (e.g., leuprolide, flutamide, aminoglutethimide).
6. New oral hypoglycemic agents (acarbose, metformin, troglitazone).
7. Stool softeners (e.g., psyllium, methylcellulose).
8. Angiotensin II receptor blockers (e.g., losartan).
9. Dermatologic agents (e.g., corticosteroids, retinoids, antifungal agents).
10. Other new pharmacologic agents (erythropoietin, RU486).

Know about:

1. Complications of empiric antibiotic use (e.g., resistance, fungal infection, pseudomembranous colitis).
2. Secondary effects of common drugs (e.g., heparin and osteoporosis, thiazides and hyperlipidemia).
3. Fundamental pharmacodynamics (e.g., partial agonists, physiologic antagonists, efficacy).
4. Drug efficacy and potency as demonstrated on dose-response curves.
5. Pharmacogenetics: drugs whose metabolism is affected by inheritance (e.g., isoniazid).
6. Anesthesia: physical properties of gaseous agents (MAC, blood:gas partition coefficient, rate of induction), different IV agents, toxicities (e.g., malignant hyperthermia).
7. Treatment of anemia (e.g., erythropoietin, B_{12}, folate, testosterone, iron supplements).
8. Prevention/treatment of cerebrovascular disease (e.g., aspirin, thrombolytics).
9. Treatment of rheumatoid arthritis.
10. Vaccines: indications, potential side effects.
11. Chemotherapeutic agents: risk of possible secondary cancer.

Pharmacokinetics

Volume of distribution (V_d)	Relates the amount of drug in the body to the plasma concentration. V_d of plasma protein-bound drugs can be altered by liver and kidney disease. $V_d = \frac{\text{amount of drug in the body}}{\text{plasma drug concentration}}$
Clearance (CL)	Relates the rate of elimination to the plasma concentration. $CL = \frac{\text{rate of elimination of drug}}{\text{plasma drug concentration}}$
Half-life ($t_{1/2}$)	The time required to change the amount of drug in the body by one-half during elimination (or during a constant infusion). A drug infused at a constant rate reaches about 94% of steady state after four $t_{1/2}$. $t_{1/2} = \frac{0.7 \times V_d}{CL}$

# of half-lives	1	2	3	3.3
Concentration	50%	75%	87.5%	90%

Dosage calculations

Loading dose = $C_p \times V_d/F$

Maintenance dose = $C_p \times CL/F$

where C_p = target plasma concentration and F = bioavailability

In patients with impaired renal or hepatic function, the loading dose remains unchanged, although the maintenance dose is decreased.

Elimination of drugs

Zero-order elimination	Rate of elimination is constant regardless of C (i.e., constant **amount** of drug eliminated per unit time). C_p decreases linearly with time. Examples of drugs: ethanol, phenytoin, and aspirin (at high or toxic concentrations).
First-order elimination	Rate of elimination is proportional to the drug concentration (i.e., constant **fraction** of drug eliminated per unit time). C_p decreases exponentially with time.

Phase I versus phase II metabolism

Phase I (reduction, oxidation, hydrolysis) yields slightly polar, water-soluble metabolites (often still active).

Phase II (acetylation, glucuronidation, sulfation) yields very polar, inactive metabolites (renally excreted).

Phase I: cyt. P450

Phase II: conjugation.

Geriatric patients lose phase I first.

Antimicrobial therapy

Mechanism of action	Drugs
Block cell wall synthesis by inhibition of peptidoglycan cross-linking	Penicillin, ampicillin, ticarcillin, piperacillin, imipenem, aztreonam, cephalosporins
Block peptidoglycan synthesis	Bacitracin, vancomycin
Block protein synthesis at 50S ribosomal subunit	Chloramphenicol, erythromycin/macrolides, lincomycin, clindamycin, streptogramins (quinupristin, dalfopristin)
Block protein synthesis at 30S ribosomal subunit	Aminoglycosides, tetracyclines
Block nucleotide synthesis	Sulfonamides, trimethoprim
Block DNA topoisomerases	Quinolones
Block mRNA synthesis	Rifampin
Disrupt bacterial/fungal cell membranes	Polymyxins
Disrupt fungal cell membranes	Amphotericin B, nystatin, fluconazole/azoles
Unknown	Pentamidine

Penicillin

Mechanism: Penicillin G (IV form), penicillin V (oral):
1. Binds penicillin-binding proteins
2. Blocks transpeptidase cross-linking of cell wall
3. Activates autolytic enzymes

Clinical use: Bactericidal for gram-positive cocci, gram-positive rods, gram-negative cocci, and spirochetes. Not penicillinase resistant.

Toxicity: Hypersensitivity reactions.

UCV Pharm.44

Methicillin, nafcillin, dicloxacillin

Mechanism: Same as penicillin. Narrow spectrum, penicillinase resistant because of bulkier R group.

Clinical use: *Staphylococcus aureus.*

Toxicity: Hypersensitivity reactions; methicillin: interstitial nephritis.

Ampicillin, amoxicillin

Mechanism: Same as penicillin. Wider spectrum, penicillinase sensitive. Also, combine with clavulanic acid (penicillinase inhibitor) to enhance spectrum. AmOxicillin has greater Oral bioavailability than ampicillin.

Clinical use: Extended-spectrum penicillin: certain gram-positive bacteria and gram-negative rods (***H**aemophilus influenzae*, ***E**scherichia coli*, ***L**isteria monocytogenes*, ***P**roteus mirabilis*, ***S**almonella*, *enterococci*).

Coverage: ampicillin/amoxicillin HELPS kill enterocci.

Toxicity: Hypersensitivity reactions; ampicillin: rash; pseudomembranous colitis.

Carbenicillin, piperacillin, and ticarcillin

Mechanism	Same as penicillin. Extended spectrum.
Clinical use	*Pseudomonas* species and gram-negative rods; susceptible to penicillinase; use with clavulanic acid.
Toxicity	Hypersensitivity reactions.

Cephalosporins

Mechanism	β-lactam drugs that inhibit cell wall synthesis but are less susceptible to penicillinases. Bactericidal.	
Clinical use	First generation: gram-positive cocci, ***P**roteus mirabilis*, ***E**. coli*, ***K**lebsiella pneumoniae*.	1st generation: **PEcK**
	Second generation: gram-positive cocci, ***H**aemophilus influenzae*, ***E**nterobacter aerogenes*, ***N**eisseria* species, ***P**roteus mirabilis*, ***E**. coli*, ***K**. pneumoniae*, ***S**erratia marcescens*.	2nd generation: **HEN PEcKS**
	Third generation: serious gram-negative infections resistant to other beta-lactams; meningitis (most penetrate the blood–brain barrier). Examples: ceftazidime for Pseudomonas; ceftriaxone for gonorrhea.	
Toxicity	Hypersensitivity reactions, increased nephrotoxicity of aminoglycosides, disulfiram-like reaction with ethanol (in cephalosporins with a methylthiotetrazole group, e.g., cefamandole).	

Penicillin

Ⓡ — C(=O) — N(H) — [β-lactam ring][5-member ring: S, N; CH_3, CH_3, COOH]; β-lactam ring =O

Ⓡ: Functional group

Cephalosporin

R_1 — C(=O) — N(H) — [β-lactam ring][6-member ring: S, N; $COO^{\ominus}$, R_2]; β-lactam ring =O

R_1: Functional group
R_2: Functional group

Aztreonam

Mechanism	A monobactam resistant to β-lactamases. Inhibits cell wall synthesis (binds to PBP3). Synergistic with aminoglycosides. No cross-allergenicity with penicillins.
Clinical use	Gram-negative rods: *Klebsiella* species, *Pseudomonas* species, *Serratia* species. No activity against gram-positives or anaerobes.
Toxicity	Usually nontoxic; occasional GI upset.

Imipenem/cilastatin

Mechanism: Imipenem is a wide-spectrum, β-lactamase-resistant carbapenem. Always administered with cilastatin (inhibitor of renal dihydropeptidase I) to ↓ inactivation in renal tubules.

With imipenem, "the kill is **lastin** with cil**astatin**."

Clinical use: Gram-positive cocci, gram-negative rods, and anaerobes. Drug of choice for *Enterobacter*.

Toxicity: GI distress, skin rash, and CNS toxicity (at high plasma levels).

Vancomycin

Mechanism: Inhibits cell wall mucopeptide formation. Bactericidal. Resistance occurs with amino acid change of D-ala D-ala to D-ala D-lac.

Clinical use: Used for serious, gram-positive multidrug-resistant organisms, including *Staphylococcus aureus* and *Clostridium difficile* (pseudomembranous colitis).

Toxicity: **N**ephrotoxicity, **O**totoxicity, **T**hrombophlebitis, diffuse flushing—"red man syndrome" (can largely prevent by pretreatment with antihistamines and slow infusion rate). Well tolerated in general: does **NOT** have many problems.

Protein synthesis inhibitors

"Buy **AT 30, CELL** at 50"

30S inhibitors:
A = Aminoglycosides (streptomycin, gentamicin, tobramycin, amikacin) [bactericidal]
T = Tetracyclines [bacteriostatic]

50S inhibitors:
C = Chloramphenicol [bacteriostatic]
E = Erythromycin [bacteriostatic]
L = Lincomycin [bacteriostatic]
L = cLindamycin [bacteriostatic]

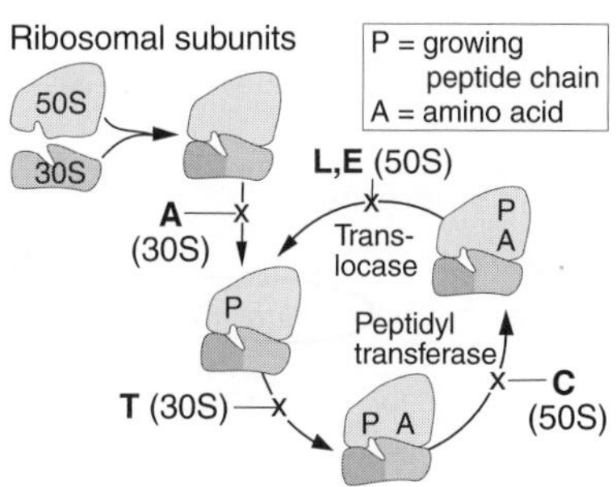

Aminoglycosides

Gentamicin, neomycin, amikacin, tobramycin, streptomycin

Mechanism: Bactericidal, inhibits formation of initiation complex and causes misreading of mRNA. Requires O_2 for uptake, therefore ineffective against anaerobes.

Clinical use: Severe gram-negative rod infections. Synergistic with β-lactam antibiotics. Neomycin for bowel surgery.

Toxicity: Nephrotoxicity (especially when used with cephalosporins), Ototoxicity (especially when used with loop diuretics). Ami**NO**glycosides.

UCV Pharm.79

Tetracyclines

Tetracycline, doxycycline, demeclocycline, minocycline

Mechanism: Bacteriostatic, binds to 30S and prevents attachment of aminoacyl-tRNA, limited CNS penetration. (Minocycline) Doxycycline fecally eliminated and can be used in patients with renal failure. Must NOT take with milk or antacids because divalent cations inhibit its absorption in the gut.

Clinical use: **V**ibrio cholerae, **A**cne, **C**hlamydia, **U**reaplasma **U**realyticum, **M**ycoplasma pneumoniae, **B**orrelia burgdorferi (Lyme disease), **R**ickettsia, tularemia.

VACUUM your Bed Room

Toxicity: GI distress, discolors teeth and inhibits bone growth in children, Fanconi's syndrome, photosensitivity. Teratogen

UCV Pharm.15

Macrolides

Erythromycin, azithromycin, clarithromycin

Mechanism: Inhibits protein synthesis by blocking translocation, binds to the 23S rRNA of the 50S ribosomal subunit. Bacteriostatic.

Clinical use: Upper respiratory tract infections, pneumonias, sexually transmitted diseases: gram-positive cocci (streptococcal infections in patients allergic to penicillin), *Mycoplasma, Legionella, Chlamydia, Neisseria.* (Intracellular organisms)

Toxicity: GI discomfort (most common cause of noncompliance), acute cholestatic hepatitis, eosinophilia, skin rashes.

Chloramphenicol

Mechanism: Inhibits 50S peptidyl transferase. Bacteriostatic.

Clinical use: Meningitis (*H. influenzae, Neisseria meningitidis, Streptococcus pneumoniae*). Conservative use due to toxicities.

Toxicity: Anemia, aplastic anemia (dose independent), gray baby syndrome (in premature infants lacking liver UDP-glucuronyl transferase). ← G-6P deficiency

UCV Pharm.39

Clindamycin

Mechanism: Blocks peptide bond formation at 50S ribosomal subunit.

Clinical use: Treat anaerobic infections (e.g., *B. fragilis, C. perfringens*).

Toxicity: Pseudomembranous colitis (*C. difficile* overgrowth), fever, diarrhea.

UCV Pharm.27

Sulfonamides

	Sulfamethoxazole (SMZ), sulfisoxazole, triple sulfas, sulfadiazine
Mechanism	PABA antimetabolites inhibit dihydropteroate synthase. Bacteriostatic.
Clinical use	Gram-positive, gram-negative, *Nocardia, Chlamydia.* Triple sulfas or SMZ for simple UTI.
Toxicity	Hypersensitivity reactions, hemolysis if G6PD deficient, nephrotoxicity, kernicterus in infants, displace other drugs from albumin.

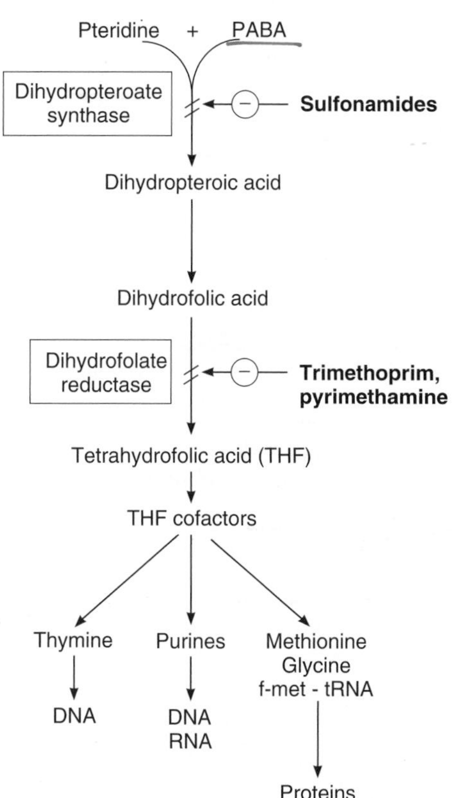

Trimethoprim

Mechanism	Inhibits bacterial dihydrofolate reductase. Bacteriostatic.	Trimethoprim = **TMP**: "**T**reats **M**arrow **P**oorly."
Clinical use	Used in combination with sulfonamides (trimethoprim–sulfamethoxazole), causing sequential block of folate synthesis. Combination used for recurrent UTI, *Shigella, Salmonella, Pneumocystis carinii* pneumonia.	
Toxicity	Megaloblastic anemia, leukopenia, granulocytopenia. (May alleviate with supplemental folinic acid.)	

Fluoroquinolones

	Ciprofloxacin, norfloxacin, ofloxacin, grepafloxacin, enoxacin (fluoroquinolones), nalidixic acid (a quinolone)	Fluoro**quinolones** hurt attachments to your **bones.**
Mechanism	Inhibits DNA gyrase (topoisomerase II). Bactericidal.	· UTI's · Sexually Transmitted · Respiratory
Clinical use	Gram-negative rods of urinary and GI tracts (including *Pseudomonas*), *Neisseria*, some gram-positive organisms.	
Toxicity	GI upset, superinfections, skin rashes, headache, dizziness. Contraindicated in pregnant women and in children because animal studies show damage to cartilage. Tendonitis and tendon rupture in adults.	

UCV Pharm.42

HIGH-YIELD FACTS

Pharmacology

Metronidazole		
Mechanism	Forms toxic metabolites in the bacterial cell. Bactericidal.	
Clinical use	Antiprotozoal. *Giardia*, *Entamoeba*, *Trichomonas*, *Gardnerella vaginalis*, anaerobes (*Bacteroides*, *Clostridium*). Used with bismuth and amoxicillin or tetracycline for "triple therapy" against *H. pylori*.	**GET** on the **Metro!**
Toxicity	Disulfiram-like reaction with alcohol, headache.	
Polymyxins	Polymyxin B, polymyxin E	
Mechanism	Bind to cell membranes of bacteria and disrupt their osmotic properties. Polymyxins are cationic, basic proteins that act like detergents.	
Clinical use	Resistant gram-negative infections.	
Toxicity	Neurotoxicity, acute renal tubular necrosis.	
Isoniazid (INH)		
Mechanism	Decreases synthesis of mycolic acids.	**INH:** Injures **N**eurons and **H**epatocytes.
Clinical use	*Mycobacterium tuberculosis*. The only agent used as solo prophylaxis against TB.	
Toxicity	Hemolysis if G6PD deficient, neurotoxicity, hepatotoxicity, SLE-like syndrome. Pyridoxine (vit. B_6) can prevent neurotoxicity.	Different INH half-lives in fast vs. slow acetylators. • Vit B_6 deficiency → neurotox.
UCV Pharm.25		
Rifampin		
Mechanism	Inhibits DNA-dependent RNA polymerase.	**R**ifampin's **4 R's:** **R**NA polymerase inhibitor; **R**evs up microsomal P450; **R**ed/orange body fluids; **R**apid resistance if used alone
Clinical use	*M. tuberculosis*, delays resistance to dapsone when used for leprosy. Always used in combination with other drugs except in the treatment of meningococcal carrier state, and chemoprophylaxis in contacts of children with *H. influenzae* type B.	
Toxicity	Minor hepatotoxicity and drug interactions ($\uparrow P_{450}$).	
UCV Pharm.45		
Anti–TB drugs	Rifampin, Ethambutol, Streptomycin, Pyrazinamide, Isoniazid (INH).	**RESPI**re. INH is used alone for TB prophylaxis.

Resistance mechanisms for various antibiotics

Drug	Most common mechanism
Penicillins/ cephalosporins	β-lactamase cleavage of β-lactam ring
Aminoglycosides	Modification via acetylation, adenylation, or phosphorylation
Vancomycin	Terminal D-ala of cell wall component replaced with D-lac; ↓ affinity.
Chloramphenicol	Modification via acetylation
Macrolides	Methylation of rRNA near erythromycin's ribosome-binding site
Tetracycline	↓ uptake or ↑ transport out of cell
Sulfonamides	Altered enzyme (bacterial dihydropteroate synthetase), ↓ uptake, or ↑ PABA synthesis

Nonsurgical antimicrobial prophylaxis

Meningococcal infection	Rifampin (drug of choice), minocycline
Gonorrhea	Ceftriaxone
Syphilis	Benzathine penicillin G
History of recurrent UTIs	Trimethoprim-sulfamethoxazole (TMP-SMZ)
PCP	TMP-SMZ (drug of choice), aerosolized pentamidine

Amphotericin B

Mechanism	Binds ergosterol (unique to fungi), forms membrane pores that disrupt homeostasis.	Amphotericin "tears" holes in the fungal membrane by forming pores.
Clinical use	Used for wide spectrum of systemic mycoses. *Cryptococcus*, *Blastomyces*, *Coccidioides*, *Aspergillus*, *Histoplasma*, *Candida*, *Mucor* (systemic mycoses). Intrathecally for fungal meningitis; does not cross blood–brain barrier.	
Toxicity	Fever/chills ("shake and bake"), hypotension, nephrotoxicity, arrhythmias ("amphoterrible"). b/c Hypokalemia	

UCV Pharm.29

Nystatin

Mechanism	Binds to ergosterol, disrupting fungal membranes.
Clinical use	"Swish and swallow" for oral candidiasis (thrush).

Fluconazole, ketoconazole, clotrimazole, miconazole, itraconazole

Mechanism	Inhibit fungal steroid (ergosterol) synthesis.
Clinical use	Systemic mycoses. Fluconazole for cryptococcal meningitis in AIDS patients and candidal infections of all types. Ketoconazole for *Blastomyces*, *Coccidioides*, *Histoplasma*, *C. albicans*; hypercortisolism.
Toxicity	Hormone synthesis inhibition (gynecomastia), liver dysfunction (inhibits cyt. P450), fever, chills.

UCV Pharm.43

Fluconazole - Penetrates CSF (cryptococcal meningitis)
candidal infections

Ketoconazole - ↑ cyclosporine levels
Blasto
Histo
coccidio
C. Albicans

Griseofulvin

Mechanism	Interferes with microtubule function, disrupts mitosis. Deposits in keratin-containing tissues (e.g., nails).
Clinical use	Oral treatment of superficial infections, inhibits growth of dermatophytes (tinea, ringworm).
Toxicity	Teratogenic, carcinogenic, confusion, headaches, ↑ coumadin metabolism.

Antiviral chemotherapy

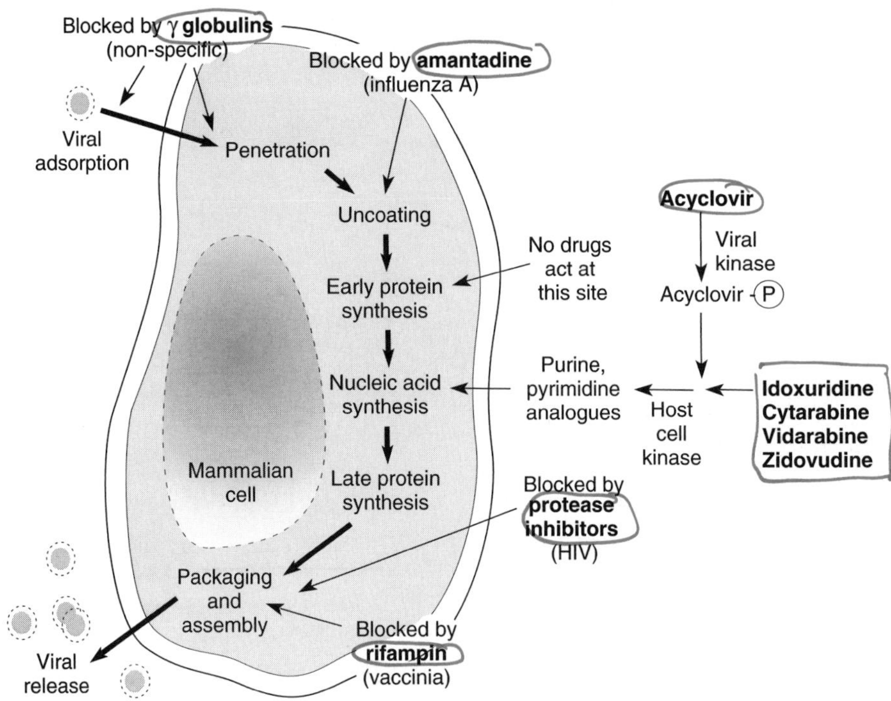

Amantadine

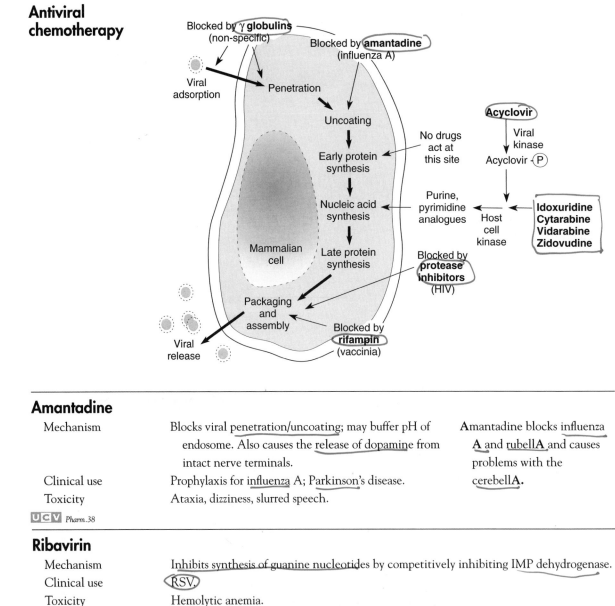

Mechanism	Blocks viral penetration/uncoating; may buffer pH of endosome. Also causes the release of dopamine from intact nerve terminals.	**A**mantadine blocks influenza **A** and rubell**A** and causes problems with the cerebell**A.**
Clinical use	Prophylaxis for influenza A; Parkinson's disease.	
Toxicity	Ataxia, dizziness, slurred speech.	

UCV Pharm.38

Ribavirin

Mechanism	Inhibits synthesis of guanine nucleotides by competitively inhibiting IMP dehydrogenase.
Clinical use	RSV.
Toxicity	Hemolytic anemia.

Acyclovir

Mechanism	Preferentially inhibits viral DNA polymerase when phosphorylated by viral thymidine kinase.
Clinical use	HSV, VZV, EBV. Mucocutaneous and genital herpes lesions. Prophylaxis in immunocompromised patients.
Toxicity	Delirium, tremor, nephrotoxicity.

Ganciclovir

DHPG (dihydroxy-2-propoxymethyl guanine)

Mechanism	Phosphorylation by viral kinase, preferentially inhibits CMV DNA polymerase.
Clinical use	CMV, especially in immunocompromised patients.
Toxicity	Leukopenia, neutropenia, thrombocytopenia, renal toxicity. More toxic to host enzymes than acyclovir.

Foscarnet

Mechanism	Viral DNA polymerase inhibitor that binds to the pyrophosphate binding site of the enzyme. Does not require activation by viral kinase.
Clinical use	CMV retinitis in immunocompromised patients when ganciclovir fails.
Toxicity	Nephrotoxicity.

Foscarnet = pyroFosphate analog.

HIV therapy

Protease inhibitors: Saquinavir, Ritonavir, Indinavir, Nelfinavir

Mechanism	Inhibits assembly of new virus by blocking protease enzyme
Toxicity	GI intolerance (nausea, diarrhea), hyperglycemia, lipid abnormalities, thrombocytopenia (indinavir).

Reverse transcriptase inhibitors

Nucleosides	Zidovudine (AZT), Didanosine (ddI), Zalcitabine (ddC), Stavudine (d4T), Lamivudine (3TC)
Non-nucleosides	Nevirapine, Delavirdine
Mechanism	Preferentially inhibit reverse transcriptase of HIV, prevent incorporation of viral genome into host DNA
Toxicity	Bone marrow suppression (neutropenia, anemia), peripheral neuropathy, lactic acidosis (nucleosides); rash (non-nucleosides); megaloblastic anemia (AZT).

Clinical use	"Triple therapy" generally entails use of two nucleoside reverse transcriptase inhibitors with a protease inhibitor, though other combinations, such as the substitution of a non-nucleoside for a protease inhibitor, are used. Initiated when patients have low CD4 counts (< 500 cells/mm^3) or high viral load. AZT used during pregnancy to reduce risk of fetal transmission.

Interferons

Mechanism	Glycoproteins from human leukocytes that block various stages of viral RNA and DNA synthesis.
Clinical use	Chronic hepatitis A and B, Kaposi's sarcoma.
Toxicity	Neutropenia.

Antiparasitic drugs

Ivermectin	Onchocerciasis ("river blindness" ⇒ rIVER-mectin).
Mebendazole/ thiabendazole	Nematode/roundworm (e.g., pinworm, whipworm) infections.
Pyrantel pamoate	Giant roundworm (*Ascaris*), hookworm (*Necator/Ancylostoma*), pinworm (*Enterobius*).
Praziquantel	Trematode/fluke (e.g., schistosomes, *Paragonimus*, *Clonorchis*) and cysticercosis.
Niclosamide	Cestode/tapeworm (e.g., *D. latum*, *Taenia* species) infections except cysticercosis.
Pentavalent antimony	Leishmaniasis.
Chloroquine, quinine, mefloquine	Malaria.
Primaquine	Latent hypnozoite (liver) forms of malaria (*P. vivax*, *P. ovale*).
Metronidazole	Giardiasis, amoebic dysentery (*E. histolytica*), bacterial vaginitis (*Gardnerella vaginalis*).
Pentamidine	*Pneumocystis carinii* pneumonia prophylaxis.
Nifurtimox	Chagas' disease (*Trypanosoma cruzi*).

Central and peripheral nervous system

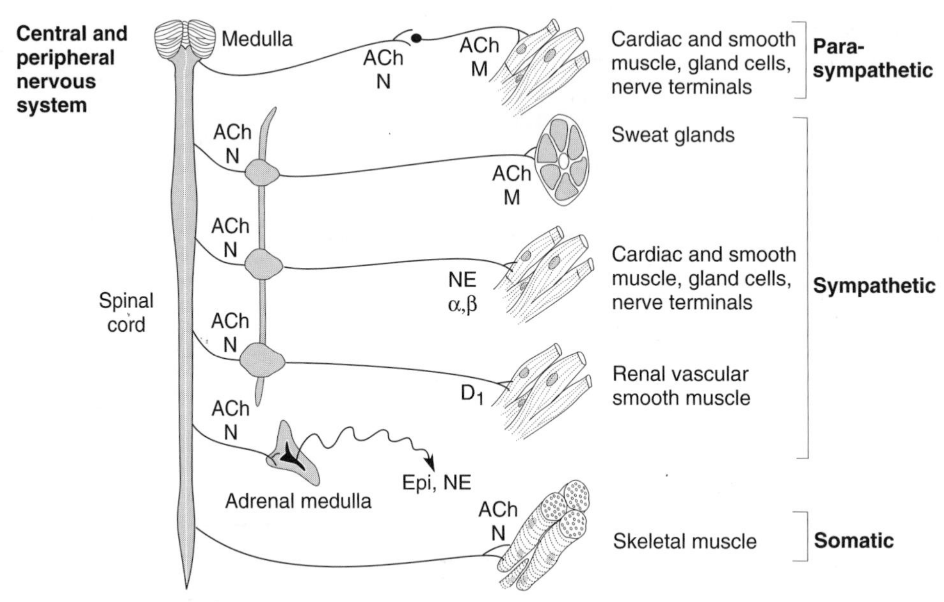

Autonomic drugs

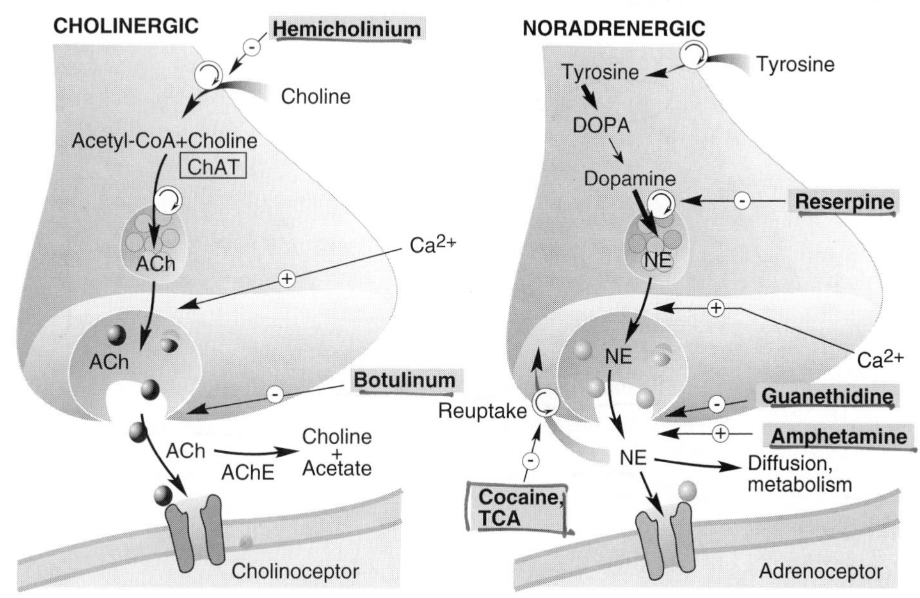

Circles with rotating arrows represent transporters; ChAT, choline acetyltransferase; ACh, acetylcholine; AChE, acetylcholinesterase; NE, norepinephrine.

UCV Pharm.41

Cholinomimetics

	Clinical applications	Action
Direct agonists		
Bethanechol	Postoperative and neurogenic ileus and urinary retention	Activates bowel and bladder smooth muscle
Carbachol, pilocarpine → enters CNS	Glaucoma	Activates ciliary muscle of eye (open angle), pupillary sphincter (narrow angle)
Indirect agonists (anticholinesterases)		
Neostigmine	Postoperative and neurogenic ileus and urinary retention, myasthenia gravis, reversal of NMJ blockade (postoperative)	↑ endogenous ACh
Pyridostigmine	Myasthenia gravis	↑ endogenous ACh; ↑ strength
Edrophonium	Diagnosis of myasthenia gravis (extremely short-acting)	↑ endogenous ACh
Physostigmine	Glaucoma (crosses blood–brain barrier → CNS) and atropine overdose	↑ endogenous ACh
Echothiophate	Glaucoma	↑ endogenous ACh

Cholinesterase inhibitor poisoning

Symptoms include: **D**iarrhea, **U**rination, **M**iosis, **B**ronchospasm, **B**radycardia, **E**xcitation of skeletal muscle and CNS, **L**acrimation, **S**weating, **S**alivation (also abdominal cramping). Treat: Atropine

DUMBBELSS

Parathion and other organophosphates. Insectacide poison

HIGH-YIELD FACTS

Pharmacology

Cholinoreceptor blockers

Muscarinic antagonists	**Atropine:** used to dilate pupil, reduce acid secretion in acid-peptic disease, reduce urgency in mild cystitis, ↓ GI motility, reduce airway secretions. Causes increased body temperature, rapid pulse, dry mouth, flushed skin, disorientation, mydriasis with cycloplegia, and constipation.	Atropine parasympathetic block side effects: Blind as a bat Red as a beet Mad as a hatter Hot as a hare Dry as a bone
Nicotinic antagonists	Hexamethonium: ganglionic blocker.	
Cholinesterase regenerator	Pralidoxime: regenerates active cholinesterase, chemical antagonist, used to treat organophosphate exposure.	Blocks **SLUD:** Salivation, Lacrimation, Urination, Defecation.

Antimuscarinic drugs

Organ system	Drugs	Application
CNS	Benztropine	Parkinson's disease
	Scopolamine	Motion sickness
Eye	Atropine, homatropine, tropicamide	Produce mydriasis and cycloplegia
Respiratory	Ipratropium	Asthma, COPD

Neuromuscular blocking drugs

Used for muscle paralysis in surgery or mechanical ventilation.

Depolarizing

Succinylcholine

Reversal of blockade:

- Phase I (prolonged depolarization)—no antidote. Block potentiated by cholinesterase inhibitors.
- Phase II (repolarized but blocked)—antidote: cholinesterase inhibitors (e.g., neostigmine).

Nondepolarizing

Tubocurarine, atracurium, mivacurium, pancuronium, vecuronium.

Reversal of blockade: neostigmine, edrophonium, and other cholinesterase inhibitors.

Dantrolene

Used in the treatment of malignant hyperthermia, which is caused by the concomitant use of halothane and succinylcholine. Also used to treat neuroleptic malignant syndrome (a toxicity of antipsychotic drugs).

Mechanism: prevents the release of Ca^{2+} from the sarcoplasmic reticulum of skeletal muscle.

Sympathomimetics

Drug	Mechanism/selectivity	Applications
Catecholamines		
Epinephrine	Direct general agonist (α_1, α_2, β_1, β_2)	Anaphylaxis, glaucoma (open angle), asthma, hypotension
Norepinephrine	α_1, α_2, β_1	Hypotension
Isoproterenol	$\beta_1 = \beta_2$	AV block (rare)
Dopamine	$D_1 = D_2 > \beta > \alpha$	Shock (↑renal perfusion), heart failure
Dobutamine	$\beta_1 > \beta_2$	Shock, heart failure
Other		
Amphetamine *Pharm.55, 66*	Indirect general agonist, releases stored catecholamines	Narcolepsy, obesity, attention deficit disorder
Ephedrine	Indirect general agonist, releases stored catecholamines	Nasal congestion, urinary incontinence, hypotension
Phenylephrine	$\alpha_1 > \alpha_2$	Pupil dilator, vasoconstriction, nasal decongestion
Albuterol, terbutaline	$\beta_2 > \beta_1$	Asthma
Cocaine *Pharm.72*	Indirect general agonist, uptake inhibitor	Causes vasoconstriction and local anesthesia

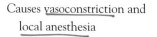

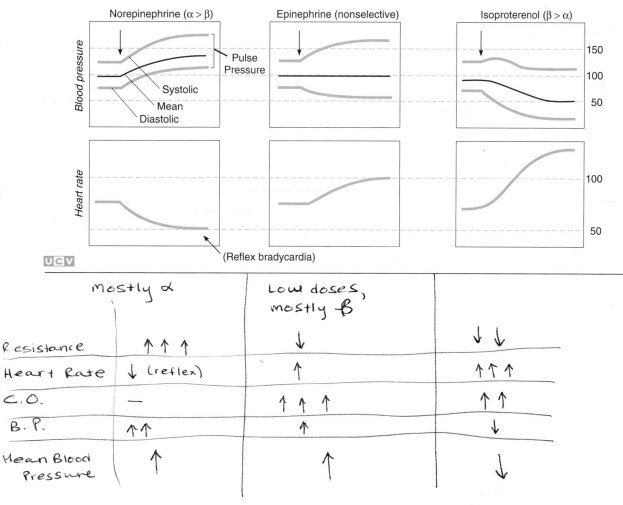

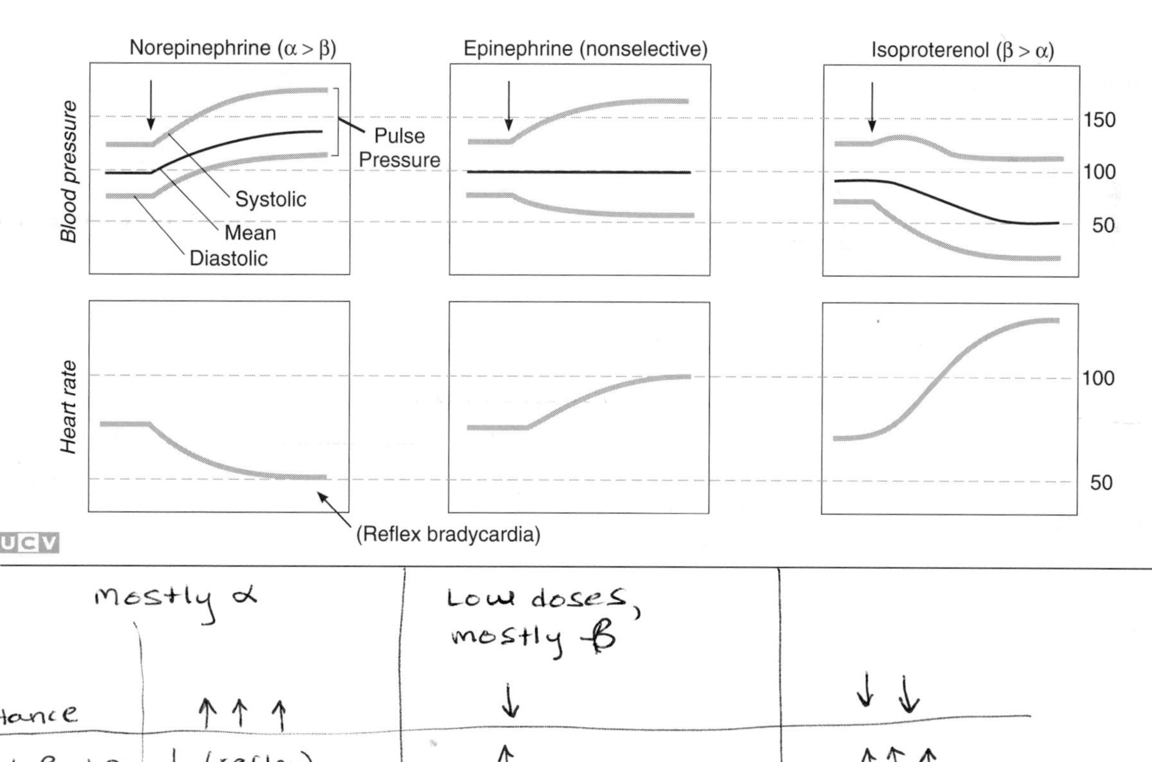

	mostly α	Low doses, mostly β	
Resistance	↑↑↑	↓	↓↓
Heart Rate	↓ (reflex)	↑	↑↑↑
C.O.	—	↑↑↑	↑↑
B.P.	↑↑	↑	↓
Mean Blood Pressure	↑	↑	↓

α-Blockers

	Application	Toxicity
Nonselective		
Phenoxybenzamine (irreversible) and phentolamine (reversible)	Pheochromocytoma	Orthostatic hypotension, reflex tachycardia
α_1-selective		
Prazosin, terazosin, doxazosin	Hypertension, urinary retention in BPH	First-dose orthostatic hypotension, dizziness, headache
α_2-selective		
Yohimbine	Impotence (effectiveness is controversial)	

β-Blockers

Propranolol, metoprolol, atenolol, nadolol, timolol, pindolol, esmolol, labetalol

Application	Effect
Hypertension	↓ cardiac output, ↓ renin secretion
Angina pectoris	↓ heart rate and contractility, resulting in decreased oxygen consumption
MI	β-blockers decrease mortality
SVT (propranolol, esmolol)	↓ AV conduction velocity
Glaucoma (timolol)	↓ secretion of aqueous humor
Toxicity	Impotence, exacerbation of asthma, cardiovascular adverse effects (bradycardia, AV block, CHF), CNS adverse effects (sedation, sleep alterations)
Selectivity	Nonselective ($\beta_1 = \beta_2$): propranolol, timolol, pindolol, nadolol, and labetalol (also blocks α_1 receptors) β_1 selective ($\beta_1 > \beta_2$): metoprolol, atenolol, esmolol (short-acting)

UCV Pharm.1

Glaucoma drugs

	Mechanism	Side effects
α agonists		
Epinephrine	↑ outflow of aqueous humor	Mydriasis, stinging. Do not use in closed-angle glaucoma.
Brimonidine	↓ aqueous humor synthesis	No pupillary or vision changes.
β blockers		
Timolol, betaxolol, carteolol	↓ aqueous humor secretion	No pupillary or vision changes.
Cholinomimetics		
Pilocarpine, carbachol, physostigmine, echothiophate	Ciliary muscle contraction, opening of trabecular meshwork; ↑ outflow of aqueous humor	Miosis, cyclospasm.
Diuretics		
Acetazolamide, dorzolamide	↓ aqueous humor secretion due to ↓ HCO_3^- (via inhibition of carbonic anhydrase)	No pupillary or vision changes.
Prostaglandin		
Latanoprost	↑ outflow of aqueous humor	Darkens color of iris (browning).

Barbiturates

Phenobarbital, pentobarbital, thiopental, secobarbital

Mechanism	Facilitate $GABA_A$ action by ↑ **duration** of Cl^- channel opening, thus ↓ neuron firing.	Barbi**DURAT**e (↑ **DURAT**ion).
Clinical use	Sedative for anxiety, seizures, insomnia, induction of anesthesia (thiopental).	Contraindicated in porphyria.
Toxicity	Dependence, additive CNS depression effects with alcohol, respiratory or cardiovascular depression (can lead to death), drug interactions owing to induction of liver microsomal enzymes (cyt. P_{450}).	

UCV Pharm.48

Benzodiazepines

Diazepam, lorazepam, triazolam, temazepam, oxazepam, midazolam, chlordiazepoxide

Mechanism	Facilitates $GABA_A$ action by ↑ **frequency of Cl^-** channel opening. Most have long half-lives and active metabolites.	**FRE**nzodiazepines (↑ **FRE**quency)
Clinical use	Anxiety, spasticity, status epilepticus (diazepam), detoxification (especially alcohol withdrawal–delirium tremens).	Short acting = **TOM** thumb = **T**riazolam, **O**xazepam, **M**idazolam
Toxicity	Dependence, additive CNS depression effects with alcohol. Less risk of respiratory depression and coma than with barbiturates. Treat overdose with flumazenil (competitive antagonist at GABA receptor).	

Antipsychotics (neuroleptics)

Thioridazine, haloperidol, fluphenazine, chlorpromazine

Mechanism	Most antipsychotics block dopamine D_2 receptors (excess dopamine effects connected with schizophrenia).	Evolution of EPS side effects: 4 h acute dystonia 4 d akinesia 4 wk akathisia 4 mo tardive dyskinesia (often irreversible).
Clinical use	Schizophrenia, psychosis.	
Toxicity	Extrapyramidal system side effects, sedation, endocrine side effects, and side effects arising from blocking muscarinic, α, and histamine receptors. **Neuroleptic malignant syndrome:** rigidity, autonomic instability, hyperpyrexia (treat with dantrolene and dopamine agonists). Pharm.57, 58 **Tardive dyskinesia:** stereotypic oral–facial movements probably due to dopamine receptor sensitization; results of long-term antipsychotic use. Pharm.59	

UCV

Atypical antipsychotics

Clozapine, olanzapine, risperidone

Mechanism	Block $5HT_2$ and dopamine receptors.
Clinical use	Treatment of schizophrenia; useful for positive and negative symptoms. **Olanzapine** is also used for OCD, anxiety disorder, and depression.
Toxicity	Fewer extrapyramidal and anticholinergic side effects than other antipsychotics. **Clozapine** may cause agranulocytosis (requires weekly WBC monitoring).

Lithium

Mechanism	Not established; possibly related to inhibition of phosphoinositol cascade.
Clinical use	Mood stabilizer for bipolar affective disorder, blocks relapse and acute manic events.
Toxicity	Tremor, hypothyroidism, polyuria (ADH antagonist causing nephrogenic DI), teratogenesis. Narrow therapeutic window requiring close monitoring of serum levels.

UCV *Pharm.56*

Tricyclic antidepressants

Imipramine, amitriptyline, desipramine, nortriptyline, clomipramine, doxepin

Mechanism	Block reuptake of norepinephrine and serotonin.
Clinical use	Endogenous depression, bedwetting (imipramine), obsessive–compulsive disorder (clomipramine).
Side effects	Sedation, α-blocking effects, atropine-like (anticholinergic) side effects (tachycardia, urinary retention). Tertiary TCAs (amitriptyline) have more anticholinergic effects than secondary TCAs (nortriptyline). Desipramine is the least sedating.
Toxicity	**"Tri-C"**s: convulsions, coma, cardiotoxicity (arrhythmias); also respiratory depression, hyperpyrexia. Confusion and hallucinations in elderly.

UCV *Pharm.60*

SSRIs

Fluoxetine, sertraline, paroxetine, italopram.

Mechanism	Serotonin-specific reuptake inhibitors.
Clinical use	Endogenous depression.
Toxicity	Fewer than TCAs. CNS stimulation: anxiety, insomnia, tremor, anorexia, nausea, and vomiting; "Serotonin syndrome" with MAOIs: hyperthermia, muscle rigidity, CV collapse.

It normally takes 2–3 wk for antidepressants to have an effect.

Heterocyclics

Second- and third-generation antidepressants with varied and mixed mechanisms of action. Used in major depressive disorders.

Trazodone	Primarily inhibits serotonin reuptake. Toxicity: sedation, nausea, priapism, postural hypotension.
Buproprion	Also used for smoking cessation. Mechanism not well known. Toxicity: stimulant effects (tachycardia, agitation), dry mouth, aggravation of psychosis.
Venlafaxine	Also used in generalized anxiety disorder. Inhibits serotonin and dopamine reuptake. Toxicity: stimulant effects (anxiety, agitation, headache, insomnia)
Mirtazapine	$Alpha_2$ antagonist (increases release of norepinephrine and serotonin) and potent $5HT_2$ receptor antagonist. Toxicity: sedation, increased serum cholesterol, increased appetite.

Monoamine oxidase (MAO) inhibitors

Phenelzine, isocarboxazid, tranylcypromine

Mechanism	Nonselective MAO inhibition.
Clinical use	Atypical depressions (i.e., with psychotic or phobic features), anxiety, hypochondriasis.
Toxicity	Hypertensive crisis with tyramine ingestion (in many foods) and meperidine; CNS stimulation. Contraindication with SSRIs or β-agonists.

UCV *Pharm.6*

MAO-B metabolize dopamine more than NE/serotonin

Selegiline (deprenyl)

Mechanism	Selectively inhibits MAO-B, thereby increasing the availability of dopamine.
Clinical use	Adjunctive agent to L-dopa in treatment of Parkinson's disease.
Toxicity	May enhance adverse effects of L-dopa.

L-dopa (levodopa)/carbidopa

Mechanism	Increases level of dopamine in brain. Parkinsonism thought to be due to loss of dopaminergic neurons and excess cholinergic function. Unlike dopamine, L-dopa can cross blood–brain barrier and is converted by dopa decarboxylase in the CNS to dopamine.
Clinical use	Parkinsonism.
Toxicity	Arrhythmias from peripheral conversion to dopamine. Carbidopa, a peripheral decarboxylase inhibitor, is given with L-dopa in order to increase the bioavailability of L-dopa in the brain and to limit peripheral side effects. Dyskinesias also occur.

Arrythmias
Dyskinesia

UCV Pharm.52

Parkinson's disease drugs

Dopamine agonists	L-dopa/carbidopa, bromocriptine (an ergot alkaloid and partial dopamine agonist), amantadine (enhance dopamine release)	BALSA:
		Bromocriptine
		Amantadine
MAO inhibitors	Selegiline (selective MAO type B inhibitor)	Levodopa
Antimuscarinics	Benztropine (improve tremor and rigidity but have little effect on bradykinesia)	Selegiline
		Antimuscarinics

Antiviral: Amantadine

Opioid analgesics

Morphine, fentanyl, codeine, heroin, methadone, meperidine, dextromethorphan

P. 69

Mechanism	Act as agonists at opioid receptors (mu - morphine, delta - enkephalin, kappa - dynorphin) to modulate synaptic transmission.
Clinical use	Pain, cough suppression (dextromethorphan), diarrhea (loperamide and diphenoxylate), acute pulmonary edema, maintenance programs for addicts (methadone).
Toxicity	Addiction, **respiratory depression,** constipation, miosis (**pinpoint pupils**), additive **CNS depression** with other drugs. Tolerance does not develop to miosis and constipation. Toxicity treated with naloxone or naltrexone (opioid receptor antagonist).

UCV Pharm.80, 91

Sumatriptan

P. 289

Mechanism	5-HT_{1D} agonist. Half-life < 2 hours. serotonin agonist
Clinical use	Acute migraine, cluster headache attacks.
Toxicity	Chest discomfort, mild tingling (contraindicated in patients with CAD or Prinzmetal's angina).

Ondansetron

P. 295

Mechanism	5-HT_3 antagonist. Powerful central-acting antiemetic.	You will not vomit, so you can go **on dancing.**
Clinical use	Control vomiting postoperatively and in patients undergoing cancer chemotherapy.	Inhibits serotonin
Toxicity	Headache, diarrhea.	

Opiod Effects: Tolerance (except for Miosis + constipation)
Dependence

1. Analgesia
2. Respiratory Depression
3. Miosis
4. Sedation/Euphoria
5. constipation
6. Antitussive
7. Emetic Effects
8. Convulsant Effects
9. Cardiovascular (Postural Hypotension)
10. ↑ circular smooth muscle: Biliary, uretral, Bronchial spasms
11. Histamine release

HIGH-YIELD FACTS
Pharmacology

Epilepsy drugs

	PARTIAL		GENERALIZED				
	Simple	Complex	Tonic-clonic	Absence	Status	TN	Notes
Phenytoin	✓	✓	✓		✓		Also a Class IB antiarrhythmic
Carbamazepine	✓	✓	✓			✓	
Lamotrigine	✓	✓	✓				See toxicity below
Gabapentin	✓	✓	✓				Adjunct in refractory seizures. Renal excretion.
Topiramate	✓	✓					Adjunct use
Phenobarbital			✓				Safer in pregnant women Crigler–Najjar II
Valproate				✓			
Ethosuximide				✓			
Benzodiazepines (Diazepam or Lorazepam)					✓		

TN = Trigeminal neuralgia

Epilepsy drug toxicities

Benzodiazepines	Sedation, tolerance, dependence.
Carbamazepine	Diplopia, ataxia, induction of cyt. P450, blood dyscrasias (agranulocytosis, aplastic anemia), liver toxicity.
Ethosuximide	Gastrointestinal distress, lethargy, headache.
Phenobarbital	Sedation, induction of cyt. P450, tolerance, dependence.
Phenytoin	Nystagmus, diplopia, ataxia, sedation, gingival hyperplasia, hirsutism, anemias, birth defects (teratogenic).
Valproic acid	Gastrointestinal distress, rare but fatal hepatotoxicity, neural tube defects in fetus (spina bifida).
Lamotrigine	Life-threatening rash, Stevens–Johnson syndrome.
Gabapentin	Sedation, movement disorders
Topiramate	Sedation, mental dulling, kidney stones, weight loss

UCV Pharm.47, 48, 49, 54

Phenytoin

Mechanism	Use-dependent blockade of Na^+ channels.
Clinical use	Grand mal seizures.
Toxicity	Nystagmus, ataxia, diplopia, lethargy. Chronic use produces gingival hyperplasia in children, peripheral neuropathy, hirsutism, megaloblastic anemia (↓ vitamin B_{12}), malignant hyperthermia (rare), teratogenic (fetal hydantoin syndrome).

UCV Pharm.54

Anesthetics—general principles

Drugs with ↓ solubility in blood = rapid induction and recovery times.

Drugs with ↑ solubility in lipids = ↑ potency = $\frac{1}{\text{MAC}}$.

Examples: N_2O has low blood and lipid solubility, and thus fast induction and low potency. Halothane, in contrast, has ↑ lipid and blood solubility, and thus high potency and slow induction.

Inhaled anesthetics

Halothane, enflurane, isoflurane, sevoflurane, methoxyflurane, nitrous oxide

Principle — The lower the solubility in blood, the quicker the anesthetic induction and the quicker the recovery.

Effects — Myocardial depression, respiratory depression, nausea/emesis, ↑ cerebral blood flow.

Toxicity — Hepatotoxicity (halothane), nephrotoxicity (methoxyflurane), proconvulsant (enflurane), malignant hyperthermia (rare).

UCV Pharm.24, 85

Intravenous anesthetics

Barbiturates — Thiopental: high lipid solubility, rapid entry into brain. Used for induction of anesthesia and short surgical procedures. Effect terminated by redistribution from brain. ↓ cerebral blood flow.

Benzodiazepines — Midazolam: used adjunctively with gaseous anesthetics and narcotics. May cause severe postoperative respiratory depression and amnesia.

Arylcyclohexylamines — Ketamine (PCP analog): dissociative anesthetic. Cardiovascular stimulant. Causes disorientation, hallucination, and bad dreams. Increases cerebral blood flow. Pharm.51

Narcotic analgesics — Morphine, fentanyl: used with other CNS depressants during general anesthesia.

Other — Propofol: used for rapid anesthesia induction and short procedures. Less postop nausea than thiopental.

UCV

Local anesthetics

Esters: procaine, cocaine, tetracaine

Amides: lidocaine, bupivacaine (amides have 2 i's in name).

Mechanism — Block Na^+ channels by binding to specific receptors on inner portion of channel. Tertiary amine local anesthetics penetrate membrane in uncharged form, then bind in charged form.

Principle

1. In infected (acidic) tissue, anesthetics are charged and cannot penetrate membrane effectively. Therefore more anesthetic is needed in these cases.
2. Order of nerve blockade: small-diameter fibers > large diameter. Myelinated fibers > unmyelinated fibers. Overall, size factor predominates over myelination, such that small unmyelinated pain fibers > small myelinated autonomic fibers > large myelinated autonomic fibers. Order of loss: pain (lose first) > temperature > touch > pressure (lose last).
3. Given with vasoconstrictors (usually epinephrine) to enhance local action.

Clinical use — Minor surgical procedures, spinal anesthesia.

Toxicity — CNS excitation, severe cardiovascular toxicity (bupivacaine), hypertension and arrhythmias (cocaine).

Antihypertensive drugs

Drug	Adverse effects
Diuretics	
Hydrochlorothiazide	Hypokalemia, slight hyperlipidemia, hyperuricemia, lassitude
Loop diuretics	Potassium wasting, metabolic acidosis, hypotension
Sympathoplegics	
Clonidine	Dry mouth, sedation, severe rebound hypertension
Methyldopa	Sedation, positive Coombs' test *Pharm.7*
Ganglionic blockers	Severe orthostatic hypotension, blurred vision, constipation, sexual dysfunction
Reserpine	Sedation, depression, nasal stuffiness, diarrhea
Guanethidine	Orthostatic and exercise hypotension, sexual dysfunction, diarrhea
Prazosin	First-dose orthostatic hypotension, dizziness, headache
β blockers	Impotence, asthma, CV effects (bradycardia, CHF, AV block), CNS effects (sedation, sleep alterations)
Vasodilators	
Hydralazine	Nausea, headache, lupus-like syndrome, tachycardia, angina, salt retention
Minoxidil	Hypertrichosis, pericardial effusion, tachycardia, angina, salt retention
Nifedipine, verapamil	Dizziness, flushing, constipation (verapamil), nausea
Nitroprusside	Cyanide toxicity (releases CN)
ACE inhibitors	
Captopril	Fetal renal toxicity. hyperkalemia Cough, Angioedema, Proteinuria, Taste changes, hypOtension, Pregnancy problems (fetal renal damage), Rash, Increased renin, Lower AII.
AII receptor inhibitors	
Losartan	Fetal renal toxicity. Hyperkalemia

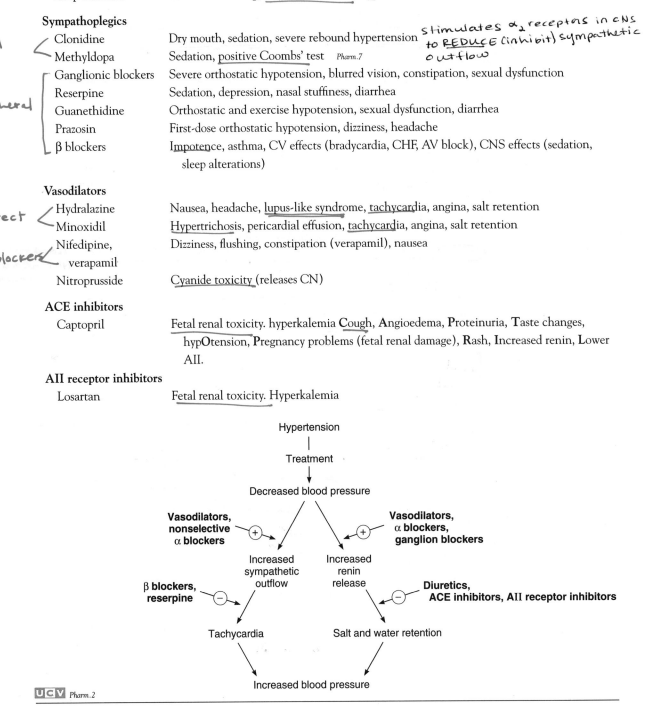

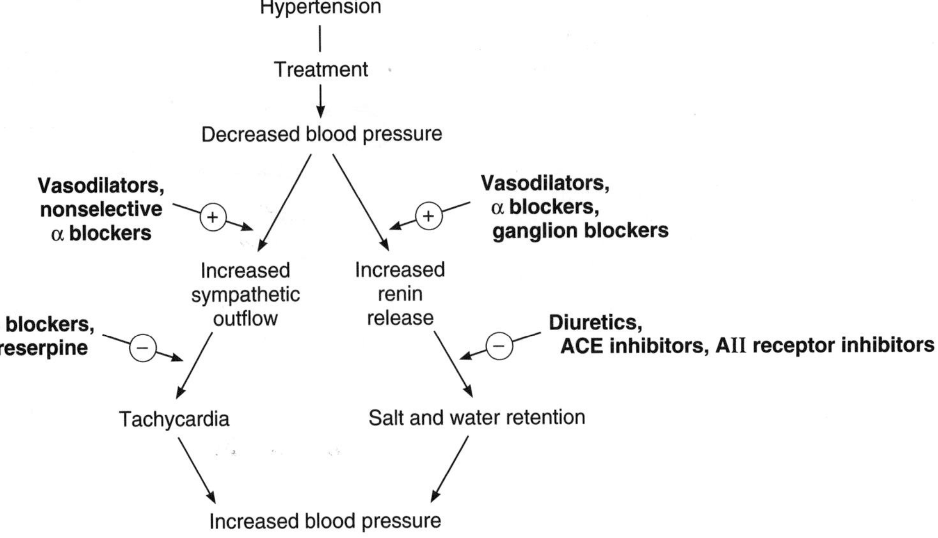

UCV *Pharm.2*

Hydralazine

Mechanism	↑ cGMP → smooth muscle relaxation. Vasodilates arterioles > veins; afterload reduction.
Clinical use	Severe hypertension, CHF.
Toxicity	Compensatory tachycardia, fluid retention. Lupus-like syndrome.

Calcium channel blockers

Nifedipine, verapamil, diltiazem

Mechanism	Block voltage-dependent L-type calcium channels of cardiac and smooth muscle and thereby reduce muscle contractility. Vascular smooth muscle: nifedipine > diltiazem > verapamil. Heart: verapamil > diltiazem > nifedipine.
Clinical use	Hypertension, angina, arrhythmias.
Toxicity	Cardiac depression, peripheral edema, flushing, dizziness, and constipation.

UCV Pharm.13

Black, elderly white

ACE inhibitors

Captopril, enalapril, lisinopril

Mechanism	Inhibit angiotensin-converting enzyme, reducing levels of angiotensin II and preventing inactivation of bradykinin, a potent vasodilator. Renin release is ↑ due to loss of feedback inhibition.	**Losartan** is an angiotensin II receptor antagonist. It is **not** an ACE inhibitor and does not cause cough.
Clinical use	Hypertension, congestive heart failure, diabetic renal disease.	
Toxicity	**C**ough, **A**ngioedema, **P**roteinuria, **T**aste changes, hyp**O**tension, **P**regnancy problems, fetal renal damage, **R**ash, **I**ncreased renin, **L**ower AII.	**CAPTOPRIL**

Young, white w/ ↑ renin

Angiotensinogen —renin→ Angiotensin I
Angiotensin I —ACE→ Angiotensin II

Acetazolamide

Mechanism	Carbonic anhydrase inhibitor. Causes self-limited $NaHCO_3$ diuresis and reduction in total-body HCO_3^- stores. Acts at the proximal convoluted tubule.	
Clinical use	Glaucoma, urinary alkalinization, metabolic alkalosis, altitude sickness.	
Toxicity	Hyperchloremic metabolic acidosis, neuropathy, NH_3 toxicity, sulfa allergy.	**ACID**azolamide causes **acid**osis.

Furosemide

Mechanism	Sulfonamide loop diuretic. Inhibits cotransport system (Na^+, K^+, 2 Cl^-) of thick ascending limb of loop of Henle. Abolishes hypertonicity of medulla, preventing concentration of urine. Increases Ca^{2+} excretion.	**L**oops **L**ose calcium.
Clinical use	Edematous states (CHF, cirrhosis, nephrotic syndrome, pulmonary edema), HTN, hypercalcemia.	
Toxicity	**O**totoxicity, **H**ypokalemia, **D**ehydration, **A**llergy (sulfa), **N**ephritis (interstitial), **G**out. (Hyperuricemia)	Toxicity: **OH DANG!**

UCV Pharm.99

Ethacrynic acid

Mechanism	Phenoxyacetic acid derivative (NOT a sulfonamide). Essentially same action as furosemide.
Clinical use	Diuresis in patients allergic to sulfa drugs.
Toxicity	Similar to furosemide except no hyperuricemia, no sulfa allergies.

Hydrochlorothiazide

Mechanism	Thiazide diuretic. Inhibits NaCl reabsorption in early distal tubule, reducing diluting capacity of the nephron. Decreases Ca^{2+} excretion.
Clinical use	Hypertension, congestive heart failure, calcium stone formation, nephrogenic diabetes insipidus.
Toxicity	Hypokalemic metabolic alkalosis, hyponatremia, hyper**G**lycemia, hyper**L**ipidemia, hyper**U**ricemia, and hyper**C**alcemia. "Hyper**GLUC**." Sulfa allergy.

K^+-sparing diuretics

Spironolactone, **T**riamterene, **A**miloride — The K^+ **STA**ys.

Mechanism	Spironolactone is a competitive aldosterone receptor antagonist in the cortical collecting tubule. Triamterene and amiloride act at same part of the tubule by blocking Na^+ channels in the CCT.
Clinical use	Hyperaldosteronism, K^+ depletion, CHF.
Toxicity	Hyperkalemia, endocrine effects (gynecomastia, anti-androgen effects).

Mannitol

Mechanism	Osmotic diuretic, ↑ tubular fluid osmolarity, producing ↑ urine flow.
Clinical use	ARF, shock, drug overdose, ↓ intracranial/ intraocular pressure.
Toxicity	Pulmonary edema, dehydration. Contraindicated in anuria, CHF.

Diuretics: electrolyte changes

Urine NaCl	↑ (all diuretics: carbonic anhydrase inhibitors, loop diuretics, thiazides, K^+-sparing diuretics)
Urine K^+	↑ (all except K^+-sparing diuretics)
Blood pH	↓ (acidosis): carbonic anhydrase inhibitors, K^+-sparing diuretics ↑ (alkalosis): loop diuretics, thiazides
Urine Ca^+	↑ loop diuretics, ↓ thiazides, ↑ spironolactone, ↓ amiloride

Diuretics: site of action

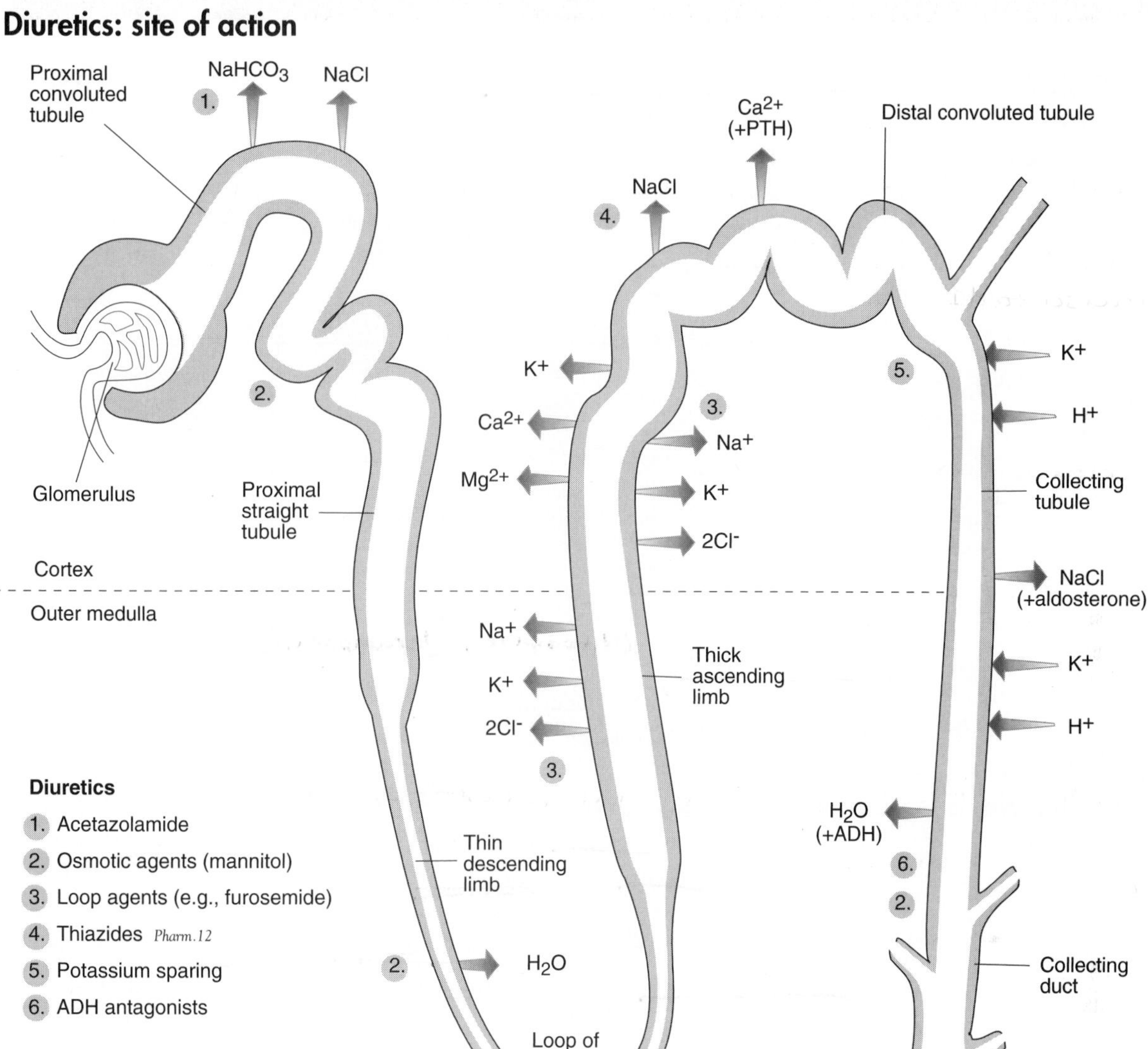

HIGH-YIELD FACTS

Pharmacology

Anti-anginal therapy

Goal: Reduction of myocardial O_2 consumption (MVO_2) by decreasing one or more of the determinants of MVO_2: end diastolic volume, blood pressure, heart rate, contractility, ejection time.

Component	Nitrates	β blockers	Nitrates + β blockers
End diastolic volume	↓	↑	No effect or ↓
Blood pressure	↓	↓	↓
Contractility	↑ (reflex response)	↓	Little/no effect
Heart rate	↑ (reflex response)	↓	↓
Ejection time	↓	↑	Little/no effect
MVO_2	↓	↓	↓↓

Calcium channel blockers:
- –Nifedipine is similar to Nitrates in effect
- –Verapamil is similar to β blockers in effect

UCV Pharm.10

Nitroglycerin, isosorbide dinitrate

Mechanism Vasodilate by releasing nitric oxide in smooth muscle, causing increase in cGMP and smooth muscle relaxation. Dilate veins >> arteries.

Clinical use Angina, pulmonary edema. Also used as an aphrodisiac and erection-enhancer.

Toxicity Tachycardia, hypotension, headache, "Monday disease" in industrial exposure development of tolerance for the vasodilating action, during the work week and loss of tolerance over the weekend, resulting in tachycardia, dizziness, and headache.

Cardiac glycosides

Digoxin: 75% bioavailability, 20–40% protein bound, $T_{1/2}$ = 40 hr, urinary excretion
Digitoxin: > 95% bioavailability, 70% protein bound, $T_{1/2}$ = 168 hrs, biliary excretion (enterohepatic recycling; no need to ↓ dose of digitoxin in renal failure)

Mechanism Inhibit the Na^+-K^+-ATPase of cell membrane, causing ↑ intracellular Na^+. Na^+-Ca^{2+} antiport does not function as efficiently, causing ↑ intracellular Ca^{2+}; leads to positive inotropy. May cause ↑ PR, ↓ QT, scooping of ST segment, T-wave inversion on EKG.

Clinical use CHF, atrial fibrillation.

Toxicity Nausea, vomiting, diarrhea. Blurry yellow vision (think Van Gogh). Arrhythmia. Toxicities of digoxin are increased by renal failure (↓ excretion), hypokalemia (potentiates drug's effects), and quinidine (↓ digoxin clearance; displaces digoxin from tissue binding sites).

Antidote Slowly normalize K^+, lidocaine, cardiac pacer, anti-dig Fab fragments.

UCV Pharm.76

Antiarrhythmics—Na^+ channel blockers (class I)

Local anesthetics. Slow or block (↓) conduction (especially in depolarized cells). ↓ slope of phase 4 depolarization and increase threshold for firing in abnormal pacemaker cells. Are state dependent (i.e., selectively depress tissue that is frequently depolarized, e.g., fast tachycardia).

Class IA

Quinidine, **A**miodarone, **P**rocainamide, **D**isopyramide. ↑ AP duration, ↑ effective refractory period (ERP), ↑ QT interval. Affect both atrial and ventricular arrhythmias. *Pharm.11*

"**Q**ueen **A**my **P**roclaims **D**iso's pyramid."

Toxicity: quinidine (cinchonism: headache, tinnitus; thrombocytopenia; torsade de pointes due to increased QT interval); procainamide (reversible SLE-like syndrome).

Class IB

Lidocaine, mexiletine, tocainide. *Pharm.5*

↓ AP duration. Affect ischemic or depolarized Purkinje and ventricular tissue. Useful in acute ventricular arrhythmias (especially post-MI) and in digitalis-induced arrhythmias.

Toxicity: Local anesthetic. CNS stimulation/depression, cardiovascular depression.

Class IC

Flecainide, encainide, propafenone.

No effect on AP duration. Useful in V-tachs that progress to VF, and in intractable SVT. Are usually used only as last resort in refractory tachyarrhythmias because of toxicities.

Toxicity: proarrhythmic.

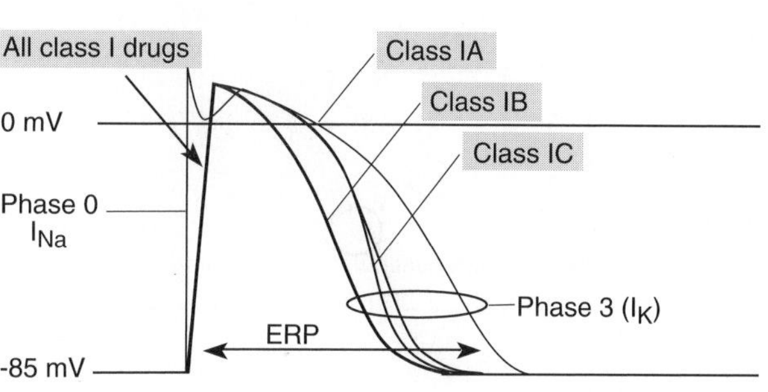

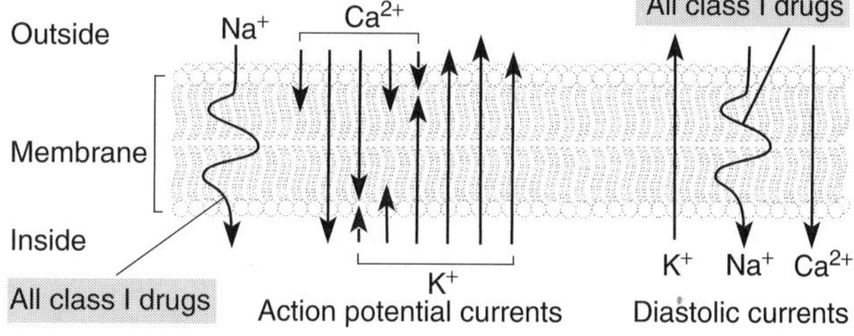

Antiarrhythmics—β blockers (class II)

Propranolol, esmolol, metoprolol, atenolol, timolol.

↓ cAMP, ↓Ca^{2+} currents. Suppress abnormal pacemakers by ↓ slope of phase 4. AV node particularly sensitive: ↑ PR interval. Esmolol very short-acting.

Toxicity: impotence, exacerbation of asthma, CV effects (bradycardia, AV block, CHF), CNS effects (sedation, sleep alterations). May mask the signs of hypoglycemia.

UCV Pharm.1

Antiarrhythmics—K^+ channel blockers (class III)

Sotalol, ibutilide, bretylium, amiodarone. Pharm.62

↑ AP duration, ↑ ERP. Used when other antiarrhythmics fail.

Toxicity: sotalol—torsade de pointes, excessive β block; ibutilide—torsade; bretylium—new arrhythmias, hypotension; amiodarone—**pulmonary fibrosis,** corneal deposits, **hepatotoxicity,** skin deposits resulting in photodermatitis, neurologic effects, constipation, CV effects (bradycardia, heart block, CHF), **hypo/hyperthyroidism.**

Remember to check **PFT**s, **LFT**s, and **TFT**s when using amiodarone.

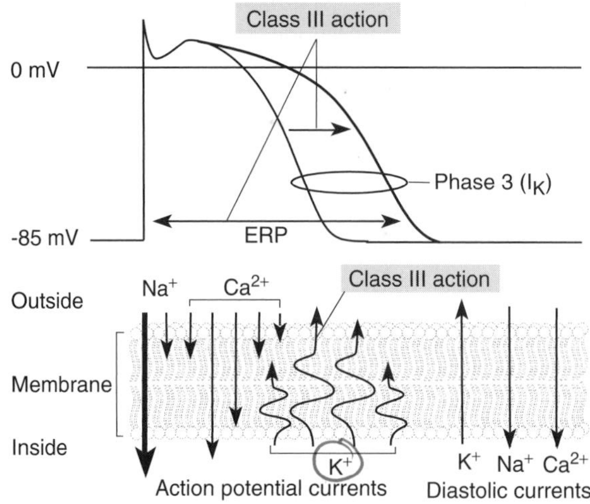

UCV

Antiarrhythmics—Ca^{2+} channel blockers (class IV)

Verapamil, diltiazem, bepridil.

Primarily affects pacemaker cells. ↓ conduction velocity, ↑ ERP, ↑ PR interval. Used in prevention of nodal arrhythmias (e.g., SVT).

Toxicity: constipation, flushing, edema, CV effects (CHF, AV block, sinus node depression); torsade de pointes (bepridil).

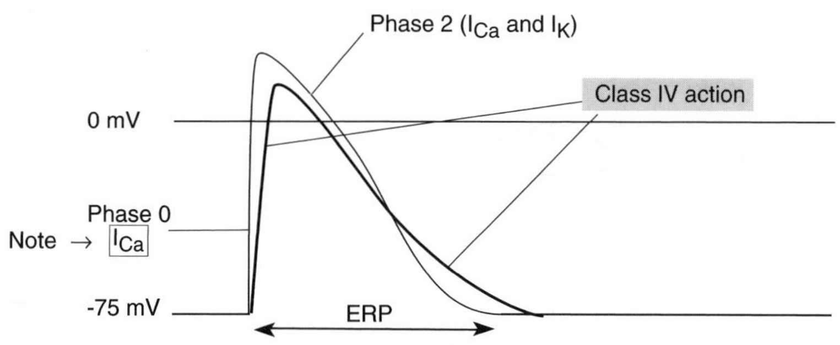

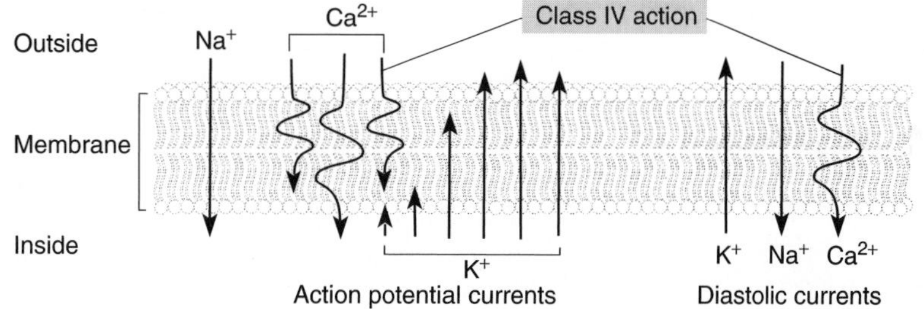

UCV Pharm.13

Antiarrhythmics—miscellaneous

Adenosine	Drug of choice in diagnosing/abolishing AV nodal arrhythmias.
K^+	Depresses ectopic pacemakers, especially in digoxin toxicity.
Mg^+	Effective in torsade de pointes and digoxin toxicity.

HIGH-YIELD FACTS

Pharmacology

Lipid-lowering agents

Drug	Effect on LDL "bad cholesterol"	Effect on HDL "good cholesterol"	Effect on triglycerides	Side effects/problems
Bile acid resins (cholestyramine, colestipol)	↓↓	No effect	Slight ↑	Patients hate it—tastes bad and causes GI discomfort
HMG-CoA reductase inhibitors (lovastatin, pravastatin, simvastatin, atorvastatin)	↓↓↓	↑	↓	Expensive Reversible ↑ LFTs Myositis
Niacin *Pharm.8*	↓↓	↑↑	↓	Red, flushed face which is ↓ by aspirin or long-term use, pruritus
Lipoprotein lipase stimulators (gemfibrozil, clofibrate)	↓	↑	↓↓↓	Myositis, ↑ LFTs
Probucol	↓	↓	No effect	↓ HDL

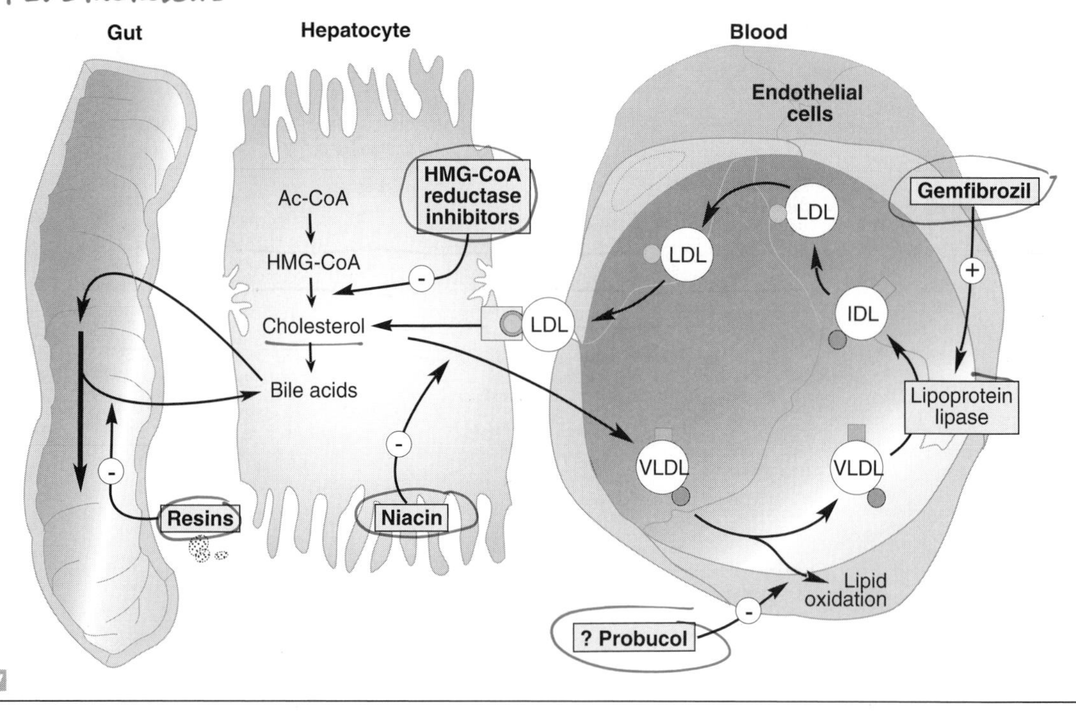

IIa, IIb — Bile acid resins
IIa, IIb — HMG-CoA reductase inhibitors
ALL — Niacin
DOC: ↓VLDL ↓chylomicron Type V — Lipoprotein lipase stimulators
IIa — Probucol ↑ LDL metabolism

I – ↑ chylomicrons
IIa – ↑ LDL
b – ↑ LDL, VLDL
III – ↑ IDL, chylomicrons ↓ LDL, HDL
IV – VLDL
V – ↑ VLDL ↑ chylomicrons

Niacin: ↓ production of VLDL's ⇒ ↓ LDL's
↑ HDL → Flushing b/c ↑ Prostaglandins

Gemfibrozil: ↑ LPL

Cancer drugs—site of action

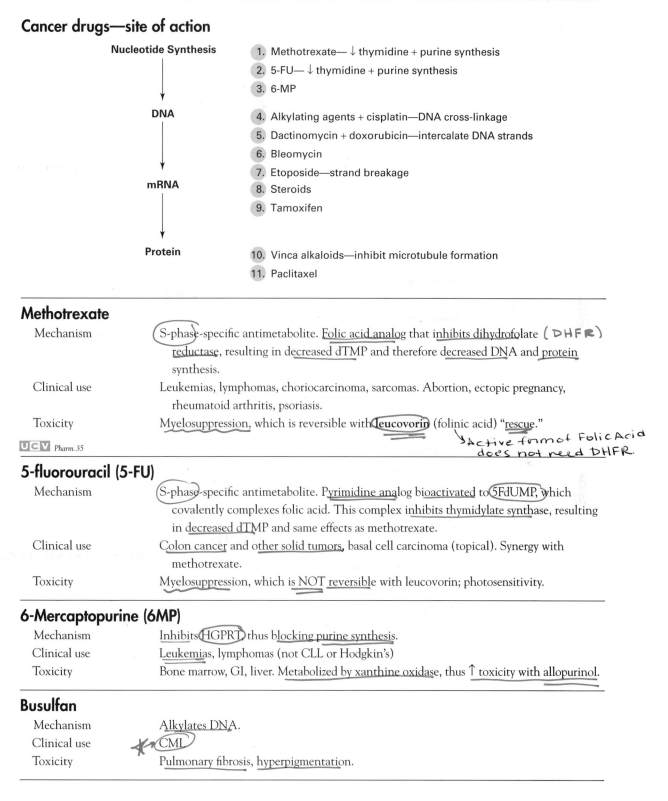

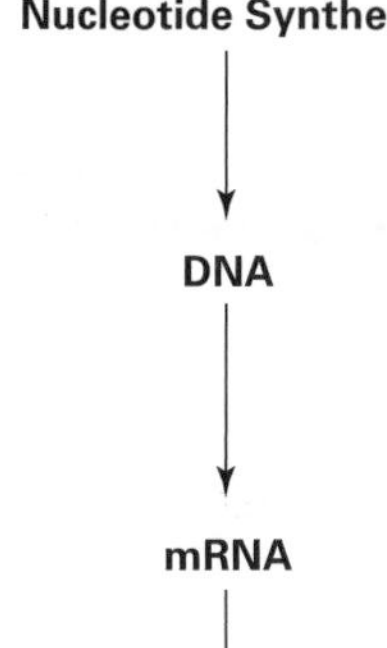

1. Methotrexate—↓ thymidine + purine synthesis
2. 5-FU—↓ thymidine + purine synthesis
3. 6-MP
4. Alkylating agents + cisplatin—DNA cross-linkage
5. Dactinomycin + doxorubicin—intercalate DNA strands
6. Bleomycin
7. Etoposide—strand breakage
8. Steroids
9. Tamoxifen
10. Vinca alkaloids—inhibit microtubule formation
11. Paclitaxel

Methotrexate

Mechanism	S-phase-specific antimetabolite. Folic acid analog that inhibits dihydrofolate reductase, resulting in decreased dTMP and therefore decreased DNA and protein synthesis.
Clinical use	Leukemias, lymphomas, choriocarcinoma, sarcomas. Abortion, ectopic pregnancy, rheumatoid arthritis, psoriasis.
Toxicity	Myelosuppression, which is reversible with leucovorin (folinic acid) "rescue."

UCV Pharm.35

5-fluorouracil (5-FU)

Mechanism	S-phase-specific antimetabolite. Pyrimidine analog bioactivated to 5FdUMP, which covalently complexes folic acid. This complex inhibits thymidylate synthase, resulting in decreased dTMP and same effects as methotrexate.
Clinical use	Colon cancer and other solid tumors, basal cell carcinoma (topical). Synergy with methotrexate.
Toxicity	Myelosuppression, which is NOT reversible with leucovorin; photosensitivity.

6-Mercaptopurine (6MP)

Mechanism	Inhibits HGPRT, thus blocking purine synthesis.
Clinical use	Leukemias, lymphomas (not CLL or Hodgkin's)
Toxicity	Bone marrow, GI, liver. Metabolized by xanthine oxidase, thus ↑ toxicity with allopurinol.

Busulfan

Mechanism	Alkylates DNA.
Clinical use	CML
Toxicity	Pulmonary fibrosis, hyperpigmentation.

Cyclophosphamide

Mechanism	Alkylating agent; covalently x-links (interstrand) DNA at guanine N-7. Requires bioactivation by liver.
Clinical use	Non-Hodgkin's lymphoma, breast and ovarian carcinomas. Also an immunosuppressant.
Toxicity	Myelosuppression, hemorrhagic cystitis.

UCV Pharm.74

Nitrosureas

Carmustine, lomustine, semustine, streptozocin

Mechanism	Alkylates DNA. Requires bioactivation. Crosses blood–brain barrier → CNS.
Clinical use	Brain tumors (including glioblastoma multiforme).
Toxicity	CNS toxicity (dizziness, ataxia).

Cisplatin

Mechanism	Acts like an alkylating agent. X-links via hydrolysis of Cl^- groups and reaction with platinum.
Clinical use	Testicular, bladder, ovary, and lung carcinomas.
Toxicity	Nephrotoxicity and acoustic nerve damage.

UCV Pharm.32

Doxorubicin (adriamycin)

Mechanism	Noncovalently intercalates in DNA creating breaks to decrease replication and transcription and generate free radicals.
Clinical use	Part of the ABVD combo regimen for Hodgkin's and for myelomas, sarcomas, and solid tumors (breast, ovary, lung).
Toxicity	Cardiotoxicity; also myelosuppression and marked alopecia. Toxic extravasation.

UCV Pharm.34

Bleomycin

Mechanism	Intercalates DNA strands, induces free radical formation, causing strand breaks.
Clinical use	Testicular cancer, lymphomas.
Toxicity	Pulmonary fibrosis, skin changes, minimal myelosuppression.

Etoposide

Mechanism	G_2-phase-specific inhibits topoisomerase II so that double-strand breaks remain in DNA following replication, with subsequent DNA degradation.
Clinical use	Oat cell carcinoma of the lung and prostate, testicular carcinoma.
Toxicity	Myelosuppression, GI irritation, alopecia.

Prednisone

Mechanism	May trigger apoptosis. May even work on non-dividing cells.
Clinical use	Most commonly used glucocorticoid in cancer chemotherapy. Used in CLL, Hodgkin's lymphomas (the "P" in the MOPP regimen). Also an immunosuppressant used in autoimmune diseases.
Toxicity	Cushing-like symptoms; immunosuppression, cataracts, acne, osteoporosis, hypertension, peptic ulcers, hyperglycemia.

UCV Pharm.19

Tamoxifen/raloxifene

Mechanism	Estrogen receptor mixed agonist/antagonist that blocks the binding of estrogen to ER+ cells.
Clinical use	Breast cancer.
Toxicity	May increase the risk of endometrial carcinoma via partial agonist effects; "hot flashes."

Vincristine and vinblastine

Mechanism	M-phase-specific alkaloid that binds to tubulin and blocks polymerization of microtubules so that mitotic spindle can't form.
Clinical use	Part of MOPP (**O**ncovin [vincristine]) combo regimen for lymphoma, Wilms' tumor, choriocarcinoma.
Toxicity	Vincristine—neurotoxicity (areflexia, peripheral neuritis), paralytic ileus. Vin**Blast**ine **Blasts B**one marrow (suppression).

Childhood tumors
Neuroblastoma
Ewings

Paclitaxel

Mechanism	M-phase-specific agent obtained from yew tree that binds to tubulin and hyperstabilizes polymerized microtubules so that mitotic spindle can't break down (anaphase cannot occur).
Clinical use	Ovarian and breast carcinomas.
Toxicity	Myelosuppression and hypersensitivity.

Specific antidotes

Toxin	Antidote/treatment
1. Acetaminophen	1. N-acetylcysteine
2. Salicylates	2. Alkalinize urine, dialysis
3. Anticholinesterases, organophosphates	3. Atropine, pralidoxime
4. Antimuscarinic, anticholinergic agents	4. Physostigmine salicylate
5. β blockers	5. Glucagon
6. Digitalis	6. Stop dig, normalize K^+, lidocaine, anti-dig Fab fragments
7. Iron	7. Deferoxamine
8. Lead	8. CaEDTA, dimercaprol, succimer, penicillamine
9. Arsenic, mercury, gold	9. Dimercaprol (BAL), succimer
10. Copper, arsenic, gold	10. Penicillamine
11. Cyanide	11. Nitrite, hydroxocobalamin
12. Methemoglobin	12. Methylene blue
13. Carbon monoxide	13. 100% O_2, hyperbaric O_2
14. Methanol, ethylene glycol (antifreeze)	14. Ethanol, dialysis, fomepizole
15. Opioids	15. Naloxone/naltrexone
16. Benzodiazepines	16. Flumazenil
17. Tricyclic antidepressants	17. $NaHCO_3$ (nonspecific)
18. Heparin	18. Protamine
19. Warfarin	19. Vitamin K, fresh frozen plasma
20. t-PA, streptokinase	20. Aminocaproic acid

UCV Pharm.63, 64, 67, 70, 73, 78, 82, 84, 86, 87

Lead poisoning

Lead Lines on gingivae and on epiphyses of long bones on x-ray.
Encephalopathy and Erythrocyte basophilic stippling.
Abdominal colic and sideroblastic Anemia.
Drops: wrist and foot drop. Dimercaprol and EDTA as first line of treatment.

LEAD
High risk in houses with chipped paint.

UCV Pharm.84

Urine pH and drug elimination

Weak acids (phenobarbital, methotrexate, aspirin) ⇒ alkalinize urine with bicarbonate to increase clearance.

Weak bases (amphetamines) ⇒ acidify urine to increase clearance (give NH_4Cl).

Drug reactions

Drug reaction	Causal agent
1. Pulmonary fibrosis	1. Bleomycin, amiodarone, busulfan *Pharm.31*
2. Hepatitis	2. Isoniazid (INH)
3. Focal to massive hepatic necrosis	3. Halothane, valproic acid, acetaminophen, *Amanita phalloides*
4. Anaphylaxis	4. Penicillin
5. SLE-like syndrome *Pharm.77*	5. Hydralazine, procainamide, INH, phenytoin
6. Hemolysis in G6PD-deficient patients	6. Sulfonamides, INH, aspirin, ibuprofen, primaquine, nitrofurantoin, pyrimethamine, chloramphenicol
7. Thrombotic complications	7. Oral contraceptives (e.g., estrogens and progestins)
8. Adrenocortical insufficiency	8. Glucocorticoids (HPA suppression)
9. Photosensitivity reactions	9. Tetracyclines, amiodarone, sulfonamides
10. Induce (↑) P450 system	10. Barbiturates, phenytoin, carbamazapine, rifampin, griseofulvin, quinidine
11. Inhibit (↓) P450 system	11. Cimetidine, ketoconazole, erythromycin, INH, sulfonamides
12. Tubulointerstitial nephritis *Pharm.98*	12. Sulfonamides
13. Hot flashes	13. Tamoxifen
14. Cutaneous flushing	14. Niacin, Ca^{2+} channel blockers, adenosine, vancomycin
15. Cardiac toxicity	15. Doxorubicin (Adriamycin)
16. Agranulocytosis	16. Clozapine, carbamazepine, colchicine
17. Stevens-Johnson syndrome	17. Ethosuximide, sulfonamides *Pharm.14*
18. Cinchonism	18. Quinidine, quinine
19. Tendonitis, tendon rupture	19. Fluoroquinolones *Pharm.42*
20. Disulfiram-like reaction	20. Metronidazole, certain cephalosporins, procarbazine, sulfonylureas
21. Ototoxicity and nephrotoxicity	21. Aminoglycosides, loop diuretics, cisplatin
22. Drug-induced Parkinson's	22. Haloperidol, chlorpromazine, reserpine, MPTP.

Alcohol toxicity

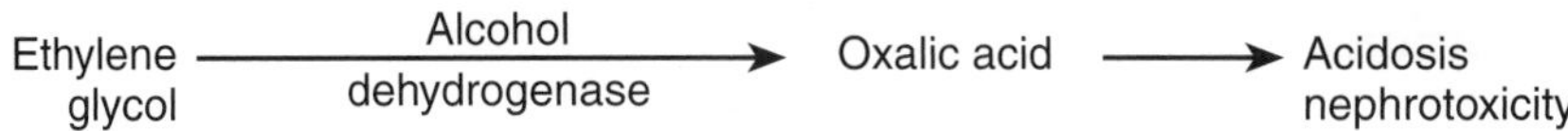

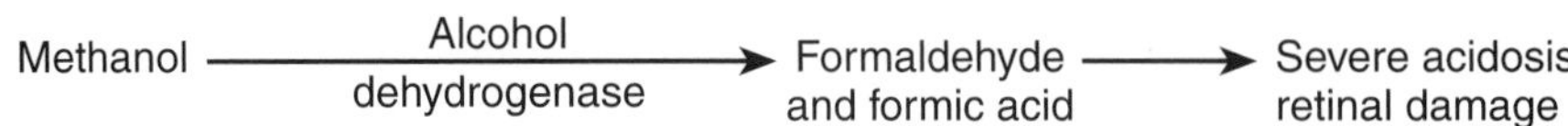

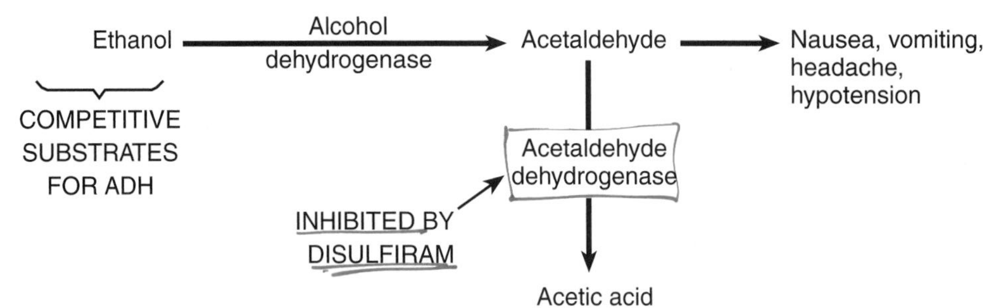

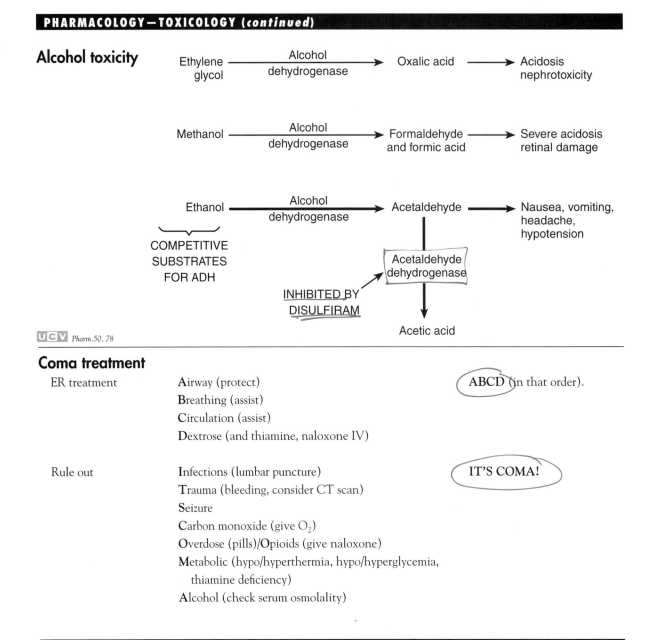

UCV Pharm.50, 78

Coma treatment

ER treatment	Airway (protect) Breathing (assist) Circulation (assist) Dextrose (and thiamine, naloxone IV)	ABCD (in that order).
Rule out	Infections (lumbar puncture) Trauma (bleeding, consider CT scan) Seizure Carbon monoxide (give O_2) Overdose (pills)/Opioids (give naloxone) Metabolic (hypo/hyperthermia, hypo/hyperglycemia, thiamine deficiency) Alcohol (check serum osmolality)	IT'S COMA!

Sildenafil (Viagra)

Mechanism	Inhibits cGMP phosphodiesterase, causing ↑ cGMP, smooth muscle relaxation in the corpus cavernosum, ↑ blood flow, and penile erection.	Sildena**fil fills** the penis.
Clinical use	Erectile dysfunction.	
Toxicity	Headache, flushing, dyspepsia, blue-green color vision. Risk of life-threatening hypotension in patients taking nitrates.	

H_2 blockers

Cimetidine, ranitidine, famotidine, nizatidine

Mechanism	Reversible block of histamine H_2 receptors.
Clinical use	Peptic ulcer, gastritis, esophageal reflux, Zollinger–Ellison syndrome.
Toxicity	Cimetidine is a potent inhibitor of P450; it also has an antiandrogenic effect and decreases renal excretion of creatinine. Other H_2 blockers are relatively free of these effects.

UCV Pharm.23

Omeprazole, lansoprazole

Mechanism	Irreversibly inhibits H+/K+ ATPase in stomach parietal cells.
Clinical use	Peptic ulcer, gastritis, esophageal reflux, Zollinger–Ellison syndrome.

Sucralfate

Mechanism	Aluminum sucrose sulfate polymerizes in the acid environment of the stomach and selectively binds necrotic peptic ulcer tissue. Acts as a barrier to acid, pepsin, and bile. Sucralfate cannot work in the presence of antacids or H_2 blockers (requires acidic environment to polymerize).
Clinical use	Peptic ulcer disease.

Misoprostol

Mechanism	A PGE_1 analog. Increases production and secretion of gastric mucous barrier.
Clinical use	Prevention of NSAID-induced peptic ulcers, maintains a PDA.
Toxicity	Diarrhea. Contraindicated in women of childbearing potential (abortifacient).

Antacid overuse

Can affect absorption, bioavailability, or urinary excretion of other drugs by altering gastric and urinary pH or by delaying gastric emptying.

Overuse can also cause the following problems:

1. Aluminum hydroxide: constipation and hypophosphatemia
2. Magnesium hydroxide: diarrhea
3. Calcium carbonate: hypercalcemia, rebound acid ↑.

All can cause hypokalemia.

AluMINIMUM amount of feces

Mg = Must go to the bathroom

Heparin

Mechanism	Catalyzes the activation of antithrombin III. Short half-life. Check the aPTT.
Clinical use	Immediate anticoagulation for PE, stroke, angina, MI, DVT. Used during pregnancy (does not cross placenta). Follow PTT.
Toxicity	Bleeding, thrombocytopenia, drug–drug interactions. Use **protamine sulfate** for rapid reversal of heparinization (positively charged molecule that acts by binding negatively charged heparin).
Note	Newer **low-molecular-weight heparins** (enoxaparin) have better bioavailability and 2 to 4 times longer half-life. Can be administered subcutaneously and without laboratory monitoring.

UCV Pharm.3

Warfarin (Coumadin)

Mechanism	Interferes with normal synthesis and γ-carboxylation of vitamin K-dependent clotting factors II, VII, IX, and X, Protein C and S via vitamin K antagonism. Long half-life.	**WEPT:** **W**arfarin affects the **E**xtrinsic pathway and **p**rolongs the **PT.**
Clinical use	Chronic anticoagulation. Not used in pregnant women (because warfarin, unlike heparin, can cross the placenta). Follow PT values.	
Toxicity	Bleeding, teratogenic, drug–drug interactions.	

UCV *Pharm.37*

Heparin vs. warfarin

	Heparin	Warfarin
Structure	Large anionic polymer, acidic	Small lipid-soluble molecule
Route of administration	Parenteral (IV, SC)	Oral
Site of action	Blood	Liver
Onset of action	Rapid (seconds)	Slow, limited by half-lives of normal clotting factors
Mechanism of action	Activates antithrombin III	Impairs the synthesis of vitamin K–dependent clotting factors II, VII, IX, and X (vitamin K antagonist)
Duration of action	Acute (hours)	Chronic (weeks or months)
Inhibits coagulation *in vitro*	Yes	No
Treatment of acute overdose	Protamine sulfate	IV vitamin K and fresh frozen plasma
Monitoring	aPTT (intrinsic pathway)	PT (extrinsic pathway)

Not used in pregnancy!

Thrombolytics

Streptokinase, urokinase, tPA (alteplase), APSAC (anistreplase)

Mechanism	Directly or indirectly aid conversion of plasminogen to plasmin which cleaves thrombin and fibrin clots. It is claimed that tPA specifically converts fibrin-bound plasminogen to plasmin.
Clinical use	Early myocardial infarction.
Toxicity	Bleeding.

Ticlopidine

Mechanism	Inhibits platelet aggregation by irreversibly inhibiting the ADP pathway involved in the binding of fibrinogen.
Clinical use	Decreases the incidence or recurrence of thrombotic stroke.
Toxicity	Neutropenia; reserved for those who cannot tolerate aspirin.

Arachidonic acid products

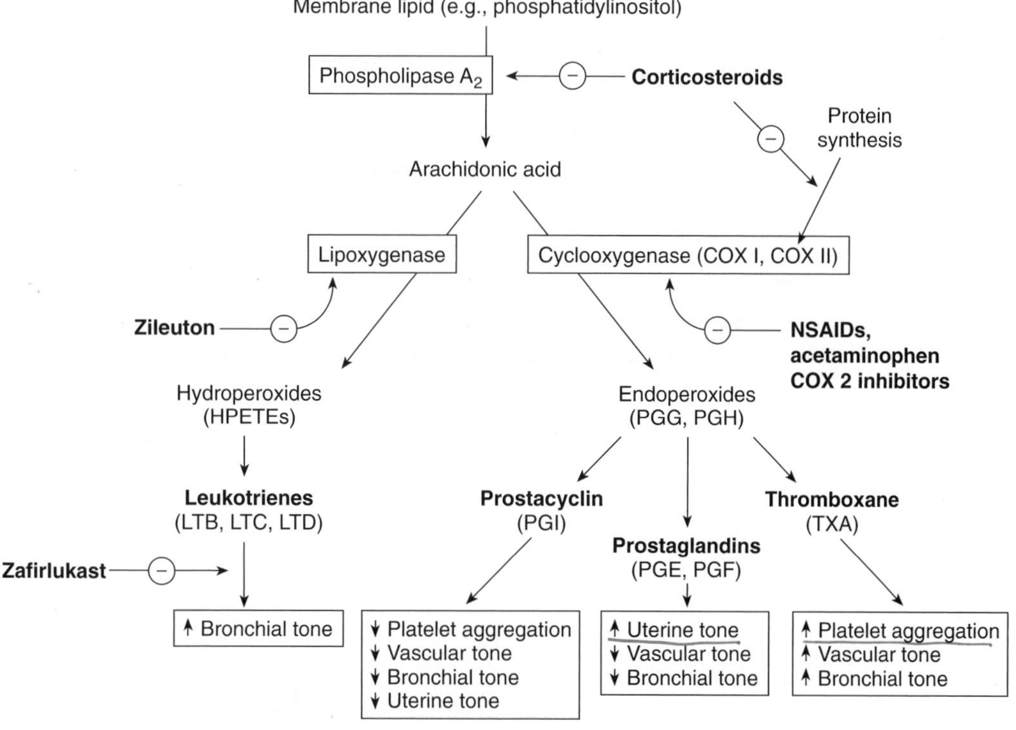

Aspirin

Mechanism	Acetylates and irreversibly inhibits cyclooxygenase (both COX I and COX II) to prevent conversion of arachidonic acid to prostaglandins.
Clinical use	Antipyretic, analgesic, anti-inflammatory, antiplatelet drug.
Toxicity	Gastric ulceration, bleeding, hyperventilation, Reye's syndrome, tinnitus (CN VIII).

UCV Pharm.95, 96

Other NSAIDs

Ibuprofen, naproxen, indomethacin

Mechanism	Reversibly inhibit cyclooxygenase (both COX I and COX II). Block prostaglandin synthesis.
Clinical use	Antipyretic, analgesic, anti-inflammatory. Indomethacin is used to close a patent ductus arteriosus.
Toxicity	Renal damage, aplastic anemia, GI distress.

UCV Pharm.95, 96

COX 2 inhibitors (celecoxib, rofecoxib)

Mechanism	Selectively inhibits cyclooxygenase (COX) isoform 2, which is found in inflammatory cells and mediates inflammation and pain; spares COX 1, which helps maintain the gastric mucosa. Thus, should not have the corrosive effects of other NSAIDs on the gastrointestinal lining.
Clinical use	Rheumatoid and osteoarthritis.
Toxicity	Similar to other NSAIDs; may have less toxicity to GI mucosa (i.e., lower incidence of ulcers, bleeding).

Acetaminophen

Mechanism	Reversibly inhibits cyclooxygenase, mostly in CNS. Inactivated peripherally.
Clinical use	Antipyretic, analgesic, but lacking anti-inflammatory properties.
Toxicity	Overdose produces hepatic necrosis; acetaminophen metabolite depletes glutathione and forms toxic tissue adducts in liver. Antidote: Acetylcysteine

UCV Pharm.63

Glucocorticoids

	Hydrocortisone, prednisone, triamcinolone, dexamethasone, beclomethasone
Mechanism	Decrease the production of leukotrienes and prostaglandins by inhibiting phospholipase A_2 and expression of COX II.
Clinical use	Addison's disease, inflammation, immune suppression, asthma.
Toxicity	Iatrogenic Cushing's syndrome: buffalo hump, moon facies, truncal obesity, muscle wasting, thin skin, easy bruisability, osteoporosis, adrenocortical atrophy, peptic ulcers.

UCV Pharm.19

Asthma drugs

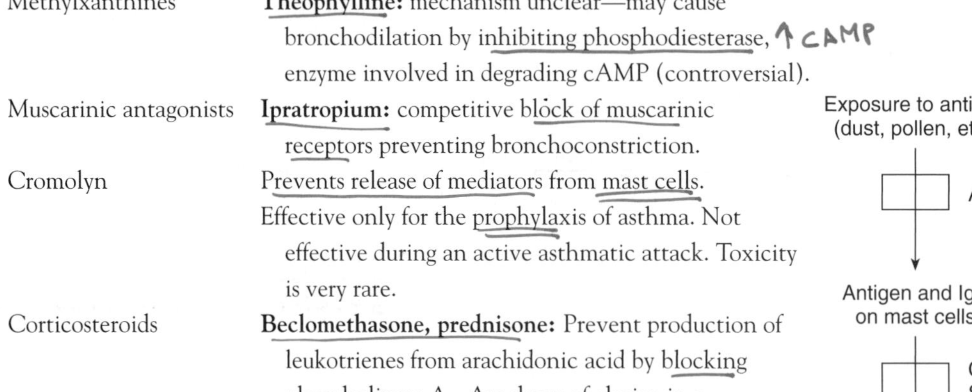

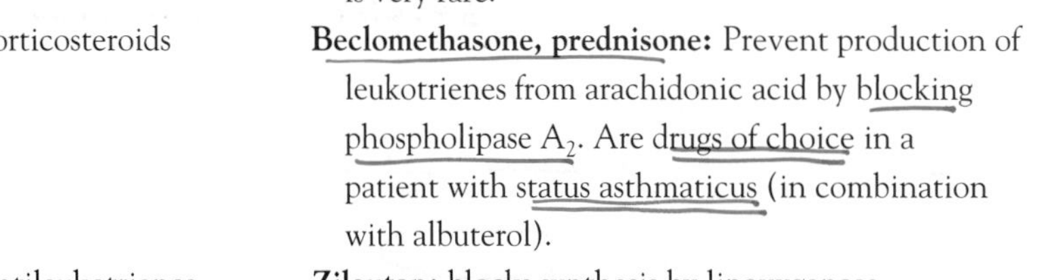

Nonspecific β agonists	**Isoproterenol:** relaxes bronchial smooth muscle (β_2). Adverse effect is tachycardia (β_1).
β_2 agonists	**Albuterol:** relaxes bronchial smooth muscle (β_2). Use during acute exacerbation. Adverse effects are tremor and arrhythmia.
Methylxanthines	**Theophylline:** mechanism unclear—may cause bronchodilation by inhibiting phosphodiesterase, ↑ cAMP enzyme involved in degrading cAMP (controversial).
Muscarinic antagonists	**Ipratropium:** competitive block of muscarinic receptors preventing bronchoconstriction.
Cromolyn	Prevents release of mediators from mast cells. Effective only for the prophylaxis of asthma. Not effective during an active asthmatic attack. Toxicity is very rare.
Corticosteroids	**Beclomethasone, prednisone:** Prevent production of leukotrienes from arachidonic acid by blocking phospholipase A_2. Are drugs of choice in a patient with status asthmaticus (in combination with albuterol).
Antileukotrienes	**Zileuton:** blocks synthesis by lipoxygenase. **Zafirlukast:** blocks leukotriene receptors.

Leukotrienes ↑ bronchial tone

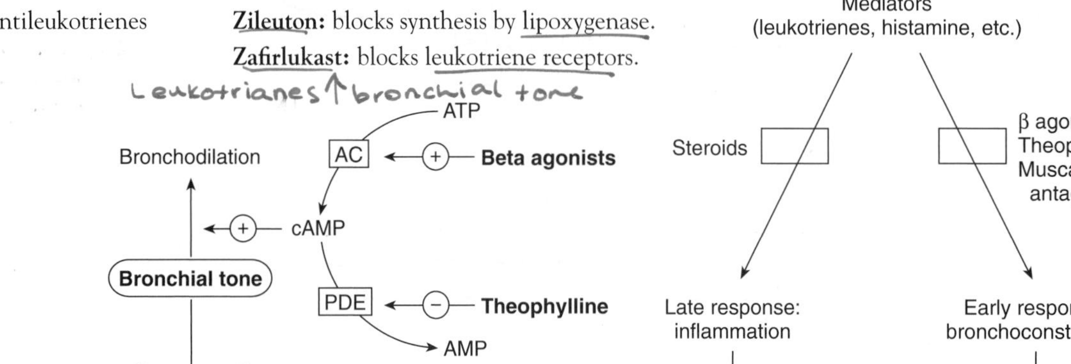

Treatment strategies in asthma

UCV Pharm.61

Gout drugs

Colchicine — Acute gout. Depolymerizes microtubules, impairing leukocyte chemotaxis and degranulation. GI side effects, especially if given orally.

Probenecid — Chronic gout. Inhibits reabsorption of uric acid (also inhibits secretion of penicillin).

Allopurinol — Chronic gout. Inhibits xanthine oxidase, decreasing conversion of xanthine to uric acid.

Diabetes drugs

Insulin — Binds insulin receptor which has tyrosine kinase activity. In liver, increases storage of glucose as glycogen. In muscle, stimulates glycogen and protein synthesis, and K+ up take. In adipose, facilitates triglyceride storage.
Clinical use includes life-threatening hyperkalemia and stress-induced hyperglycemia.
Toxicities are hypoglycemia and hypersensitivity reaction.

Sulfonylureas — Tolbutamide, chlorpropamide, glyburide, glipizide.
Oral hypoglycemic agents used to stimulate release of endogenous insulin in NIDDM (Type II).
Close K+ channels in β cell membrane → cell depolarizes → insulin release triggered.
Inactive in IDDM (Type I) because requires some residual islet function.
Toxicities includes hypoglycemia (more common with 2nd generation drugs: glyburide, glipizide) and disulfiram-like effects (not seen with 2nd generation drugs: glyburide, glipizide).

Metformin — Mechanism unknown; decreases serum glucose levels.
Used as an oral hypoglycemic. Can be used in patients without islet function.
Most grave adverse effect is lactic acidosis.

"Glitazones" — Pioglitazone, rosiglitazone, troglitazone.
Increase target cell response to insulin. Used as monotherapy in Type II diabetes, or in combination with above agents.
Toxicity: weight gain.

α-glucosidase inhibitors — Acarbose, miglitol.
Inhibit intestinal brush border α-glucosidases; delayed hydrolysis of sugars and absorption of glucose lease to ↓ postprandial hyperglycemia.
Used as monotherapy in Type II diabetes, or in combination with above agents.
Toxicity: GI disturbances.

UCV Pharm.20

Leuprolide

Mechanism — GnRH analog with agonist properties when used in pulsatile fashion and antagonist properties when used in continuous fashion.

Clinical use — Infertility (pulsatile), prostate cancer (continuous: use with flutamide), uterine fibroids.

Toxicity — Antiandrogen, nausea, vomiting.

When used in continuous fashion, it causes a transient initial burst of LH and FSH.

Propylthiouracil

Mechanism — Inhibits organification and coupling of thyroid hormone synthesis. Also decreases peripheral conversion of T_4 to T_3.

Clinical use — Hyperthyroidism.

Toxicity — Skin rash, agranulocytosis (rare), aplastic anemia.

Antiandrogens

Finasteride	A 5α-reductase inhibitor (↓ conversion of testosterone to dihydrotestosterone). Useful in BPH.
Flutamide	A nonsteroidal competitive inhibitor of androgens at the testosterone receptor. Used in prostate carcinoma.
Ketoconazole, spironolactone	Inhibit steroid synthesis, used in the treatment of polycystic ovarian syndrome to prevent hirsutism.

Immunosuppressive agents: sites of action

Agent	Site
Prednisone	2, 5
Cyclosporine	2, 3
Azathioprine	2
Methotrexate	2
Dactinomycin	2, 3
Cyclophosphamide	2
Antilymphocytic globulin and monoclonal anti-T-cell antibodies	1, 2, 3
Rh_3(D) immune globulin	1
Tacrolimus	4

① Antigen recognition
② Proliferation
③ Differentiation synthesis
T cells or antibody
④ Cytokine secretion
Inter-action
Complement
Antigen
⑤ Tissue injury

Cyclosporine

Mechanism	Binds to cyclophilins (peptidyl proline *cis-trans* isomerase), blocking the differentiation and activation of T cells mainly by inhibiting the production of IL-2 and its receptor.
Clinical use	Suppresses organ rejection after transplantation; selected autoimmune disorders.
Toxicity	Predisposes patients to viral infections and lymphoma; nephrotoxic (preventable with mannitol diuresis).

UCV Pharm.75

Azathioprine

Mechanism	Antimetabolite derivative of 6-mercaptopurine that interferes with the metabolism and synthesis of nucleic acid. Toxic to proliferating lymphocytes after antigenic stimulus.
Clinical use	Kidney transplantation, autoimmune disorders (including glomerulonephritis and hemolytic anemia).

Tacrolimus (FK506)

Mechanism	Similar to cyclosporine; binds to FK-binding protein, inhibiting secretion of IL-2 and other cytokines.
Clinical use	Potent immunosuppressive used in organ transplant recipients.
Toxicity	Significant: nephrotoxicity, peripheral neuropathy, hypertension, pleural effusion, hyperglycemia.

Drug name

Ending	Category	Example
-ane	Inhalational general anesthetic	Halothane
-azepam	Benzodiazepine	Diazepam
-azine	Phenothiazine (neuroleptic, antiemetic)	Chlorpromazine
-azole	Antifungal	Ketoconazole
-barbital	Barbiturate	Phenobarbital
-caine	Local anesthetic	Lidocaine
-cillin	Penicillin	Methicillin
-cycline	Antibiotic, protein synthesis inhibitor	Tetracycline
-ipramine	Tricyclic antidepressant	Imipramine
-navir	Protease inhibitor	Saquinavir
-olol	Beta antagonist	Propranolol
-operidol	Butyrophenone (neuroleptic)	Haloperidol
-oxin	Cardiac glycoside (inotropic agent)	Digoxin
-phylline	Methylxanthine	Theophylline
-pril	ACE inhibitor	Captopril
-terol	β_2 agonist	Albuterol
-tidine	H_2 antagonist	Cimetidine
-triptyline	Tricyclic antidepressant	Amitriptyline
-tropin	Pituitary hormone	Somatotropin
-zosin	α_1 antagonist	Prazosin

NOTES

SECTION II

Physiology

"When I investigate and when I discover that the forces of the heavens and the planets are within ourselves, then truly I seem to be living among the gods."
—*Leon Battista Alberti*

The portion of the examination dealing with physiology is broad and concept oriented and does not lend itself as well to fact-based review. Diagrams are often the best study aids from which to learn, especially given the increasing number of questions requiring the interpretation of diagrams. Learn to work with basic physiologic relationships in a variety of ways (e.g., Fick equation, clearance equations). You are seldom asked to perform complex calculations. Hormones are the focus of many questions. Learn their sites of production and action as well as their regulatory mechanisms.

A large portion of the physiology tested on the USMLE Step 1 is now clinically relevant and involves understanding physiologic changes associated with pathologic processes (e.g., changes in pulmonary function testing with chronic obstructive pulmonary disease). Thus, it is worthwhile to review the physiologic changes that are found with common pathologies of the major organ systems (e.g., heart, lungs, kidneys, and gastrointestinal tract).

High-Yield Topics
Cardiovascular
Respiratory
Gastrointestinal
Renal
Endocrine/Reproductive

Cardiovascular

1. Basic electrocardiographic changes (e.g., Q waves, ST segment elevation).
2. Effects of electrolyte abnormalities (e.g., potassium or calcium imbalances).
3. Physiologic effects of the Valsalva maneuver.
4. Cardiopulmonary changes with pregnancy.
5. Responses to hemorrhage.
6. Responses to changes in position.

Pulmonary

1. Alveolar-arterial oxygen gradient and changes seen in lung disease.
2. Mechanical differences between inspiration and expiration.
3. Characteristic pulmonary function curves for common lung diseases (e.g., bronchitis, emphysema, asthma, interstitial lung disease).
4. Gas diffusion across alveolocapillary membrane.
5. Responses to high altitude.

Gastrointestinal

1. Sites of absorption of major nutrients (e.g., ileum: vit. B_{12}).
2. Bile production and enterohepatic circulation.
3. Glucose cotransport into cells of gut.
4. Fat digestion and absorption.
5. Secretion and actions of GI hormones.

Renal/Acid-Base

1. Differences among active transport, facilitated diffusion, and diffusion.
2. Differences between central and nephrogenic diabetes insipidus.
3. Major transporter in each nephron segment.
4. Clearance calculation.
5. Effects of afferent and efferent arteriolar constriction on GFR and RPF.

Endocrine/Reproductive

1. Physiologic features of parathyroid diseases, associated laboratory findings; physiology and pathophysiology of PTHrP.
2. Clinical tests for endocrine abnormalities (e.g., dexamethasone suppression tests, glucose tolerance tests, TSH measurement).
3. Diseases associated with adrenocortical abnormalities (e.g., Cushing's, Addison's, Conn's).
4. Sites of hormone production during pregnancy (e.g., corpus luteum, placenta).
5. Regulation of prolactin secretion.
6. All aspects of diabetes mellitus.

General

1. Role of calmodulin, troponin C, and tropomyosin in muscle contraction.
2. Role of ions (e.g., calcium, sodium, magnesium, potassium) in skeletal muscle, cardiac muscle, and nerve cells (e.g., muscle contraction, membrane and action potentials, neurotransmitter release).
3. The clotting cascade, including those factors which require vitamin K for synthesis (II, VII, IX, X).
4. Regulation of core body temperature.

Myocardial action potential

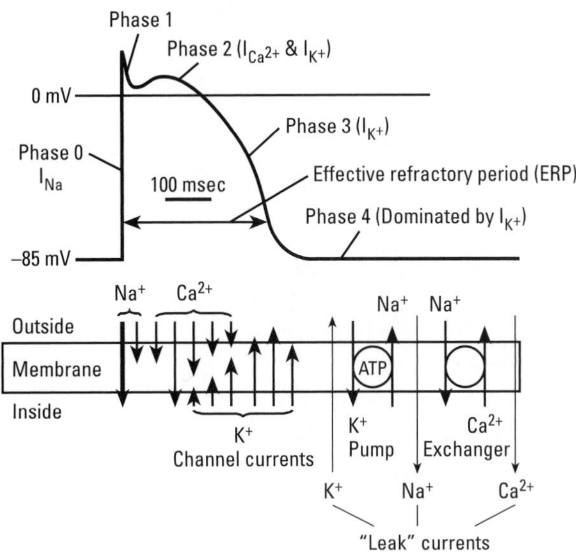

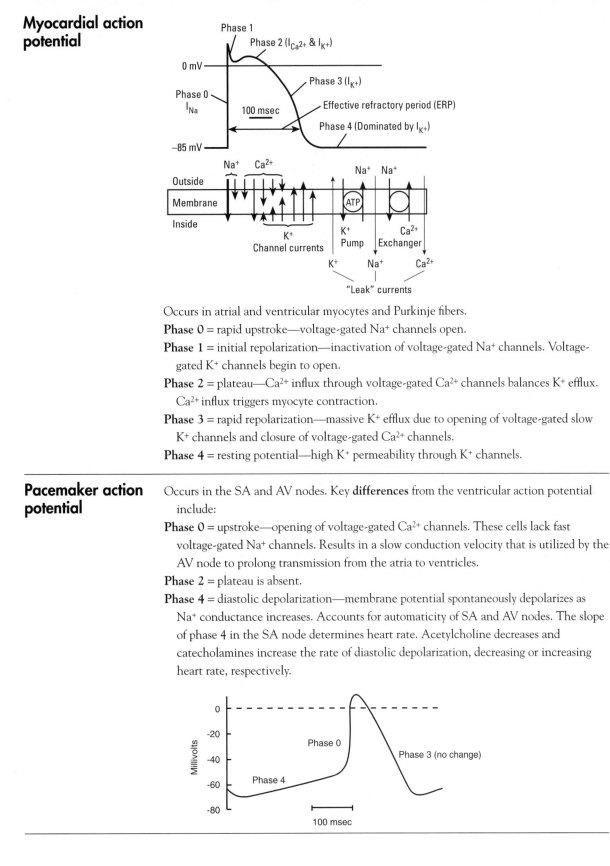

Occurs in atrial and ventricular myocytes and Purkinje fibers.

Phase 0 = rapid upstroke—voltage-gated Na^+ channels open.

Phase 1 = initial repolarization—inactivation of voltage-gated Na^+ channels. Voltage-gated K^+ channels begin to open.

Phase 2 = plateau—Ca^{2+} influx through voltage-gated Ca^{2+} channels balances K^+ efflux. Ca^{2+} influx triggers myocyte contraction.

Phase 3 = rapid repolarization—massive K^+ efflux due to opening of voltage-gated slow K^+ channels and closure of voltage-gated Ca^{2+} channels.

Phase 4 = resting potential—high K^+ permeability through K^+ channels.

Pacemaker action potential

Occurs in the SA and AV nodes. Key **differences** from the ventricular action potential include:

Phase 0 = upstroke—opening of voltage-gated Ca^{2+} channels. These cells lack fast voltage-gated Na^+ channels. Results in a slow conduction velocity that is utilized by the AV node to prolong transmission from the atria to ventricles.

Phase 2 = plateau is absent.

Phase 4 = diastolic depolarization—membrane potential spontaneously depolarizes as Na^+ conductance increases. Accounts for automaticity of SA and AV nodes. The slope of phase 4 in the SA node determines heart rate. Acetylcholine decreases and catecholamines increase the rate of diastolic depolarization, decreasing or increasing heart rate, respectively.

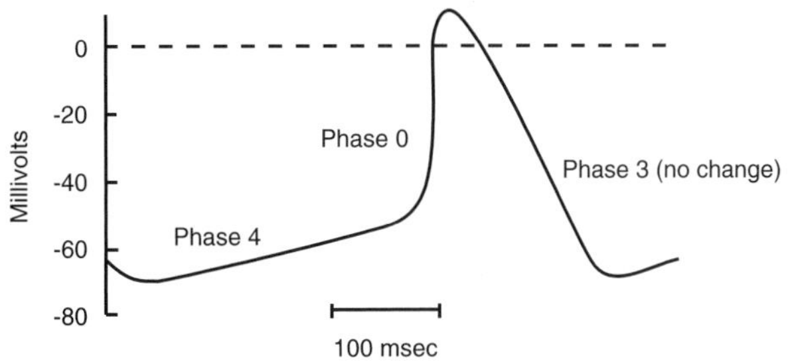

Cardiac output (CO)	Cardiac output = (stroke volume) × (heart rate)	During exercise, CO increases initially as a result of an increase in SV. After prolonged exercise CO increases as a result of an increase in HR.
Fick principle:	$CO = \dfrac{\text{rate of } O_2 \text{ consumption}}{\text{arterial } O_2 \text{ content} - \text{venous } O_2 \text{ content}}$	If HR is too high, diastolic filling is incomplete and CO drops (e.g., ventricular tachycardia).
	$\text{Mean arterial} = \left(\text{cardiac}\right) \times \left(\text{total peripheral}\right)$ Similar to Ohm's law: voltage = (current) × (resistance) MAP = diastolic + ⅓ pulse pressure Pulse pressure = systolic – diastolic Pulse pressure ≈ stroke volume	
UCV Path1.7		
Cardiac output variables	Stroke volume affected by **C**ontractility, **A**fterload, and **P**reload. Contractility (and SV) increased with: 1. Catecholamines (↑ activity of Ca^{2+} pump in sarcoplasmic reticulum) 2. ↑ intracellular calcium 3. ↓ extracellular sodium 4. Digitalis (↑ intracellular Na^+, resulting in ↑ Ca^{2+}) Contractility (and SV) decreased with: 1. β_1 blockade 2. Heart failure 3. Acidosis 4. Hypoxia/hypercapnea	SV **CAP** Stroke volume increases in anxiety, exercise, and pregnancy. A failing heart has decreased stroke volume. Myocardial O_2 demand is ↑ by: ↑ afterload (∝ diastolic BP) ↑ contractility ↑ heart rate ↑ heart size (↑ wall tension)
Preload and afterload	Preload = ventricular end-diastolic volume. Afterload = diastolic arterial pressure (proportional to peripheral resistance). Venous dilators (e.g., nitroglycerin) decrease preload. Vasodilators (e.g., hydralazine) decrease afterload. ↑ SV when ↑ preload, ↓ afterload or ↑ contractility.	Preload increases with exercise (slightly), increased blood volume (overtransfusion), and excitement (sympathetics). Preload pumps up the heart.

Starling curve

Force of contraction is proportional to initial length of cardiac muscle fiber (preload).

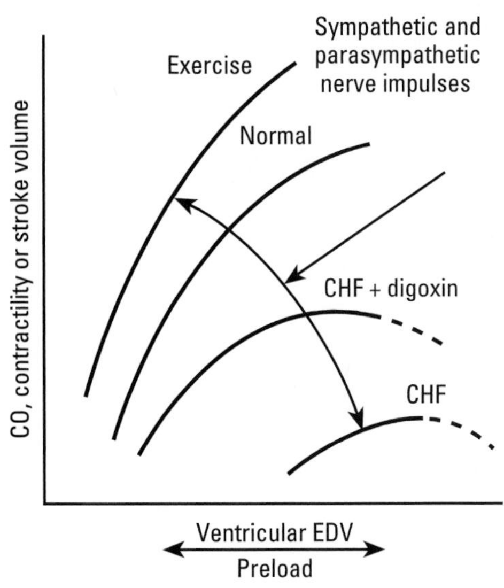

CONTRACTILE STATE OF MYOCARDIUM

⊕	⊖
Circulating catecholamines	Pharmacologic depressants
Digitalis	Loss of myocardium (MI)
Sympathetic stimulation	Parasympathetic stimulation

Ejection fraction

$$\text{Ejection fraction} = \frac{\text{end-diastolic volume} - \text{end-systolic volume}}{\text{end-diastolic volume}}$$

Ejection fraction is an index of ventricular contractility.

Ejection fraction is normally 60–70%.

Resistance, pressure, flow

$$\text{Resistance} = \frac{\text{driving pressure } (\Delta P)}{\text{flow}} \propto \frac{\text{viscosity } (\eta) \times \text{length}}{\textbf{(radius)}^4}$$

Viscosity depends mostly on hematocrit.

Viscosity increases in:

1. Polycythemia
2. Hyperproteinemic states (e.g., multiple myeloma)
3. Hereditary spherocytosis

Remember: resistance is directly proportional to viscosity and inversely proportional to the radius to the 4th power.

Blood

Normal adult blood composition. Note that serum = plasma – clotting factors (e.g., fibrinogen).

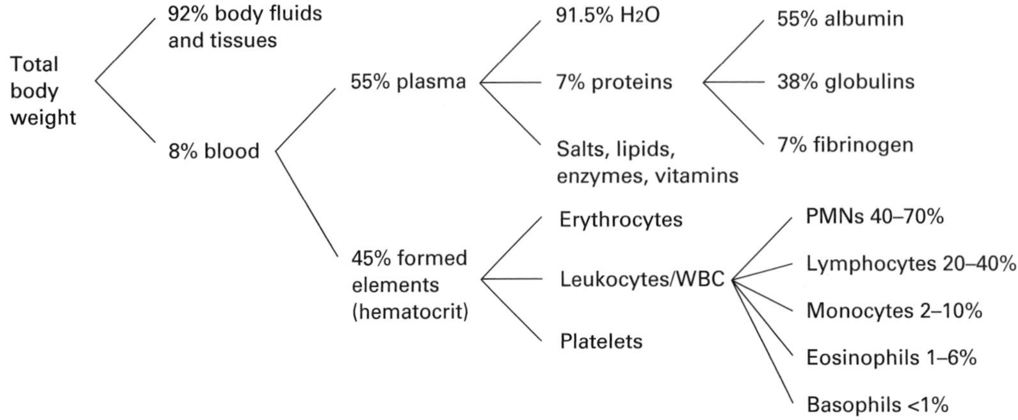

Capillary fluid exchange

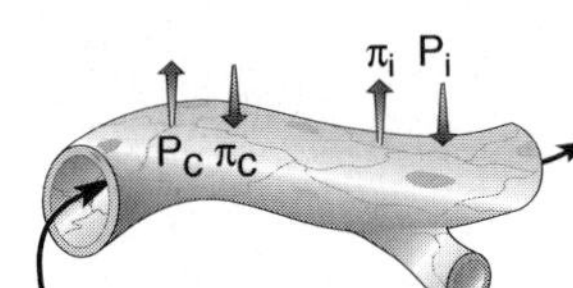

Four forces known as Starling forces determine fluid movement through capillary membranes:

P_c = capillary pressure—tends to move fluid out of capillary

P_i = interstitial fluid pressure—tends to move fluid into capillary

π_c = plasma colloid osmotic pressure—tends to cause osmosis of fluid into capillary

π_i = interstitial fluid colloid osmotic pressure—tends to cause osmosis of fluid out of capillary

Thus net filtration pressure = $P_{net} = [(P_c - P_i) - (\pi_c - \pi_i)]$

K_f = filtration constant (capillary permeability)

Net fluid flow = (P_{net}) (K_f)

Edema: excess fluid outflow into interstitium that is commonly caused by:

1. ↑ capillary pressure (↑ P_c; heart failure)
2. ↓ plasma proteins (↓ π_c; nephrotic syndrome, liver failure)
3. ↑ capillary permeability (↑ K_f; toxins, infections, burns)
4. ↑ interstitial fluid colloid osmotic pressure (↑ π_i; lymphatic blockage)

Cardiac cycle

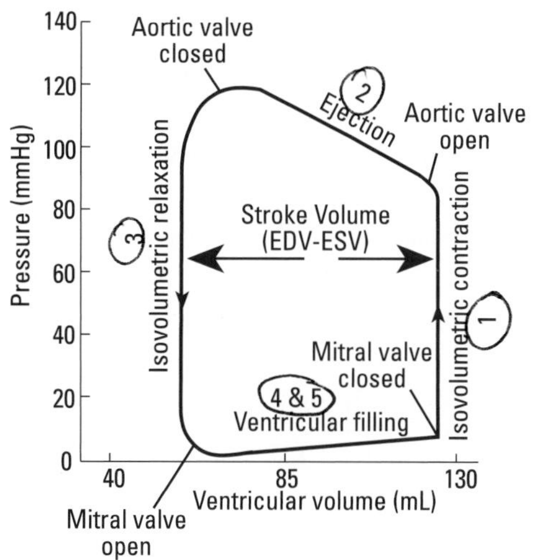

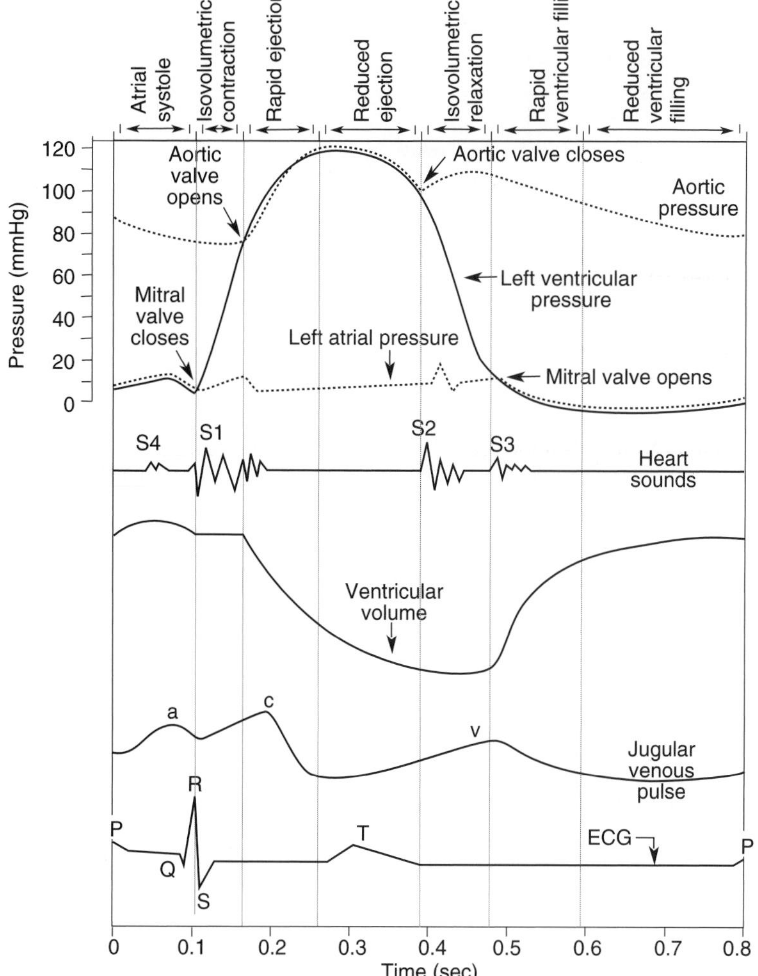

Phases:

1. Isovolumetric contraction—period between mitral valve closure and aortic valve opening; period of highest oxygen consumption
2. Systolic ejection—period between aortic valve opening and closing
3. Isovolumetric relaxation—period between aortic valve closing and mitral valve opening
4. Rapid filling—period just after mitral valve opening
5. Slow filling—period just before mitral valve closure

Sounds:
S1—mitral and tricuspid valve closure
S2—aortic and pulmonary valve closure
S3—end of rapid ventricular filling
S4—high atrial pressure/stiff ventricle

S3 is associated with dilated CHF
S4 ("atrial kick") is associated with a hypertrophic ventricle

a wave: **a**trial contraction
c wave: RV **c**ontraction (tricuspid valve bulging into atrium)
v wave: ↑ atrial pressure due to **fi**lling against closed tricuspid **v**alve

Jugular venous distention is seen in right-heart failure.

Electrocardiogram

P wave—atrial depolarization.

P-R interval—conduction delay through AV node (normally <200 msec).

QRS complex—ventricular depolarization (normally <120 msec).

Q-T interval—mechanical contraction of the ventricles.

T wave—ventricular repolarization.

Atrial repolarization is masked by QRS complex.

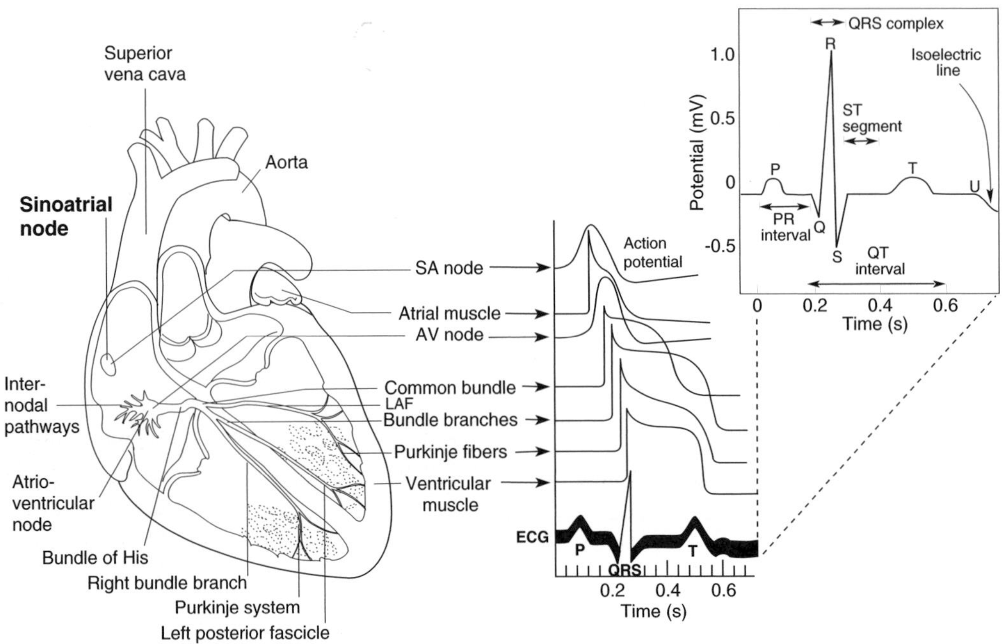

SA node "pacemaker" inherent dominance with slow phase of upstroke
AV node - 100-msec delay-atrial-ventricular delay

AV block (heart block)

First degree	Prolonged P-R interval (>200 msec).
Second degree	Type I (Wenckebach) shows a progressive prolongation of P-R interval until a P wave is blocked and not followed by a QRS complex ("dropped" beat).
	Type II (Mobitz) shows sporadic/episodic "dropped" QRS complex.
Third degree	Complete AV block with P waves completely dissociated from QRS complexes.

Cardiac myocyte physiology

Cardiac muscle contraction is dependent on extracellular calcium, which enters the cells during plateau of action potential and stimulates calcium release from the cardiac muscle sarcoplasmic reticulum (calcium-induced calcium release).

In contrast to skeletal muscle:

1. Cardiac muscle action potential has a plateau, which is due to Ca^{2+} influx.
2. Cardiac nodal cells spontaneously depolarize, resulting in automaticity.
3. Cardiac myocytes are electrically coupled to each other by gap junctions.

Control of mean arterial pressure

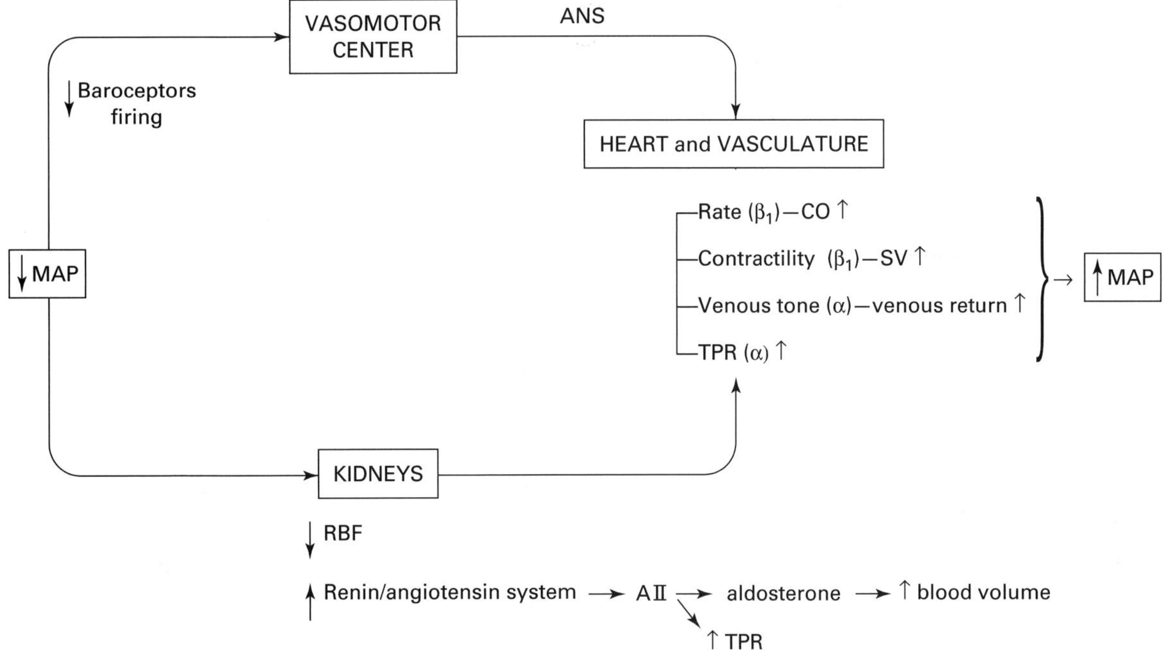

Arterial baroreceptors

Receptors:

1. **Aortic arch:** transmits via vagus nerve to medulla (responds **only** to ↑ blood pressure).
2. **Carotid sinus:** transmits via glossopharyngeal nerve to medulla.

Hypotension: ↓ arterial pressure → ↓ stretch → ↓ afferent baroreceptor firing → ↑ efferent sympathetic firing and ↓ efferent parasympathetic stimulation → vasoconstriction, ↑ HR, ↑ contractility, ↑ BP. Important in the response to severe hemorrhage.

Carotid massage: increased pressure on carotid artery → ↑ stretch . . . ↓ HR.

Chemoreceptors

Peripheral — **Carotid and aortic bodies:** respond to decreased P_{O_2}, increased P_{CO_2}, and decreased pH of blood. Response to P_{CO_2} is small.

Central — Respond to changes in pH and P_{CO_2} of brain interstitial fluid, which in turn are influenced by arterial CO_2. Do not directly respond to P_{O_2}. Responsible for Cushing reaction to increased intracranial pressure: hypertension and bradycardia.

Circulation through organs

Liver: largest share of systemic cardiac output.

Kidney: highest blood flow per gram of tissue.

Heart: large arteriovenous O_2 difference. Increased O_2 demand is met by increased coronary blood flow, not by increased extraction of O_2.

Normal pressures

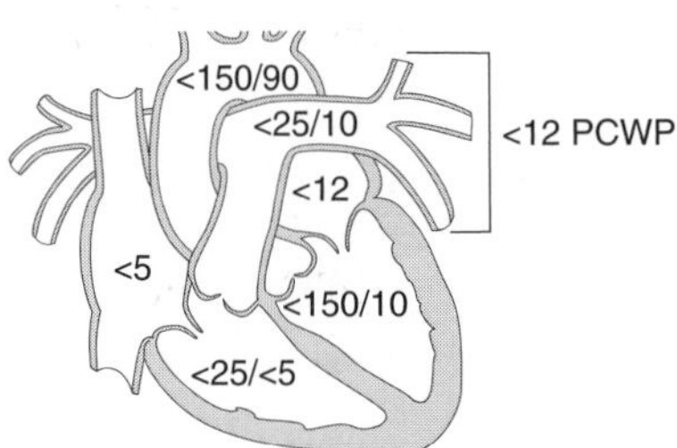

PCWP = pulmonary capillary wedge pressure (in mmHg) is a good approximation of left atrial pressure.

Autoregulation

Mechanism: blood flow is altered to meet demands of tissue via local metabolites (e.g., nitric oxide, adenosine).

Organ	Factors determining autoregulation
Heart	Local metabolites, $-O_2$, adenosine, NO
Brain	Local metabolites, ΔCO_2 (pH)
Kidneys	Myogenic and tubuloglomerular feedback
Lungs	Hypoxia causes vasoconstriction
Skeletal muscle	Local metabolites, sympathetic (α, β_2) innervation, lactate, adenosine, K^+

Note: the pulmonary vasculature is unique in that hypoxia causes vasoconstriction (in other organs hypoxia causes vasodilation).

Response to high altitude

1. Acute increase in ventilation
2. Chronic increase in ventilation
3. ↑ erythropoietin → ↑ hematocrit and hemoglobin (chronic hypoxia)
4. Increased 2,3-DPG (binds to Hb so that Hb releases more O_2)
5. Cellular changes (increased mitochondria)
6. Increased renal excretion of bicarbonate to compensate for the respiratory alkalosis
7. Chronic hypoxic pulmonary vasoconstriction results in right ventricular hypertrophy

Important lung products

1. Surfactant: ↓ alveolar surface tension, ↑ compliance
2. Prostaglandins
3. Histamine
4. Angiotensin converting enzyme (ACE): AI → AII; inactivates bradykinin (ACE inhibitors ↑ bradykinin and cause cough, angioedema)
5. Kallikrein: activates bradykinin

Surfactant: dipalmitoyl phosphatidylcholine (lecithin) deficient in neonatal RDS.

Lung volumes

1. Residual volume (RV) = air in lung at maximal expiration
2. Expiratory reserve volume (ERV) = air that can still be breathed out after normal expiration
3. Tidal volume (TV) = air that moves into lung with each quiet inspiration
4. Inspiratory reserve volume (IRV) = air in excess of tidal volume that moves into lung on maximum inspiration
5. Vital capacity (VC) = TV + IRV + ERV
6. Functional reserve capacity (FRC) = RV + ERV (volume in lungs after a normal respiration)

7. Inspiratory capacity (IC) = IRV + TV
8. Total lung capacity = TLC = IRV + TV + ERV + RV

Vital capacity is everything but the residual volume.

A capacity is a sum of ≥2 volumes.

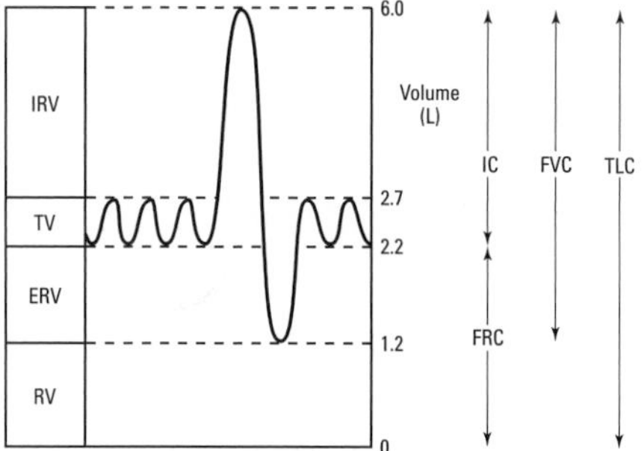

Oxygen dissociation curve

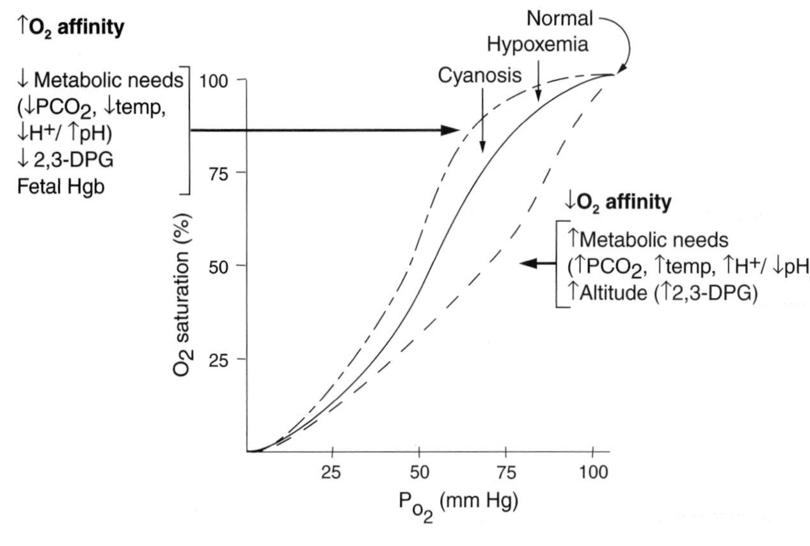

When curve shifts to the right, ↓ affinity of hemoglobin for O_2 (facilitates unloading of O_2 to tissue).

An ↑ in all factors (except pH) causes a shift of the curve to the right.

A ↓ in all factors (except pH) causes a shift of the curve to the left.

Pulmonary circulation

Normally a low-resistance, high-compliance system. P_{O_2} and P_{CO_2} exert opposite effects on pulmonary and systemic circulation. A ↓ in P_{AO_2} causes a hypoxic vasoconstriction that shifts blood away from poorly ventilated regions of lung to well-ventilated regions of lung.

A consequence of pulmonary hypertension is cor pulmonale and subsequent right ventricular failure (jugular venous distention, edema, hepatomegaly).

V/Q mismatch

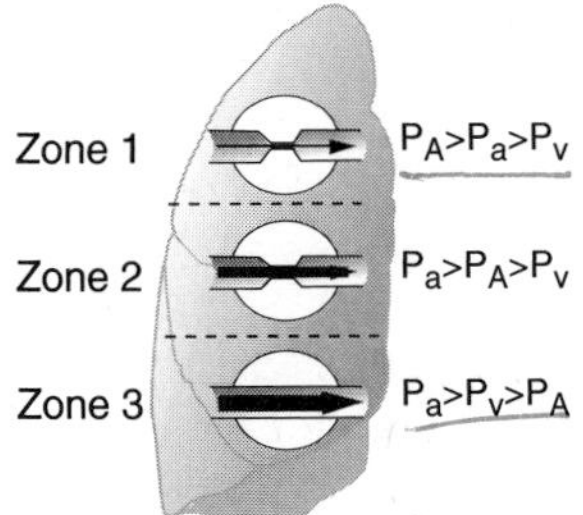

Ideally, ventilation is matched to perfusion (i.e., V/Q = 1) in order for adequate oxygenation to occur efficiently.
Lung zones:
Apex of the lung: V/Q = 3 (wasted ventilation)
Base of the lung: V/Q = 0.6 (wasted perfusion)
Both ventilation and perfusion are greater at the base of the lung than at the apex of the lung.

With exercise (increased cardiac output), there is vasodilation of apical capillaries, resulting in a V/Q ratio that approaches one.
Certain organisms that thrive in high O_2 (e.g., TB) flourish in the apex.
$V/Q \rightarrow 0$ = shunt
$V/Q \rightarrow \infty$ = dead space

CO_2 transport

Carbon dioxide is transported from tissues to the lungs in 3 forms:

1. **Bicarbonate (90%)**

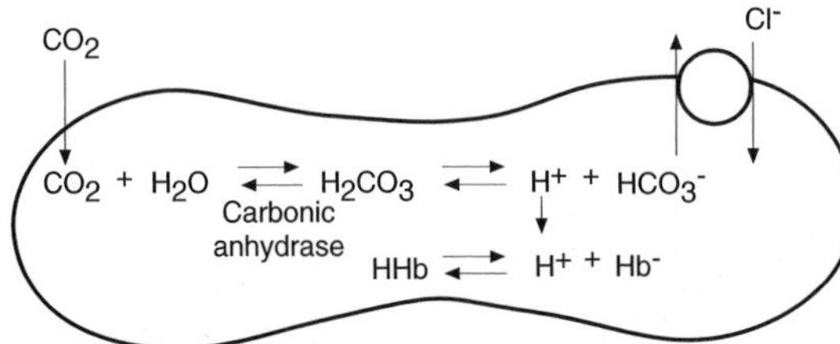

2. Bound to hemoglobin as carbaminohemoglobin (5%)
3. Dissolved CO_2 (5%)

In lungs, oxygenation of Hb promotes dissociation of CO_2 from Hb.
In peripheral tissue, ↑H^+ shifts curve to right, unloading O_2 (Bohr effect).

PHYSIOLOGY—GASTROINTESTINAL

Salivary secretion

Source	Parotid, submandibular, and sublingual glands.	Salivary secretion is stimulated by both sympathetic and parasympathetic activity.
Function	1. Alpha-amylase (ptyalin) begins starch digestion 2. Neutralizes oral bacterial acids, maintains dental health 3. Mucins (glycoproteins) lubricate food	

Stomach secretions

	Purpose	Source
Mucus	Lubricant, protects surface from H^+	Mucous cell
Intrinsic factor	Vitamin B_{12} absorption (in small intestine)	Parietal cell
H^+	Kills bacteria, breaks down food, converts pepsinogen	Parietal cell
Pepsinogen	Broken down to pepsin (a protease)	Chief cell
Gastrin	Stimulates acid secretion	G cell

GI secretory products

Product	Source	Function	Regulation	Notes
Intrinsic factor	Parietal cells (stomach)	Vitamin B_{12} binding protein required for vitamin's uptake in terminal ileum		Autoimmune destruction of parietal cells → chronic gastritis → pernicious anemia
Gastric acid	Parietal cells	Lowers pH to optimal range for pepsin function. Sterilizes chyme	Stimulated by histamine, ACh, gastrin. Inhibited by prostaglandin, somatostatin, and GIP	Not essential for digestion. Inadequate acid → ↑ risk of *Salmonella* infections
Pepsin	Chief cells (stomach)	Begins protein digestion; optimal function at pH 1.0–3.0	Stimulated by vagal input, local acid	Inactive pepsinogen converted to pepsin by H^+
Gastrin	G cells of antrum and duodenum	1. Stimulates secretion of HCl, IF and pepsinogen 2. Stimulates gastric motility	Stimulated by stomach distention, amino acids, peptides, vagus (via GRP); inhibited by secretin and stomach acid pH < 1.5	Hypersecreted in Zollinger–Ellison syndrome → peptic ulcers. Phenylalanine and tryptophan are potent stimulators.
Bicarbonate	Surface mucosal cells of stomach and duodenum	Neutralizes acid; present in unstirred layer with mucus on luminal surface, preventing autodigestion	Stimulated by secretin (potentiated by vagal input, CCK)	
Cholecystokinin (CCK)	I cells of duodenum and jejunum	1. Stimulates gallbladder contraction 2. Stimulates pancreatic enzyme secretion 3. Inhibits gastric emptying	Stimulated by fatty acids, amino acids	In cholelithiasis, pain worsens after eating fatty foods due to CCK release
Secretin	S cells of duodenum	Nature's antacid: 1. Stimulates pancreatic HCO_3^- secretion 2. Inhibits gastric acid secretion	Stimulated by acid and fatty acids in lumen of duodenum	Alkaline pancreatic juice in duodenum neutralizes gastric acid, allowing pancreatic enzymes to function
Somatostatin	D cells in pancreatic islets, gastrointestinal mucosa	Inhibits: 1. Gastric acid and pepsinogen secretion 2. Pancreatic and small intestine fluid secretion 3. Gallbladder contraction 4. Release of both insulin and glucagon	Stimulated by acid; inhibited by vagus	Very inhibitory hormone; anti-growth hormone effects (↓ digestion and ↓ absorption of substances needed for growth)

HIGH-YIELD FACTS

Physiology

Regulation of gastric acid secretion

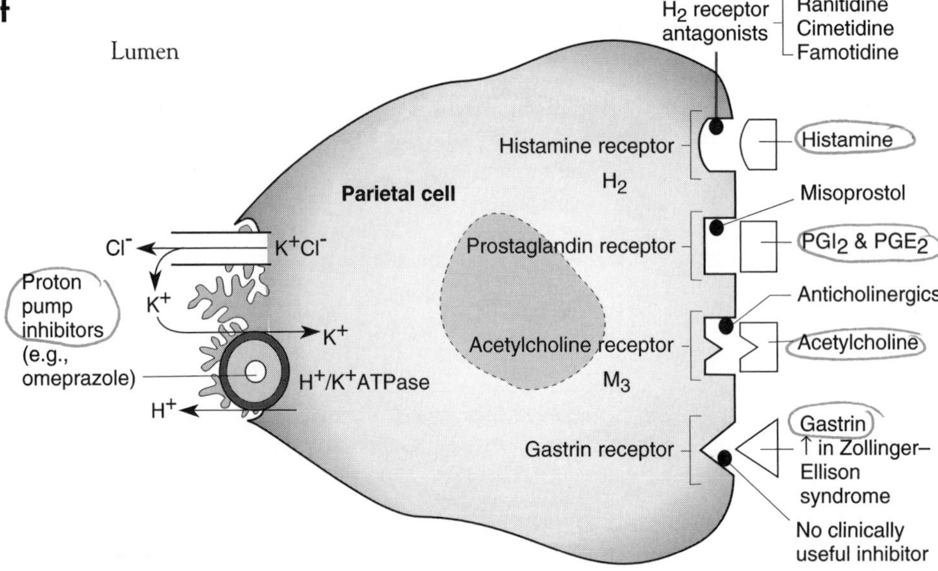

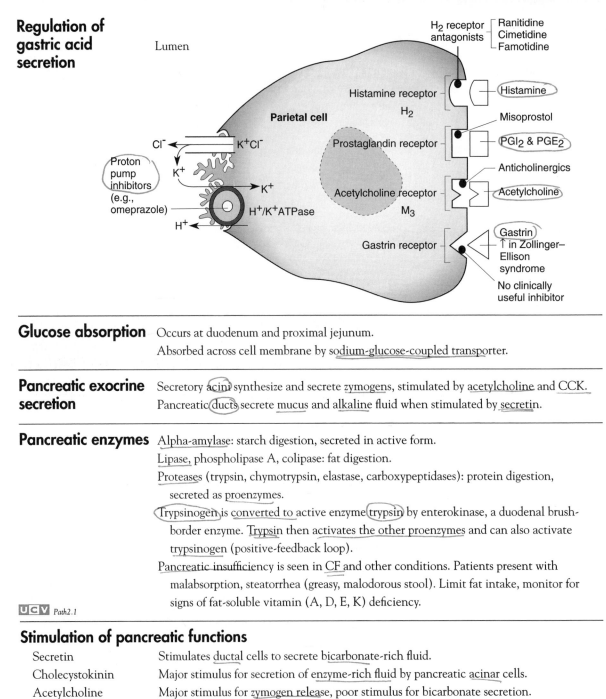

Glucose absorption	Occurs at duodenum and proximal jejunum. Absorbed across cell membrane by sodium-glucose-coupled transporter.
Pancreatic exocrine secretion	Secretory acini synthesize and secrete zymogens, stimulated by acetylcholine and CCK. Pancreatic ducts secrete mucus and alkaline fluid when stimulated by secretin.
Pancreatic enzymes	Alpha-amylase: starch digestion, secreted in active form. Lipase, phospholipase A, colipase: fat digestion. Proteases (trypsin, chymotrypsin, elastase, carboxypeptidases): protein digestion, secreted as proenzymes. Trypsinogen is converted to active enzyme trypsin by enterokinase, a duodenal brush-border enzyme. Trypsin then activates the other proenzymes and can also activate trypsinogen (positive-feedback loop). Pancreatic insufficiency is seen in CF and other conditions. Patients present with malabsorption, steatorrhea (greasy, malodorous stool). Limit fat intake, monitor for signs of fat-soluble vitamin (A, D, E, K) deficiency.

UCV Path2.1

Stimulation of pancreatic functions

Secretin	Stimulates ductal cells to secrete bicarbonate-rich fluid.
Cholecystokinin	Major stimulus for secretion of enzyme-rich fluid by pancreatic acinar cells.
Acetylcholine	Major stimulus for zymogen release, poor stimulus for bicarbonate secretion.
Somatostatin	Inhibits the release of gastrin and secretin.

Carbohydrate digestion

Only monosaccharides are absorbed.

Salivary amylase	Starts digestion, hydrolyzes alpha-1,4 linkages to give maltose, maltotriose, and α-limit dextrans.
Pancreatic amylase	Highest concentration in duodenal lumen, hydrolyzes starch to oligosaccharides, maltose, and maltotriose.
Oligosaccharide hydrolases	At brush border of intestine, the rate-limiting step in carbohydrate digestion, produce monosaccharides (glucose, galactose, fructose).

Bilirubin

Product of heme metabolism, actively taken up by hepatocytes. Conjugated version is water soluble. Jaundice (yellow skin, sclerae) results from elevated bilirubin levels.

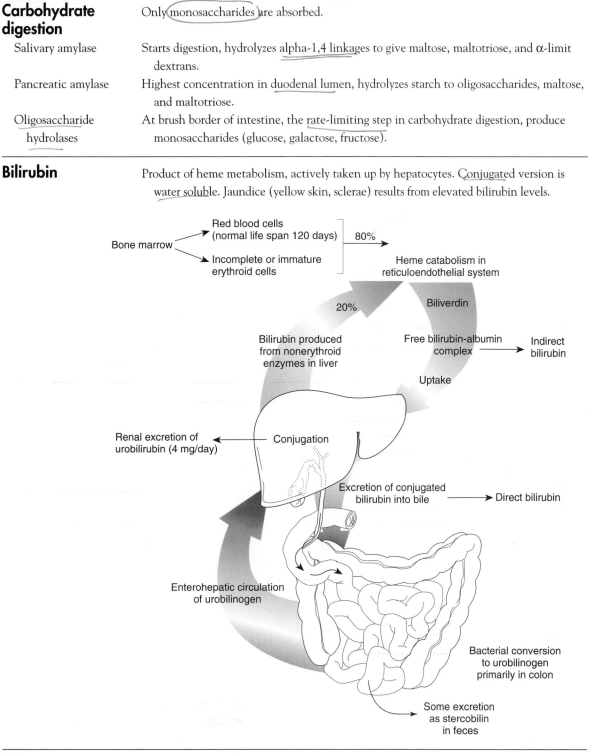

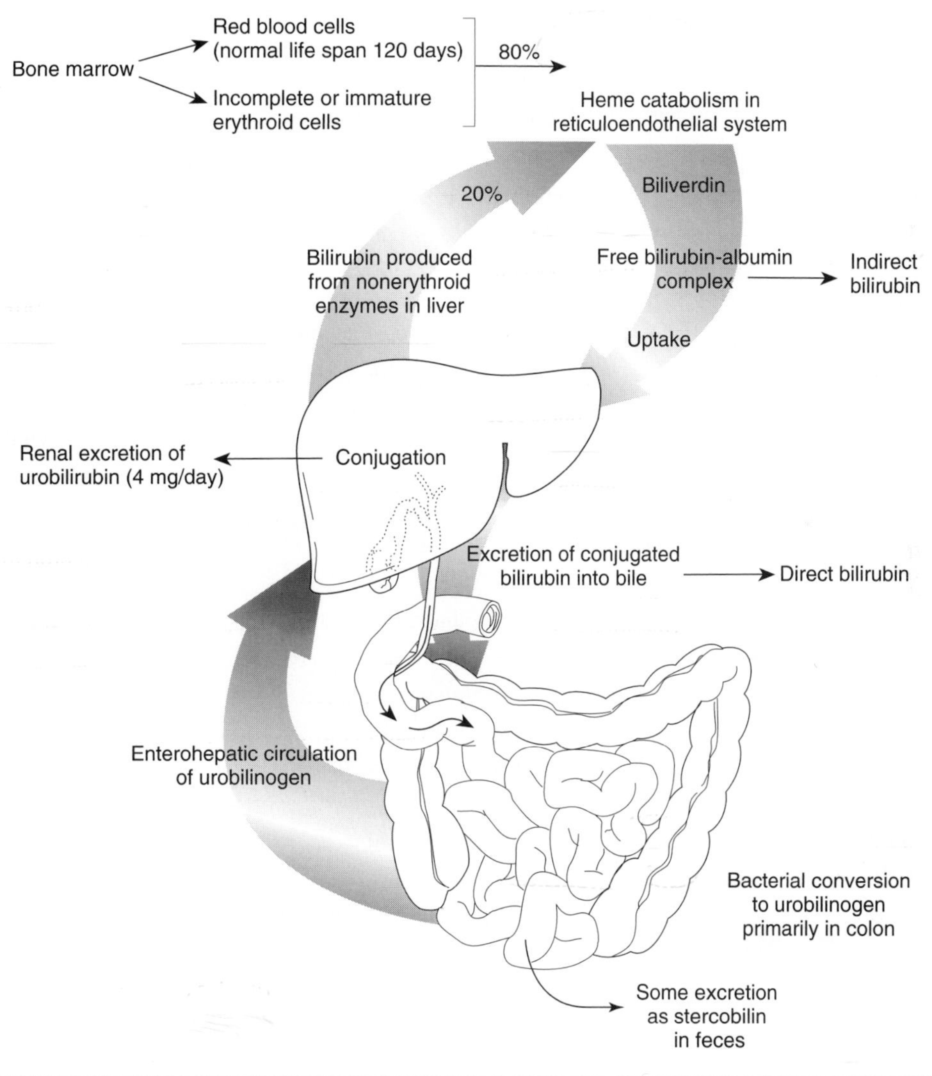

Bile

Secreted by hepatocytes. Composed of bile salts, phospholipids, cholesterol, bilirubin, water (97%). Bile salts are amphipathic (hydrophilic and hydrophobic domains) and solubilize lipids in micelles for absorption.

HIGH-YIELD FACTS

Physiology

Measuring fluid compartments

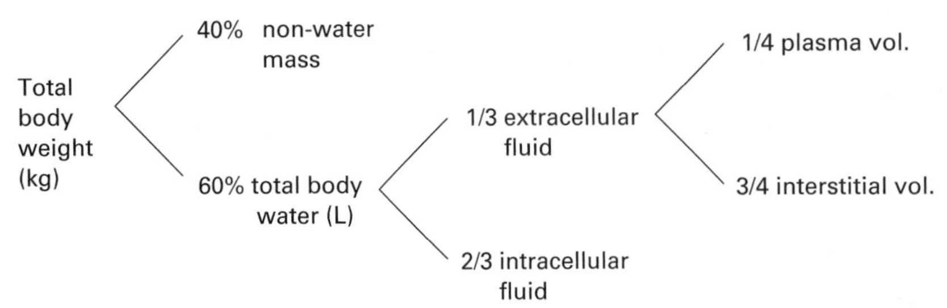

TBW – ECF = ICF
ECF – PV = interstitial volume

Renal clearance

$C_x = U_xV / P_x$ = volume of plasma from which the substance is cleared completely per unit time.
If C_x < GFR, then there is net tubular reabsorption of X.
If C_x > GFR, then there is net tubular secretion of X.
If C_x = GFR, then there is no net secretion or reabsorption.

Be familiar with calculations.

Glomerular filtration barrier

Composed of:
1. Fenestrated capillary endothelium (size barrier)
2. Fused basement membrane with heparan sulfate (negative charge barrier)
3. Epithelial layer consisting of podocyte foot processes

The charge barrier is lost in nephrotic syndrome, resulting in albuminuria, hypoproteinemia, generalized edema, and hyperlipidemia.

Glomerular filtration rate

$GFR = U_{Inulin} \times V / P_{Inulin} = C_{Inulin}$
$= K_f [(P_{GC} - P_{BS}) - (\pi_{GC} - \pi_{BS})]$
(GC = glomerular capillary; BS = Bowman's space)

Inulin is freely filtered and is neither reabsorbed nor secreted.

PAH

Secreted in proximal tubule.
Secondary active transport.
Mediated by a carrier system for organic acids, competitively inhibited by probenecid.

Effective renal plasma flow

$ERPF = U_{PAH} \times V / P_{PAH} = C_{PAH}$
$RBF = RPF / 1 - Hct$

PAH is filtered and secreted.

Filtration fraction

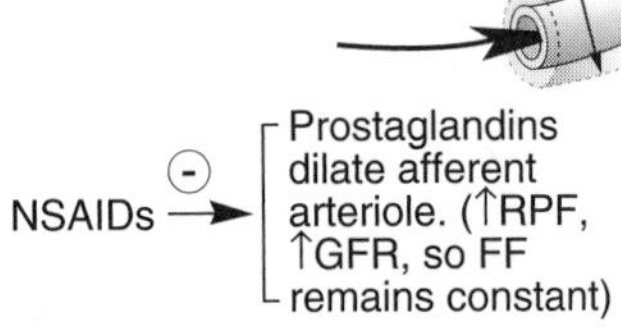

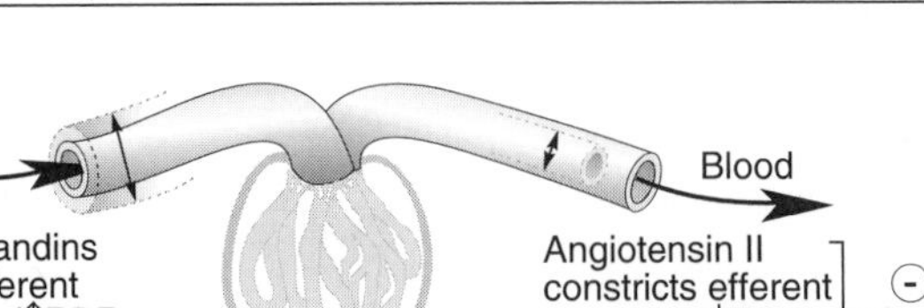

FF = GFR/RPF
$GFR = C_{inulin} \approx C_{creatinine}$
$RPF = C_{PAH}$

Free water clearance

Given urine flow rate, urine osmolarity, and plasma osmolarity, be able to calculate free water clearance:
$C_{H_2O} = V - C_{osm}$
V = urine flow rate; $C_{osm} = U_{osm}V/P_{osm}$

Glucose clearance	Glucose at a normal level is completely reabsorbed in proximal tubule. At plasma glucose of 200 mg/dL, glucosuria begins. At 300 mg/dL, transport mechanism is completely saturated.	Glucosuria is an important clinical clue to diabetes mellitus.
Amino acid clearance	Reabsorption by at least 3 distinct carrier systems, with competitive inhibition within each group. Secondary active transport occurs in proximal tubule and is saturable.	

Nephron physiology

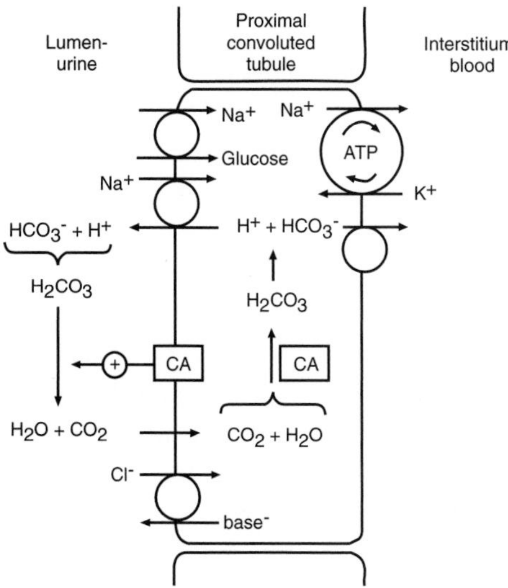

A. **Early proximal convoluted tubule**—"workhorse of the nephron." Reabsorbs all of the glucose and amino acids and most of the bicarbonate, sodium, and water. Secretes ammonia, which acts as a buffer for secreted H^+.

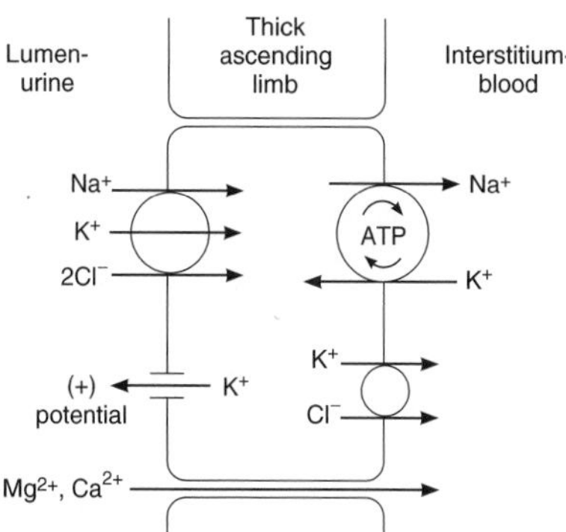

B. **Thin descending loop of Henle**—passively reabsorbs water via medullary hypertonicity (impermeable to sodium).

C. **Thick ascending loop of Henle**—actively reabsorbs Na^+, K^+, Cl^- and indirectly induces the reabsorption of Mg^{2+} and Ca^{2+}. Impermeable to H_2O.

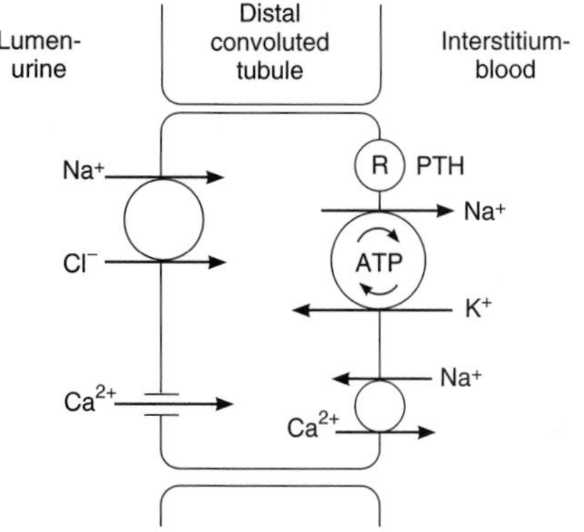

D. **Early distal convoluted tubule**—actively reabsorbs Na^+, Cl^-. Reabsorption of Ca^{2+} is under the control of PTH.

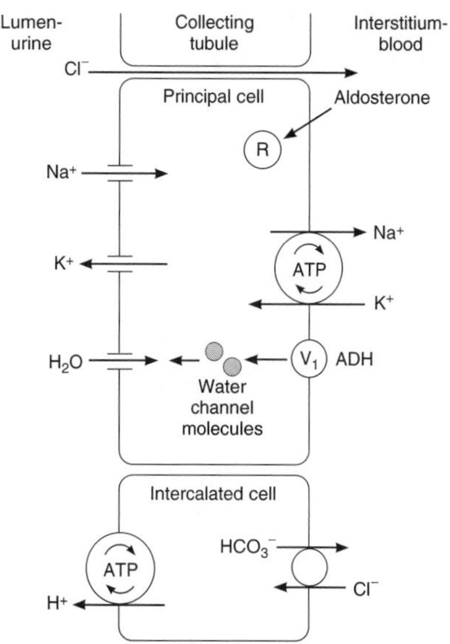

E. **Collecting tubules**—reabsorb Na^+ in exchange for secreting K^+ or H^+ (regulated by aldosterone). Reabsorption of water is regulated by ADH (vasopressin). Osmolarity of medulla can reach 1200–1400 mOsm.

Relative concentrations along renal tubule

$\frac{TF}{P} = \frac{[\text{Tubular fluid}]}{[\text{Plasma}]}$

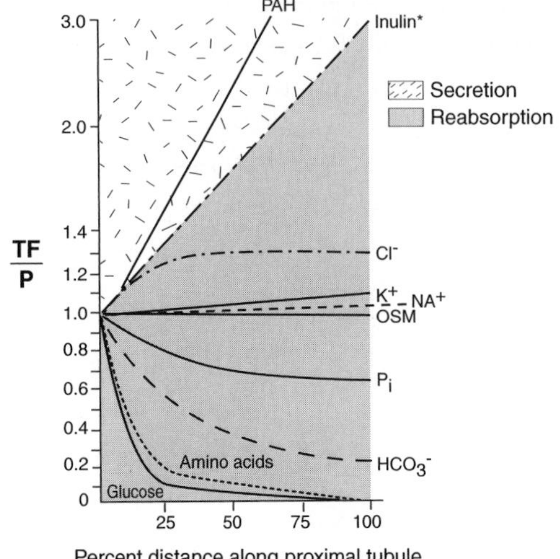

* Neither secreted nor reabsorbed; concentration increases as water is reabsorbed.

Kidney endocrine functions

Endocrine functions of the kidney:

1. Endothelial cells of peritubular capillaries secrete erythropoietin in response to hypoxia
2. Conversion of 25-OH vit. D to 1,25-$(OH)_2$ vit. D by 1α-hydroxylase, which is activated by PTH
3. JG cells secrete renin in response to ↓ renal arterial pressure and ↑ renal nerve discharge
4. Secretion of prostaglandins that vasodilate the afferent arterioles to increase GFR

NSAIDs can cause renal failure by inhibiting the renal production of prostaglandins, which normally keep the afferent arterioles vasodilated to maintain GFR.

Hormones acting on kidney

	Stimulus for secretion	Action on kidneys
Vasopressin (ADH)	↑ plasma osmolarity ↓↓ blood volume	↑ H_2O permeability of principal cells in collecting ducts ↑ Urea absorption in collecting duct ↑ $Na^+/K^+/2Cl^-$ transporter in thick ascending limb
Aldosterone	↓ blood volume (via AII) ↑ plasma $[K^+]$	↑ Na^+ reabsorption, ↑ K^+ secretion, ↑ H^+ secretion in distal tubule
Angiotensin II	↓ blood volume (via renin)	Contraction of efferent arteriole → ↑ GFR ↑ Na^+ and HCO_3^- reabsorption in proximal tubule
Atrial natriuretic peptide (ANP)	↑ atrial pressure	↓ Na^+ reabsorption, ↑ GFR
PTH	↓ plasma $[Ca^{2+}]$	↑ Ca^{2+} reabsorption, ↓ PO_4^{3-} reabsorption, ↑ 1,25 $(OH)_2$ vitamin D production

Renin–angiotensin system

Mechanism	Renin is released by the kidneys upon sensing ↓ BP and serves to cleave angiotensinogen to angiotensin I (AI, a decapeptide). AI is then cleaved by angiotensin-converting enzyme (ACE), primarily in the lung capillaries, to angiotensin II (AII, an octapeptide).
Actions of AII	1. Potent vasoconstriction 2. Release of aldosterone from the adrenal cortex 3. Release of ADH from posterior pituitary 4. Stimulates hypothalamus → ↑ thirst Overall, AII serves to ↑ intravascular volume and ↑ BP. ANP released from atria may act as a "check" on the renin-angiotensin system (e.g., in heart failure).

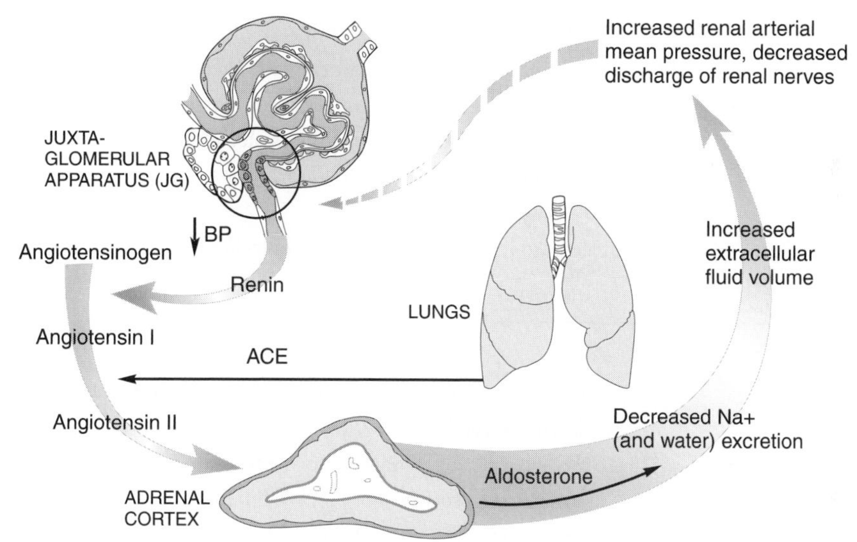

Pituitary gland

Posterior pituitary → vasopressin and oxytocin, made in the hypothalamus and shipped to pituitary. Derived from neuroectoderm.

Anterior pituitary → **F**SH, **L**H, **A**CTH, **G**H, **T**SH, Melan**O**tropin, **P**rolactin. Derived from oral ectoderm. — **FLAGTOP**

α subunit – common subunit to TSH, LH, FSH and hCG. — **T.S.H.** and **TSH** = The Sex Hormones and **TSH**

β subunit – determines hormone specificity.

PTH

Source: Chief cells of parathyroid.

Function:
1. Increases bone resorption of calcium
2. Increases kidney reabsorption of calcium in DCT
3. Decreases kidney reabsorption of phosphate
4. Increases 1,25 $(OH)_2$ vit. D (cholecalciferol) production by stimulating kidney 1α-hydroxylase

PTH: increases serum Ca^{2+}, decreases serum PO_4^{3-}, increases urine PO_4^{3-}.

PTH stimulates both osteoclasts and osteoblasts.

Regulation: Decrease in free serum Ca^{2+} increases PTH secretion.

PTH = **P**hosphate **T**rashing **H**ormone

UCV Path2.31, 2.36

Vitamin D

Source: Vitamin D_3 from sun exposure in skin. D_2 from plants. Both converted to 25-OH vit. D in liver and to 1,25-$(OH)_2$ vit. D (active form) in kidney.

If you do not get vit. D, you get rickets (kids) or osteomalacia (adults).

Function:
1. Increases absorption of dietary calcium
2. Increases absorption of dietary phosphate
3. Increases bone resorption of Ca^{2+} and PO_4^{3-}

24,25-$(OH)_2$ vit. D is an inactive form of vit. D.

Regulation: Increased PTH causes increased 1,25-(OH_2) vit. D formation.

Decreased phosphate causes increased 1,25-$(OH)_2$ vit. D conversion. 1,25-$(OH)_2$ vit. D feedback inhibits its own production.

Calcitonin

Source: Parafollicular cells (C cells) of thyroid.

Function: Decreases bone resorption of calcium

Regulation: Increase in serum Ca^{2+} increases secretion.

Calcitonin opposes actions of PTH and acts faster than PTH. It is probably not important in normal calcium homeostasis.

Thyroid hormone (T_3/T_4)

Source	Follicles of thyroid.	T_4 Functions: **4Bs**
Function	1. Bone growth (synergism with GH) 2. CNS maturation 3. β-adrenergic effects 4. ↑ Basal metabolic rate via ↑ Na^+/K^+ ATPase activity = ↑ O_2 consumption, ↑ body temp 5. ↑ glycogenolysis, gluconeogenesis, lipolysis 6. CV: ↑ CO, HR, SV, contractility, RR	**B**rain maturation **B**one growth **B**eta-adrenergic effects **B**MR ↑
Regulation	TRH (hypothalamus) stimulates TSH (pituitary), which stimulates follicular cells. Negative feedback by T3 to anterior pituitary ↓ sensitivity to TRH. TSI, like TSH, stimulates follicular cells (Graves' disease).	

Steroid/thyroid hormone mechanism

The need for gene transcription and protein synthesis delays the onset of action of these hormones.

Steroid/thyroid hormones:
- Cortisol
- Aldosterone
- Testosterone
- Estrogen
- Progesterone
- Thyroxine

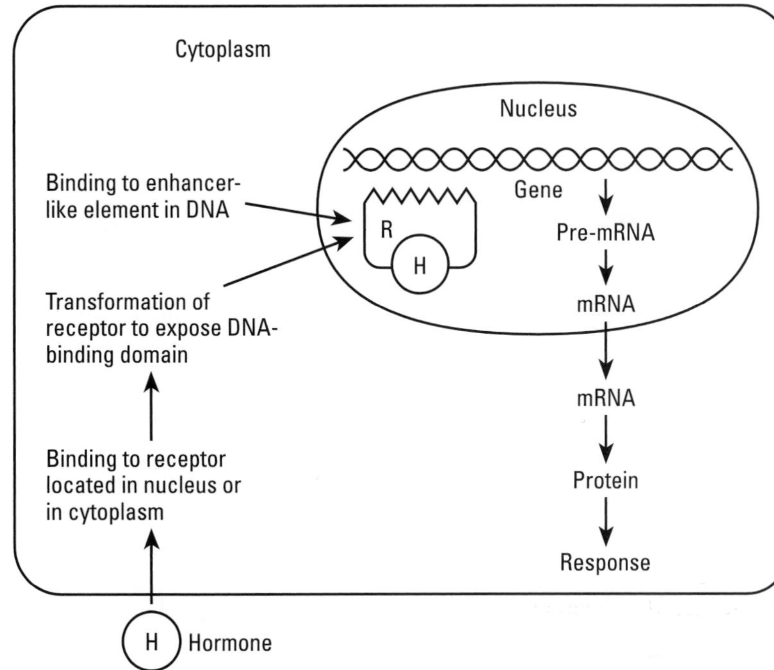

Steroid hormones are lipophilic and insoluble in plasma; therefore they must circulate bound to specific binding globulins (e.g., thyroid-binding globulin), which ↑ solubility and allow for ↑ delivery of steroid to the target organ.

Adrenal steroids

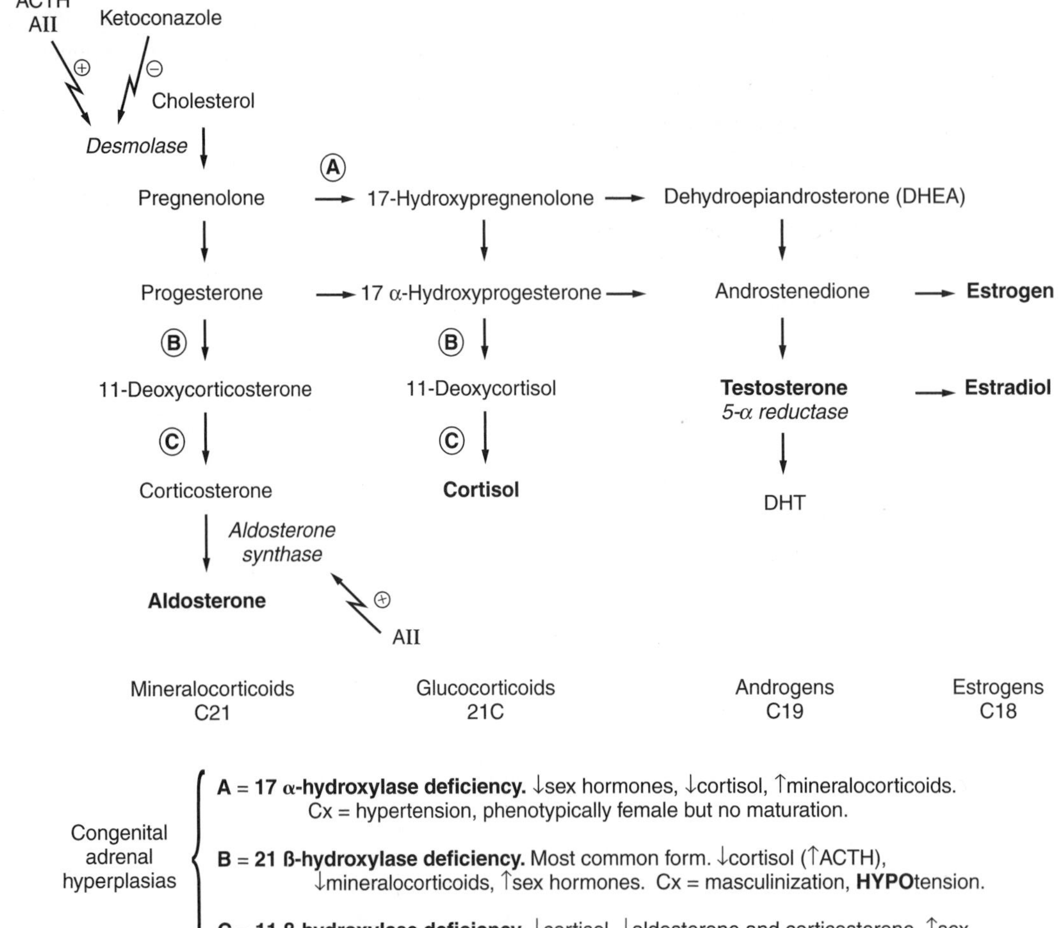

Congenital adrenal hyperplasias

- **A = 17 α-hydroxylase deficiency.** ↓sex hormones, ↓cortisol, ↑mineralocorticoids. Cx = hypertension, phenotypically female but no maturation.
- **B = 21 ß-hydroxylase deficiency.** Most common form. ↓cortisol (↑ACTH), ↓mineralocorticoids, ↑sex hormones. Cx = masculinization, **HYPO**tension.
- **C = 11 ß-hydroxylase deficiency.** ↓cortisol, ↓aldosterone and corticosterone, ↑sex hormones. Cx = masculinization, **HYPER**tension (11-deoxycorticosterone acts as a weak mineralocorticoid).

UCV Bio.1, 2

Insulin-independent organs	Muscle and adipose tissue depend on insulin for increased glucose uptake. Brain and RBCs take up glucose independent of insulin levels.	Brain and RBCs depend on glucose for metabolism under normal circumstances. Brain uses ketone bodies in starvation.

Estrogen

Source

Ovary (estradiol), placenta (estriol), blood (aromatization), testes.

Potency: estradiol > estrone > estriol

Function

1. Growth of follicle
2. Endometrial proliferation, myometrial excitability
3. Genitalia development
4. Stromal development of breast
5. Fat deposition
6. Hepatic synthesis of transport proteins
7. Feedback inhibition of FSH
8. LH surge (estrogen feedback on LH secretion switches to positive from negative just before LH surge)
9. Increased myometrial excitability

Estrogen hormone replacement therapy after menopause: ↓ risk of heart disease, ↓ hot flashes, and ↓ postmenopausal bone loss.

Unopposed estrogen therapy: ↑ risk of endometrial cancer; use of progesterone with estrogen ↓ those risks.

Progesterone

Source

Corpus luteum, placenta, adrenal cortex, testes.

Elevation of progesterone is indicative of ovulation.

Function

1. Stimulation of endometrial glandular secretions and spiral artery development
2. Maintenance of pregnancy
3. Decreased myometrial excitability
4. Production of thick cervical mucus, which inhibits sperm entry into the uterus
5. Increased body temperature (0.5 degree)
6. Inhibition of gonadotropins (LH, FSH)
7. Uterine smooth muscle relaxation

Menstrual cycle

Follicular growth is fastest during second week of proliferative phase.

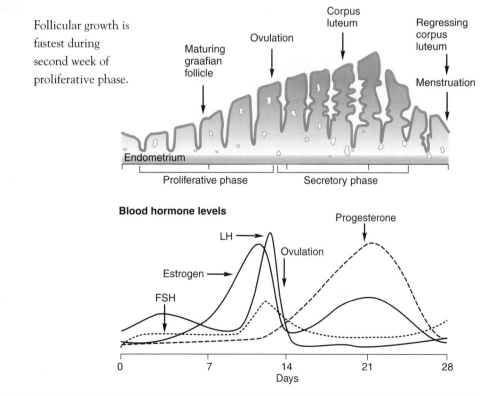

Maturing graafian follicle
Ovulation
Corpus luteum
Regressing corpus luteum
Menstruation
Endometrium
Proliferative phase
Secretory phase

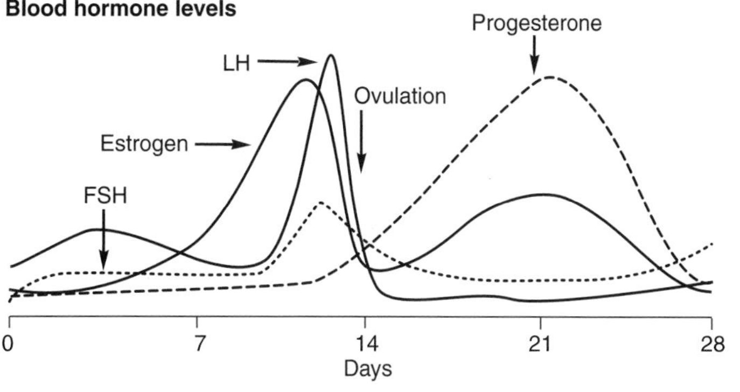

hCG

Source	Trophoblast of placenta	
Function	1. Maintains the corpus luteum for the 1st trimester because it acts like LH but is not susceptible to feedback regulation from estrogen and progesterone. In the 2nd and 3rd trimester, the placenta synthesizes its own estrogen and progesterone. As a result, the corpus luteum degenerates. 2. Used to detect pregnancy because it appears in the urine 8 days after successful fertilization (blood and urine tests available). 3. Elevated hCG in women with hydatidiform moles or choriocarcinoma.	

Menopause

	Cessation of estrogen production with age-linked decline in number of ovarian follicles. Average age of onset is 51 y (earlier in smokers). Therapy = estrogen replacement therapy.	Hormonal changes: ↓ estrogen, ↑↑ FSH, ↑ LH (no surge), ↑ GnRH. Menopause causes **HAVOC:** **H**ot flashes, **A**trophy of the **V**agina, **O**steoporosis, **C**oronary artery disease.

UCV Path1.34

Androgens

	Testosterone, dihydrotestosterone (DHT), androstenedione	
Source	DHT (prostate, peripheral conversion) Testosterone (testis, adrenal) Androstenedione (adrenal)	Potency DHT > testosterone > androstenedione
Targets	Skin, prostate, seminal vesicles, epididymis, liver	Testosterone is converted to DHT by the enzyme 5α-reductase, which is inhibited by finasteride.
Function	1. Differentiation of wolffian duct system into internal gonadal structures. 2. Secondary sexual characteristics and growth spurt during puberty. 3. Requirement for normal spermatogenesis. 4. Anabolic effects: ↑ muscle size, ↑ RBC production. 5. ↑ Libido	Testosterone and androstenedione are converted to estradiol and estrogen in adipose tissue by enzyme aromatase.

Male spermatogenesis

Pituitary	Testes	Products	Functions of products

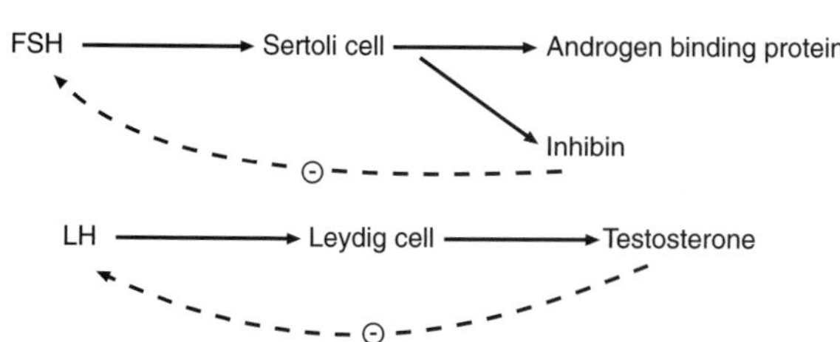

Ensures that testosterone in seminiferous tubule is high

Inhibits FSH

Differentiates male genitalia, has anabolic effects on protein metabolism, maintains gametogenesis, maintains libido, inhibits LH, and fuses epiphyseal plates in bone

FSH → Sertoli cells → Sperm production
LH → Leydig cells

NOTES

SECTION III

Database of Basic Science Review Resources

HOW TO USE THE DATABASE

This section is a database of current basic science review books, sample examination books, software, websites and commercial review courses marketed to medical students studying for the USMLE Step 1. At the end of this section is a list of publishers and independent bookstores with addresses and phone numbers. For each book, we list the **Title** of the book, the **First Author** (or editor), the **Series Name** (where applicable), the **Current Publisher,** the **Copyright Year,** the **Number of Pages,** the **ISBN Code,** the **Approximate List Price,** the **Format** of the book, and the **Number of Test Questions.** The entries for most books also include **Summary Comments** that describe their style and overall utility for studying. Finally, each book receives a **Rating.** The books are sorted into a comprehensive section as well as into sections corresponding to the seven traditional basic medical science disciplines (anatomy, behavioral science, biochemistry, microbiology, pathology, pharmacology, and physiology). Within each section, books are arranged by Rating, and alphabetically by Title within each Rating group.

For the 2000 edition of *First Aid for the USMLE Step 1*, the database of review books has been expanded and updated, with more than 30 new books and software. New this year is a section on websites that contain review and self-assessment materials. A letter rating scale with ten different grades reflects the detailed student evaluations. Each resource receives a rating as follows:

A+	Excellent for boards review.
A A–	Very good for boards review; choose among the group.
B+ B B–	Good, but use only after exhausting better sources.
C+ C C–	Fair, but there are many better books in the discipline; or low-yield subject material.
D	Avoid like the plague.
N	Not rated.

The **Rating** is meant to reflect the overall usefulness of the resource in preparing for the USMLE Step 1 examination. This is based on a number of factors, including:

- The cost.
- The readability of the text.
- The appropriateness and accuracy of the material.
- The quality and number of sample questions.
- The quality of written answers to sample questions.
- The quality and appropriateness of the illustrations (e.g., graphs, diagrams, photographs).
- The length of the text (longer is not necessarily better).
- The quality and number of other resources available in the same discipline.
- The importance of the discipline on the USMLE Step 1 examination.

Please note that the rating does **not** reflect the quality of the resources for purposes other than reviewing for the USMLE Step 1 examination. Many books with low ratings are well written and informative but are not ideal for boards preparation. We have not listed or commented on general textbooks available in the basic sciences.

Evaluations are based on the cumulative results of formal and informal surveys of thousands of medical students at many medical schools across the country. The summary comments and overall ratings represent a consensus opinion, but there may have been a broad range of opinion or limited student feedback on any particular resource. When necessary, we have identified the exceptional entry with limited student feedback.

Please note that the data listed are subject to change in that:

- Publishers' prices change frequently.
- Bookstores often charge an additional markup.
- New editions come out frequently, and the quality of updating varies.
- The same book may be reissued through another publisher.

We actively encourage medical students and faculty to submit their opinions and ratings of these basic science review materials so that we may update our database. (*See* How to Contribute, p. xvii.) In addition, we ask that publishers and authors submit review copies of basic science review books, including new editions and books not included in our database for evaluation. We also solicit reviews of new books or suggestions for alternate modes of study that may be useful in preparing for the examination, such as flashcards, computer-based tutorials, commercial review courses, and World Wide Web sites.

Disclaimer/Conflict of Interest Statement

No material in this book, including the ratings, reflects the opinion or influence of the publisher. All errors and omissions will gladly be corrected if brought to the attention of the authors through the publisher. Please note that the book *Underground Step 1 Answers to the NBME Retired and Self-Test Questions* (p. 337) and the entire *Underground Clinical Vignette* series are independent publications by the authors of this book; their ratings are based solely on data from the student survey and feedback forms.

Medical Study Guides Page

Review

Goodman

http://www.kumc.edu/AMA-MSS/study/study.htm

Contains extensive notes for first- and second-year courses that are in outline form. Useful as both companion to courses and for review. Many great tables and a section devoted to boards review.

A−

WebPath The Internet Pathology Laboratory

Review/Questions

Klatt

http://www-medlib.med.utah.edu/WebPath/webpath.html

Features a wealth of gross and microscopic illustrations, clinical vignette questions and case studies. Contains many classic, high-quality illustrations. Questions reflect current boards format and difficulty level but are typically shorter. Online exam lacks illustrations and a timer. A WebPath CD-ROM is available for $60.00 and features the online Website plan supplemented with photos and questions. Ideal for computers with slow or no internet access. May be ordered directly from website.

B+

Digital Anatomist Interactive Atlases

Review

University of Washington

http://www9.biostr.washington.edu/da.html

Good site containing an interactive neuroanatomy course along with a three-dimensional atlas of the brain, thorax, and knee. Atlases have computer-generated images along with cadaver dissections. Each atlas also has a useful quiz in which users identify structures in the slide images.

B+

Medical Pharmacology

Review/Questions

Gordon

http://www.kumc.edu/research/medicine/pharmacology/mgordon/learning1.htm

Contains online guides that are useful as tools for both learning and reviewing drug classes, mechanisms, and uses. Many short, multiple-choice questions useful for self-quizzing and memorizing drugs. Also has a limited number of short cases.

B

Active Learning Center

Questions

Turchin

http://www.med.jhu.edu/medcenter/quiz/home.cgi

A quiz engine site based upon a large database that has an extensive list of bugs, drugs, and vaccines. The questions generated test the basic characteristics of each element in the database in a multiple-choice, matching, or essay format that the user selects. The questions are not boards-style but are useful for learning the memory intensive subjects of microbiology and pharmacology.

B | ## The Whole Brain Atlas | Review

Johnson

http://www.med.harvard.edu/AANLIB/home.html

A collection of high-quality brain MR and CT images with views of normal, aging, and diseased brains (CVA, degenerative, neoplastic, and inflammatory diseases). The interface is technologically impressive but also complex. The guided tours and image correlation to cases are especially useful. Although not all of the images are particularly high-yield for the boards, this is an excellent introduction to neuroimaging.

B− | ## Introduction to Clinical Microbiology Table of Contents | Review

http://medic.med.uth.tmc.edu/path/00001450.htm

A very basic introduction/review of the fundamentals of microbiology. The site has a useful review of the different types of media and lab tests. The information on bugs is shallow but a quick read.

Buzzwords for the Boards: USMLE Step 1 Recall — $26.00 — Review only

Reinheimer

Lippincott Williams & Wilkins, 1999, 400 pages, ISBN 0683306391

Quizzes on main topics and key points in a two-column question-answer format. Good for self-testing and quick review. Use as a change of pace; hits many important clinical features but is not comprehensive or tightly organized.

NMS Review for USMLE Step 1 Examination — $35.95 — Test/1000+ q

Lazo

Lippincott Williams & Wilkins, 1998, 350 pages, ISBN 0083304909

Very good source of practice questions and answers. Features updated clinical questions with a limited number of vignettes. Some questions are too picky or difficult. Good explanations, but occasionally offers unnecessary detail. Good buy for the number of questions. Organized as four 200-question booklets; good for simulating exam conditions, yet clinical vignettes with multiple questions per case description do not reflect current boards format. Helpful color plates.

Appleton & Lange's Review for the USMLE Step 1 — $36.95 — Test/1200 q

Barton

Appleton & Lange, 1999, 331 pages, ISBN 0838502652

Features seven subject-based tests and two 150-question comprehensive exams. Good buy for the number of questions. Thorough explanations of right and wrong answers. A decent, straightforward, question-based review to assess your strengths and weaknesses. Testing includes references to diagrams, images, and a few color plates. Revised and updated to current USMLE format.

Board Simulator Series — $25.95 (each) — Test/770 q

Gruber

Lippincott Williams & Wilkins

Body Systems Reviews I: 1997, 338 pages, ISBN 0683302981

Body Systems Reviews II: 1997, 350 pages, ISBN 068330299X

Body Systems Reviews III: 1997, 298 pages, ISBN 0683303007

General Principles in the Basic Sciences: 1997, 306 pages, ISBN 0683302965

Normal and Abnormal Processes in the Basic Sciences: 1997, 304 pages, ISBN 0683302973

Four exams per book with approximately 160 questions each. Follows USMLE content outline. Numerous vignettes reflect clinical slant of the exam. Good black-and-white photographs. Comprehensive systems-based approach. Most effective if all three "Reviews" books are used. For the motivated student. Questions tend to be more "picky" than those of the actual USMLE exam. Explanations discuss important concepts. *General Principles* has some overlap with *Normal and Abnormal Processes*. *Normal and Abnormal Processes* can be used independently of the other books, as it covers all seven major subject areas.

B+ **Crashing the Boards: USMLE Step 1** **$17.95** Review only

Yeh

Lippincott Williams & Wilkins, 1999, 168 pages, ISBN 0397584091

Brief coverage of high-yield topics. Great diagrams and a good sense of humor. No photos. Good organization (bulleted facts and highlighted boxing). Useful for supplementary, last-minute review. Incomplete book reviews in the back. New edition retains outdated strategies for paper-and-pencil exam. Compare with Carl's *Medical Boards—Step 1 Made Ridiculously Simple*.

B+ **NMS USMLE Step 1** **$44.95** Software/1000+ q

Lazo

Lippincott Williams & Wilkins, 1998, ISBN 0683300954

Windows/Mac-based testing software. Features questions from Lazo's *Review for USMLE Step 1 Examination*. Organized as four comprehensive tests. Flexible test modes. Well-written questions with frequent clinical vignettes. Illustrations poorly reproduced. Does not accurately reflect CBT format.

B+ **PreTest USMLE Step 1 Clinical Vignettes** **$24.95** Test/350 q

McGraw-Hill

McGraw-Hill, 1999, 280 pages, ISBN 0071351337

Questions relating to clinical vignettes with very detailed explanations. Covers all the basic sciences. Good self-evaluation tool, though questions may not be exactly like those on the actual USMLE exam.

B+ **Underground Step 1 Answers to the NBME Retired and Self-Test Questions** **$22.95** Review/1600 a

Le

S2S Medical, 1996, 463 pages, ISBN 1890061018

Concise explanatory study guide to 1600+ *NBME Retired* and *Self-Test* questions. Easy read, good review; not for last-minute use. Useful with or without NBME questions (not included). Referenced to current textbooks. Second edition features expanded and updated explanations.

B+ **USMLE Step 1 Starter Kit** **$31.95** Test/360 q

Kaplan Educational

Appleton & Lange, 1998, 208 pages, ISBN 0838586651

Two 180-question sample exams. Customers can have their answers analyzed over the Internet, at a Kaplan Center, or by mail. Analysis includes a diagnostic profile and study-plan summary. Questions accurately reflect clinical slant of the current boards, and answers are thorough. High-quality questions, but expensive for the amount of material.

B

Ace Basic Sciences: USMLE Step 1

$31.95 Test/800 q

Mosby

Mosby-Yearbook, 1996, 206 pages, ISBN 0815169043

Some clinically focused vignettes interspersed with basic science questions. Answers explain why each choice is right or wrong rather than focusing on didactic teaching of main concepts. Four comprehensive exams with 200 questions each. Money-back guarantee if you fail. Questions can be done in book or on diskette. Compare with Lazo (*Review for USMLE Step 1 Examination*) and Barton (*Appleton & Lange's Review for the USMLE Step 1)*. No photomicrographs. Very limited student feedback.

B

Boards & Wards USMLE Step 1 Quickie: From Horses to Zebras

$24.95 Review only

Ayala

Emrani Publication, 1999, 287 pages, ISBN 0965468763

System-based outline, with a focus on pathology. Text-dense, but not complete or well organized. Clinical scenarios and a few questions at end of each chapter. A few memory tools; no diagrams. Appendix has brief, helpful overview of neurology, immunology, "zebras," syndromes, and pearls.

B

Cracking the Boards: USMLE Step 1

$34.95 Review/400 q

Stein

Princeton Review, 1999, 760 pages, ISBN 0375754717

Comprehensive text review based on the USMLE content outline. Wordy, broad spectrum but few details. Many diagrams and photos. Student opinion varies widely. New edition now available.

B

Gold Standard Prep Set for USMLE Step 1

$259.00 Audio tapes

Knouse

Gold Standard, 1999

Set of 48 approximately 90-minute audio tapes covering USMLE Step 1 material. Limited, but positive, feedback on updated and expanded set of audiotapes. Popular among some students as a way to review while driving, while working out, and during down time. Has some inaccuracies. Available only by mail order at (740) 592-4124, fax: (740) 592-4045 or http://www.boardprep.net.

B

Integrated Basic Sciences

$29.95 Review only

Brown

McGraw-Hill, 1999, 578 pages, ISBN 007052551X

Great clinical review questions. Each vignette is followed by a group of three questions testing anatomy, normal and abnormal function. Answers discussed in detail. Covers many core diseases, organized by system. Time consuming.

B **Medical Boards—Step 1 Made Ridiculously Simple** **$24.95** Review only

Carl

MedMaster, 1999, 367 pages, ISBN 0940780399

Quick and easy reading. Table and chart format is organized by subject. Excellent pathology section. Very mixed reviews. Some charts are poorly labeled. Consider as an adjunct. Compare with Yeh's *Crashing the Boards*.

B **Passing the USMLE Steps 1, 2, & 3 Photo Diagnosis, Vols. I and II** **$30.00 (each)** Test/100 q

Gold

Vol. I: Southland Tutorial, 1996, 77 pages, ISBN 1888628235

Vol. II: Southland Tutorial, 1996, 75 pages, ISBN 1888628243

One hundred picture-based questions with thorough explanations. Pictures include high-quality CTs, x-rays, MRIs, angiograms, EKGs, etc. May be helpful if used in conjunction with other question books. Limited student feedback. Very expensive for the number of questions.

B **Preparation for USMLE Step 1 Basic Medical Sciences, Volumes A, B, C** **$15.00 (each)** Test/315 q

Waintrub

Maval Medical Education, 1999, 78 pages, ISBN 1884083137 (Vol. A), 1884083143 (Vol. B), 1884083153 (Vol. C)

Three tests with appropriate-format straightforward questions and explanatory answers. Suggested time frame for test simulation. Fairly clinically focused. Good color photographs. Moderately expensive for the number of questions.

B **Preparation for the USMLE Step 1 Basic Medical Sciences, Volumes D, E** **$15.00 (each)** Test/210 q

Waintrub

Maval Medical Education, 1995, 57 pages, ISBN 1884083161

Same format and comments as for Volumes A, B, and C, but even more expensive for the number of questions.

B **Preparation for the USMLE Step 1, Basic Medical Sciences, Volume F** **$18.00** Test/540 q

Waintrub

Maval Publishing, 1997, ISBN 1884083080

Six practice tests and answers; otherwise same comments as for Volumes A–E. Free with purchase of USMLE Review Book (listed separately) from the Maval publishing website.

B

Rapid Preparation for the USMLE Step 1

$36.00 Test/926 q

Johnson

J&S Publishing, 1997, 406 pages, ISBN 1888308028

A "best of J&S" compendium. Questions are organized by subject and are drawn as exact duplicates from other books in the series. Thorough explanations with key concepts in boldface; however, some are incomplete or inaccurate. High-quality black-and-white MRIs, CTs, line drawings, histology, and gross photo illustrations. Clinical vignette-based questions. Mixed student feedback.

B

Retired NBME Basic Medical Sciences Test Items

— Test/993 q

NBME

NBME, 1991, 136 pages, out of print

Contains "retired" questions in all seven areas of basic science. Good topics. Letter answers only with no explanations. Content is still relevant, but format is outdated. Contains old K-type questions. No clinical vignettes. Limited utility for test simulation. Out of print, so try to find an old copy. Not available in bookstores. Explanatory study guide is available as a separate publication (*Underground Step 1 Answers;* see below).

B

Self-Test in the Part I Basic Medical Sciences

— Test/630 q

NBME

NBME, 1989, 91 pages, out of print

Outdated question format, although the material is relevant. Ninety items are given per discipline. Letter answers are given with no explanations. No clinical vignettes. Limited utility for test simulation. Some repeated questions from "Retired Items." Out of print, so try to find an old copy. Explanatory study guide is available as a separate publication (*Underground Step 1 Answers;* see below).

B

USMLE Success

$20.00 How-to/360 q

Zaslau

FMSG, 1999, 150 pages, ISBN 1886468303

Broad overview of all three Steps. Has a useful "what to study" section with a list of classic slides, x-rays, and gross specimens that have appeared on previous USMLE exams; however, no pictures or diagrams. Mnemonic section is helpful. Includes a 180-question mock Step 1 exam with explanations. Appropriate for the IMG student preparing to take all three Step exams in a short time period.

B-

A&LERT USMLE Step 1 Deluxe

$89.95 Software/3600 q

Appleton & Lange

Appleton & Lange, 1998, ISBN 0838503497

Windows/Mac-based testing software. Includes all the same features of the Standard Edition plus an additional question bank of 1200 questions and answers for each of the basic science topics. Some answers are incomplete or inaccurate. Equal emphasis on all subjects.

B– **Basic Science Question Bank** **$19.00** Test/500 q

Zaslau

FMSG, 1997, 141 pages, ISBN 1886468176

Three sections designed to simulate the three-hour time periods of the exam. Includes letter answers with explanations and some clinical vignettes. Questions adequately reflect the clinical slant of the USMLE. Includes 90 poor photo quality pictures and diagrams. Repeated questions from other books in the series. Limited student feedback.

B– **Exam Master Step 1 & 2** **$99.00** Software/8000 q

Exam Master

Exam Master Corporation

Windows/Mac-based testing software with access up to 8000 Step 1 questions. Questions are relatively simple. Ability to hide multiple-choice options. New version eliminates K-type, nonclinical questions and provides compatibility with Windows 98.

B– **MEPC USMLE Step 1 Review** **$32.95** Test/1200 q

Fayemi

Appleton & Lange, 1996, 455 pages, ISBN 0838562698

Features questions with explanatory answers. Offers mixed-quality questions with some incomplete or inaccurate explanations. Includes clinical vignettes with multiple questions per vignette, which is unlike the format of the 1998 USMLE.

B– **Rypin's Basic Sciences Review, Vol. I** **$34.95** Review/1000+ q

Frohlich

Lippincott Williams & Wilkins, 1997, 848 pages, ISBN 0397514883

Multitopic textbook with few figures and tables. A good general reference, but should be used with other subject-specific sources. Well priced for the number of pages and questions. Requires extensive time commitment.

B– **Rypin's Questions and Answers for Basic Science Review** **$29.95** Test/1640 q

Frohlich

Lippincott Williams & Wilkins, 1997, 256 pages, ISBN 0397515456

Questions with detailed answers to supplement *Rypin's Basic Sciences Review*. Decent overall question-based review of all subjects. Requires time commitment. Limited and mixed reviews.

B–

Step 1 Success | $26.00 | Test/720 q

Zaslau

FMSG, 1999, 198 pages, ISBN 1886468079

Full-length practice examination with four 180-question booklets with explanations (same as 1998 USMLE). Features many clinically focused questions similar to USMLE format. Offers small number of black-and-white photographs of moderate quality but no color pictures. Limited student feedback. Also available on CD-ROM.

B–

"Virtual Reality" Step 1 | $19.00 | Test/370 q

Zaslau

FMSG, 1998, 136 pages, ISBN 1886468230

Includes two "virtual" practice tests. Simple, straightforward questions; few images but in poor quality black-and-white photocopy. Explanations of both correct and incorrect answers.

B–

"Virtual Reality" Step 1 Update 1998 | $10.00 | Test/130 q

Zaslau

FMSG, 1998, 69 pages, ISBN 1886468265

Includes updated questions following administration of the 1997 USMLE.

C+

A&LERT USMLE Step 1 | $59.95 | Software/2500 q

Appleton & Lange

Appleton & Lange, 1998, ISBN 0838584462

Windows/Mac-based testing software. Includes six simulated USMLE-type tests featuring 2500 questions with explanations. Friendly interface does not accurately reflect CBT format. Some answers are incomplete or inaccurate. Also provides timing, scoring, searching, note-taking, and bookmarking functions. Equal emphasis on all subjects.

Basic Science Bank—"NBME" | $50.00 | Test/3500 q

FMSG

FMSG, 1991, 372 pages

Advertised as questions "remembered" from past NBME exams. Variable-quality questions with letter answers only. Poor photo quality. Contains outdated K-type and C-type (A/B/both/neither) items. Not available in bookstores. Can be ordered at (904) 774-5277; nonrefundable.

Basic Science Review Success

$18.00 Review only

Zaslau

FMSG, 1997, 138 pages, ISBN 1886468184

A very cursory presentation of high-yield facts in all seven basic science topics. However, much more knowledge is required for actual success on the USMLE. No pictures or diagrams. Includes sections on test-taking pointers and a bonus section on the Match, internship, and residency. Limited student feedback.

Clinical Anatomy and Pathophysiology for the Health Professional

$18.95 Review only

Stewart

MedMaster, 1997, 260 pages, ISBN 0940780062

Written for non-MD professionals. Not boards oriented. Simplistic, but may be a good place to start for some students. Good diagrams.

Medical Student's Guide to Top Board Scores: USMLE Steps 1 and 2

$15.95 Review only

Rogers

Lippincott Williams & Wilkins, 1996, 146 pages, ISBN 0316754366

Easy to read, but information is low yield and coverage of topics is spotty. Contains some good mnemonics in basic and clinical sciences, but not necessarily boards-relevant. Incomplete and outdated list of recommended books for boards review.

PASS USMLE Step 1: Practice by Assessing Study Skills

$19.95 How-to/500 q

Schwenker

Lippincott Williams & Wilkins, 1995, 140 pages, ISBN 0316776009

Detailed review of study and testing strategies for standardized exams and medical school. Worth considering if you have study or testing difficulties. Includes diagnostic test.

Study Skills and Test-Taking Strategies for Medical Students

$19.95 How-to only

Oklahoma Notes, Shain

Springer-Verlag, 1995, 204 pages, ISBN 038794396X

Very detailed discussion of study skills for medical school. May be useful for some students seeking a structured approach, but probably not necessary for most medical students.

New Rudman's Questions and Answers on the USMLE — **$49.95** — Test/280 q

Rudman

National Learning Corporation, 1991, 200 pages, ISBN 0837358043

Combines Step 1 and Step 2 questions but with no explanations. Lacks clinical vignettes and references. Some errors. Very expensive for the amount of material. Limited review of anatomy and physiology at the end of the book.

USMLE Step 1 Review: The Study Guide — **$32.95** — Review only

Goldberg

Sage, 1996, 473 pages, ISBN 0803972849

A comprehensive review that often reads like a textbook. Does not organize ideas in a way that is useful for review purposes. No mnemonics, no questions, and very few diagrams or pictures. Requires a large time commitment and is low yield.

NEW BOOKS—COMPREHENSIVE

Step Up: A Systems-Based Review for the USMLE — **$22.95** — Review only

Mehta

Lippincott Williams & Wilkins, 1999, 250 pages, ISBN 068330755X

Comprehensive review text highly dependent on outlines, charts, tables, and diagrams. Appendix includes 40 clinical cases and an alphabetical section on pharmacology.

USMLE Review Book, Step 1 Basic Medical Sciences — **$18.00** — Review

Walling

Maval Publishing, 1999, 239 pages, ISBN 1884083218

Detailed summaries of important information, organized by USMLE content outline. Mostly text, with some tables, photos, diagrams. Requires a time commitment; not for quick review. Not yet reviewed.

N

USMLE Step 1 Simulated Test 1 & 2 — **$18.00 (each)** — Test/180 q (each)

Walling

Maval Publishing, 1999, 87 pages, ISBN 1884083188 & 1884083196

Two 90-question simulated exams in each booklet, covering all the basic science topics. Reasonably clinically oriented but simplistic questions. Good images. Moderately expensive for amount of material. Not yet reviewed.

USMLE Step 1: The Stanford Solutions to the NBME Computer-Based Sample Test Questions — **$18.95** — Answers

Kush

J & S, 1999, 120 pages, ISBN 1893730077

Explanations, with references, for the NBME practice CD-ROM. Not yet reviewed.

ANATOMY

High-Yield Embryology

$15.95 Review only

Dudek

Lippincott Williams & Wilkins, 1996, 50 pages, ISBN 068302714X

Excellent, concise review of embryology for USMLE. Excellent organization with clinical correlations. High-yield list of embryologic origins of tissues. Expensive for amount of material. No index.

High-Yield Gross Anatomy

$15.95 Review only

Dudek

Lippincott Williams & Wilkins, 1997, 144 pages, ISBN 0683182153

Excellent, concise review with clinical correlations. Contains well-labeled, high-yield radiologic images, yet may be useful to supplement with an atlas. No index.

High-Yield Neuroanatomy

$15.95 Review only

Fix

Lippincott Williams & Wilkins, 1999, 128 pages, ISBN 0683307215

Clean, easy-to-read outline format. Straightforward text with excellent diagrams and illustrations. Compare with Goldberg's *Clinical Neuroanatomy Made Ridiculously Simple*. No index.

Underground Clinical Vignettes: Anatomy

$14.95 Review only

Bhushan

S2S Medical, 1998, 100 pages, ISBN 1890061107

Concise clinical cases illustrating approximately 100 frequently tested diseases with an anatomic basis. Cardinal signs, symptoms, and buzzwords are highlighted. Use as a supplement to other sources of review.

Anatomy: Review for USMLE Step 1

$25.00 Test/560 q

Johnson

J & S, 1998, 275 pages, ISBN 1888308036

Easy reading. Clinical case-based questions with detailed explanations. Good superficial overview of cell biology, histology, gross anatomy, embryology, and neuroanatomy. Discusses clinically relevant anatomic science with good explanations, illustrations, and pictures; also covers many clinically relevant genetic diseases. Some key topics are not covered. Includes good photomicrographs, cross-sectional imaging-based questions, and patient photos.

Clinical Anatomy Made Ridiculously Simple

$19.95 Review only

Goldberg

MedMaster, 1991, 175 pages, ISBN 094078002X

Easy reading, simple diagrams, lots of mnemonics and amusing associations. Incomplete. This style has variable appeal to students, so browse before buying. Good coverage of selected topics. Best if used during the course.

Clinical Neuroanatomy Made Ridiculously Simple

$12.95 Review/Few q

Goldberg

MedMaster, 1997, 87 pages, ISBN 0940780003

Easy to read, memorable, and simplified, with clever hand-drawn diagrams. Very quick, high-yield review of clinical neuroanatomy. Good emphasis on clinically relevant pathways, cranial nerves, and neurologic diseases. Spotty coverage of some key boards topics. No CT or MRI images. Compare to Fix's *High-Yield Neuroanatomy*.

Liebman's Neuroanatomy Made Easy & Understandable

$34.00 Review/Few q

Gertz

Aspen, 1996, 176 pages, ISBN 0834207303

Easy to read. Contains excellent diagrams. A fast, straightforward, high-yield review. Some humor and interesting facts to help the student remember pathways. Expensive. Incomplete, but more thorough than Goldberg's *Clinical Neuroanatomy Made Ridiculously Simple*.

MEPC Anatomy

$19.95 Test/700 q

Wilson

Appleton & Lange, 1995, 251 pages, ISBN 0838562183

Many clinical vignettes followed by questions. Includes gross anatomy, neuroanatomy, cell biology, and embryology. Worth considering as an alternative to J&S *Anatomy*. Good value. Mixed-quality questions with concise answers. More detailed than required for USMLE.

B

Ace Anatomy

$30.00 Review/300+ q

Moore

Mosby-Year Book, 1996, 400 pages, ISBN 0815169051 (Windows), ISBN 0815186711 (Mac)

Thorough coverage of gross anatomy only. Good but non-boards-style questions with explanations. Helpful summary tables. Detailed coverage of a low-yield topic. More appropriate for coursework. No radiographs. Test software included with text. Money-back guarantee with proof of failure.

B **Ace Neuroscience** **$32.00** Review/235 q

Castro

Mosby-Year Book, 1996, 464 pages, ISBN 0815114796 (Windows), ISBN 081511480X (Mac)

Outline format with some good photomicrographs. Covers neuroanatomy, neurophysiology, and neuropathology. Separate chapters on clinical correlations are very high-yield. Limited student feedback. Test software included with text. Money-back guarantee if you fail. For the motivated student.

B **BRS Embryology** **$25.95** Review/500 q

Dudek

Lippincott Williams & Wilkins, 1998, 250 pages, ISBN 0683302728

Outline-based review of embryology that is typical for books in this series. Good review of important embryology, but too detailed. Good discussion of congenital malformations at the end of each chapter. The comprehensive exam at the end of the book is the most high-yield part of the book.

B **BRS Neuroanatomy** **$24.95** Review/500 q

Fix

Lippincott Williams & Wilkins, 1995, 416 pages, ISBN 0683032496

Updated text. Covers anatomy and embryology of the nervous system. Complete but lengthy; requires a time commitment. Compare with *High-Yield Neuroanatomy* by the same author.

B **Cell Biology: Review for New National Boards** **$25.00** Review/524 q

Adelman

J&S, 1995, 203 pages, ISBN 0963287389

Question-based review format like other J&S books. Covers classic topics in cell biology. Contains some high-quality micrographs. Recycles some questions and illustrations from J&S *Anatomy*. Not as useful as other books in series.

B **Clinical Neuroanatomy: A Review with Questions and Explanations** **$29.95** Review/440 q

Snell

Lippincott Williams & Wilkins, 1997, 336 pages, ISBN 0316803154

Comprehensive review book requiring time commitment. Frequent clinical correlations. Many clear diagrams. Questions cover a lot of ground, but format is outdated.

B **High-Yield Histology** $15.95 Review only

Dudek

Lippincott Williams & Wilkins, 1997, 110 pages, ISBN 0683027204

Quick and easy review of relatively low-yield subject. Tables with some high-yield information. Good pictures. Appendix contains classic EMs. New edition due in 2000.

B **PreTest Anatomy** $18.95 Test/500 q

April

McGraw-Hill, 1999, 260 pages, ISBN 0070526834

Difficult questions with detailed answers. Some illustrations. Requires extensive time commitment. Includes high-yield section that highlights clinically relevant relationships and lessons.

B **Review Questions for Neuroanatomy** $19.95 Test/965 q

Mosenthal

Parthenon, 1996, 200 pages, ISBN 1850706530

Good, non-boards-style questions with explanations. Some diagrams with quesions on lesions scattered throughout. Includes embryology of nervous system. Best of series. Some clinical vignettes.

B **Wheater's Functional Histology** $54.95 Review only

Burkitt

Churchill-Livingstone, 1993, 407 pages, ISBN 0443046913

Color atlas with pictures of normal histology and accompanying text. Useful as a text for course; skim through photomicrographs for USMLE review.

B- **BRS Gross Anatomy** $25.95 Review/500 q

Chung

Lippincott Williams & Wilkins, 1995, 400 pages, ISBN 068301563X

Detailed, lengthy text in outline format with illustrations and tables. Perhaps better for coursework than quick boards review. Good clinical correlation section. New edition due in 2000.

B- **Clinical Anatomy: An Illustrated Review with Questions and Explanations** $27.95 Review/500+ q

Snell

Lippincott Williams & Wilkins, 1996, 308 pages, ISBN 0316803073

Text is a well-organized summary of Snell's major book. Great diagrams and tables. Questions incorporate radiographs, CT scans, and MRIs. Does not cover neuroanatomy or embryology. Neither text nor questions are as clinical as the title implies. Only some of the answers have explanations, most of which are too short.

Embryology: Review for New National Boards

$25.00 Test/569 q

Gasser

J&S, 1997, 221 pages, ISBN 188830801X

Typical format for this series. Occasional vignettes somewhat reflect the clinical slant of the USMLE. The question format does not reflect the format of the USMLE. However, the pictures are high quality. Too long for boards review for such a low-yield topic. Limited student feedback.

Oklahoma Notes Anatomy

$17.95 Review/70 q

Papka

Springer-Verlag, 1995, 231 pages, ISBN 0387943951

Covers embryology, gross anatomy, neuroanatomy, and histology. Broad coverage, but dense text is somewhat difficult to read. Very few illustrations. The student is "encouraged to thoughtfully engage the narrative . . . and incorporate mental images of structures."

Oklahoma Notes Neuropathology and Basic Neuroscience

$18.95 Review/101 q

Brumback

Springer-Verlag, 1996, 289 pages, ISBN 0387946357

Utilizes organ system approach by integrating CNS anatomy, pathology, physiology, and some pharmacology. Easy to read. High-quality line drawings. Use either with organ system review or as a supplement to a subject review. Limited student feedback.

PreTest Neuroscience

$17.95 Test/509 q

Siegel

McGraw-Hill, 1999, 273 pages, ISBN 0070526907

Detailed questions and answers. Includes photographs of CT/MRIs and drawings of brain sections. Useful after studying from other sources. For the motivated student. Picky questions. High-yield section in back summarizes pathways and function. Few helpful diagrams.

Ace Histology and Cell Biology

$29.95 Review/286 q

Ace, Burns

Mosby-Year Book, 1996, 250 pages, ISBN 0815113382 (Windows), ISBN 0815113358 (Mac)

Good diagrams of tissues, but no actual photomicrographs. Packaged with questions on a floppy disk. Outline format with dense text. Icons are more distracting than helpful. Non-boards-style review questions are given at the end of each chapter with detailed explanations. Too much detail in some areas. Limited feedback on software. Money-back guarantee if you fail.

BRS Cell Biology & Histology

$25.95 Review/500 q

Gartner

Lippincott Williams & Wilkins, 1997, 377 pages, ISBN 0583361039

Nice format with mixed-quality reproductions, but too detailed. Nineteen chapters with detailed answers. For the motivated student.

Histology QuizBank Vols. 1 & 2

$49.95 (each) Software/800+ q

Downing

MedTech Publishing, 1995, ISBN 1573492302 & 1573492361 (Mac), ISBN 1573492337 & 1573492396 (Windows)

Database of boards-style questions arranged by subject area. Explanations on demand. Questions cross-referenced to Junqueira's *Histology Text Stack* (sold separately). Expensive for limited-yield topic; discounts available by reaching the publisher directly (800 260 2600 or www.medtech.com).

IMS Medical Neuroscience

$25.95 Review/150 q

Prichard

Fence Creek, 1998, 448 pages, ISBN 1889325295

Similar to others in the series. Readable but very lengthy and detailed text. Many excellent diagrams. Simple questions with good explanations.

Langman's Medical Embryology

$36.00 Review only

Sadler

Lippincott Williams & Wilkins, 1995, 460 pages, ISBN 068307489X

Long text. Good for reference, but too detailed for boards review. Concise summary pages. Good pictures with useful clinical correlations.

Molecular Biology QuizBank

$59.00 Software/500+ q

Case Western Reserve

Keyboard Publishing, 1995, ISBN 1573493422 (Mac), ISBN 1573493430 (Windows)

Software database of boards-style questions. Expensive for limited-yield topic.

NMS Histology

$27.00 Review/312 q

Henrickson

Lippincott Williams & Wilkins, 1997, 425 pages, ISBN 0683062255

Good black-and-white images. No color plates. Outline format is easy to read for main points; however, too dense for boards review. Best used with course.

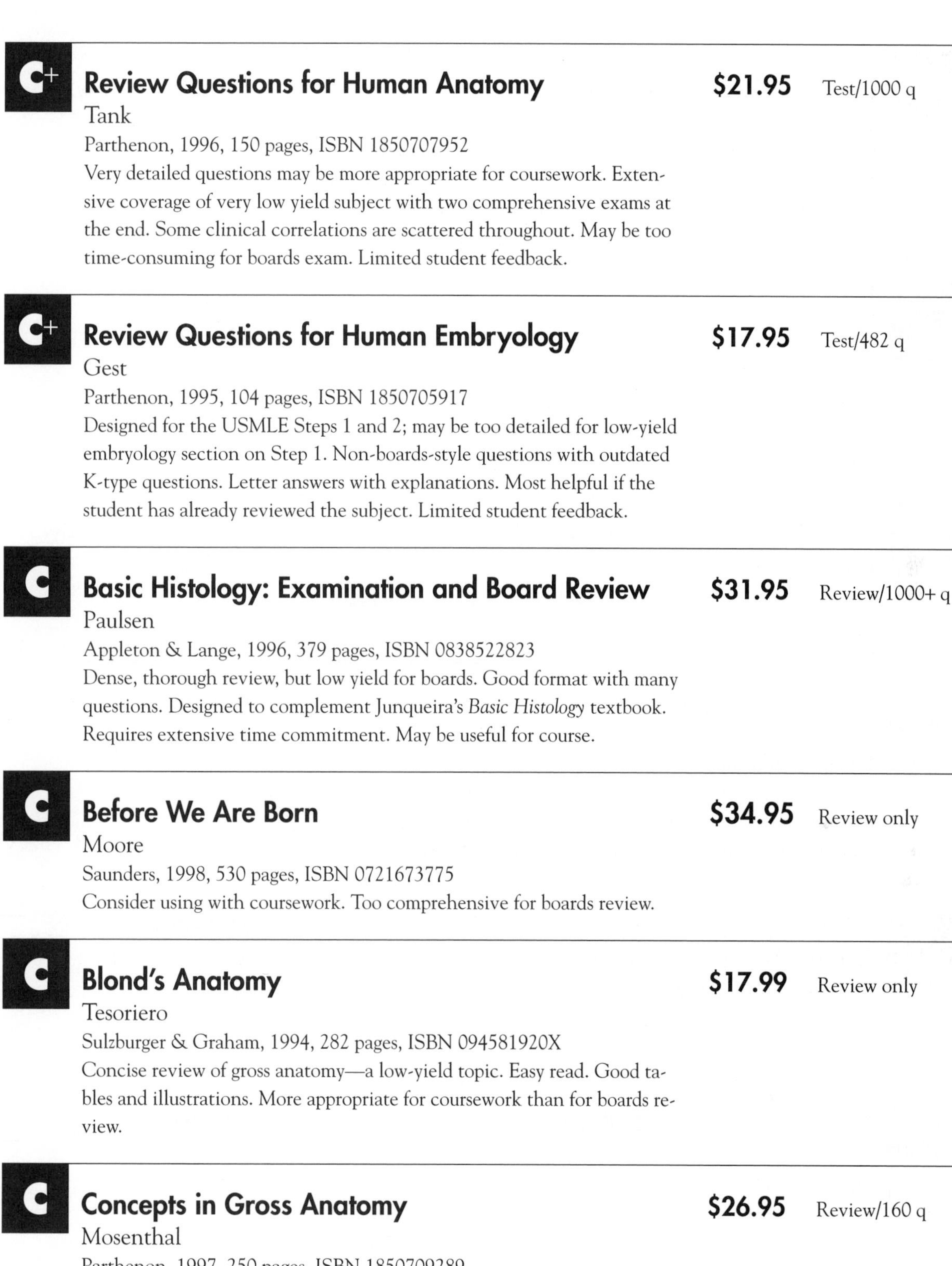

C+

Review Questions for Human Anatomy

$21.95 Test/1000 q

Tank

Parthenon, 1996, 150 pages, ISBN 1850707952

Very detailed questions may be more appropriate for coursework. Extensive coverage of very low yield subject with two comprehensive exams at the end. Some clinical correlations are scattered throughout. May be too time-consuming for boards exam. Limited student feedback.

C+

Review Questions for Human Embryology

$17.95 Test/482 q

Gest

Parthenon, 1995, 104 pages, ISBN 1850705917

Designed for the USMLE Steps 1 and 2; may be too detailed for low-yield embryology section on Step 1. Non-boards-style questions with outdated K-type questions. Letter answers with explanations. Most helpful if the student has already reviewed the subject. Limited student feedback.

C

Basic Histology: Examination and Board Review

$31.95 Review/1000+ q

Paulsen

Appleton & Lange, 1996, 379 pages, ISBN 0838522823

Dense, thorough review, but low yield for boards. Good format with many questions. Designed to complement Junqueira's *Basic Histology* textbook. Requires extensive time commitment. May be useful for course.

C

Before We Are Born

$34.95 Review only

Moore

Saunders, 1998, 530 pages, ISBN 0721673775

Consider using with coursework. Too comprehensive for boards review.

C

Blond's Anatomy

$17.99 Review only

Tesoriero

Sulzburger & Graham, 1994, 282 pages, ISBN 094581920X

Concise review of gross anatomy—a low-yield topic. Easy read. Good tables and illustrations. More appropriate for coursework than for boards review.

C

Concepts in Gross Anatomy

$26.95 Review/160 q

Mosenthal

Parthenon, 1997, 250 pages, ISBN 1850709289

Long, detailed narrative format with review questions may be more appropriate for coursework. In-depth coverage of a relatively low-yield subject. Clinical correlations hidden in dense text. Some line drawings and fill-in-the-blank drawings are of questionable value for review. Limited student feedback.

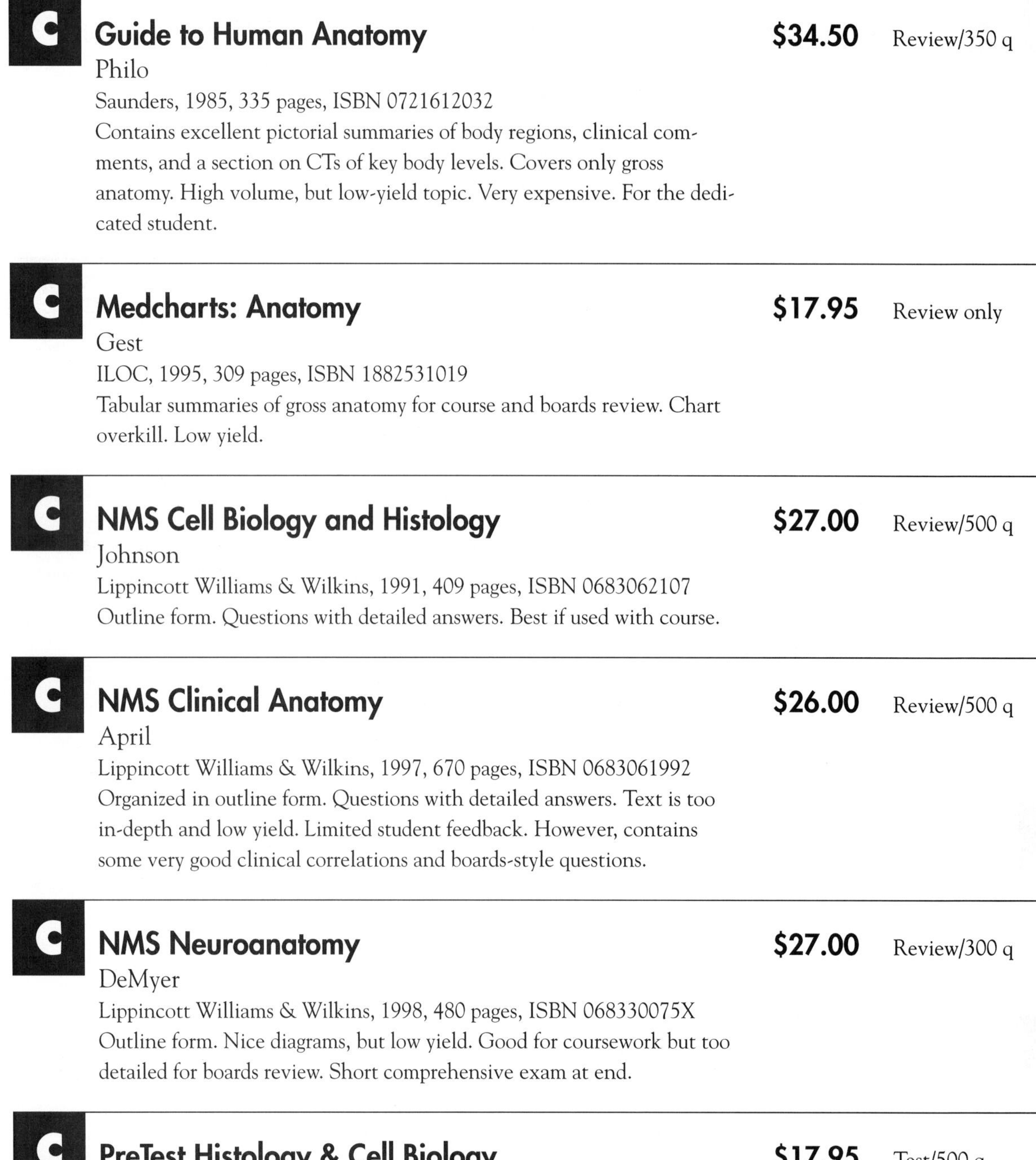

C **Guide to Human Anatomy** **$34.50** Review/350 q

Philo

Saunders, 1985, 335 pages, ISBN 0721612032

Contains excellent pictorial summaries of body regions, clinical comments, and a section on CTs of key body levels. Covers only gross anatomy. High volume, but low-yield topic. Very expensive. For the dedicated student.

C **Medcharts: Anatomy** **$17.95** Review only

Gest

ILOC, 1995, 309 pages, ISBN 1882531019

Tabular summaries of gross anatomy for course and boards review. Chart overkill. Low yield.

C **NMS Cell Biology and Histology** **$27.00** Review/500 q

Johnson

Lippincott Williams & Wilkins, 1991, 409 pages, ISBN 0683062107

Outline form. Questions with detailed answers. Best if used with course.

C **NMS Clinical Anatomy** **$26.00** Review/500 q

April

Lippincott Williams & Wilkins, 1997, 670 pages, ISBN 0683061992

Organized in outline form. Questions with detailed answers. Text is too in-depth and low yield. Limited student feedback. However, contains some very good clinical correlations and boards-style questions.

C **NMS Neuroanatomy** **$27.00** Review/300 q

DeMyer

Lippincott Williams & Wilkins, 1998, 480 pages, ISBN 068330075X

Outline form. Nice diagrams, but low yield. Good for coursework but too detailed for boards review. Short comprehensive exam at end.

C **PreTest Histology & Cell Biology** **$17.95** Test/500 q

Klein

McGraw-Hill, 1999, 351 pages, ISBN 00706877

Similar to others in the PreTest series. Some difficult questions with explanations that are often too detailed. Requires extensive time commitment. High-yield section at end discusses select concepts.

Review of Gross Anatomy — $39.95 — Review/500+ q

Pansky

McGraw-Hill, 1996, 688 pages, ISBN 0071054464

Outline format with pictures on opposite page. New color illustrations and imaging correlations. Very detailed review of only gross anatomy, so low overall yield. Contains good illustrations and a few tables. For the dedicated student.

Review Questions: Gross Anatomy and Embryology — $21.95 — Test/2500+ q

Gest

Parthenon, 1993, 401 pages, ISBN 1850705038

Contains outdated K-type questions and has no matching questions or clinical vignettes. Huge collection of questions covers only gross anatomy and embryology.

C

Rypins' Intensive Reviews: Anatomical Sciences — $19.95 — Review/219 q

Pratt

Lippincott Williams & Wilkins, 1999, 330 pages, ISBN 0397515529

Friendly text but quite lengthy for boards review purposes. Relatively few pictures or clinical tie-ins. Covers gross anatomy, embryology, histology, and neuroanatomy. One comprehensive exam at the end, with brief explanations. Focused review possible with use of "must-know topics" at the end as a check-list.

C–

Appleton & Lange's Review of Anatomy — $32.95 — Test/1400+ q

Montgomery

Appleton & Lange, 1995, 340 pages, ISBN 0838502466

High volume of questions with brief explanations, no text, and few diagrams. Limited student feedback.

C–

Essentials of Human Histology — $29.95 — Review/100 q

Krause

Lippincott Williams & Wilkins, 1996, 452 pages, ISBN 0316503363

Review text with some boards-style questions and letter answers. May be more appropriate as a course text than as a review book. Limited student feedback.

C–

Gross Anatomy: A Review with Questions and Explanations — $28.95 — Review/430+ q

Snell

Lippincott Williams & Wilkins, 1990, 345 pages, ISBN 0316801976

Dense but thorough; requires time commitment. Good diagrams. Some questions are outdated. Low-yield with few clinical correlations.

Neuroanatomy: A Review with Questions and Explanations

$29.95 Review/400+ q

Snell

Lippincott Williams & Wilkins, 1992, 298 pages, ISBN 0316802468

Reasonably easy to read; contains some clinical correlations. Book is too long in relation to the small portion of the exam devoted to neuroanatomy.

NEW BOOKS—ANATOMY

Anatomy Recall

$26.00 Review only

Blackbourne

Lippincott Williams & Wilkins, 2000, 500 pages, ISBN 0683304364

Not yet reviewed.

Digging Up the Bones: Anatomy

$18.95 Review only

Linardakis

McGraw-Hill, 2000, 117 pages, ISBN 0070384150

Hits the high points of gross anatomy. Not very in depth. Clear diagrams. Clinical tie-ins throughout but no vignettes. Not yet reviewed.

Digging Up the Bones: Neuroscience

$18.95 Review only

Linardakis

McGraw-Hill, 2000, 117 pages, ISBN 0070383693

Due in 2000. Not yet reviewed.

IMS Cell Structure and Function

$22.95 Review

Davis

Fence Creek, 1998, ISBN 1889325252

Text to be written.

N

Study Guide to Accompany: The Human Brain

$21.95 Review

Nolte

Mosby, 1999, 189 pages, ISBN 0815189931

Designed as a companion to Nolte's text, *The Human Brain*, this guide covers the main topics in concise language. Includes neuroembryology. Well-illustrated. Diagrams and clinically oriented study questions at the end of each chapter, as well as comprehensive quiz in the back of the book. Not yet reviewed.

High-Yield Behavioral Science — $15.95 — Review only

Fadem

Lippincott Williams & Wilkins, 1996, 115 pages, ISBN 0683029401

Clear, concise, quick review of behavioral science. Logical presentation with crammable charts, graphs, and tables. Short but adequate statistics chapter. No index.

B+

BRS Behavioral Science Review — $25.95 — Review/500 q

Fadem

Lippincott Williams & Wilkins, 1999, 352 pages, ISBN 0683306812

Easy-to-read outline format with boldfacing of key terms. Good, detailed coverage of high-yield topics. Lengthy; gives more information than may be needed for USMLE. Great tables and charts. Short but complete statistics chapter. Good review questions.

B+

Underground Clinical Vignettes: Behavioral Science — $14.95 — Review only

Bhushan

S2S Medical, 1998, 100 pages, ISBN 1890061115

Concise clinical cases illustrating commonly tested diseases in behavioral science. Cardinal signs, symptoms, and buzzwords are highlighted. Use as a supplement to other sources of review. Some cases lack details.

B+

USMLE Behavioral Science Made Ridiculously Simple — $16.95 — Review only

Sierles

MedMaster, 1998, 171 pages, ISBN 0940780348

Easy reading; reasonable yield for the amount of text. Includes medical sociology and strong on psychopathology with illustrative examples. No biostatistics. At times too much detail on low-yield topics.

B

A & L's Review of Epidemiology and Biostatistics — $24.95 — Review/100 q

Hanrahan

Appleton & Lange, 1994, 109 pages, ISBN 083850244X

Excellent, concise overview of epidemiology with complete explanations and diagrams. Does not include other behavioral science subtopics. Expensive and limited yield. Good for the motivated student.

B

Ace Behavioral Science — $30.00 — Review/217+ q

Cody

Mosby-Year Book, 1996, 200 pages, ISBN 0815118449 (Windows), ISBN 0815114877 (Mac)

Concise content review with boards-style questions and explanations. Includes floppy disk of questions. Thorough, easy-to-read format with numerous tables. Icons may be more distracting than helpful. No biostatistics. Test software is included with text. Money-back guarantee if you fail.

B	**Behavioral Science: Review for New National Boards** Frank J&S, 1998, 248 pages, ISBN 1888308001 Answers given in text format with additional information to help teach and expand on concepts.	**$25.00**	Test/500+ q
B	**Digging up the Bones: Biostatistics and Epidemiology** Linardakis McGraw-Hill, 1998, 111 pages, ISBN 0070382220 A fairly concise review with clinical applications. Most effective as a quick refresher. Heavy on low-yield equations. No self-testing opportunities.	**$18.95**	Review
B	**High-Yield Biostatistics** Glaser Lippincott Williams & Wilkins, 1995, 96 pages, ISBN 0683035665 Well-written book with extensive coverage of biostatistics. Good review exercises and tables. Still, low-yield topic. For the motivated student; not for last-minute cramming. Suitable for a course.	**$15.95**	Review only
B	**NMS Behavioral Sciences in Psychiatry** Wiener Lippincott Williams & Wilkins, 1995, 375 pages, ISBN 0683062034 Detailed multidisciplinary outline. Neatly organized. Incorporates DSM-IV. Probably more detailed than necessary. For the motivated student starting early, or to be used as a reference. Biostatistics chapter is inadequate. Incomplete coverage of some boards topics.	**$27.00**	Review/300 q
B−	**Digging Up the Bones: Behavioral Sciences** Linardakis McGraw-Hill, 1998, 88 pages, ISBN 0070382182 Concise narrative review of behavioral sciences; disorganized format covers some high-yield topics. Choppy style.	**$18.95**	Review only
B−	**Oklahoma Notes Behavioral Sciences** Krug Springer-Verlag, 1995, 311 pages, ISBN 0387943935 Typewritten; easy reading. Outline format. Questions of mixed quality. Good tables. For the motivated student.	**$19.95**	Review/169 q

B– **PreTest Behavioral Science** **$17.95** Test/500 q

Pattishall

McGraw-Hill, 1999, 321 pages, ISBN 0070526893

Detailed answers cross-referenced with other resources. Good test questions. Requires time commitment. Brief high-yield section in back.

C **A Review of Biostatistics** **$25.00** Review only

Leaverton

Lippincott Williams & Wilkins, 1995, 144 pages, ISBN 0316518832

Review of biostatistics that does not focus on high-yield topics for the USMLE. Last two chapters cover material relevant to USMLE review. More appropriate for coursework than for USMLE review.

C **NMS Clinical Epidemiology and Biostatistics** **$27.00** Review/300 q

Knapp

Lippincott Williams & Wilkins, 1992, 435 pages, ISBN 0683062069

Overkill for a limited-yield topic.

C **STARS Epidemiology, Biostatistics and Preventive Medicine Review** **$20.95** Review/385 q

Katz

Saunders, 1997, 241 pages, ISBN 0721640842

Detailed and dense text that is excessive for USMLE Step 1 review. May be useful for an in-depth biostatistics course.

C– **Medical Biostatistics and Epidemiology: Examination and Board Review** **$32.95** Review/100+ q

Essex-Sorlie

Appleton & Lange, 1995, 359 pages, ISBN 0838562191

Too in-depth for USMLE biostatistics. Requires time commitment. Consider using with a course. Sample questions may not be representative of the USMLE Step 1.

NEW BOOKS—BEHAVIORAL SCIENCE

N **Rypins' Intensive Reviews: Behavioral Science** **$19.95** Review/158 q

Tucker

Lippincott Williams & Wilkins, 1996, 197 pages, ISBN 0397515537

Text-heavy, with few tables or memory tools. Only rudimentary statistics. Comprehensive test in the back. "Must Know Topics" section may focus studying.

Underground Clinical Vignettes: Biochemistry — $14.95 — Review only

Bhushan

S2S Medical, 1999, 101 pages, ISBN 1890061344

Concise clinical cases illustrating approximately 100 frequently tested diseases with a biochemical basis. Cardinal signs, symptoms, and buzzwords are highlighted. Useful supplement to other sources of review.

High Yield Cell & Molecular Biology — $15.95 — Review only

Dudek

Lippincott Williams & Wilkins, 1999, 110 pages, ISBN 06833033597

Cellular and molecular biology presented in outline format, with good diagrams and clinical correlations. Brief but complete. Includes description of laboratory techniques and genetic disorders. No questions or vignettes.

Lippincott's Illustrated Reviews: Biochemistry — $29.95 — Review/250+ q

Champe

Lippincott Williams & Wilkins, 1994, 443 pages, ISBN 0397510918

Excellent book, but requires time commitment, so an early start is necessary. Best used while taking the course. Excellent diagrams. Emphasizes "big picture" concepts. Good clinical correlations. Comprehensive review of biochemistry, including low-yield topics. Skim high-yield diagrams to maximize USMLE review.

BRS Biochemistry — $25.95 — Review/500 q

Marks

Lippincott Williams & Wilkins, 1998, 350 pages, ISBN 0683304917

Easy-to-read outline with very good boldfaced chapter summaries. Very thorough; at times too detailed. Mixed-quality diagrams. High-yield clinical correlations are given at the end of each chapter. Questions with short answers.

High Yield Biochemistry — $15.95 — Review only

Wilcox

Lippincott Williams & Wilkins, 1999, 106 pages, ISBN 0683304593

Concise and crammable. Outline format with good clinical correlations at end of each chapter. Lots of diagrams and tables. Good as a study supplement.

B+

IMS Metabolism

$25.95 Review/170+ q

Coffee

Fence Creek, 1998, 409 pages, ISBN 18893325260

Detailed coverage of general metabolic functions. Good diagrams, tables, and clinical correlations. Most chapters begin with a relevant clinical case and end with its resolution. Review questions after every chapter. Very readable. Compare with *Lippincott's Illustrated Reviews: Biochemistry*.

B

Ace Biochemistry

$29.95 Review/326 q

Pelley

Mosby-Year Book, 1997, 371 pages, ISBN 0815186525 (Windows), ISBN 0815186681 (Mac)

Concise content review with good clinical correlations. Outdated test-taking tips. Easy-to-read format. Test software is included with text. Money-back guarantee if you fail. Limited student feedback.

B

Biochemistry: An Illustrated Review with Questions and Explanations

$29.95 Review/220+ q

Friedman

Lippincott Williams & Wilkins, 1995, 240 pages, ISBN 0316294284

Good-quality, concise text review. Metabolism section is well illustrated. Molecular biochemistry section fails to emphasize important concepts and has few illustrations. Good coverage of vitamin deficiencies and genetic disorders. Too few pathways; too many structures. Questions favor basic biochemistry over clinical correlation. Gives letter answers with occasional short explanations. No vignettes.

B

Biochemistry Illustrated

$38.95 Review only

Campbell

Churchill-Livingstone, 1994, 304 pages, ISBN 0443045739

Excellent diagrams with explanations but no questions. Good for students who prefer learning by diagrams. Readable. Expensive. Requires time commitment.

B

Biochemistry: Review for New National Boards

$25.00 Test/505 q

Kumar

J & S, 1993, 211 pages, ISBN 0963287311

Quick question-based review of biochemistry. Includes clinical vignettes and extended matching questions; few diagrams. Use in conjunction with other resources.

B Clinical Biochemistry Made Ridiculously Simple

$23.95 Review only

Goldberg

MedMaster, 1999, 95 pages, ISBN 0940780305

Conceptual approach to clinical biochemistry, with humor. Casual style does not appeal to all students. Mnemonics tend to be somewhat complicated. Good overview and integration for all metabolic pathways. Includes a 23-page clinical review that is very high yield and crammable. Also contains a unique foldout "road map" of metabolism. For students with firm biochemistry background.

B Molecular Biology QuizBank

$49.95 Software/500+ q

MedTech, 1995, ISBN 1573493422 (Mac); ISBN 1573493430 (Win)

Many good questions with clear explanations. Expensive for student purchase; discount available by contacting publishers directly (1 800 260-2600 or www.medtech.com). Limited student feedback.

B PreTest Biochemistry

$18.95 Test/500 q

Chlapowski

McGraw-Hill, 1999, 273 pages, ISBN 0070526842

Difficult questions with detailed, referenced explanations. Best for the motivated student who uses this together with a review book. Contains some questions on biochemical disorders but no clinical vignettes. Six pages of high-yield facts focusing on genetically based disease.

B STARS Biochemistry Review

$20.95 Review/600 q

Roskoski

Saunders, 1996, 242 pages, ISBN 0721651755

Content review in dense outline format with small type. Chapters are short and include only relevant pathways. Good for students who prefer outline-based review. Parallels a core text by the same authors. Comprehensive exam at end of book has some questions with a clinical slant.

B- Biochemistry: Examination and Board Review

$32.95 Review/500+ q

Balcavage

Appleton & Lange, 1995, 433 pages, ISBN 0838506615

Comprehensive review of biochemistry. Requires time commitment. Appropriate as a course text. Has some clinical correlations.

B- Digging Up the Bones: Biochemistry

$18.95 Review only

Linardakis

McGraw-Hill, 1998, 115 pages, ISBN 0071159452

Collection of high-yield biochemistry facts. Use for last-minute review or in conjunction with another review book. Some lists are helpful. Few clinical correlations. Limited student feedback.

B−

IMS Medical Molecular Genetics — **$25.95** — Review/150+ q

Hoffee

Fence Creek, 1998, 384 pages, ISBN 1889325287

Detailed coverage of molecular biology and medical genetics. Includes photographs. Easy reading with good explanations and diagrams. Chapters begin and end with clinical cases. Highly clinical but very lengthy for board review; focus on chapter outline and review questions.

MEPC Biochemistry — **$19.95** — Test/700 q

Glick

Appleton & Lange, 1995, 228 pages ISBN 0838557791

Picky questions with brief explanations. Few clinical vignettes.

Oklahoma Notes Biochemistry — **$19.95** — Review/549+ q

Briggs

Springer-Verlag, 1995, 287 pages, ISBN 0387943986

Dense text with many hand-drawn diagrams. Good chapter on medical genetics. Non-clinically oriented questions with brief explanations in margin. Multiple authors; inconsistent style. Easy reading, but not thorough.

Rypins' Intensive Reviews: Biochemistry — **$19.95** — Review/229 q

Vrana

Lippincott Williams & Wilkins, 1999, 283 pages, ISBN 0397515464

Thorough text but difficult to use for quick boards review. Does not emphasize which concepts are most clinically relevant. Questions in the back of the book. "Must Know Topics" listed at the end are non-specific.

Blond's Biochemistry — **$19.99** — Review only

Guttenplan

Sulzburger & Graham, 1994, 269 pages, ISBN 0945819498

Easy reading. Requires moderate time commitment. Some topics are covered only superficially. Lacks clinical correlations. Not boards oriented; may be more appropriate with coursework.

Color Atlas of Biochemistry — **$29.90** — Review only

Koolman

Thieme, 1996, 435 pages, ISBN 0865775842

Excellent four-color diagrams with accompanying explanatory text. Very little clinical information. Not designed for boards review. Limited student feedback.

EBS Essentials of Biochemistry — $32.95 — Review/100 q

Schumm

Lippincott Williams & Wilkins, 1995, 382 pages, ISBN 0316775312

Review text with some boards-style questions and letter answers. May be more appropriate as a course text than as a review book.

NMS Biochemistry — $28.00 — Review/500 q, CD-ROM

Davidson

Lippincott Williams & Wilkins, 1999, 485 pages, ISBN 0683062050

Very long, detailed outline. Questions with detailed answers. Good pathway illustrations, but too much chemical structure detail. Concise review of genetics. Overall, too detailed to use as a review text unless previously used during coursework. For the motivated student.

Basic Concepts in Biochemistry: A Student's Survival Guide — $25.95 — Review only

Gilbert

McGraw-Hill, 1992, 298 pages, ISBN 0070234493

Presents concise summaries of difficult biochemical concepts and principles. Ignores much high-yield material and thus it is not very useful for boards review. Oriented toward undergraduate courses.

NMS Genetics — $27.00 — Review/300 q

Friedman

Lippincott Williams & Wilkins, 1995, 304 pages, ISBN 0683062174

Highly detailed outline format supplemented by numerous charts and diagrams. Low yield. Some chapters are not relevant for boards review. For the highly motivated student.

PreTest Genetics — $18.95 — Test/500 q

Wilson

McGraw-Hill, 1999, 249 pages, ISBN 0070526850

Detailed questions and answers. Questions of mixed quality. Not consistently boards-relevant. New edition includes two pages of high-yield facts at the end.

Clinical Biochemistry

$31.00 Review only

Gaw

Churchill Livingstone, 1999, 175 pages, ISBN 0443061831

Biochemistry and physiology presented in a clinical framework. Visually pleasing. Focuses on adult medicine; skimpy on inherited disorders, genetics, and molecular biochemistry. Case studies throughout but no standard question–answer exercises. May be more wards- than boards-oriented.

N

Human Genetics

$42.95 Review

Korf

Blackwell Science, 1996, 363 pages, ISBN 0865423539

Learning in an almost entirely clinical context; each subject is introduced and discussed around an engaging clinical vignette. Many images, diagrams. Includes description of modern molecular diagnostic techniques. A few review questions at chapter end with brief answers in the back. Excellent study tool, but requires time; not for last-minute review.

Clinical Microbiology Made Ridiculously Simple

$23.95 Review only

Gladwin

MedMaster, 1999, 272 pages, ISBN 0940780321

Very good chart-based review of microbiology. Clever and humorous mnemonics. Best of this series. Text easy to read. Excellent antibiotic review helps for pharmacology as well. "Ridiculous" style does not appeal to everyone. Requires supplemental source for immunology. Excellent if you have limited time or are "burning out."

Medical Microbiology & Immunology: Examination and Board Review

$31.95 Review/692 q

Levinson

Appleton & Lange, 1998, 547 pages, ISBN 0838562876

Clear, concise writing with excellent diagrams and tables. Excellent immunology section. Forty-three-page "Summary of Medically Important Organisms" very crammable. Requires time commitment. Sometimes too detailed and dense. Best if started early with the course. Covers all topics, including low-yield ones. Good practice questions and comprehensive exam, but questions have letter answers only.

Microbiology Companion

$27.95 Review/Cards

Topf

Alert and Oriented, 1997, 253 pages, ISBN 0964012413

Chart format is well organized; spiral binding makes it easy to read and carry. Most relevant to microbiology topics. Ties in relevant drugs. Very little immunology. High-yield flash cards (180) are a plus.

Underground Clinical Vignettes: Microbiology

$14.95 (each) Review only

Bhushan

S2S Medical

Microbiology Vol I: 1999, 109 pages, ISBN 1890061166

Microbiology Vol II: 1999, 105 pages, ISBN 1890061301

Concise clinical cases illustrating approximately 100 frequently tested diseases in microbiology and immunology. Cardinal signs, symptoms, and buzzwords are highlighted. Use as a supplement to other sources of review.

B+

Appleton & Lange's Review of Microbiology and Immunology

$34.95 Test/995 q

Yotis

Appleton & Lange, 1997, 288 pages, ISBN 0838502733

Large number of questions with detailed answers. Well referenced. Inadequate as a primary source, but a very good supplement. For the motivated student.

B+ **Cases in Medical Microbiology and Infectious Disease** **$34.95** Review/200 q

Gilligan

ASM Press, 1997, 336 pages, ISBN 155581106X

Seventy cases are presented and discussed in detail. Cases test pathogenesis and lab diagnosis of organisms, clinical presentations, epidemiology, and treatment. Over one hundred full color images demonstrate laboratory and clinical diagnosis of disease. Excellent for integrating basic and clinical concepts.

B+ **Case Studies in Immunology—A Clinical Companion** **$19.95** Review/100 q

Rosen

Garland, 1996, 134 pages, ISBN 0815321740

Originally designed as a clinical companion to Janeway's *Immunobiology*, this text provides an excellent synopsis of the major disorders of immunity in a clinical vignette format. Integrates basic and clinical science. Wonderful images, illustrations, questions, and discussion.

B+ **Clinical Microbiology Review** **$35.75** Review only

Warinner

Wysteria, 1998, 152 pages, ISBN 0965116212

Concise yet comprehensive review in chart form with some clinical correlations. Each page is devoted to a single organism with ample space for adding notes during class. No immunology. Spatial organization, color coding, and bulleting of facts facilitate review of subject. Great cross-reference section groups organisms by general characteristics. New edition includes color plates of significant microbes. Limited but positive student feedback. Compare with Topf's *Microbiology Companion*.

B+ **STARS Microbiology Review** **$19.95** Review/600 q

Walker

WB Saunders, 1997, 255 pages, ISBN 0721646425

Parallels core text by same authors. Learning objectives are clearly defined. Includes numerous questions throughout as well as 160-question comprehensive exam with answers and detailed discussion. Immunology not included.

B **Ace Microbiology & Immunology** **$30.00** Review/262+ q

Rosenthal

Mosby-Year Book, 1996, 320 pages, ISBN 0815173490 (Windows), ISBN 0815186703 (Mac)

Concise but comprehensive review of microbiology and immunology in outline format. Good diagrams and tables. Icons are designed to help classify information, but overabundance may confuse some students. Additional questions are given on test software included with text. Money-back guarantee if you fail. Limited student feedback.

B

BRS Microbiology & Immunology

$25.95 Review/500 q

Johnson

Lippincott Williams & Wilkins, 1996, 297 pages, ISBN 0683180053

Outline-format, well-organized, organ-based approach. Good questions at the ends of chapters. Too few diagrams. Includes chapters on bacterial genetics and laboratory methods. Immunology section is concise. Compare with Levinson *(Medical Microbiology & Immunology: Examination and Board Review)*.

B

Buzzwords in Microbiology

$19.95 Review only

Hurst

Bryan Edwards, 1997, 155 pages, ISBN 1878576089

Spiral-bound flash cards contain important facts about the most medically relevant bacteria and fungi. Directed toward boards review. Bullet presentation of information affords easy and quick review. Excellent pictures and buzzwords. Useful as a speedy pocket-sized review after you have studied from a more complete text. Does not cover virology, parasitology, or immunology.

B

Concepts in Microbiology, Immunology, and Infectious Disease

$17.95 Review/100+ q

Gupta

Parthenon, 1997, 150 pages, ISBN 1850707979

Brief paragraphs in outline form on each disease cover most of the important points. Good clinical questions at the end of each section. Good section on immunologic disorders. Format may not appeal to all students. No illustrations. Best for the well-prepared student. For quick review. Many answers not sufficiently explained.

B

Digging Up the Bones: Microbiology and Immunology

$17.95 Review/Cards

Linardakis

McGraw-Hill, 1998, 107 pages and flash cards, ISBN 0071159436

Easy to read. Brief collection of phrases and associations. A few tables and simple diagrams. Expensive for the amount of material given. Features detachable flash cards. Limited student feedback.

B

IMS Immunology

$24.95 Review/170 q

Anderson

Fence Creek, 1999, 194 pages, ISBN 1889325341

Integrates clinical cases and questions into each chapter. Answers and explanations provided. Some chapters contain more detail than necessary for boards preparation.

B

Medical MicroCards

$19.95 150 Cards

Orlando

Medfiles, 1996, 150 pages, ISBN 0965537307

Concise flash cards cover bacteriology, virology, mycology, and parasitology. Designed for fast review. No extraneous information. Covers disease characteristics, treatment, prevention, and clinical findings. Mixed reviews. Compare with Topf's *Microbiology Companion*.

B

Microbiology & Immunology: An Illustrated Review with Questions and Explanations

$31.95 Review/450+ q

Hentges

Lippincott Williams & Wilkins, 1995, 304 pages, ISBN 0316357847

Comprehensive review takes time commitment. Revised edition has updated tables and charts. Improved format and organization. Summation chapter at end of book is of limited value. Limited student feedback.

B

Microbiology: Review for New National Boards

$25.00 Test/507 q

Stokes

J & S, 1993, 194 pages, ISBN 096328732X

Easy reading. Covers many high-yield topics and includes case-based questions and extended matching questions. Very good question-and-answer–based review of clinically relevant microbiology and immunology, but lacking somewhat in detailed information. Helpful as a supplement to a review book.

B

Oklahoma Notes Microbiology and Immunology

$19.95 Review/312+ q

Hyde

Springer-Verlag, 1995, 229 pages, ISBN 0387943927

Easy to read, but not adequate as sole study source. Good summary statements are given at end of each chapter. Extended matching questions. Poor typeface and diagrams. Unequal coverage.

B

STARS Microbiology

$31.50 Review

Walker

WB Saunders, 1998, 504 pages, ISBN 0721646417

Pathogens are presented in a consistent outline format—from pathogenicity to treatment. Numerous multi-color tables and illustrations. No questions. Consider using as a course supplement.

B−

Basic Concepts in Immunology

$25.95 Review only

Clancy

McGraw-Hill, 1998, 328 pages, ISBN 0070113718

Review book similar to other Student's Survival Guide series. Not sufficiently high-yield for boards review. However, appropriate for coursework. Limited student feedback.

B− **Blond's Microbiology** | **$19.99** | Review only

Alcamo

Sulzberger & Graham, 1994, 181 pages, ISBN 0945819412

Text review. Spotty coverage of some key topics. Below average for this series.

B− **Essential Immunology Review** | **$21.95** | Test/422 q

Roitt

Blackwell Science, 1995, 319 pages, ISBN 0865424586

Boards-style questions with explanations that also discuss incorrect answers. Required text at some medical schools. Mixed reviews.

B− **Flash Micro** | **$28.00** | 131 Cards

Ting

Stanford Ink

Concise flash cards designed for boards review. Includes 190 pathogens. No immunology. Color coded. Compare with Orlando's *Medical Micro Cards*. Mixed student feedback.

B− **Immunology Quizbank** | **$49.95** | Software/700 q

Roitt

MedTech, 1995, ISBN 157349321X (Mac), ISBN 1573491969 (Windows).

Multiple-choice questions with detailed feedback. Questions are conveniently cross-linked to *Essential Immunology Textstack*. Available for PC and Macintosh. Good learning tool. Discount available by contacting publisher directly (1 800 260 2600 or www.medtech.com).

B− **MEPC Microbiology** | **$19.95** | Test/770 q

Kim

Appleton & Lange, 1995, 257 pages, ISBN 0838563082

Includes clinical vignettes. Good infectious-disease questions. Variable-quality questions. Easy read. Explanations are brief and direct.

B− **Microbiology QuizBanks Vols. 2 & 3** | **$49.95 (each)** | Software/800+ q

Gotts

MedTech, 1995, ISBN 1573490873 & 1573492213 (Mac), ISBN 1573491470 & 1573492248 (Windows)

Computer-based questions with explanations. Helpful to gauge strengths and weaknesses. Questions are electronically referenced to Sherris *Microbiology Text Stack* (sold separately). Expensive. Discount available by contacting publisher.

B–

NMS Immunology
$27.00 Review/300 q

Hyde

Lippincott Williams & Wilkins, 2000, 316 pages, ISBN 068306231X

Outline form. Very detailed. Good figures and explanations of laboratory methods. Lengthy for immunology alone. Requires time commitment.

NMS Microbiology and Infectious Disease
$27.00 Review/500 q

Virella

Lippincott Williams & Wilkins, 1996, 575 pages, ISBN 0683062352

Outline form. Too detailed in some areas. Insufficient immunology; NMS has a separate immunology book. Lacks good explanation of bacterial genetics. Updated material on AIDS. Useful only if previously used as a textbook. Limited student feedback.

PreTest Microbiology
$18.95 Test/500 q

Tilton

McGraw-Hill, 1999, 199 pages, ISBN 0070526885

Mixed-quality questions with detailed, often verbose explanations. Useful for additional question-based review in bacteriology and virology, but not high yield. Includes two pages of high-yield facts.

C+

Microbiology & Immunology Casebook
$19.95 Review/185 q

Barrett

Lippincott Williams & Wilkins, 1995, 272 pages, ISBN 0316081329

Uses case examples to cover major concepts. Cases do not resemble typical boards vignettes. Useful only as a supplement to a review.

C

Immunology Illustrated Outline
$19.95 Review only

Male

Lippincott Williams & Wilkins, 1991, ISBN 0397448252

Pocket-sized booklet that is well organized and concise. Quick to read and review. Not targeted for boards review.

NEW BOOKS—MICROBIOLOGY

N

Basic Immunology
$32.95 Review/150 q

Sharon

Lippincott Williams & Wilkins, 1998, 300 pages, ISBN 0683077295

Well organized text with many figures and tables. Unique images of clinical presentations. Includes section on organ transplantation.

N **BUGCARDS: The Complete Microbiology Review for Class, the Boards, and the Wards** **$26.50** Cards

Levine and Bhalla

BL Publishing, 1998, 154 flash cards, ISBN 0967165504

High quality flash cards (similar to "Pharm Cards") designed for rapid class and USMLE microbiology review. Covers all medically relevant bacteria, viruses, fungi, and parasites. Includes important "buzzwords," mnemonics and clinical vignettes to aid in recall. Unique "disease process cards" summarize all organisms for a particular disease (e.g., UTI or Pneumonia). Helpful for formulation of a differential diagnosis.

N **Clinical Immunology Cases** **$49.95** Software

Chapel

MedTech, 1995, ISBN 157349190x (Mac), 1573491926 (Windows)

89 vignettes outlining a clinical case, with review of treatment and results. Links to Immunology Textstack (sold separately). Not yet reviewed.

N **Diagnostic Picture Tests in Clinical Infectious Disease** **$19.75** Test/178 q

Beeching

Mosby, 1996, 124 pages, ISBN 0723424519

178 infectious disease images (including MRIs, CT, X-ray, and gross) presented with a brief clinical description and questions. Includes answers and index.

N **High-Yield Immunology** **$15.95** Review only

Johnson

Lippincott Williams & Wilkins, 1999, 125 pages, ISBN 068330614

Typical of this series. No index.

N **High-Yield Microbiology and Infectious Disease** **$15.95** Review only

Hawley

Lippincott Williams & Wilkins, ISBN 068330277

Expected in early 2000.

N **IMS Microbial Pathogenesis** **$25.95** Review/150+ q

McClane

Fence Creek, 1999, 350 pages, ISBN 1889325279

Not yet reviewed.

Lippincott's Illustrated Reviews: Microbiology — $32.98 — Review only

Strohl

Lippincott Williams & Wilkins, 2000, 448 pages, ISBN 0397515685

Features a comprehensive, highly illustrated review of microbiology similar in style to Champe's *Lippincott's Illustrated Reviews: Biochemistry*.

Medical Microbiology Made Memorable — $24.95 — Review only

Myint

Churchill Livingstone, 1999, 138 pages, ISBN 0443061351

Presents material in brief two-page summaries. Contains numerous charts, tables, and illustrations. Seven case studies are presented with very brief discussion.

Quick Look Medicine: Immunology — $19.95 — Review/100+ q

Mamula

Fence Creek, 1999, 130 pages, ISBN 1889325384

Not yet reviewed.

Rypin's Intensive Review: Microbiology and Immunology — $19.95 — Review/200 q

Luftig

Lippincott Williams & Wilkins, 1998, 352 pages, ISBN 0397515472

Presentation of microbiology and immunology in detailed format. Includes exams with answers and discussion. Answers are cross-referenced to other sections of the text for convenience.

BRS Pathology

$25.95 Review/500 q

Schneider

Lippincott Williams & Wilkins, 1993, 412 pages, ISBN 0683076086

Excellent, concise review with appropriate content emphasis. Outline-format chapters with boldfacing of key facts. Excellent questions with explanations at the end of each chapter and a comprehensive exam at the end of the book. Well-organized tables and diagrams. Some good black-and-white photographs representative of classic pathology. Correlate with color photographs from an atlas. Short on clinical details for vignette questions. Consistently high student recommendations. Very worthwhile to master this book. Most effective if started early and then reviewed during study period.

Underground Clinical Vignettes: Pathophysiology, Vol. 1

$14.95 Review only

Bhushan

S2S Medical
Pathophysiology, Vol. I: 1999, 102 pages, ISBN 1890061174
Pathophysiology, Vol. II: 102 pages, ISBN 1890061182
Pathophysiology, Vol. III: 109 pages, ISBN 1890061328

Concise clinical cases illustrating approximately 100 frequently tested pathology and physiology concepts. Cardinal signs, symptoms, and buzzwords are highlighted. Use as a supplement to other sources of review.

B+

Colour Atlas of Anatomical Pathology

$55.00 Review only

Cooke

Churchill-Livingstone, 1995, 261 pages, ISBN 0443050627

Beautifully photographed atlas of gross pathology. Expensive, but definitely worth browsing.

B+

Digging Up the Bones: Pathology

$18.95 Review only

Linardakis

McGraw-Hill, 1997, 130 pages, ISBN 0071159444

Easy reading. Brief collection of phrases and associations often based on answers to assorted multiple-choice questions. Expensive for the amount of material. Features photomicrographs (gross and microscopic).

B+

Pathophysiology of Disease: An Introduction to Clinical Medicine

$34.95 Review/Few q

McPhee

Appleton & Lange, 1997, 521 pages, ISBN 0838576788

Interdisciplinary course text useful for understanding the pathophysiology of clinical symptoms. Excellent integration of basic sciences with mechanisms of disease. Great graphs, diagrams, and tables. Most helpful if used during coursework due to length. Few non-boards-style questions. Clinical emphasis nicely complements *BRS Pathology*.

B+

Pathology: Review for New National Boards

$25.00 Test/509 q

Miller

J & S, 1993, 222 pages, ISBN 0963287338

Question-and-answer–based review of pathology. Includes many case-based questions. Focuses on high-yield topics. Good black-and-white photographs. Some picky questions with incomplete answers. Inadequate as sole source of review. Expensive for number of questions.

B+

PreTest Pathophysiology

$18.95 Test/500 q

Mufson

McGraw-Hill, 1999, 172 pages, ISBN 0070526923

Includes 500 questions and answers with detailed explanations. Questions may be more difficult than the boards. Includes very brief section of "High Yield" student-reviewed pathology topics.

B+

STARS Pathology

$29.95 Review only

Goljan

WB Saunders, 1998, 528 pages, ISBN 0721670237

Well organized, concise and easy-to-read explanations of pathology. Illustrated with diagrams; lacks photos and imaging. Excellent charts and tables. Some students use this text as a primary source.

B+

STARS Pathology Review

$19.95 Review/500+ q

Goljan

WB Saunders, 1998, 352 pages, ISBN 0721670245

Companion book to *STARS Pathology*. It uses a concise outline to summarize key concepts. Includes chapter questions with answers and detailed explanations as well as a comprehensive 150-question practice exam. Features over 100 illustrations and includes photos and histological images.

B

Ace Pathology

$29.95 Test/414 q

Wurzel

Mosby-Year Book, 1996, 400 pages, ISBN 0815192762 (Windows), ISBN 0815194285 (Mac)

Features a detailed content review with good photomicrographs. Test software with additional questions is included with text. Money-back guarantee if you fail.

B

Appleton & Lange's Review of General Pathology

$34.95 Test/896 q

Lewis

Appleton & Lange, 1993, 197 pages, ISBN 0838501613

Short text sections followed by lots of questions with answers. Some very useful high-yield tables at the beginning of each section. Good photomicrographs. Covers only general pathology (i.e., no organ-based pathology). Can be used as a supplement to more detailed texts. Good review when time is short.

B **Basic Concepts in Pathology** — $25.95 — Review only

Brown

McGraw-Hill, 1998, 437 pages, ISBN 0070083215

Good review of basic concepts. No images. Not entirely suitable for USMLE review.

B **EBS Essentials of Pathophysiology** — $39.95 — Review/69 q

Kaufman

Lippincott Williams & Wilkins, 1996, 650 pages, ISBN 0316484059

Review book with few questions. Features clinical descriptions of important diseases, but too detailed for high-yield review. Good diagrams, tables, and black-and-white photographs. More appropriate as a course text and reference. For the highly motivated student. Limited student feedback.

B **MEPC Medical Exam Review: Pathology** — $19.95 — Test/600 q

Fayemi

Appleton & Lange, 1994, 317 pages, ISBN 0838584411

High-quality questions with explanations. Good case-study chapter with some vignettes. Use as a supplement to other review books.

B **NMS Pathology** — $27.00 — Review/500 q

LiVolsi

Lippincott Williams & Wilkins, 1994, 508 pages, ISBN 0683062433

Outline form. Comprehensive review of large amount of material. Sometimes too detailed. Slow reading. Best if used with course.

B **Oklahoma Notes Pathology** — $19.95 — Review/140 q

Holliman

Springer-Verlag, 1994, 279 pages, ISBN 0387943900

Dense text. Few diagrams and tables. No illustrations. Questions with letter answers only. Good when you have no time for comprehensive review books.

B **Pathology: Examination and Board Review** — $29.95 — Review/Few q

Newland

Appleton & Lange, 1995, 314 pages, ISBN 0838577199

Concise text review with some high-quality charts and photomicrographs. Non-boards-style questions at the end of each chapter with letter answers only.

B

Pathology Notes

$26.95 Review only

Chandrasoma

Appleton & Lange, 1992, 788 pages, ISBN 0838551645

Lengthy but well organized and easy to read. Requires considerable time commitment. Good tables. No photographs. Good line drawings. Compare the format with *Pocket Companion to Robbins'* as to which best suits your style. Companion to *Concise Pathology* by same authors.

B

Pathophysiology of Heart Disease

$29.00 Review only

Lilly

Lippincott Williams & Wilkins, 1998, 401 pages, ISBN 0683302205

A collaborative project by medical students and faculty at Harvard. Well organized, easy-to-read and concise, it offers comprehensive coverage of cardiovascular pathophysiology from the medical student perspective. Provides an excellent bridge between the basic and clinical science. Very good for review of this subject, but does not cover other areas of pathology tested on the boards.

B

Pocket Companion to Robbins' Pathologic Basis of Diseases

$26.95 Review only

Robbins

Saunders, 1995, 620 pages, ISBN 0721657427

Good for reviewing associations between keywords and specific diseases. Very condensed and easy to understand. Explains most important diseases and pathologic processes. No photographs or illustrations. Useful as a quick reference.

B

PreTest Pathology

$18.95 Test/500 q

Brown

McGraw-Hill, 1999, 467 pages, ISBN 0070526869

Picky, difficult questions with detailed, complete answers. Often obscure or esoteric questions. Good-quality black-and-white photographs; no color photographs. Can be used as a supplement to other review books. For the motivated student who desires challenging exposure to lots of photographs. 28 pages of high-yield facts are very useful for concept summaries.

B-

Essential Pathology

$49.95 Review only

Rubin

Lippincott Williams & Wilkins, 1995, 814 pages, ISBN 0397514875

Thin book with excellent color illustrations and pictures that are useful for second year and beyond. Use as a text for coursework; too detailed for boards review. Limited student feedback.

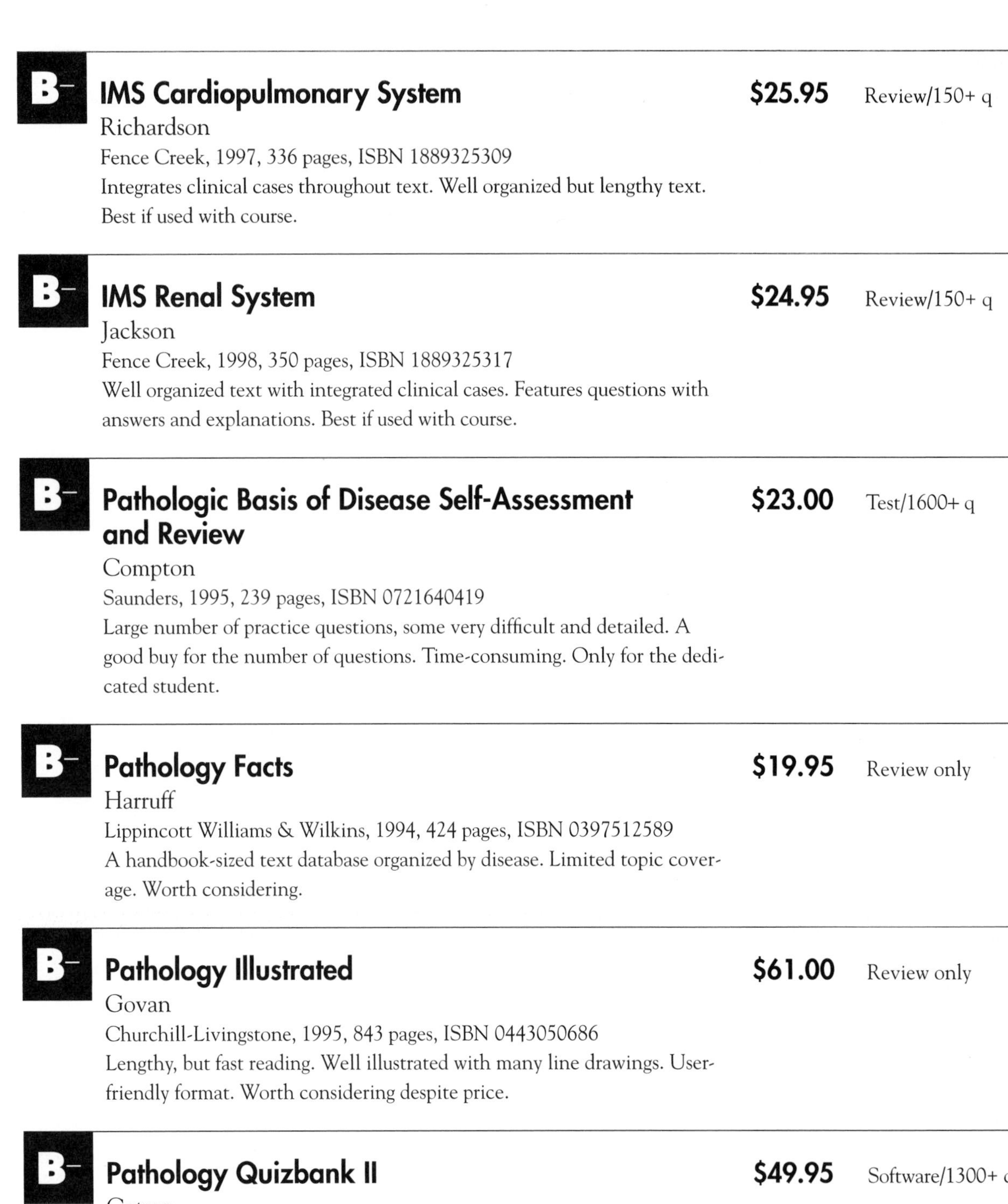

B− **IMS Cardiopulmonary System** — **$25.95** — Review/150+ q

Richardson

Fence Creek, 1997, 336 pages, ISBN 1889325309

Integrates clinical cases throughout text. Well organized but lengthy text. Best if used with course.

B− **IMS Renal System** — **$24.95** — Review/150+ q

Jackson

Fence Creek, 1998, 350 pages, ISBN 1889325317

Well organized text with integrated clinical cases. Features questions with answers and explanations. Best if used with course.

B− **Pathologic Basis of Disease Self-Assessment and Review** — **$23.00** — Test/1600+ q

Compton

Saunders, 1995, 239 pages, ISBN 0721640419

Large number of practice questions, some very difficult and detailed. A good buy for the number of questions. Time-consuming. Only for the dedicated student.

B− **Pathology Facts** — **$19.95** — Review only

Harruff

Lippincott Williams & Wilkins, 1994, 424 pages, ISBN 0397512589

A handbook-sized text database organized by disease. Limited topic coverage. Worth considering.

B− **Pathology Illustrated** — **$61.00** — Review only

Govan

Churchill-Livingstone, 1995, 843 pages, ISBN 0443050686

Lengthy, but fast reading. Well illustrated with many line drawings. User-friendly format. Worth considering despite price.

B− **Pathology Quizbank II** — **$49.95** — Software/1300+ q

Cotran

MedTech, 1995, ISBN 1573493295 (Mac), ISBN 1573493317 (Windows)

Multiple-choice questions with detailed explanations and links to related materials in Robbins' *Pathologic Basis of Disease* on CD-ROM (sold separately). Very good if used as reference or with course. Not boards-type questions. Expensive for students, discounts available through publisher.

B−

Review Questions for Human Pathology

$19.95 Test/1300+ q

Jones

Parthenon, 1997, 180 pages, ISBN 1850705992

Includes over thirteen hundred questions with answers and discussion. Many questions are in outdated USMLE format. Step 1 level questions are interspersed with questions at Step 2 and Step 3 level. Good value for the price.

B−

Wheater's Basic Histopathology

$49.00 Review only

Burkitt

Churchill-Livingstone, 1996, 252 pages, ISBN 0443050880

Color atlas with text. Contains pictures of pathologic histology. Not directed to boards-type review. May be more useful for photomicrograph-based questions.

C+

Pathology QuizBank Vol. 2

$99.00 Software/1000 q

Faculty, UC Davis

MedTech, 1995, ISBN 1573493295 (Mac), ISBN 1573493317 (Windows)

Expensive software database of board-style questions with good, detailed explanations. Some repetitive questions. Requires time commitment. Electronically referenced to Robbins' *Pathology Text Stack*. Quizzer has no timer or ability to custom-generate tests. Good product, but expensive. Best for library acquisition.

NEW BOOKS—PATHOLOGY

N

Cardiovascular Pathophysiology

$27.95 Review/100+ q

Kusomoto

Fence Creek, 1998, 353 pages, ISBN 1889325007

Numerous charts and illustrations. Each chapter offers summary questions.

N

Case Studies in General and Systemic Pathology

$30.00 Review/300+ q

Underwood

Churchill Livingstone, 1996, 172 pages, ISBN 0443050961

Sixty cases are presented with excellent images and integrated questions/answers. Full color images include gross specimens, histology and MRIs. Closely linked to *General and Systemic Pathology* by Underwood.

Endocrine Pathophysiology

$27.95 Review/100+ q

Niewoehner

Fence Creek, 1999, 270 pages, ISBN 1889325023

Well organized and easy to read with integrated clinical cases.

N **Gastrointestinal and Hepatobiliary Pathophysiology** **$27.95** Review/100+ q

Rose

Fence Creek, 1998, 451 pages, ISBN 1889325015

Well organized, however, lengthy. For the motivated student.

N **Hematologic Pathophysiology** **$25.95** Review/100+ q

Rubin

Fence Creek, 1998, 129 pages, ISBN 188932504X

Emphasis on clinical aspects of disease and treatment.

N **Outlines in Pathology** **$49.25** Review only

Sinard

WB Saunders, 1996, 228 pages, ISBN 0721663419

No index, images or questions are provided with this detailed outline of pathology. Short glossary of terms included as an appendix. Very expensive for the amount of material presented.

N **Pulmonary Pathophysiology** **$27.95** Review/100+ q

Criner

Fence Creek, 1998, 418 pages, ISBN 1889325058

Typical of this series. Well organized with integrated clinical case presentations.

N **Rypin's Intensive Reviews: Pathology** **$21.95** Review/220+ q

Damjanov

Lippincott Williams & Wilkins, 1998, 432 pages, ISBN 0397515553

Typical of this series. Includes comprehensive exam with answers and explanations. Illustrated with simple diagrams; no photos included.

N **USMLE Pathology Review: The Study Guide** **$25.95** Review/300+ q

Hassanein

Sage, 1998, 398 pages, ISBN 0761905170

Key pathology concepts are presented in an outline format. Numerous questions with answers and explanations. Includes a comprehensive 184 question exam. No index.

A−

Lippincott's Illustrated Reviews: Pharmacology $29.95 Review/230+ q

Harvey

Lippincott Williams & Wilkins, 1997, 475 pages, ISBN 0397515677

Outline format with practice questions and many excellent and memorable illustrations and tables. Cross-referenced to *Lippincott's Biochemistry*. Good for the "big picture." Good pathophysiologic approach. Detailed, so use with course and review for USMLE. For the motivated student. Ten illustrated case studies with questions and answers in the appendix.

A−

Pharmacology: Examination and Board Review $29.95 Review/800 q

Katzung

Appleton & Lange, 1998, 560 pages, ISBN 0838577083

Text is well organized in a narrative format with concise explanations. Good charts and tables. Good for drug interactions and toxicities. Features two practice exams and 17 case studies with questions and detailed answers. Includes some low-yield/obscure drugs. The 40-page crammable list of "top boards drugs" is especially high yield. Compare closely with *Lippincott's Illustrated Reviews: Pharmacology*.

B+

Basic Concepts in Pharmacology $25.95 Review only

Stringer

McGraw-Hill, 1996, 288 pages, ISBN 0070631654

Presents summaries of "elusive" concepts in pharmacology, from simple to complex. No questions. Limited student feedback.

B+

Digging Up the Bones: Pharmacology $18.95 Review/Cards

Linardakis

McGraw-Hill, 1998, 99 pages and 100+ flash cards, ISBN 007038214X

Easy reading. Brief collection of phrases and drug associations. Contains more than 100 flash cards of top drugs with clinical use, mechanisms, and side effects. Use as a supplement.

B+

Pharm Cards: A Review for Medical Students $26.95 Cards

Johannsen

Lippincott Williams & Wilkins, 1995, 195 cards, ISBN 0316465496

Highlights important features of major drugs/drug classes. Perfect for class review; also offers a quick, focused review for the USMLE. Lacks pharmacokinetics. Good charts and diagrams. Highly rated by students who enjoy flash-card-based review. Somewhat dated; lacks new drug classes.

B+ **Pharmacology: An Illustrated Review with Questions and Explanations** **$31.00** Review/400+ q

Ebadi

Lippincott Williams & Wilkins, 1996, 336 pages, ISBN 0316199575

Comprehensive review of pharmacology, with many illustrations and tables. Content and emphasis do not always reflect high-yield topics. Some emphasis on neuropharmacology. Good for the student who likes comprehensive chart/illustration–based review. Requires time commitment. Includes clinical case-based questions.

B+ **Pharmacology: Review for New National Boards** **$25.00** Test/539 q

Billingsley

J & S, 1995, 186 pages, ISBN 0963287370

Question-and-answer book typical for this series. Includes clinical vignettes. Good explanations cover many high-yield pharmacology topics. Easy, fast reading. Questions about drug structures probably low yield. Useful adjunct to a review book. Limited student feedback.

B+ **Underground Clinical Vignettes: Pharmacology** **$14.95** Review only

Bhushan

S2S Medical, 1999, 102 pages, ISBN 1890061352

Concise clinical cases illustrating approximately 100 frequently tested pharmacology concepts. Cardinal signs, symptoms, and buzzwords are highlighted. Clinical vignette style less effective for pharmacology. Use as a supplement to other sources of review.

B **Ace Pharmacology** **$29.95** Review/462 q

Enna

Mosby-Year Book, 1996, 394 pages, ISBN 0815131127 (Windows), ISBN 0815131526 (Mac)

Concise content review with some boards-style questions. Very thorough explanations. Test software included with text. Money-back guarantee if you fail.

B **Blond's Pharmacology** **$19.99** Review only

Kostrzewa

Sulzburger & Graham, 1995, 398 pages, ISBN 094581948X

Concise review of pharmacology. Many good diagrams. Some key topics are inadequately covered.

B **Clinical Pharmacology Made Ridiculously Simple** **$19.95** Review only

Olson

MedMaster, 1998, 162 pages, ISBN 0940780178

Includes general principles and many drug summary charts. Particularly strong in cardiovascular drugs and antimicrobials; incomplete in other areas. Mostly tables; lacks the humorous illustrations and mnemonics typical of this series. Well organized, but occasionally too detailed. Effective as a chart-based review book but not as a sole study source. Must supplement with a more detailed text.

B **EBS Essentials of Pharmacology** **$29.95** Review/250+ q

Theoharides

Lippincott Williams & Wilkins, 1996, 444 pages, ISBN 0316839361

Review text with some boards-style questions and letter answers. May be more appropriate as a course text than as a review book. New edition has many good tables that summarize important drug mechanisms and toxicities. Good text but not focused enough for boards.

B **MEPC Pharmacology** **$19.95** Test/700 q

Krzanowski

Appleton & Lange, 1995, 267 pages, ISBN 0838562272

Questions with brief, direct explanations. Well-referenced answers.

B **NMS Pharmacology** **$27.00** Review/450+ q

Jacob

Lippincott Williams & Wilkins, 1996, 373 pages, ISBN 0683062514

Outline format. More tables and diagrams in new edition. Often too detailed. Lacks emphasis on high-yield material. Has a lengthy USMLE-type exam. Requires time commitment. Typical for this series.

B **Oklahoma Notes Pharmacology** **$19.95** Review/560+ q

Moore

Springer-Verlag, 1995, 235 pages, ISBN 0387943943

Conceptual approach. Features USMLE-type questions with brief explanations. A concise and readable review book.

B **Pharmacology Companion** **$27.95** Review/Cards

Gallia

Alert and Oriented, 1997, 339 pages, ISBN 096401243X

Spiral bound with high-yield flash cards. Chart format illustrating mechanisms, uses, and side effects of each drug or class of drugs. However, few diagrams, and format does not seem to work as well as it does in Topf's *Microbiology Companion*. Limited student feedback.

B **PreTest Pharmacology** **$18.95** Test/500 q

Stern

McGraw-Hill, 1999, 258 pages, ISBN 007052694X

Picky, difficult questions with detailed answers. New high-yield chapter is a comparison chart intended only as a sample learning tool.

B− **The Phunny Pharm** **$21.00** Review only

Reidhead

Hanley & Belfus, 1997, 207 pages, ISBN 1560531142

Pharmacology review based on memory devices and illustrations. Sometimes too intricate. For the student who likes this approach; somewhat similar to the *Ridiculously Simple* series. Examine carefully.

C+ **BRS Pharmacology** **$24.95** Review/450 q

Rosenfeld

Lippincott Williams & Wilkins, 1997, 357 pages, ISBN 0683180509

Outline format. Good use of boldface, although few tables. Questions are of moderate difficulty with short answers. Worse than average for this series.

C+ **Med Charts, Pharmacology** **$14.95** Review only

Rosenbach

ILOC, 1993, 171 pages, ISBN 1882531000

Contains tables and summaries. Good for quick review, but requires previous reading from other sources. May be helpful for students who prefer studying charts.

C+ **Medical PharmFile** **$22.95** Cards

Feinstein

Medfiles, 1998, ISBN 0965537315

High-yield pharmacology in flash-card format similar to *Medical Micro-Cards*. Cards have printing on one side only. Not conducive to self-testing.

NEW BOOKS—PHARMACOLOGY

N **Color Atlas of Pharmacology** **$29.90** Review

Lullmann

Thieme, 1990, 369 pages, ISBN 0865774552

Highly visual approach to pharmacology. No questions. 149 color plates are accompanied by brief descriptions.

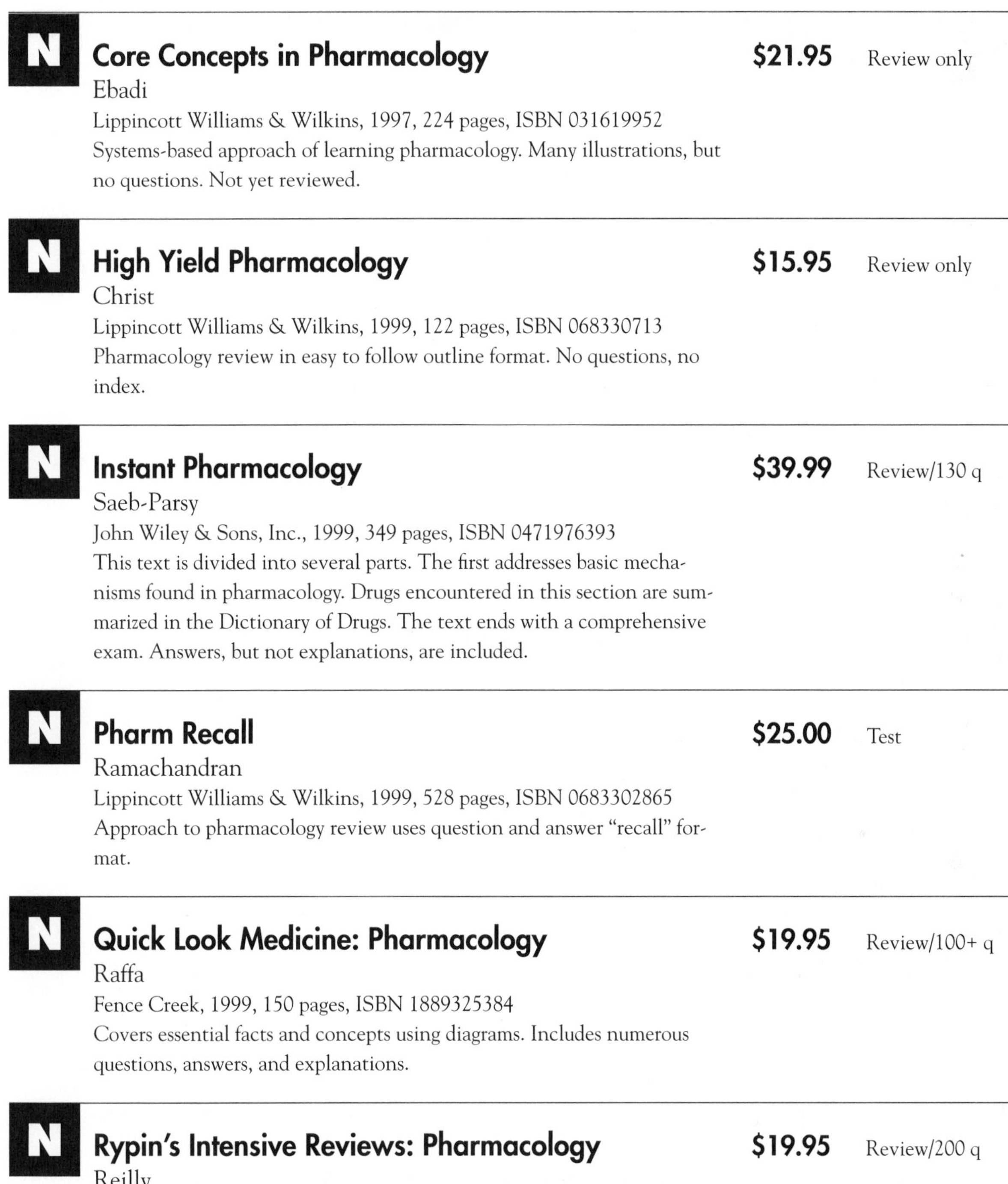

N **Core Concepts in Pharmacology** — **$21.95** — Review only

Ebadi

Lippincott Williams & Wilkins, 1997, 224 pages, ISBN 031619952

Systems-based approach of learning pharmacology. Many illustrations, but no questions. Not yet reviewed.

N **High Yield Pharmacology** — **$15.95** — Review only

Christ

Lippincott Williams & Wilkins, 1999, 122 pages, ISBN 068330713

Pharmacology review in easy to follow outline format. No questions, no index.

N **Instant Pharmacology** — **$39.99** — Review/130 q

Saeb-Parsy

John Wiley & Sons, Inc., 1999, 349 pages, ISBN 0471976393

This text is divided into several parts. The first addresses basic mechanisms found in pharmacology. Drugs encountered in this section are summarized in the Dictionary of Drugs. The text ends with a comprehensive exam. Answers, but not explanations, are included.

N **Pharm Recall** — **$25.00** — Test

Ramachandran

Lippincott Williams & Wilkins, 1999, 528 pages, ISBN 0683302865

Approach to pharmacology review uses question and answer "recall" format.

N **Quick Look Medicine: Pharmacology** — **$19.95** — Review/100+ q

Raffa

Fence Creek, 1999, 150 pages, ISBN 1889325384

Covers essential facts and concepts using diagrams. Includes numerous questions, answers, and explanations.

N **Rypin's Intensive Reviews: Pharmacology** — **$19.95** — Review/200 q

Reilly

Lippincott Williams & Wilkins, 1997, 352 pages, ISBN 0397515502

Includes numerous tables and 200-question practice exam with answers and explanations. Features an appendix of "must know" topics.

BRS Physiology | **$24.95** | Review/400 q

Costanzo

Lippincott Williams & Wilkins, 1998, 326 pages, ISBN 0683303961

Clear, concise review of physiology. Fast, easy reading. Comprehensive and efficient. Great charts and tables. Good practice questions with explanations and a clinically oriented final exam. Excellent review book, but may not be enough for in-depth coursework. Comparatively weak respiratory and acid–base sections. New edition for 1999.

STARS Physiology | **$29.95** | Review only

Costanzo

WB Saunders, 1998, 429 pages, ISBN 0721666116

Comprehensive coverage of concepts outlined in *BRS Physiology*. Excellent diagrams and charts. Each systems-based chapter includes a detailed summary of objectives and a boards-relevant clinical case. Time commitment is greater than for *BRS Physiology*.

Appleton & Lange's Review of Physiology | **$32.95** | Test/700+ q

Penney

Appleton & Lange, 1998, ISBN 0838502741

Boards-style questions with letter answers and explanations. No vignettes. Questions somewhat picky. Limited review.

B+

High-Yield Acid Base | **$12.95** | Review only

Longnecker

Lippincott Williams & Wilkins, 1998, 100 pages, ISBN 0683303937

Concise and well-written description of acid/base disorders. Includes chapters discussing differential diagnosis and 12 clinical cases. Introduces multistep approach to material. Bookmark with useful factoids included with text. No index or questions.

PreTest Physiology | **$18.95** | Test/500 q

Ryan

McGraw-Hill, 1999, 291 pages, ISBN 0070526915

Questions with detailed, well-written explanations. Some questions too difficult or picky. May be useful for the motivated student following extensive review from other sources. Includes 34 pages of high-yield facts.

B **Ace Physiology** **$29.95** Review/250 q

Ackermann

Mosby-Year Book, 1996, 285 pages, ISBN 081510054X (Windows), ISBN 0815109334 (Mac)

Concise yet thorough content review with some boards-style questions. Outline format is easy to read. Good illustrations. Test software included with text. Money-back guarantee if you fail.

B **Blond's Physiology** **$20.00** Review only

Grossman

Sulzburger & Graham, 1995, 439 pages, ISBN 0945819420

Comprehensive but easy-to-read review text of physiology. Clear and simple classic diagrams and charts. Better than average for this series. Strong endocrine chapter. Good hormone list.

B **Clinical Physiology Made Ridiculously Simple** **$19.95** Review only

Goldberg

MedMaster, 1999, 160 pages, ISBN 0940780216

Easy reading with many amusing associations. Style does not work for everyone. Not as well illustrated as the rest of series. Use as a supplement to other review books.

B **Color Atlas of Physiology** **$29.00** Review only

Despopoulos

Georg Thieme Verlag, 1991, 369 pages, ISBN 0865773823

Compact, with more than 156 colorful but complicated diagrams on the right and dense explanatory text on the left. Some translation problems. A unique, highly visual approach worthy of consideration. Useful as an adjunct to other review books.

B **Concepts in Physiology** **$17.95** Review/100+ q

Gupta

Parthenon, 1996, 135 pages, ISBN 1850707308

System-based review in paragraph form. Some sections have clinical questions at the end of the chapter with explanations. Format may not appeal to all students. Limited student feedback.

B **MEPC Physiology** **$19.95** Test/700 q

Penney

Appleton & Lange, 1996, 257 pages, ISBN 0838562221

Questions with brief, direct answers. Reflects USMLE Step 1 format. Compare with *PreTest Physiology*. Good as an adjunct to other review texts. Limited student feedback.

B **NMS Physiology** $27.00 Review/300 q

Bullock

Lippincott Williams & Wilkins, 1995, 641 pages, ISBN 068306259X

Very complete text in outline form. Often too detailed, but some good diagrams. Moderately difficult questions with detailed answers. Provides some pathophysiology and clinical correlations. More useful if used as a course text and reference; too long as a review text. Inexpensive for the amount of material. For the motivated student.

B **Physiology: A Review for the New National Boards** $25.00 Test/506 q

Jakoi

J & S, 1994, 214 pages, ISBN 0963287346

Good review book, but inadequate as sole source of review. Quick reading. Below-average question quality for this series. Answer discussions cover many important topics.

B **Physiology: An Illustrated Review with Questions & Explanations** $32.00 Review/320 q

Tadlock

Lippincott Williams & Wilkins, 1995, 333 pages, ISBN 0316827649

Features updated text with superb illustrations and tables. Format and organization improved. Quite detailed. Best used with the course. Some questions include complex calculations not typical for the USMLE. Requires time commitment.

B- **Digging Up Bones: Physiology** $21.50 Review only

Linardakis

McGraw-Hill, 1998, 146 pages, ISBN 1878576089

Organ-based collection of facts. Text includes tables, graphs, and some illustrations.

B- **EBS Essentials of Physiology** $35.95 Review/100 q

Sperelakis

Lippincott Williams & Wilkins, 1996, 680 pages, ISBN 0316806285

Dense review text with some boards-style questions and letter answers. Numerous diagrams, including some that are not particularly helpful. May be more appropriate as a course text than as a review book. Requires significant time commitment.

B- **Linardakis' Illustrated Review of Physiology** $37.95 Review/200 q

Linardakis

Michaelis Medical, 1998, 340 pages, ISBN 1884084176

Comprehensive, illustration-based review of medical physiology. Color illustrations integrated into text.

Review Questions for Physiology
$19.95 Test/600 q

Pasley

Parthenon, 1997, 180 pages, ISBN 1850706018

Few clinical vignette-type questions. Answers on same page so easy to move through questions and check answers at the same time.

B−

Rypin's Intensive Reviews: Physiology
$19.95 Review/305 q

Hall

Lippincott Williams & Wilkins, 1997, 416 pages, ISBN 0397515499

Covers material using a systems-based approach. Sample examination includes answers and detailed explanations to all 305 questions. Features a "Must Know Topics" list.

Oklahoma Notes Physiology
$19.95 Review/345 q

Thies

Springer-Verlag, 1995, 280 pages, ISBN 0387943978

Dense text. Inconsistent quality of sections. Emphasizes general concepts, but incomplete. Boards-type questions with short answers. Some errors.

NEW BOOKS—PHYSIOLOGY

N

Memorix Physiology
$35.25 Review

Schmidt

Chapman & Hall, 1997, 281 pages, ISBN 041271440X

Systems-based coverage of key concepts in easy-to-carry handbook. Similar in format to the *Color Atlas of Physiology*. Contains over 200 color illustrations and tables. Expensive for the amount of material.

Quick Look Medicine: Cardiopulmonary System
$19.95 Review/117 q

Richardson

Fence Creek, 1999, 164 pages, ISBN 1889325422

Presents concepts in diagram format. Includes questions, answers, and detailed explanations for self-assessment. Discussion covers cardiovascular and pulmonary physiology as well as cardiopulmonary pathophysiology.

Respiratory Physiology—The Essentials
$28.00 Review/100+ q

West

Lippincott Williams & Wilkins, 2000, 171 pages, ISBN 068307347

Comprehensive coverage of respiratory physiology. Limited student feedback. New edition includes appendices with over 100 questions and answers with explanations.

NOTES

SECTION III

Commercial Review Courses

Commercial preparation courses can be helpful for some students, but these courses are expensive and require significant time commitment. They are usually effective in organizing study material for students who feel overwhelmed by the volume of material. Note that the multiweek courses may be quite intense and may thus leave limited time for independent study. Also note that some commercial courses are designed for first-time test takers while others focus on students who are repeating the examination. Some courses focus on foreign medical graduates who want to take all three Steps in a limited amount of time. Student experience and satisfaction with review courses are highly variable. We suggest that you discuss options with recent graduates of review courses you are considering. Course content and structure can evolve rapidly. Some student opinions can be found in discussion groups on the World Wide Web.

Kaplan Educational Centers

Kaplan Medical

Kaplan Educational Centers, National Medical School Review (NMSR), and Compass Medical Education Network have recently merged to form KAPLAN MEDICAL. All program offerings are designed around the new computer-based USMLE.

Live Lectures

Kaplan Medical offers the IntensePrep™ live lecture program created by Compass. This 19-day live course is designed specifically for second-year students and is offered on over 25 US Medical School campuses across the nation. Its fast pace and high-yield structure make it suitable for (and restricted to) first-time takers of the exam. Many of the lecturers have authored USMLE review books and all are experienced instructors. The course includes a full set of lecture notes, hundreds of practice questions, an organ-system based CD-ROM, and a full-length simulated exam on CD-ROM. The course lecture notes are available before the start of the actual lectures for advanced preparation. Tuition for this course is $999.

Longer live lecture program options include a Prep version (approximately 7 weeks) and Extended-Prep version (approximately 14 weeks) for repeaters of the exam, or for students or physicians wanting more time to prepare. These courses include course lecture notes and texts where appropriate, hundreds of practice questions, and a full-length (350 questions) simulated exam on CD-ROM. Tuition for the 7-week course is $2700 and for the 14-week course is $5000.

ComputerPass

The ComputerPass program gives you the opportunity to go to a Kaplan Center and sit for two full-length computer simulated exams. You take two, one-day, 350-question exams that are reflective of the USMLE-style question format and USMLE computer interface. After sitting for the two full-length exams, you may review the questions and comprehensive explanations for another two full days at the Kaplan Centers. ComputerPass also includes a 360-question CD-ROM divided into organ-system-based quizzes. The fee for ComputerPass is $199.

MedPass

This center-based study program is offered at over 120 Kaplan Centers across the country, and is designed for and restricted to 2nd-year medical students. It includes 30 visits to the Kaplan Centers and access to its varied resources, including diagnostic testing and an individual study plan that takes into account available study time and level of preparation. Center resources include more than 100 hours of lectures on video. The video lecture modules may be reviewed by organ system or discipline. Materials include a 7-volume organ system review series, as well as an organ-system based CD-ROM and a full length simulation on CD-ROM. Included in MedPass is the above mentioned ComputerPass program, complete with 2 full-length in-center computer USMLE simulations. The fee for MedPass is $599.

Books and Software

You may purchase Kaplan's Organ-Based Review Books and CD-ROMs separately by calling 1-800-KAP-ITEM. The books and software package is $399 and includes all 7 Organ-system based books, a test-taking and strategy guide, and 2 Step 1 CD-ROMs (one with 360 questions divided by organ system and one with a full-length simulation). The software can also be purchased separately for $79 for both CDs.

For more information call 1-800-533-8850 or 949-567-4499.

Kaplan Medical can be found on-line at www.kaptest.com

Northwestern Learning Center

Northwestern Learning Center offers live-lecture review courses for both the USMLE Step 1 and the COMLEX Level 1 examinations. Two types of courses are available for each exam: NBI 100—Primary Care for the Boards and NBI 300—Intensive Care for the Boards. NBI 100 is an on-site, 15-hour live-lecture review offered in two- or three-day formats that uses Northwestern Learning Center's TALLP techniques in conjunction with a systematic review of high-yield USMLE facts and concepts. This course is designed to organize students and to help them focus on the most essential aspects of their boards preparation. NBI 300 is a comprehensive, live boards-preparation review conducted by a team of university faculty and authors of review notes. It also includes organized lecture notes, a large pool of practice questions, and simulated exams. NBI 300 is offered each year in 15- or 18-day formats both across the country and overseas. NBI 300 is also available in a customized, on-site format for groups of second-year students from individual American medical schools. Sites are East Lansing and Detroit, Michigan, Kansas City, Philadelphia, Los Angeles, and New York–Long Island. International sites in 2000 are in India, Saudi Arabia, the West Indies, and Tehran.

Tuition for NBI 100 ranges from $130 to $250 and for NBI 300 from $500 to $950 per student, depending on group size and early enrollment discounts. NBI 100 home-study materials are also available for $110. The Center also offers a retake option and a liberal cancellation policy. For more information, call 800-837-7737 or 517-332-0777, or write to:

Northwestern Learning Center
4700 S. Hagadorn
East Lansing, MI 48823

E-mail should be sent to: testbuster@aol.com or northwestern@voyager.net

The Center may also be found online at: http://www.northwesternlearning.com/nw

Postgraduate Medical Review Education

Postgraduate Medical Review Education (PMRE) has twenty-three years of experience with medical licensing exam preparation.

PMRE offers a complete home-study course for USMLE Step 1 in the form of audio cassettes and concise books beginning at $300. PMRE has packages of 4200 questions and answers for both basic and clinical sciences for $220.

Every month, PMRE offers video reviews for $300 and live reviews for $990. PMRE guarantees that if a student does not pass the USMLE, he or she will receive a free additional live or video or audio three-week review. The home study course also comes with study materials totaling over $900.

PMRE advertises professors who write questions for USMLE exams and profesionally recorded materials.

For more information, call 1-800-ECFMG-30 or write to:

PMRE
407 Lincoln Road, Suite 12E
Miami Beach, FL 33139

E-mail should be sent to: PMRE@aol.com

PMRE can also be found online at www.PMRE.com

The Princeton Review

Several preparation options are available from The Princeton Review for USMLE Steps 1 and 2. Medical students and graduates who thrive in a structured, classroom environment are likely to be more interested in The Princeton Review's Total Prep and Premium Prep courses, while its Exam Review and Self-study options are more likely to appeal to those who wish to augment their own study plans with one or two of the benefits that review courses offer.

Premium Prep (207 hours live instruction) provides an extensive review of content tested on Step 1 for physicians who completed their undergraduate medical training several years previously. Total Prep (110 hours live instruction) provides a short, intensive review of the material for medical students who plan to sit for Step 1 or Step 2 shortly after completing the relevant curriculum. Exam Review (25–39 hours live instruction) provides and reviews The Princeton Review's diagnostic exams. A Self-Study Option (complete set of review manuals and workbooks plus 5 hours of class) is available for students and graduates who are unable to fit a review course into their schedules or otherwise prefer to study alone.

Students in Premium Prep, Total Prep and Exam Review complete two full-length simulated computer-based tests and a battery of computer-based subject tests. Students in Premium Prep, Total Prep or the Self-study option receive a complete set of review and practice materials for in and out of the classroom.

The Princeton Review recruits and trains medical students and physicians who have achieved high USMLE scores to teach its preparation courses and contribute to its materials and tests. Classes are small, with no more than 30 students in each Exam Review section or 20 in each Total or Premium Prep course section.

You may request more information from The Princeton Review about its USMLE preparation options by calling 1.800/USMLE84 or by sending an e-mail message to info.medlic@review.com. Information is also available at www.review.com on the Internet.

Youel's Prep, Inc.

David Bruce Youel, MD, has specialized in medical board preparation programs for 22 years. Youel's Prep provides comprehensive sets of preparation books and videotapes and offers live-lecture and preparation programs for the USMLE Step 1 and for the NBOME COMLEX Level 1. Programs are held at selected medical schools, upon invitation by the school and students.

Youel's courses are all live-lecture and are all taught by physicians to reflect the clinical slant of the boards. Youel's phones are answered by professionals to provide students with instant answers to their questions and concerns.

Youel's offers three complete and continuously updated book sets to allow students to tailor their study to review needs and available study time. The *Quick Study Series* includes three volumes: *Youel's Jewels I and II* and *Case Studies*, a book of questions and answers. This is a shorter version of the Home Study program that is designed for current medical students, well-prepared recent graduates, and those with limited time. It prepares students for all three USMLE steps.

The FUNdaMENTALS program includes five volumes broken down by disciplines: *Pathology I and II*, *Molecular Medicine*, *Big & Little Parts Book*, and *Case Studies*. FUNdaMENTALS is designed for those who prefer to study by disciplines and is preparation for Step 1 only.

The *Home Study Program* includes ten volumes: eight *Multi-Systems Books*, the *Prepper's Manual*, and *Case Studies*. The *Home Study Program* is designed for students who are preparing early, test repeaters, and US and foreign medical graduates. It prepares students for all three USMLE steps.

Contact Youel's Prep, Inc., at 1-800-645-3985 or 1-561-795-1555, fax 1-561-795-0169, or write to:

Youel's Prep, Inc.
701 Cypress Green Circle
Wellington, FL 33414.

E-mail should be sent to: YouelsPrep@aol.com

Youel's Prep can also be found online at: http://www.youelsprep.com

Publisher Contacts

If you do not have convenient access to a medical bookstore, consider ordering directly from the publisher.

Alert & Oriented
13025 Candela Place
San Diego, CA 92130-1866
(888) 253-7844
joel@alertandonline.com
www.alertandonline.com

Appleton & Lange
P.O. Box 545
Blacklick, OH 43004-0545
(800) 722-4726
Fax: (614) 755-5645
www.appletonlange.com

BL Publishing
3614 North Raven Wash Drive
Tucson, Arizona 85745
(520) 743-1711
blpublishing@hotmail.com

Blackwell Science
350 Main Street
Malden, MA 02148
(800) 759-6102
(781) 388-8255
Fax: (781) 388-8250
www.blacksci.co.uk

Churchill Livingstone
300 Lighting Way
Secaucus, NJ 07094
(800) 553-5426
(973) 319-9800
Fax: (201) 319-9659

FMSG Publishing Co.
35 Hollow Pine Dr.
DeBary, FL 32713
(904) 774-5277
Fax: (904) 774-5563
fmsgco@n-jcenter.com

Gold Standard Board Prep.
6374 Long Run Rd.
Athens, OH 45701
(740) 592-4124
Fax: (740) 592-4045
www.boardprep.net

ILOC Inc.
P.O. Box 232
Granville, OH 43023
(740) 587-2658
Fax: (740) 587-2679

J&S Publishing
1300 Bishop Lane
Alexandria, VA 22302
(703) 823-9833
Fax: (703) 823-9834
Jandspub@ix.netcom.com
www.jandspub.com

Lippincott Williams & Wilkins
P.O. Box 1580
Hagerstown, MD 21741
(800) 777-2295
Fax: (301) 824-7390
www.lww.com

Maval Publishing, Inc.
567 Harrison St.
Denver, CO 80206

McGraw-Hill Customer Service
P.O. Box 545
Blacklick, OH 43004-0545
(800) 722-4726
Fax: (614) 755-5645
www.mghmedical.com

MedMaster, Inc.
P.O. Box 640028
Miami, FL 33164
(800) 335-3480
(305) 653-3480
Fax: (954) 962-4508
mmbks@aol.com

MedTech USA
6310 San Vicente Blvd.
Suite #425
Los Angeles, CA 90048
(800) 260-2600
Fax: (301) 824-7390
mail@medtech.com
www.medtech.com

Mosby-Year Book
11830 Westline Industrial Drive
St. Louis, MO 63146
(800) 325-4177 ext. 5017
Fax: (800) 535-9935
www.mosby.com

National Learning Corporation
212 Michael Drive
Syosset, NY 11791
(800) 645-6337
Fax: (516) 921-8743

Parthenon Publishing
One Blue Hill Plaza
P.O. Box 1564
Pearl River, New York 10965
(914) 735-9363
(800) 735-4744
usa@parthpub.com
www.parthpub.com

Southland Tutorials
(distributed by Technical Book Co.)
2056 Westwood Boulevard
Los Angeles, CA 90025
(310) 475-5711
(800) 233-5150
tbcbkstore@aol.com
www.medicalbooks-online.com

Springer-Verlag, NY Inc.
P.O. Box 2485
Secaucus, NJ 07096
(800) 777-4643
Fax: (201) 348-5405
www.Springer-NY.com
orders@Springer-NY.com

W.B. Saunders
6277 Sea Harbor Drive
Orlando, FL 32887
(800) 545-2522
Fax: (800) 874-6418

Sulzburger & Graham
165 West 91st Street
New York, NY 10024
(212) 947-0100

APPENDIX

Abbreviations and Symbols

Abbreviation	Meaning
AA	amino acid
AAV	adeno-assisted virus
Ab	antibody
ACE	angiotensin-converting enzyme
ACh	acetylcholine
AChE	acetylcholinesterase
ACL	anterior cruciate ligament
ACTH	adrenocorticotropic hormone
AD	autosomal dominant
ADA	adenosine deaminase, Americans with Disabilities Act
ADH	antidiuretic hormone (vasopressin)
ADHD	attention-deficit hyperactivity disorder
ADP	adenosine diphosphate
Ag	antigen
AIDS	acquired immunodeficiency syndrome
ALA	aminolevulinate synthase
ALL	acute lymphocytic leukemia
ALS	amyotrophic lateral sclerosis
ALT	alanine transaminase
AML	acute myelogenous leukemia
ANA	antinuclear antibody
ANOVA	analysis of variance
ANP	atrial natriuretic peptide
ANS	autonomic nervous system
AOA	American Osteopathic Association
AP	arterial pressure
APC	antigen-presenting cell
APKD	adult polycystic kidney disease
APSAC	anistreplase
aPTT	activated partial thromboplastin time
ARC	Appalachian Regional Commission
ARDS	acute respiratory distress syndrome
ASD	atrial septal defect
ASO	antistreptolysin O
AST	aspartate transaminase
ATP	adenosine triphosphate
ATPase	adenosine triphosphatase
AV	atrioventricular
AVM	arteriovenous malformation
AZT	azidothymidine
BAL	British anti-Lewisite (dimercaprol)
BM	basement membrane
BP	blood pressure
BPG	bis phosphoglycerate
BPH	benign prostatic hyperplasia
BUN	blood urea nitrogen
CAD	coronary artery disease
cAMP	cyclic adenosine monophosphate
CAST	computer-adaptive sequential testing
CBT	computer-based testing
CCK	cholecystokinin
CCT	cortical collecting tubule

Abbreviation	Meaning
CD	cluster of differentiation
CDC	Centers for Disease Control
CDP	cytidine diphosphate
CE	cholesterol ester
CEA	carcinoembryonic antigen
CETP	cholesteryl-ester transfer protein
CF	cystic fibrosis
CFTR	cystic fibrosis transmembrane regulator
CFX	circumflex (artery)
cGMP	cyclic guanosine monophosphate
ChAT	choline acetyltransferase
CHF	congestive heart failure
CIN	cervical intraepithelial neoplasia
CJD	Creutzfeldt–Jakob disease
CL	clearance
CLL	chronic lymphocytic leukemia
CM	chylomicron
CML	chronic myelogenous leukemia
CMT	Computerized Mastery Test
CMV	cytomegalovirus
CN	cranial nerve
CNS	central nervous system
CO	cardiac output
CoA	coenzyme A
COMLEX	Comprehensive Osteopathic Medical Licensing Examination
COMT	catechol-O-methyltransferase
COPD	chronic obstructive pulmonary disease
COX	cyclooxygenase
C_p	concentration in plasma
CPK-MB	creatine phosphokinase, MB fraction
CRH	corticotropin-releasing hormone
CSA	Clinical Skills Assessment (exam)
CSF	cerebrospinal fluid
CT	computed tomography
CV	cardiovascular
CXR	chest x-ray
D	dopamine
DAG	diacylglycerol
ddC	dideoxycytidine
DEA	Drug Enforcement Agency
DES	diethylstilbestrol
DG	data gathering
DHT	dihydrotestosterone
DI	diabetes insipidus
DIC	disseminated intravascular coagulation
DIMS	disorder in initiating and maintaining sleep
DIP	distal interphalangeal joint
DKA	diabetic ketoacidosis
DMD	Duchenne muscular dystrophy
DMN	dorsal motor nucleus
DNA	deoxyribonucleic acid
2,4-DNP	2,4-dinitrophenol
DO	Doctor of Osteopathy

Abbreviation	Meaning
DOES	disorder of excessive somnolence
DOPA	dihydroxyphenylalanine (methyldopa)
DPG	diffuse proliferative glomerulonephritis; diphosphoglycerate
DPM	Doctor of Podiatric Medicine
DPPC	dipalmitoyl phosphatidylcholine
ds	double stranded
DSM	Diagnostic and Statistical Manual
dTMP	deoxythymidine monophosphate
DTR	deep tendon reflex
DTs	delirium tremens
EBV	Epstein–Barr virus
ECF	extracellular fluid
ECFMG	Educational Commission for Foreign Medical Graduates
ECT	electroconvulsive therapy
EDRF	endothelium-derived relaxing factor
EDTA	ethylenediamine tetraacetic acid
EDV	end-diastolic volume
EEG	electroencephalogram
EF-2	elongation factor 2
EGF	epidermal growth factor
EKG	electrocardiogram
ELISA	enzyme-linked immunosorbent assay
EM	electron microscopy
EMB	eosin–methylene blue
EOM	extraocular muscle
epi	epinephrine
EPS	extrapyramidal symptoms
ER	endoplasmic reticulum; emergency room
ERP	effective refractory period
ERV	expiratory reserve volume
ESR	erythrocyte sedimentation rate
ESV	end-systolic volume
EtOH	ethyl alcohol
FAD	oxidized flavin adenine dinucleotide
$FADH_2$	reduced flavin adenine dinucleotide
FAP	familial adenomatous polyposis
FDA	Food and Drug Administration
FEV	forced expiratory volume
FF	filtration fraction
FFA	free fatty acid
FFP	fresh frozen plasma
FH_x	family history
FLEX	Federal Licensing Examination
FMG	foreign medical graduate
FMN	flavin mononucleotide
FMR	fragile X mental retardation
FSH	follicle-stimulating hormone
FSMB	Federation of State Medical Boards
FTA-ABS	fluorescent treponemal antibody—absorbed
5-FU	5-fluorouracil
FVC	forced vital capacity
G3P	glucose-3-phosphate
G6PD	glucose-6-phosphate dehydrogenase
GABA	γ-aminobutyric acid
GBM	glomerular basement membrane
GFAP	glial fibrillary acidic protein
GFR	glomerular filtration rate
GGT	γ-glutamyl transpeptidase
GH	growth hormone
GI	gastrointestinal
G_i	G protein, inhibitory
GM-CSF	granulocyte-macrophage colony-stimulating factor
GMP	guanosine monophosphate
GN	glomerulonephritis
GnRH	gonadotropin-releasing hormone
GRP	gastrin-releasing peptide
G_s	G protein, stimulatory
GTP	guanosine triphosphate
HAV	hepatitis A virus
Hb	hemoglobin
HBsAG	hepatitis B surface antigen
HBV	hepatitis B virus
hCG	human chorionic gonadotropin
HCV	hepatitis C virus
HDL	high-density lipoprotein
HDV	hepatitis D virus
H & E	hematoxylin and eosin (stain)
HEV	hepatitis E virus
HGPRT	hypoxanthine-guanine phosphoryltransferase
HHS	Department of Health and Human Services
HHV	human herpesvirus
5-HIAA	5-hydroxyindoleacetic acid
HIV	human immunodeficiency virus
HLA	human leukocyte antigen
HMG	human menopausal gonadotropin
HMG-CoA	hydroxymethylglutaryl-CoA
HMP	hexose monophosphate
HNPCC	hereditary nonpolyposis colorectal cancer
HPSA	Health Professional Shortage Area
HPV	human papillomavirus
HR	heart rate
HSV	herpes simplex virus
5-HT	5-hydroxytryptamine (serotonin)
HTLV	human T-cell lymphotropic virus
HUS	hemolytic uremic syndrome
HTN	hypertension
IC	inspiratory capacity
ICE	integrated clinical encounter
ICF	intracellular fluid
ICU	intensive care unit
ID_{50}	median infectious dose
IDDM	insulin-dependent diabetes mellitus
IDL	intermediate-density lipoprotein
I/E	inspiratory/expiratory
IF	intrinsic factor; immunofluorescence
IFN	interferon
Ig	immunoglobulin
IHSS	idiopathic hypertrophic subaortic stenosis
IL-1, -2, -3, -4, -5	interleukin-1, 2, 3, 4, 5
IM	intramuscular
IMA	inferior mesenteric artery
IMG	international medical graduate
IMP	inosine monophosphate
IND	investigational new drug
INH	isonicotine hydrazine (isoniazid)
INS	Immigration and Naturalization Service
IP_3	inositol triphosphate
IPS	interpersonal skills
IPV	inactivated polio vaccine
IRV	inspiratory reserve volume
ITP	idiopathic thrombocytopenic purpura

Abbreviation	Meaning
IVC	inferior vena cava
JCV	JC virus
JGA	juxtaglomerular apparatus
KPV	killed polio vaccine
KSHV	Kaposi's sarcoma–associated herpesvirus
LA	left atrium
LAD	left anterior descending; left atrial defect
LAF	left anterior fascicle
LCA	left coronary artery
LCAT	lecithin-cholesterol acyltransferase
LCL	lateral collateral ligament
LCME	Liaison Committee on Medical Education
LCV	lymphocytic choriomeningitis virus
LDH	lactate dehydrogenase
LDL	low-density lipoprotein
LES	lower esophageal sphincter
LFT	liver function test
LH	luteinizing hormone
LLQ	left lower quadrant
LM	light microscopy
LMN	lower motor neuron
LPS	lipopolysaccharide
LSE	Libman–Sacks endocarditis
LT	leukotriene; long thoracic
LV	left ventricle; left ventricular
MAC	*Mycobacterium avium–intracellulare* complex; membrane attack complex; minimum alveolar anesthetic concentration
MAO	monoamine oxidase
MC	musculocutaneous
MCHC	mean corpuscular hemoglobin concentration
MCL	medial collateral ligament
M-CSF	macrophage colony stimulating factor
MD	muscular dystrophy
MEN	multiple endocrine neoplasia
MEOS	microsomal ethanol oxidizing system
MHC	major histocompatibility complex
MI	myocardial infarction
MLF	medial longitudinal fasciculus
MMR	measles, mumps, rubella
MPTP	1-methyl-4-phenyl-1, 2, 3, 6-tetrahydropyridine
MRI	magnetic resonance imaging
MS	multiple sclerosis
MSH	melanocyte stimulating hormone
MTP	metatarsal–phalangeal
MVA	motor vehicle accident
NAD	oxidized nicotinamide adenine dinucleotide
NADH	reduced nicotinamide adenine dinucleotide
NADP	oxidized nicotinamide adenine dinucleotide phosphate
NADPH	reduced nicotinamide adenine dinucleotide phosphate
NBME	National Board of Medical Examiners
NBOME	National Board of Osteopathic Medicine Examiners
NBPME	National Board of Podiatric Medical Examiners
NE	norepinephrine

Abbreviation	Meaning
NIDA	National Institute on Drug Abuse
NIDDM	non-insulin-dependent diabetes mellitus
NMJ	neuromuscular junction
NREM	non–rapid eye movement
NSAID	nonsteroidal anti-inflammatory drug
OAA	oxaloacetic acid
OBS	organic brain syndrome
OD	overdose
OMT	osteopathic manipulative technique
OPV	oral polio vaccine
OR	operating room
PABA	para-aminobenzoic acid
PAH	para-aminohippuric acid
PALS	periarterial lymphoid sheath
PAN	polyarteritis nodosa
P-ANCA	perinuclear pattern of antineutrophil cytoplasmic antibodies
PAS	periodic acid–Schiff (stain)
PCAT	phosphatidylcholine-cholesterol acyltransferase
PCI_2	prostacyclin I_2
PCL	posterior cruciate ligament
PCP	*Pneumocystis carinii* pneumonia; phencyclidine hydrochloride
PCR	polymerase chain reaction
PCWP	pulmonary capillary wedge pressure
PD	posterior descending
PDA	patent ductus arteriosus
PDE	phosphodiesterase
PDGF	platelet-derived growth factor
PEP	phosphoenolpyruvate
PFK	phosphofructokinase
PFT	pulmonary function tests
PG	prostaglandin
PID	pelvic inflammatory disease
PIP	proximal interphalangeal joint
PIP_2	phosphatidylinositol 4,5-bisphosphate
PK	pyruvate kinase
PKU	phenylketonuria
PML	progressive multifocal leukoencephalopathy
PMN	polymorphonuclear
PN	patient note
PNH	paroxysmal nocturnal hemoglobinuria
PNS	peripheral nervous system
POMC	pro-opiomelanocortin
PP	pyrophosphate
PPRF	parapontine reticular formation
PR	pulmonic regurgitation
PRPP	phosphoribosylpyrophosphate
PSA	prostate-specific antigen
PSS	progressive systemic sclerosis
PT	prothrombin time
PTH	parathyroid hormone
PTT	partial thromboplastin time
PVR	pulmonary vascular resistance
RA	right atrium
RBC	red blood cell
RBF	renal blood flow
RCA	right coronary artery
RDS	respiratory distress syndrome
REM	rapid eye movement
RER	rough endoplasmic reticulum
RES	reticuloendothelial system
RPF	renal plasma flow

Abbreviation	Meaning
RPR	rapid plasma reagin
RR	respiratory rate
RSV	respiratory syncytial virus
RUQ	right upper quadrant
RV	residual volume; right ventricle; right ventricular
RVH	right ventricular hypertrophy
SA	sino-atrial
SAM	S-adenosylmethionine
SC	sickle cell, subcutaneous
SCID	severe combined immunodeficiency disease
SD	standard deviation
SEM	standard error of the mean
SER	smooth endoplasmic reticulum
SES	socioeconomic status
SGOT	serum glutamic oxaloacetic transaminase
SGPT	serum glutamic pyruvate transaminase
SLC	Sylvan Learning Center
SLE	systemic lupus erythematosus
SLL	small lymphocytic lymphoma
SMA	superior mesenteric artery
SMX or SMZ	sulfamethoxazole
SOMA	Student Osteopathic Medical Association
SP	standardized patient
SRP	sponsoring residency program
SRS-A	slow-reacting substance of anaphylaxis
ss	single stranded
SSPE	subacute sclerosing panencephalitis
STC	Sylvan Testing Center
STD	sexually transmitted disease
SV	stroke volume
SVC	superior vena cava
SVT	supraventricular tachycardia
$t_{1/2}$	half-life
T_3	triiodothyronine
T_4	thyroxine
TAT	thematic apperception test
TB	tuberculosis
TBW	total body water
TCA	tricarboxylic acid
TCR	T-cell receptor
TG	triglyceride
TGF	transforming growth factor
TGV	transposition of great vessels
TIBC	total iron binding capacity
TLC	total lung capacity
TMP-SMX	trimethoprim-sulfamethoxazole
TN	trigeminal neuralgia
TNF	tissue necrosis factor
TNM	tumor, node, metastasis
ToRCHeS	toxoplasmosis, rubella, CMV, herpes, syphilis
tPA	tissue plasminogen factor
TPP	thiamine pyrophosphate
TPR	total peripheral resistance
TRH	thyrotropin-releasing hormone
TSH	thyroid-stimulating hormone
TSS	toxic shock syndrome
TSST	toxic shock syndrome toxin
TTP	thrombotic thrombocytopenic purpura
TV	tidal volume
TXA	thromboxane
UDP	uridine diphosphate
UMN	upper motor neuron
URI	upper respiratory infection
USIA	United States Information Agency
USMLE	United States Medical Licensing Examination
UTI	urinary tract infection
VA	Veterans Administration
VC	vital capacity
V_d	volume of distribution
VDRL	Venereal Disease Research Laboratory
VF	ventricular fibrillation
VHL	Von Hippel Lindau (disease)
VLDL	very low-density lipoprotein
VMA	vanillylmandelic acid
V/Q	ratio of ventilation to perfusion
VSD	ventricular septal defect
VWF	Von Willebrand factor
VZV	varicella-zoster virus
WBC	white blood cell
$\bar{X}$	statistical mean
ZE	Zollinger–Ellison (syndrome)

Symbol	Meaning
↑	increase(s)
↓	decrease(s)
→	leads to
1°	primary
2°	secondary
3°	tertiary
≈	approximately; homologous
≡	defined as
⊖	negative effect
⊕	positive effect

Vikas Bhushan, MD

Tao Le, MD

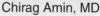

Chirag Amin, MD

Antony Chu

Esther Choo

Vikas Bhushan, MD Dr. Bhushan is a world-renowned author, publisher, entrepreneur, and board-certified diagnostic radiologist who resides in Los Angeles, California. Dr. Bhushan conceived and authored the original First Aid for the USMLE Step 1 in 1992, which, after ten consecutive editions, has become the most popular medical review book in the world. Following this, he co-authored and led three additional First Aid books as well as the development of the highly acclaimed 17-title Underground Clinical Vignettes series. He was an active researcher in medical informatics and digital radiology and completed his training in diagnostic radiology at the University of California, Los Angeles. Dr. Bhushan has more than 12 years of entrepreneurial experience and started two successful software and publishing companies prior to co-founding Medschool.com. Over the course of his career, he has worked directly with dozens of medical school faculty members, colleagues, and consultants and corresponded with well over a thousand medical students from around the world. Dr. Bhushan earned his bachelor's degree in biochemistry from the University of California, Berkeley, and his MD with thesis from the University of California, San Francisco.

Tao Le, MD Dr. Le has led multiple medical education projects over the past six years. As a medical student, he was editor-in-chief of the University of California, San Francisco Synapse, a university newspaper with a weekly circulation of 9,000. Subsequently, he authored First Aid for the Wards and First Aid for the Match and led the most recent revision of First Aid for the USMLE Step 2. At Yale, he was a regular guest lecturer on the USMLE review courses and an adviser to the Yale University School of Medicine curriculum committee. Dr. Le earned his medical degree from the University of California, San Francisco in 1996 and recently completed his residency training and board certification in internal medicine at Yale-New Haven Hospital. Dr. Le subsequently went on to co-found Medschool.com and currently serves as its Chief Medical Officer.

Chirag Amin, MD Dr. Amin has extensive experience in the field of medical education and has served as a co-author with Drs. Bhushan and Le on the entire First Aid and Underground Clinical Vignettes series. He also led the completion of The Insider's Guide to the MCAT, published by Lippincott Williams & Wilkins. In addition to his contributions in the field of medical education, Dr. Amin has an extensive background in Internet-related enterprises; he actively follows a number of development-stage Internet companies and serves as a staff writer and chief trading strategist for Internet Stock News (www.internetstocknews.com), an online financial content website with over 400,000 users worldwide. Dr. Amin earned his BS in biology at the University of Illinois in 1992. He then went on to get his MD with Research Distinction from the University of Miami School of Medicine in 1996 and completed three years of residency training in orthopedic surgery at Orlando Regional Medical Center.

Antony Chu Antony is a third-year medical student at Yale University and active FOE ("Friend of Esther"). A graduate of the University of Wisconsin at Madison, Mr. Chu graduated with degrees in Russian and genetics. He has completed fellowships with the United States Information Agency (Moscow, Russia), United States Senator Russell Feingold, and large mechanical sausages (Oscar Mayer Foods). He was a 1999 Howard Hughes Medical Fellow. Despite a rigorous q365 call schedule, he is earnestly pursuing rights for a "scratch and sniff" series of pathology texts. For more, engage antony.chu@yale.edu

Esther Choo Esther is a fourth-year Yale medical student taking time to develop an online student community at Medschool.com's sunny Santa Monica, CA office. She is planning to apply to residency in Emergency Medicine. Other interests include examining the social patterns of Rhesus monkeys, finding perfect combinations at Diddy Reese, acquiring a new ACL, and aspiring after Joan Didion. Enneagram-wise, she remains a Loyalist-Trooper.

Jean Shein Jean is a third-year medical student at NYU School of Medicine. Much of her life experience has been shaped by her years at her beloved alma mater, Dartmouth College. She is drawn to the wonders of priceline.com and often finds herself getting locked into buying things she doesn't really need. Her rabbit is her pride and joy, although he often indulges in coprophagy and urinates in random places in her apartment. If anyone knows where she can get Taiwanese shaved ice in the States, please contact her at sheinj01@popmail.med.nyu.edu.

About the Authors